18/8/05.

Happy Birthday Brian, and may your sails
be always full of happiness, good health,
and joy, for many years.

Love,

Mom & Dad.

THE STORY OF SAIL

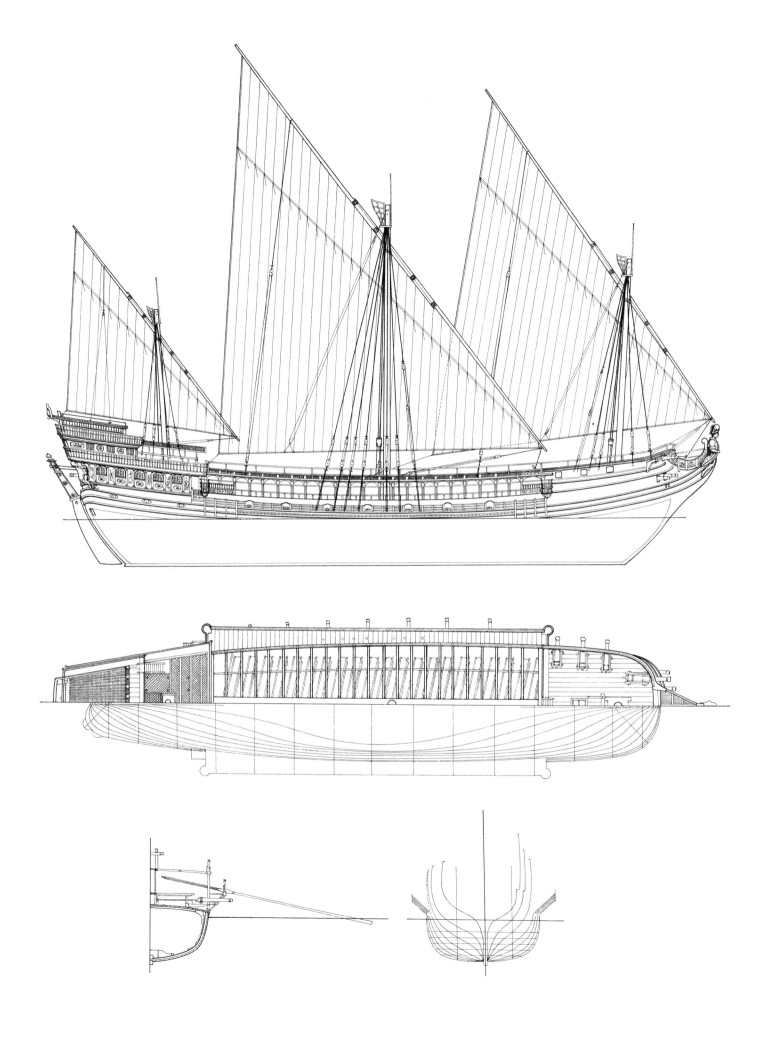

THE STORY OF SAIL

ILLUSTRATED WITH 1000 SCALE DRAWINGS

VERES LÁSZLÓ &
RICHARD WOODMAN

CHATHAM PUBLISHING

LONDON

Frontispiece A French galleasse of the late seventeenth century, based on information contained in *Souvenirs de Marine* by Admiral Paris, a great compilation of plans and drawings that inspired *The Story of Sail. (167)*

© All illustrations Veres László 1999
© Text Richard Woodman 1999

First published in the United Kingdom in 1999 by
Chatham Publishing, 61 Frith Street,
London W1V 5TA

Chatham Publishing is an imprint of
Gerald Duckworth & Co Ltd

British Library Cataloguing in Publication Data
A catalogue record for this book is available from the
British Library

ISBN 1 86176 075 2

Typeset and designed by Tony and Matthew Hart

Printed and bound in Great Britain by Hillman Printers
(Frome) Ltd

Contents

Introduction

WE CAN ONLY GUESS at how and why primitive man first went afloat, though it is fairly certain that a rotten tree, floating in some lake or river, first tempted him. Simple craft still exist in the remoter corners of our modern world, providing evidence of a tangible sort, while the achievements and exploits of once powerful or legendary people, give us further clues in pictographic form on sources as diverse as shards of pottery or the tombs of monarchs. In addition, descriptions of early boats are to be found in classical histories from several cultures.

The first logs to be bestriden by man were probably no more than objects of experimental curiosity, but the notion of travel to the far side of a lake or river must soon have crystallised into purpose, bringing with it the extended possibilities of a means to raid an otherwise inaccessible enemy, to transport negotiable commodities, or to better hunt fish. As soon as man decided to *use* his craft, he had to develop a means of propulsion better than his hands. No doubt the advantage of paddles soon occurred to him, but it would not have taken him long to discover the tiring nature of this method, particularly if he ventured on a river with a contrary current against which he had to strive. It was not long before he discovered the advantages of the oar, which conferred a power and range unobtainable by paddle.

By this time man was *constructing* his craft, bending materials to his will in order to further his ambitions to travel. The pursuit of war provided warriors willing to row, while victory and the acquisition of slaves enabled the warriors to conserve their energies for fighting, leaving the slaves to provide propulsion. The considerable abilities of the resultant galley led to its retention as a warship until the early years of the nineteenth century, but the galley was incapable of voyages of a long duration, or of venturing across the world's oceans. Even when its banks of oars were supplemented by sails, the galley remained a vessel of limited applications. But the sail, introduced to relieve the wretched slaves when the wind was fair, was to provide the answer of how to propel a hull beyond the endurance of men's strength. It was to endure in this capacity for two thousand years.

From the simple concept of the wind propelling a floating object, the variety of craft developed through these millennia is astonishing. The story of sail runs concurrently with mankind's experience of the wind and although a proper understanding of this natural resource is relatively recent, he has been quick to take advantage of the benefits of this powerful phenomenon. Empirical development has, therefore, governed the greater part of the history of ships, the drive for this deriving from mankind's strong desires to enquire and explore.

The story of sail is thus a protracted one with a tentative and uncertain beginning. In the earliest times the motivation of food-gathering, rivalry, power, escape, war and trade were closely inter-twined, but like a length of rope unravelling to expose first its strands and then its myriad individual fibres, development gradually quickens, dividing first into vessels capable of venturing offshore, then to sea and finally across oceans. The specialist categories of man-of-war and merchantmen next emerge, then quickly split into sub-groups, each striving to acquire that fitness-for-purpose that provides the dynamic for further improvement. Many of the basic concepts which still dominate merchant ship development were in place before the final demise of sail. While there were no container sailing ships, sailing vessels were bulk-carriers and there were sailing tankers carrying oil and these were fitted with electric lighting. Moreover, those specialised vessels which today quest for oil and gas, have their origins in the auxiliary men-of-war, whalers and sealers whose steam engines gave them power to drive through ice, or to beat a calm, but whose sail-plans gave them the endurance necessary for protracted voyaging.

Local wind systems such as prevail in the Mediterranean, were known of to the first true sailors, but understanding the global winds was a matter largely ignored. The monsoons of the north Indian Ocean and China Seas were used by early

European voyagers to the Orient and kept the voyages of East Indiamen to a stately schedule, but despite the seventeenth century observations of William Dampier, which he enshrined in his *Discourse of Winds, Breezes, Storms, Tides and Currents,* such elemental studies were the hobbies of devoted data-catchers like the British whaling captain, William Scoresby. It was not until 1830 that James Rendell published collected information on the world's winds and ocean currents and this work was continued by Lieutenant Matthew Maury of the United States Navy, who promulgated seasonal data, so that ocean voyaging could be planned to take advantage of favourable prevailing winds. This coincided with a general upswing in the education of sea-officers and the establishment of seafaring as a more thoroughly professional undertaking than had hitherto been the case.

Long after the first tentative study of meteorology, then called, not inappropriately, 'atmosphereology', came the development of the sciences of hydrodynamics and, later still, aerodynamics. These further influenced sailing ship design and once science had made its impact, matters changed rapidly. Hull design in deep-water shipping was, until the first quarter of the nineteenth century, largely governed by a shipowner's desire to maximise cargo carrying capacity and minimise the effects of customs and tonnage dues. This restricted experimentation, so that whilst the small craft of the world burgeoned in remarkably diverse form according to the demands of their operational locality, the round bow, splendidly buoyant though it was, remained the dominant feature of large European ocean-going vessels. Between about 1814 and 1820, at the end of the Napoleonic War, it was the hollow hulls of the parvenu Yankees that shook British complacency and led to rapid reassessment of design parameters. Breaking the grip of outmoded regulation by rendering it obsolescent in the face of superior competition, the pioneers of free trade initiated an extraordinary explosion of enterprise. British and other European shipbuilders met this challenge with enthusiasm and vessels ceased to be generally characterised by their hull form, and were described by the configuration of their rig.

With no major European war to disrupt commerce, the nineteenth century saw the foundation of the technological age at sea. The greatest spin-off, migrating from land applications to marine use, was of course the steam engine, but it is often forgotten that the steam ship did not oust the sailing ship overnight. Difficulties with its own development, the simultaneous rapid expansion of the world's economy and the requirement for low cost freighting, ensured the merchant sailing ship co-existed profitably alongside the steam ship for a century before the disasters of war finally disposed of the last, oceanic sailing traders. It was, in fact, the inability of sail to conform to the modern convoy system, though it had done so admirably in the past, which ensured its demise when confronted with the submarine and torpedo. Notwithstanding this, sail was to linger on where commercial conditions favoured the economic advantages of the low running costs which sail still conferred. Coastal sailing vessels endured in European waters until well within living memory, and linger yet in some quarters of the world, while fishing in sailing vessels prevailed on the coast of China until recently, and may still be found in many parts of the so-called Third World. But such vestigial remnants lack the investment of new ideas and are vanishing slowly as the reliability, availability and economic advantages of the diesel engine supervene.

And yet, despite the economic imperatives which overwhelmed the sailing ship as a global carrier, experimentation does still continue. The increasing fascination with the natural world and the sustainable if erratic resource of the wind, the wide appeal of physical sports and the ever-present urge in men and women to compete, has ensured sail an enduring place into the next millennium. The challenges posed by the omnipotent power of natural forces, ensures that sailing craft continue to develop in the form of hi-tech racing yachts which, apart from their natural motive power, embrace the most sophisticated materials and technologies available to modern mankind. The story of sail, though largely fulfilled in its broadest commercial sense, continues to stimulate the same primitive endeavours that first made man curious as he contemplated a log, sporting perhaps an upthrust branch with a few dried leaves still upon it, as the wind blew it across a lake.

A Note on the Drawings

In the illustration pages following, the master scale of the drawings is generally shown by a rule in both metric and imperial measures. Variations have been kept to a minimum, in order to make the comparative sizes of the vessels more obvious, and scales are mostly in simple multiples of a hundred – 1/200, 1/300, and so on. Some details within the drawing may be reproduced to a different scale for clarity, but these and other variations from the master scale are indicated in the captions. The numbers *in italics* within parentheses at the ends of the captions indicate the principal source(s) for the drawing, which can be found by reference to the numbered list at the end of the book (beginning on page 348).

Primitive Sail and the Birth of Seafaring

THE EARLIEST FORMS of boat barely justify the name, being nothing more than buoyancy aids or crude rafts. Yet they contributed to the nascent story of sail by providing primitive man with a platform for traversing water, and he cannot have been insensible, being a sentient creature, to the fact that the wind affected his path across the lake or lagoon he wished to traverse. Perhaps it was first to combat the tendency of the wind to frustrate him, that he devised the paddle, since he would have found even a light breeze defeated his own feeble efforts to provide motive power by his hands or feet. Soon he must have realised the advantage conferred by using this force, possibly from observing the different track followed by a log with a branch full of leaves. After this he might have carried his own branch with him, noticing perhaps that he was losing energy through the rustling leaves, something which did not happen if he spread a cloak with his arms – he did not even have to go afloat to experience the effect of the wind in a cloak or blanket. On applying the principle to his early boat, he might now have remarked that his craft accelerated, even that it buried itself or rolled over even more menacingly than before. Such empirical development led, in due course, to the concept of the displacement hull, though our early waterman can have understood nothing of the principles enshrined in his pre-Archimedean naval architecture. His fast, paddleable dugout would roll without an out-rigger, while his reed raft proved superbly stable, though slow. By careful adaptation, using the natural materials to hand, he would have tentatively progressed towards something that better answered his needs.

Thus, by means of slow, evolutionary development, a simple sail plan emerged, to be harnessed to advantage particularly where a prevailing wind blew contrary to the current of a river, such as the mighty Nile. As hull forms improved, man wanted to push beyond the rivers of Egypt, Mesopotamia, India, China, or South America, where a greater challenge lay. The Persian Gulf and the Mediterranean Sea in particular, being land-locked, are subject to a system of winds which in some areas are predictable and in others conform to certain observable weather patterns and are thus deductible by a shrewd observer. These enabled seasonal voyages to be made under sail so that both war and trade could be pursued by successive civilisations and societies from the predynastic Egyptians to those first major commercial seafarers, the Phoenicians.

Where aboriginal societies required nothing more than the simple performance of simple craft, many such boats have survived into the present century, particularly among the descendants of the earliest civilisations, such as the Marsh Arabs of Iraq, or the riverine Chinese. Such people, still using reed-boats and hide rafts, provide us with our most convincing evidence of how and why our forefathers went afloat. These relics of prehistory initiate the story of sail.

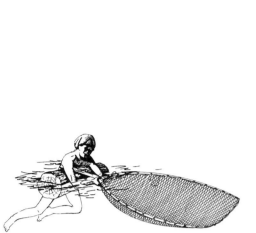

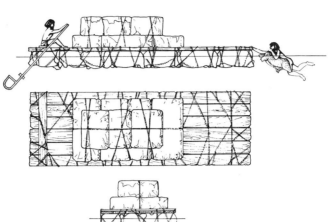

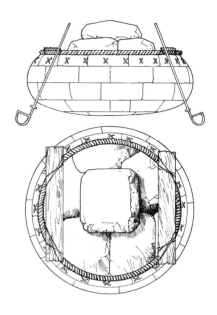

River Kaveri fishing float, early twentieth century. In the rivers of southern India, fishing methods used into the present century employed a floating log of wood to enable the fisherman to guide his hand-held net. *(88)*

Assyrian *kelek*, about 700 BC. A raft in almost any form is stable enough to allow heavy weights to be conveyed with considerable ease when compared with a similar load committed to ox-drawn carts. This Assyrian 'kelek' is based upon animal skins, rendered with salt and grease, and either inflated or stuffed with straw or reeds. Lashed to a framework of wooden staves, such a raft could be made to a considerable size, while

remaining light and portable. Suitable for carrying anything from bundles and bales, to horses, cattle and siege engines, the kelek was an early cargo-carrier, displaying the superiority of water over land transport to shift major loads. Depicted in relief carvings dating to *circa* 700 BC, keleks have been widely used across southern Asia, surviving on the Tigris and Euphrates until recent times. *(244)*

Assyrian *quffa*, about 450 BC. The circular reed-boat of Mesopotamia is mentioned by Herodotus around 450 BC. Known as a 'quffa' it had probably already been in use for 5000 years when the historian observed it. Made of reed well payed with bitumen, the quffa came in assorted sizes and was used for fishing as well as a cargo-carrier. Truly adaptable, the craft, which was sometimes given a hide skin, could be used for bridging rivers. *(244)*

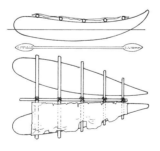

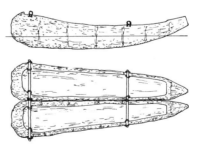

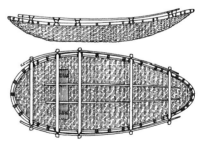

South American *caballito*, 1565. Observed by the *Conquistadores* in 1565, the caballito from modern Ecuador and Peru was a simple raft made of balsa planks or whole trunks and undoubtedly predated the arrival of the Spaniards by several centuries. The inherent stability of the trio of lashed planks, marks it as a considerable technological advance on the simple log, allowing a man to draw in fishing nets from a steady platform. Larger balsa rafts, based on this principle, are believed to have made trans-Pacific voyages as replicated in 1947 by Thor Heyerdahl in *Kon Tiki*. *(243)*

Chilean seal skin raft, 1732. By combining the stability of the raft, the buoyancy of the inflated dressed animal skin and a roughly hydrodynamic shape, the fisherfolk of northern Chile produced the seal skin raft observed and reported by Europeans in 1732. *(187)*

Indian double dugout, twentieth century. The dugout, although possessing the directionally stable advantages of a ship-shape, capsized easily and had little transverse stability. However, by lashing two together and tapering the shape, an early displacement craft begins to produce the advantages of a raft. Much less vulnerable to damage, this double dugout canoe was constructed from coconut palms and could be found on the Kistna and Godavari rivers of Andhra Pradesh in southern India into the twentieth century. *(88)*

Vietnamese basket boat, early twentieth century. The reed or 'basket-boat' has many forms and is found in many places. Like the quffa and the Welsh coracle, this boat from Vietnam is of a primitive but enduring type, still being used in the twentieth century. *(88)*

Guyanese dugout, 1883. An observer in Guyana recorded the use of a bush as a sail on a dugout in 1883. The way conferred by the wind in the bush on the canoe, could be further controlled by the steering oar. *(244)*

Chinese inflated skin, early twentieth century. Believed to be one of the earliest ways of crossing a river, the inflated animal skin is no more than a glorified buoyancy-aid, a temporary means of assisting men and women desirous of crossing an obstacle. Yet these survived for thousands of years, used by Tibetan nomads in the Himalayas and by the Chinese to cross the upper reaches of the Huang-ho river in the twentieth century. *(227)*

Tasmanian raft, 1824. The worldwide similarity of aboriginal solutions to the problem of flotation is seen here by this boat made from eucalyptus bark by the now extinct indigenous natives of Tasmania and recorded by an English observer in 1824 before its builders were exterminated. *(244)*

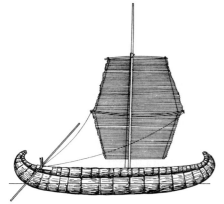

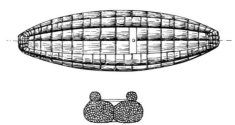

Totora reed raft, Peru, twentieth century. A more sophisticated form of sail, made like the raft, of local reeds, was reported in Lake Titicaca, Peru, in the mid-twentieth century. The sail is spread partly by its material, but also by a stiff yard and controlled by two braces, which swivel the yard about the mast.

The construction of the Titicaca reed boat shows the heavy bundles necessary to give buoyancy to the load and a form of bulwark provided by side bundles which improved freeboard. The buoyant quality of a reedboat deteriorated with age, while the waves generated on a large lake, required some form of deterrent to swamping. *(244)*

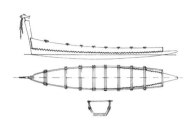

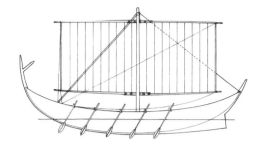

Aegean boat, third millenium BC. About 2800 BC, boats such as this were in use around the Aegean Sea. A simple dugout has been given greater freeboard and thus increased seaworthiness by extending its sides upwards by means of flat, split planks, stitched on by hide thongs and stiffened by cross battens. The raised sternpost may initially have had little more than a totemic significance. *(43)*

Cretan vessel, about 2200 BC. Iconographic evidence from Crete dated to the latter part of the Third Millennium BC shows a sail-driven, high-sterned hull. This was partly derived from the necessity of stitching timbers and then drawing them together at bow and stern where the totem device proved useful and could

be repeated forward as a stempost. This gave a pleasing and useful sheer, but it was equally necessary to protect a hull usually employed running down-wind with a following sea. The projecting forefoot gave directional stability and, while suggestive as a ram, cannot have originally been intended as such. *(43)*

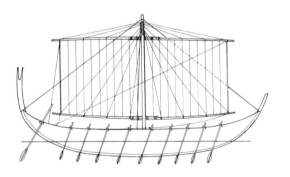

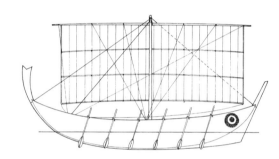

Cretan vessel, about 2000 BC. Of similar age, Cretan vase fragments suggest the fitting of vertically lashed, but swivelling stern paddles to act as rudimentary steering devices and mounted on either quarter. *(43)*

Cretan vessel, about 2200 BC. Strengthened by ribs, Cretan ships of the era between circa 2200-2000 BC also had thwarts for the crew, whose oars could pass through rope loops secured to the gunwale. Stem- and sternposts were now a necessary fea-

ture of construction, enabling free-board to be increased by stitching on additional side strakes, while the any totemic image or artefact could be shifted to the bow as a painted device. *(43)*

Earliest Ships

We know that prehistoric man was traversing water by means of boats at an early period, as early as 30,000 BC in the case of *Homo sapiens sapiens* who crossed what has since become the Bering Strait. We know also that it was soon appreciated that large weights could be carried by raft and that a favourable current and helpful prevailing wind could be used to advantage. With these endeavours came the need to form a hull more able to cope with the disturbed surface of more open water, and with this hull form moves away from the merely buoyant, to the displacement craft with its hollow shape. Central to the story of sail is a by-product of this new hull form. Not only did a vessel that sat *in* water facilitate the task of the paddlers or oarsmen, it had *bite*, and was less susceptible to drift, making control under sail more effective. Such vessels still made a large amount of leeway, but when the chosen direction was largely down-wind, this did not greatly matter.

Nordic skin boat, about 2000 BC. A roughly contemporaneous hull from Scandinavian rock drawings from Nord Trøndelag, Norway, dated around 2000 BC, suggests an early form of the Inuit 'umiak', or 'kayak'. Although a simple skin of stitched hides stretched over a light framework of wood, the hull form, with its pointed bow and stern, and low sheer, has pretensions of elegance. Its long life attests to its suitability for its task of fishing in enclosed fjords or waters protected by broken ice. *(43)*

Nordic skin boat, about 2000 BC. To increase its size and render the umiak more suitable for the transport of large cargoes, or to facilitate portages over land or ice, rock pictographs show a long wooden runner fitted along the bottom and lashed to the extended gunwales by short vertical timber struts. Early decorative terminals seem to have been fitted to the stem and stern. *(43)*

1/300 30 20 10 0 ft
8 4 0 m

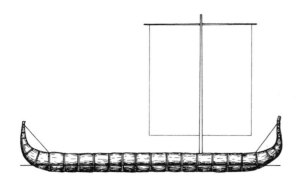

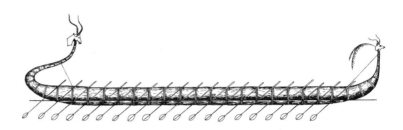

Predynastic reed boat. Predynastic Egyptian societies existing along the banks of the Nile before 3400 BC, the date of the founding of the Old Kingdom, ventured onto the great river in reed boats of papyrus which grew in profusion along the banks.

Depictions of boats believed to date from as early as 6000 BC show early sail forms, paddles and steering 'oars'. Bow and stern were gathered together, making beaching and launching easier and giving some 'sea-kindliness' to the otherwise basic hull. *(113) Scale 1/150*

Predynastic reed boat. Iconographic images on pottery, rocks and graves show versions of the predynastic papyrus reed-boat, here decorated with the skulls of antelope or bull. *(113) Scale 1/150*

Egyptian Vessels

The early Egyptian civilisations owed their existence to the cyclical flooding of the flood plain of the lower reaches of the River Nile. These annual inundations have been recorded since 3600 BC and the fecundity of the land depends upon them. The Nile also provides a great highway through Egypt, while its constant northward current facilitates traffic in that direction. Travel upstream was possible by using the counter-current close to the banks when the river was not in spate. More effective, however, was harnessing the northerly wind known as the *Bai*, meaning 'the ram', to overcome the strength of the river. It is not therefore surprising that the early Egyptians took to the Nile, nor that they were soon able to make use of sail, though the inconstant nature of favourable winds meant that manpower provided a means of propulsion for much of the time. Nevertheless, the availability of the Nile encouraged development of ever larger hulls, so that when the Pharaohs wished for the transport of large, stone obelisks, Egyptian technology was able to provide the means. In addition to iconographic sources which provide such evidence as the Pharaoh Ity eating whilst aboard a reed-boat on a fishing expedition, the tombs of these kings have revealed models of their riverine craft.

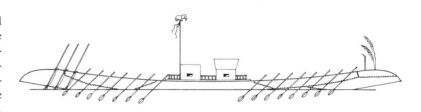

Predynastic boat. Such craft were suitable for basic commercial traffic, but hide covered versions seem to have been constructed for persons of rank and dignity, propelled by many oars and with multiple steering paddles. *(113) Scale 1/150*

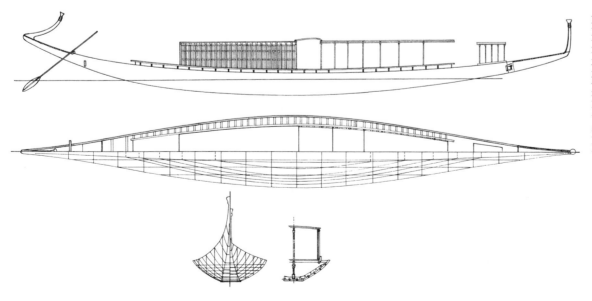

Royal ship, about 2650 BC. Pharaoh Khufu, or Cheops of the Old Kingdom, who reigned about 2650 BC, is thought to have ventured on the Nile in a boat constructed of planks held together by pegs and stiffened by ribs. The hull shape thus obtained is long and elegant. This is a reconstruction of the vessel discovered in 1952 alongside the Great Pyramid at Giza. It is probably the world's oldest relatively intact ship *(113) Scale 1/300*

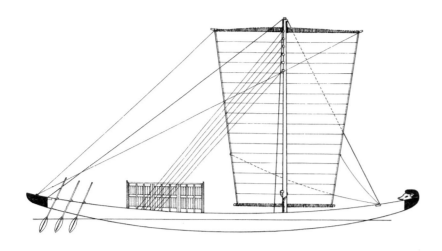

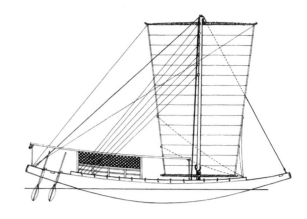

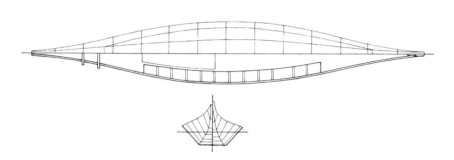

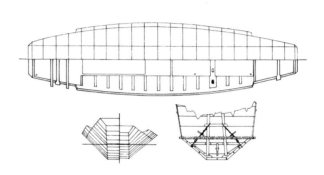

Old Kingdom passenger vessel. The appearance of sail shown on a relief of about 3000 BC shows a bipod mast supported by several backstays, spreading a braceable yard. The planked construction has an after platform upon which several helmsmen steer, while a shelter on deck indicates some form of shade for the passengers. *(113)*

Old Kingdom boat. From a different but roughly contemporary source at the time of the Old Kingdom, this sailing boat is substantially similar. The bipod mast, set on the central, flat, longitudinal planking, is steadied by heavy fibre rope set tight by inserting a stave and tensioning it by twisting, a method later known to seamen as a 'Spanish windlass'. *(113)*

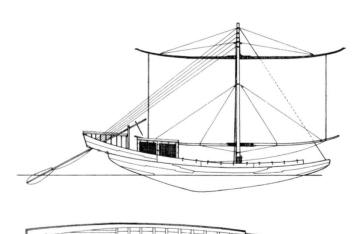

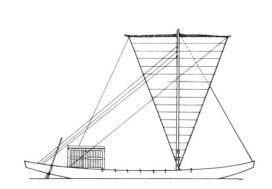

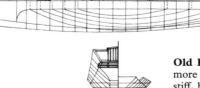

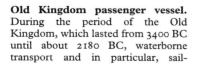

Old Kingdom passenger vessel. During the period of the Old Kingdom, which lasted from 3400 BC until about 2180 BC, waterborne transport and in particular, sail-powered vessels, became commonplace. Interpretations of graphic evidence show a variety of craft of which this is a simple version. *(113)*

Old Kingdom passenger vessel. A more complex vessel, still with the stiff, bipod mast well stayed from aft, shows a steering oar set at a shallow angle which would make it very efficient. The sail is spread by yards top and bottom, both of which are controlled by braces, though the bottom pair might be regarded as sheets. *(113)*

1/300   30   20   10   0 ft
          8   4   0 m

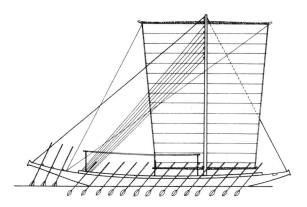

Old Kingdom boat. A papyrus vessel, with paddles and sail retains the standard form of the Old Kingdom. *(113)*

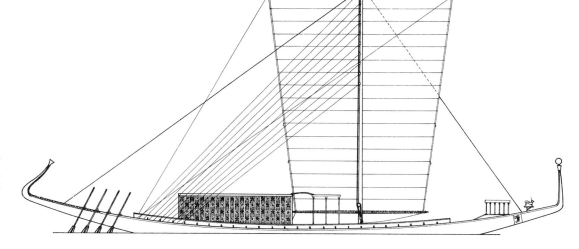

Sea-going ship, about 2400 BC. Early sea-going voyages were made by the Egyptians in the reign of Sneferu around 2600 BC, but Sahure in about 2400 BC nursed real naval ambitions. This is a royal ship from the time of his reign. *(113)*

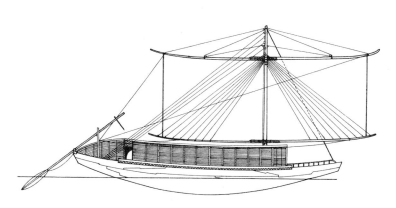

Old Kingdom merchant vessel. Passengers and merchandise were carried on the Nile Delta and perhaps beyond, in merchant vessels such as this sturdy craft of the Old Kingdom. *(113)*

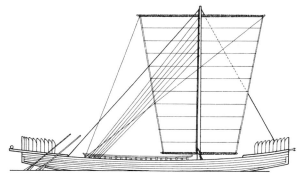

Old Kingdom river vessel. A stout riverine cargo-carrying craft of the same period. *(113)*

30   20   10   0 ft
1/300
8   4   0 m

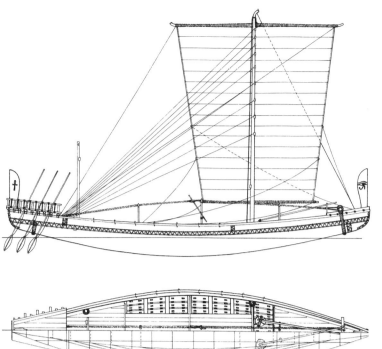

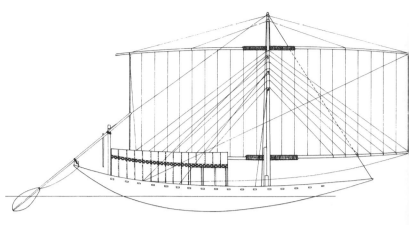

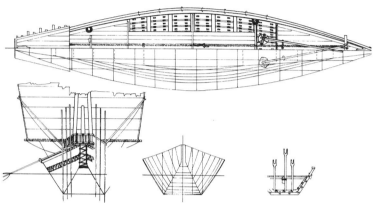

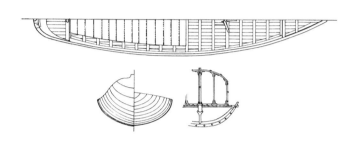

Sea-going ship, about 2400 BC. In the sea-going vessels of Sahure, dated from a detailed relief of 2400 BC, are seen the characteristics of the riverine craft with modifications to enable them to take the greater stresses of sea-going. Here the length of the wooden hull, built of thick pegged blocks and further held by water pressure, is also girt by two ropes, wracked together, while overall a twisted rope runs from stem to stern, tensioned by twisting. The sail could be removed and stowed, and the bipod mast lowered, converting the craft into an oared galley, doubtless for war, for Sahure's fleet laid waste the Syrian coast and brought home Phoenician prisoners. Religious emblems decorated the stem and sternpost, the eye of Horus being the most ancient decorative form to linger on into modern times. *(113)*

Riverine ship, about 2180 BC. Something of a breakdown in law and order occurred in Egypt around 2180 BC and although trade was probably affected, life in this transitional period went on. This river craft, based on models from the tomb of Mehemkvetre, vizier to the Pharaoh Mentuhotep, has a mast made from a single pole. It could be lowered and its base had a stone counter-weight to facilitate this, from the mast lines extended from the mast to support the very wide lower yard which is constructed in two sections. The models show the forestay securing to a short spar, forming a bowsprit. The hull has a rounded bilge and would be heavily loaded or ballasted to confer stability. The very large steering oar is braced against the stern and a vertical spar to which the lowered yard was lashed. Steering is accomplished by a tiller lashed at right-angles to the loom of the steering oar. Also visible are the cross beams which, protruding through the hull, were pegged and held the sides together, dispensing with the rope girding in the Sahure ship left. *(113)*

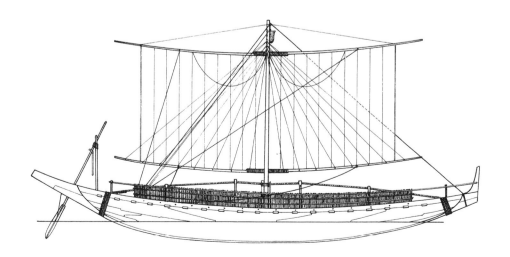

Sea-going merchant ship, Middle Kingdom. The New, or Middle Kingdom, emerged out of the disruption of the transitional period. By now coastal voyages were possible, using the technology first revealed, though probably developed earlier in merchant vessels, of combating the tendency of the hull to hog at sea by using a longitudinal tensioned rope brace. The block construction, though clumsy, would have served well as a cargo carrier. Clearly the tiller has become a feature of Egyptian ship technology. *(113)*

1/300

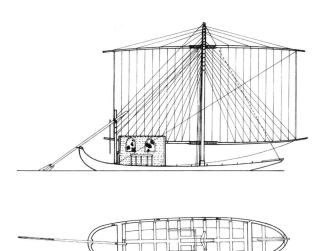

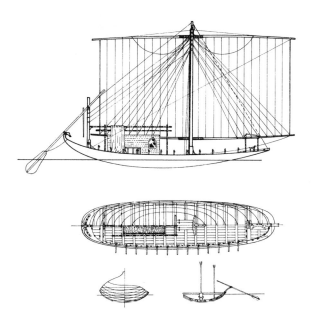

Middle Kingdom estuary vessels. These craft, built for the sheltered waters of the Nile Delta or the lower reaches of the river during the period of the Middle Kingdom embrace the advances found elsewhere in craft built for a more challenging environment. They demonstrate the standard form Egyptian vessels had achieved by about 2000 BC. *(113)*

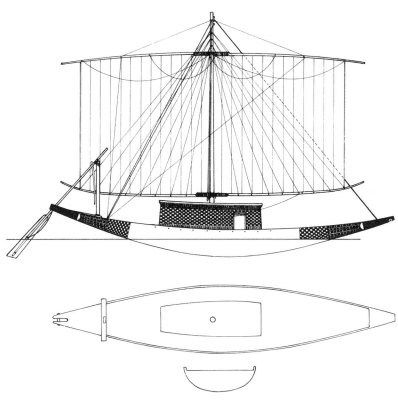

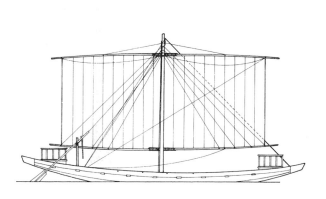

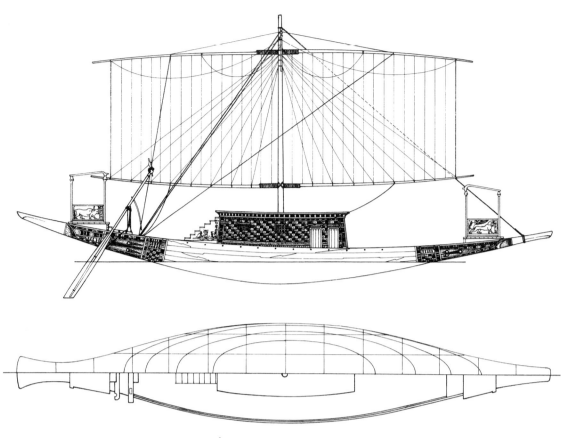

Royal vessel, New Kingdom. This beautiful reconstruction of a Pharaonic royal vessel is an early example of the notion of state splendour being shown afloat. It is a theme that was to be found irresistible by the projectionists of power of all ages. *(113) Scale 1/150*

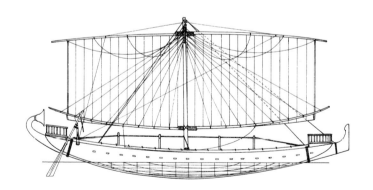

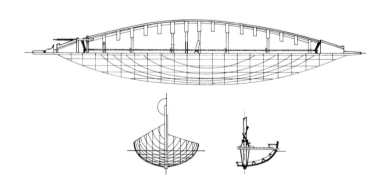

Sea-going merchant ship, about 1500 BC. Contemporary with the obelisk ship opposite is this example of a fleet of merchant ships, sent by Queen Hatshepsut, co-regent and sister of Thotmes II, to the land of Punt to bring back supplies of ebony, ivory, myrrh-resin, gold, incense, coursing dogs and apes. Punt is thought to have been on the African coast at the southern end of the Red Sea, so the ship marks the highest achievement of Egyptian naval architecture, fitted out for a major expedition. *(113) Scale 1/300*

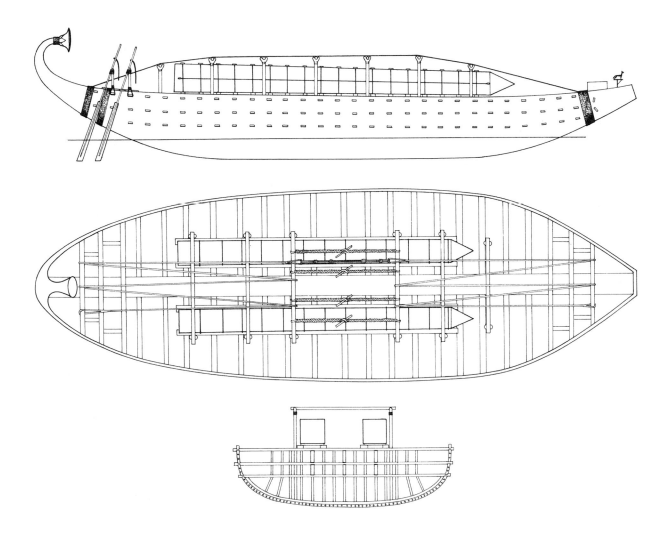

Queen Hatshepsut's obelisk transport, about 1500 BC. The building of temples at Heliopolis and Luxor in about 1500 BC, required the transport of two large obelisks from the place of their quarrying and fashioning upstream near Aswan. One was intended to commemorate Queen Hatshepsut's father, the second the queen herself.

To accomplish this task a huge barge was built, using the basic block construction, with three rows of retaining cross-beams and held by no less than four longitudinal tensioned ropes. Although manned by oarsmen, clearly visible in the rock reliefs in the temple of Deir el-Bahri, the queen's burial place, and not sailed, the importance

of these vessels is the realisation that Queen Hatshepsut's order called into being hulls capable of bearing great weights. No other means of transport produced by the hand of man has exceeded the load-bearing capability of a ship's hull. *(112)*

40   30   20   10   0 ft

1/400

10   5   0 m

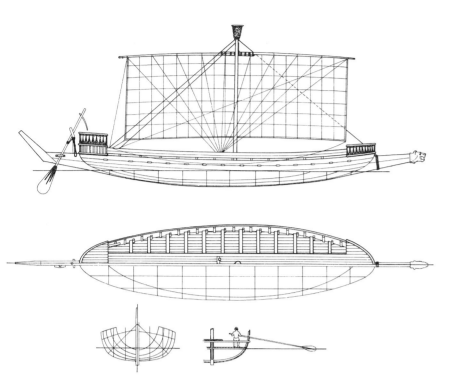

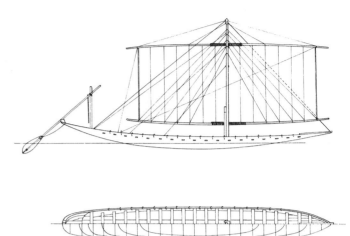

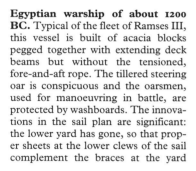

Egyptian warship of about 1200 BC. Typical of the fleet of Ramses III, this vessel is built of acacia blocks pegged together with extending deck beams but without the tensioned, fore-and-aft rope. The tillered steering oar is conspicuous and the oarsmen, used for manoeuvring in battle, are protected by washboards. The innovations in the sail plan are significant: the lower yard has gone, so that proper sheets at the lower clews of the sail complement the braces at the yard arms, and the sail is brailed up to the heavy yard which is steadied by several lines. Other interesting features are manifest: the top at the head of the mast from which a lookout could be maintained and which in battle might have supported archers; the extending timbers which provide a ram, and the barriers at bow and stern, in which might be discerned forerunners of the fore and after castles which were to feature in later ship design. *(163)*

Egyptian vessel, Middle Kingdom. This light, dispatch boat is an auxiliary, featuring in Ramses's fleet. Its estuarine derivation is clear, for the Egyptians were not, by nature, seafarers. *(113)*

The First War Vessels

The Egyptians had encountered rival societies in the eastern Mediterranean as early as 3000 BC and vessels were trading with Egypt by around 1500 BC from the islands in and around the Aegean. Here a war between the Greeks and Minoans had resulted in the latter being driven out of their Cretan homeland. It is possible that the Minoans are the enemy known to the Egyptians as the Sea People, or the People from the Sea. Other suggestions are that they were Mycenaeans, Phoenicians or Therans, but whatever their origins they invaded Egypt and precipitated war with Ramses III. The battle, the first recorded naval engagement, is depicted on the victorious Pharaoh's tomb and marks the entry of the warship into the story of sail.

Ramses failed to follow up his victory by making Egypt a sea-power and his country fell into a long decline. Meanwhile the Phoenicians prosecuted a vigorous trade, founding a commercial empire extending the length of the Mediterranean, passing the Straits of Gibraltar and reaching Britain. But this dominance was soon challenged by a less advanced but more rapacious people, the Greeks who quickly populated the archipelagos of the Aegean and Ionian Seas and swiftly developed the oared galley, a potent and uncompromising weapon of war.

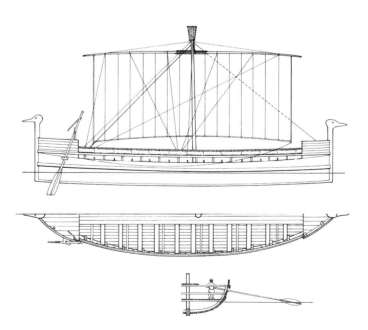

Ship of the Sea People, about 1200 BC. The similarity of the vessels opposing the Egyptian fleet is marked. It is believed that it was from the mysterious Sea People that the Egyptian shipbuilders copied many features. However, although conjectural, the Sea People did not appear to build their hulls on the same principle of block construction as the Egyptians, and this may have made them superior in manoeuvring. *(215)*

1/300   30   20   10   0 ft

8   4   0 m

Greek vessel, about 3300 BC. The oared vessels of the Dorians, a Bronze-Age tribe who, about 3300 BC invaded Greece and established the beginnings of Greek civilisation, developed large dugout craft. This made the incorporation of the ram bow a matter of ease, though the fulcrums for the oars had to be provided by an extended framework. *(112)*

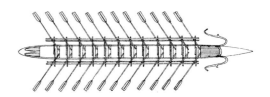

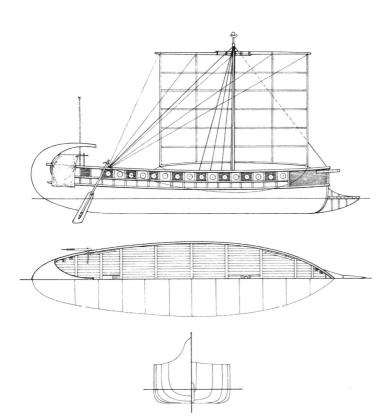

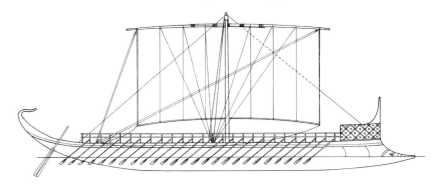

Single-banked *Pentecontor*. The *Pentecontor* had variants, such as this single-tiered sailing version. Lesser galleys were also named for the number of oarsmen, such as the 30-oared *Triacontor*. *(63)*

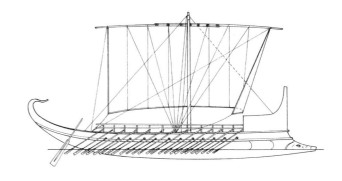

Phoenician warship, 500-400 BC. The earliest civilisation to cultivate a maritime culture, was that of the Phoenicians, whose oared warships of the fifth to fourth centuries BC were technologically advanced, having oarsmen places on two tiers, but employing a brailed and braceable sail. *(138)*

Double-banked *Pentecontor*. A shorter, two-tiered *Pentecontor* exhibits the standard Greek ram bow and forward protection to archers and spearmen massed at the point of attack. *(63)*

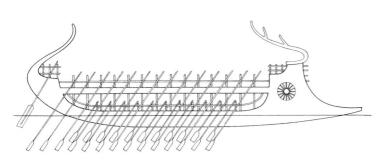

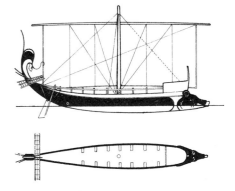

Pentecontor of about 760-710 BC. The Greek *Pentecontor* of this period followed Phoenician design and was pulled by fifty oarsmen, hence its name. *(63)*

Greek galley, about 400 BC. Somewhat stylised and extravagant versions of the Greek galleys of the fourth century BC figure on pottery, yet it is clear that warships at this period had already acquired a metaphysical dimension, invested as they were with the pretentious ambitions of their commanders. This example invokes the hydrodynamics of the fish to prosper its purpose. *(242)*

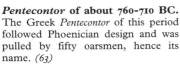

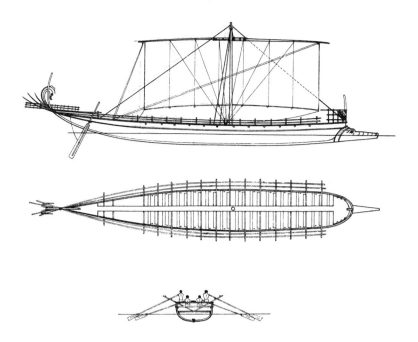

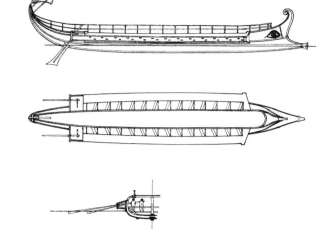

Greek bireme galley, about 500 BC. This two-tiered galley of the fourth century BC was known as a bireme and has a storming bridge running the length of the vessel and enabling fast reinforcement of a boarding party. The crocodile-headed ram was probably not an integral part of the keel, but detached after a lodgement in an enemy's side to avoid irreparable damage to the attacking craft. *(112)*

Greek bireme galley, about 400 BC. Another Greek bireme of the same period has a wide, stable hull. Mast, yard and sail would have been lowered during battle. Note the tripartite finned bronze ram of a form that was to remain standard for hundreds of years. A large, later example of such a ram was discovered at Athlit in 1980. Its design made ramming, even at glancing angles of attack, a very potent tactic *(112)*

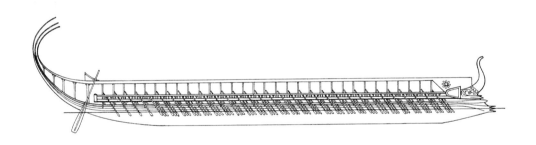

Greek trireme, about 500 BC. The 'secret weapons' of the Athenian fleet which defeated the Persians at Salamis in 480 BC were three-tiered triremes, the largest and most powerful warships of their day. A fortuitous discovery of silver enabled the Athenians to build a fleet of 200 triremes to confront the ships of the Persian King Xerxes. *(157)*

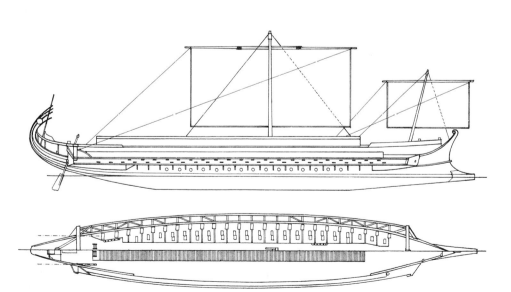

Greek *Trihemiola*, about 190 BC. This was a variant galley with two full and one half row of oarsmen on each side. Evidence suggests the vessel was a fast, light galley, clearly as suitable for use by lawless elements, as for the formal navies of the Greek states. They became common in the eastern Mediterranean and this one, from about 190 BC, sets a forward mast. *(63)*

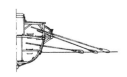

Speculative reconstructions of trireme layout. The arrangements necessary to work three rows of oars have challenged scholars for some time and a number of solutions have been suggested. The upper row were known as *thranites*, the middle row *zygite* and the lower row, *thalamites*. The ascending order was well enough understood at the time for the playwright Aristophanes to indicate the *thranites* and *zygites* 'made wind into the face of the *thalamites*'. *(39)*

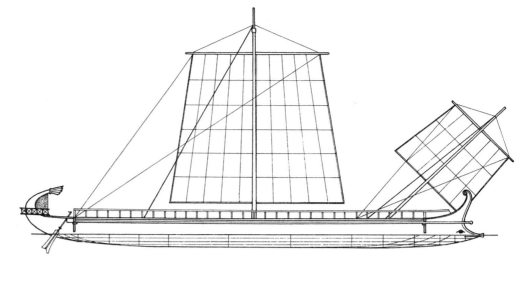

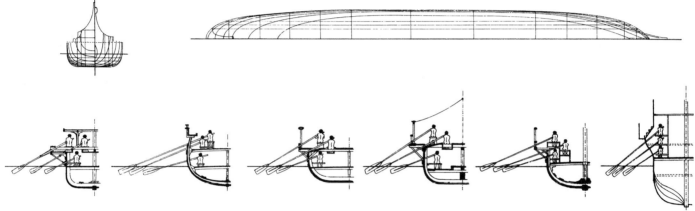

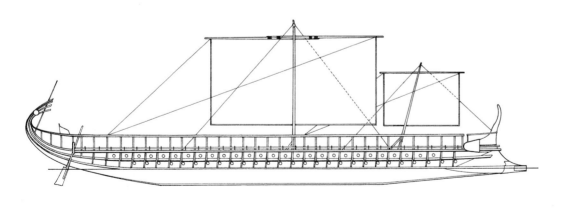

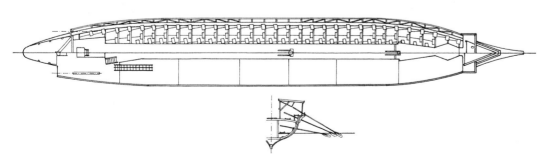

***Olympias*, trireme reconstruction, 1987.** Speculation as to the practicalities of operating a trireme have largely been laid to rest by this modern reconstruction. The *Olympias* was built by the Hellenic Navy. Based on ancient accounts, iconographic evidence and academic research, *Olympias* verifies the abilities and achievements of the galley as claimed by contemporary sources. *(63)*

1/300 30 20 10 0 ft
        8   4   0 m

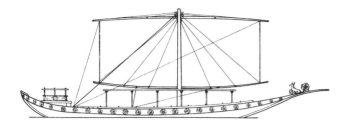

Cretan ship, seventeenth to sixteenth centuries BC. This trading vessel shows an early, controlled sail. *(141)*

Cretan ship, seventeenth to sixteenth centuries BC. This Minoan ship from the Thera frieze shows a splendidly decorated vessel with canopied accommodation for someone of great importance. *(66)*

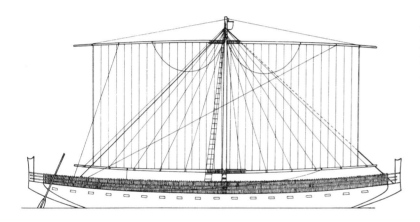

Syrian ship, contemporary with the 18th Egyptian Dynasty. This ship would have traded with the Nile Delta. The 'through-beam' construction of the Levant is clearly shown, as is the lookout position and ratlined shrouds enabling access to be gained in what was then the primary aid to navigation, the human eye. Freeboard is increased for an offshore passage by reed bulwarks. The easy removal of these would facilitate the loading and discharge of cargo. *(113)*

Sail Traders of the Ancient Levant

The ancient civilisations which grew up around the shores of the eastern Mediterranean were more often engaged in trade than war, developing strong and capacious ribbed and carvel-planked hulls for the carriage of cargo. Unable to employ oarsmen or unwilling to purchase slaves, merchant vessels had to harness the wind out of a more pressing necessity than state-owned men-of-war. The need to earn profits therefore drove the development of efficient sails and the means of controlling a sailing ship in a seaway.

Early forms of such ships are largely conjectural and derive from iconographical evidence which is stylised, resulting in distortions and embellishments probably in excess of the reality, though opulent decoration cannot be ruled out in the case of craft belonging to rich merchants or officers of state whose duties took them afloat in pursuit of customs dues and other tolls.

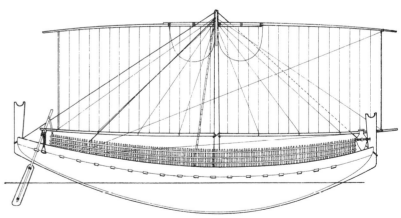

Phoenician merchant ship of about 1500 BC. Similar characteristics are to be seen in this later vessel. Such craft would have been very beamy and, if off the wind to any extent, would have made leeway. The amphora forward probably held drinking water, much in demand when she was rowed in calm weather or when proceeding through sheltered waters. *(113)*

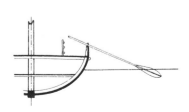

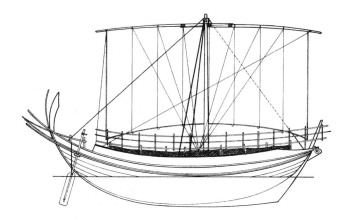

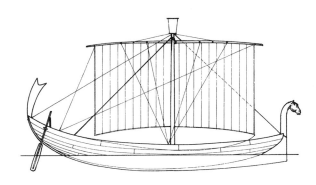

Greek merchant ship of about the eighth century BC. The city-states of the emerging Greek world engaged in trade using vessels such as this. Carvel planking on a framework of stout timbers, or ribs, provided a strong, beamy hull, with plenty of room for cargo. The sail is loose-footed and the flat stem indicates the ship was designed to do little more than run before the prevailing wind. *(112)*

Phoenician merchant ship, about 700 BC. It was the Phoenicians who first traded extensively and developed a primitive sea-going ship. Though largely making coastal passages, voyages out of sight of land were often carried out in such a vessel as this merchantman of circa 700 BC. Both lookout position atop the mast and the loose-footed sail increasingly characterise practical rig configurations. *(112)*

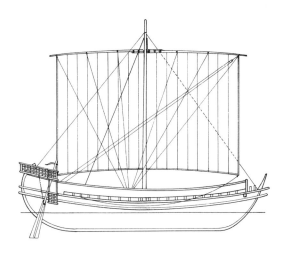

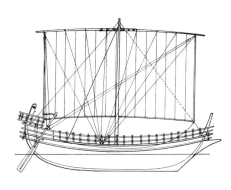

Cypriot merchant ships, fifth century BC. A standard form can be seen emerging in these Cypriot traders of around 500 BC. Both exhibit a fitness-for-purpose that reflects the best practice in the naval architecture of their day, combining a strong, hollow hull, with a workable sail plan. A commanding position is assumed aft, where, on the starboard quarter, the steering oar is positioned. *(114)*

The Kyrenia ship, about 300 BC. The sturdiness characteristic of successful merchant ships throughout history is to be seen in this Greek example of the late fourth century BC, based on the wreck excavated off Kyrenia, Cyprus, in 1968-69. The high stern still shows the prevailing danger as being pooped by a following sea and therefore such a vessel never tried to do more than harness favourable winds when making a passage. *(244)*

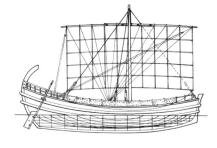

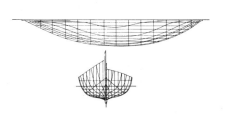

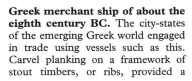

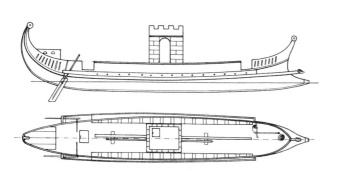

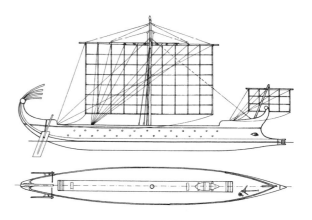

Hellenistic trireme of 323 BC. In the years following the death of Alexander the Great a naval arms race took place among the Hellenistic successor states, and it was this kind of large multi-banked galley that Rome adopted for its early naval forces. This example bears a curious castle-like structure, almost certainly of wood, which is confirmed from several pictorial sources. This was obviously a strong point from which to launch an attack, with the added advantage of providing a citadel from which a counter-attack could be launched in the case of being boarded. *(213)*

Roman bireme, about 150 BC. The Romans relied heavily upon a fleet of ageing Greek galleys to challenge the might of Carthage at sea. Unsurprisingly, this produced biremes of similar appearance to those of Athens, this example being of 150 BC. Shown in this drawing is an anchor, an efficient form of which was known to the Romans. The small forward sail was of use as much to manoeuvre such a long and heavy hull, as to give it forward motion and may well have been used in conjunction with the oars when the mainsail was doused. *(213)*

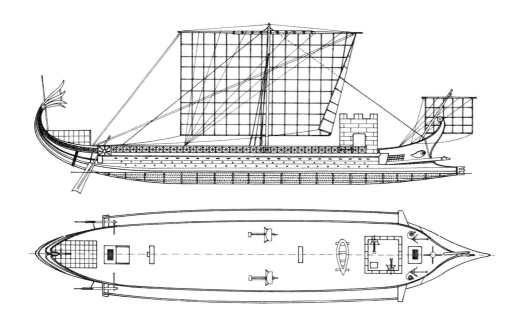

Roman trireme of 36 BC. This large trireme of the pre-Augustan period combines all the lessons of Greek and Phoenician experience. *(213)*

Shipping of the Roman Empire

The supercession of the Greek and Phoenician civilisations by that of Rome in the centuries before the birth of Christ saw a dramatic shift of power away from the Levant towards Europe and the west. The great military empire built by the Romans was largely land-based, though of course the cross-Channel incursion into Britain in 55 BC, followed by full scale invasion about a century later, required war galleys and military transports. It was however, the domination of the Mediterranean by the power of Rome which, thanks to the ensuing *Pax Romana*, enabled trade to thrive largely free of disruptive piracy. The defeat of Carthage, a consequence of Phoenician colonisation in modern Tunisia, during the Punic Wars established Rome as the dominant power in the Mediterranean, with even Egypt becoming a province of the Roman empire. Thereafter trans-Mediterranean trade flourished to the extent that the Roman market became the principal destination of the annual harvest of Egyptian grain, establishing a regular commerce in a bulk commodity.

1/300

30   20   10   0 ft

8   4   0 m

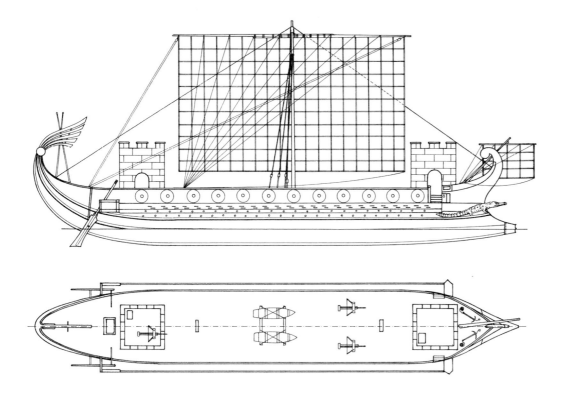

Quadrireme of 38 BC. Increases in power and speed required increased manpower and oars were no longer pulled by a single oarsman. Now several men were put to work on a single loom, something facilitated by the slave system and while no more than three rows of oars were ever practical, these multi-manned galleys were known by ascending numeric names, indicating the number of rowers on an oar-group. This would translate as a 'four'. *(213)*

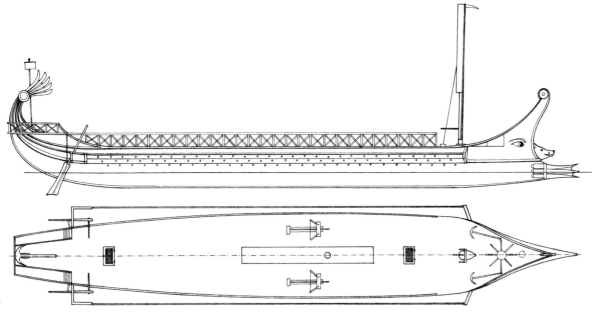

Quinquereme of 260 BC. This 'five' shows the increased beam necessary to accommodate the additional galley slaves. The formidable ram, similar to the example discovered at Athlit, was a bronze fitting designed to penetrate the waterline of an enemy craft. However, even the disablement of a row of oars could render a galley inoperable. This galley carries the great Roman invention, the *corvus*, a hinged boarding bridge which turned sea warfare into the kind of land battle in which the Romans excelled. *(213)*

30   20   10   0 ft
1/300
8   4   0 m

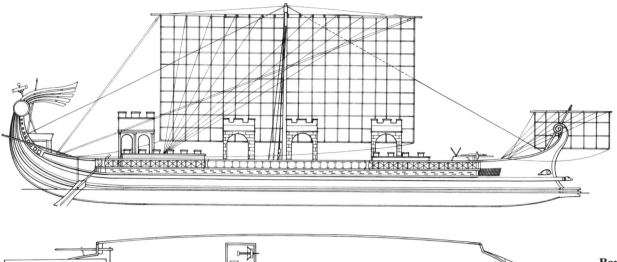

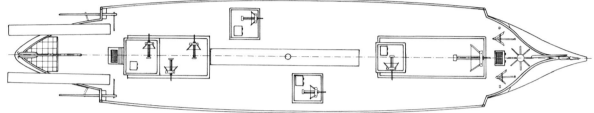

Roman galley of AD 118. Archaeological evidence confirms the considerable size of many Roman galleys. This is a *hexeris*, or 'six', a capital ship of the Augustan age, it mounts catapults capable of hurling Greek fire, an inextinguishable mixture chiefly containing naptha. *(213)*

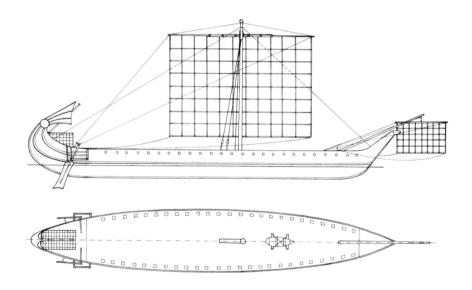

Lembus, **third-second century BC.** Used for reconnaissance, the *lembus*, or 'liburnian', was similar to the *hemiola* and derived from the craft used by the Illyrians inhabiting the eastern shores of the middle Adriatic. Usually powered by a single bank of oars the Romans adopted the type during the Punic Wars, about 240 BC. The most interesting feature is the shifting of the small foresail onto a bowsprit, where its effect used in conjunction with the rudder would have been dramatic and was probably valuable to a small, vulnerable warship in escaping from an attack by a superior vessel. *(213)*

Cargo vessel of the Rhine, second and third centuries BC. This depiction shows a remarkable development, the sprit rig. Such a boat would have been capable of using the wind to greater advantage, working to windward and even upstream against a current, since it falls within the generic family of the fore-and-aft rig. As such, this small *oraria navis* is the forerunner of scores of types of sprit-rigged craft, successive generations of which emanated from the Low Countries of the Lower Rhine. This may be the type known from written sources as a *caudicaria*. *(213)*

Navis lusoria **of the fourth century AD.** The defence of an empire required the patrolling of borders, particularly those along the river frontiers in the north, beyond which stretched the 'barbarian' lands of the Germanic tribes. At the height of the Roman Empire's greatest expansion, such a task was undertaken on the Rhine by small vessels like this. Under sail or oars, this is a river warship. *(213)*

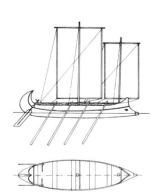

30   20   10   0 ft

1/300

8   4   0 m

Cargo vessel of the Rhine, Roman era. A similar small cargo-carrier from the Rhine, this *oraria navis*, or coastal vessel, appears to have existed over some six centuries, from the first century BC until the fifth century AD. This may be the type known from written sources as a *musculus*. *(213)*

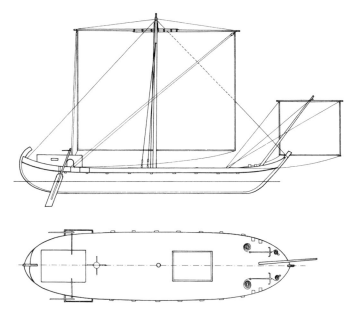

Cargo vessel, fifth century AD. The diversity of ship-types used within the Roman Empire reflects both its extent and the degree to which it was susceptible to many influences. This marine transport from the Levant, dating from the break-up of the Empire, shows strong Arab characteristics, predominantly in the huge lateen yard and its triangular sail which, like the sprit-rig in Northern Europe, was not only a fellow member of the fore-and-aft family, but was to have a profound effect upon the small craft of the Mediterranean for a thousand years. *(213)*

Coastal trader of the fourth century AD. This vessel appears capable of modest voyages, with accommodation aft for her passengers. She is decked, with a hatch, broad of beam and has a forward sail making her handy manoeuvring in confined waters such as rivers. The increasing sheer forward suggests she was able to sail across the wind, perhaps even point slightly to windward, since the windward clew of her mainsail could be led well forward. *(213)*

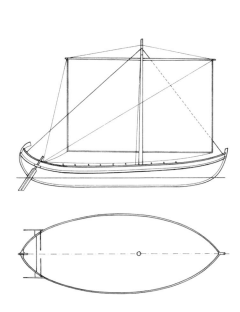

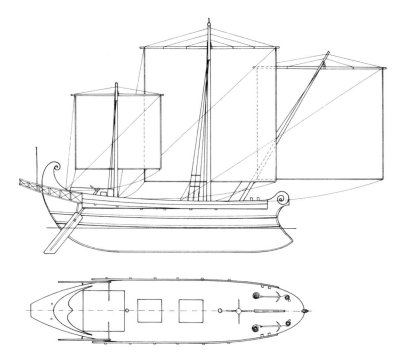

Cargo vessel, third to the fifth centuries AD. Further diversity is shown by this more conventional coastal cargo carrier of the last centuries of the western Empire, plying her trade in the Mediterranean. The generic term *oraria navis*, of which this is one, signified a coastal ship and they were subdivided by function, shape or some other characteristic (this may be the type known as a *lenunculus*). The broad beam makes this an ample and serviceable workhorse. *(213)*

Coastal trader of the second century AD. This more complex coaster was probably used for short-sea voyages. Her rig, suggesting the first stirrings of a three-masted configuration would, in differing combinations, be able to sail upon several headings relative to wind direction. Note the increasingly spade-like profile of the steering oars and its ever more robust securing arrangements. *(213)*

1/300 30 20 10 0 ft
8 4 0 m

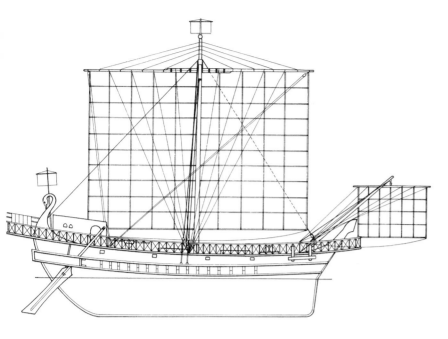

Roman merchant ship, first century BC. This ship is an example of the large Roman merchant vessel such as forged a supply bridge for grain between the fields of the Nile basin and the granaries of Rome. A short-sea trader built for capacity, her heavy mast supports a single sail and is set up with rigging tensioned with deadeyes. The sails in such craft were brailed up and triangular topsails, or rafees, were set above them. Accommodation is again provided by a deckhouse, while an awning set over a platform running out over the stern is either quarters for the master, or may be a latrine. As a grain-carrier, she would be called a *corbita* after the basket carried as a masthead signal of her cargo. *(213)*

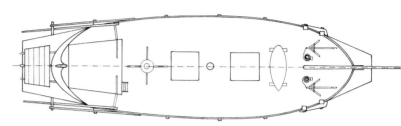

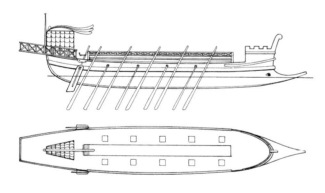

Three classes of liburnians, first century AD. The lower reaches of the wide rivers throughout the Roman Empire provided a highway for trade and required policing. Such craft as are depicted here were named after the Liburni, a piratical Illyrian tribe from Dalmatia. The eponymous term spawned a variety of craft, all loosely known as *Lembi*, or Liburnians, noted chiefly for their light construction and speed. These examples were used in river, estuary and coastal work during the last century BC. *(213/63)*

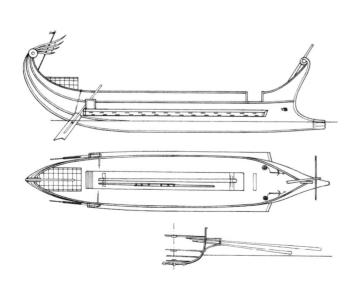

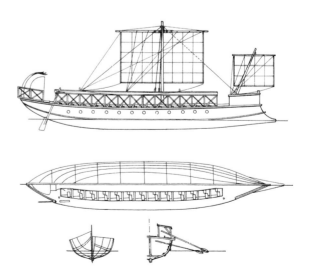

30   20   10   0 ft
1/300
8   4   0 m

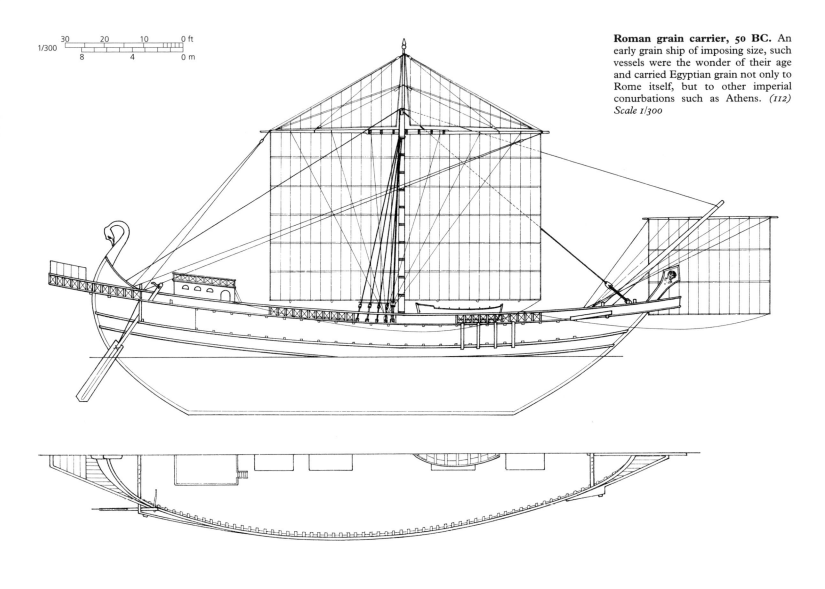

1/300 30 20 10 0 ft
8 4 0 m

Roman grain carrier, 50 BC. An early grain ship of imposing size, such vessels were the wonder of their age and carried Egyptian grain not only to Rome itself, but to other imperial conurbations such as Athens. *(112) Scale 1/300*

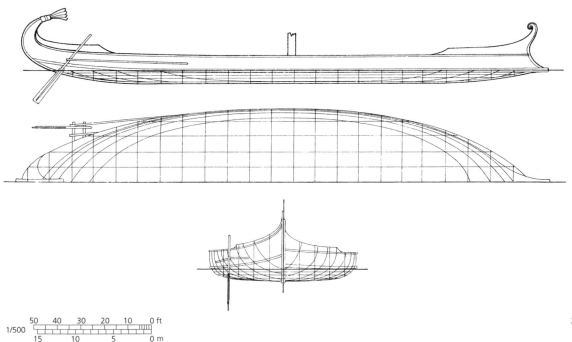

The Nemi barges. Hauled from Lake Nemi in 1932, two huge Roman-built hulls revealed the abilities of Roman shipbuilders both in terms of construction methods and size. Originally thought to have been built by Caligula (AD 12-41), coins found on site suggested a later period, perhaps even AD 165. The burning of the recovered hulls during the Second World War prevented carbon dating being applied. The larger hull was 70 metres in length, of carvel construction with inner ribs. It was also fitted with transverse beams of iron and an anchor weighing 1400kgs. Tarred woollen fabric sheathed in lead formed an outer skin. Whatever their origin, their function was probably to remain static as floating palaces. *(139) Scale 1/500*

1/500 50 40 30 20 10 0 ft
15 10 5 0 m

Shipping of the Roman Empire 31

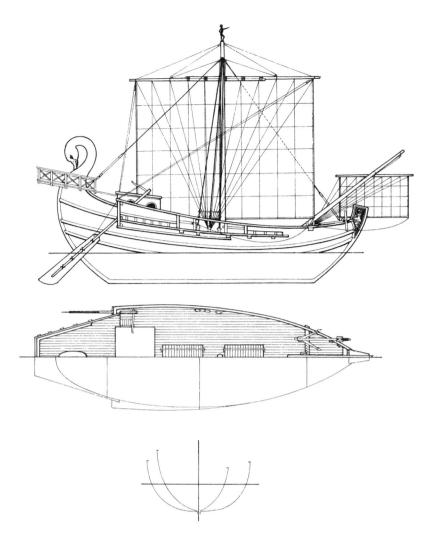

Judean merchant ship of about AD 150. A fore-and-aft rigged vessel which would perform well on a run or reach when traversing the coasts of the Levant from modern Turkey to Egypt. *(150)*

Roman merchant ship, second century AD. The proliferation of such images suggests they were a common, though imposing, sight. There can be little doubt but that such vessels were well known to the inhabitants of the Roman ports during the imperial centuries. Sturdy, sea-worthy and capacious, they represent a fully-fledged seagoing merchant vessel of handsome proportions. *(138)*

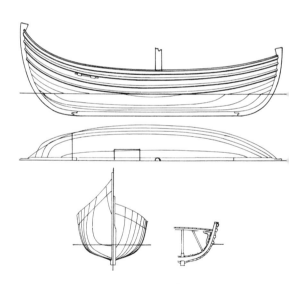

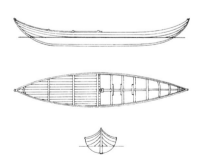

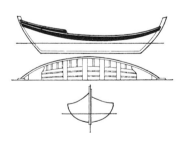

The Golo boat. This boat was found on the bed of the Golo River in northeast Corsica during the eighteenth century. Being entirely constructed with wooden pegs, its lack of iron fastenings suggests an origin in classical times and is probably Roman. *(167)*

Roman ship's boat. A second century boat of the kind carrried by the merchant ships of the period. *(138)*

Byzantine merchant ship, about AD 625. Located off the Turkish coast at Yassi Ada, this wrecked vessel was excavated between 1960 and 1964. The hull was heavily framed, with carvel planking, suggesting the ship was a merchantman, but also demonstrating the move from classical shell-first construction to a less labour-intensive method of raising the frames first. She had eleven anchors, probably for mooring offshore to work her cargo and it was conjectured that she had a lateen rig upon her single mast. The wreck was documented but not preserved. *(11)*

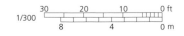

Sea-going Sail

ALTHOUGH IT IS KNOWN that the Phoenicians voyaged beyond the Strait of Gibraltar as far as the Azores and to the remoter coasts of Britain, as far as we can tell, their ships remained vessels designed for the Mediterranean. But the great stirrings of migration in Asia were to force the inhabitants of northern Europe to become the first maritime colonisers, just as they were to threaten, and in due course destroy, the might of the Roman Empire. The Scandinavians, in taking to the sea, were to develop a beautiful, sea-going ship, capable in time of making long voyages, for the Norse longship was both a trading and a raiding vessel.

The primitive peoples of northern Europe had, by about AD 500, adapted the hide-covered, wooden framework form into a long boat shape. In the course of this evolution, the hide had been replaced by thin, flat planks split from felled trees and sewn together, giving greater strength and rigidity to the resultant hull. Later, planks would be nailed to each other to produce the lapstrake, or clinker-built longship.

The genesis of the longship was to run concurrently with that of the larger merchant traders of the Mediterranean in which the lateen sail became the principal driving engine. Oars remained important to both these northern and Mediterranean traditions, and the war galley continued to dominate warship design, being the only form of specialised war vessel built.

In the aftermath of the demise of the Roman Empire, an era regarded as a Dark Age in western Europe, the emergence of Norse sea-power and the foundations of European feudalism under the aegis of the Pope at Rome, were to produce an inevitable collision between Christianity and Islam, for the new faith of the Arab peoples had soon created an empire extending from modern Turkey, along the North African coast and into Spain. The wars of the Crusades were to produce a fusion of the hitherto distinct methods of ship construction of northern and Mediterranean Europe. The importance of this was both a contributor to the Renaissance in Europe, for as the coalescing nation-states of Christendom emerged from the Medieval era, ships had changed radically. Not only had a method of construction been found in which an increasing degree of control over hull shape could be asserted, but a sail-plan capable of going to windward became the norm. Most significantly, European builders had adopted the centreline rudder. The means by which they did so is unknown, though the device was already known to the Chinese, but it is quite logical that the idea simply occurred to someone.

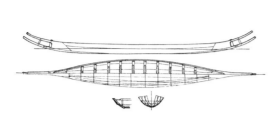

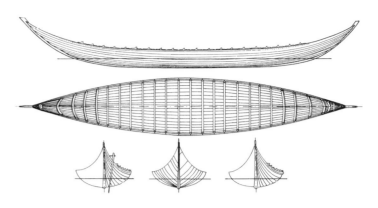

The Hjortspring boat, fourth-third century BC. Found in 1921, in a bog at Hjortspring on the Danish island of Als, the remains of a plank-on-frame hull reveals the extent to which northern Europeans had initiated a new technique by 350 BC. Some 15 metres in length, with a central keel, a garboard strake and single side planks of split lime, the hull is strengthened by longitudinal gunwales and transverse, internal hazel frames, which were lashed to the planks. *(54)*

The Sutton Hoo ship, about 600 AD. Studies of the sixth-century burial ship found in 1939 at Sutton Hoo in Suffolk, England, show a more sophisticated longship of some 27 metres, with a central keel to which a tall beakhead and a sternpost were bolted. Nine tapered and scarphed planks were fitted on each side of this keel, with a reinforced section on the starboard quarter for a steering oar. Transverse strength was given by fashioned ribs, inserted after the hull form had taken shape from the natural curve of the planking. *(48)*

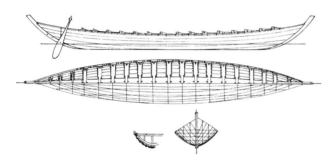

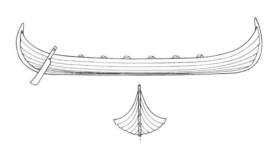

The Nydam boat, later fourth century. Dating from AD 350, the hull of an early, oared longship was found in a peat bog at Nydam in southern Denmark in 1863. A triumph of ingenuity, the 25-metre hull consisted of only fifteen pieces. Each overlapping strake was secured to its neighbour by iron rivets, the hull being stiffened by oak branches lashed to cleats on the planks and providing the basis for rowlocks against which the oars could be pulled. A steering oar and ballast were found in the excavation, and although it is unlikely that such a longship was sailed, she was capable of making an extended voyage, probably in stages. *(54)*

'Viking age ship'. This reconstruction shows the likely form of vessel in which the peoples of Scandinavia first voyaged across the North Sea to the British Isles in the fifth century, harassing the remnant Romano-British and establishing Anglo-Saxon kingdoms. They were later to be followed by a Danish invasion. Such incursions also extended down the coast of the modern Netherlands to France, establishing a Norse 'colony' in what came to be called Normandy. Oared at first, in such ships the utility of a sail must soon have become obvious. **NB.** Twice Scale *(20)*

The Norse Tradition

As early as the first century, the Roman historian Tacitus wrote of the ships of the Sviones of the north, that they were the same at both bow and stern. The sharp, double-ended 'Viking' longship, with its decorative shields and dragon's head bow, is one of the most enduring images in the iconography of ships. The evidence for the hanging of shields along the vessels' sides is flimsy, but there is no doubt that the longship not only took the Norsemen to Iceland, Greenland and Vinland, in North America, founding maritime colonies in those remote locations, but became the standard major ship-type in the cultures that resulted from the Norse diaspora. It is thus in longships that Duke William of Normandy, himself descended from the Norse chieftain Rollo who had struck a settlement bargain with the King of the Franks a century earlier, invaded southern England in 1066. William, known to history as 'The Conqueror', defeated the incumbent Saxons, whose own ancestors had themselves previously voyaged across the North Sea from Denmark and what is now North Germany. The British Isles in particular, were subject to successive waves of tribal incursion and invasion by Jutes, Angles, Saxons and Danes, and the ships in which these people came are remarkably beautiful creations.

The development of lapstrake construction, perfected by AD 400, had, by the end of the first millennium after Christ, incorporated the keel and produced a hull not merely capable of voyaging abroad, but doing so under sail, over the open sea and making ground against a foul wind. The origins of the Norse rig are obscure, but logical, and it was somewhat hampered mainly by using woollen homespun, a baggy material. For fighting at sea, platforms were built in the bow for the *stafnbui*, or 'stem-dwellers', the fighting elite of a longship.

30   20   10   0 ft
1/300
8   4   0 m

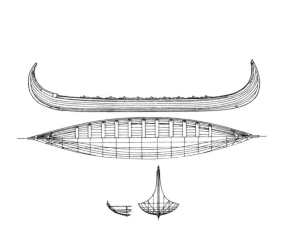

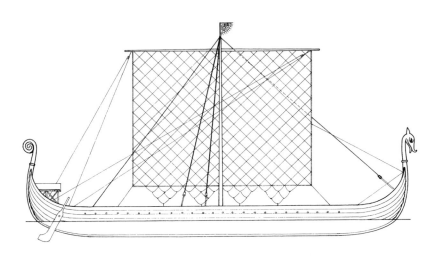

The Kvalsund boats, about AD 700. In 1920 the remains of two vessels were found at Kvalsund in Norway. Dating from about AD 700, the larger was a 16-metre hull over 3 metres in beam and capable of bearing a mast and sail; there is extant, contemporary iconographic evidence of such hulls with a single mast and square sail. The smaller (below) was about 9.5 metres long and was rowed with two pairs of oars. **NB.** Smaller boat, below, is twice scale. *(54)*

Viking *drakkar*, eighth century AD. By the eighth century, the classic Norse longship was approaching its peak with the *drakkar*, or dragon-ship. As with Mediterranean war-boats, bow and stern are obvious places for intimidating decoration, but most significant are representations of the sails, made of weak homespun wool and therefore reinforced with doubling strips, probably of leather. Rock carvings clearly show a sheeting arrangement consisting of bridles, while the long yard spreads the sail aloft. *(112)*

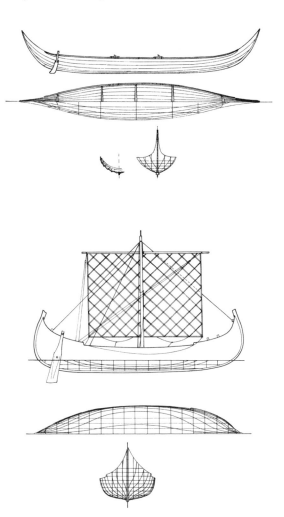

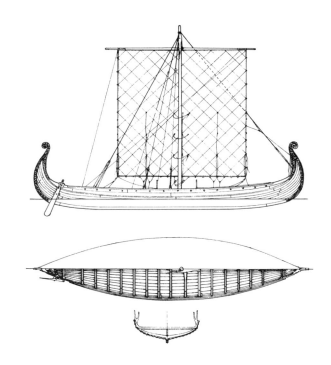

The Äskekärr ship, about AD 800. In 1933 a Norse merchant ship of the eighth century was found near Äskekärr, on the Gota River in southern Sweden. Full-hulled for capacity, such a ship worked her cargo clear of the 'steerboard', using the opposite or lading side, so that starboard and larboard became the terms to distinguish each side of a vessel. *(114)*

The Oseberg ship, about AD 820. The hull of burial ship found in 1904 at Oseberg in southern Norway was 21 metres in length, had a beam of 5 metres, and dated from the early ninth century. Twelve oak planks were fitted either side of a keel, the ninth of which is heavy, a combined plank and stringer, known as the *meginhufr*. The clenched planks sheer upwards to elaborately carved stem- and sternposts. The sheer strake is pierced for oars, but most important is the clear evidence of a mast-step, indicating the former presence of a mast and sail. *(22)*

30   20   10   0 ft
1/300
8   4   0 m

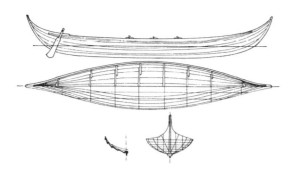

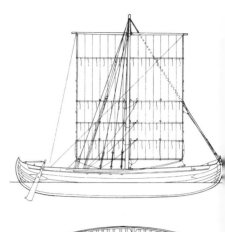

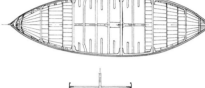

The Gokstad ship of about AD 890.
A find in 1880 at Gokstad, also in southern Norway, of a rather later ship, shows a more seaworthy hull of 24 metres in length, with a beam of 5 metres (below). As in the Oseberg ship, the hull was strongly constructed and pierced for oars, though no thwarts were present. The oarsmen, it is thought, sat upon wooden chests containing their effects, utensils, stores and weapons. A heavy mast step

and other evidence of blocks and a forward timber, called the *beitass*, which enabled the weather clew of the sail to be drawn forward and 'tacked down', is taken as evidence that such a ship could work to windward. This was demonstrated when, in 1893, a replica was sailed across the Atlantic in 28 days. The burial mound also contained the remains of three smaller boats, one of which is illustrated above at twice scale. *(54)*

Saga Siglar, **replica of Skuldelev 1, 1983.** A number of hulls, presumed sunk for defensive purposes before the ancient town of Roskilde in the Danish island of Sjælland in the eleventh century, were discovered in 1956. Seven years later excavations revealed five ships, named after the adjacent village of Skuldelev. A replica of Skuldelev 1, the *Saga Siglar*, was built later in order to learn more about Norse shipbuilding and seamanship, though the tradition of lapstrake building in Denmark remains unbroken. Skuldelev 1 was a broad, cargo-carrier with a bluff bow, known from the sagas as a *knarr*, but experiment showed *Saga Siglar* could beat to windward. She was a sea-going craft and in fact the replica has circumnavigated the globe. *(96)*

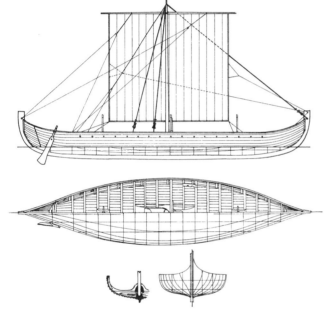

Roar Ege, **replica of Skuldelev 3, 1984.** This was a finer-lined coaster, probably used for carrying farm produce and similar to small boats used in the Baltic until the twentieth century. She also demonstrated a windward sailing capability. *(96)*

The Graveney boat, about AD 950.
An Anglo-Saxon hull dating from the tenth century was found at Graveney in Kent, England in 1971. A broad, lapstrake hull of 12 metres length and clearly typical of her time, demonstrates the widespread use of the Norse technique and its success. *(66)*

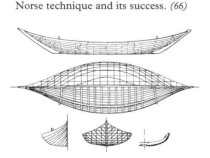

Ralswiek II boat, tenth century AD. An example of the smaller craft of the Viking era is the so-called Ralswiek II boat, a tenth century coaster, the remains of which were discovered on the German Baltic island of Rügen in

1967. The clinker-built vessel was 9.5 metres long overall and 2.5 metres in breadth; the sail-plan and steering oar are reconstructions. **NB.** Twice Scale *(52)*

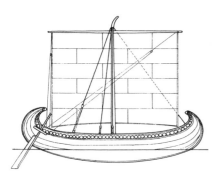

Sixth century Mediterranean coaster. The square sail continued to dominate Mediterranean sailing vessels until about the sixth century, when Arab influence began to impact upon the Mediterranean littoral. Eastern influence is here clear in both hull and sail-plan. *(152)*

Ninth century Mediterranean coaster. The Arab culture that spread with Islam along the North African coast, brought a modified hull form and the lateen sail to the Mediterranean by the end of the first Christian millennium. *(112)*

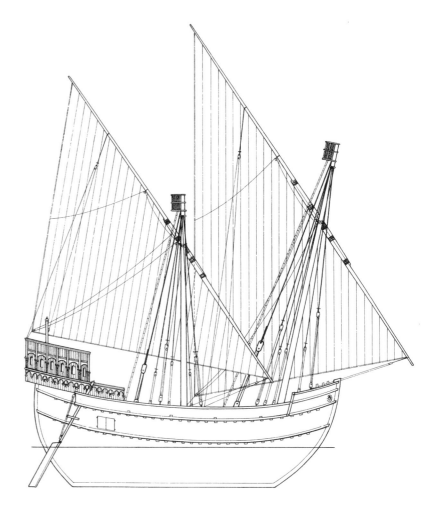

Venetian merchantman of 1268. The increasing importance of trade by sea was a pan-European phenomenon which, in the Mediterranean basin, grew out of centres of banking such as Venice. This Venetian merchant ship has an elaborate after cabin, but her hull is that of a craft capable of windward work, with its lateen sails. Note the tackles controlling the lower end of the heavy yards. *(112)*

Mediterranean Lateen

To what extent the presence of banks of oarsmen along the sides of a galley inhibited the operation of a square sail can now only be conjectured, but the setting of a yard along the longitudinal line of a vessel must have recommended the adoption of the Arab sail, known to northern Europeans as the 'lateen', a corruption of 'latin', and signifying Mediterranean, denoting its belonged to the culture of the Middle Sea. Although the sail seems to have been known in late antiquity, it was the vigorous proponents of Islam who popularised its use, bringing it to the southern and eastern shores of the Mediterranean, one of many manifestations of a scientifically-superior civilisation to that of Europe to the north. Versed in mathematics and astronomy, from which the art of navigation gradually emerged, the Arab contribution to the maritime history of European states emergence is often overlooked.

The superiority of the lateen rig must soon have commended itself to European seamen, especially the rising trading centres of Genoa and

Venice. The lateen yard was often made of two or three spars, lashed together, giving both length (often greater than the ship it served), and a flexibility which allowed the triangular sail set from this spar to form a naturally aerodynamic shape. The bowsing down of the forward end prevented the fitting of a forestay, so often the comparatively short mast was not only a heavy spar, but was stepped with forward rake. Although able to drive a ship to windward, the lateen was an extremely difficult sail to handle when manoeuvring in a seaway, the huge yard being liable to swing and take charge when tacking. It thus had to be treated with caution and handled with great skill and judgement – and preferably by a large crew.

Increased trade with the east brought about the development and increase of merchantmen sent to sea from several major ports in southern Europe, such as Venice, Genoa, Marseilles and Barcelona. These ships encouraged piracy, and the need for their protection against it.

30   20   10   0 ft
1/300
8   4   0 m

Genoese merchant vessel, thirteenth century. The city-states of thirteenth century Italy produced large numbers of merchant ships such as this Genoese vessel which plied in multiple commodities between her home port and the Levant. Note the fore and after structures, the crow's nests for lookouts and the rake of the foremast. *(112)*

Thirteenth century Mediterranean merchant vessel. Arab influence extended beyond the sail-plan and was adopted in decoration of the hull, the degree of which may well have served as an indicator of the success of the merchant house owning the vessel and thus as an advertisement. This ship, reconstructed from a very stylised contemporary illustration, may well have had Levantine owners. *(152)*

Mediterranean merchant vessel, mid-thirteenth century. Trade, with its possible advantages of profit, employment and expansion, encouraged the building of larger ships. To maintain sail-plans of manageable proportions, additional masts appeared, as in this three-master of the thirteenth century. *(152)*

30   20   10   0 ft
1/300
8   4   0 m

Fourteenth century single-masted vessel. Even small coasters, such as this, were capable of lifting cargoes larger than could be managed by a train of ox-carts and carriage of such quantities reduced the prices of commodities, thus speeding up and amalgamating local economies. The stowage of a cargo below decks in a covered hold was both secure and protective. A lateen-rigged hull like this, could be managed by a relatively small crew. *(228)*

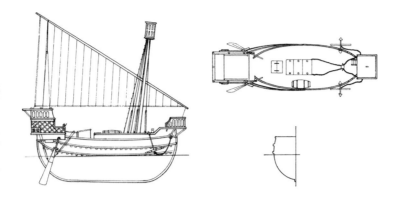

Fourteenth century Venetian ship. With the puissance of her owner proclaimed by the richness of ornamentation, this three-masted cargo vessel has a protective guard built over her steering arrangement, suggesting that she regularly lay alongside a quay. *(114)*

30   20   10   0 ft
1/300
8   4   0 m

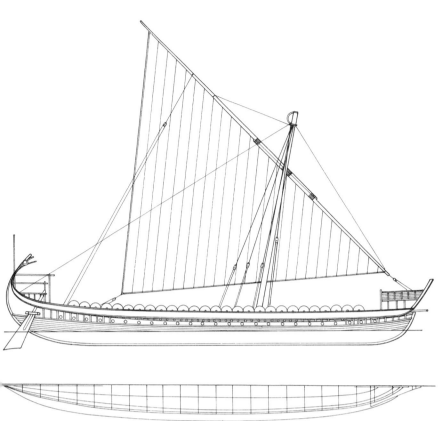

Medieval Galleys

As a means of power-projection, the galley was to exist as an arm of Mediterranean polity into the eighteenth century. Galleys came in several forms, but were specific warships, sent against the enemy by most major states on the shores of the Mediterranean, from the French in the west to the Saracen rulers of Syria in the east. The Greek concept of the citizen soldier, who would pull his oar before drawing his sword or hefting bow or spear, had long vanished. The Moslem despots of the Levant, the tyrannous feudal monarchs of central Europe, the Byzantine Emperors and the Dukes and Doges of city-states, found political undesirables and plain criminals a useful and economic form of propulsion. Even such charitable institutions as the Knights of Malta did not scruple to send men to the galleys, and the characteristic of these men-of-war was said to be the dreadful smell that accompanied them. In propelling these ships, it is clear that short, stabbing oar-strokes were necessary and a galley could make a passage speed of 4 knots, accelerating to double that during an attack.

Extant records of the Arsenale at Venice dated 1571 reveal that building and maintaining the state galleys employed over 15,000 people; that work was carried out at night when, in two days, the battle-fleet of 38 galleys could be readied for sea.

But galleys were not only important as men-of-war. They reached their largest form in the merchant *galea grossa*, the largest cargo carrier of her age. These merchant galleys were, moreover, sent beyond the Mediterranean and made voyages across the Bay of Biscay to the Rhine and Schelde, visiting the great northern port of Antwerp.

Byzantine *dromon*, twelfth century. Despite numerous descriptions of the prime Byzantine fighting ship, the *dromon* (a word derived from the Greek meaning 'runner'), visual evidence is very thin, and scholarly interpretations are very varied. This reconstruction of a twelfth-century example is some 35 metres in length. Fighting platforms or castles for archers, or catapults, are fitted at either end and a continuous overseeing deck runs from stem to stern. Greek fire, a much feared liquid incendiary the recipe for which was kept a secret, could not only be catapulted, but ejected through a pump mechanism the spout of which extends ahead of the stem. An auxiliary lateen sail is fitted. *(63)*

Byzantine *dromon*, twelfth century. Large bireme *dromons* of up to 50 metres, pulled by two rows of 25 oars a side, each manned by a single oarsman, were built for the rulers of Byzantium up to the twelfth century. Note the heavy timbers extending forward of the raked bow and forming an above-water spur rather than a traditional ram. *(114)*

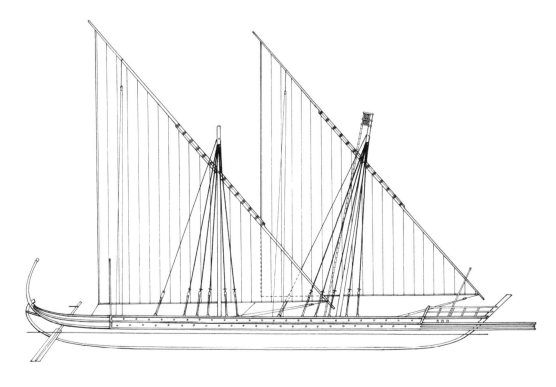

1/300

30   20   10   0 ft

8   4   0 m

Genoese galley of about AD 1200.
This reconstruction is based on pictorial evidence. The craft it represents is single-banked, with a heavy spur, or ram. A light, fast ship, with a forward fighting platform, it was clearly intended to make hit and run attacks and not built for endurance. It epitomises the tactical advantages, but strategic disadvantages, of the galley as a man-of-war. *(151)*

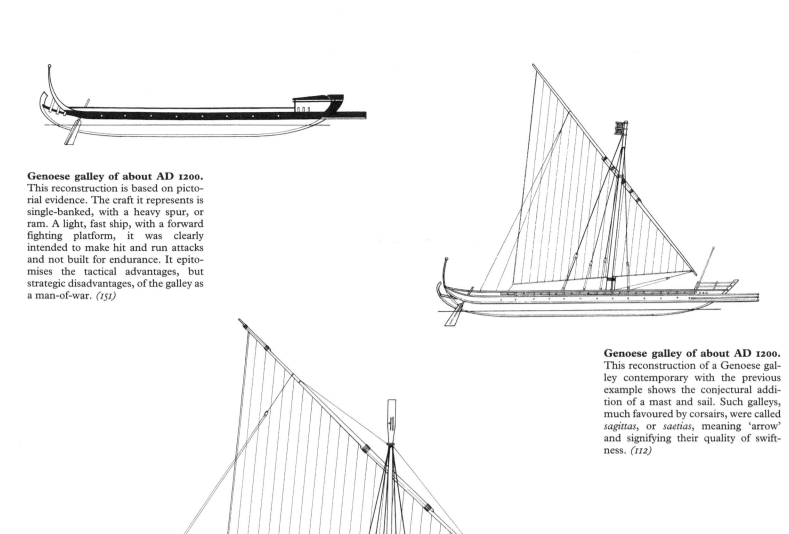

Genoese galley of about AD 1200.
This reconstruction of a Genoese galley contemporary with the previous example shows the conjectural addition of a mast and sail. Such galleys, much favoured by corsairs, were called *sagittas*, or *saetias*, meaning 'arrow' and signifying their quality of swiftness. *(112)*

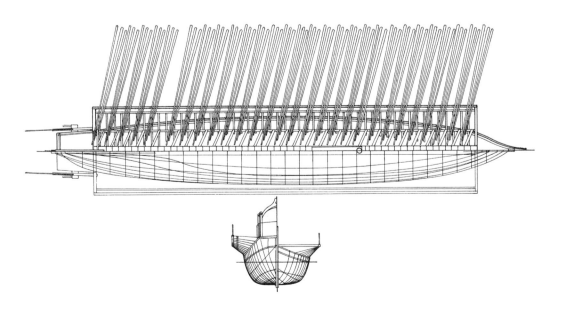

Venetian Flanders galley, 1410.
This *Galea de Fiandra*, or galley of Flanders, was a Venetian merchant craft fitted for service to the Rhine and Schelde. The rowing arrangements deployed the oarsmen for maximum effect. Three oars were pulled from each angled rowing bench. The thole pins against which each oar transmitted its effort to the hull were fitted along a framework extended out from the galley's side. This also served to bear the weight of the oar. Long after the fitting of rudders, this galley still carries two steering 'oars' in case the rudder was damaged. *(63)*

1/300

30   20   10   0 ft

8   4   0 m

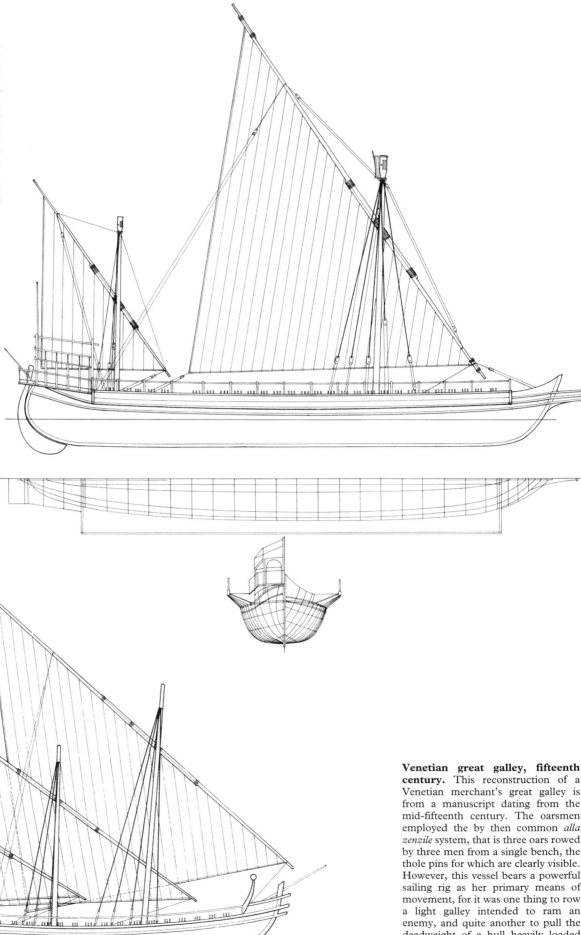

Venetian great galley, thirteenth century. Introduced by the Venetians in the thirteenth century, the 'great galley', or *galea grossa*, was a cargo vessel which sat 75 oarsmen a side. Her importance lies in the fact that, despite the oarsmen, she was primarily a sailing vessel, employing her oars in calms, or to escape corsairs. To this end, and having a large crew, she carries a huge mainsail, the yard of which is controlled by a number of tackles. Her after, or mizen, sail would enable her to manoeuvre, particularly during the protracted process of tacking. *(63)*

Venetian great galley, fifteenth century. This reconstruction of a Venetian merchant's great galley is from a manuscript dating from the mid-fifteenth century. The oarsmen employed the by then common *alla zenzile* system, that is three oars rowed by three men from a single bench, the thole pins for which are clearly visible. However, this vessel bears a powerful sailing rig as her primary means of movement, for it was one thing to row a light galley intended to ram an enemy, and quite another to pull the deadweight of a hull heavily loaded with cargo. The light spar projecting from her bow is a flagstaff. *(151)*

30   20   10   0 ft
1/300
8   4   0 m

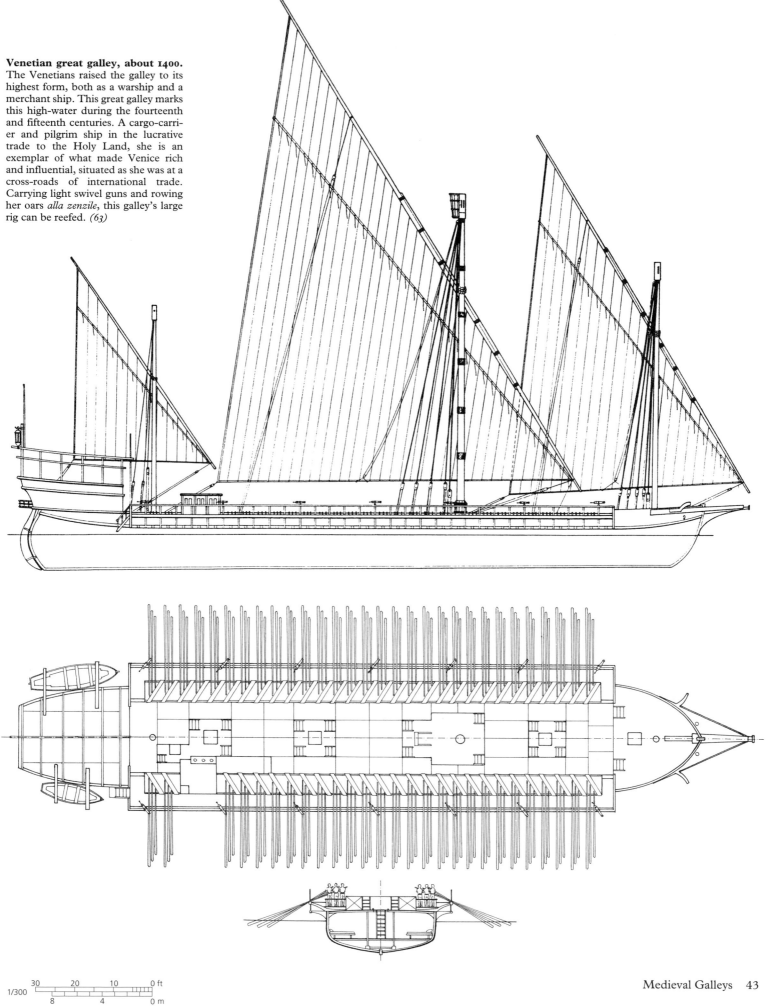

Venetian great galley, about 1400.
The Venetians raised the galley to its highest form, both as a warship and a merchant ship. This great galley marks this high-water during the fourteenth and fifteenth centuries. A cargo-carrier and pilgrim ship in the lucrative trade to the Holy Land, she is an exemplar of what made Venice rich and influential, situated as she was at a cross-roads of international trade. Carrying light swivel guns and rowing her oars *alla zenzile*, this galley's large rig can be reefed. *(63)*

30 20 10 0 ft

1/300

8 4 0 m

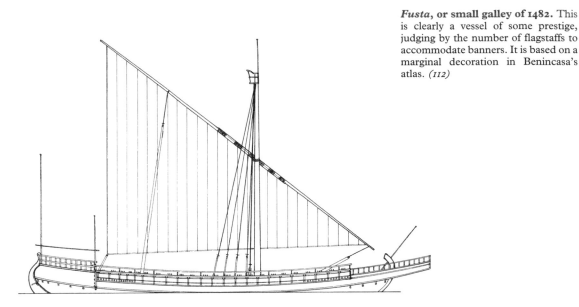

Fusta, or small galley of 1482. This is clearly a vessel of some prestige, judging by the number of flagstaffs to accommodate banners. It is based on a marginal decoration in Benincasa's atlas. *(112)*

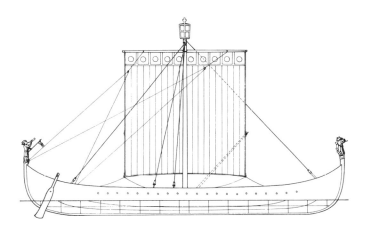

Norman longship, 1066. The fleet of Duke William of Normandy, who invaded England in 1066, was composed of ships largely indistinguishable from those of earlier invaders of the country. It is clear from the Bayeux Tapestry that such vessels as the *Mora* depicted here, were beamy and well able to carry the horses of the Normans which marked them militarily distinct from the Saxon defenders. *(53)*

Fighting Castles and Superstructure

The Norse longship was to metamorphose during the twelfth century into a number of variants in north European waters. From the eighth century the cargo-carrying *knarr* had contrasted with the *drakkar*, or dragon warship of the so-called Vikings. As the Norse diaspora progressed, reaching as far as Sicily with the establishment of a Norman Kingdom there, the descendants of the 'Vikings' adopted and adapted desirable elements of local vessels they encountered, particularly features of Saracen or Arabic vessels. Thus, like the lateen sail, the fighting platforms of the galleys, similar to planks laid in the bows of longships to accommodate the *stafnbui*, were incorporated, modified and

enlarged. They became dominant features of all subsequent sailing warship design until the eighteenth century. Such forecastles and aftercastles provided stations not only for archers and catapults, but command platforms. In merchant vessels they enclosed the traditional home of a ship's master and his mates, as well as accommodation for passengers, leaving the greater part of the hull for revenue-earning cargo. The most important innovation, however, was the rudder, which became commonplace in European shipbuilding from the thirteenth century.

1/300   30   20   10   0 ft
8   4   0 m

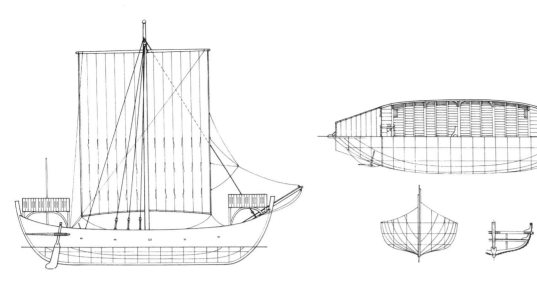

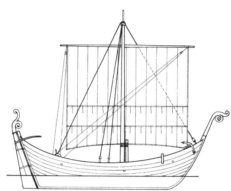

Winchelsea ship, thirteenth century. The seal of the seaport of Winchelsea in southern England shows a ship with prominent fore and after castles. The seal also shows men weighing an anchor (using one of the earliest recorded windlasses), steering and ascending the rigging to let fall the sail while trumpeters on the aftercastle announce the fact that the vessel is getting under weigh. The longship form is clearly discernible, though whether the shortened hull is truly representative or a result of distortion, is uncertain. *(53)*

The Fide ship, about AD 1200. In a church in Fide, on the Swedish island of Gotland, a scratched graffito confirms mural evidence elsewhere in Scandinavia that by the end of the twelfth century the steering of a sailing hull was accomplished by means of a stern-hung rudder. The tiller had to be curved to work round the sternpost, but pintles and gudgeons are clearly visible. The rig retains the traditional Norse square sail. *(112)*

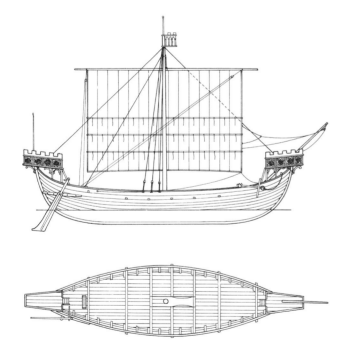

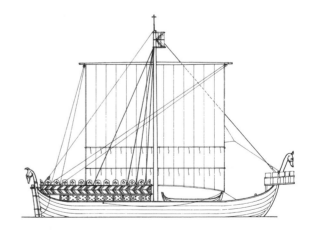

The Dover ship, 1305. The seal of the English town of Dover, important in 1305 as a Cinque Port bound to provide ships to the king in case of war with neighbouring France, shows what must have been a typical early fourteenth century ship. Normally a trading vessel, a war-muster would have requisitioned her for naval service, though this would probably have been confined to acting as a military transport. Nevertheless she possesses fully integrated castles fore and aft. *(114)*

The Skamstrup ship, late fourteenth century. On the ceiling of the church at Skamstrup, Denmark, there are paintings of two ships believed to date from the end of the fourteenth century. They possess rudders, the smaller clearly showing a tiller curving around the sternpost. The larger, shown here, has a small forecastle, but a very long aftercastle. This, with the variegated hull-paint indicates she is a man-of war. Rigging details show the standard single square sail, clearly crossed by two rows of reef points. The original image has a conspicuous anchor forward, hoisted under the forecastle. *(112)*

30   20   10   0 ft
1/300
8   4   0 m

The Højby ship, fifteenth century.
The derivation of small north European ships from the longship is clearly seen as late as the fifteenth century in this depiction of a single-masted ship, found in a church in Højby, Denmark. Although an aftercastle is fitted, the bow, supporting a small bowsprit to which the forestay leads, still sports a dragon head. This is probably a cargo vessel and the lack of innovation must show her as a standard type, with reef points on her single sail. Though a revolution in sailing rig was about to occur, it is not visible yet. *(112)*

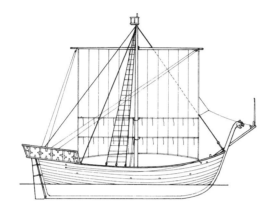

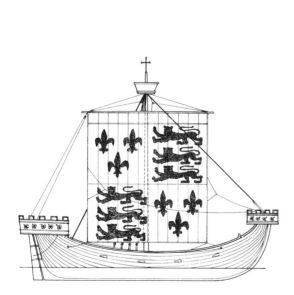

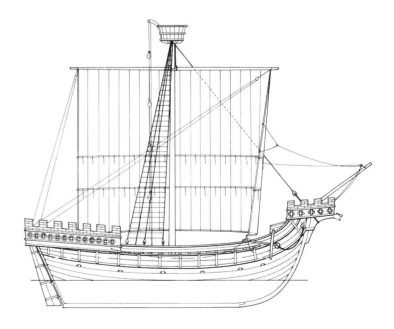

The ship of Richard, Duke of Gloucester, about 1480. Representing the other end of the spectrum of marine status, the seal of King Richard III of England when he was Duke of Gloucester, a title he held until 1483, shows a late Medieval warship. The stern-hung rudder rises inside the aftercastle, protecting the helmsman and allowing the head of the rudder post to superimpose above the stern-post. The rig however, remains simple, although the Duke's arms are emblazoned upon it and the seal shows a brazier burning on the forecastle. As Duke of Gloucester, Richard held the office of admiral of England to his brother, King Edward IV, and this is thus a badge of his high office. *(112)*

Danzig ship, 1400. By the beginning of the fourteenth century the great trading enterprise of confederated northern ports known as the Hanseatic League was established. One such port was Danzig (modern Gdansk), whose seal of 1400 shows this high-bowed merchantman. Due to the integration of the forecastle into the hull structure, the dragon's head has migrated to become a decorative figurehead and thus able to hold cargo, by vertical outer frames. Other innovations include the running of the anchor cable through a hawse-pipe and the fitting of ratlines across the shrouds. *(114)*

1/300   30   20   10   0 ft
         8   4   0 m

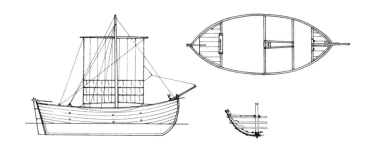

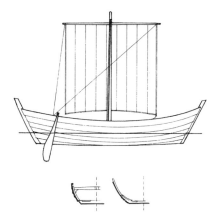

Kalmar boat, mid-thirteenth century. The discovery of a medieval boat near the castle of Kalmar in Sweden in 1932 showed a lapstrake hull, built of wood with deck beams projecting through the planking. Notched ribs, fitting the joggled form of the interior of the hull, were riveted through the strakes. Shaped knees also held the deck beams to the hull sides. Eleven metres long, the Kalmar boat is 4.6 metres in the beam and clearly bore a mast and sail, for a crutch for the lowered mast is fitted forward. She was half-decked forward and aft. *(112)*

Brügge boat, fifth-sixth centuries AD. This simple Frisian proto-cog of the fifth to sixth centuries was a lap-straked craft with the familiar steering arrangement and square sail of the Norse tradition. *(52)*

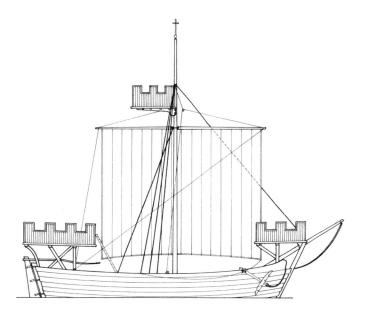

Danzig cog of 1299. This interpretation derives from the city's seal. The elevated castles, apart from facilitating the operation of the tiller aft, suggest her to be a man-of-war, prestigious enough to represent a visual image of Danzig's importance as a leading member of the Hanse. The bowsprit permitted the stiffening of the leading edge of the mainsail by means of bowlines when beating. *(231)*

The Cog Tradition

The development of a purely cargo-carrying hull in the waters of the North and Baltic Seas during the Medieval era reached an apogee in the cog. Such vessels became, so to speak, the standard carrier for the vast trade carried out by the ports of the Hanseatic League. This great confederated monopoly not only extended trade routes, but made them reliable, answering the demands of Europe's growing population by means of supply by cog.

The cog as a distinct type is said to have first emerged among the Frisian Islands and is mentioned in AD 948. She consisted of a simple, but relatively deep-draughted hull with a long, straight keel. Her end posts were more nearly vertical than hitherto and in due course the cog became fully decked. The long stem supported a small forecastle and a bowsprit, the importance of which lies in the fact that bowlines – ropes tensioned to stiffen the leading edge, or windward luff, of a square sail – could be hove taut when the cog was working to windward. This improved the efficiency of the single sailed rig, which could not only be reduced in bad weather by reefing, but extended in calms by lacing a bonnet along its foot. It is known that by 1242 cogs bore a rudder, hung on a sternpost and that this was later cut short enough to allow the tiller to swing above it.

Hull construction, which was full bilged, beamy and stable, allowed the decks to shed water. Transverse beams extended through holes in the appropriate strake, where they were pegged to give added strength, for cargo-carrying stressed a hull. The conjectural presence of windlasses in earlier ship-types is confirmed by archaeological evidence in the cog. Such machines gave added mechanical advantage to heavy tasks such as raising the anchor and hoisting the yard, for these merchant ships had to be economically manned.

Customs records from Lübeck indicate several classes of cog, from quite small vessels of 10 tons capacity, tonnage being reckoned as a measure of volume, to those of about 25 tons. The upper tonnage increased over time, so that by 1360 only two classes existed, those over, and those under, 120 tons. At this time, almost 850 vessels cleared out of Lübeck, with about 600 leaving Hamburg, most of which were cogs.

Although occasional voyages were made to the Mediterranean, the cog was essentially a north European craft and sailed often in convoy, escorted by a military version sporting castles and a banner denoting the city from which she came. From the end of the fourteenth century, light cannon were carried in the castles.

30   20   10   0 ft
1/300
8   4   0 m

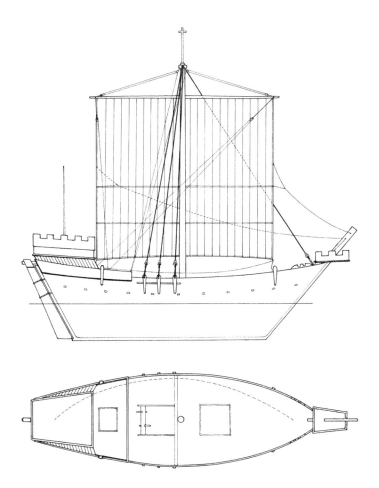

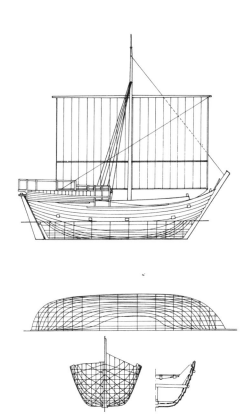

Elbing cog, 1367. Based on a seal, the lateral projection of the deck beams is conspicuous, as are reinforcing timbers to bear the local stress of the shrouds. Some form of post to which the clew of the sail is hauled when going to windward is also shown. In this example, the stempost appears to be extended in place of a bowsprit to take the bowlines. *(112)*

Bremen cog replica. In 1962, the remains of a cog of 1380 were discovered in the River Weser in northern Germany. She contained some notable features, including a lavatory situated in the extension over the stern, a windlass for hoisting the anchor, and a capstan aft for hoisting the heavy yard. This replica of the 'Bremen cog' has since been constructed and successfully sailed. *(84)*

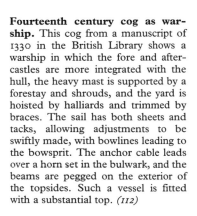

Fourteenth century cog as warship. This cog from a manuscript of 1330 in the British Library shows a warship in which the fore and aftercastles are more integrated with the hull, the heavy mast is supported by a forestay and shrouds, and the yard is hoisted by halliards and trimmed by braces. The sail has both sheets and tacks, allowing adjustments to be swiftly made, with bowlines leading to the bowsprit. The anchor cable leads over a horn set in the bulwark, and the beams are pegged on the exterior of the topsides. Such a vessel is fitted with a substantial top. *(112)*

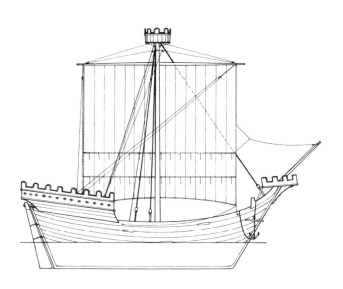

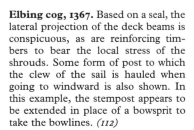

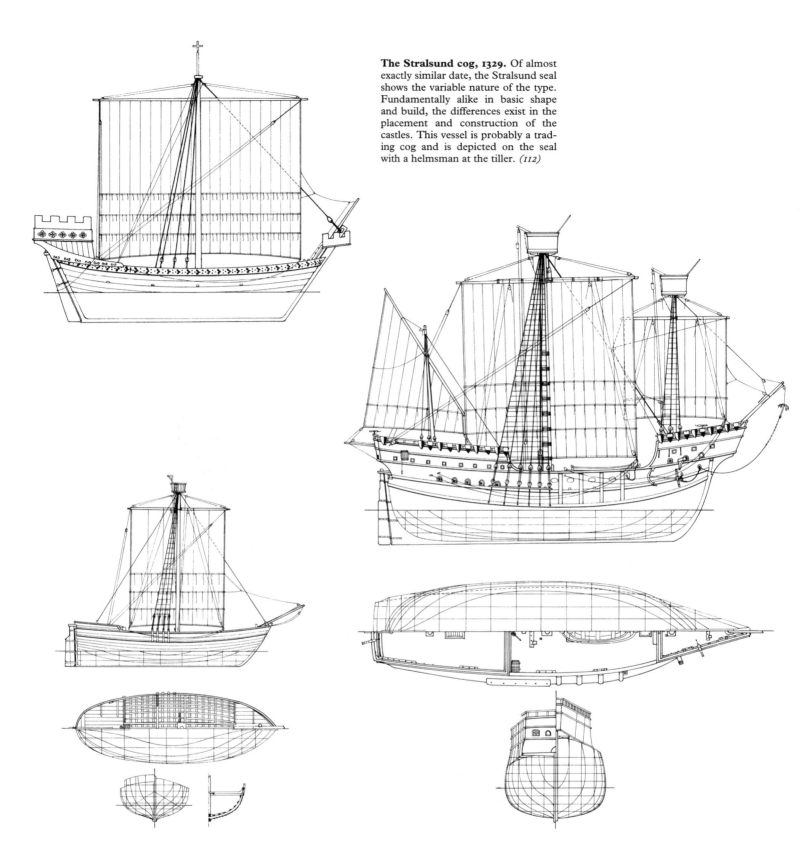

The Stralsund cog, 1329. Of almost exactly similar date, the Stralsund seal shows the variable nature of the type. Fundamentally alike in basic shape and build, the differences exist in the placement and construction of the castles. This vessel is probably a trading cog and is depicted on the seal with a helmsman at the tiller. *(112)*

The Kalmar cog, thirteenth century. Among the excavations at Kalmar, another hull, known as Kalmar V, is an interesting variant, with a vertical sternpost and slightly curving stem, dated around the thirteenth century. Such a hull would have very dissimilar waterlines fore and aft. This drew in the natural geometry of the after 'run', making it finer than the bluffer 'entry' of the bow. This, seen here for the first time in north European shipbuilding, was to establish a tradition which would later dominate naval architecture. It was also to have an important impact upon the development of the rig of sailing ships. *(231)*

Fifteenth century cog. The consequences of the raked stem and vertical sternpost were to drive a large hull away from the wind, requiring the application of lee helm. To counter this a large cog of 1470, seen here, fitted with a second square sail on a foremast, would require a third sail set well aft. This is an adapted lateen sail, cut with a small vertical luff making it a proto-'setee' sail. In this late form of cog, can be seen the genesis of something very new. *(223)*

Ocean-going Sail

IN THE AFTERMATH of the Crusades, during which the Mediterranean had become a cultural melting pot, the necessity of transporting armies from the north-west of Europe to the Holy Land had encouraged shipbuilding and the adoption of the southern method of constructing the frame of a hull first and then planking it, the strakes being laid edge-to-edge and caulked, a system known to northern Europeans as 'carvel'. The influence of Arab culture, particularly in Spain, and the increase in trade between the Mediterranean and northern Europe rapidly spread this new technique, enabling larger hulls to be built. This was a revolution in shipbuilding, which was drawn in to serve the increasing rivalry and ambition of European princes. The great conflict between the Catholic and Protestant faiths now began to create a number of engines driving ship design, and the warship became increasingly distinct from the more capacious merchantman.

This turbulent period inspired the intellectual quest of the Renaissance, with its concomitant interest in navigation and exploration. Ships had to be better fitted for sea-keeping, able to stay at sea for many days and to endure bad weather without running for shelter. Adept at this was a vessel developed on the margins of the tempestuous Atlantic, the caravel. For many generations the seamen of the Biscay and Iberian coasts had been going to sea in search of fish and whales and the outcome of their empirical design was a fine, adaptable craft. But the caravel was always a small vessel, and a larger was required to cross 'the Ocean-Sea' in safety and take advantage of the possession of overseas territories that Europeans considered theirs by right of 'discovery'. For this a new type emerged, the true 'ship' of three masts and in such ships, or *nãos*, as they were called in Spanish, the power of the kings of a united Aragon and Castile was carried to the Americas.

At the practical level, seamen were devising better methods of ship-handling, demanding improved materials for sails and ropes, and, in the case of their officers, improving their ability to navigate. Knowledge of foreign coasts, the run of tides and currents, the location of shoals and rocks, became state secrets. Geographers, astronomers, cartographers, and ship-masters came together at Sagres on the Atlantic coast of Portugal under the aegis of Prince Henry, known to history as 'the navigator' for his promotion of exploration. It was, however, King Ferdinand and Queen Isabella of Spain who underwrote the small fleet of the Genoese mariner Cristoforo Columbo (or Columbus, in his preferred Latinised form) for his first voyage in 1492 in which he reached the islands of the Caribbean. The sailing ship had, in fact, become an important component in the political argument, standing alongside an army as a means by which the powerful manipulated the affairs of the world.

The development of the cog into a rounded form, known as the 'hulk' soon assumed the characteristics of the true ship and, increasing in tonnage, became an 'orrible, greete and stoute' vessel called the *kraek*, or 'carrack'. Such huge carracks were symbols of temporal puissance and Henry VIII of England imported shipwrights and caulkers to build plank-on-frame men-of-war. These, the nascent Royal Navy, were intended to combat the growing maritime might of France and Spain, whose courts were also building large warships, or galleons, capable of mounting rows of guns along their pierced sides. The age of broadside naval war beckoned and the divergence of warship design from that of merchantmen was now established. While the galley, particularly those of the Venetian Republic, continued to exercise sea-power in the Mediterranean, a new power-base was rising in the north. Rebelling against their Catholic Spanish overlords, the Dutch were engaged in a long war which would see them utterly overthrow their hitherto all-powerful overlords and emerge as the dominant sea-power of the era.

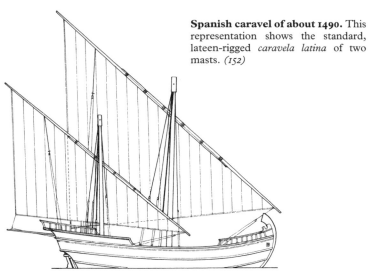

Spanish caravel of about 1490. This representation shows the standard, lateen-rigged *caravela latina* of two masts. *(152)*

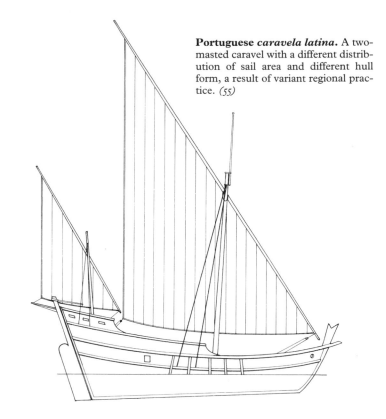

Portuguese *caravela latina*. A two-masted caravel with a different distribution of sail area and different hull form, a result of variant regional practice. *(55)*

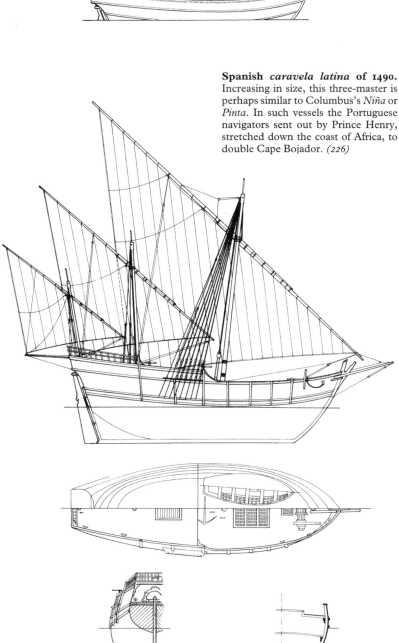

Spanish *caravela latina* of 1490. Increasing in size, this three-master is perhaps similar to Columbus's *Niña* or *Pinta*. In such vessels the Portuguese navigators sent out by Prince Henry, stretched down the coast of Africa, to double Cape Bojador. *(226)*

1/300

Caravel and Não

The fusion of the building methods of north and south Europe resulted in the skeletal construction of plank-on-frame becoming the norm for large ship construction. That the butting and caulking of planks bears the name 'carvel' to this day, reveals its origins, deriving from the caravel. Round-bilged, carvel hulls proved superior to the cog as cargo carriers, more easily accepting the additions of castles, and resulted in a type known as the 'hulk', not then a pejorative term, but deriving from a towed vessel of the Roman era. Like many nautical terms, its application and history is loose and imprecise, varying from place to place. In due course the tonnage of hulks rose to about 300, and she ousted the cog as a cargo carrier.

But it was the caravel that spearheaded European exploration in the fifteenth century. Originally a carvel-built, fine-lined fishing and coastal boat of Portugal with two lateen-rigged masts, the first mention of a caravel dates from 1255. Seaworthy and weatherly, she could sail to windward, though possessed of no great draught and was thus excellent for surveying. Columbus took two caravels on his first voyage. But the caravel had its limitations, and these lay in the unwieldy yards, dangerous to handle and often replaced by square yards when the wind was favourable. Thus, when men did not make great passages to windward, but voyaged with the prevailing winds whenever possible, regarding this as revealing divine purpose, the windward-performing square-rigged 'ship' proved ultimately more suitable.

The latin for ship, *navis*, became widespread with a variety of meanings and was corrupted into several variants, most notably in Spanish *não* and in French *nef*. Both refer to substantial vessels and as the size of ships grew after the Crusades, the generic terms moved with them, with no very specific limitations. By the end of the fifteenth century, the generally accepted *nao* was a three-masted vessel such as the *Santa Maria*, Columbus's flagship.

Four-masted Portuguese *caravela redonda*, late sixteenth century. The adaptation of the caravel to incorporate square sails allowed larger hulls to be built without a consequent increase in the size of the yards, and improved endurance. This is a late example from the end of the sixteenth century and displays the by then common spritsail. *(55)*

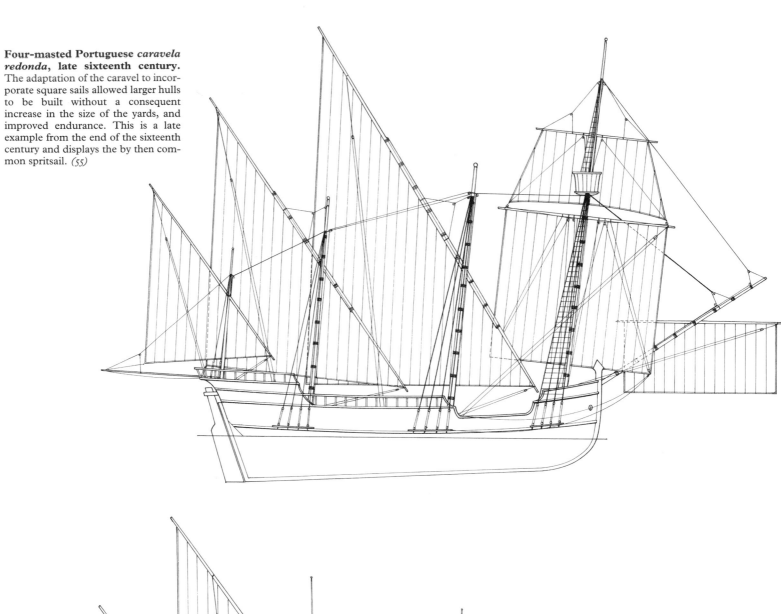

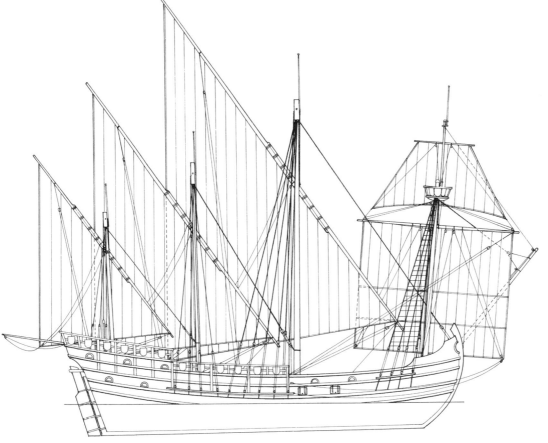

Caravela de armada, **1545.** This large four-masted adaptation of the *caravela redonda* was a naval vessel with increased capacity and stability. The hull form has additions derived from other sources. Thought to have been French or Flemish, she was a not uncommon vessel in the sixteenth century and, fitted for war, was known as a *caravela de armada*. *(114)*

1/300

30   20   10   0 ft

8   4   0 m

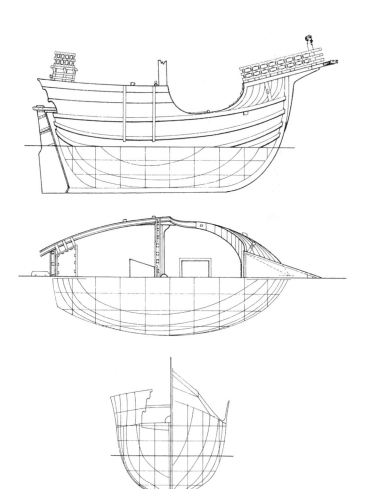

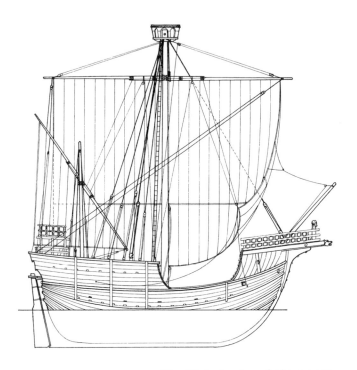

The Mataró *não*, of about 1450 – hull. This represents a mid-fifteenth century Catalan ship model originally from a church at Mataró, near Barcelona. She is a *não*, of stubby proportions, the hull bound with heavy exterior stringers and vertical strengthening timbers. The aftercastle and forecastle are entirely part of the hull, indeed the former has become a half-deck, with a small additional castle raised above it. The low waist is pierced by a hatch to the hold. Although not to scale, the details in this votive model are generally convincing. *(225)*

The Mataró *não*, of about 1450 – rig. This reconstruction of the rig of the Mataró *não* is based upon evidence present in the original model, and attempts to make the proportions more realistic. Modern academic opinion, with its need to categorise, tends to regard the vessel as an early carrack, and make her two-masted. The mizen would be needed to drive such a ship with even a beam wind. Anchor handling, always a difficult procedure, is facilitated by a stubby timber, or cathead, extending outwards at the break of the forecastle. *(112)*

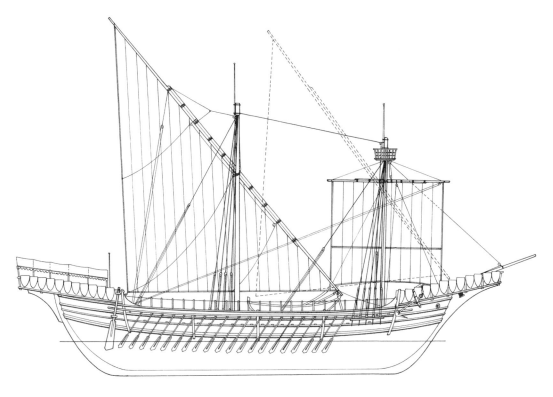

Catalan *uxer*. This Catalan *uxer, usciere* or *hussier* of the sixteenth century, shows the extent to which ideas migrated and 'ship-types' were difficult to pigeon-hole. This vessel derives from the Roman horse-transport and was a broad-beamed Mediterranean cargo-carrier, capable of being pulled in a calm, and possessing the adaptable rig of the *caravela redonda*. *(127)*

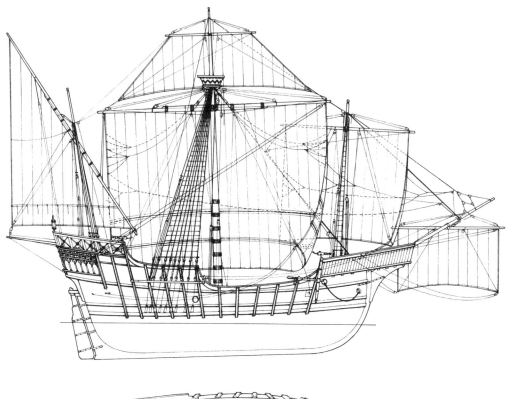

Santa Maria in 1492 (i). Interpretations based on the hull of the contemporaneous Mataró ship provide valuable clues as to the likely appearance of the *Santa Maria* in 1492. Combined with Columbus's own mention of the sails, it appears that the flagship was a sophisticated vessel, as befitted a royal vessel sent out on a voyage pregnant with possibilities. Note the additional raised deck aft. This was to become the poop. *(226)*

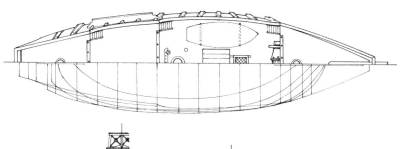

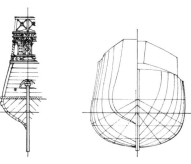

Santa Maria in 1492 (ii). This simpler analysis shows a rectangular topsail handled from the large top. *(112)*

Columbus' Ships – Changing Interpretations

We know very little about the three vessels of Columbus's first voyage. That two were caravels is indisputable, but beyond some references to the *Santa Maria* as '*la não*', the admiral's writings referred in detail only to her sails. Of these Columbus said that he 'set all the sails, the main course with two bonnets, the fore course, the sprit sail, the mizen the [main] topsail and the boat's sail on the half-deck'. The allusion to the sprit sail, the topsail and the half-deck are valuable clues, almost the only available for scholarly interpretation, but they argue in favour of the *Santa Maria* being a carrack.

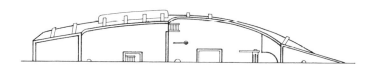

30   20   10   0 ft
1/300
8   4   0 m

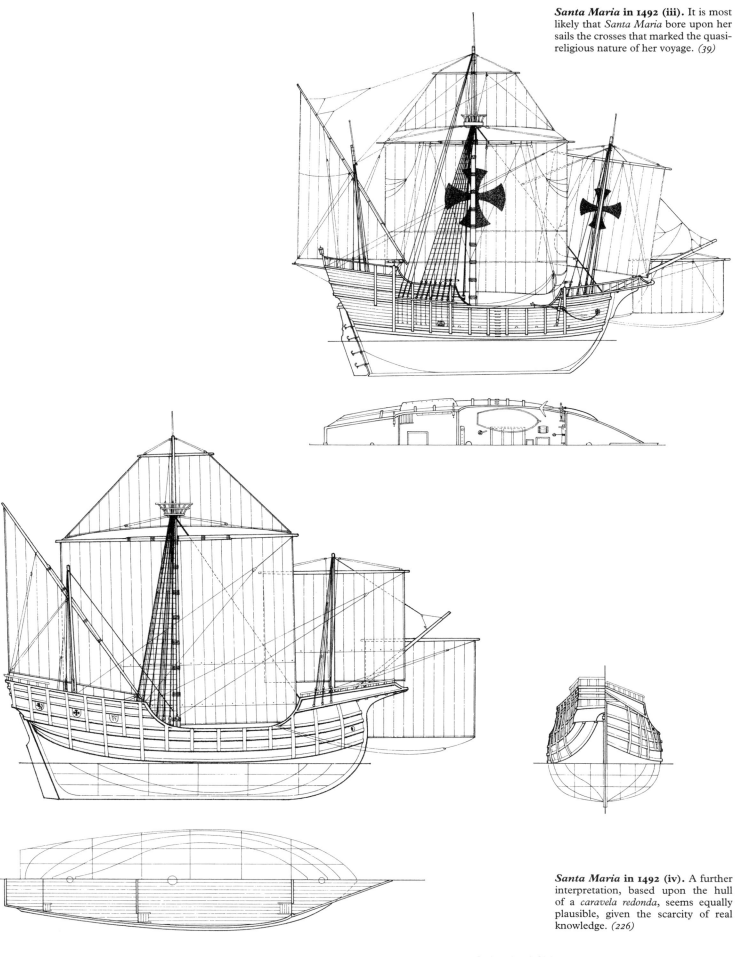

***Santa Maria* in 1492 (iii).** It is most likely that *Santa Maria* bore upon her sails the crosses that marked the quasi-religious nature of her voyage. *(39)*

***Santa Maria* in 1492 (iv).** A further interpretation, based upon the hull of a *caravela redonda*, seems equally plausible, given the scarcity of real knowledge. *(226)*

30 20 10 0 ft
1/300
8 4 0 m

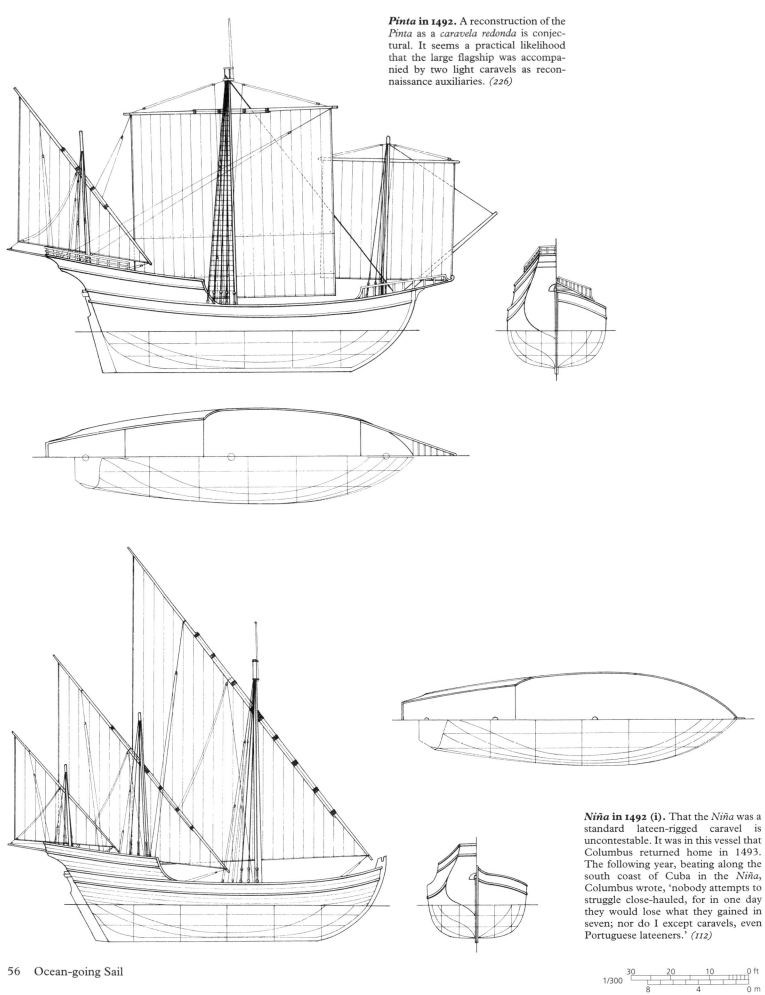

Pinta in 1492. A reconstruction of the *Pinta* as a *caravela redonda* is conjectural. It seems a practical likelihood that the large flagship was accompanied by two light caravels as reconnaissance auxiliaries. *(226)*

Niña in 1492 (i). That the *Niña* was a standard lateen-rigged caravel is uncontestable. It was in this vessel that Columbus returned home in 1493. The following year, beating along the south coast of Cuba in the *Niña*, Columbus wrote, 'nobody attempts to struggle close-hauled, for in one day they would lose what they gained in seven; nor do I except caravels, even Portuguese lateeners.' *(112)*

1/300   30   20   10   0 ft
        8   4   0 m

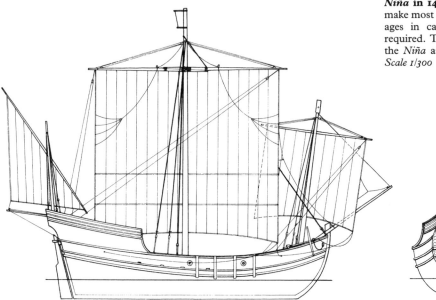

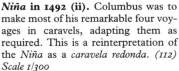

***Niña* in 1492 (ii).** Columbus was to make most of his remarkable four voyages in caravels, adapting them as required. This is a reinterpretation of the *Niña* as a *caravela redonda*. *(112) Scale 1/300*

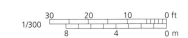

30 20 10 0 ft
1/300
8   4   0 m

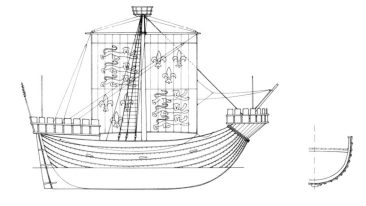

The Bristol 'hulc', 1446. This seal of the Admiralty Court of the important English port of Bristol shows a royal vessel, but the hull construction is that of the hulk, or hulc. The successful hulk had ousted the cog as the cargo-vessel of the Hanseatic League; she sailed better and allowed greater quantities of cargo to be carried in her round-bilged, full-ended hull. She remained, however, a single-masted, medieval ship. *(66) Scale 1/400*

The Full-Rigged Carrack

The somewhat woolly definitions applied to various types of vessel were to coalesce in the sixteenth century. As the standard rig for substantial sea-going craft became three-masted, with two square sails, a bowsprit and sail, a lateen sail on the mizen and, in the course of time, topsails on all three masts, it became known as 'a ship', or more correctly, a full-rigged ship. The rig became paramount, born on many types of hull of varying size, but it is significant in that it was able to drive the largest hull, though some early four-masters, following the tradition established by the *caravela da armada*, set an additional lateen 'bonaventure'.

The term used for the largest of these ships was 'carrack', then the grandest vessels built in Europe and synonymous with size in the popular imagination. Like the great cathedrals, the carrack became a symbol of temporal might. At the marriage of Charles, Duke of Burgundy, to the English princess, Margaret of York, in 1348, thirty large models of carracks were borne in the procession to overawe the populace.

The carrack's hull was heavily built, massively framed and planked, though the lines of her hull were finer and more sea-kindly that contemporary renditions of the type might suggest. In the tidal waters of northern Europe, she could rest on the bottom at low water without stress, in order to discharge her cargo. Her mainmast was a massive, laminated spar, supported by an immense web of standing rigging spread to the sides of the ship and necessary to bear the vast spread of the unwieldy mainsail. Yet this very quality was to demand a relatively complex control system, with clew- and buntlines, tacks, sheets and bowlines, in addition to the halliards and braces necessary to work the yard. Despite this, by about 1470, the mainsail had grown so cumbersome that its size was limited and the topsail appeared above it, its sheets leading into the heavy mast-top. The bowsprit, developed to take the lead of the bowlines, was now to offer a securing point for the heavy forestay, and to set its own sail.

40 30 20 10 0 ft
1/400
10   5   0 m

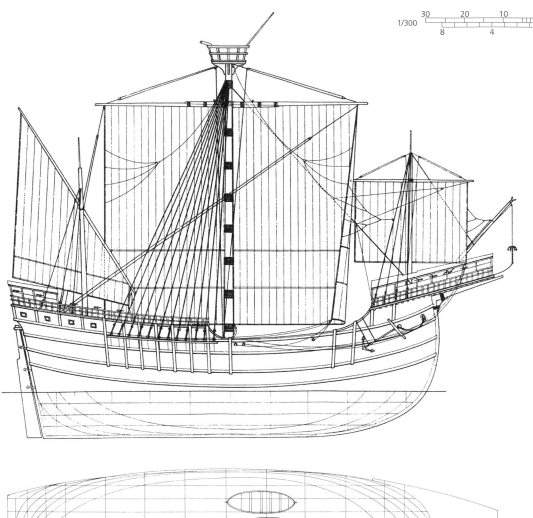

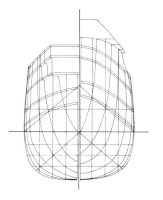

Peter von Danzig, 1462. Early northern exponents of the plank-on-frame building method of the Mediterranean, were the shipbuilders of the French Atlantic coast. In 1462, a merchantman, the *Pierre de la Rochelle* was abandoned at Danzig. The ship was seized, renamed the *Peter von Danzig*, also called *Das Grosse Kraweel*, and fitted out in 1470 for the war of the Hanseatic League against England. A three-masted, carvel-built ship with a robust frame of keel, hog and ribs, after her refit she bore a score of light-weight cannon. *(123)*

1/300
30   20   10   0 ft
8   4   0 m

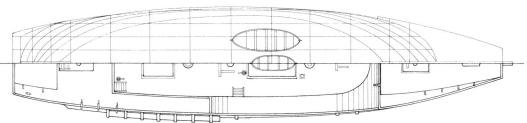

Carrack of about 1470. The cumbersome nature of the mainsail clearly dominates this representation. Even with the yard lowered, the windage of the mast and rigging would render the ship difficult to handle in bad weather, though the much smaller fore and mizen sails would allow her commander a degree of control. Such were the new generation of large merchantmen fulfilling the increasing demands of distant markets. *(112)*

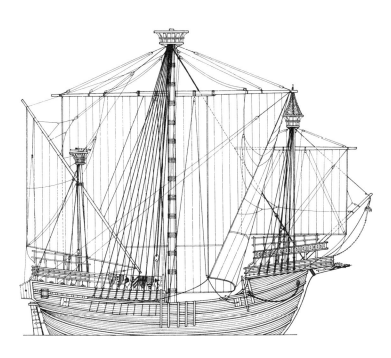

1/400
40   30   20   10   0 ft
10   5   0 m

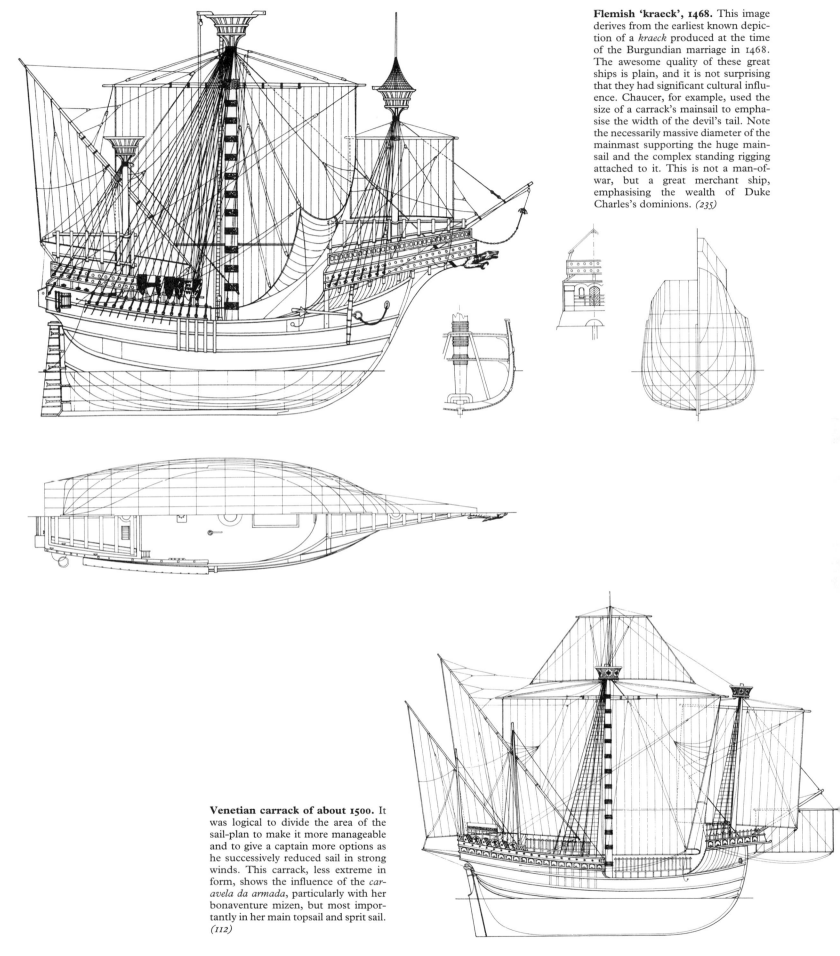

Flemish 'kraeck', 1468. This image derives from the earliest known depiction of a *kraeck* produced at the time of the Burgundian marriage in 1468. The awesome quality of these great ships is plain, and it is not surprising that they had significant cultural influence. Chaucer, for example, used the size of a carrack's mainsail to emphasise the width of the devil's tail. Note the necessarily massive diameter of the mainmast supporting the huge mainsail and the complex standing rigging attached to it. This is not a man-of-war, but a great merchant ship, emphasising the wealth of Duke Charles's dominions. *(235)*

Venetian carrack of about 1500. It was logical to divide the area of the sail-plan to make it more manageable and to give a captain more options as he successively reduced sail in strong winds. This carrack, less extreme in form, shows the influence of the *caravela da armada*, particularly with her bonaventure mizen, but most importantly in her main topsail and sprit sail. *(112)*

1/400

40   30   20   10   0 ft

10   5   0 m

The Full-Rigged Carrack   59

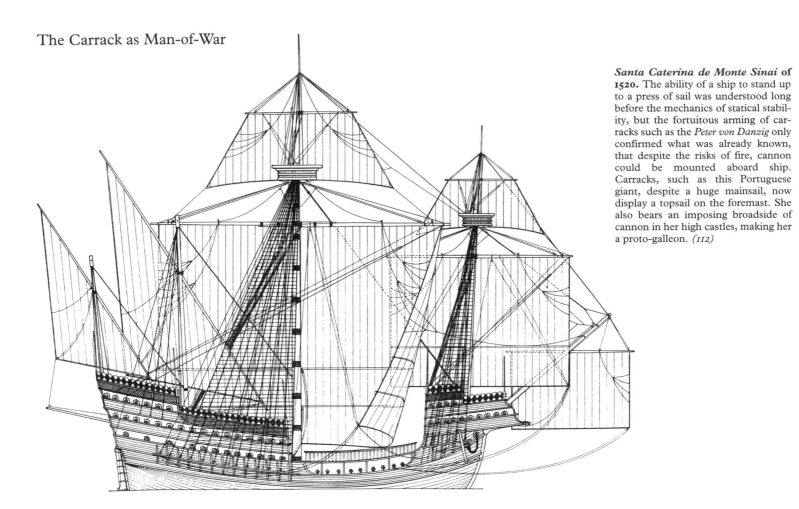

Santa Caterina de Monte Sinai of **1520.** The ability of a ship to stand up to a press of sail was understood long before the mechanics of statical stability, but the fortuitous arming of carracks such as the *Peter von Danzig* only confirmed what was already known, that despite the risks of fire, cannon could be mounted aboard ship. Carracks, such as this Portuguese giant, despite a huge mainsail, now display a topsail on the foremast. She also bears an imposing broadside of cannon in her high castles, making her a proto-galleon. *(112)*

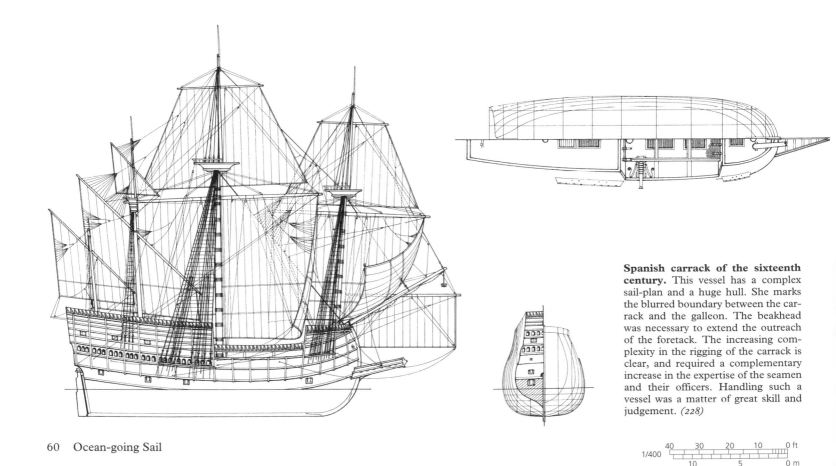

Spanish carrack of the sixteenth century. This vessel has a complex sail-plan and a huge hull. She marks the blurred boundary between the carrack and the galleon. The beakhead was necessary to extend the outreach of the foretack. The increasing complexity in the rigging of the carrack is clear, and required a complementary increase in the expertise of the seamen and their officers. Handling such a vessel was a matter of great skill and judgement. *(228)*

1/400

40   30   20   10   0 ft

10   5   0 m

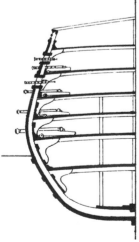

Henri Grâce à Dieu, 1514. This vessel was perhaps the ultimate carrack, for she took the metaphor of temporal power and enshrined it as a symbol of monarchical might. This was a deliberate political statement by King Henry VIII of England, a statement enshrined in the ship's name, in her armament, her cost and the splendour of her decoration. She was built to impress, a proto-battleship with the high forecastle of a carrack, but the narrow towering transom of a galleon. She bore 21 heavy bronze guns, 130 light guns and 100 hand guns. To overawe his rival, King Francis of France, Henry had her fitted out with yellow sails to convey the impression of gold. Her tall rig with its proliferation of lateen yards was doubtless an attempt to intimidate, but the appearance of topgallant sails with braces on those lofty spars is evidence of increasing confidence and it was necessary to appoint to her a sailing master of proven ability. *(112)*

1/400
40 30 20 10 0 ft
10   5   0 m

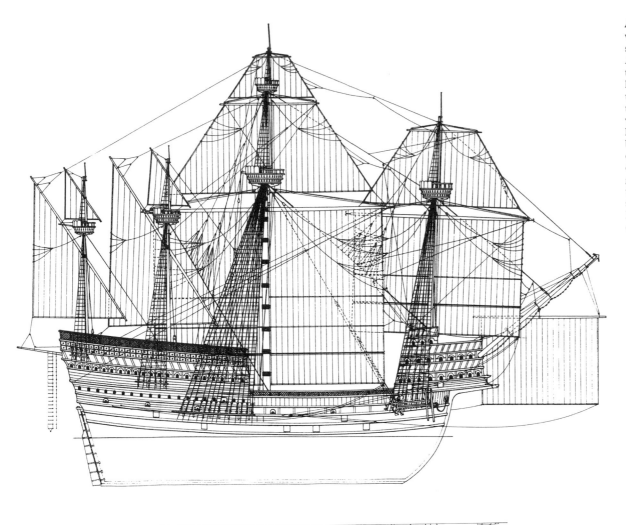

***Mary Rose*, 1545.** Although a lesser
warship than what the English themselves called the *Great Harry*, the *Mary
Rose* was one of the largest warships in
the English fleet. Built in 1510, with a
keel length of 32 metres, the *Mary Rose*
underwent a refit in 1536 when it is
thought she was rearmed, being fitted
with low, opening gunports, which
had appeared around the time of her
building. Sailing from Portsmouth to
engage the French with her guns run
out on 15 July 1545, she heeled to a
gust of wind. Water flooded in through
the lee gunports and she rapidly capsized within sight of the watching King
Henry. Note the grappling iron at the
end of the bowsprit. *(146)*

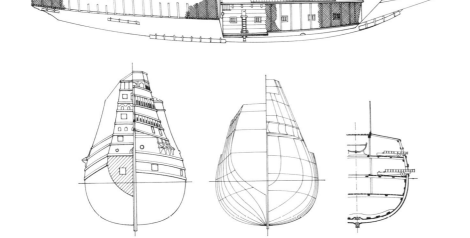

**A small English man-of-war from
around 1560.** This shows the complete adoption of what was to become,
importantly, the 'ship rig'. Lightly
armed, though with their cannon well-
served, it was small vessels such as this
– many converted merchantmen – that
attacked larger Spanish warships during the Anglo-Spanish wars of the second half of the sixteenth century. *(184)*

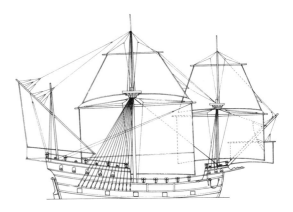

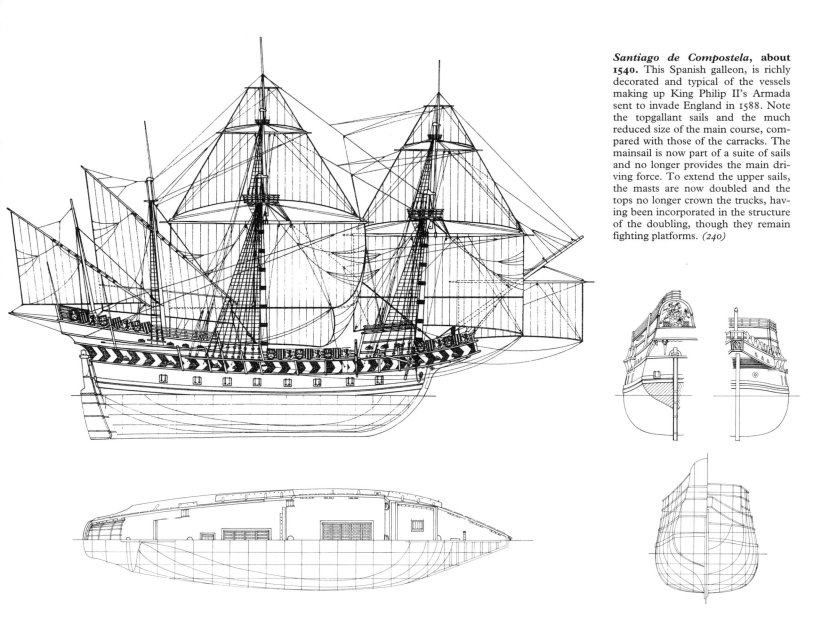

The Evolution of the Galleon

The expansion of national navies and the evolution of fleet procedures soon called for a variety of ship-types for specific tasks. Fast, scouting pinnaces (a pinnace being the early form of a word replaced by the Dutch imposition 'yacht' in the seventeenth century), fast, intercepting commerce raiders, and the heavier forms of proto-battleships, designed to force upon an enemy a decisive action. Such an exerter of power might take the form of the broadside-bearing descendant of the carrack, the galleon, or in the Mediterranean, remain the heavy war galley, with her forward pointing guns.

Although the war galley could outmanoeuvre a carrack or galleon in a calm, the defence of several single such ships against a number of galleys, persuaded the Venetian admirals in particular to try and combine the virtues of both types, increasing the armament, but without sacrificing manoeuvrability. At first larger galleys were built, but they proved too heavy for long passages, and in due course the resultant compromise was the galeasse. The galeasse possessed greater draught and improved sea-keeping, her oarsmen were better protected and her value in battle was as five to one, when compared with the standard oared galley. At the battle of Lepanto in 1571, the fleet of the Christian allies had among its vessels a number of galleasses which proved decisive against the Turkish galleys. The galleasse became a major fleet weapon,

reached 1000 tons and four served in Medina Sidonia's Spanish Armada in 1588.

This was defeated in a running battle by English galleons, smaller than those in the Spanish fleet, whose gunnery was superior to the enemy's. The tactics of the English in plying their guns with great effect, deprived the Spanish of the opportunity to board, upon which they had been relying. The greatest demonstration of English gunnery, however, occurred in 1591, when a single English galleon, the *Revenge*, held a Spanish fleet at bay.

The galleon was little more than an enlarged and seaworthy version of the carrack, and the name is a generic title covering a wide variation in ship size. The difference lies largely in application, for while the word carrack applied to merchantman and man-of-war, galleon tended to denote a warship. In its largest form the galleon was both, the Spanish 'Manila galleon' being a large, naval ship designed to carry specie annually from the Spanish colonies of South America, across the Pacific for onward carriage to Spain. It was, however, the English who perfected the galleon as a fast, manoeuvrable and well-armed warship, producing what were called 'race-built' galleons which benefited from improved and standardised artillery.

1/400   40   30   20   10   0 ft
         10   5   0 m

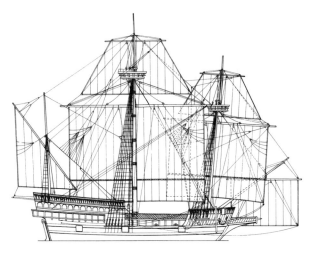

Greyhound, 1545. The success of the galleasse in the Mediterranean encouraged its development elsewhere. Here, one of Henry VIII's 'galeasses' shows very little of her ancestry. Ship-rigged, she possesses a low profile and light armament and was intended for reconnaissance. *(243)*

Sixteenth century Venetian galleon. Although substantially similar to the galleons of Spain, France and England, this vessel shows her Mediterranean ancestry. The high poops that distinguish galleons, appear top-heavy but were probably lightly built and therefore did not pose the threat to stability that at first seems unavoidable. *(170)*

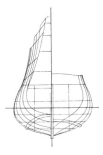

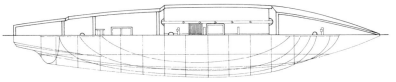

1/400   40   30   20   10   0 ft
10   5   0 m

Golden Hind, 1576. In this galleon the English adventurer Francis Drake circumnavigated the globe in 1577-80. Originally the *Pelican*, Drake renamed his ship in honour of his patron, Sir Christopher Hatton, whose arms were a golden hind. On his return, Drake was knighted by Elizabeth I, and the ship was put into dock and opened to the public, the money raised going to charity. She should not be confused with the smaller 50-ton *Golden Hind* which first sighted the approaching Spanish Armada off the Lizard in July 1588. *(202)*

Revenge, 1577. A 441-ton galleon mounting 34 guns, the *Revenge* was Drake's flagship as vice-admiral of the English fleet attacking the Spanish Armada. The following year, 1589, Drake attacked Spanish ships on the coast of Portugal. A year later, under Sir Martin Frobisher, she was again off the Spanish coast. But it was in 1591 that the *Revenge* became immortal, passing her name to successive generations of British warships, for she was attacked by a fleet of fifty-three Spanish warships at Flores in the Azores. Sir Richard Grenville fought for fifteen hours before his officers persuaded him to surrender. Mortally wounded, Grenville reluctantly agreed, to die a prisoner two days later. The Spanish failed to bear their prize home, for she foundered in a storm, taking with her the 200 Spanish seamen put aboard as prize-crew. *(82)*

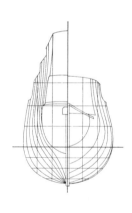

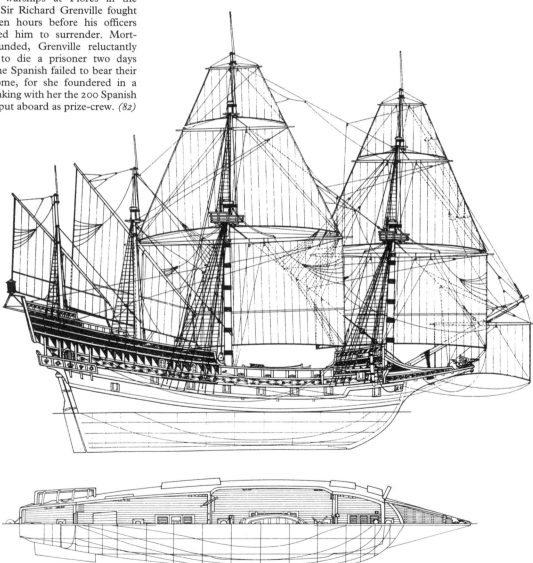

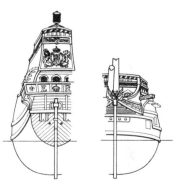

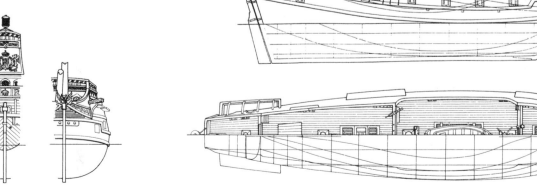

40　30　20　10　0 ft

1/400

10　　　5　　　0 m

The Evolution of the Galleon　65

Race-built English galleon *White Bear*, about 1599. Race-built denoted a lower hull form dedicated to presenting an enemy with a broadside, and eschewing the exaggerated castles of many Spanish galleons. Sir John Hawkins is generally attributed with the promotion of this form of building. *(82)*

English pinnace of about 1570. This light, scouting craft displays similar characteristics to the *caravela redonda*. This example is wearing decorative arming cloths over her topsides, a token of mourning when the ship was used to bring home the body of Sir Philip Sidney, who was killed fighting at Zutphen in 1586. *(82)*

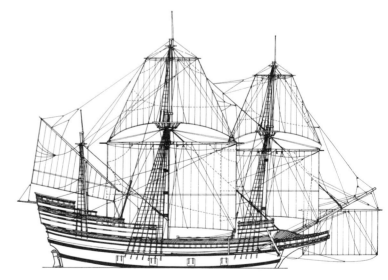

English merchant ship, 1532. This shows the small carrack form, though the sail plan is that of the full-rigged ship. *(82)*

***Mayflower*, 1620.** The success of the fighting galleon was bound to influence merchant ship design. This is the *Mayflower*, a ship of 180 tons, a ton being the space needed to stow a 'tun', or large barrel, of wine. In 1620, the *Mayflower* crossed the Atlantic with about 100 religious dissidents who, landing in what is now Massachusetts, founded the Plymouth colony on 21 December. *(231)*

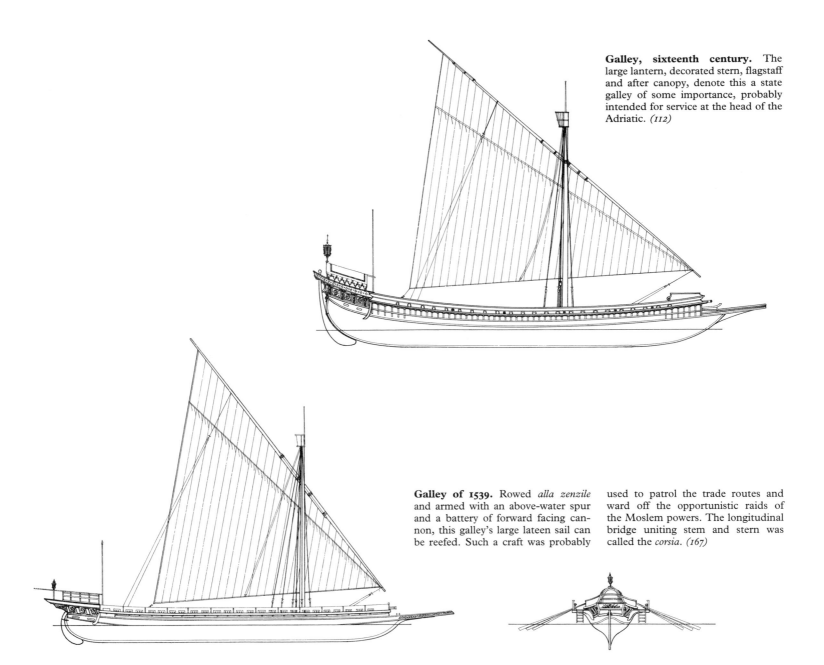

Galley, sixteenth century. The large lantern, decorated stern, flagstaff and after canopy, denote this a state galley of some importance, probably intended for service at the head of the Adriatic. *(112)*

Galley of 1539. Rowed *alla zenzile* and armed with an above-water spur and a battery of forward facing cannon, this galley's large lateen sail can be reefed. Such a craft was probably used to patrol the trade routes and ward off the opportunistic raids of the Moslem powers. The longitudinal bridge uniting stem and stern was called the *corsia*. *(167)*

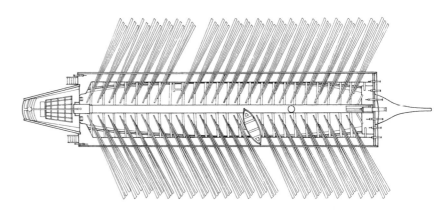

Ships of La Serenissima

The Venetian Republic was reaching its apogee as a Mediterranean seapower during the sixteenth century. Originally a fishing village, Venice's position at the head of the Adriatic encouraged trade with the hinterland to the north. Attracting raids by Dalmatians, a system of defence was constructed and a navy was founded. Independent from about AD 600, it acted as a major entrepôt for a thousand years after the Doge Pietro Orscolo II defeated the Dalmatians in 1000. During the Crusades it was a major staging post, gradually increasing in wealth, attracting the envy of Genoa and the emperor in Constantiople. Finally defeating the Genoese in 1380, defence of the rich Levantine trade brought war with the Turks, which ended with the victory of Lepanto in 1571. But the explorations of the Portuguese had opened an alternative route to the east when Bartholomew Diaz doubled the Cape of Good Hope, and Venice's fortunes began to ebb. Nevertheless, the influence of 'The Serene Republic' in the Mediterranean was enormous, as was the innovation of her shipbuilders and mariners.

40   30   20   10   0 ft
1/400
10   5   0 m

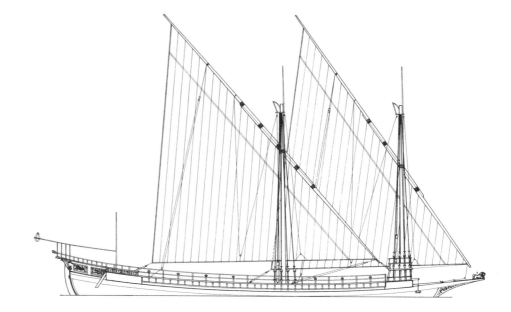

Galley, about 1500. The lion of St Mark, patron saint of La Serenissima, stands upon the extended prow of this two-masted, late fifteenth century galley. Low and fast, this craft may well have been a dispatch vessel, used to attend the flagship, or the conveyance of an important Venetian official. *(39)*

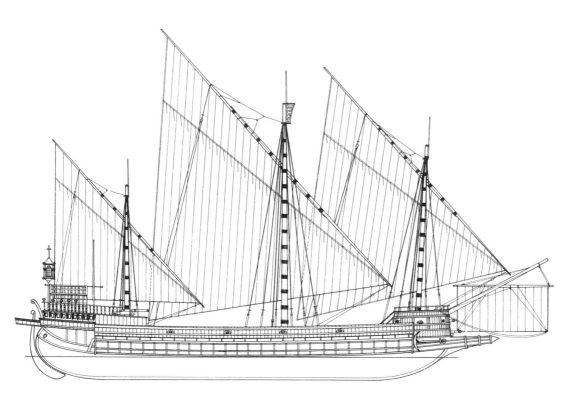

Galleasse, mid-sixteenth century. The attempts of the Venetians to produce a hybrid warship for the Mediterranean are clear in this magnificent war galleasse of the sixteenth century. Such vessels played an important part in the battle fought by the combined fleet commanded by Don Juan of Austria against the Turks at Lepanto. The Turkish commander, Ali Pasha, relied upon his archers, but the guns of the galleasses, seen here both pointing forward in the rounded forecastle, and along the upper gundeck, proved superior. Note the powerful, bronze-tipped ram, a primitive but still effective weapon which, even if it failed to strike an enemy hull, could wreck its oars and thus its manoeuvrability. *(112)*

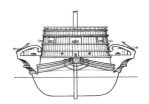

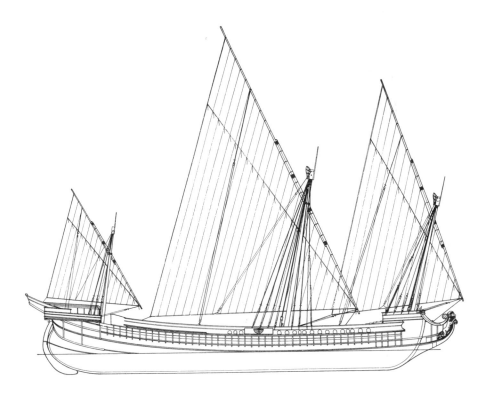

Merchant galleasse, seventeenth century. Apart from its decorated figurehead, the almost obligatory lion of St Mark, this is a sturdy, commodious and relatively simple vessel, with an efficient sailing rig, far less reliant upon her oars than former Venetian merchant galleys. *(170)*

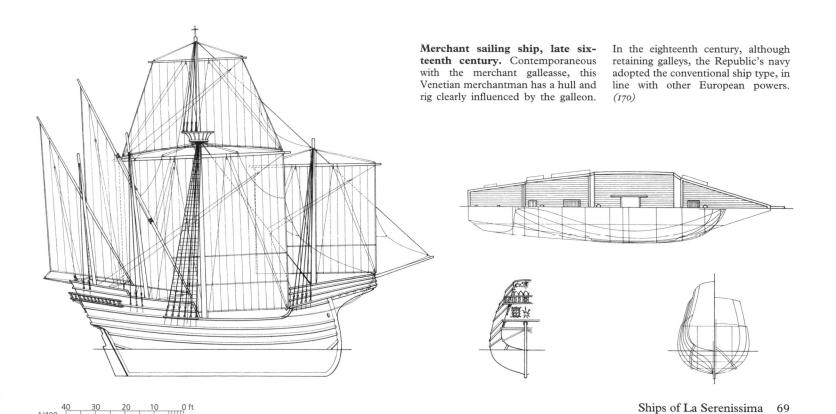

Merchant sailing ship, late sixteenth century. Contemporaneous with the merchant galleasse, this Venetian merchantman has a hull and rig clearly influenced by the galleon. In the eighteenth century, although retaining galleys, the Republic's navy adopted the conventional ship type, in line with other European powers. *(170)*

40 30 20 10 0 ft
1/400
10 5 0 m

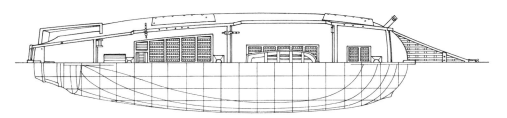

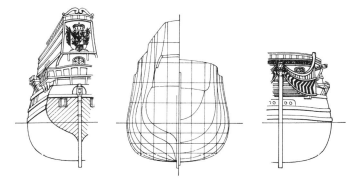

Roter Löwe, **1597.** Like many terms, that of 'frigate' has a non-specific and changing etymology, the only constant being a concept of speed. Derived from the oared sailing warship of Arabic North Africa, the name when applied to the sailing navies came to signify a warship of the second rank, developing from the smaller galleon. This is a Dutch example of 1597, built to engage the warships of Philip of Spain. *(82)*

The Beginnings of Dutch Sea-Power

The rebellion of the Protestant Dutch against the Spanish monarchy provoked a long, savage and intermittent war in the Low Countries. Insofar as the history of the sailing ship was concerned, it was the need to discover new sources of wealth that drove the Dutch, deprived of their traditional Iberian markets, to follow the Portuguese lead round the African cape and into the Indian Ocean. Since earliest times the Dutch, in their low and watery country, had been conditioned to the sea in all its moods, surviving the floods of nature and the military inundations occasioned by war. From North Sea fishermen, Dutch maritime expansion swiftly encompassed Arctic whaling in the Barents Sea (named after a Dutch mariner), and the colonisation of the East Indies. This brought them into collision with the weaker, but significant sea-power of England.

The plethora of Dutch ship-types beggars description, but the importance of Antwerp as a northern entrepôt imitated the importance of Venice and attracted foreign ships, elements of which were absorbed by the practical Dutch. They had, however, a native talent which had long exploited the channels bisecting their lands; in particular they favoured the fore-and-aft mainsail supported diagonally by a 'sprit'. Moreover, such a rig, with a stout mainmast, required a forestay upon which triangular staysails could be set. Further triangular sails, set flying and tensioned by their halliard, appeared on bowsprits, and these jibs produced an effective rig for windward work. Their smaller vessels are dealt with later.

30   20   10   0 ft
1/300
8   4   0 m

Dutch *cromster*, late sixteenth century. Meaning small ship, the *cromster* was a minor trading coasting vessel of the sixteenth century. Although carrying a lateen mizen, which makes her technically a ketch, her chief interest lies in her large sprit mainsail. By contrast with the lateen, such a sail performs well to windward and requires little handling, being self-tacking. The sprit, controlled at its outer end by vangs, is a standing spar and the sail is reduced or furled by brailing in to the mast, a simple task. During the war of independence such craft were often armed with a few heavy guns as makeshift warships. *(89)*

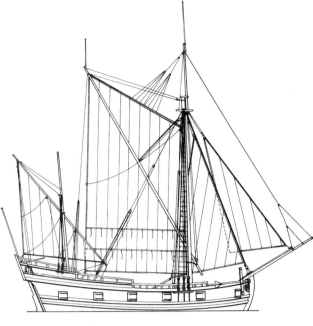

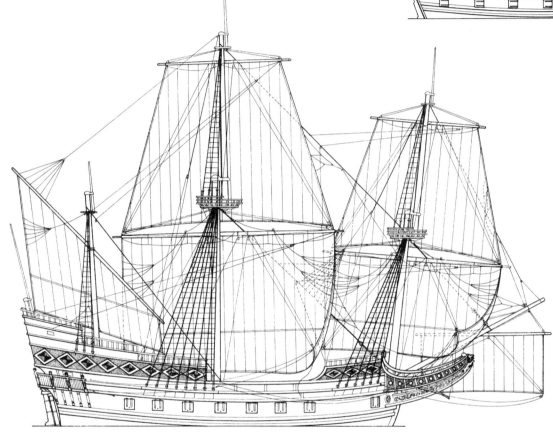

Galleon of about 1600. This vessel bears upon her poop the device of the Amsterdam admiralty. The increasing size of the topsails in relation to the main course makes for a more manageable rig, allowing the ship to be manoeuvred under her upper canvas, with her courses clewed up. *(112)*

Dutch *boyer*, late sixteenth century. The *botter, boyer* or *boier*, was a small Dutch coaster. This sixteenth century example is similar in rig to the *cromster*. The name *boyer* was to metamorphose over time, producing a variety of derivative types. *(45)*

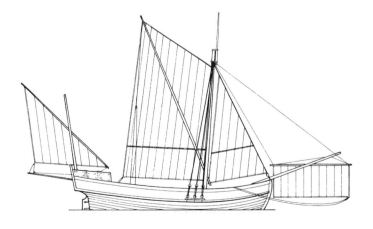

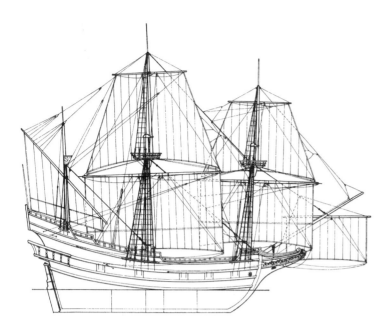

Dutch *patache*, 1616. In the sixteenth century the term meant a small armed vessel, often used as a reconnaissance vessel or a dispatch boat and as such a precursor of the French corvette or English sloop-of-war. This Dutch version would be modelled on Spanish *pataches*, several of which, of some 60 tons, sailed with the Armada as tenders. *(94)*

Dutch 'flute' of 1620. The flute was one of the most important and influential developments in the history of sail. An adaptable, low cost, high return merchantman, the flute could switch trades in reaction to market demands. One form was used to hunt the Greenland Right Whale, another, armed against the corsairs of Barbary, traded through the Straits of Gibraltar into the Mediterranean. With a characteristic high poop atop a round sterned, shallow-draughtcd but long, narrow hull, the flute, *fluit*, or *fluyt* bore a tall rig with the doubled masts that were now characteristic of Dutch ships. The tall topsails, without topgallants, kept crew-size and hence operating costs, down, making the flute a highly viable cargo-carrier. The poop was set over an opening for the tiller that ran in over the stern post. *(141)*

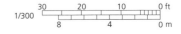

Sea-Power

THE ESTABLISHMENT of great European nation states, many of them Protestant and deaf to the central mediation of the Pope in Rome, initiated a series of maritime wars between countries competing for trade and overseas possessions. The most significant of these were the Anglo-Spanish wars of the sixteenth century, the Anglo-Dutch Wars of the seventeenth century and the Anglo-French wars of the eighteenth century. However, the development of the sailing ship also owes something to other conflicts, such as the Russo-Swedish war of the early eighteenth century and the later American Revolution, which embroiled Britain in a further war with France as well as the armed hostility of other European powers.

While commerce continued, more-or-less interrupted by assaults on it by the warring factions, the main developments in the history of sail took place within the opposing naval fleets. Initially, as in the Anglo-Spanish confrontation, matters were somewhat haphazard, but the success of sea-borne artillery was best capitalised by lining one's ships up, stem to stern. The massed cannon thus assembled on the broadsides was a formidable weapon and protected the sailing warship's two weak spots, her bow and stern. Such a concept of battle-fleet action became a shibboleth, but prompted admiralties, particularly the French, to build large men-of-war to conform to varying ranks or rates, producing a complicated structure upon which numbers of guns, sizes of complements and captains' pay depended. In practice, battle-lines were a good deal less formal, and British admirals in the wars with France between 1793 and 1814 finally destroyed the sanctity of the line-of-battle by seeking to break an enemy line, roll up a portion and annihilate it.

In their approach to warship design in the eighteenth century, the French were to establish an ascendancy, initially by carrying on with their established tradition of building larger ships rate for rate than those of their enemies, but also by encouraging a more scientific attitude to design. Although the superiority of individual French warships was to frustrate British commanders, the Royal Navy's seamanship invariably gained the upper hand, while the British strategy of blockade largely contained the French fleets throughout the successful wars of 1756-63 and 1793 to 1815. When sea control was lost and blockade could not be applied, the French navy gained notable strategic victories. The contribution of De Grasse's French fleet off the Carolinas in 1781 to Washington's victory at Yorktown is often overlooked. By depriving Great Britain of her sea-power at that crucial moment, De Grasse prevented the relief of the beleaguered Cornwallis and ensured the independence of the United States. This was the high-water mark of the Bourbon French navy.

During this long period, the greater pressure exerted upon the British was by enemy privateers. These were sent to sea by the French and their allies, particularly the Danes. With British wealth resting upon her trade, this threat was serious, and the British adopted the expedient of convoy. For escort the British developed small cruisers, most notably ship- and brig-sloops, and also frigates. These types were also employed wrecking enemy trade and were generically known as 'cruisers'. Frigates were also attached to fleets to act as lookouts and repeat signals in battle. Apart from her ship rig and single gun-deck, one of the chief characteristics of the frigate was her long endurance, allowing her to make protracted cruises against the enemy. Indeed, 'keeping the sea' was the key to British naval supremacy at the end of the era of sailing warfare; the British gained the ascendancy by producing an all-weather, all-seasons battle-fleet, a marked contrast with the campaigning-season only conflicts of two centuries earlier. With a large fleet and an ethos of sea-keeping, it ensured the final victory of British sea-power which was summed up by Napoleon, in reflective mood in exile on St Helena: 'wherever there was water to float, there you would find an English ship'.

Prestige Flagships

Following the example of King Henry VIII of England's great warship *Henri Grâce à Dieu*, it became a matter of monarchical prestige to build major men-of-war richly decorated with elaborate, carved gilded work. Skills in such decorative work were released onto the market by the austere reactions of Protestantism banning such fol-de-rols from churches, and even minor warships carried some decoration, even if only the standard lion rampant of the British Royal Navy's minor cruisers. The extent to which this extravagance could be taken was perhaps best exemplified by the *Sovereign of the Seas*, build on the orders of King Charles I of a now united kingdom of Great Britain. A king dogged by the sin of hubris, Charles's great pride led to civil war and his execution; his great ship was to end in a similar fashion, as was that of the Swedish King, Gustavus Vasa.

Prince Royal, 1610. Considered at her building by Phineas Pett to be the most magnificent ship in the world, the lavish decorations of the *Prince Royal* mask the significance of her three gun decks, later the mark of a 'First Rate line-of-battle ship'. Although only mounting 56 guns, at £1309, her decorations formed about one eighth of her total cost. Her sail plan, bearing the now standard topgallants, shows two interesting features, the small fourth mast, and the 'sprit topsail', both very necessary in handling such a large vessel, particularly when tacking. The adherence to an awkward square sail at the extremity of the bowsprit was an apparent anachronism, but modern replicas of the ships of this period have proved the sail remarkably effective when tacking. The stern shows the royal arms surmounting the initials 'HP', for Prince Henry of Wales, eldest son of King James I, who died young. *(114)*

Vasa, 1628. Built by Dutch shipwrights in Stockholm, the 800-ton *Vasa* was completed in 1628. According to tradition, King Gustavus Vasa had ordered her length to be four times her beam, on a shallow draught, possibly in emulation of the flute-form. But she carried no cargo and although ballasted, bore her lower gunports close to the water. Setting sail in full view of the king, his court and an excited populace, the mighty *Vasa* heeled to a gust of wind, drove her gunports below the waterline and down-flooded with spectacular rapidity. Her capsize into the mud of Stockholm preserved her, and her remains, raised and restored, may be seen there today. **NB.** Sail plan is 1/600 scale. *(116)*

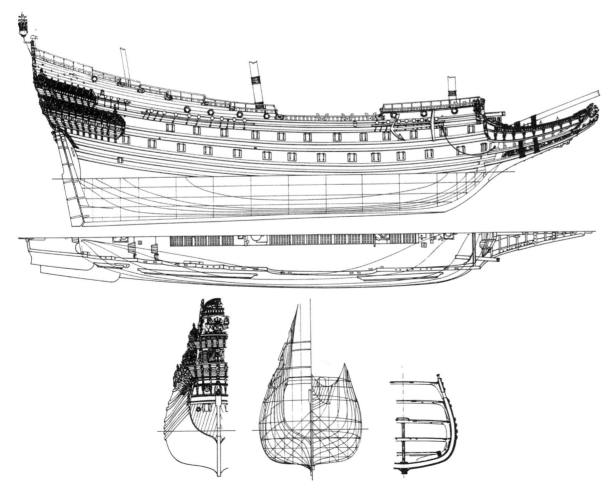

1/400   40   30   20   10   0 ft

10   5   0 m

La Couronne, 1636. One of the French fleet built in the reign of Louis XIII, *La Couronne* of 1636 was built as a response to the *Sovereign of the Seas* and commissioned a year earlier. Of similar dimensions, the French ship, displacing 2000 tons, had only 72 guns borne on two decks, and therefore failed in comparative grandiloquence with her British rival. She was, however, a more seaworthy man-of-war and was the precursor of the most successful form of wooden warship, the two-decked 74-gun Third Rate. The turreted structures on the ship's bows and quarters are splendid privies, and the unusual strengthening members incorporated by her Dutch builders, give added support to her load-bearing gun-decks. The stern lanterns carried on the poop marked the presence of an admiral and were intended to allow a fleet to maintain station on the flagship at night. **NB.** Sail plan is 1/600 scale. *(169)*

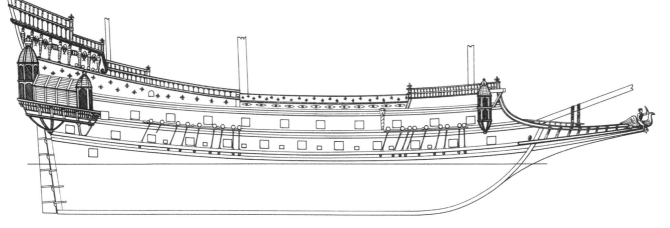

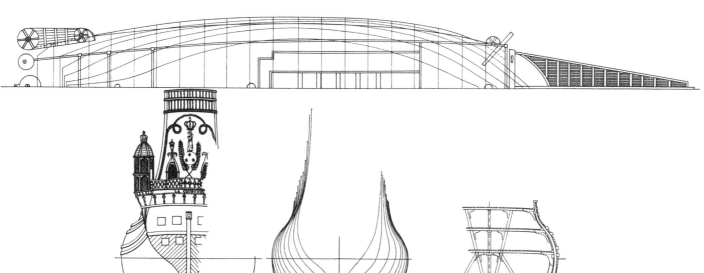

1/400

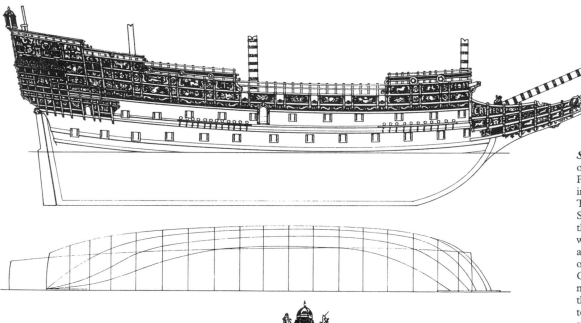

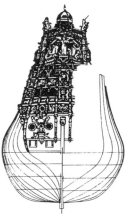

***Sovereign of the Seas*, 1637.** Much of the ornate decoration of Phineas Pett's *Sovereign of the Seas*, launched in 1637, was symbolic of British unity. The lion of England and unicorn of Scotland surmounted the poop and there were Irish and Welsh icons elsewhere; in fact there was scarcely an image from the whole pantheon of European mythology that King Charles did not desire for her. Of 38 metres, her hull bore 100 guns on three decks and she measured 1400 tons. Her cost was £65,587, a sum of staggering magnitude in the political climate of the time. Riding dangerously low in the water, she was stripped of much of her glory after the establishment of the Puritan Republic, but preserved enough to be dubbed 'the Golden Devil' by the Dutch during the first of their wars with Britain. She became the *Royal Sovereign* at the time of the restoration of the monarchy in 1660 and met her end when, in 1696, an overset candle set her ablaze. Her tall rig, that of a three-masted, full-rigged ship, boasts sails above the top-gallants; these were called 'royals'. **NB.** The sail plan is 1/600 scale *(112)*

1/400

40 30 20 10 0 ft

10 5 0 m

Prince Maurice's *jacht*, 1600. This relatively simple precursor of more elaborate state-yachts was built for Prince Maurice of Orange in 1600. *(94)*

State yacht, mid seventeenth century. This later example of a Dutch-built state-yacht, also well furnished with flagstaffs, including one at the extremity of the gaff, dates from the mid seventeenth century. It shows several differences, most notably a more rounded hull form, a square topsail and a loose-footed mainsail set on a standing gaff, not a sprit, but still brailing in to the mast. She is pierced for small cannon and possesses an elaborate cabin aft. The gaff main and square topsail were characteristics of English adaptation. *(112)*

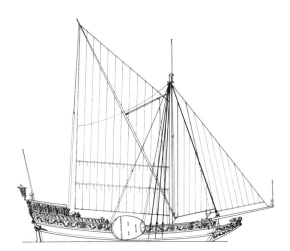

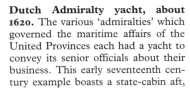

Dutch Admiralty yacht, about 1620. The various 'admiralties' which governed the maritime affairs of the United Provinces each had a yacht to convey its senior officials about their business. This early seventeenth century example boasts a state-cabin aft, and sufficient flagstaffs to display the national ensign, a jack and the official's banner at the masthead. The sprit rig differs from earlier examples by having a high peak, but the efficient headsails are prominent, as are her leeboards. *(112)*

The Origins of the Yacht

The origins of the yacht are only in part associated with pleasure. As far as competition is concerned, it was not initially that between friendly rivals, but as between pursuer and pursued, for the term originates from a Germanic root meaning 'hunter'. The presentation of a Dutch yacht to King Charles II on his restoration in London in 1660 transferred the word into English, eclipsing the native word 'pinnace', but it is the quest for speed and windward efficiency that secures the yachts of the seventeenth century a position in the history of sail. Incorporating the lessons and techniques of the small, able cargo-carriers of the Zuider Zee and Dutch waterways, the sprit rig was to be a familiar sight on the Thames in the succeeding three centuries.

The Dutch in particular pioneered yacht development, their officials requiring water-transport in the great ports of the United Provinces of the Netherlands. The *Stadtholder*, or head of state, was provided with a state-yacht of considerable splendour, and this concept migrated elsewhere in Europe.

The ability of these craft to work to windward was made possible not only by their rig, but by leeboards. Faced with the problem of shallow water preventing a deep draughted, long-keeled hull form, the Dutch fitted heavy, iron-shod oak boards on each side. These could be lowered on the lee side when beating, to inhibit leeward drift. They were, moreover, so shaped that their cross-section was hydrodynamic, and in passing through the water conferred 'lift', assisting the hull laterally to windward. Leeboards were raised when lying alongside, or running before the wind.

Dutch *besanjacht*, seventeenth century. The *besanjacht* was a small tender or auxiliary used throughout the seventeenth century, such as might be used to convey passengers about the waterways. She was characterised by a small gaff and a boomed, loose-footed mainsail. The form was common for a number of differing applications. The bowsprit could be lifted, or 'steeved' to reduce length when berthing. *(112)*

Dutch yacht, seventeenth century. The term *besanjacht* was loosely applied, suggesting function, rather than rig. Many bore two masts, the foremost being well forward to dispense with a bowsprit and reduce length amid the crowded quays of the Dutch cities. Modern twin-masted una-rigs attest to the efficiency of this configuration. *(112)*

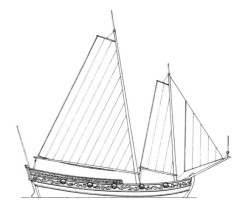

Dutch yacht, about 1700. This *besanjacht* suggests why the term later referred to early Dutch ketch and yawl forms, for the name 'schooner' had yet to be invented. The example shows the diversity of basic forms that the ingenious Dutch used, many being merely variations established by local tradition, or on the orders of owners. This two-master, with jib and bowsprit, may have been a warship's tender, for she mounts ten small guns. *(112)*

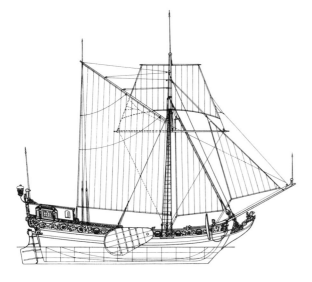

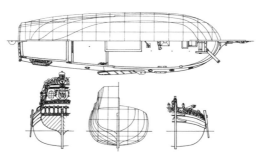

'The Elector's Large Yacht', 1678. The stirrings of Prussian naval ambition might be discerned in this splendid state-yacht of 1678 from Brandenburg-Prussia. The Elector of Brandenburg had his first yacht built in Amsterdam in 1652 and this was his second, known as 'The Elector's Large Yacht'. Although built in Kolberg, her Dutch ancestry is obvious, with leeboards for sailing in the Baltic shallows. The ornate stern cabin, lantern and guns, mark her as 'royal', but an interesting feature is the projecting cat-head, facilitating the handling of her anchor. Her hull was 20 metres in length and she mounted ten guns. She was broken up in 1721. *(82)*

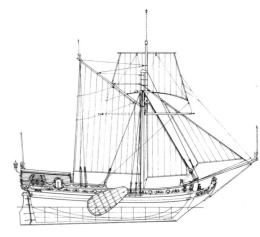

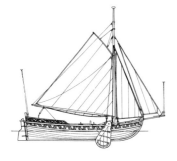

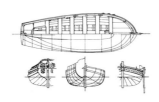

Peter the Great's boat, 1688. The naval ambitions of Tsar Peter the Great of Russia grew after his 'great embassy' of 1697-1698 during which he visited the shipyards of Amsterdam and London. The Tsar's interest in sailing had been aroused much earlier when, in exile, he learned to sail on a 6-metre long boat on the royal estate at Ismailovskovo. Attributed to both Dutch and English builders, the small boat displays the leeboards typical of the time, and her true origins are obscure, though it was a Dutchman, Karl Brandt, who taught Peter to sail. **NB.** Twice scale *(231)*

Brandenburg yacht, 1694. A somewhat later example of one of three further Dutch *stadtjachts* exported to Brandenburg Prussia. Dating from 1694, the square topsail was to become a feature of the fast naval 'cutter' which developed, particularly in England, from the yacht. *(192)*

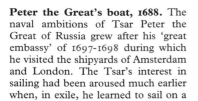

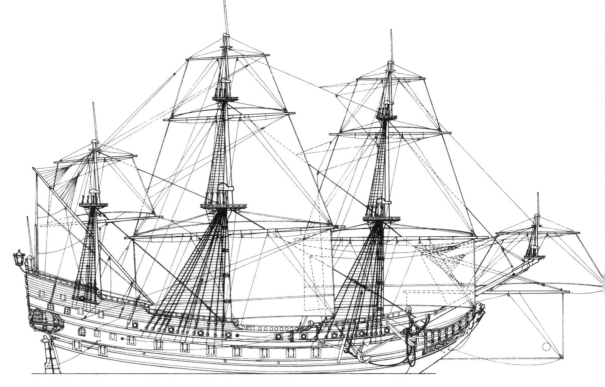

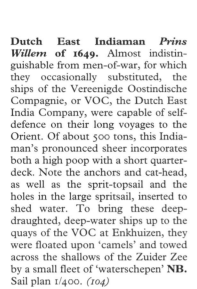

Dutch East Indiaman *Prins Willem* of 1649. Almost indistinguishable from men-of-war, for which they occasionally substituted, the ships of the Vereenigde Oostindische Compagnie, or VOC, the Dutch East India Company, were capable of self-defence on their long voyages to the Orient. Of about 500 tons, this Indiaman's pronounced sheer incorporates both a high poop with a short quarter-deck. Note the anchors and cat-head, as well as the sprit-topsail and the holes in the large spritsail, inserted to shed water. To bring these deep-draughted, deep-water ships up to the quays of the VOC at Enkhuizen, they were floated upon 'camels' and towed across the shallows of the Zuider Zee by a small fleet of 'waterschepen' **NB.** Sail plan 1/400. *(104)*

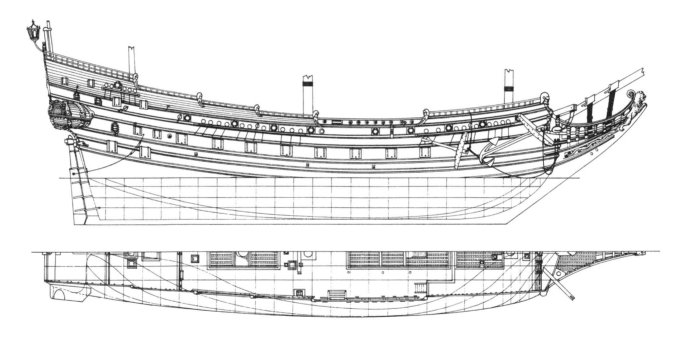

Ships of the Low Countries

The spectacular rise of Dutch sea-power, based upon wealth generated from commerce, led to an expansion of shipbuilding in the yards around Amsterdam, the creation of a vast infrastructure of canals, dykes and locks, a regulatory authority and a banking system. In addition to a battle-fleet, Dutch shipping included every class of vessel, from the tiny cargo-carriers of the waterways, to large Indiamen which ventured as far as Java and China in their quest for spices, rare woods, precious metals, jewels, tea and coffee.

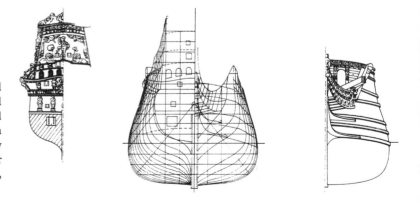

1/300

30   20   10   0 ft

8   4   0 m

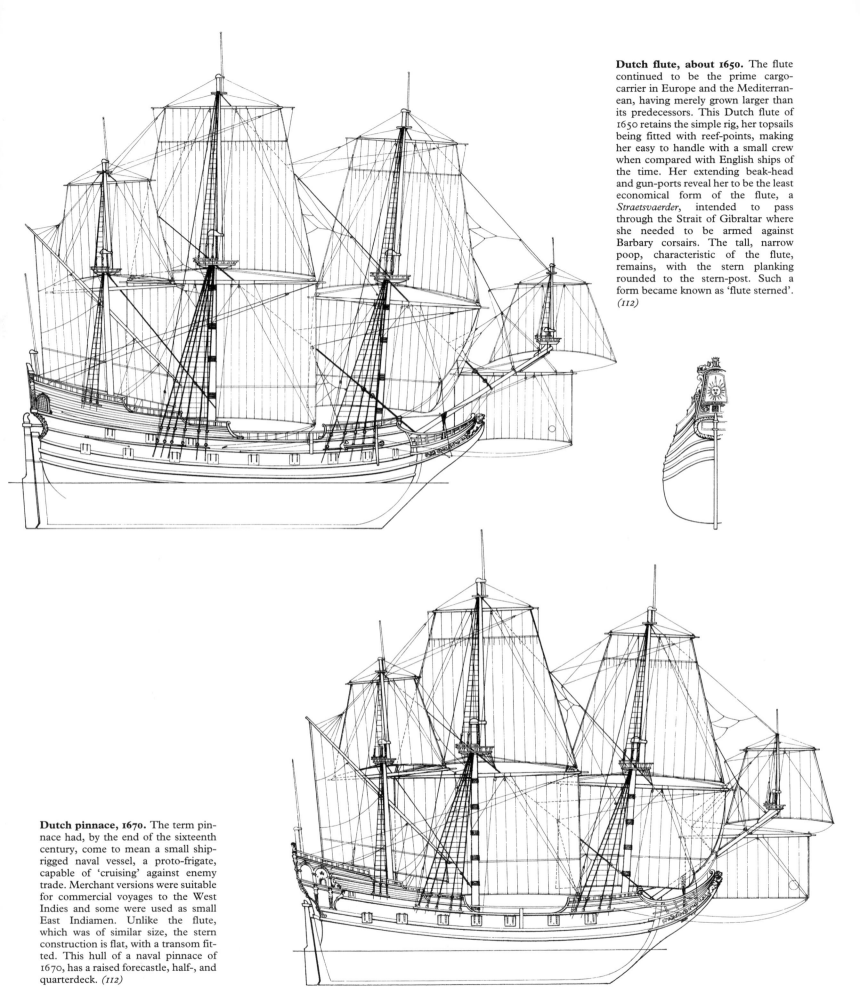

Dutch flute, about 1650. The flute continued to be the prime cargo-carrier in Europe and the Mediterranean, having merely grown larger than its predecessors. This Dutch flute of 1650 retains the simple rig, her topsails being fitted with reef-points, making her easy to handle with a small crew when compared with English ships of the time. Her extending beak-head and gun-ports reveal her to be the least economical form of the flute, a *Straetsvaerder*, intended to pass through the Strait of Gibraltar where she needed to be armed against Barbary corsairs. The tall, narrow poop, characteristic of the flute, remains, with the stern planking rounded to the stern-post. Such a form became known as 'flute sterned'. *(112)*

Dutch pinnace, 1670. The term pinnace had, by the end of the sixteenth century, come to mean a small ship-rigged naval vessel, a proto-frigate, capable of 'cruising' against enemy trade. Merchant versions were suitable for commercial voyages to the West Indies and some were used as small East Indiamen. Unlike the flute, which was of similar size, the stern construction is flat, with a transom fitted. This hull of a naval pinnace of 1670, has a raised forecastle, half-, and quarterdeck. *(112)*

30   20   10   0 ft

1/300

8   4   0 m

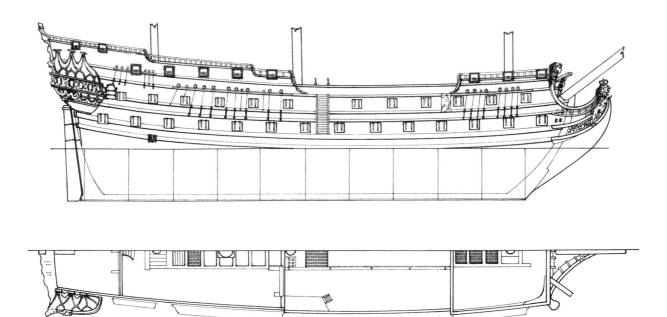

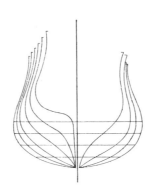

Willem Rex, 1698. This Dutch man-of-war carries two continuous decks of guns, with weapons of lighter calibre on her forecastle, half- and quarter-decks. Although still richly decorated, especially about her stern, the home of her senior officers, the ship is a more practical proposition than the prestige flagships of earlier in the century. Note the projecting cat-head and the side 'chain-wales', extending the supporting platform for the shrouds and backstays. This reconstruction is based on a contemporary model. *(170)*

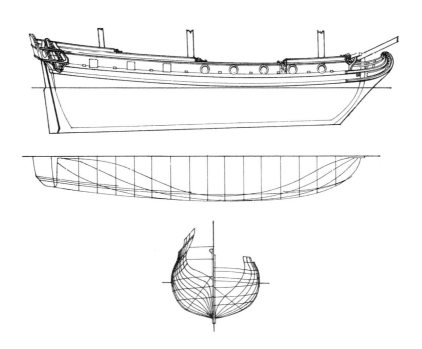

Ostend privateer Neptunus, about 1690. The commerce of a trading nation is always vulnerable to attack and in time of war needed the protection afforded by convoy. Governments licensed private vessels with 'letters of marque and reprisal' to legally attack enemy merchant ships for profit. Certain ports derived considerable wealth from this practice, one of which was Ostend, then part of the Austrian Netherlands, from which this 'privateer' hailed. These privateers were generally fast, armed and heavily manned vessels. This example, has a low sheer and relatively fine hull, making the overhauling of a slower merchantman only a matter of time. The vessel is of interest because it was the subject of the earliest known drawing by the infant F H Chapman, who grew up to be one of the greatest naval architects of the eighteenth century. *(34)*

30   20   10   0 ft
1/300
8   4   0 m

Wappen von Hamburg of 1667.
This powerful man-of-war was a form
of prestigious flagship for the city she
represents, designed to deter any vessel from interfering with the trade that
was so vital to the prosperity of the
Hamburgers. Her figurehead and
stern bear the heraldic gateway that is
the device of the great city dominating
the River Elbe. Similar to major Dutch
warships, she shows considerable tumblehome to support two continuous
decks mounting 66 heavy guns. Her
ship-rig, with single-reefed topsails
and topgallants, spritsail and sprit topsail is the standard sailing rig of her
generation. *(176)*

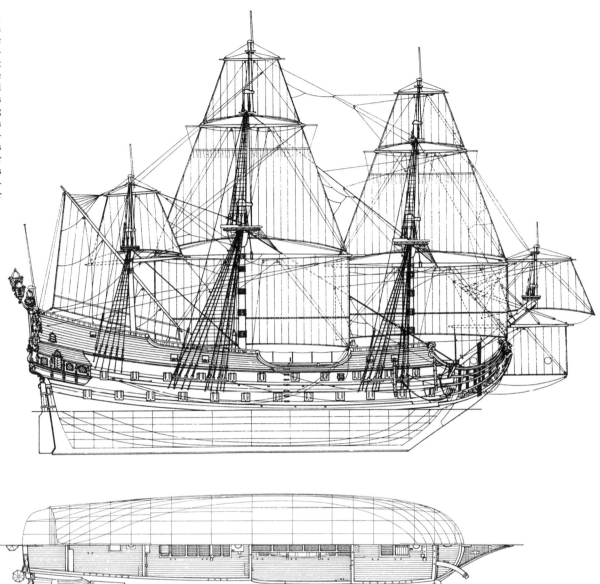

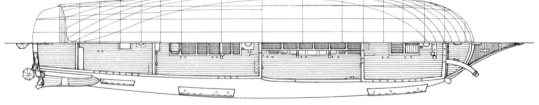

The Influence of Dutch Shipbuilding

The Dutch not only dominated world commerce, owning the largest
merchant fleet ever seen, but exported their shipbuilding expertise, in
particular to the small, fragmented states of what later became
Germany. The most powerful of these, Brandenburg-Prussia, with
ports on the southern shores of the Baltic and a system of waterways
reaching into the hinterland, maintained a small fleet to protect its convoys of neutral merchant ships from the depredations of hostile powers.
Quasi-independent cities, such as the ancient Hanseatic foundation of
Hamburg, also maintained the integrity of its seaward approaches by
building a small but powerful naval force. These men-of-war exhibited
the characteristics of Dutch shipbuilding.

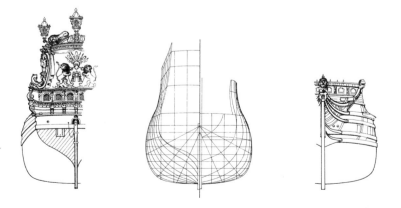

40   30   20   10   0 ft
1/400 ├┼┼┼┼┼┼┼┤
        10   5   0 m

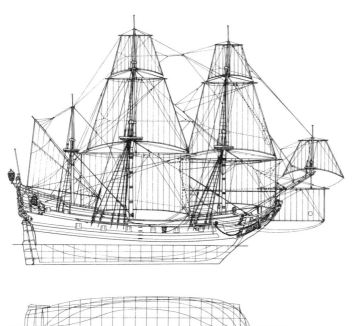

Brandenburg frigate *Berlin*, 1674.
The term 'frigate', signifying a lesser warship, begins to emerge in the late seventeenth century. In due course it was to be hull-specific, denoting a flush-decked and fast ship, both merchant and naval, before returning to the purpose of identifying a major cruiser-type, with her guns on a single deck. This Brandenburg man-of-war is therefore a precursor of the true naval frigate of the classical era of naval sail, but conforms to the specification of possessing a substantial armament on a single gun-deck, with lines fine enough to turn in a creditable speed. She still retains the long beakhead necessary to handle the headsails and the high half- and quarterdecks. *(82)*

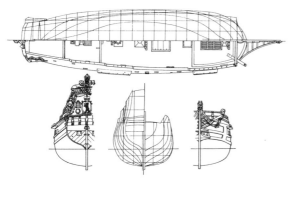

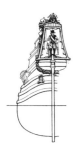 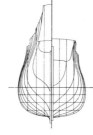

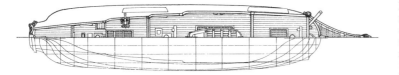

Brandenburg flute *Derfflinger*, 1684. Like other former Hanseatic cities, Danzig (modern Gdansk) possessed armed ships. One, a flute named the *Wolkensäule* and built in 1675, was acquired by the Great Elector of Brandenburg-Prussia in 1684. She was renamed after the Prussian Marshal Derfflinger and used as an armed merchantman, bearing 16 guns and a small, economic crew of about 20 men. The *Derfflinger* made voyages to West Africa and India until her capture by a French privateer in 1693. Recaptured by a British cruiser, she was returned to Brandenburg and then sold to Emden interests in 1694. Note the narrow hull, the round stern and tiller-entry, all characteristic of the flute. The port low on the quarter is for cargo-access, not a gun-port. *(82)*

40	30	20	10	0 ft

1/400

| 10 | | 5 | | 0 m |

Brandenburg frigate *Friedrich Wilhelm zu Pferde*, **1684.** Although termed a frigate, this small warship bears her main armament on two continuous decks. She shows the limitations of Dutch men-of-war, limitations which were to prove fatal to Dutch naval ambition, for shallow draught warships, which could bear no more than two decks of relatively small calibre weapons, would soon be unable to compete with the increasing sizes of guns carried in the large French and particularly British line-of-battle ships which would emerge in the eighteenth century. *(82) Scale 1/400*

The French Navy of Louis XIV

Under Louis XIV, the Sun King, the French monarchy was to reach a pinnacle of extravagance. The navy established by Richelieu had fallen into decay under his successor Mazarin, and the new minister, Colbert, had to begin again in 1663. At the beginning of the new reign, Colbert wrote that 'nothing...so befits the Majesty of the King than that his ships bear the finest ornament on the high seas' and with this air of grandiloquence, Louis' minister set out to build up a massive battle-fleet based upon a system of rating so complex that it had to be modified in 1684. French finances, however, were quite inadequate to maintain this and in order to conserve the new ships, they remained largely unexercised, the consequence of which was decline.

This was not immediately apparent and for the British, the challenge of a French fleet-in-being became a major strategic problem for the succeeding century. Using Dutch, Maltese and Spanish skills, but building larger, deeper draught men-of-war, Colbert's fleet became the most powerful in Europe. Of broader beam and greater freeboard than their British counterparts, they mounted heavier batteries and on a visit to Portsmouth in 1673, the French two-decked, 74-gun *Superbe* inspired the British to enlarge their designs.

Royal Louis **of 1668.** A simplified drawing of a first class French flagship, first of Colbert's super-First Rates, which by virtue of her 120 guns belonged to *le premier rang extraordinaire*. Although Colbert built the first of his new fleet in The Netherlands, the *Royal Louis* was laid down in the great dockyard at Toulon and registered 2000 tons (this figure was official propoganda, and by the British system she came out at about 1650 tons). In *le premier rang extraordinaire* with the *Royal Louis*, were *Le Soleil Royal* of 120 guns, *La Reine* of 104, and *Le Royal Dauphin* of 100 guns. *Royal Louis* was 50 metres in length but was replaced with a ship of the same name in 1697. *(169) Scale 1/800*

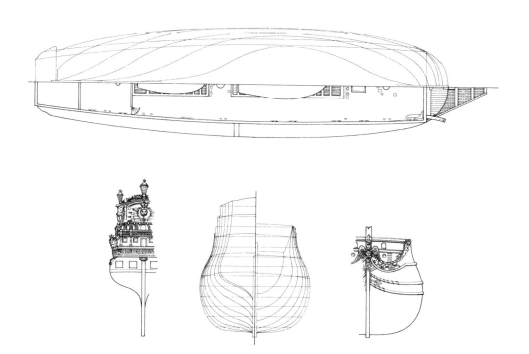

Le Phenix, **86 guns, 1664.** This draught represents the ships mounting between 80 and 100 guns. The ranking band was subdivided into subsidiary classes, an 80-gun ship being of the First Rate, but of the Third Class within it. Designed as standard line-of-battle ships they registered between 1500 and 1800 tons and mounted 36-pounders on their lower gun decks. Although fitted with guns on her quarterdeck and forecastle, *Le Phenix* is a two-decker, an early example of this successful type. Her sail plan, with its sprit-topsail, is rooted in the seventeenth century, but this drawing shows triangular, fore-and-aft staysails. *(237)*

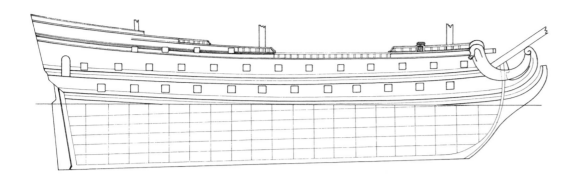

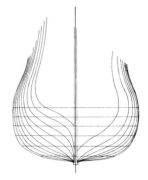

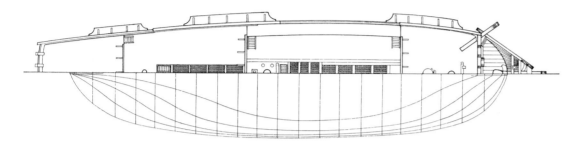

A Second Rate, Second Class, about 1670. Supporting the three classes of the First Rate, came the two-deckers mounting between 60 and 80 guns. The impressive 70-gun *Superbe*, which caused a sensation when she visited Portsmouth, measured 1300 tons and was in the first class of this rate. *(169)*

A Third Rate, First Class, about 1670. French Third Rates mounted between 50 and 60 guns on two decks. These were the weakest rate to be considered fit for the line-of-battle. In time these subdivisions proved unrealistic in terms of gun-power and the French fell broadly in line with the British practice. *(169)*

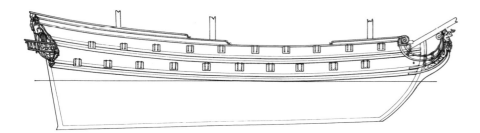

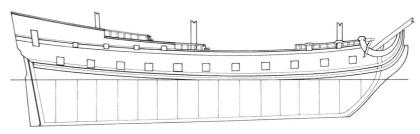

L'Amphitrite, a Fourth Rate, First Class, 1700. Vessels of less than 50 guns were not considered suitable for the battle-line. This draught shows a two-decker used in support of a battle-fleet or as a cruiser, sent against the enemy's trade. *(169)*

Le Capricieux, 1689. This smaller, Second Class, Fourth Rate may be regarded as a proto-frigate, designed to act in support of the main fleet. *(169)*

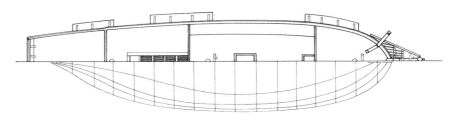

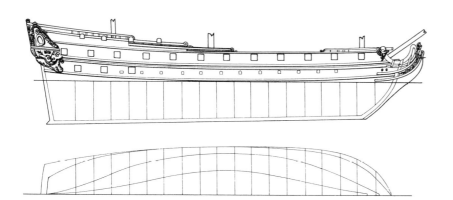

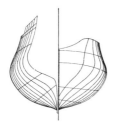

La Gloire of 1707. Built specifically as a commerce raider, the French *demi-batterie* ship was introduced in the late seventeenth century. This example was captured by the British in 1709 during the War of the Spanish Succession. However, under the command of the corsair Duguay-Trouin, she had scored notable successes. Originally built with three lower-deck gunports cut in the quarters (as shown), these had been increased to five at the time of her capture. The lower deck was otherwise pierced for its entire length by ports for sweeps, long oars which enabled *La Gloire* to be pulled when in pursuit of becalmed merchantmen. Armed with 40 French 8-pounder guns, small anti-personnel 4-pounders were mounted on her quarterdeck. *(169)*

40   30   20   10   0 ft
1/400
10   5   0 m

Fifth Rate, 24 guns, about 1680.
Ports for guns and sweeps on the
lower deck are seen in this draught of a
small cruiser. Such ships were soon
outmoded, replaced by the single-
decked corvette and frigate during the
eighteenth century. *(169)*

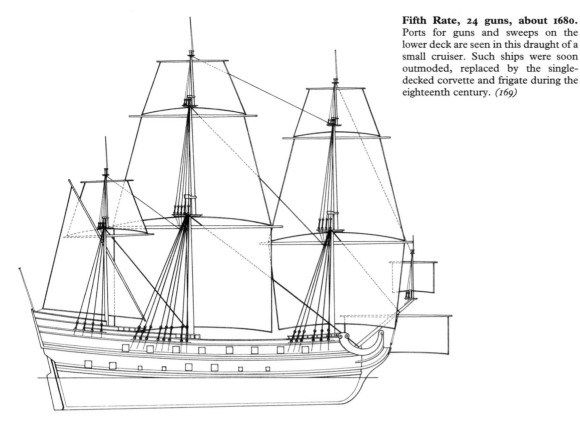

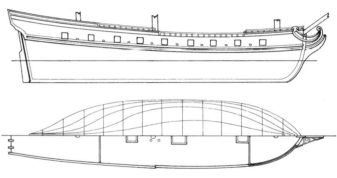

Bomb ketch, 1679. In the late seventeenth century the French invented the
bomb vessel, a new type specifically
designed for shore bombardment with
heavy mortars. The ketch rig (called in
French a *galiote* or galliot) enabled a
pair of heavy mortars to be located
athwartships on an uncluttered deck
forward of the mainmast. Built with
extremely heavy scantlings to absorb
the recoil of her mortars, the bomb galliot was first employed by Du Quesne
against Algiers in 1682. To enable the
mortar shells to be accurately aimed, a
bomb galliot was brought to a single
anchor, upon the cable of which
another rope was clapped. By heaving
and veering these and setting steadying
sails, the entire vessel could be pointed
at the target. Range was achieved by
the size of the charge, the timing of the
explosion by the length of the fuse. To
avoid damaging her forward standing
rigging, it was of chain. Note the jib
and staysail. *(112)*

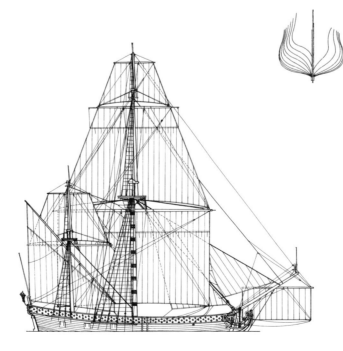

Fregate légère, **about 1690.** Although denominated a *Fregate légère*
this small 16-gun cruiser is closer in
function to a sloop-of-war than the
later frigate. Nevertheless, the tasks
upon which this vessel, like the Fifth
Rate, would be employed were to be
similar, consisting of commerce raiding, trade protection, patrol and
reconnaissance. *(169)*

40   30   20   10   0 ft
1/400
10   5   0 m

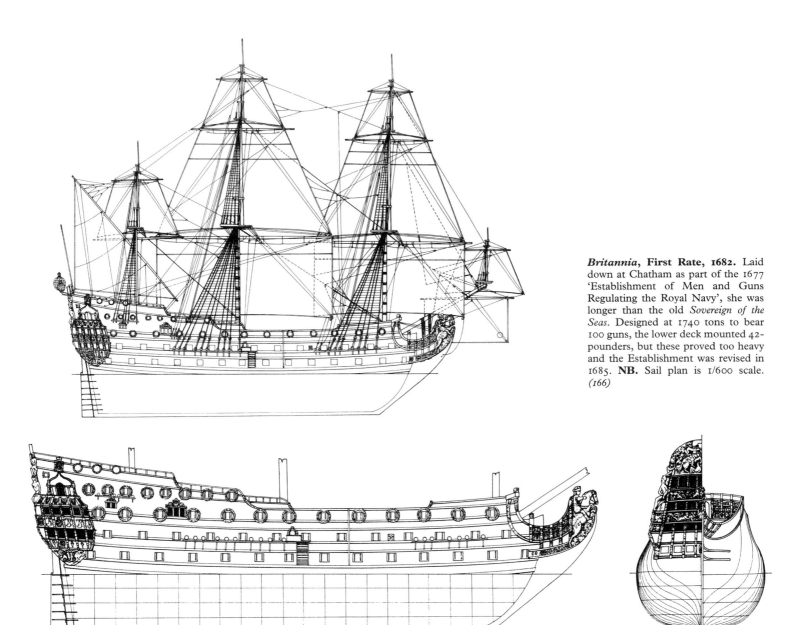

***Britannia*, First Rate, 1682.** Laid down at Chatham as part of the 1677 'Establishment of Men and Guns Regulating the Royal Navy', she was longer than the old *Sovereign of the Seas*. Designed at 1740 tons to bear 100 guns, the lower deck mounted 42-pounders, but these proved too heavy and the Establishment was revised in 1685. **NB.** Sail plan is 1/600 scale. *(166)*

The British Restoration Navy

The restoration of King Charles II in 1660 ended the dissension that had riven Britain for a generation. The newly united kingdom now had to confront the rising threat of the Dutch as well as containing the greater power of France. France sought domination over Europe, the Dutch the unchallenged dominance of sea-borne trade. The British position was weak, the country's finances being in a ruinous condition thanks to the English Civil War, and the contest with The Netherlands was hard-fought. Despite the humiliations of defeat, and not for the last time, British sea-power emerged in better shape. The ships of her navy were better fitted for their tasks and the naval administration was better organised under the guiding genius of such men as Samuel Pepys and Sir Anthony Deane. Several influential men took an interest in the navy,

chief among whom was the king's brother James, Duke of York, a commander of distinction in his own right.

Like the French, the British introduced a system of rating and although this needed an overhaul to avoid overloading ships with too great a weight of artillery, it proved a simpler one than Colbert's, dispensing with intermediate classes. Ships of less than 50 guns were not considered suitable to stand in the line-of-battle, and whenever possible they were excluded, being used as independent cruisers.

Though it was to suffer from a degree of mismanagement and neglect, the fleet of Charles II might be said to have properly founded the institution of the British Royal Navy which was to be so important an exemplar of sea-power in the succeeding two centuries.

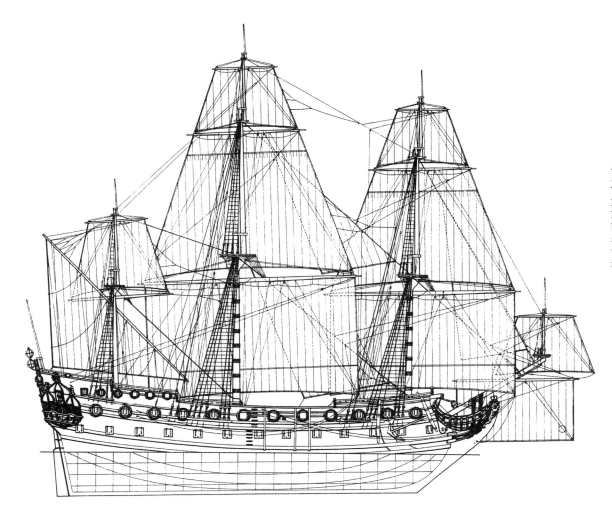

Resolution, 70 guns, 1667. Built by Sir Anthony Deane, this two-decked Third Rate measured 45 metres. Of her design, it is said that Charles II himself insisted on her having a large beam. Whether or not this is true, she acquired a fine reputation for seaworthiness. Note that staysails and jibs now feature as standard. *(228)*

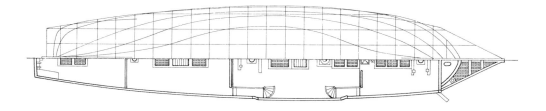

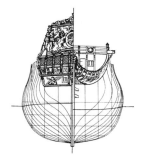

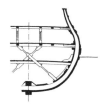

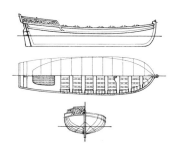

Resolution's longboat. The boats of men-of-war were numerous and important, used not only for the conveyance of officers, but in making attacks, landing troops and the domestic tasks of bringing off wood, water, stores and provisions. This example is the longboat of the *Resolution*, the largest boat, which was usually towed when the ship was at sea. **NB.** 1/300 scale *(228)*

1/400

40 30 20 10 0 ft

10 5 0 m

Fourth Rate, 50 guns, of about 1680. The late seventeenth century ship rig is shown here without topgallants. Although the lower courses are provided with reef points, the huge topsails have double reefing, revealing their increasing importance. Men-of-war clewed up their lower sails to manoeuvre and fight, the ships being more manageable in this state, but when encountering strengthening winds all ships shortened down to reefed topsails, their being so much easier to control than the large loose-footed courses. The 'crowsfeet' extending from the leading edges of the tops to the appropriate forestay are to protect the valuable topsails. Note the gap between the main and foremasts. This area is 'the waist' and was open, allowing ventilation to the gun-deck below. The space was beamed over and the ship's boats were stowed here, hoisted outboard by means of tackles on the main stay and the main and fore yardarms. *(112)*

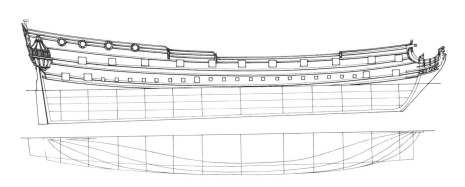

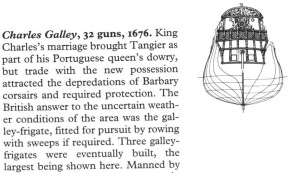

Charles Galley, **32 guns, 1676.** King Charles's marriage brought Tangier as part of his Portuguese queen's dowry, but trade with the new possession attracted the depredations of Barbary corsairs and required protection. The British answer to the uncertain weather conditions of the area was the galley-frigate, fitted for pursuit by rowing with sweeps if required. Three galley-frigates were eventually built, the largest being shown here. Manned by 160 impressed Thames watermen in addition to their seamen, they were rigged as ships to give good performance under sail. Regarded as Fourth Rates, they mounted 30 guns and were capable of independent operations. *(89)*

Saudadoes, **20 guns, 1673.** One of the undertakings made to a suspicious parliament to induce them to finance naval rearmament under Charles II was to remove the King's actual title to 'his' fleet. Nevertheless, Charles found money particularly for the Royal Yachts, about two dozen of which were built in Britain following the gift of one by the Dutch. Charles and his brother James enjoyed gambling on the result of races, among the consequences of which were improvements in hull and rig. Several of the Royal Yachts were engaged on Admiralty business, including acting as dispatch boats and small cruisers. They were rated as Sixth Rates and manned by the Royal Navy. Conversely, several ship-rigged Sixth Rates acted as Royal Yachts and one of these was the *Saudadoes* seen here. Carrying 20 guns, she was the equivalent of the later ship-sloop. *(166)*

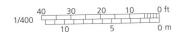

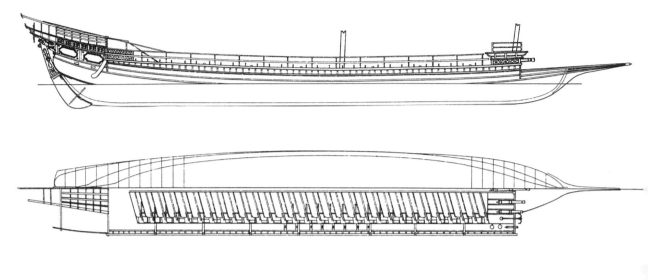

Maltese *capitana*, mid eighteenth century. The flagship of the Captain of the Galleys of the Knights of Malta was named *La Capitana* after that officer, the galley of the Grand Master being known as *La Magistrale*. This example of a 'capitana' from the mid eighteenth century was 55 metres between stem and sternpost and mounted a single, heavy 36-pounder, flanked by a pair of 8-pounders, and a pair of 6-pounders. A number of smaller anti-personnel swivel guns were situated elsewhere along her length. No longer pulled *alla zenzile*, the oars were longer and fewer, 30 per side in this case, each being worked by five or sometimes six men. The amount of energy expended, particularly by the slaves operating the inner looms must have been incredible, for synchronisation was crucial and these craft moved at a staggering pace. This method of rowing was known as *a scaloccio*. (34)

The Last of the Mediterranean Galley Fleets

It was not until the nineteenth century that the day of the galley finally passed, the type having existed as a warship in the Mediterranean since the dawn of European civilisation. France, Venice, Genoa, Spain, Portugal, the Papal States and the Knights of Malta continued to operate them well into the 1700s, buying slaves when there were insufficient local malefactors to fill up the rowing benches. The repressive regimes of the kings of Spain and Portugal, the Popes, the Doge, the Grand-Masters at Valletta and the pre-Revolutionary French monarchs, using *lettres de cache* to root out any opposition, consigned dissidents to the living death of the galleys. Although propelled by sail when the wind served, the galley remained primarily powered by human toil. She was never entirely ousted by the sailing warship, being replaced when steam power made redundant the labour of wretched men.

To the end the galley manifested the hubristic ornamentation of despotic power, beautifully embellished with carved and gilded allegorical decorations, brightly painted and sporting the gonfalon or the oriflamme of her principal, she stank from the misery of the hundreds of men cooped up in her, chained to their benches and dying slowly from indescribable inhumanity, disease and starvation. It comes as no surprise that Le Roi Soleil, Louis XIV, in ordering Colbert to overhaul his navy, revived the French galley fleet. Colbert, in sycophantic mood, agreed: 'there is no more powerful a sign of the greatness of a prince than his show of galleys, which guarantee his good reputation abroad.'

In order to bring her heavy cannon to bear, a galley had to be aimed at her adversary, a slow business in so long a hull, but in a calm she could take up a position astern of a sailing man-of-war and rake her. In a breeze, on the other hand, a skilful commander in a sailing ship could bring his broadside to bear and rake a galley the length of her deck, decimating her oarsmen and wrecking her oars. Several spirited fights were put up against galleys, most notable being a drawn engagement between the 26-gun *Lion Couronné* and eleven galleys in 1651 and the defeat of thirty-five galleys by the ship *Le Bon* in 1684. But despite this demonstrable superiority, kings, popes, doges and grand-masters retained their galleys, an intimidating deterrent to their subject people, if not their enemies, and their successors continued to maintain the galley fleet. These most durable of warships, also proved the cheapest to build and maintain.

The last major action between galleys was fought off Cape Matapan on 19 July 1717, when a mixed force of fifty-seven Venetian, Spanish, Portuguese and Papal vessels, included galleys, engaged a Turkish fleet of similar strength. The Turks withdrew after a hard fight. King Ferdinand of the Two Sicilies had two half-galleys built in 1804 and to be pulled by freemen. They took part in an attack on the island of Caprera in 1815. Only in the Baltic did the oared warship continue to linger, the very last in action being the Russians at Åbo in 1854 during the misnamed Crimean War.

1/400 40 30 20 10 0 ft
10 5 0 m

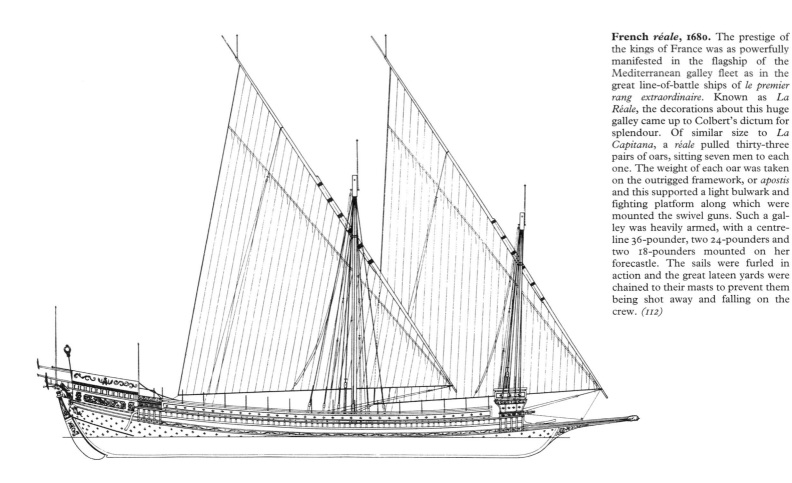

French *réale*, 1680. The prestige of the kings of France was as powerfully manifested in the flagship of the Mediterranean galley fleet as in the great line-of-battle ships of *le premier rang extraordinaire*. Known as *La Réale*, the decorations about this huge galley came up to Colbert's dictum for splendour. Of similar size to *La Capitana*, a *réale* pulled thirty-three pairs of oars, sitting seven men to each one. The weight of each oar was taken on the outrigged framework, or *apostis* and this supported a light bulwark and fighting platform along which were mounted the swivel guns. Such a galley was heavily armed, with a centre-line 36-pounder, two 24-pounders and two 18-pounders mounted on her forecastle. The sails were furled in action and the great lateen yards were chained to their masts to prevent them being shot away and falling on the crew. *(112)*

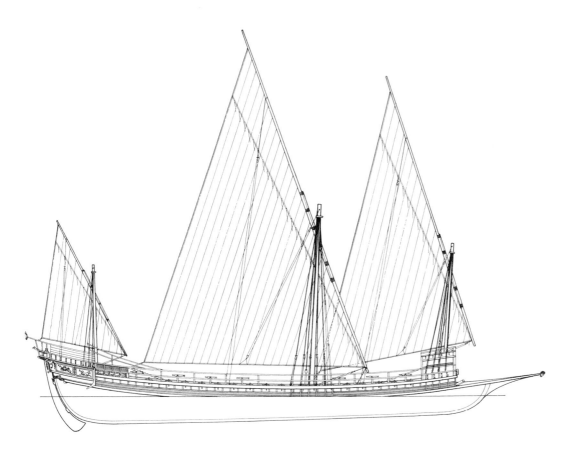

La Ferme, **1690.** To this vessel belongs the dubious honour of being the last French galley. Long disused and discredited as a symbol of despotic abuse, she was broken up on the orders of Napoleon. *(167)*

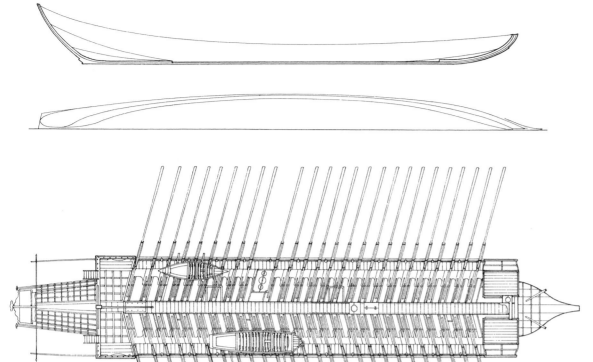

French galley, 1697. This detailed plan of the hull is of a French *ordinaire*, or regular galley, of 1697. The space taken up by the 'missing' oar on the port side is the location of the vessel's cooking area. *(167)*

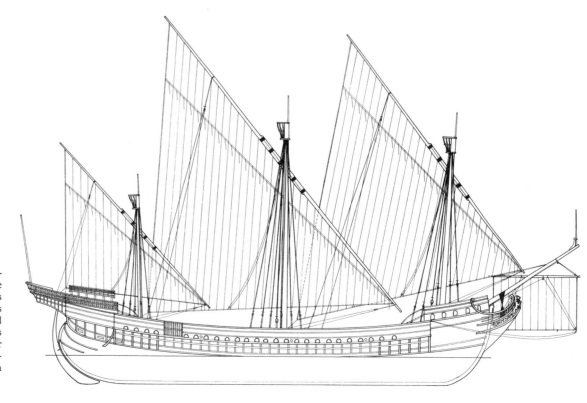

Venetian *galleasse*, 1669. The *galleasse* had altered little in appearance and this late Venetian example is almost identical to her predecessors which fought at Lepanto. The hybrid nature of the craft remained, but its broadside, strong enough to counter the mixed calibre armament of the sixteenth century galleon, was already an anachronism. *(112)*

1/400

The Last of the Mediterranean Galley Fleets 95

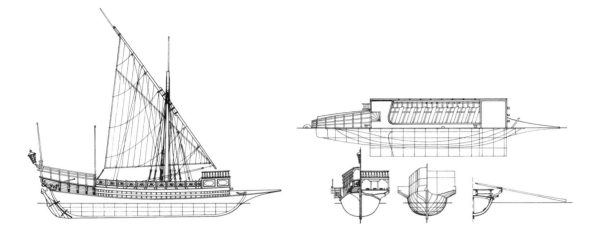

Brandenburg half-galley, 1692.
The association between galleys and national prestige reached as far north as the Baltic, where the Elector had a highly decorated 'half-galley' built for Berlin in 1692. Only 20 metres long and armed with six small guns, she was more a state yacht than a fighting ship, although she could function as a command ship in wartime. *(192)*

French flute, 1684. This flute-built storeship served as a tender to the French galley fleet and represents the final flowering of the true flute-sterned craft, most closely resembling the old *straetsvaerder*. In both the French and British navies, to be armed 'en flûte' came to mean any naval vessel with her armament reduced and acting as a store-ship or a naval transport. Redundant classes or ageing frigates were often used in this role. *(62)*

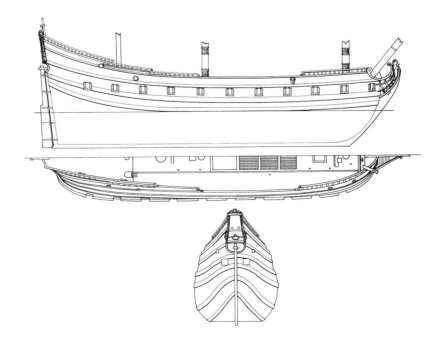

40   30   20   10   0 ft

1/400

10   5   0 m

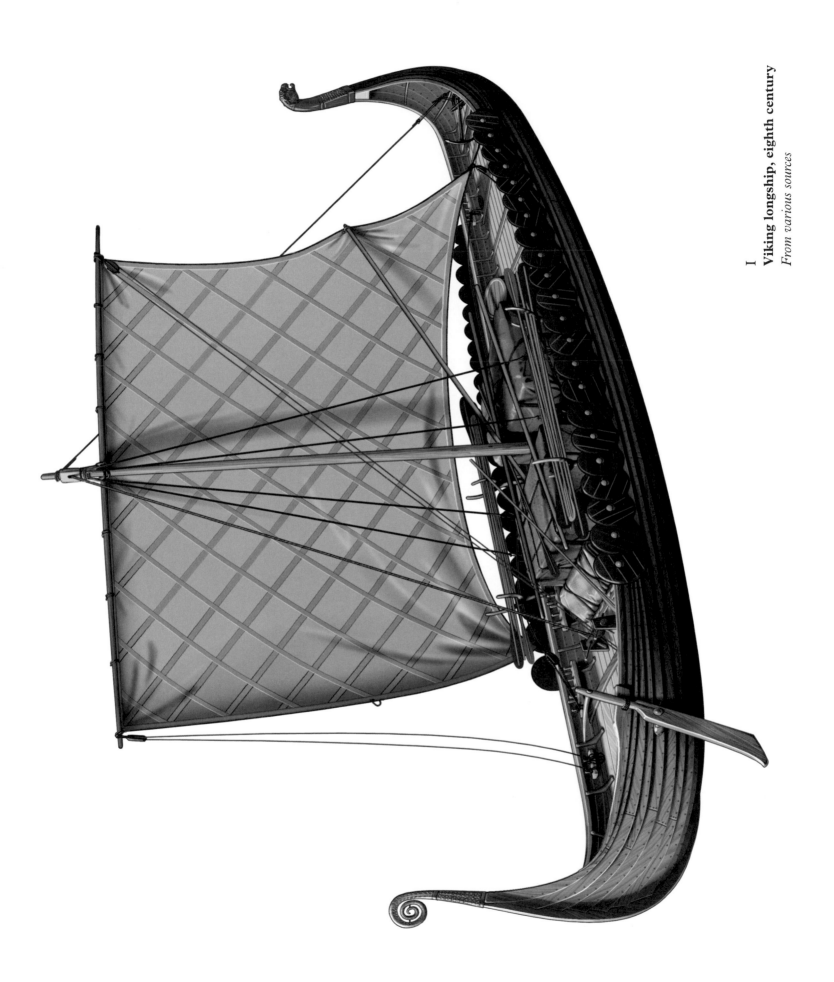

I
Viking longship, eighth century
From various sources

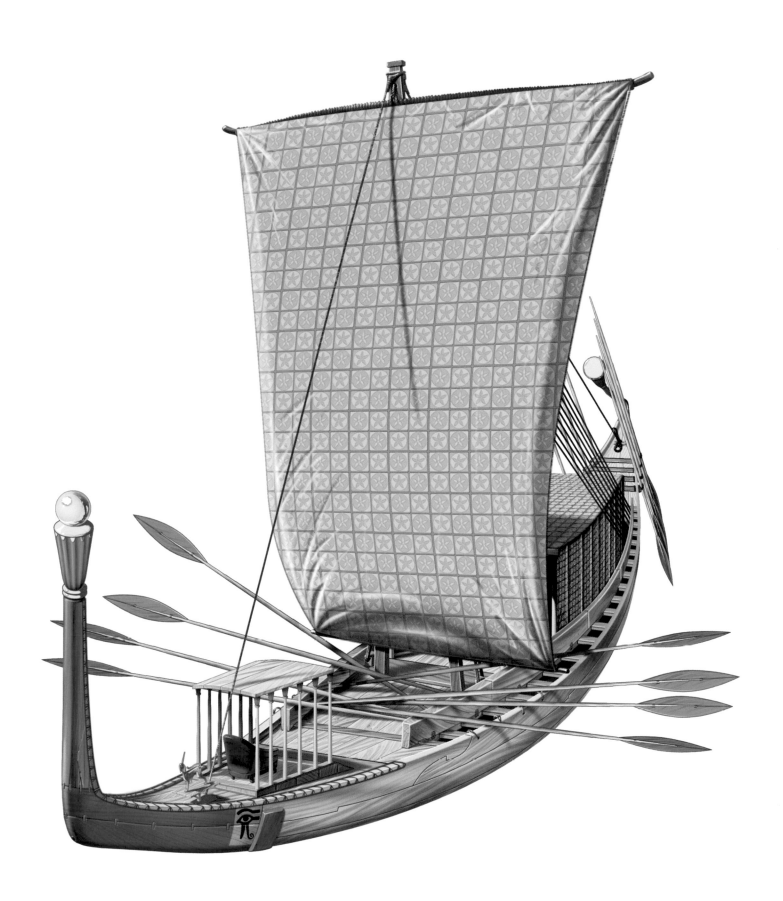

II
Royal ship of Pharaoh Sahure, 5th Dynasty
Based on a contemporary relief, reproduced in 113

III
Athenian trireme, about 500 BC
From various sources, including 112

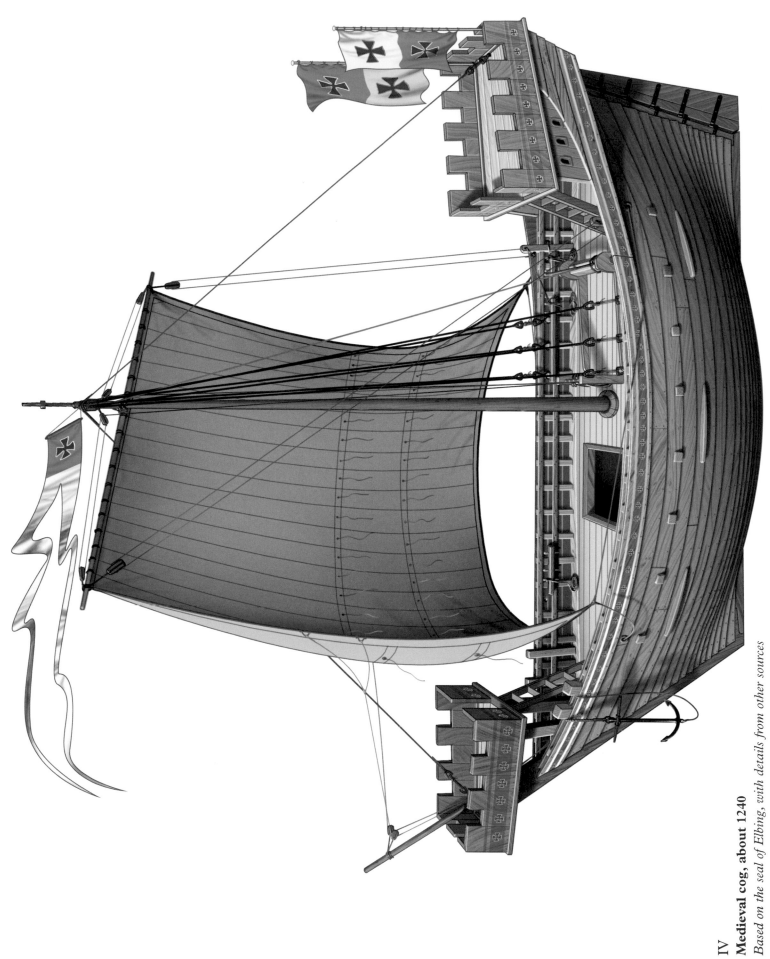

IV
Medieval cog, about 1240
Based on the seal of Elbing, with details from other sources

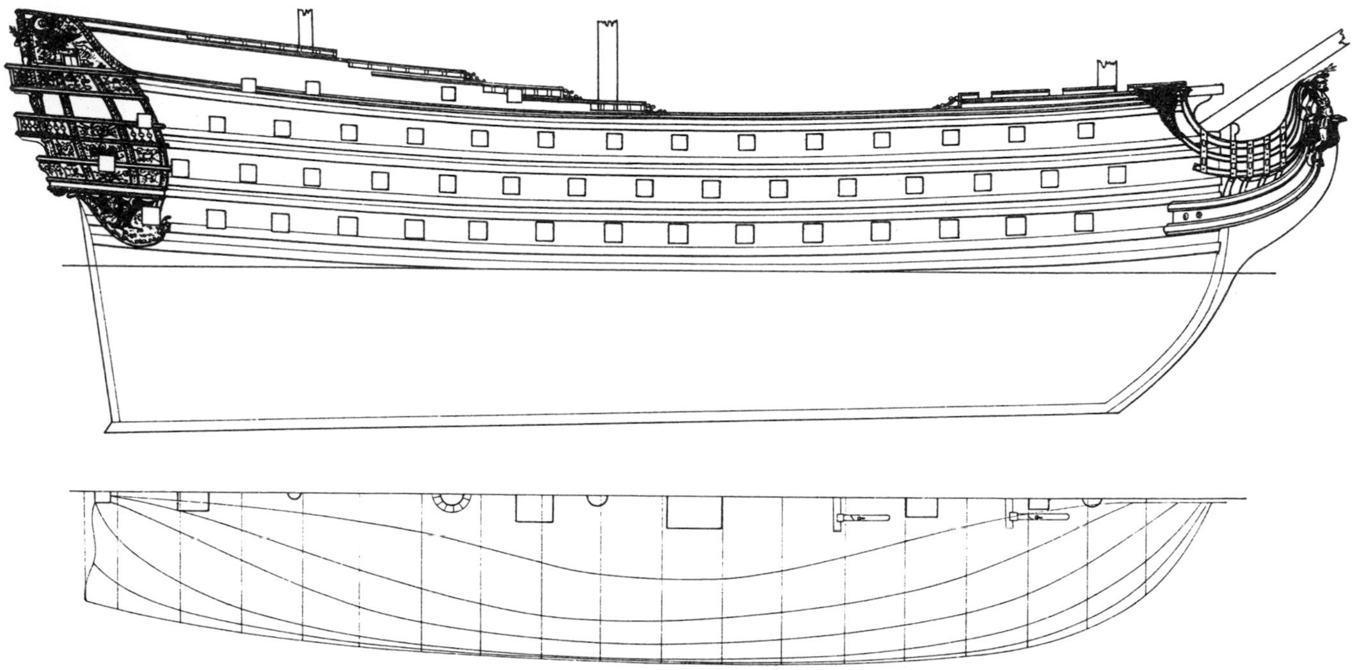

French *Le Foudroyant*, 120 guns, 1691. Built at Toulon, she was one of the last of a big programme of three-deckers, preceding both a decline in the size of the French navy and an attempt to do without such ships altogether. At about 55 metres on the gundeck she would have been one of the largest ships of her day and represents the state of First Rate design around 1700. Such ships would not grow dramatically in size for nearly a century to follow. *(168)*

The Three-Decked Man-of-War

Warship design underwent subtle, rather than radical change, with longer hulls, despite a crisis in shipbuilding timber, and heavier armament. Although dynamical stability and hydrodynamics were imperfectly understood, empiric development based upon experience and performance guided innovation and pushed matters forward. Large men-of-war were still difficult to handle and never outgrew the basic ship-rig, but small numbers of three-deckers were built by the major powers to act as flagships and centres of resistance in the battle-line. On occasion a good sailer, such as Slade's *Victory*, was produced and as a consequence she was a favourite flagship, but the bulk of the battle-fleet came to be composed of the two-decked 74-gun Third Rate line-of-battle ship.

The huge expense of three-deckers resulted in their periodic decline, and, at times, France attempted to do without them altogether; but the tactical and moral disadvantage of facing British three-deckers in battle always prompted a return to the construction of ever-larger ships. The Seven Years War, for example, produced a new wave of building these massive and impressive men-of-war. Most, however, sailed badly, and the structure of the largest examples like the French *Commerce de Marseilles* was too weak, being effectively beyond the wooden technology of the time.

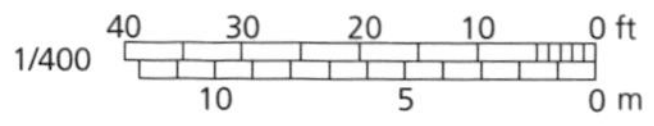
1/400
40 30 20 10 0 ft
10 5 0 m

British *Victory*, 100 guns, 1765. The *Victory* was unusual among First Rates in being a good sailer. Built at Chatham between 1759 and 1765 to a design by Sir Thomas Slade, she mounted 100 guns and measured 2162 tons. Successively the flagship of many admirals including Kempenfelt, Howe, Nelson and Saumarez, *Victory* underwent a number of major refits and this shows her appearance at Trafalgar. Her sail plan was modernised for, by the end of the eight-eenth century, the spanker had become a much larger, gaff-rigged sail, its long, loose-foot extended beyond the stern by a boom. By this time too, the studding sails set on the fore and main masts extending the leeches of the square sails, had become standard and the British fleet set them to close the combined fleets of France and Spain off Trafalgar on 21 October 1805. **NB.** The sail plan is 1/600 scale. *(112)*

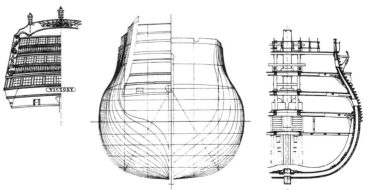

1/400   40   30   20   10   0 ft

10   5   0 m

French _Royal Louis_, 100 guns, 1759. One of a new class of three-deckers built for the French navy and very similar to British First Rates, _Royal Louis_ displays the significant changes that had occurred in replacing the ageing ships of Louis XIV's fleet. The hull sheer is much flatter and less emphasis is placed upon decoration; the quarterdeck is extended, while increased draught and beam have made a more stable gun-platform and a more weatherly hull with higher freeboard. There have been significant alterations in the basic ship-rig, too. The sprit-topsail has gone, the bowsprit is extended by doubling it with a jib-boom. This retains its square sails, often useful for pulling a dismasted battle-ship out of the line, but now supports a series of jibs which are complemented by staysails set between the masts. Above the deepgored topsails with three rows of reefing points, are set topgallants and royals. Most interesting is the spanker with its vertical leech, which, although it retains its long, vestigial lateen yard (carried as a spare lower yard), has shed the area of sail forward of the mast. **NB.** Sail plan is 1/600 scale. (168)

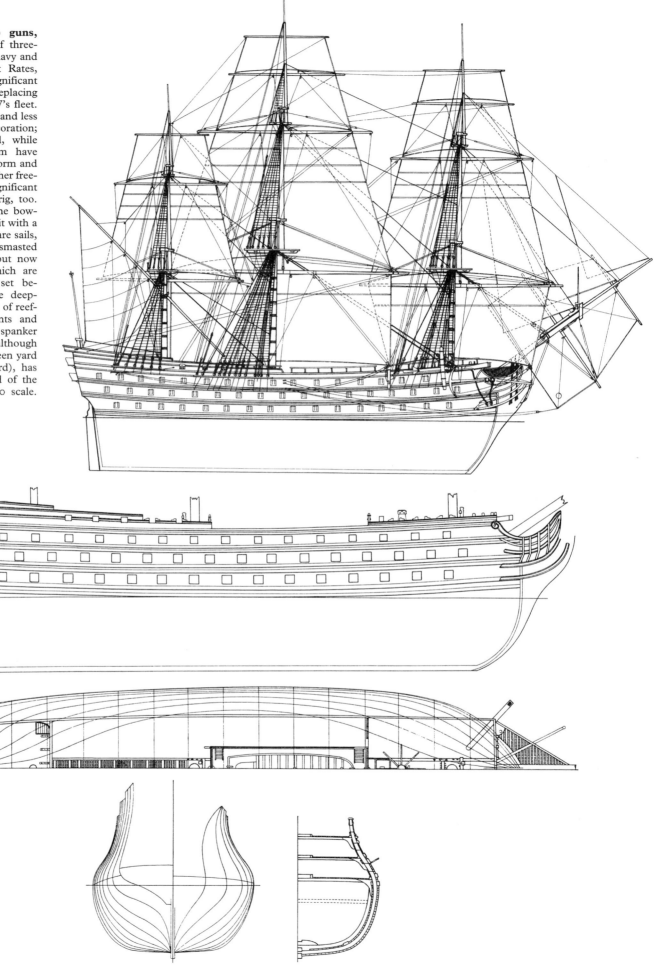

1/400 40 30 20 10 0 ft

10 5 0 m

The Three-Decked Man-of-War 99

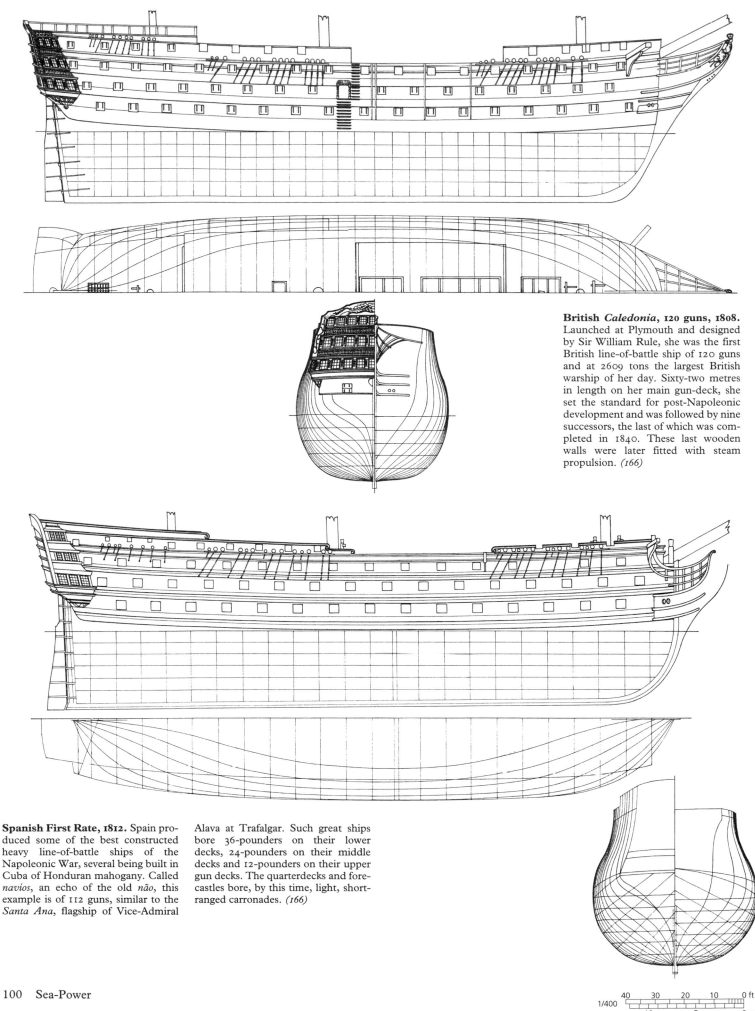

British *Caledonia*, 120 guns, 1808.
Launched at Plymouth and designed
by Sir William Rule, she was the first
British line-of-battle ship of 120 guns
and at 2609 tons the largest British
warship of her day. Sixty-two metres
in length on her main gun-deck, she
set the standard for post-Napoleonic
development and was followed by nine
successors, the last of which was completed in 1840. These last wooden
walls were later fitted with steam
propulsion. *(166)*

Spanish First Rate, 1812. Spain produced some of the best constructed
heavy line-of-battle ships of the
Napoleonic War, several being built in
Cuba of Honduran mahogany. Called
navíos, an echo of the old *não*, this
example is of 112 guns, similar to the
Santa Ana, flagship of Vice-Admiral
Alava at Trafalgar. Such great ships
bore 36-pounders on their lower
decks, 24-pounders on their middle
decks and 12-pounders on their upper
gun decks. The quarterdecks and forecastles bore, by this time, light, short-
ranged carronades. *(166)*

40   30   20   10   0 ft
1/400
10   5   0 m

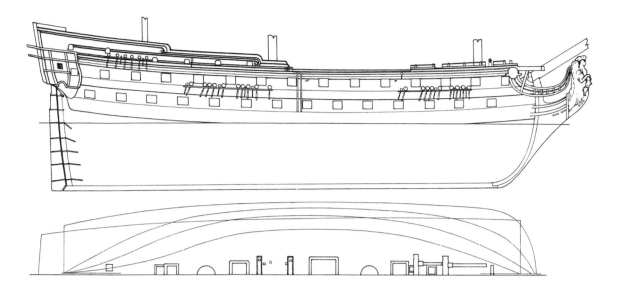

Spanish *Princessa*, 70 guns, 1730.
During the War of the Austrian Succession, this vessel fought a fierce action in 1740 against three British ships of nominally similar force. The British ships were smaller and the captured *Princessa* was a highly influential vessel. Of 1709 tons burthen and measuring 50 metres on the gun-deck, the *Princessa*'s superior capability when compared with her three adversaries, was chiefly due to her size, and thus her freeboard and ability to provide a more stable gun-platform; she was also strongly built and well able to resist damage. *(166)*

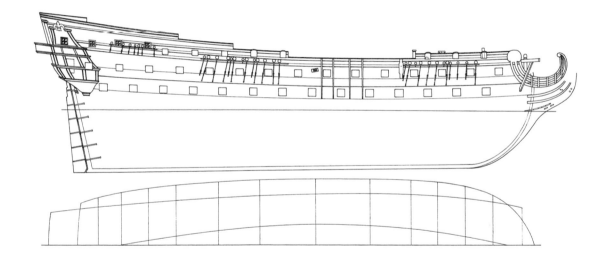

French *Terrible*, 74 guns, 1739. Similar qualities were built into the new 74s building for the French navy, the first of which was this ship built at Toulon in 1739. Of a larger hull size than previous French 74s, being 50 metres in length, *Terrible* had heavier guns concentrated in her principal batteries, carrying twenty-eight 36-pounders on her lower, and thirty 18-pounders on her upper gun-decks. *(166)*

Large Two-Deckers

The expansion of the main rivals, Britain and France produced a proliferation of the two-decked man-of-war – the most useful all-round battle ships – varying between 50 and 80 guns. However, the weaker ships were gradually excluded from the battle line, the 50s by the middle of the century and the 60s by the 1780s. By the 1750s it was the 74-gun two-decker which became the standard back-bone of the contending fleets which, in the great wars with France and her allies, sought the mastery of the sea and the domination of the world. They were a good compromise between gun-power (they generally had the same calibre main batteries as the largest First Rate) and sailing qualities, being lower and more weatherly than three-deckers. As with the three-deckers there was a trend towards greater average tonnage, and the big two-deckers also grew in length and firepower as more guns were fitted into the heavier-calibre lower batteries, while the lighter armament on the upper-works was reduced. Much of this development was driven by the French and Spanish, the British not disdaining to learn from captured enemy vessels.

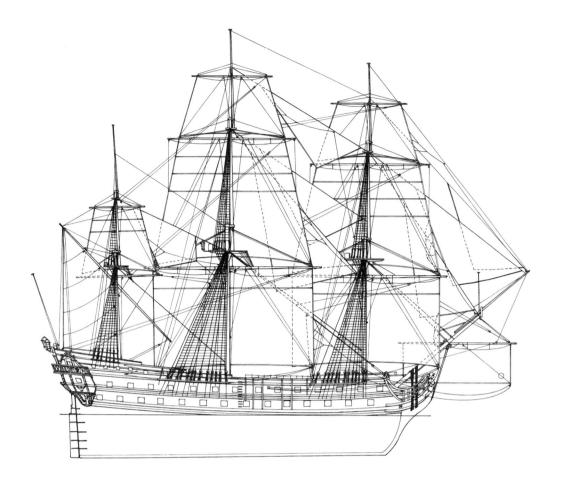

French *Invincible*, 74 guns, 1744.
The *Terrible* was not an unqualified success and was followed by the slightly longer *Magnanime* and *Invincible*, shown here. Both built at Rochefort, these ships proved the value of extending the waterlines and producing a faster hull, powered by a tall rig. *Invincible* was 52 metres in length and, in addition to her immediate sister, *Magnanime*, was followed by fifteen successors before the end of the Seven Years War. Captured by the British in 1747, *Invincible* was as influential in the Royal Navy of Great Britain as she had been in that of France. Although lost off the coast of Norfolk in 1758, the ship was the inspiration for the first British 74s, and her lines were also used as an exact model for the *Valiant* and *Triumph* in 1757, the first British 'Large Class' 74-gun ships. **NB.** Sail plan is 1/600 scale. *(166)*

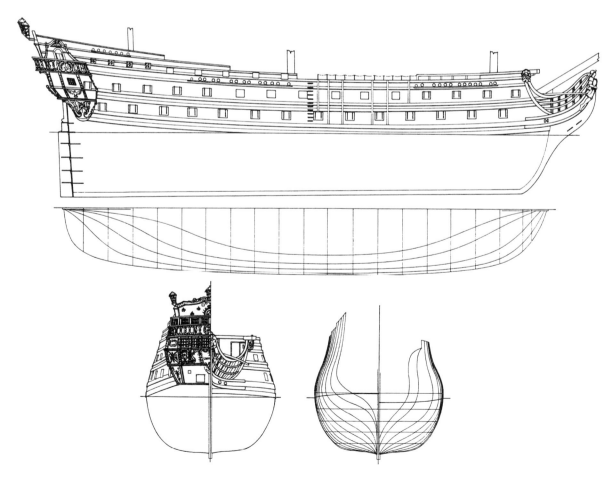

40   30   20   10   0 ft
1/400
10   5   0 m

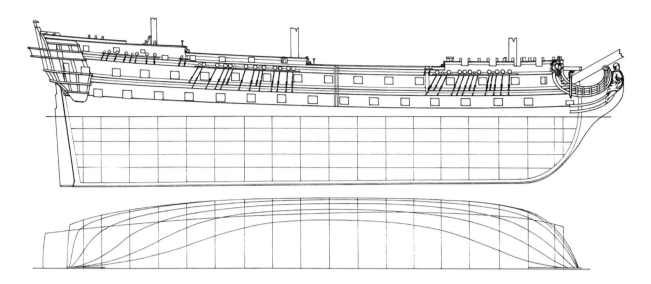

French *Foudroyant*, 80 guns, 1750.
Captured in 1758 by the weaker 64-gun *Monmouth*, the *Foudroyant* measured 55 metres on the gun-deck and mounted 80 guns. This superb ship, the first of the new style 80-gun two-deckers in the Royal Navy, served first as Rodney's flagship in the West Indies and was later commanded by John Jervis, afterwards Earl St Vincent, and took the new French 74, *Pegase* during the American Revolution. Nelson's flagship after the Nile was a replacement of the same name. *(166)*

British *Valiant*, 74 guns, 1759. The first British attempts at a French-style 74 resulted in the *Dublin* class, but these were too small and *Invincible* was more closely copied in the *Valiant* and *Triumph*, of which this is the former. Built at Chatham, *Valiant* was launched in 1759 and not broken up until 1850. She mounted twenty-eight 32-pounders on the lower gun-deck, thirty 24-pounders on her upper gun-deck, ten 9-pounders on her quarterdeck and two long 9-pounder chase guns on her forecastle. *Valiant* was of 1800 tons burthen and measured 52 metres on the gun-deck, slightly larger than the numerous *Bellona* class and its derivatives, and the design was revived as late as the 1790s for *Ajax* and *Kent*. *(166)*

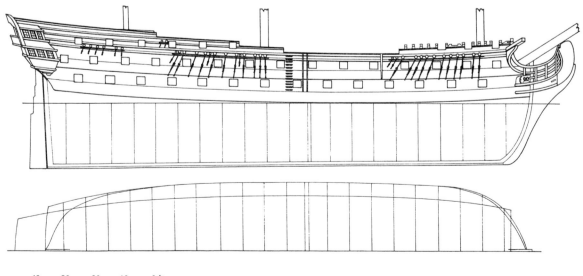

1/400

40 30 20 10 0 ft

10 5 0 m

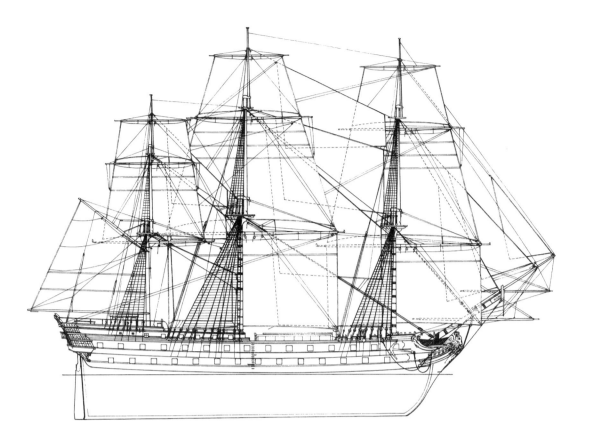

French *Superbe*, 74 guns, 1785.
This represents an equivalent French 74 built in 1785 and shows the decoration typical of the type. Note the tumblehome which conferred considerable stability as well as strength, the short poop and the continuous level of the quarterdeck and forecastle, united across the waist by fore-and-aft gangways. The deckhome (or *dunette*) is a French feature, not found in British ships of the period. Her sail plan, typical of both opposing navies, shows the now universal gaff-rigged, boomed spanker and the reefing tackles necessary to draw up the reefing cringles of the topsails. **NB.** Sail plan is 1/600 scale. *(237)*

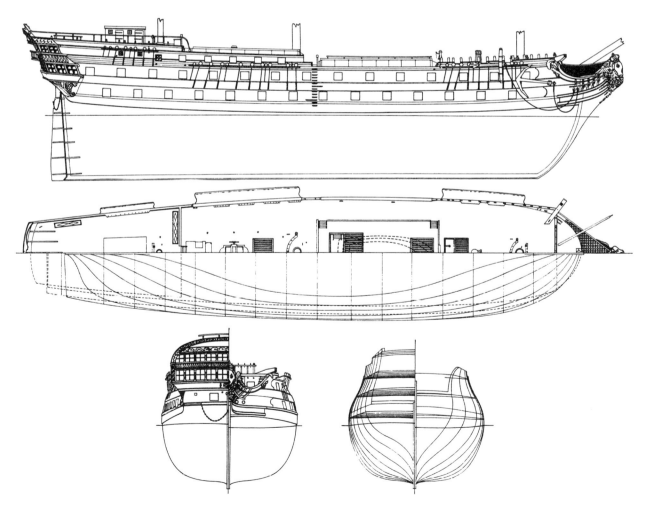

40   30   20   10   0 ft
1/400
10   5   0 m

Dutch *Stadt en Lande*, 74 guns, 1790. The rapprochement of The Netherlands with Britain which had grown out of their alliance against Louis XIV, disintegrated during the American Revolution into open war. This was due to British insistence on the right to search neutral shipping to prevent military supplies reaching the American rebels. The Dutch, who had been content with a navy of trade-defence ships, were compelled to build a fleet of largely 74-gun ships, such as this. *(100)*

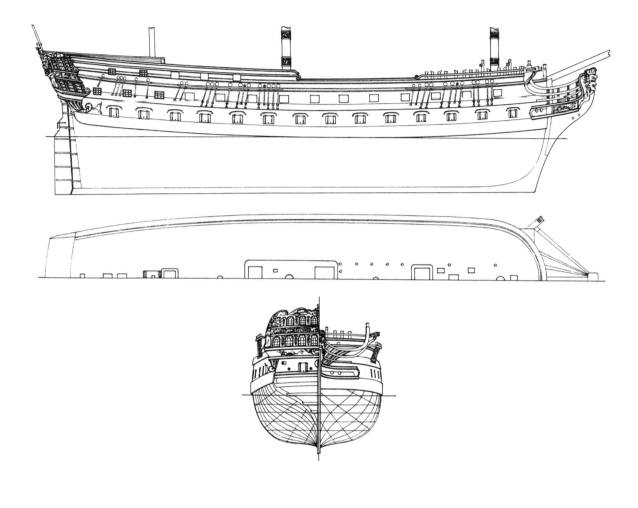

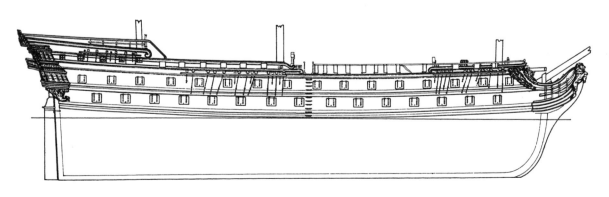

French 80-gun ship, about 1790. To avoid the poor sailing qualities of three-deckers, both the British and French experimented with larger two-deckers, like this French 80-gun ship. The first was the *Tonnant*, built at Toulon in 1740, but a powerful derivative was the *Soleil Royal* which, measured 55.5 metres on her lower gun-deck where she mounted thirty 36-pounders, with 24-pounders on the deck above. A large vessel, the French 80s were superior to anything in the British fleet of that time except First Rates. *(168)*

40 30 20 10 0 ft
1/400
10   5   0 m

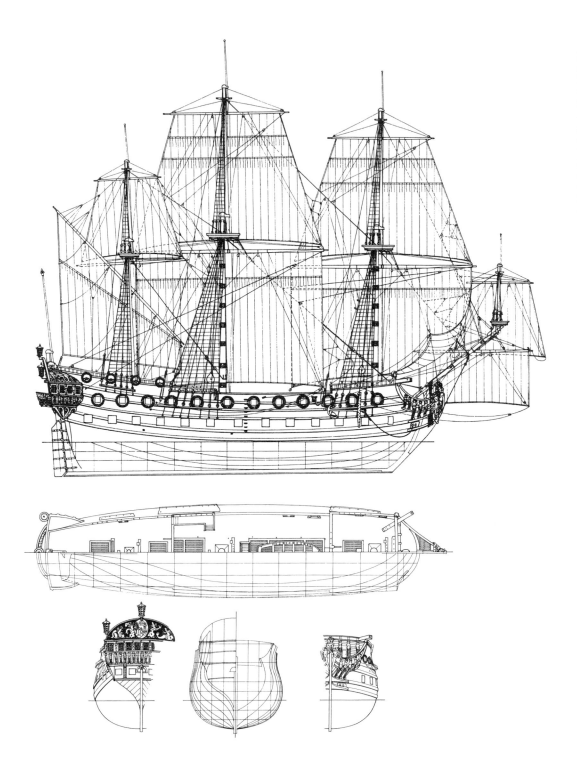

Russian *Priediestinacja*, 58 guns, about 1708. The national navies of lesser maritime powers, such as those of Denmark, Sweden and Russia, favoured the smaller, more economical two-decker. This example, suitable for the Baltic, was built for the embryonic navy of Tsar Peter the Great, who was then engaged in war with Sweden. Evidence of the Tsar's visit to Amsterdam and Deptford are visible in this small, but powerful man-of-war which has a low rig typical of the first quarter of the eighteenth century. *(235)*

Small Two-Deckers

The smaller types of two-deckers, mounting between 50 and 64 guns, had formed the backbone of national fleets at the beginning of the eighteenth century, but by the end they were outmoded, although in emergencies they were taken into the British line-of-battle as late as Trafalgar in 1805. The French abandoned the 50-gun class at the end of the Seven Years War when their defeat forced them to reassess their warship policy. The French 64s went the same way at the end of the American Revolution. The British, however, with increasingly global commitments retained both 50s and 64s, leaving the latter in the battle-fleets opposing the second rank navies, with the 50s serving as large cruisers or flagships on distant stations, such as Newfoundland, the

Cape of Good Hope or the Red Sea. To this end the class survived, a few being built until 1815. During the eighteenth century the Dutch fleet declined, along with Dutch fortunes. Concentrating upon protecting their trade with the east, the limitations of their home waters coupled with their shrinking economic power to cause this. Close alliance with Britain seemed to offer vicarious protection, so the Dutch concentrated on small two-deckers for trade defence, but a rupture during the American Revolution followed by more serious hostilities in the wake of the French Revolution meant the Dutch had to rebuild their battle-fleet with 74-gun ships.

French *Le Fendant*, 60 guns, 1701.
A vaisseau de 3me rang of Louis XIV's fleet, she carries topgallants above her deep topsails. Her steeply angled mizen yard shows the strong influence of the Mediterranean lateen, an influence which was to wane completely before the century was out. *(169)*

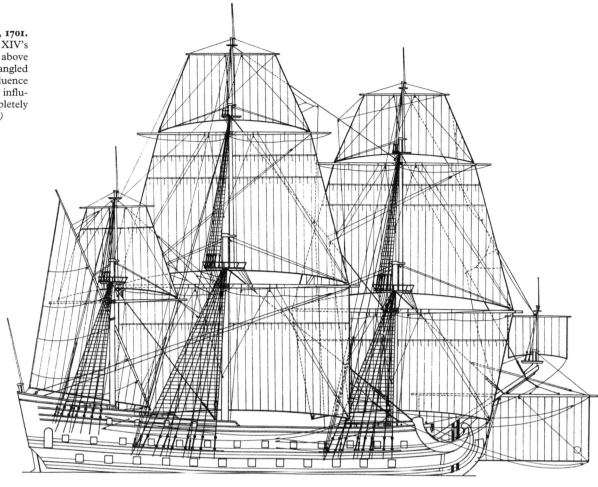

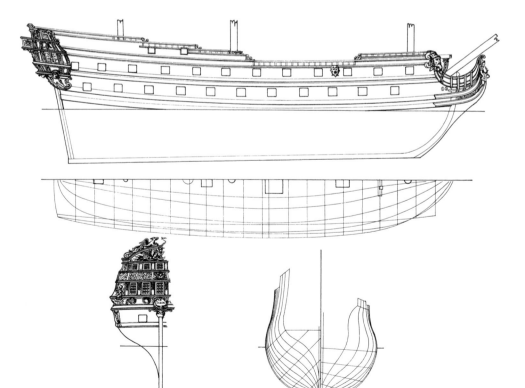

French *Le Jazon*, 50 guns, 1723. Of similar overall size to *Le Fendant*, she mounted 12-pounders on the lower deck. She retains rich embellishments at bow and stern with a figurehead depicting her eponymous hero, Jason. *(168)*

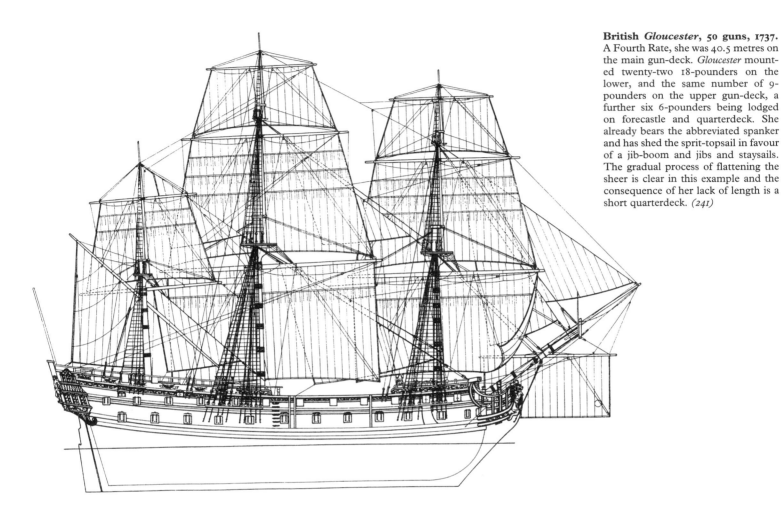

British *Gloucester*, 50 guns, 1737.
A Fourth Rate, she was 40.5 metres on the main gun-deck. *Gloucester* mounted twenty-two 18-pounders on the lower, and the same number of 9-pounders on the upper gun-deck, a further six 6-pounders being lodged on forecastle and quarterdeck. She already bears the abbreviated spanker and has shed the sprit-topsail in favour of a jib-boom and jibs and staysails. The gradual process of flattening the sheer is clear in this example and the consequence of her lack of length is a short quarterdeck. *(241)*

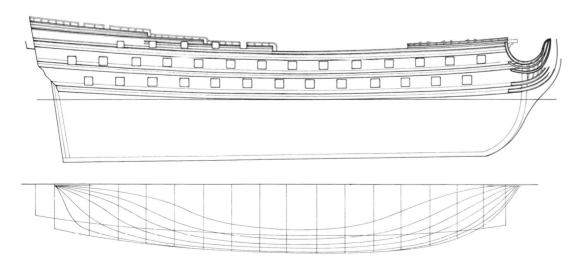

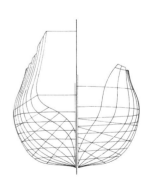

French *Dauphin Royal*, 64 guns, 1736. Almost contemporary with the *Gloucester*, her waterlines suggest she was probably a fast ship. *(168)*

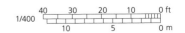

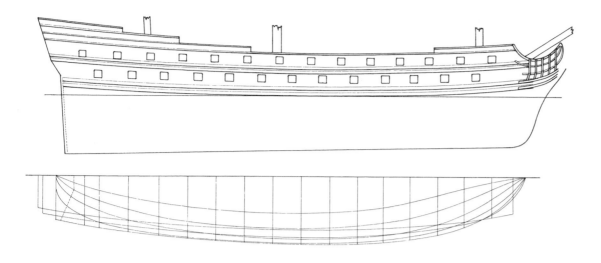

French 54-gun ship, 1761. This draught represents one of the last of her type, ultimately regarded as too large and expensive for a commerce-raider yet too feeble to stand in the line of battle. Three built at Bordeaux between 1762 and 1764 were the last of the class. *(168)*

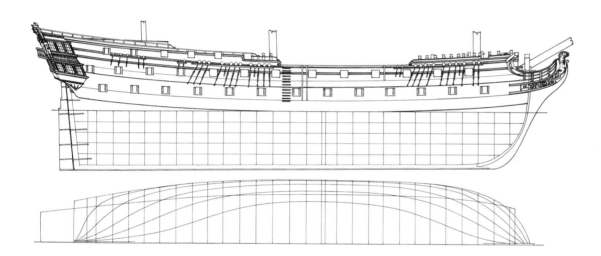

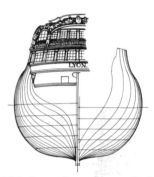

British *Lyon*, 64 guns, 1777. Built at Portsmouth to a design by Slade this 64-gun Third Rate belonged to the final generation of such ships built by the British. A contemporary drawing of her shows her setting topgallants, but with a boomed spanker which retains the lateen yard. Having served in the Mediterranean, *Lyon* was dispatched to the Indian Ocean and the East Indies squadron. *(166)*

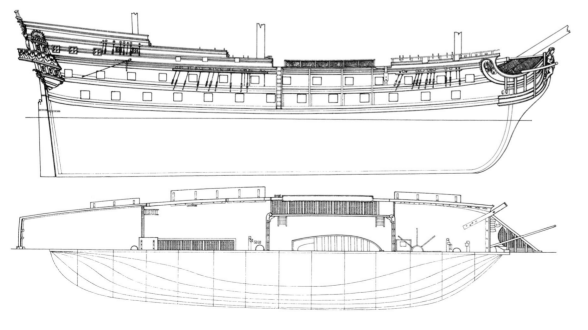

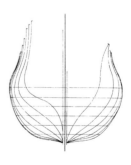

French *Le Protecteur*, 64 guns, about 1755. Directly comparable with *Lyon* in terms of armament, she represents a slightly earlier French design. *Le Protecteur* carries slightly more of her guns on her forecastle. Comparison of the waterlines shows a distinctly narrower form on a lighter draught. *(170)*

40   30   20   10   0 ft

1/400

10   5   0 m

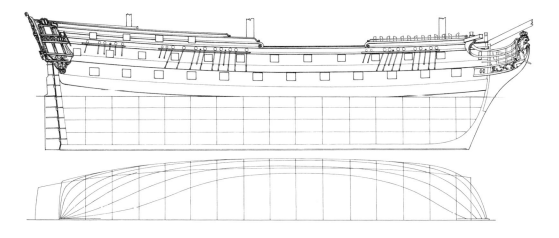

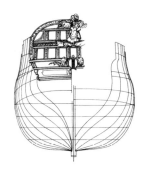

Dutch *Delft*, 50 guns, 1783. Completed at the end of the war with Britain associated with events in America, this small Dutch two-decker retains what may now be called an old-fashioned spanker. The *Delft* was taken by the British at the Battle of Camperdown, but was so badly shattered that she sank a few days later. **NB.** Sail plan is 1/600 scale. *(166)*

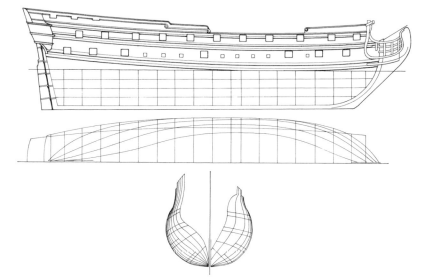

British *Sweepstakes*, 32 guns, 1708. The British revival of the *demi-batterie* ship sought to create a vessel capable of effective trade protection by being fast, well-armed and weatherly. Classed as Fifth Rates these 'one-and-a-half' decked ships proved a disappointment. The lower deck guns were too few to be effective, and could not be used in any sort of a seaway. Such ships were often fast, but their overall freeboard made them less than weatherly. Captured by the French, *Sweepstakes* was retaken by a British squadron, but not recommissioned. *(166)*

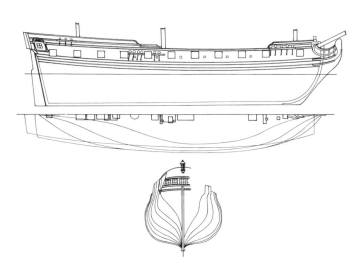

British *Greyhound*, 20 guns, 1712. The prototype 1706 Establishment did not include Sixth Rates, and a number of designs were tried. This class, mounting 20 guns on a single gun-deck, sailed well, but were too small to be effective if anything of a sea was running. Rather than precursors of the frigate, they are really embryonic ship-sloops. *(166)*

British Sixth Rate of the 1719 Establishment. One of twenty slightly varying vessels, this 20-gun ship measured 32 metres on the gun-deck with a burthen of 374 tons. Reverting to Torrington's concept, the lower deck was pierced only with sweep ports, and the superstructure was kept to a minimum, making them effective small cruisers. *(166)*

Ancestors of the Frigate

Perhaps more than any other generic name, with the single exception of 'sloop', the frigate has undergone a long metamorphosis, the only common denominator being an association with speed. The word itself appears to be of Arab origin and attached itself to an oared Algerine lateen-rigged pursuit craft. In the 1650s the new lighter warships of the English Parliament were called 'frigates', but as they grew into two-deckers, the term reverted to a more general application to small cruisers. William III's accession to the throne of Britain precipitated war with Louis XIV, and with it the need to defend British overseas trade from raiders based in the French Atlantic ports. This requirement for a more seaworthy escort produced a new style of frigate, a vessel which 'should have but one tier of ordnance flush and that to be on the upper deck whereby they will be able to [fire] . . . them in all weathers'. To achieve this specification of 1688 proposed by Admiral Lord Torrington, the new type of ship was to have a freeboard of 2 metres and, of great benefit, the crew were to be accommodated in a lower deck, which was to be pierced only for sweeps. Naval conservatism,

however, compromised this objective, and initially a form of the *demi-batterie* ship was revived, it proving impossible to resist the temptation of arming the lower deck. More conventional ships followed, but, as with a class of larger contemporary French Fifth Rates, insufficient freeboard was provided. Losses of British trade to powerful French corsairs provoked the Admiralty to build small two-deckers for trade protection, but these proved poor sailers. After the Peace in 1715, a new type of British Sixth Rate reverted to Torrington's concept, but again, as time passed, gunports were cut in the lower deck and upperworks were increased, so that the advantages of the layout were lost. In 1719, under the Surveyorship of Sir Jacob Acworth, the British Royal Navy introduced the first full 'Establishment', a set of standard specifications which prescribed the dimensions and scantlings of all classes of major warship, from First to Sixth Rates; this rigidity was to hamper the development of British warships for thirty years. Contemporary French developments were little better, but the Great Northern War between Sweden and Russia produced some innovative cruisers in the Baltic.

40 30 20 10 0 ft
1/400
10   5   0 m

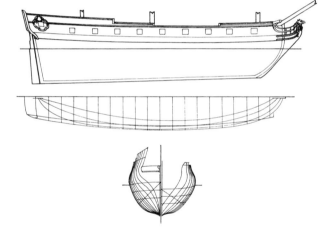

Danish *Blaa Heyren*, 20 guns, about 1734. Smaller cruisers continued to favour the single deck with only platforms below. Lacking the fuller hull form of her British counterparts, her leaner midships section suggests an attempt at producing a fast hull on a short waterline, but stiff though she might prove, it was probable that she heeled too much to enable her to employ her guns effectively in moderate to heavy weather. *(34)*

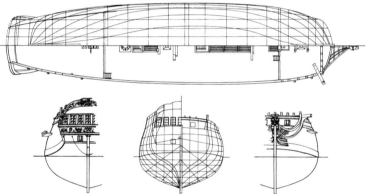

British *Lyme*, 24 guns, 1740. Modifications in the succeeding Establishment of 1733 enhanced the habitability of the hull, with enlarged upperworks, but again adding gunports to the apertures for sweeps on the lower deck.

Raising the height of the topside made them more leewardly, and produced another unsatisfactory compromise. It is perhaps no surprise that *Lyme* foundered at sea. *(238)*

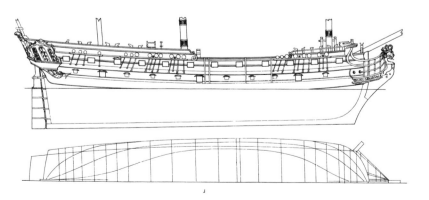

Dutch *Eendracht*, 24 guns, 1770. Unable to emulate the French and British in building ever-bigger ships, and with their extensive trade still requiring convoy, the Dutch retained the *demi-batterie* ship longer than other navies, accepting a high freeboard, with its attendant disadvantages. *(100)*

40 30 20 10 0 ft
1/400
10   5   0 m

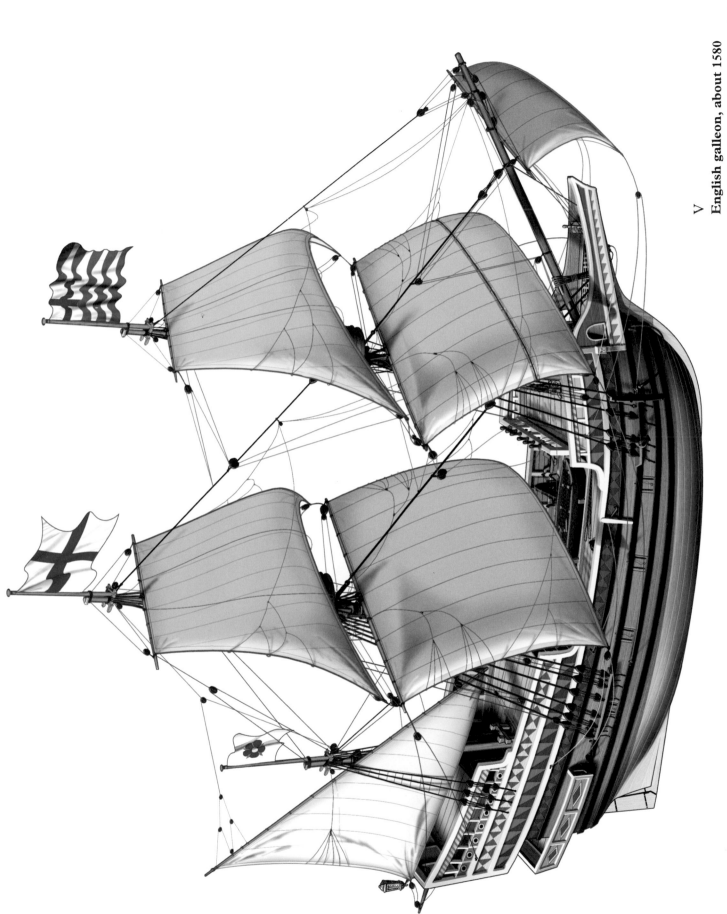

V

English galleon, about 1580
*Loosely based on reconstruction of Golden
Hind in 82, but with added details*

VI

Spanish carrack, first half of sixteenth century

An interpretation of an engraving by Pieter Brueghel, reproduced in 47, with additional details from other sources

VII

Dutch flute, about 1650

An interpretation of an engraving by Wenzel Hollar, reproduced in 47, with additional details from other sources

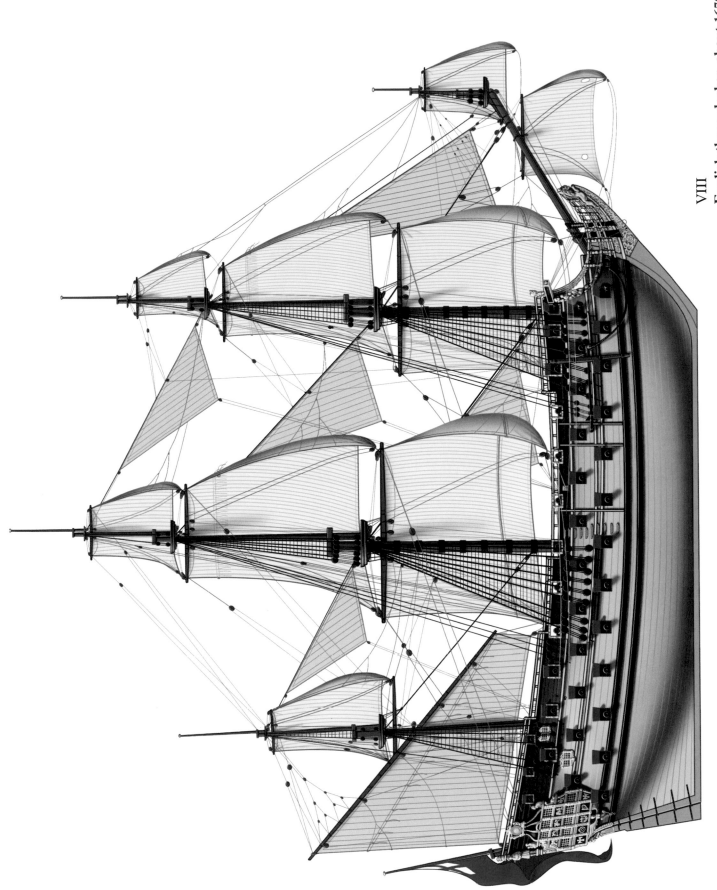

VIII

English three-decker, about 1670
Based on the First Rate in Anthony
Deane's Treatise (118)

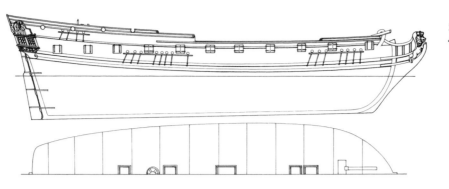

Swedish *Hvide Ørn*, 30 guns, 1711. The British shipwright William Smith built this single gun-decked cruiser for the Swedish navy at Karlscrona in 1711. She mounted 30 guns in all, carrying her main battery on one continuous deck. Below this was a second deck, giving the crew a 'berth-deck' which not only improved their day-to-day living conditions, but improved the endurance of the type, later a prerequisite of frigate design. *(166)*

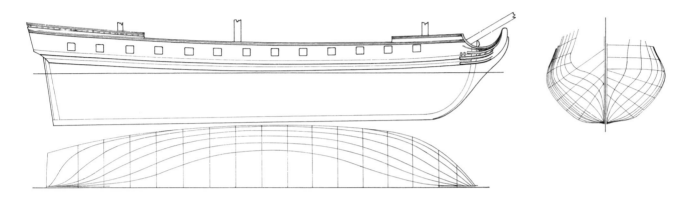

French *Medée*, 26 guns, 1744. The French were less inhibited by orthodoxy than the British and in the *Medée*, built by Blaise Ollivier at Brest, produced a 'true' frigate. The ship and many of her consorts were soon captured by the British who recognised the weaknesses inherent in their light construction, size and cost. Armed with twenty-six French 8-pounders, *Medée* had proved no match for her opponents and was not purchased into the Royal Navy, but sold and fitted out as a privateer. Nevertheless some thirty derivatives were built in the period up to 1774. *(168)*

The 'True Frigate'

The resolution of the problem of how to bear a heavy enough armament on a fast, seaworthy hull was solved by the middle of the eighteenth century, when a layout that came to be regarded as the 'true frigate' was evolved. The lower deck of the old-style *demi-batterie* ship was not only stripped of its exiguous armament but reduced in height and placed at or below the waterline, producing a relatively low and weatherly topside but an upper-deck battery freeboard that allowed the guns to be fought in all weathers. The credit is customarily accorded to the French, though it was the Swedish navy which actually built the first 'true' frigate. Perhaps it was the swift emulation of the British in copying and adapting French designs in such profusion, which secured the plaudit of history for the Bourbon Royal Navy, but ironically it was an expatriate Briton who built the *Hvide Ørn*. Moreover, this was followed by a class of similar but larger Swedish cruisers, of over 900 tons burthen, with 18-pounder guns which anticipated the heavy frigates developed much later in parallel by the contesting navies of Britain and France.

To overcome conservatism in their Navy Board, the authority actually responsible for ship construction, the British Admiralty had to compel a new Establishment and ordered new tonnage outside controlling restrictions. Fortunately too, the ageing Surveyors, Acworth and Allin retired, ushering in Bately and Slade whose alternative designs for potential cruisers were compared before a class was ordered in numbers.

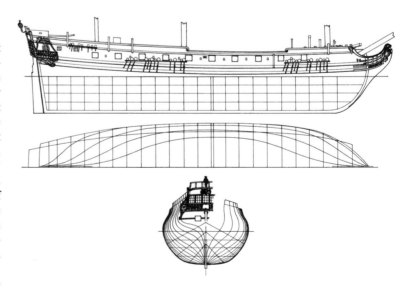

French *Panthère*, 20 guns, 1744. The French also produced a smaller class, mounting 6-pounder guns, of which this ship, built by Coulomb at Brest in 1744, is typical. Again, the lightness of their scantlings made them vulnerable and she too fell a prize to the British 74, *Monarch*, herself French-built. Taken into the Royal Navy, *Panthère* was renamed *Amazon*, rated as a Sixth Rate whose hull-form was afterwards the basis for numerous sloops and specialist fireships. *(166)*

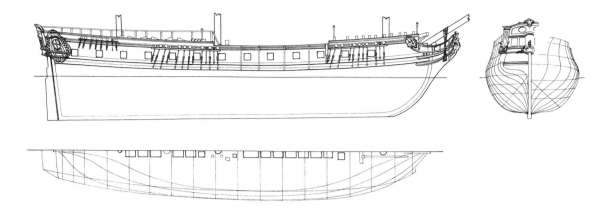

French *Sirène*, 30 guns, 1744.
Although a fine, weatherly class, the *Sirène* and her 8-pounder armed sisters suffered in that the fineness of their entrance provided little reserve buoyancy and could not tolerate the weight of forward chase guns. At about 38 metres on the gun-deck, *Sirène*'s calculated tonnage was around 580-600. Ironically, *Sirène*'s captor in 1760, the frigate *Boreas*, was herself a product of British development of French prizes. *(34)*

British *Unicorn*, 28 guns, 1748.
Pressure on the Admiralty to combat the inroads of the French war on British trade resulted in Their Lordships circumventing their traditional designers and ordering two ships to be built on the lines of a captured French privateer, the *Tygre*. These, *Unicorn* and *Lyme*, became the prototype 28-gun, 9-pounder, frigates for a large class, spawning fifty successors built as adaptations by Bately and Slade. These two new vessels compared very favourably with two more conservative ships, *Seahorse* and *Mermaid*, designed by Acworth and Allin. *(34)*

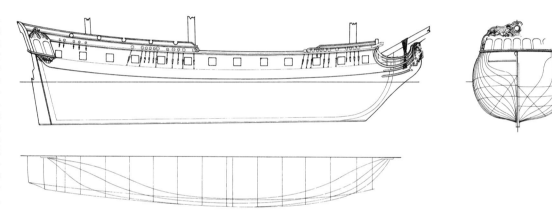

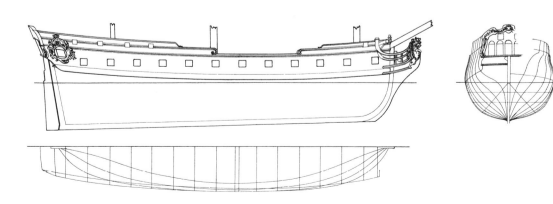

Swedish *Jarramas*, 36 guns, 1759.
The advanced concept promoted by William Smith, building single gun-decked men-of-war at Karlscrona for the Swedes, resulted in the 36-gun *Illerim* being the largest single-decker of her day, when built in 1716. This example, the *Jarramas*, was built later in the century by which time the 'true frigate' layout had become common. *(34)*

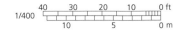

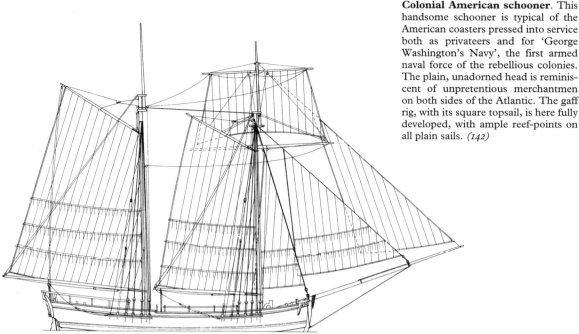

Colonial American schooner. This handsome schooner is typical of the American coasters pressed into service both as privateers and for 'George Washington's Navy', the first armed naval force of the rebellious colonies. The plain, unadorned head is reminiscent of unpretentious merchantmen on both sides of the Atlantic. The gaff rig, with its square topsail, is here fully developed, with ample reef-points on all plain sails. *(142)*

Ships of the American Revolution

By the mid eighteenth century, the Thirteen Colonies of British North America had developed their basic economy so that a thriving trade existed not merely between individual colonies, but with the West Indies. Inexhaustible supplies of softwood enabled small shipbuilding yards to be established in almost every creek and river, while the off-shore prevailing winds soon established the effectiveness of small, two-masted fore-and-afters which, though their forbears came from The Netherlands and England, soon became a native, North American type. At the launching of one such coaster in 1714, an admirer exclaimed how the hull 'scooned' upon the water. 'Then a sc(h)ooner she shall be,' agreed her enthusiastic owner. Fast and weatherly, the schooner's abilities were soon appreciated and she became small naval cruiser, slaver and privateer.

At the outbreak of the rebellion against Great Britain, Congress hired a number of ships to attack British trade, which they did with great success on both sides of the Atlantic, though the hand-to-mouth nature of Congress's finances made the establishment of a proper navy of the United States a somewhat uncertain matter during these difficult years when, under terrific pressure from the rebels' allies, the British navy continued to dominate the North Atlantic for most of the time. Congress's most favoured expedient was to leave the expense of fitting out ships for war to its richer citizens, authorising them to act as privateers with 'letters of marque and reprisal', licences which in British eyes were illegal and exposed the holders to charges of piracy. At the height of the war in 1781 when 449 American privateers, mounting 6700 guns were at sea, the so-called 'Continental' Navy had only three men-of-war at sea. The weakness of the privateering war lay in the fact that prizes were usually sold in Europe and the British often bought back their own property, so the economic impact was felt mainly on British insurance markets, although much political capital was made by the Government's opposition at the failure of the Royal Navy to cope with this threat.

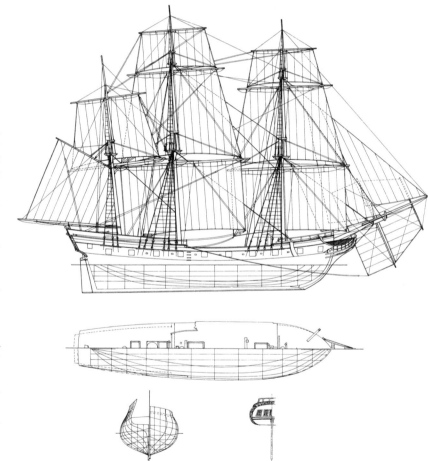

Privateer *Rattlesnake*, 12 guns, 1781. By the end of the war the exploits of American privateers had established a fierce tradition of fighting sail which was to be subsumed into the history of the United States Navy. Equating to a ship-rigged sloop-of-war, this privateer of 1781 was named *Rattlesnake* after a popular emblem of American independence. American privateers took about 600 British vessels, including 16 men-of-war. *Rattlesnake* was outstanding among these in that in a single cruise against the important and numerous British trade in the Baltic, she took prizes valued at $1 million. *(27)*

40 30 20 10 0 ft

1/400

10 5 0 m

Hancock, **32 guns, 1776.** Named after John Hancock, a rich and leading luminary of rebellion, *Hancock* was one of the first thirteen frigates built for the Continental Navy. Laid down at Newburyport, Massachusetts, she was 42 metres on the gundeck, of 760 tons burthen and mounted 32 guns. Quality did not extend to early American naval crews, for *Hancock* was captured in July 1777 and it was the British who, renaming her *Iris*, better appreciated her virtues. *Iris* became renowned as one of the fastest sailers in the navy, before being taken by De Grasse's fleet when the French entered the Chesapeake to throttle Cornwallis at Yorktown in the autumn of 1781. *(27)*

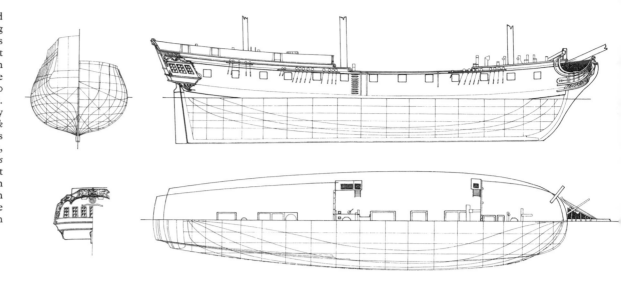

Confederacy, **36 guns, 1778.** The impoverished Continental Congress attempted to overcome their numerical disadvantage by building a few powerful cruisers of which the most outstanding was the *Confederacy*. Built at Norwich, Connecticut, she measured 49 metres on the gundeck, was of 960 tons burthen and mounted twenty-eight 12-pounders on her upper deck. Her lower deck was pierced for sweeps, as in the old galley-frigates. Thus was American naval thinking settled upon the large frigate, a type that was to catch the British at a disadvantage a generation later. **NB.** Sail plan is 1/600 scale. *(26)*

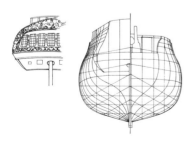

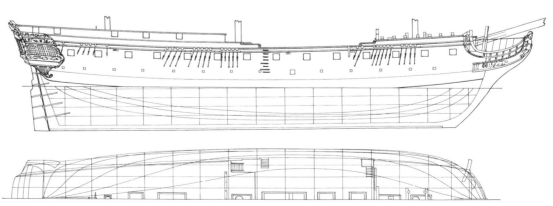

1/400

40   30   20   10   0 ft

10   5   0 m

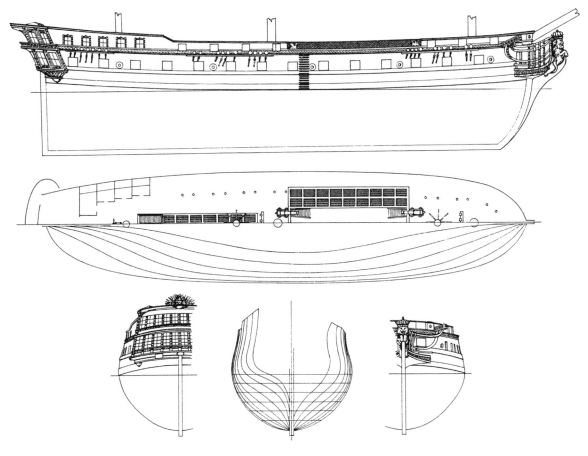

South Carolina, 40 guns, 1782. One solution to a deficiency in ships was purchase abroad and in the French and Dutch, Congress found sympathetic suppliers. Designed by the Chevalier Boux in an attempt to convince the French that they should build very large frigates, *L'Indien* was built as a speculation in The Netherlands. Not unlike the East Indiaman inspiring her name, she was 52 metres in length and having been purchased by the Americans as a commerce raider, was fitted out as the *South Carolina*. She mounted twenty-eight French 36-pounders, ten 12-pounders and two 9-pounder chase guns when she was captured in 1782 after a fiercely contested action with three British ships. Despite their losses, American naval vessels took 196 British ships during the war. *(168)*

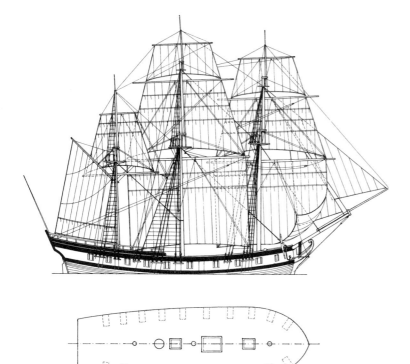

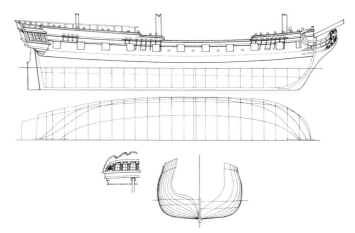

British *Inflexible*, 18 guns, 1776. Thought to have been specially designed and built by an inventive British naval officer named Schank, this misnamed 20-gun, shallow-draught but fully-rigged sloop, the *Inflexible*, was manhandled from the St Lawrence to Lake Champlain, to be built as the flagship of the British squadron sent to clear Benedict Arnold's vessels from its waters. Schank commanded her and she mounted eighteen 12-pounders. *(27)*

British *Royal George*, 26 guns, 1777. Built at St John's for service on Lake Champlain in 1777, she replaced a similar vessel sunk and later salved by the Americans. She was intended to maintain British dominance of the Lake and was armed with twenty 12-pounders, and six 6-pounders. Note the flat bottom and beam necessary to provide a stable platform on a shallow draught *(166)*

Lake Champlain Flotilla

The strategic importance of the corridor between New York and Montreal had been realised since the first stirrings of what the English colonists of North America called 'the French and Indian Wars'. From New York, the Hudson valley ran due north. Beyond this, descent to the Laurentian Shield was by way of the Chambly River. At the watershed, athwart this route, lay Lake Champlain, command of which was contested by both sides and resulted in the formation of small squadrons of warships of minor size, but major military importance. A precipitate American invasion of Canada in 1775 had ended disastrously and the consequent counter-attack by the British was stalled brilliantly on the Lake by Benedict Arnold at Valcour Island in October the following year. The British, dismantling a ship and two schooners, dragged them up the Chambly and reassembled them on Lake Champlain, augmenting them with locally-built boats. The power of the British squadron was ultimately successful, but Sir Guy Carleton had lost the initiative and the renewal of the campaign in 1777 ended in the surrender of Burgoyne's British force at Saratoga.

American schooner from Lake Champlain, 1777. Possibly the *Revenge*, built by Arnold at Ticonderoga and which took part in the action at Valcour Island. *(27)*

1/400

40 30 20 10 0 ft

10 5 0 m

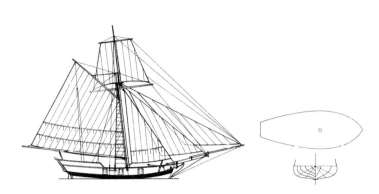

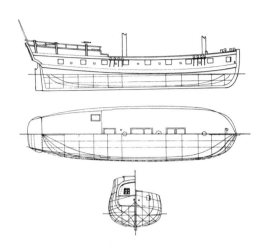

American sloop from Lake Champlain, 1780. The fixed bowsprit of this single-masted vessel marks her as an armed sloop of about 1780, built for service on Lake Champlain by the Americans after the victory of Saratoga to secure their northern border against further incursions from Canada. *(27)*

American galley Washington, 1776. The energetic Arnold had a small shipbuilding yard established at Skenesboro where, in 1776, a cutter and four large galleys were swiftly built. This, the *Washington*, was 22 metres long and mounted one 18-pounder, two 9-pounders and six 6-pounders, together with small swivels. Simply rigged with two lateen sails, *Washington* was captured after the action. *(27)*

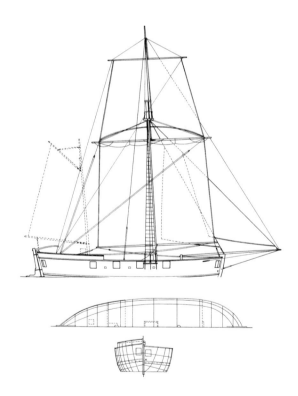

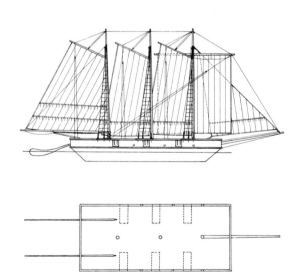

Gundalow Loyal Convert, 1776. The 'gundalow', a corruption of gondola, was the simplest of such hurriedly built vessels, double-ended and flat-bottomed. This, the *Loyal Convert*, was actually built on the St Lawrence as the *Convert*, by the invading Americans in 1775. Taken by the British and renamed in 1776, she was armed with 9-pounders and substantially similar to those built by Arnold on Lake Champlain the following year. *(26)*

British radeau Thunderer, 1776. Another extempore craft was the even more basic 'radeau'. Notwithstanding her simple construction, the radeau *Thunderer* bore six heavy 24-pounders on a lower gun-deck and eight 12-pounders on her upper deck along with two mortars. This made her very low in the water and vulnerable when under sail. The simple steering system is of interest. *(27)*

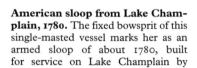

Russian galley, 1743. The Russian naval victory at Gangut during the Great Northern War was fought largely between galleys, and these were retained in the Russian fleets, being very successful against the Turks on the Sea of Azov. As was common in Russia, foreign expertise was imported, the advice of the Knights of Malta being taken in the matter of galley management. This large galley of 1743 was both a warship and a military transport able to stow horses in her hold. *(72)*

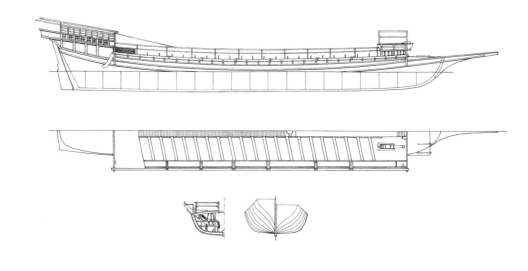

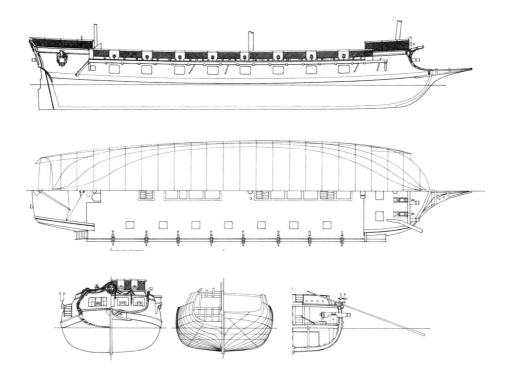

Swedish praam. This 'praam' was essentially a sailing vessel, oars being used in calm weather and shipped when the main battery went into action. She appears to date from the pre-Chapman era when both Baltic powers had huge galley fleets. Beamy enough not to require the outrigged apostis, the great beam could support broadside guns. *(72)*

Chapman's Archipelago Fleet

The Great Northern War at the beginning of the eighteenth century ended Swedish domination of the Baltic, but the Finnish coast remained an uneasy frontline between the Swedes and the increasingly ambitious Russians. The relatively calm, island- and skerry-studded waters off the Finnish coast were not ideal for deep-draughted sailing ships, so rowing craft were often employed. However, a brief war between 1741 and 1743 raised concerns over epidemic disease which infected many of the galley crews. The Swedish naval architect Fredrik

Henrik af Chapman designed and built an oared, sail-assisted fleet specifically intended to meet these conditions. The Finnish Archipelago Fleet was part of the army, not the Swedish navy, and its units were often required to land troops. The 'galley-frigates' were not suitable to this task, but at the rout of the Russians at Svenskund in 1790, Chapman's 'galley-frigates' overwhelmed their enemy with gunfire, smashing the Russian galleys' oars and decimating the unfortunate oarsmen.

1/400   40 30 20 10   0 ft

10   5   0 m

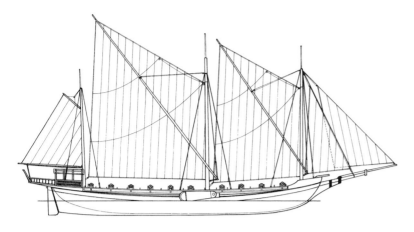

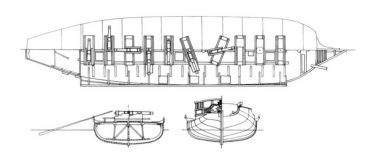

Chapman 'galleasse' design, 1760. Chapman's Finnish Archipelago Fleet began in 1760 with a conceptual design that was never actually built, but was to have been rowed by 72 men at 18 pairs of oars. Sailed by a simply handled sprit rig, supplemented by a small gaff mizen and two headsails, the galley was to be shoal-draught and fitted with leeboards. She was to be armed with ten centrally mounted guns. These, on swivelling carriages, would be fired on either side and the ideas were in due course to be adopted in the *udema*. *(72)*

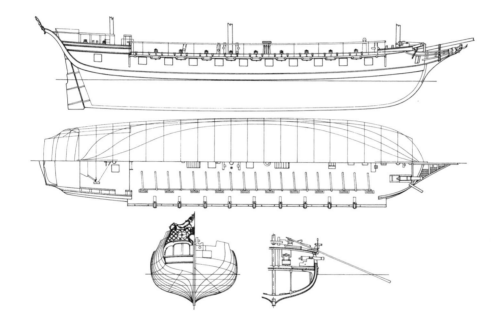

The *turunmaa Lodbrok*, 1771. In the event, Chapman built a fleet consisting of four highly original classes of vessel, the *udema, pojamaa, hemmema* and *turunmaa*, named after the provinces of Finland. They were principally sailing vessels, the oars being auxiliary. This is the *Lodbrok*, a *turunmaa*, a twin-broadsided shallow-draught sailing warship launched in 1771. The *Lodbrok* was rigged with square sails and armed with 12-pounder broadside and 18-pounder chase guns. The *turunmaa* put out nineteen pairs of oars, each manned by four men. The chief innovation in Chapman's design was the longitudinal stiffening in the hull, which made the *turunmaa* and her sisters, very strong. Four sister-ships were built to this design. *(72)*

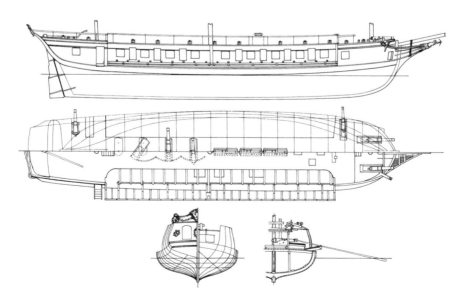

The *udema Torborg*, 1770. The lateen-rigged *udema*, her sail split to avoid the necessity of moving the yard from one side of the mast to the other, mounted a central battery of nine 12-pounders 'en barbette' as had first been envisaged by Chapman. An additional four conventionally broadside guns were mounted forward and aft. This was primarily a sailing vessel, but could deploy twenty pairs of oars each pulled by four men. *(62)*

40 30 20 10 0 ft
1/400 |—————————————|
10 5 0 m

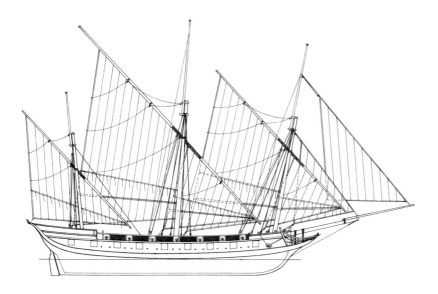

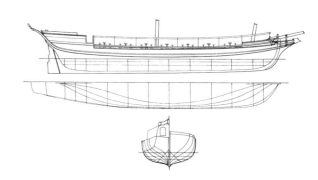

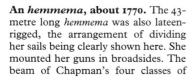

An *hemmema*, about 1770. The 43-metre long *hemmema* was also lateen-rigged, the arrangement of dividing her sails being clearly shown here. She mounted her guns in broadsides. The beam of Chapman's four classes of vessel indicates their ability to sail and use their guns, but they were often too deep-draughted for offensive operations which, being army vessels, often included landing troops. *(112)*

A *pojamma*, about 1770. The smallest class of Chapman's Archipelago Fleet was the *pojamaa*. Sail power was based on the ketch-rig with a square main topsail, with 16 pairs of oars provided auxiliary propulsion. *(74)*

Archipelago hospital ship. The ravages of disease in war and the difficulties of persuading Swedish recruits into an army which required them to man oars in the chilly Baltic, increased awareness of the health of soldiers and sailors. This hospital ship provided the additional accommodation missing from an army galley. *(74)*

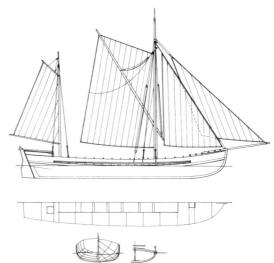

Archipelago horse-carrier. Fully fitted with stalls and stowage for hay, blacksmith's and farrier's stores, this was designed to provide the facilities of a floating stable for a cavalry squadron. *(74)*

Archipelago water-carrier. Fitted with tanks, this craft shows the sophistication necessary to wage war in an area such as the archipelagos of the Baltic. The sprit rig enabled a small crew to handle this craft. *(74)*

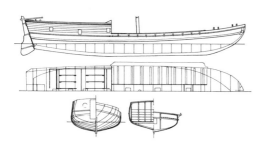

1/400
40   30   20   10   0 ft
10   5   0 m

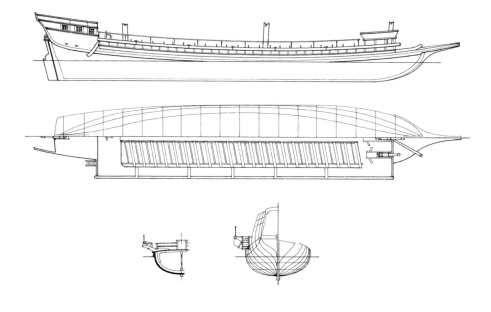

Russian Black Sea galley, 1796.
Russian claims to domination of the
Black Sea and Sea of Azov were based
upon the large fleet of galleys maintained in Crimean waters by the navy
of the Tsars. Well provided with
oarsmen from criminals, dissenters
and prisoners of war, the Russians
were in almost constant collision with
Turkish interests. *(170)*

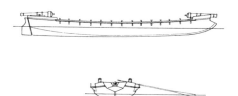

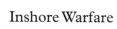

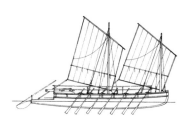

Chapman's *kanonslup*, 1775. This
'gunsloop' was demonstrated before
the king, who was enthusiastic and
made the designer a lieutenant-colonel
for his efforts. Produced in large numbers during the Napoleonic Wars, the
design spread widely through the
Baltic, Danish units being very effective when employed against British
merchant ships endeavouring to pass
The Sound, the Little or the Great
Belts. To make the boats more stable
under sail, the guns could be slid into
the bottom, amidships. *(74)*

Chapman's *kanonjolle*, 1789. The
smaller *kanonjolle*, or gunboat, was
designed in November 1789 and went
into production that winter prior to a
surprise spring attack on the Russian
positions. A floating gun-platform, the
single 24-pounder was on a fixed carriage. Two deep, longitudinal oak
bulkheads of solid oak ran forward

from the stern-pointing gun-mounting
to absorb recoil. These small and
seemingly insignificant craft with their
simple lugsails, oars and primitive
steering proved very effective as arms
of the Danish navy against British
merchant ships and men-of-war after
their conventional fleet had been
destroyed by the British in 1807. *(112)*

**Swedish mortar boat, late eigh-
teenth century.** The mortar – a high-
trajectory shell-firing weapon – could
be mounted in small craft such as this
sprit-rigged Baltic gunboat of the late
eighteenth century. Note the small
guns fore and aft, and the stowage for
the oars when under sail. Such low
cost craft could bombard shore batteries and other military targets, sea-ports
and anchored ships and were of particular use in insular warfare when cover
was available over which they could
throw their shells. *(112)*

Inshore Warfare

In order to land troops, Chapman invented two additional classes of
craft suitable for this task, the *kanonslup* and the smaller *kanonjolle*.
Although the Swedish Archipelago Fleet was the most ingenious, many
other navies built specialist small craft for combined operations or
coastal defence. A blue-water navy like the British generally adapted the
various boats of their conventional warships, but other countries developed task-related and often substantial hulls. Although almost all were
fitted to use oars, sail was invariably used to close the objective,
demountable masts causing many contemporary images of such boats
to give the appearance of being exclusively oar-propelled.

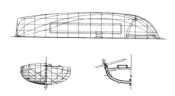

US Navy Gunboats Nos 2-5, 1805.
The tradition established by Benedict
Arnold had, despite his defection to
the British, endured in the form of
these United States Navy gunboats.
This lateen-rigged version mounts a
single heavy 32- or 24-pounder. The

United States had attacked the
Barbary pirates at the turn of the century and used borrowed Neapolitan
gunboats. This experience tempted
President Jefferson to substitute such
craft for a blue-water navy. *(27)*

40 30 20 10 0 ft
1/400
10 5 0 m

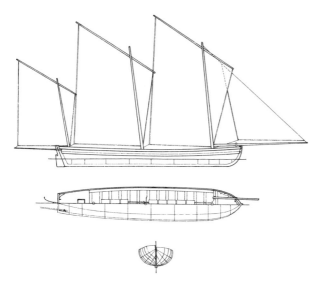

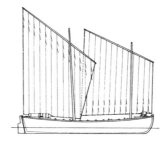

French *caïque*, 1809. Invasion craft were built in places far from the Straits of Dover and painfully worked along the coast to the ports of embarkation. This *caïque*, or gunboat, was built at Rochefort in 1809 and is effectively an enlarged ship's launch with lugsail rig. Such craft were also useful in sheltered areas such as the Morbihan, on the south coast of Brittany, often trapping small British cruisers who penetrated these waters in pursuit of the French coastal trade and fell victims in their turn when the wind dropped away. Like the Danish gunboats, they were heavily armed and could lay off their hapless prey and batter them with guns of 32- or 24-pound shot. *(170)*

French invasion *péniche*, 1805. The French built a huge number of craft to standardised designs intended for the invasion of England in many Channel ports. Although Napoleon abandoned his main enterprise in the autumn of 1805, he continued to regard the invasion as a long-term objective and the threat was maintained to the end of the First Empire. Organised by port of departure, this is a *peniche* of the Boulogne flotilla, one of over 450 such craft deployed between the Schelde and Cherbourg, all built at ruinous and useless expense. As an open lugger, its efficacy as an infantry transport is suspect. *(170)*

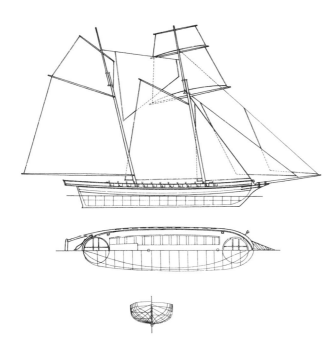

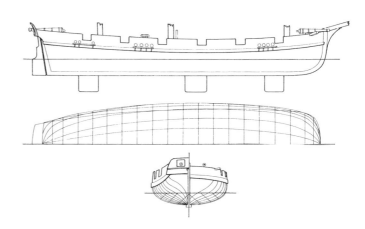

Venetian gunboat, 1812. The Venetian navy was subsumed into that of France, but by 1812, when this gunboat was built, the British were masters of the Adriatic. A creeping coastal trade was maintained when possible and for this, light sailing escorts were built. Rakish and fast she could make good her escape when the patrolling British frigates fell upon the small, local trading vessels. As with an increasing number of small warships, her armament consisted of two heavy guns mounted 'en barbette', capable of traversing over a wide arc. *(170)*

Dutch gunboat, 1806. The protection of coastal trade and suppression of smuggling occupied the Napoleonic authorities throughout the French Empire which included The Netherlands. This Dutch gunboat is fitted with sliding keels which had been introduced to Europe by Captain Schank of the Royal Navy from his experience in North America. *(170)*

40 30 20 10 0 ft
1/400
10   5   0 m

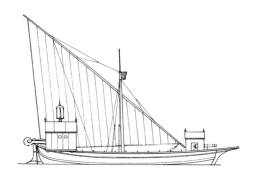

Hungarian *naszád*, sixteenth century. Right at the end of the fifteenth century a new type of warship was introduced on the Danube by the Hungarians. It was adopted from a German design from Nassau, whence it was called a *naszád* in Hungarian. It was a fine-lined galley type craft that could be propelled by eight or ten pairs of oars or a lateen sail when the wind was favourable. A forward-firing gun was protected by a small deckhouse and another aft covered the helmsman and commander. They were widely used in the wars against the Turks during the sixteenth and seventeenth centuries. *(38)*

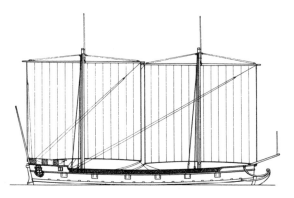

Austrian galley *Santa Theresa*, 1736. Although pierced for oars between the guns, the large sail plan of this 12-gun galley demonstrates the primary motive force employed. The low freeboard is raised by defensive nettings and an ornate after cabin accommodates the galley's officers. She was one of five old but still battle-worthy galleys that were repaired for the campaigns of 1736-39 against the Turks. *(38)*

Warships of the Danube

The importance of great rivers as highways has, as we have seen, been of great importance since early times. The development of Roman craft on the Rhine in the early Christian era is mirrored in a later age by the naval forces maintained by the dual monarchy of Austria-Hungary (the Austrian emperor was also King of Hungary) on the Danube, the valley of which was of high strategic importance during the dynastic wars of the early eighteenth century and the Napoleonic conflict at the beginning of the next. From the dissolution of the Roman Empire until the mid sixteenth century, south-east Europe was the disputed frontier with the Turks and it is therefore unsurprising to see the influence of the galley form in the various gun-vessels designed and built to patrol this vital waterway. The significant influence on the movement of such craft is the strong current prevailing in the Danube as it flows east towards the Black Sea. For this reason would-be exponents of maritime power seeking to use its waters had to rely mainly upon sail and this offshoot of mainstream sea-power merits consideration. Also of interest is the exploitation of the steering oar which, using the river current, could prove very effective in manoeuvring in a river.

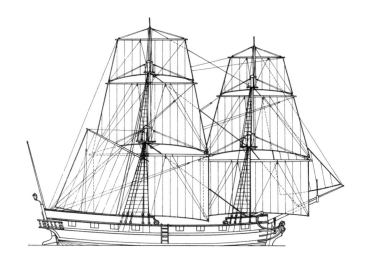

Austrian river frigate *Maria Theresa*, 1769. From 1740 more ship-like warships began to appear on the Danube, and these were referred to as 'frigates'. Two were laid down in 1763 and 1769, this representing the latter vessel, named *Maria Theresa* after the queen of Austria-Hungary. Masted as a conventional sea-going brig, this remarkably sophisticated rig was clearly intended to carry out complex manoeuvres and its abilities to work upstream in a river are well attested. Built as flagship of the Danube fleet, in 1787 the 26-metre long vessel carried four 18-pounders, twelve 12-pounders and twenty-four smaller guns and two howitzers on deck, with a crew of 127 including 45 soldiers. *(38)*

40 30 20 10 0 ft
1/400
10   5   0 m

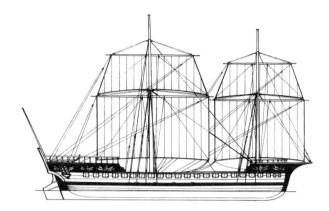

Austrian galley-frigate, 1768. There is evidence that Danube warship design drew on Swedish experience with the Archipelago Fleet, and Chapman's colleague Erik Åhrsberg certainly went to Vienna about 1768 to advise on shipbuilding. He is usually credited with this galley-frigate, a model of which survives in the Viennese military museum. Unlike the *Maria Theresa*, the simple but adaptable square rig on this large, shallow draft vessel suggests it was never intended to work to windward within the confines of the Danube's banks; such vessels took the maximum advantage of a favourable wind. The model shows fourteen pairs of long sweeps amidships between the gunports. *(38)*

Hungarian double *sajka*, 1769. During the seventeenth century the *naszád* tended to become longer and lower, and from the middle of the century the developed form came to be called a *sajka* (possibly from the Italian *saetta* or the Russian *csajka*, both of which were small galley types). Eventually, they were subdivided into 'double', 'full', 'half' and 'quarter' *sajkas*. This 'double *sajka*' of 1769 has her battery well embrasured behind a casemate. Well supplied with oars, sail is clearly here only employed when the wind was abaft the beam. With the disappearance of traditional galleys, these became the largest warships on the Danube, measuring up to 27.5 metres in length. *(38)*

Hungarian half *sajka*, 1771. This small gunboat, or 'half *sajka*', has a shallow draught and low freeboard. Propelled by oars when required, the oarsmen shelter behind a defensive casemate. About 12 metres long, she was armed with two ½-pounders, firing over the bow and stern. *(38)*

Hungarian gunboat, 1819. By the nineteenth century the river flotilla included large *Kanonenboote*, or gunboats, divided into three classes. This Third Class boat of 1819 could be propelled by fifteen pairs of oars, but also incorporated a form of the standing lugsail which combined an ability to work to windward as well as use a prevailing favourable wind. *(38)*

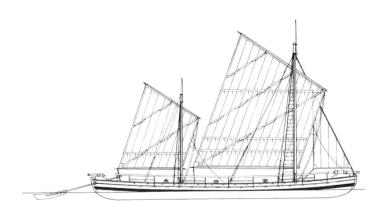

1/400
40 30 20 10 0 ft
10 5 0 m

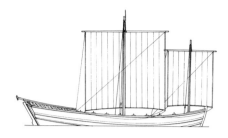

French *barque longue*, 1679. The longboat, *barca longa* or *barque longue*, such as this French example from 1679, was basically a sea-going off-shore tender used to take provisions to men-of-war riding to their anchors in the roads of Calais and Dunkirk. Their English equivalents are the Deal punts and galleys whose terminology only adds to the confusion. Oars were of course of equal importance when the winds were light and it was not long before such craft were manned by armed men and used to seize anchored or becalmed merchant ships in enemy anchorages. The origins of the frigate are, of course, identical. *(62)*

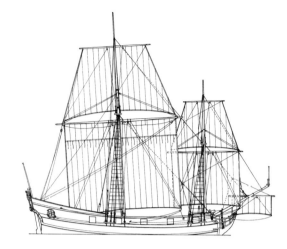

French *chaloupe* of around 1710. Insofar as any defining characteristic governed the early development of either the sloop or the corvette, the two-masted rig was probably it. The graduation of the sloop-type from mere boat to small naval cruiser was accomplished in France by the beginning of the eighteenth century. This example shows the two-masted configuration, still all square-rigged, but with topsails, plus the usual attributes of larger warships – beakhead, bowsprit, forecastle and quarterdeck, and a cabin for the commanding officer. *(62)*

The Sloop-of-War and Corvette

No term has such a confusing history as that of the 'sloop'. The passage of time, shifts in fashion, imprecision of usage in an age untroubled by Linnean categorisation and tolerant of regional differences, make matters difficult in a history of sail. The term took on a specific meaning when used for a whole range of un-rated small British naval vessels and was used for administrative purposes, but it existed outside this naval application. What may be said with certainty is that the term originally referred to a general type, rather than a rig, that there have for many years been two sloops, the naval form being quite different from the civilian interpretation, and the latter has finally fixed upon rig as the defining quality. The word itself derives from 'shallop', for which the French equivalent is *chaloupe*. Of parallel etymology is the French word *corvette* which derived from the word for basket and meant a small cargo-carrier, and is defined in a dictionary of 1711 as a longboat with two masts used as tenders to fleets. In turn the notion of a basket derives from the latin *corvis*, a name applied to Roman grain-carriers who bore a wicker basket aloft as a sign of their lading.

After the Napoleonic Wars the adoption of the word corvette into Royal Naval parlance was a matter of fashion. Along with 'corvette' and 'frigate', usage of the word 'sloop' continued to undergo evolutionary change up to and including modern times.

It is from these humble beginnings that an equally humble but important man-of-war developed.

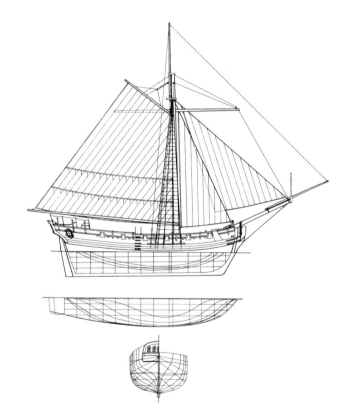

British sloop *Ferret*, 1711. A shift in task occurred when the French pursued a vigorous war on trade and the Admiralty ordered some lightly armed 'sloops' to be built to combat privateers penetrating The Downs and other British anchorages. One of the first was the *Ferret*, depicted here. Built at Deptford in 1711, *Ferret* bore 10 small guns, measured 19.6 metres in length, and was of 113 tons burthen.

The fore-and-aft rig was adopted, though a yard was retained to set a single square course in fair winds. The single-masted rig was unusual in naval circles, but the large boomed mainsail – a contrast to the lateen mizen of larger ships and interesting when set against the retention of the lateen-rig in larger warships – proved unwieldy and *Ferret* bore a two-masted snow rig from 1716. *(27)*

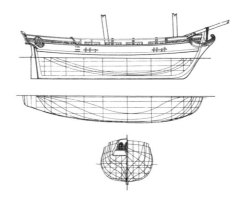

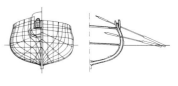

British sloop *Swift*, 1721. The two-masted rig tended to prevail in these small warships, the snow being adopted for the *Swift* of 1721. This entailed providing a small spar running parallel with the main (after) mast, upon which the spanker was hooped but which was otherwise broadly similar to the brig. *Swift* was of 91 tons burthen and reported as over-canvassed. She had very exposed decks protected by rough-tree rails and her light guns fired over her sheer-strake. *(27)*

British sloop *Spence*, 1730. By contrast the near contemporaneous *Spence* of 1730 was a much longer vessel, almost a galley-frigate, of 26.5 metres and 206 tons burthen, fitted for two rows of sweeps. Her precise rig is unknown, but her hull form is designed to maximise efficiency under sweeps, while producing speed under sail. *(31)*

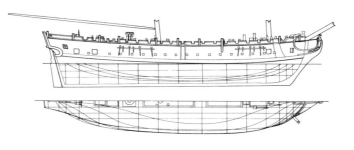

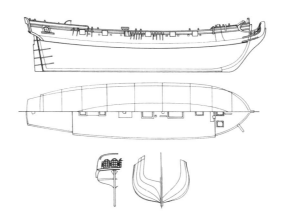

British sloop *Speedwell*, 1744. The rig of the *Speedwell* of 1744 was known to have been that of a ketch, a rig more popular in the seventeenth than the eighteenth century Royal Navy. Despite this, the more integrated hull form, with its fore and aft platforms and midships bulwarks, is tending towards the light frigate that was to be the naval sloop's ultimate destiny. *(166)*

British sloop *Favourite*, 1757. The concept of the sloop-as-frigate came of age in 1757 when Thomas Slade designed a small, 16-gun ship-rigged class. Initially denominated a 'frigate', the first of these, the *Favourite*, mounted 6-pounders on a 29-metre gun-deck and measured 309 tons burthen. The adoption of ship rig extended the quarterdeck and produced a more accommodating hull, able to keep the sea longer. A smaller, 14-gun class was also built. *(166)*

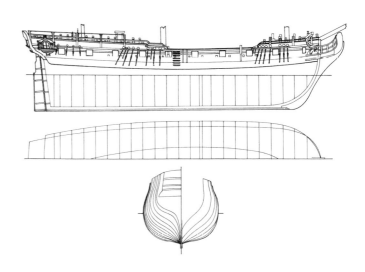

```
           40     30     20     10      0 ft
  1/400  ├────┼────┼────┼────┼┼┼┼┤
               10          5          0 m
```

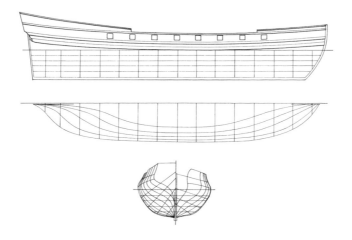

French corvette of 1765. This is built for a shallower draught and her lines have not yet thrown off her descent from an offshore boat. *(62)*

British *Merlin* class ship-sloop, 1795. By the start of the Revolutionary War with France in 1793 the concept of the sloop-of-war was well established. Her role consisted of those multifarious tasks undertaken by a small to medium-sized cruiser. Classes proliferated, but the sloop, like the French corvette, had resolved her naval development and appeared in two guises, as a brig (usually mounting 12 to 18 guns) and a ship (mounting from 16 to 20). The *Merlin* class of ship-sloop, measuring 365 tons, bore sixteen 6-pounders. In conformance with the practice of the day, she also carried four 12-pounder carronades on her quarterdeck and two on her forecastle. These were omitted from her 'official' gun-power. *(62)*

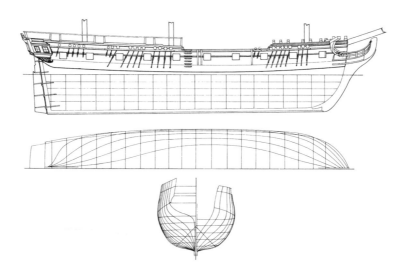

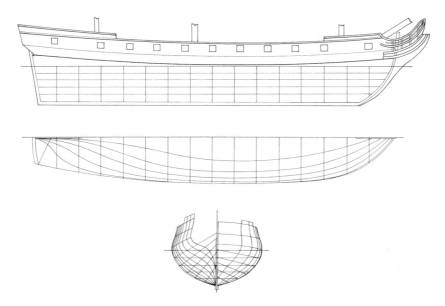

French corvette of 1793. This is of a larger type mounting a heavier armament. A pair of such vessels was often attached to a frigate squadron sent out to harry British trade, pursuing 'la guerre de course' as far as the Indian Ocean with considerable success. *(62)*

1/400   40 30 20 10 0 ft
        10   5   0 m

French *Hermione*, 30 guns, 1748. The first 12-pounder frigate was the *Hermione*, launched at Rochefort in 1748, and this vessel's deeper, more heavily constructed hull set the trend for further evolution. Deep-draughted but low and weatherly, measuring 812 tons burthen, *Hermione* was built by Morineau, the constructor of the 74-gun *Invincible* a few years earlier. The notion of providing similar hull strength in a cruiser enabled French naval strategy to become increasingly stretched towards blue-water. *(166)*

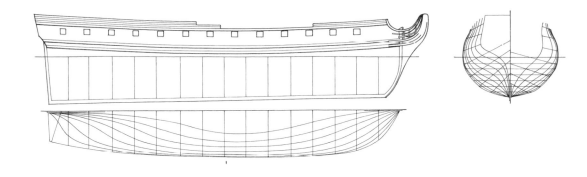

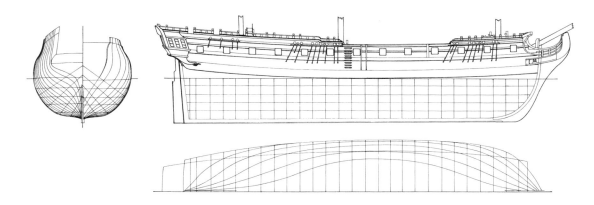

British *Southampton*, 32 guns, 1756. The British countered with Thomas Slade's *Southampton* class, of which this is the name-ship. Numerous derivatives followed from the board of Slade and his colleague Bately. *Southampton* and her close sisters were Fifth Rates mounting 32 guns, twenty-six 12-pounders on the gun-deck and six 6-pounder on the quarterdeck; carronades were later added from about 1780. Ship-rigged and of lesser size than *Hermione*, Slade's hull, of 672 tons burthen, is of greater strength and depth than Morineau's. *(166)*

French *Charmante* and *Junon*, 32 guns, 1778. The French dockyards soon produced significantly larger 12-pounder frigates. The superiority of this class was not slow to impact on the Royal Navy who were then engaged in a world-wide war without allies, attempting to suppress armed rebellion in the American colonies and ward off a host of opportunistic European powers happy to join in the dismemberment of the British Empire. This was the apogee of the Bourbon Navy of France. *(168)*

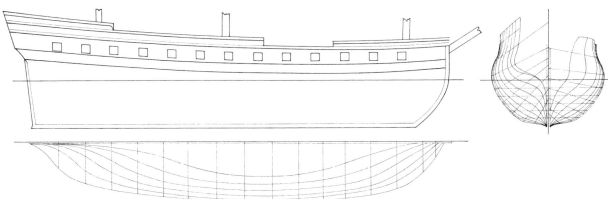

The Evolution of the Frigate

The wars of the eighteenth century increasingly became global maritime conflicts and it was after the struggle over the Austrian Succession that rapid development of the frigate occurred. The massing of the frigate's main armament on a single gun-deck produced a stable, snug and weatherly hull form, making it easy to increase the calibre of the guns. A minor arms race ensued: by 1748 the French had produced the 12-pounder frigate; this was matched by the British during the Seven Years War, who then trumped the French by adopting 18-pounders in the 1770s. As weight of metal increased, so did battery size – the 32-gun frigate was superseded by the 36, then the 38. In the 1780s Chapman contemplated 24-pounders for Swedish frigates, and the French and then the Americans built a few of these 'super frigates' in the 1790s.

The French Revolutionary War was, by the time of the Peace of

Amiens, effectively a French victory. Although suffering several major fleet defeats at home, the strategic advantage was held by France and the British Royal Navy had to do much of its work all over again when war resumed two years later in 1803. The annihilating victory at Trafalgar masks the continuing difficulties the over-stretched Royal Navy had in order to contain their enemies during the following decade of the Napoleonic War. Much of the opposition was provided by the heavy frigates of the French which, operating in squadrons, plagued the trade route from India from bases in Mauritius. The superiority of British seamanship generally overpowered these French ships and many ended their days as British men-of-war, highly regarded by their captors. Others formed the basis for British imitative improvements.

1/400
40   30   20   10   0 ft
10   5   0 m

British *Flora*, 36 guns, 1778. Although the French had considered the 18-pounder for frigates in 1775, it was a highly pressurised British Admiralty who, in 1778 introduced three classes, two of 36-guns and one of 38. The *Flora* was class-ship of one of the first. Built at Deptford and launched in 1781, *Flora* was 42 metres on the gundeck and was of 870 tons burthen. After the renewal of war with Republican France in 1793, *Flora* was one of a number of crack frigates operating in the Channel as a 'flying squadron' and took part in the capture of the *Pomone*. (166)

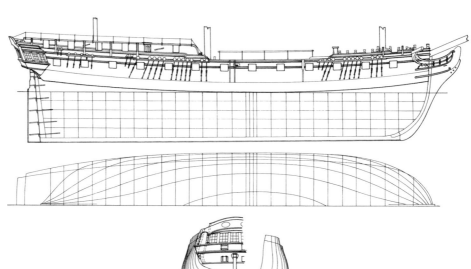

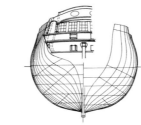

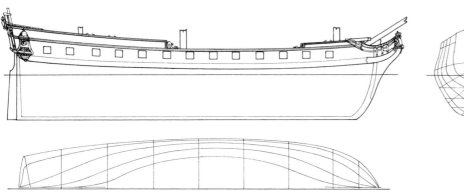

French 32-gun frigate, 1785. The Bourbon French Navy continued to build large 12-pounder 32-gun frigates, often characterised by a rising after sheer and a more angular midships section. (168)

Dutch *Mars*, 32 guns, 1781. Smaller European navies with overseas possessions and foreign trade such as The Netherlands and Denmark followed France and Britain in building large frigates. The Dutch frigate *Mars*, of 700 tons burthen, was built in 1769 as a 38-gun frigate, but because of the weight of her battery, afterwards reduced to a 12-pounder 32 when captured by the British in 1781. (166)

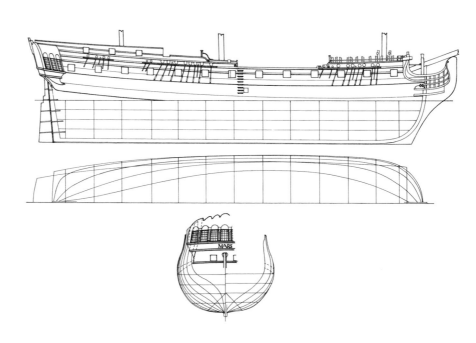

40 30 20 10 0 ft
1/400
10 5 0 m

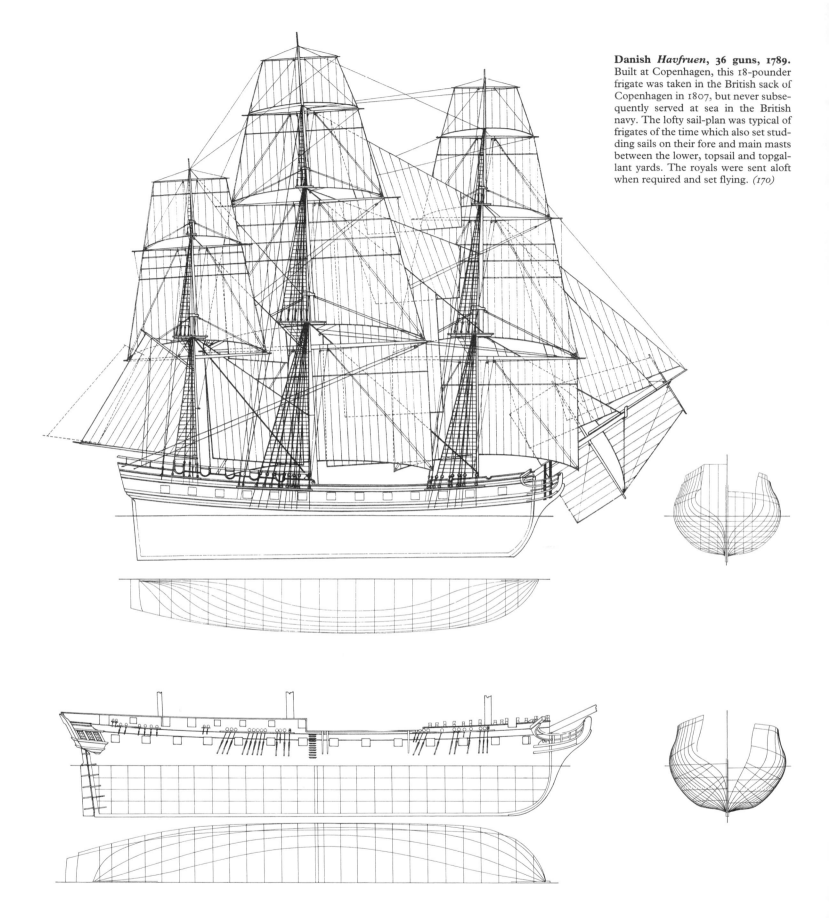

Danish *Havfruen*, 36 guns, 1789.
Built at Copenhagen, this 18-pounder
frigate was taken in the British sack of
Copenhagen in 1807, but never subse-
quently served at sea in the British
navy. The lofty sail-plan was typical of
frigates of the time which also set studding sails on their fore and main masts
between the lower, topsail and topgallant yards. The royals were sent aloft
when required and set flying. *(170)*

French *Pomone*, 40 guns, 1785.
Captured by a flying squadron in
1794, this frigate was found to be
armed with 24-pounders. As a consequence three British 64-gun ships-of-
the-line were razéed to produce formidable 44-gun frigates, and a direct
copy of *Pomone* was ordered. The
resultant copy was the handsome
Endymion of 1797, a ship still regarded
as a prime sailer in the 1830s. Built
by Randall at Rotherhithe on the
Thames, she measured 48.5 metres on
the gun-deck and was almost 1240
tons burthen. *(166)*

40   30   20   10   0 ft
1/400
10   5   0 m

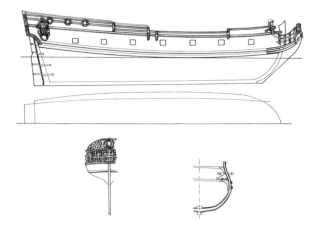

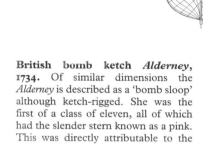

British ship-rigged bomb *Mortar* of 1693. This early British bomb vessel betrays little of her purpose in this simplified draught. She was two decked and rigged, unusually, as a three-masted ship. Measuring 26 metres in length, she was of 300 tons burthen. *(216)*

British bomb ketch *Alderney*, 1734. Of similar dimensions the *Alderney* is described as a 'bomb sloop' although ketch-rigged. She was the first of a class of eleven, all of which had the slender stern known as a pink. This was directly attributable to the influence of the Dutch flute and was found in contemporary merchantmen. Her mortar beds are clear and enabled the weapons to be traversed. Much of the recoil was taken by heavy beams between which oakum was stuffed as a shock-absorbent. *(216)*

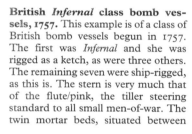

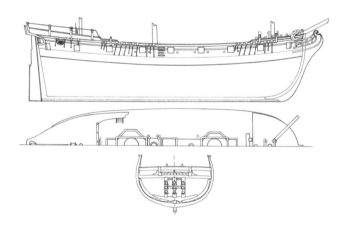

British *Infernal* class bomb vessels, 1757. This example is of a class of British bomb vessels begun in 1757. The first was *Infernal* and she was rigged as a ketch, as were three others. The remaining seven were ship-rigged, as this is. The stern is very much that of the flute/pink, the tiller steering standard to all small men-of-war. The twin mortar beds, situated between the masts, are shown in the cross section. The heavy supporting structure, resting on heavy floors on top of the futtocks, provide stowage for the shell cases or 'carcasses' (incendiary shells). Although pierced for a number of carriage guns, most of these were removed when the vessel was assigned to bombardment duties when they were exchanged for mortars. *(216)*

Bomb Vessels and Fireships

Confusingly listed as 'sloops' in the British navy, because when not required for their specialist purpose both bomb vessels and fireships were used for general fleet tasks, most notably convoy escort, these smaller warships were of occasional significance. As has already been noted, the mortar-armed *galiote* had been first used by the navy of Louis XIV, but by 1693 the British had followed suit. The advantage of the mortar was two-fold: it could theoretically throw a projectile over defences; and the projectile *exploded* at the expiry of its fuse. For these reasons mortars were generally handled by artillery experts rather than naval gunners, and to achieve the best results some form of spotting the fall of the shells was necessary. The early method of aiming by turning the whole vessel to align the mortar with the target was abandoned with the introduction of the revolving mortar. This enabled the weapon to be laid on the target independent of the ship's head and thus, about 1750, the ketch rig was replaced by that of the ship. Immense strength was built into these vessels to absorb the recoil of the mortars. At the end of the Napoleonic War the British cut down several bomb vessels to barque-rig, fitted steam engines and prepared them for Arctic exploration.

Navies interested in simple home defence did not need to produce complex sea-going ships, so mortar boats became useful to several powers.

The vulnerability of wooden ships to fire was known from earliest times and this weakness was first exploited by the use of Greek fire. Ships fitted out for attacking enemy fleets by means of fire were often improvised, but a few were purpose-built against just such an eventuality. Their construction encouraged the swift progress of the fire and, provided they were accurately laid on course, there was a good chance of entanglement with the enemy target. Opportunities to use them, however, diminished and in their attack on Copenhagen in 1807 the British used the fireship *Prometheus* as a lightvessel off The Skaw, the Danes having extinguished the lighthouse there. In 1809, during his attack on the French squadron in the Basque Road, Captain Lord Cochrane preferred his explosion vessels to the fireships provided by the fleet, taking the concept one stage further to some effect.

40 30 20 10 0 ft
1/400
10 5 0 m

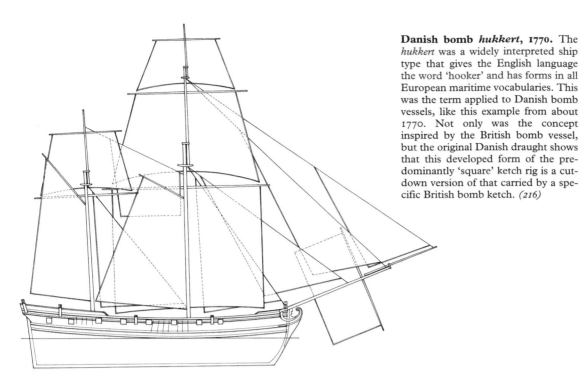

Danish bomb _hukkert_, 1770. The _hukkert_ was a widely interpreted ship type that gives the English language the word 'hooker' and has forms in all European maritime vocabularies. This was the term applied to Danish bomb vessels, like this example from about 1770. Not only was the concept inspired by the British bomb vessel, but the original Danish draught shows that this developed form of the predominantly 'square' ketch rig is a cut-down version of that carried by a specific British bomb ketch. _(216)_

Danish bomb galliot, late eighteenth century. The smaller type is based on a local coaster, though the ketch rig is retained and the craft is immensely strong. Mortars came in a number of sizes, some being quite small and they were usually fired at an elevation of 45°. Achieving range depended on the size of the powder charge for which tables were available for the artillerist. _(166)_

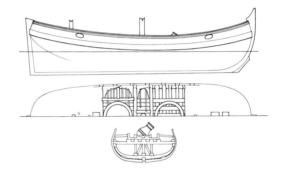

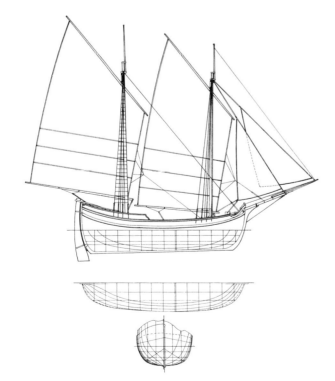

US Navy converted _trabaccolo_, 1804. An all-purpose coastal craft of the Adriatic, the _trabaccolo_ was temporarily adopted by the United States Navy when it attacked the Barbary States in retaliation for their abuses of American merchant ships and seamen. Upon the loss of the frigate _Philadelphia_, the Americans had to hire Neapolitan native craft, including oared galleys and several _trabaccolos_ like this example. They were fitted out with mortars for inshore operations against the corsairs' stronghold of Tripoli in 1804. The natural strength of these native craft made them suitable for bombardment. _(26)_

40   30   20   10   0 ft
1/400
10   5   0 m

British bomb vessel *Vesuvius*, 1812. Adopting the contemporary form of the small sloop-of-war, the ship-rigged *Vesuvius* of 1812 was 31 metres in length and 325 tons burthen. She mounted two mortars, the heavier of the two located amidships and capable of throwing a shell of 13 inches in diameter, the forward one smaller, suitable for shells of 10 inches. Her sister-ship, *Terror*, was lost in the Arctic in search of the North West passage. *(216)*

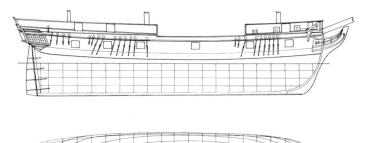

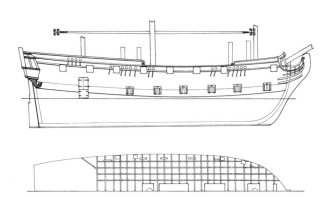

British fireship, about 1700. In 1688 the British had twenty-six fireships and some were used to attack and destroy a portion of the French fleet at La Hogue and Cherbourg after their defeat off Barfleur in 1692. The craft used had lower ports which opened downwards and thus did not close like conventional gun-ports when their lanyards burnt through. This increased the upward draught, encouraging conflagration in the spaces between decks which were stuffed with combustible materials including tar, turpentine and wood-shavings. The ship's yards were fitted with grapnels, irons intended to foul the rigging of the target and prevent the shoving off of the burning fireship. *(166)*

British fireship *Vulcan*, 1780. She was a merchant ship chartered as an armed ship, or transport, then later converted to a fireship in 1780. A central trunking is laid to provide forced draught and the ports again fall open. Escape by the crew was usually achieved by dropping into a towed boat when the fireship was steadied on course towards the target vessel. *Vulcan* was lost at Yorktown in 1782. *(166)*

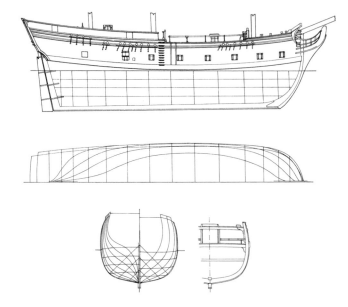

40   30   20   10   0 ft
1/400
10   5   0 m

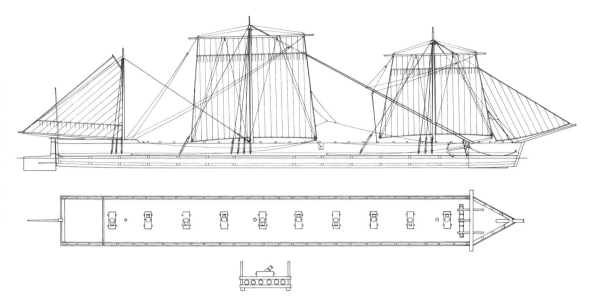

Swedish battery *Lange Maren*, 1719. Defensive measures taken by the Swedes against the possibility of Russian attack during the closing phases of The Great Northern War resulted in this extraordinary floating battery. Known as a *flottpram*, the derivation of 'pram' or 'praam' is obscure, but is just another word for a simple hull-form. The prefix 'flott' indicates the craft is a military, or fleet, vessel. Shoal-draughted, the *flottpram* is a form of bomb vessel, armed with mortars and fitted with a simple, low rig. (72)

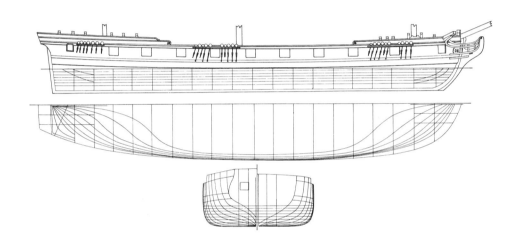

Danish coast defence ship, 1787. The Danes possessed considerable numbers of shoal-draught craft. Despite its name as a *defensionsfregate*, this example was ship-rigged and could be employed in an offensive role in sheltered waters. (16)

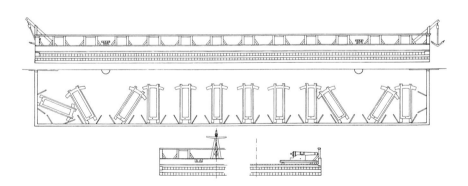

Blockships and Floating Batteries

The use of floating batteries, or blockships, is a means of providing cheap and powerful defences, denying access to an enemy fleet. They were used against the British by the Danes at Copenhagen in 1801 and by the Americans in 1815. The British themselves formed a line of defensive blockships across the Thames during the French invasion scare of 1803-5, though laid-up frigates were employed, but the Spanish sought to probe and weaken British defences of Gibraltar in the siege of 1779-1783 using classic floating batteries.

Danish floating battery, 1789. The simplest form of floating battery was little more than a pontoon on which guns were mounted on slides. Extensive lines of these were moored off Copenhagen to defend the city against Nelson's squadron in 1801. They were devoid of sail and were warped and towed into their station. (16)

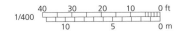

1/400
40 30 20 10 0 ft
10   5   0 m

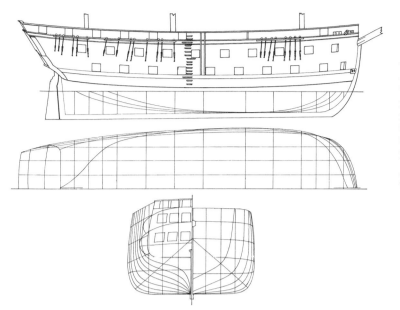

US blockship design, 1806. It was the policy of President Jefferson between 1801 and 1809 to maintain neutrality. Unwilling to further expand the United States Navy, he sought to deter units of the British fleet from entering the many rivers and creeks of the eastern seaboard of the United States by providing the cheap expedient of gunboats and defensive blockships. An example of this policy is to be seen in this manoeuvrable two-decked monster proposed for the defence of New York in 1806, a period of rising tension between Britain and the United States. An armament of 32-pounders and 42-pounder carronades combined with a shallow draught would have made it very difficult for sea-going ships of the line to attack. These blockships were fitted with a simple ship-rig. (26)

US block-sloop, 1812. The outbreak of hostilities between Britain and the United States in 1812 is usually remembered for the series of brilliant victories scored by American frigates over their British adversaries. What is forgotten is that the American coast was extremely vulnerable. Although committed to the maintenance of the blockade of Europe, the Royal Navy increasingly applied a tourniquet to American trade and raided several American towns, including Washington. To oppose these humiliations, the blockship policy proved inadequate, but individual vessels gave good account of themselves. This American block-sloop, built in 1812, is again a basic craft, with the crew under covered shelter. The rig is simple and, with the foot of the squaresail fitted with a Bentinck's boom, can be handled from cover. Note the large cat-head for anchor handling. (26)

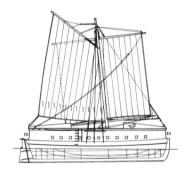

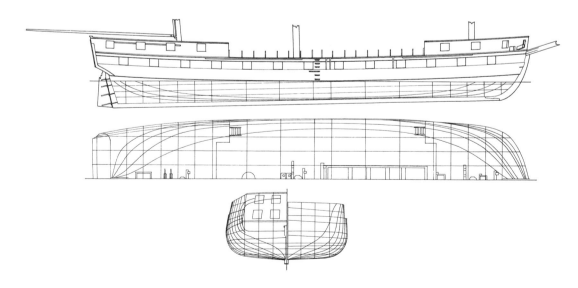

US battery *Tchifonta*, 1815. The bayous and islands of the Mississippi delta were defended by a small fleet of shallow-draught gun vessels, but it was planned to block the passage to New Orleans with a powerful floating battery called *Tchifonta*. However, when the British attack was launched in 1815 – after peace had been signed in Ghent – the blockship was still incomplete. (26)

40 30 20 10 0 ft
1/400
10   5   0 m

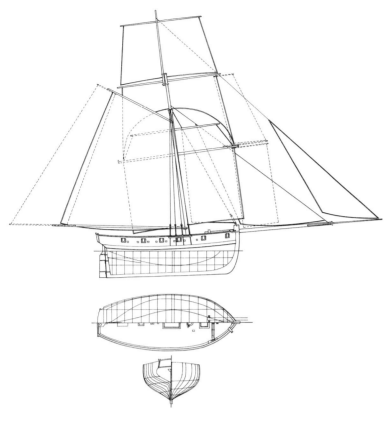

British cutter *Fly*, 1763. The tall masted cutter with its long, running bowsprit entered naval service after the mid eighteenth century tenders were outrun by cutter-rigged smuggling craft. The running bowsprit was theoretically forbidden to private vessels, but this had little impact, since many British naval cutters were hired in from private owners complete with long bowsprit. Known familiarly if a little inaccurately as 'Folkestone cutters', they were ideal for the choppy, tidal waters of the English Channel and southern North Sea. In fact British naval cutters cruised as far as the Mediterranean. This is the *Fly*, purchased in 1763, and she set an amazing array of sails when the wind was light. With a hull 15 metres long, the bowsprit was of almost equal length and a feature of the cutter was that she carried all plain sail, which included a single topsail, upon a pole mast. The topgallant mast and jib-boom were generally fair-weather extensions. Although pierced for 12 guns, she also bore a dozen swivel guns. *(129)*

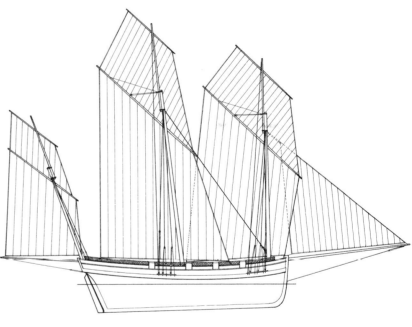

Naval Small Craft

The elevation of the sloop to the duties of a cruiser left to smaller vessels a multitude of lesser duties such as reconnaissance, the conveyance of dispatches, the escort of small coastal convoys and patrolling inshore against both privateers and enemy coastal trade. For such tasks small, fast vessels were required. The British tended to use cutters as against the French, who generally favoured the lugger, while the Americans used the schooner, particularly as a privateer. Brig-sloops were also much favoured by all navies, requiring less maintenance and fewer men than a ship-rigged sloop, while able to bear almost as heavy an armament. By the end of the Napoleonic War there were more brigs in British service than any other type of vessel, and these included a simple brig-rigged armed vessel, capable of being pulled by oars, the gun-brig.

French lugger *Coureur*, 1775. Of similar size, the French *chasse marée* was a fast, weatherly competitor to the British cutter, much favoured by the corsairs of Dunkirk and St Malo. Capable of setting an equally extravagant amount of sail, such craft were potent privateers, highly suitable in hit-and-run raids. Lying with sails down off headlands used as landfalls by homeward-bound merchantmen, enemy luggers caused tremendous problems to the British naval authorities. *(170)*

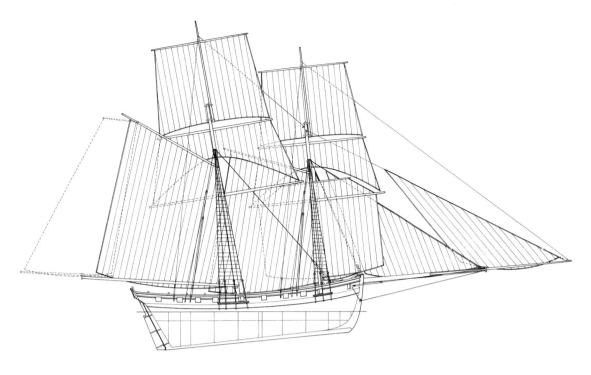

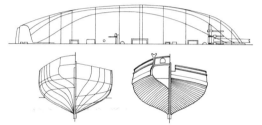

British schooner *Helena*, 1778.
Before the rupture with the American colonies, the schooner had made its impact upon British naval orthodoxy. Used not only as small naval cruisers, schooners were used by the colonial revenue officers on the American coast. The seizure of the *Gaspee* in 1772 was a pivotal act in the breakdown of British authority in the American colonies. Despite her square sails, the principal sail-plan is fore-and-aft and in the period preceding the denomination of type by rig, such a craft as the *Helena* of 1778, was unequivocally a schooner, though the clinker build of her hull, the customary method of construction in cutters, causes her to have been called 'cutter-built'. *(129)*

French brig *L'Atalante*, 1796. The brig as a small sloop was favoured by almost all the protagonists in the wars of 1793-1815. This example is a 16-gun French brig, or *brick*. She is flush-decked, the usual configuration, although there were a few quarter-decked brig-sloops. *(170)*

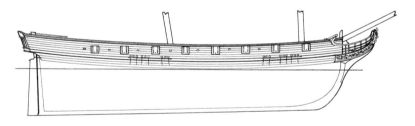

Dutch brig *Echo*, 1796. This Dutch example is flush-decked and pierced for sweeps. *(100)*

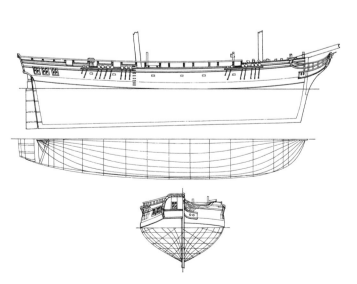

1/400 40 30 20 10 0 ft
10 5 0 m

British *Cruizer* class brig, 1802.
Pierced for twenty guns, the forward
ports were usually unarmed, leaving
sixteen 32-pounder carronades and
two 6-pounder chase guns. The
exceptionally tall rig, with skysails
above royals, was unusual, but the
long-boomed spanker was typical of
the later brig-rig. This too is a flush-
decked vessel and was a very successful design. With over 100 vessels built
to this draught, it was the largest single
class of warship in the age of sail.
French versions of fast brigs were
called by the French *corvette-avisos*, a
retention of the old term synonymous
with 'advice-boat', meaning a reconnoitring dispatch-carrier. *(170)*

British lugger *Lark*, 1799. The 170-
ton craft carried an armament of fourteen guns, two long 4-pounder chase
guns forward and a dozen 12-pounder
carronades. Her deep-heeled, fine-
lined hull form, with its sharp deadrise, was typical of both French and

British cutters at the turn of the eighteenth century. Note the complicated
timbering forming the stem. She is
thought to have been captured by the
Danes while operating in the Baltic
about 1808/9 and renamed *Larken*.
(31)

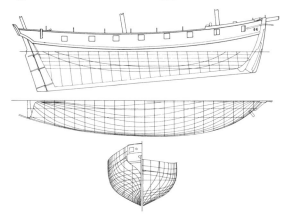

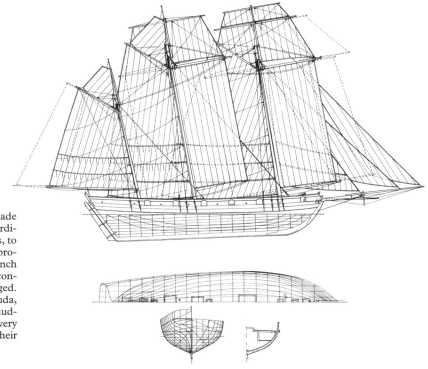

**United States' schooner *Revenge*,
1805.** A dramatic shift in schooner
design in noticeable in this vessel, built
at Baltimore, Maryland. The raked
sternpost and cut-away spoon bow
was adopted from the pilot schooners
of Chesapeake Bay. She appears to
have been purchased by the French
and then captured by the British, soon
after her building, to become HMS
Flying Fish and the model for a class of
six schooners. The low deck was com-
pensated for by high bulwarks, but the

mass of her 10-12 carronades made
her low in the water. Her extraordinary rig is based on tall lower masts, to
which short topmasts are fitted to provide sparring for kites. The French
built similar hulls from the same concept, some of which were brig-rigged.
The resulting class, built in Bermuda,
were colloquially known as 'Bermud-
ians'. Very fast, they were also very
wet and the topweight of wind in their
high kites made them tender. *(31)*

1/400

40   30   20   10   0 ft

10   5   0 m

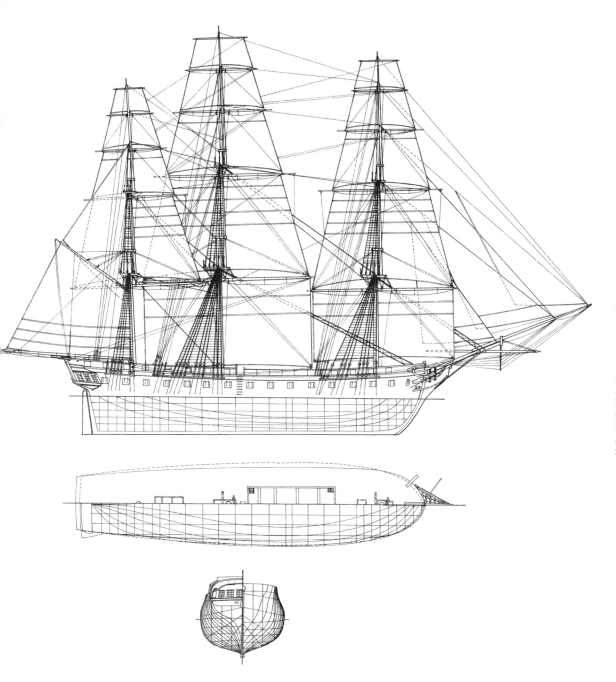

The United States Navy, 1794-1815

After Independence the Continental Navy was disbanded, but the new country relied heavily upon overseas trade and that with the former enemy Great Britain was soon amicably re-established. However, this shipping was now entirely undefended, and the depredations of the piratical Barbary states led to the establishment of a regular state navy in 1794. Ironically, the new force was first deployed against France, the quondam ally of the United States. In the 'quasi-war' that followed, actions between United States and French men-of-war were fought without a formal declaration of hostilities. In the longer term, more damage was done to American trade by the British grand strategy of controlling economic resources entering the French Empire which, between 1806 and 1812, covered most of Europe. American insistence on free trade was in direct opposition to Britain's right of search, and in due course war was declared. This began with a series of defeats of individual British frigates, a bad blow to British prestige, but strategically insignificant, given the immense size of the British fleet.

The reason for this American superiority was in part due to the quality of the ships of the new navy. Unable to build ships-of-the-line, the Americans had built three very heavy frigates, *Constitution*, *United States* and *President*, which were far more powerful than European models, or the other conventional US frigates built from public subscription. These were supplemented by similarly powerful ship-sloops and some lesser vessels, mostly brigs.

Ambitious American eyes were turned on Canada, seeking to take advantage of British distractions in Europe, and the Great Lakes became a theatre of war, flotillas again being built by both sides, between which some fierce actions were fought. Although the United States achieved only partial success in this conflict, its navy was not allowed to deteriorate after the war and the building of its first-line-of-battle ship was a mark of its coming of age as a blue-water force.

60 50 40 30 20 10 0 ft
1/600
15 10 5 0 m

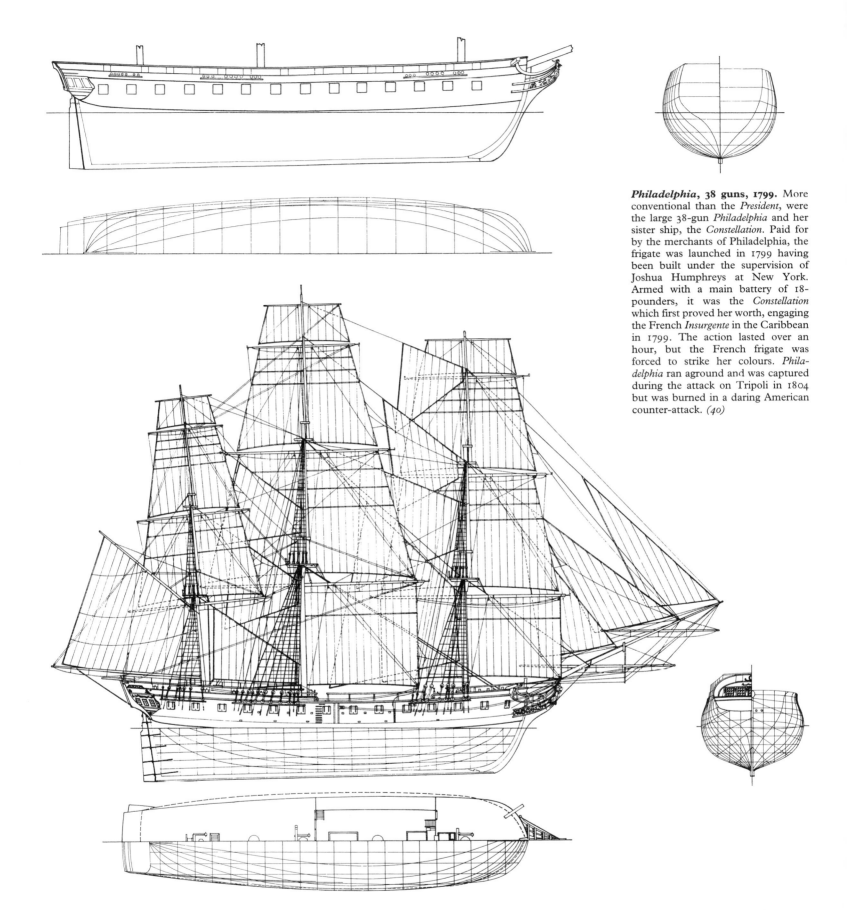

Philadelphia, 38 guns, 1799. More conventional than the *President*, were the large 38-gun *Philadelphia* and her sister ship, the *Constellation*. Paid for by the merchants of Philadelphia, the frigate was launched in 1799 having been built under the supervision of Joshua Humphreys at New York. Armed with a main battery of 18-pounders, it was the *Constellation* which first proved her worth, engaging the French *Insurgente* in the Caribbean in 1799. The action lasted over an hour, but the French frigate was forced to strike her colours. *Philadelphia* ran aground and was captured during the attack on Tripoli in 1804 but was burned in a daring American counter-attack. *(40)*

Essex, 32 guns, 1799. The tall ship-rig favoured by the Americans is seen in this profile of the *Essex*. Built in 1799 by public subscription at Salem, Massachusetts, *Essex* was designed for speed but proved an inferior sailer.

Nevertheless, in 1812 she captured the first British warship, the sloop *Alert*. By the end of the war, she had been armed with forty carronades, with only six long 12-pounders as chase guns. She fell victim to the long guns of the

British frigate *Phoebe* in 1814 after a very successful cruise against British whalers in the Pacific. *Essex* ended her days as a prison hulk in Cork, Ireland. The extreme depth of the topsails with their three rows of reef points, marks

them as much larger than the courses and the topgallants are also of considerable size. The staying of so powerful and lofty a rig required a hull of great rigidity. *(27)*

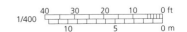

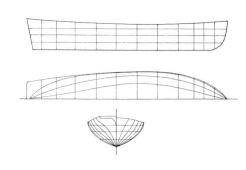

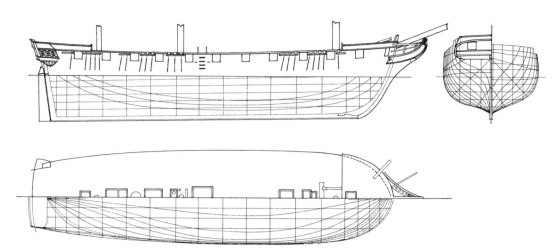

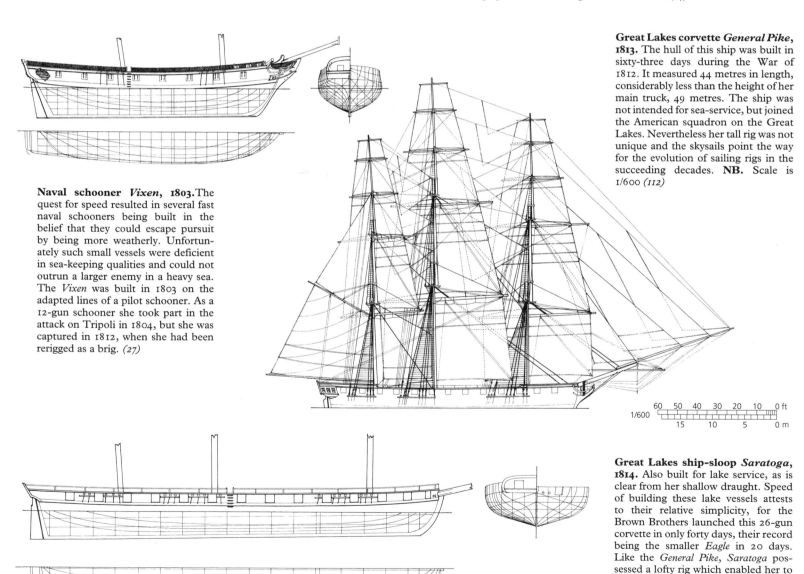

Ship-sloop *Wasp*, 1794. American preoccupation with speed, which often failed to take into consideration the stresses induced by a high sea and/or carrying too much sail in a chase, nevertheless bore fruit after the War of 1812-1814. These are the lines of a fast sloop, the *Wasp*, built in 1794 and not to be confused with two later naval sloops of the same name. *(40)*

Ship-sloop *Peacock*, 1813. Two designs, one fine-lined and based upon the pilot-schooner hull, the other fuller and more seaworthy, were produced by William Doughty. *Peacock* belonged to the latter group, which were larger than British equivalents and proved capable ships. Mounting twenty 32-pounder carronades and two long guns of either 12-pounder or 18-pounder calibre, *Peacock* was 36.5 metres on the gun-deck, of 540 tons burthen and ship-rigged. She took one British brig-sloop on her first cruise, fourteen merchantmen on her second, and ranged as far as the Indian Ocean on her third and final sortie. *(27)*

Naval schooner *Vixen*, 1803. The quest for speed resulted in several fast naval schooners being built in the belief that they could escape pursuit by being more weatherly. Unfortunately such small vessels were deficient in sea-keeping qualities and could not outrun a larger enemy in a heavy sea. The *Vixen* was built in 1803 on the adapted lines of a pilot schooner. As a 12-gun schooner she took part in the attack on Tripoli in 1804, but she was captured in 1812, when she had been rerigged as a brig. *(27)*

Great Lakes corvette *General Pike*, 1813. The hull of this ship was built in sixty-three days during the War of 1812. It measured 44 metres in length, considerably less than the height of her main truck, 49 metres. The ship was not intended for sea-service, but joined the American squadron on the Great Lakes. Nevertheless her tall rig was not unique and the skysails point the way for the evolution of sailing rigs in the succeeding decades. **NB.** Scale is 1/600 *(112)*

Great Lakes ship-sloop *Saratoga*, 1814. Also built for lake service, as is clear from her shallow draught. Speed of building these lake vessels attests to their relative simplicity, for the Brown Brothers launched this 26-gun corvette in only forty days, their record being the smaller *Eagle* in 20 days. Like the *General Pike*, *Saratoga* possessed a lofty rig which enabled her to be swung right round in battle on Lake Champlain, to bring her unengaged broadside into action when the other was wrecked. *(27)*

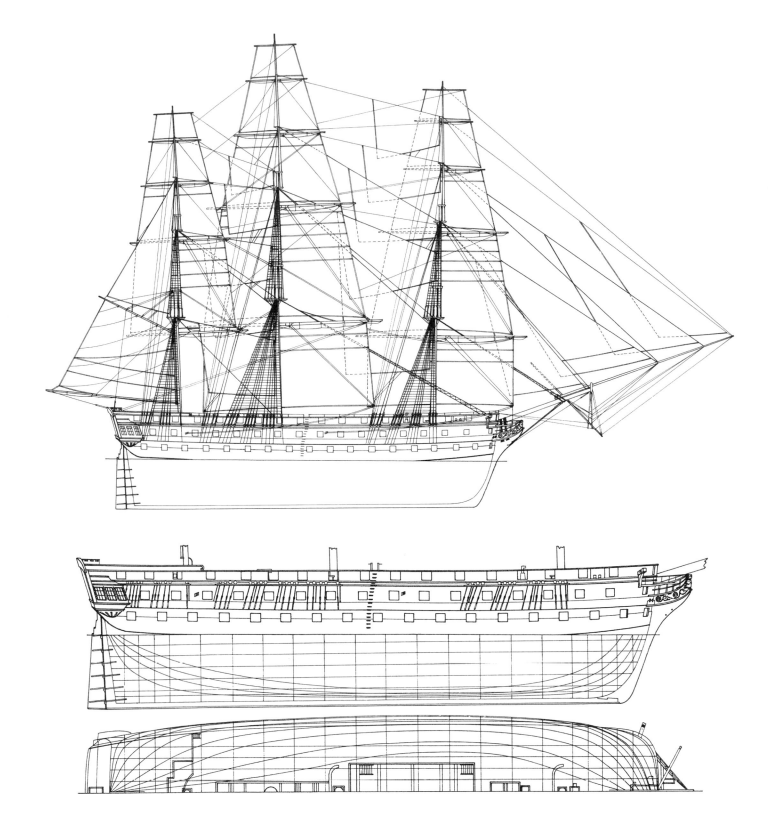

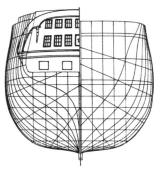

***Columbus*, 74 guns, 1815.** After the war with Great Britain, the United States embarked upon a somewhat half-hearted programme to build 74-gun line-of-battle ships. One of these, the *Columbus*, was laid down by Doughty at the Washington Navy Yard in 1815, but was not commissioned until 1820 (a sister-ship, the *Alabama*, was not launched until 1864!), whereafter she took the first American ambassador to Constantinople. Longer than contemporary British 74-gun ships, *Columbus* bore 32-pounders of varying weights, long guns on the lower gun-deck, short-barrelled weapons on the upper gun-deck and carronades on the forecastle and quarterdeck. These threw a weight of metal almost 500 pounds heavier than British equivalents. The sail plan, like those of the large post-war British and French line-of-battle ships was lofty in the extreme. As there were no flag-officers in the United States Navy, a senior captain being appointed commodore for an operation involving more than one ship, the *Columbus* was built without a poop cabin. **NB.** Sail plan is 1/600 scale *(26)*

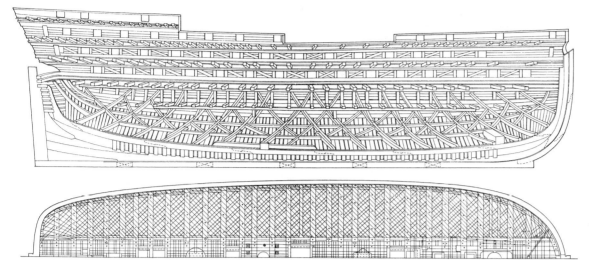

The Seppings system. This drawing shows the diagonal strengthening introduced by Seppings, along with the use made of iron knees. These proved exceptionally durable, but the diagonal deck planking was found superfluous and not adopted in later ships. *(166)*

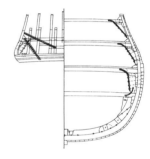

The Seppings circular stern. The traditional stern, seen here on the left, of a man-of-war was vulnerable to raking fire from a vessel firing a broadside along the length of her decks, or from galling fire on the quarters. Stern chase guns could not be massed in any numbers to respond, so Seppings addressed this problem by constructing the round, or 'lighthouse' stern, seen on the right. This made large gunports of the windows of the wardroom and captain's cabin, allowing a wide traverse to guns placed in these apertures. Seppings' construction method also strengthened the extremities of the hull, an important development as length increased to accommodate large gun-batteries. The design was unpopular with officers, and Symonds went on to produce a more traditional looking stern without losing Seppings's advantages. *(166)*

Sailing Warships – the Final Generation

During the wars of 1793-1815 the British in particular had experienced a severe shortage of shipbuilding timber. The forests of English oak had been decimated and other sources were often under threat from enemy commerce raiders. In the post-war period this shortage became acute even though warship construction was severely curtailed. Moreover, it coincided with an ever increasing demand for longer hulls, France especially concentrating on very large two-deckers in an attempt to offset British superiority in three-decked ships. When timber for such massive hulls was available it was rarely of sufficient quality or length, while the grown curves, the 'compass-timber' thought to be the best means of providing angled knees for the support of beams and frames, became increasingly scarce. The solution was found by Sir Thomas Seppings, who on becoming Surveyor in 1813 introduced to the Royal Navy a system of hull construction that used smaller timber lengths and incorporated additional intercostal strengthening by means of diagonal stiffening. To obviate the need for 'grown' knees, iron was increasingly employed for brackets and supports.

A war largely spent pursuing a reluctant enemy led the British on a quest for speed, and in due course Seppings was superseded by Sir William Symonds, who refined the entrance to the hull, steepened the rise of floor and produced a deeper 'vee' form. This enabled a large line-of-battle ship to make 13 knots, but such ships were uneasy in their motions and therefore failed to make good gun-platforms. Huge and inelegant compared with their ancestors, the last major British sailing warships were fitted with steam engines and able to make way to windward at eleven knots. But they were increasingly obsolescent and foreign developments forced the British to abandon the wooden sailing fleet. Steam, steel, shells, breech-loading guns and torpedoes were to revolutionise sea-warfare in the nineteenth century.

40 30 20 10 0 ft

1/400

10 5 0 m

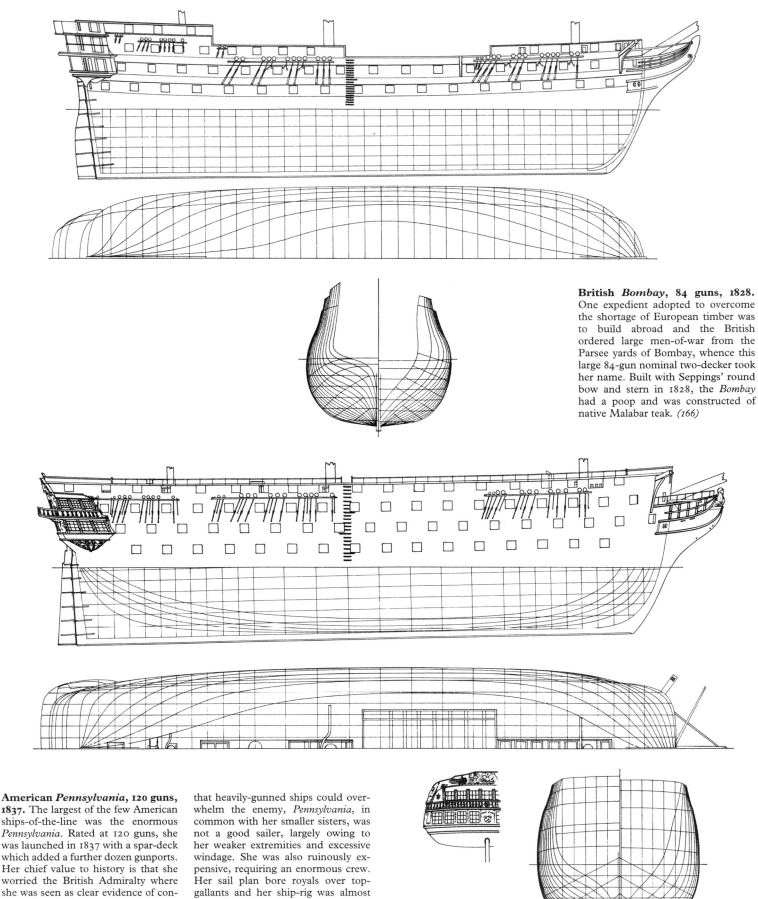

British *Bombay*, 84 guns, 1828.
One expedient adopted to overcome the shortage of European timber was to build abroad and the British ordered large men-of-war from the Parsee yards of Bombay, whence this large 84-gun nominal two-decker took her name. Built with Seppings' round bow and stern in 1828, the *Bombay* had a poop and was constructed of native Malabar teak. *(166)*

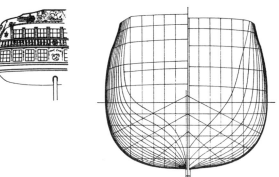

American *Pennsylvania*, 120 guns, 1837. The largest of the few American ships-of-the-line was the enormous *Pennsylvania*. Rated at 120 guns, she was launched in 1837 with a spar-deck which added a further dozen gunports. Her chief value to history is that she worried the British Admiralty where she was seen as clear evidence of continuing blue-water ambitions. Despite her size and the general assumption that heavily-gunned ships could overwhelm the enemy, *Pennsylvania*, in common with her smaller sisters, was not a good sailer, largely owing to her weaker extremities and excessive windage. She was also ruinously expensive, requiring an enormous crew. Her sail plan bore royals over topgallants and her ship-rig was almost too large to be manageable. *(26)*

1/400   40 30 20 10 0 ft

10   5   0 m

French *Suffren*, 90 guns, 1829 After the defeat of France in 1815, the restored Bourbon monarchy sought to rebuild their navy with a number of line-of-battle ships. Only one proper three-decker, the *Valmy*, was built, but a number of large two-deckers were laid down, such as the *Suffren*, seen here. Following the American practice of fitting a spar-deck, the *Suffren* was virtually a three-decker and while being rated as a 90-gun ship, she was pierced with 96 gunports. The problem of producing a manoeuvrable and speedy hull was in part solved by a large sail-plan, and in part by improvements in hull form. However, the mass of the hull and the carriage of guns so high up, frequently made such huge vessels crank and leewardly. **NB.** Sail plan is 1/600 scale. *(166)*

1/400

40 30 20 10 0 ft

10 5 0 m

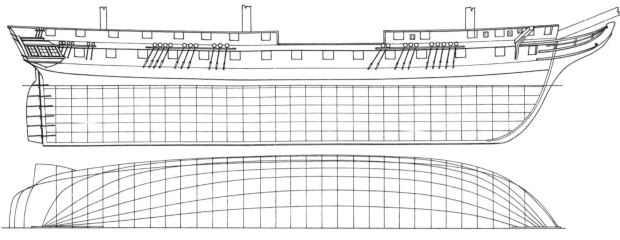

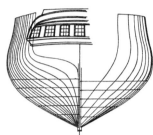

British frigate *Vernon*, 1834.
Displaying the mid-section Symonds introduced to the Royal Navy, the *Vernon* of 1832 only partially adopted the armed spar-deck. The *Vernon* was built as an experiment with a continuous weather deck, but as British naval orthodoxy held, with some justice, that mounting guns along its entire length over-strained the hull, the waist was left clear. Fifty-three metres in length and with an exceptional freeboard, the ship proved fast. She mounted fifty 32-pounders and measured over 2000 tons burthen. *(166)*

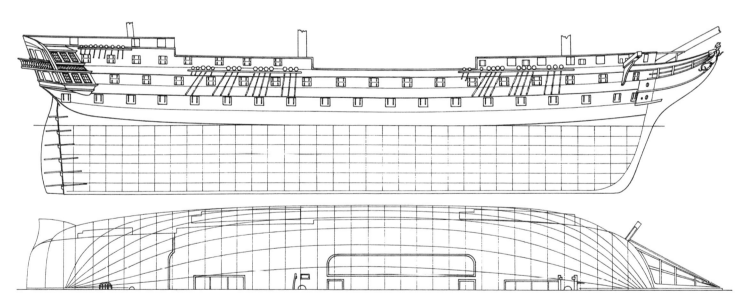

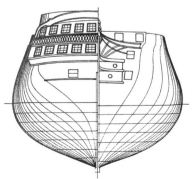

British *Albion*, 90 guns, 1842.
Similar in concept to the French *Suffren*, Symonds's *Albion* was a large, nominal two-decker of 90 guns. As with all Symonds's ships, irrespective of size, she proved fast in trials, due to her beam and her section, but she rolled badly and it was clear that speed could not be at the expense of gunnery efficiency, a factor hard to determine in peace. Admiralty decisions indicated a return to conventional hulls and a disappointed Symonds resigned in 1847. However, the days of the sailing warship were already numbered. Like so many of her contemporaries, the size of the *Albion* makes her as ungainly as the dinosaur she was shortly to become. *(166)*

British brig *Columbine*, 1834. Originally an ordinary naval officer, William Symonds was a speed enthusiast with an interest in yacht design. He succeeded in pressing the British Admiralty into building his design for a fast, 18-gun brig. The *Columbine* of 1826 possessed the long-established virtues of being cod headed and mackerel tailed, with a short entrance and a long run on a deep, 'vee'-formed hull. She was successful in trials held in 1827 and five years later Symonds was promoted to official naval Surveyor. The lines of *Columbine*'s hull provide an interesting comparison with American brigs based upon the pilot-schooner hull. *(195)*

American corvette *Germantown*, 1843. As the large frigate became as long as a line-of-battle ship, a vacancy arose for a smaller, more economical cruiser to 'show' the national flag throughout the world during the long period of peace. It was the sloop, now undergoing fashionable metamorphosis into a 'corvette' such as the *Germantown* of 1843 which carried out this duty on behalf of the United States. Such vessels broke little new ground and were soon adopting steam, relegating sail to an auxiliary role. **NB.** Sail plan is 1/600 scale *(26)*

American razée corvette *Macedonian* of 1852. Smaller frigates made redundant by this shift, were cut down and reclassified as corvettes. The American *Macedonian* was razéed in this way. *(26)*

40 30 20 10 0 ft
1/400
10 5 0 m

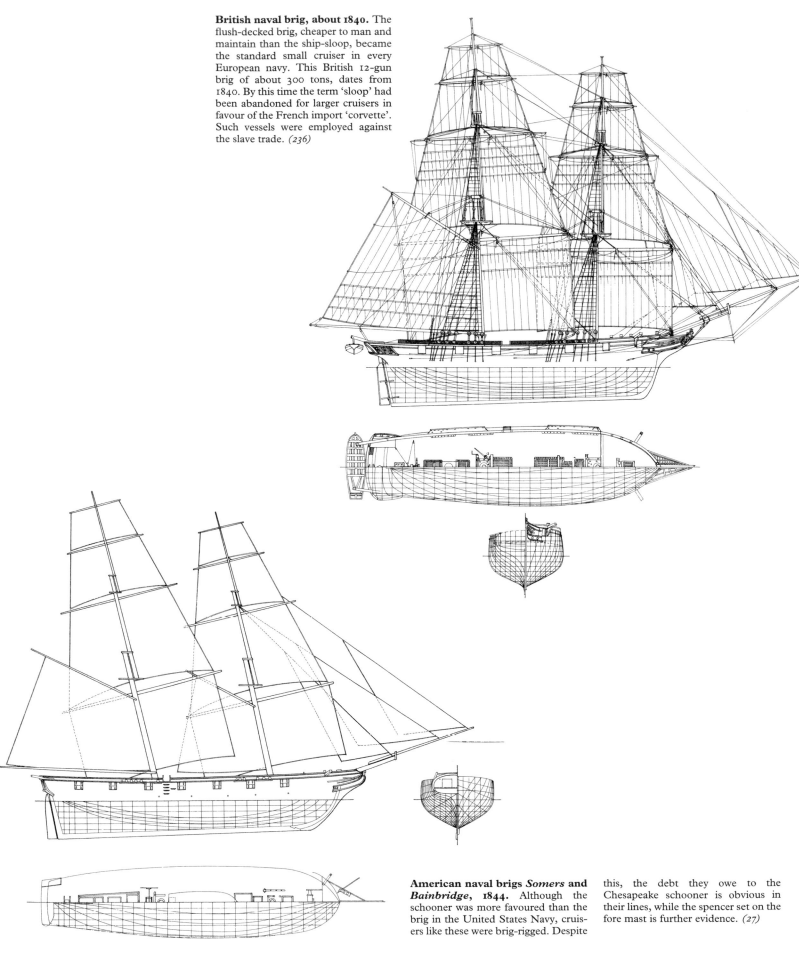

British naval brig, about 1840. The flush-decked brig, cheaper to man and maintain than the ship-sloop, became the standard small cruiser in every European navy. This British 12-gun brig of about 300 tons, dates from 1840. By this time the term 'sloop' had been abandoned for larger cruisers in favour of the French import 'corvette'. Such vessels were employed against the slave trade. *(236)*

American naval brigs *Somers* and *Bainbridge*, 1844. Although the schooner was more favoured than the brig in the United States Navy, cruisers like these were brig-rigged. Despite this, the debt they owe to the Chesapeake schooner is obvious in their lines, while the spencer set on the fore mast is further evidence. *(27)*

40   30   20   10   0 ft
1/400
10   5   0 m

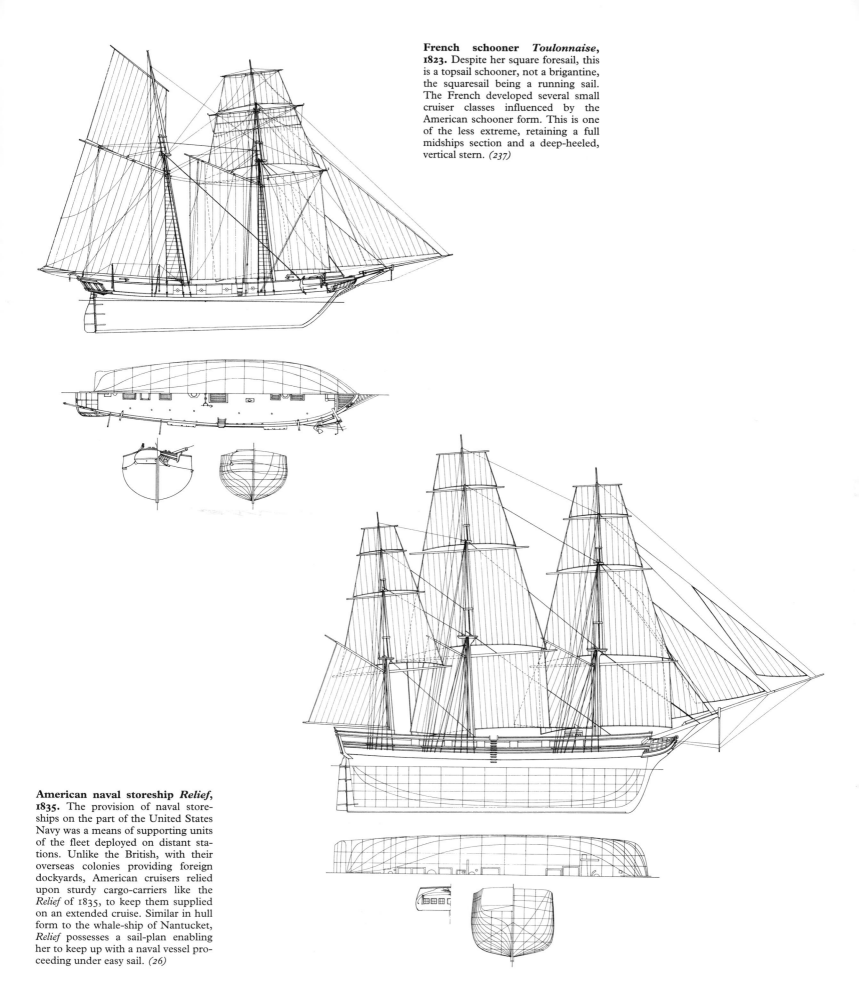

French schooner *Toulonnaise*, 1823. Despite her square foresail, this is a topsail schooner, not a brigantine, the squaresail being a running sail. The French developed several small cruiser classes influenced by the American schooner form. This is one of the less extreme, retaining a full midships section and a deep-heeled, vertical stern. *(237)*

American naval storeship *Relief*, 1835. The provision of naval storeships on the part of the United States Navy was a means of supporting units of the fleet deployed on distant stations. Unlike the British, with their overseas colonies providing foreign dockyards, American cruisers relied upon sturdy cargo-carriers like the *Relief* of 1835, to keep them supplied on an extended cruise. Similar in hull form to the whale-ship of Nantucket, *Relief* possesses a sail-plan enabling her to keep up with a naval vessel proceeding under easy sail. *(26)*

1/400   40   30   20   10   0 ft
        10   5   0 m

SECTION SIX Trading Sail

ALTHOUGH THE LORDLY East Indiaman was to steadily increase in size during the eighteenth century, reaching 1000 tons, the majority of merchant vessels were of little more than 200-300 tons burthen. Ships of such a size were handy enough to carry manageable sail-plans and small crews, being able to serve most ports where they might have to lie on the bottom at low water to handle their cargoes. Indeed the word 'wharf' derives from a tidal strand upon which ships could ground at low water, enabling horse-drawn carts to take off their cargo. By the end of the century several ports possessed wet-docks where ships could lie afloat while loading and discharging and this was particularly important with large vessels, such as Indiamen, which would otherwise be irretrievably strained if they were subject to excessive stress.

Because of the paucity of statistics about coasting sail, the exact size of merchant fleets in this period is largely a matter of conjecture, though that under the British flag was huge. During the Napoleonic War it was not unusual for convoys leaving the Baltic to number 1000 sail, most of which were British, and in addition to this important commerce, British ships were trading across the Atlantic to the United States and the West Indies, as well as to India and China. Commitment to supplying the British army in the Iberian Peninsula encouraged an increase in American tonnage to supply the deficiency, and for which British Navigation Laws were specifically relaxed.

The ship types within this multitude of vessels were numerous and were commonly differentiated by hull-form and by rig. The latter came to be increasingly favoured and in the following century entirely eclipsed the former. But in the eighteenth century it was usual in common parlance for a ship's name to be succeeded by a qualification, plus her port of registry. This qualification might take the form of a reference to her hull, such as in James Cook's '*Endeavour*, Bark'; or in her rig, such as 'the *John*, Brig, of Boston'; or in her trade, such as '*Laertes*, Guineaman of Liverpool', referring to a slaver. Categorisation was not prescrip-

tive and in an age of laxity this quality reflected the society in which it was used.

The rivalry between European states which erupted into a series of wars throughout the eighteenth century also promoted an increase in world trade. Both cause and consequence of conflict, the predominance of one mercantile fleet over another was closely related with the exercise of sea-power. At the end of the seventeenth century the Dutch were dominant, but the commercial and financial advantage shifted inexorably in favour of Great Britain which, in the aftermath of a final victory over France in 1815, left Britain in an unprecedented position of superiority. The envy which this engendered and the difficulties experienced by the British in maintaining this ascendancy had an impact upon the story of sail in that technological development in warships required the abandonment of sail. Matters were rather different insofar as sailing ships engaged in trade were concerned.

For many generations British governments, seeking only to raise revenue on their own account, had used restrictive Navigation Laws to protect British trade. The criteria for levying dues thus rested upon certain dimensions in a merchant vessel's hull and this had stultified development, since it encouraged bluff, box-like hull-forms that gave the maximum carrying capacity within the dutiable measurements. Speed was not a consideration, since frequent periods of hostility required merchantmen to sail in slow convoys. But the triumph of British seapower in 1815 resulted in a period of peace and expansion in world trade. All nations owning ocean-going merchant fleets benefited from this, not least that of the United States of America, where decades of embargo, blockade and war had already focused design and development on speed. Simultaneously there was a huge increase in passenger trade. Emigration from the overcrowded towns of Europe became a social phenomenon of the age. The Irish famine, anti-Semitic pogroms, the rumour and lure of gold in several locations, all fuelled the imperial ambitions of advanced societies. To serve this explosion of aspiration in rich and poor alike, the merchant sailing ship reached a peak of development, for it was not until well into the second half of the nineteenth century that steam vessels had themselves acquired the engines, boilers and bunker capacity to make long voyages.

Under the *Pax Britannica* it was thus not only the British merchant marine which grew. Powerful merchant fleets were operated under the flags of the United States and, by the end of the nineteenth century, the newly unified nations of Germany and Italy. Other countries with long maritime traditions such as Denmark, Norway/Sweden and Britain's old rival France also built up merchant fleets.

The design lead was initially taken by the Americans, but iron and steel hulls introduced during the mid and late nineteenth century restored the advantage to Europe. As the British abandoned sail at the end of the period, the Germans, and to a lesser but significant extent the French, continued to invest in it, producing what must be regarded as the apogee of the commercial sailing ship. The durability of the sailing ship was due to the increased costs in running steam vessels which, unless they could be offset by fast passages, passenger fares, government mail subsidies or high freight rates, simply could not compete. Thus the large commercial sailing ship, with her low overheads, was able to earn her keep in tramping trades until the disruption of the First World War. The post-war slump which followed depressed world trade and saw the eclipse of trading sail.

Sloop rig. Single-masted and even some small two-masted decked cargo vessels were almost invariably called 'sloops' during the eighteenth century. It was a word deriving from *chaloupe* and simply meant a small vessel. The difference between the single-masted sloop and the cutter was technically in the fact that the former had a long standing bowsprit and functionally in that, although the sloop might be used in naval service, the cutter was rarely a commercial vessel, though it might be used as a smuggler. The commercial sloop was much used for cargo and passengers in the inter-island trade in the West Indies and along the coasts of Colonial North America. This example is from 1760. *(27)*

Eighteenth Century Rigs

The variety of small vessels, hailing from hundreds of ports and reflecting diverse building traditions, produced many forms of sail plan. By the time hulls were being built for regular trades, these increasingly reflected the profitability of the trade and thus in consequence, the crew size. Prevailing conditions had some influence, but less so in short-sea trades where almost any conditions could be met. Examples of the contemporary ship rig are elsewhere in this volume, but the other principal rigs are shown here.

Bilander rig. The bilander was the third two-masted rig which failed to outlast the century. Similar in most respects to the brig and snow, the bilander only differed in the shape of its 'main' sail which takes the quadrilateral form of a 'settee', a common sight in Mediterranean craft. Originating in The Netherlands but used throughout northern Europe, the bilander rig tended to be fitted to a coaster's hull, as in this example. *(142)*

30 20 10 0 ft
1/300 ⊢—┼—┼—┼—┼—┼—┤
8   4   0 m

Snow (above) and brig rigs. The snow (above) and brig were the most popular rigs for small and medium-sized merchantmen, both requiring smaller crews than the ship, but both proving exceptionally handy when manoeuvring in confined waters, which include the shoal-girt channels of an estuary like that of the Thames or the Elbe. Both rigs were two-masted, where deep reefed topsails were borne, but the snow carried a square main course and this necessitated her spanker, sometimes called a 'driver', being hooped to a subsidiary spar set up abaft the main lower mast. This gaff-rigged sail was loose-footed and was reduced or furled by brailing. In the case of the brig, the 'main' sail was the spanker, which is proportionately larger, boomed and had reef points. Note the diagonal reef points on the snow's sprit sail, showing the angle to which the yard was canted in practice. *(142)*

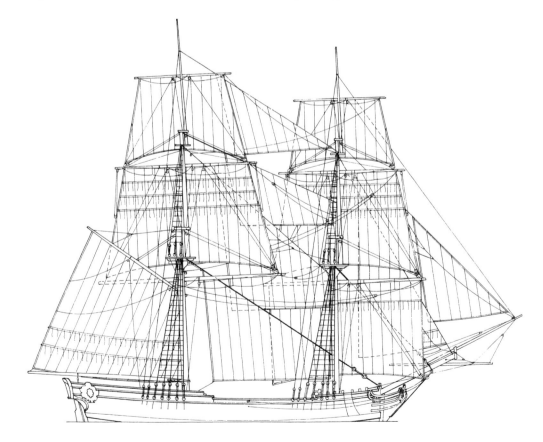

1/300

30   20   10   0 ft

8   4   0 m

Ketch rig. The ketch was essentially an enlargement of the single-masted rig on a small hull, though ketches of moderate size were built. The mizen mast is stepped well forward of the rudder post and bears a tall, vertically leeched and loose-footed driver, or spanker. Note the reef points of this sail, the course, both topsails and the staysail. *(142)*

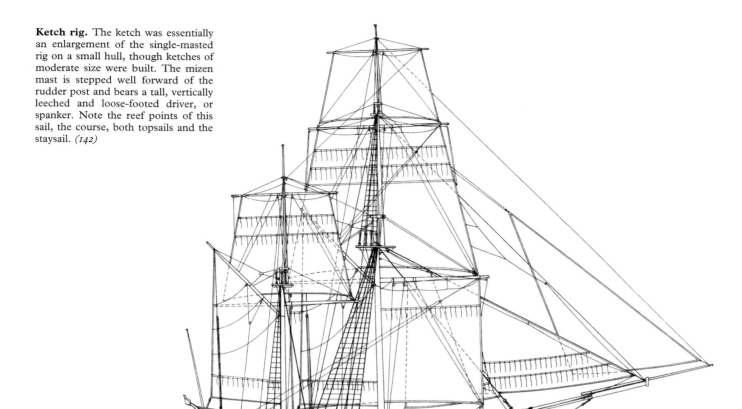

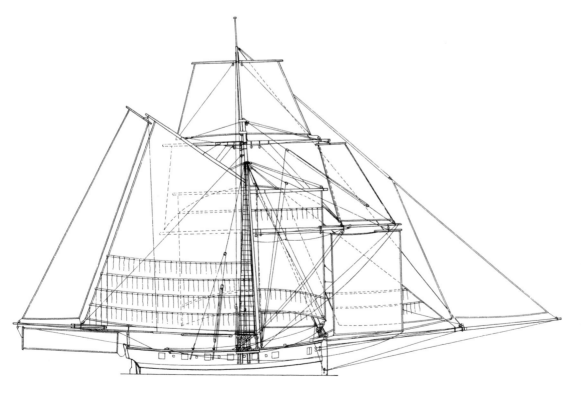

Cutter rig. The cutter is perhaps the most quintessentially English of all rigs. In addition to being small naval cruisers and auxiliaries, cutters were used by the Revenue Officers to pursue vessels thought to be smuggling. They were also employed as Post Office Packets and by the Trinity House as lighthouse and buoy tenders. Such craft were invariably armed, but were most distinguished by the extravagance of their sail plans. In addition to a topgallant, a deep-gored topsail and narrow square course which was set flying, an upper and lower studding sail are shown. Forward of the fore-staysail, a jib and flying jib are set on the long bowsprit. This was drawn in, or reefed, in bad weather. The mainsail is further extended by a watersail, set under the long boom and an additional bumpkin which also takes the clew of the ring-tail. Despite the flamboyance of this rig, the extensive reef points attest to the cutter being far from a fair-weather craft and they carried large and skilled crews. *(142)*

30   20   10   0 ft

1/300

8   4   0 m

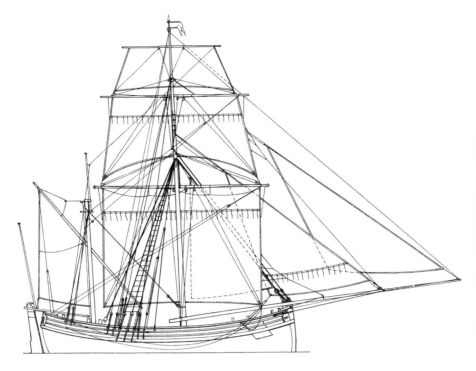

Hooker rig. The hooker derives from a Dutch fishing craft, the *huker*, and is known variously as 'hoeker' or 'hukker'. The rig is similar to the ketch, though somewhat simpler, and in this, though not all cases, a full lateen-type yard is carried on the mizen, though the sail is quadrilateral and hooped to the short mizen. To some extent the name hooker refers to hull-form, which signified a broad, shallow-draughted coaster. The use of the sea-going hooker for the herring fishery in the eighteenth century, where it acquired characteristics of strength and somewhat bulbous ugliness, probably explains the pejorative nature of the word in sailors' slang. *(142)*

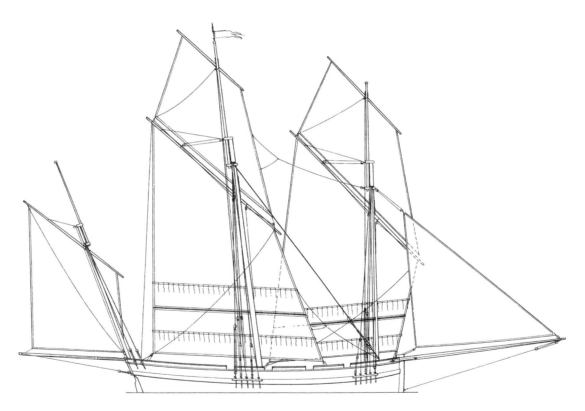

Lugger rig. The lugger was an uncompromisingly fore-and-aft rig which nevertheless possessed tremendous power with the wind free. With its long spars, including a bowsprit and stern bumpkin, the rig is tall, yet capable of being shortened down and was intended for all weathers. In addition to a naval auxiliary, smuggling and privateering, the lugger was employed as a cargo-carrier of up to some 130 tons, and as a fishing vessel. Developed in France it has, like its English counterpart the cutter, a deep, fine-lined hull. In many luggers intended for fishing, the fore and mainmasts lower so that the vessel can lie to her nets. The lugsail itself took several forms and this example shows dipping lugs on the forward masts. As the lugger went about, the forward end of the yard, as the upper spar is called, was dipped round abaft of its mast by means of the line clearly shown running across the sail. The mizen shows a standing lug which was, as its name implies, left to stand without adjustment. *(142)*

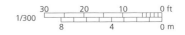

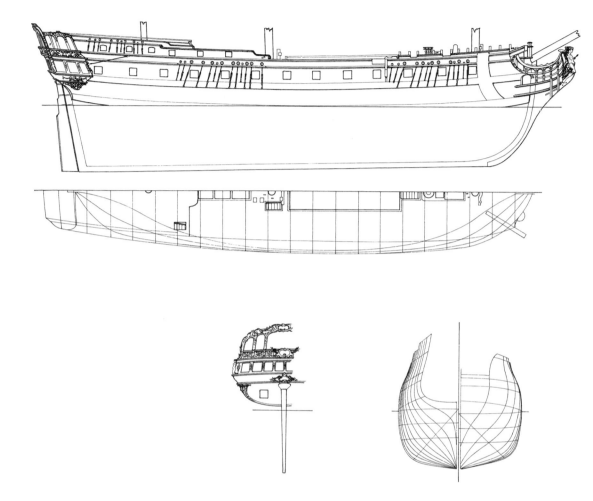

I. Merchant 'frigate' ship rig – large Indiaman type. *(34)*

Eighteenth Century Hull Forms – the Merchant 'Frigate'

It was the Swedish naval architect Fredrik Henrik af Chapman who first sought to classify merchant ship types as he studied the variety of forms these took. Finding the difference resided chiefly in the construction of the stern, he resolved the matter to his satisfaction with a number of groups which used this as the criterion, but then added those which possessed a different and simpler bow. Most merchant vessels of this period were armed, their officers and seamen as familiar with gunnery, if not as skilful, as their naval cousins. The depredations of privateers in time of war, of pirates, especially the corsairs of the Barbary coast, and the dangers inherent in some trades, particularly that of slaving, required them to do so. The provision of gunports, however, does not necessarily indicate that guns were carried behind them.

Most British merchant vessels intended for foreign service tended to become increasingly 'frigate-built' as time passed. These were vessels of some consequence, having full heads, after cabins and decorated sterns. Frigate-building consisted of using a flat stern in which the upper plank-

ing ends on a lower counter under the elaborate stern windows; at the waterline the hull curved into a 'round-tuck' stern.

The method was used in large, ship-rigged Indiamen (**I**) and is, in principle, little different from that of a contemporary man-of-war. Another large example (**II**) has a deckhouse mounted on the poop. The smallest ship-rigged example (**III**) shows a series of rising transoms, while the heavy single lower counter is clear in the tiller-steered snow. A shallower draught schooner rig example is also shown. The frigate-build easily accommodated a low hull which, when the single gun-deck was its naval objective, is not surprising, but is the secret of its success. This is clearly of advantage, even in the short, single-masted hull of a merchant sloop. Such vessels were used extensively as small passenger and mail packets, requiring a cabin aft, for which the frigate-build proved most appropriate. All these hulls show a bill-board, a panel protecting the topsides from damage by the anchor flukes.

40 30 20 10 0 ft
1/400
10 5 0 m

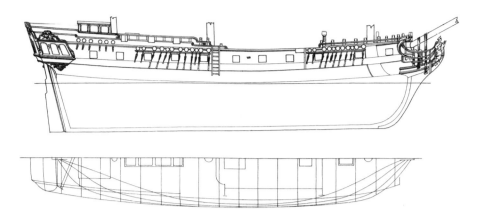

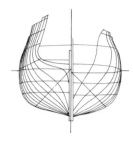

II. Merchant 'frigate' ship rig–
large. *(34)*

III. Merchant 'frigate' ship rig–
small. *(34)*

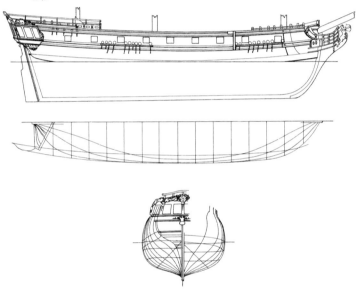

IV. Merchant 'frigate', snow rig.
(34)

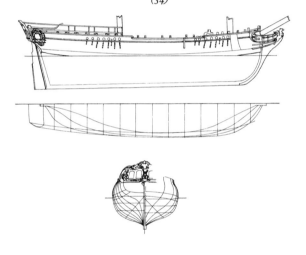

V. Merchant 'frigate', schooner
rig. *(34)*

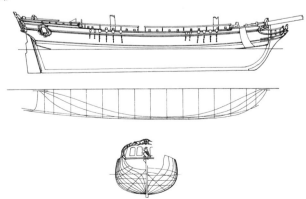

VI. Merchant 'frigate', sloop rig.
(34)

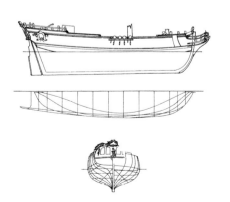

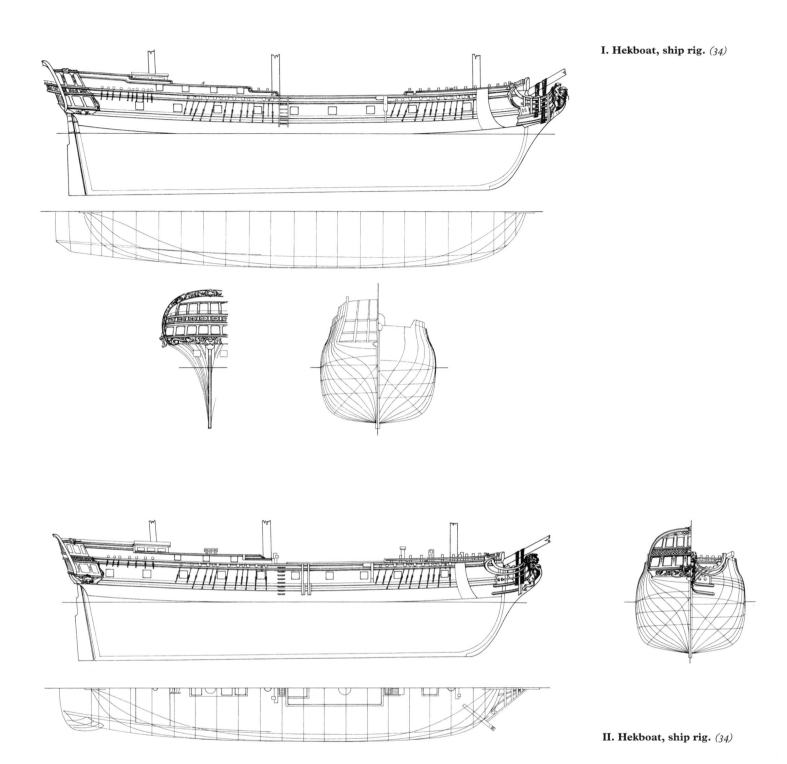

Eighteenth Century Hull Forms – the Hag, or Hekboat

An alternative method and, on the face of it, somewhat difficult to distinguish from frigate-building, the hekboat's name derives from the Dutch for stern and is essentially the northern European variant of the 'English' merchant frigate. The hull was usually of lesser draught and flatter bottom than the English type, but kept the lines expected of a deep-water vessel. Most also retained the tiller aperture in the lower stern characteristic of the flute, whereas the frigate accommodated this slightly higher, above the transom timbers.

Two hulls such as might have been found on a Dutch East Indiaman

are shown in **I** and **II**. Comparison with the Indiaman type 'frigate' shows the difference in the run of planking round the stern. The flatter, squarer midship section of **III** marks this example as a cargo-carrier and her plain head shows her as a more modest vessel, a 'cat' in fact. The narrow section of the stern shows the ancestry of the flute, which is less obvious in **IV**. This vessel, however, shows a conspicuous forward bulkhead across the bow, probably containing privies for passengers. The timbering of the stern is shown in **V**, where the planking runs right up under the stern, with a modest gallery above it.

1/400   40   30   20   10   0 ft
         10   5   0 m

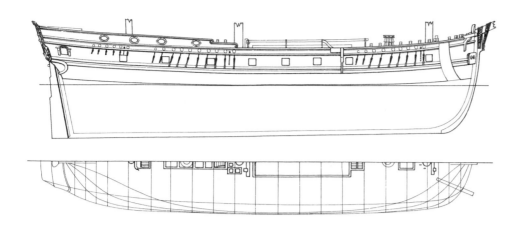

III. Hekboat, ship rig. *(34)*

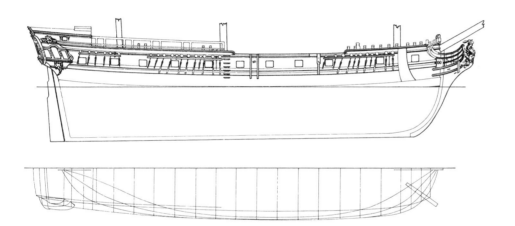

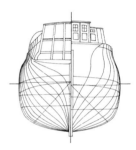

IV. Hekboat, ship rig. *(34)*

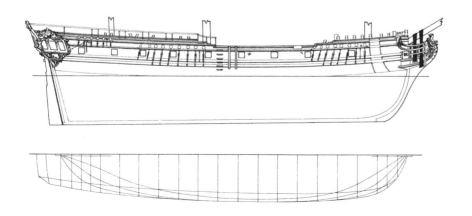

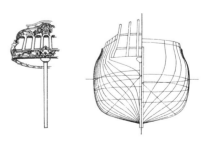

V. Hekboat, ship rig. *(34)*

160   Trading Sail

1/400

40   30   20   10   0 ft

10   5   0 m

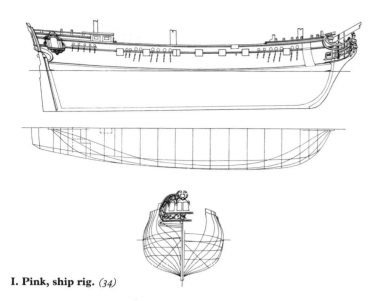

I. Pink, ship rig. *(34)*

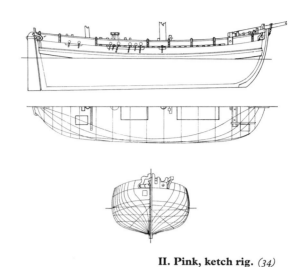

II. Pink, ketch rig. *(34)*

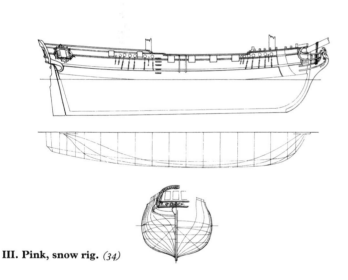

III. Pink, snow rig. *(34)*

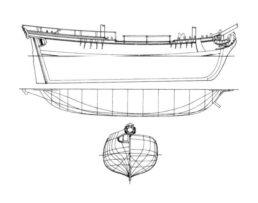

IV. Pink, brig rig. *(34)*

Eighteenth Century Hull Forms – the Pink

Like the hekboat, the pink owes much to the flute; unlike the hekboat the pink more closely conforms to the old flute, the stern being very round and terminating in a much narrower and tapering taffrail. The tiller aperture is, moreover, much more obvious and although the pink stern persisted in quite substantial ship-rigged vessels, as in **I**, smaller, flush-decked coasters such as the ketch-rigged cat in **II** were also considered to be pink-built. This example, incidentally, appears to be fitted for handling moorings and is probably a tender to one of the Dutch admiralties. Most commonly found on medium-sized merchantmen, such as the snow in **III**, the flute influence remains in the very narrow, overhung sterns of the small brig in **IV** and the sloop-rigged yacht, **V**.

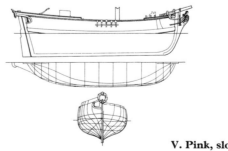

V. Pink, sloop rig. *(34)*

1/400 40 30 20 10 0 ft
10 5 0 m

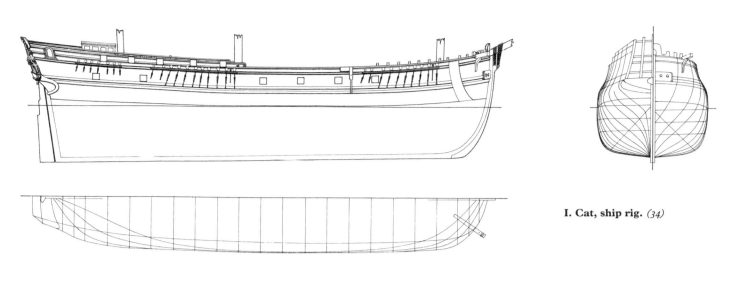

I. Cat, ship rig. *(34)*

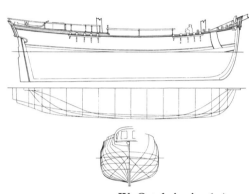

IV. Cat, brig rig. *(34)*

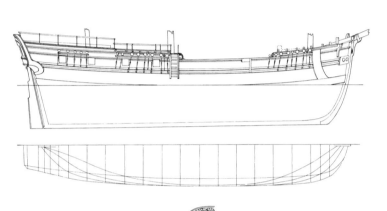

II. Cat, ship rig. *(34)*

V. Cat, sloop rig. *(34)*

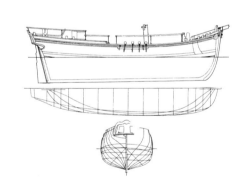

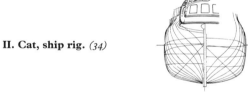

III. Cat, ship rig. *(34)*

Eighteenth Century Hull Forms – the Kat, or Cat

It was not always the stern which defined name, nor were the terms exclusive, as in the ketch-rigged pink and the ship-rigged hekboat (above). When the stem was plain and lacked a beak-head, a vessel was considered a kat, or cat. The differences between a hekboat and a cat become indistinguishable when comparing the ship-rigged cat here (**I**) with the ship-rigged hekboat (page 160), and only contemporary usage could determine the correct name, but the more elaborate vessel **II** is quite clearly a cat, as is the ship-rigged **III**. The plain brig-rigged coaster in **IV** and the sloop-rigged **V** are cats by virtue of their plain bows and consideration of their sterns becomes secondary.

1/400

40   30   20   10   0 ft

10   5   0 m

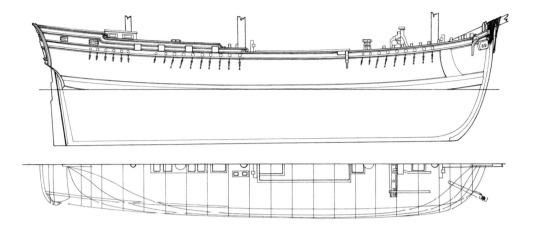

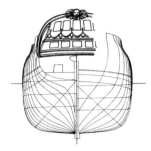

I. Bark, ship rig. *(34)*

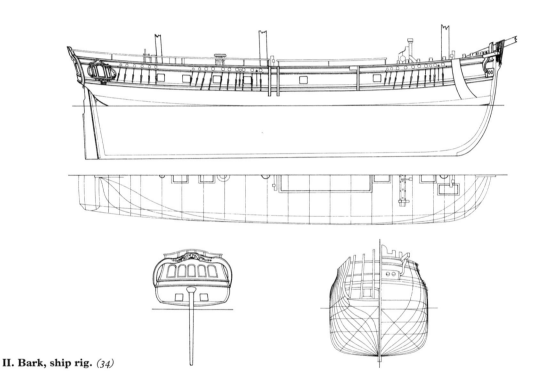

II. Bark, ship rig. *(34)*

Eighteenth Century Hull Forms – the Bark

The water muddies still further when we come to consider the bark, which is not to be confused with the later French import 'barque' and which refers to rig. The bark was a generally more austere craft with markedly less embellishment around her stern, as in **I**, a ship-rigged bark. She is generally considered to have been cat-headed and with a flatter bottom than the pure cat, as in **II**, a ship-rigged example, and the smaller schooner-rigged **VII**. This was to enable the bark to take the ground and sit on the bottom without a pronounced heel, in order to work cargo. It is interesting to note that James Cook's first vessel, commissioned as His Majesty's Bark *Endeavour*, was generically known under her previous name *Earl of Pembroke* as a common Whitby cat, similar to **III**. In its simple form, the cat could be ship-rigged, as in **IV**, snow-rigged as in **V**, or rigged as a brig, as in **VI**. A variation of rig, which was similar to a fore-and-aft ketch and was known in The Netherlands and the Baltic as a galeass or galiot, could be used on a cat, as in **VIII**, while the small, plain cat seen in **IX** is sloop-rigged.

40 30 20 10 0 ft
1/400
10 5 0 m

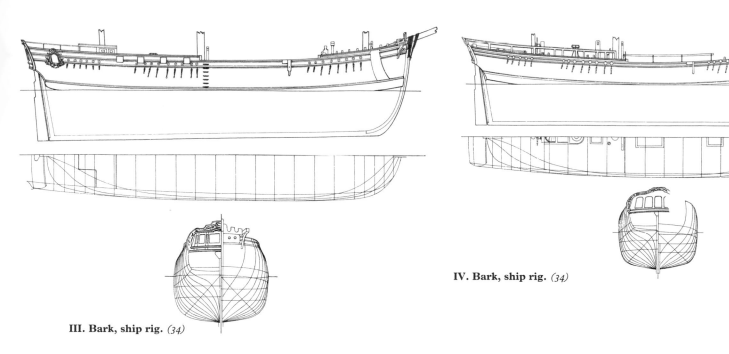

III. Bark, ship rig. *(34)*

IV. Bark, ship rig. *(34)*

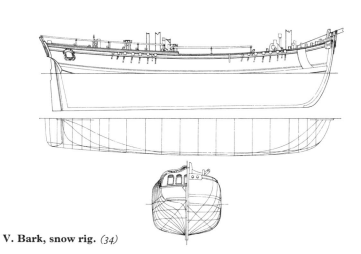

V. Bark, snow rig. *(34)*

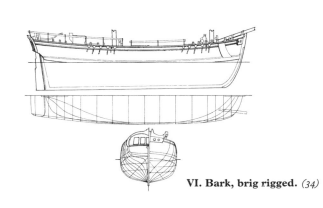

VI. Bark, brig rigged. *(34)*

VII. Bark, schooner rig. *(34)*

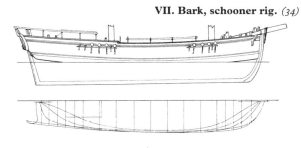

VIII. Bark, galeass rig. *(34)*

IX. Bark, sloop rigged. *(34)*

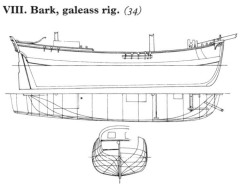

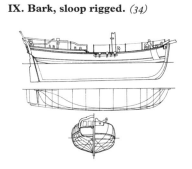

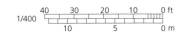

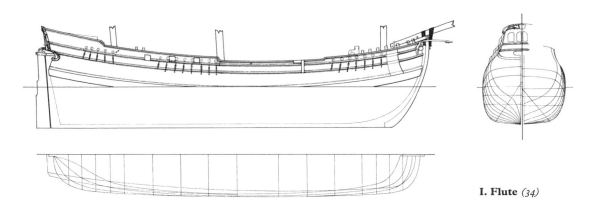

I. Flute *(34)*

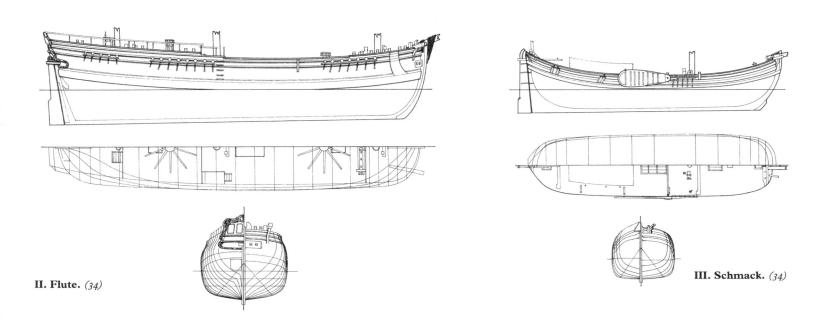

II. Flute. *(34)*

III. Schmack. *(34)*

Dutch Hull Forms

As befitted the great shipbuilding nation responsible for the basic concept of the influential flute, the Dutch wrought their own variations upon af Chapman's patient classification. It was in the building of small ships and vessels that nomenclature becomes ever more confusing, due largely to local etymological usage favouring one term over another, rather like the modern tradition of calling all submarines, no matter how monstrous, 'boats'. Thus by the mid-eighteenth century the term flute had come to mean a lower-sterned hull than its eponymous originator, but the rounded midship section, with its severe tumblehome, still bears a relationship to its predecessor, as can be seen in **I** and **II**. The small carrier of the Dutch waterways was called a schmack, **III**, usually single-masted, but often with a small mizen. Interpretations of the rig/hull denomination alter, often when a hull form takes the name of a favoured rig and then this changes, leaving the hull unmodified. The rounded hull of the Dutch galiot, **IV**, with a simple fore-and-aft rig, is a modest vessel. In such unpretentious craft, of which the largest eighteenth century examples were of about 120 tons, Dutch mariners ventured into the Arctic, across the Atlantic, or as far as the East Indies. The name was to persist, a sort of bastard-schooner or ketch, until well into the nineteenth century.

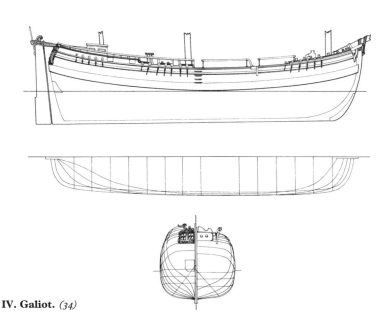

IV. Galiot. *(34)*

40 30 20 10 0 ft
1/400
10   5   0 m

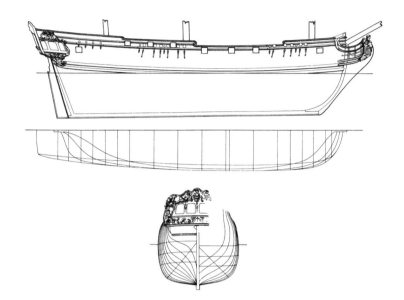

West Indiaman, about 1750. With the exception of the East Indiamen, the largest merchant ships of Britain and other major maritime nations traded across the Atlantic to North America and the West Indies. The West Indiaman, seen here, rarely exceeded 450 tons burthen, most measuring considerably less, though tonnage of most ship-types increased gradually throughout the century. Pierced for a light armament and decorated at bow and stern as a means of emphasising the innate worth of the trading house owning the ship, the hull is otherwise austere, though full-bodied to bear a profitable lading of sugar. *(34)*

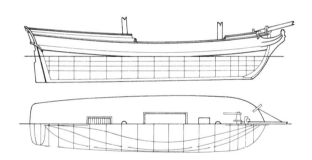

Schooner, late eighteenth century. This schooner might also have crossed the Atlantic, engaged in the triangular trade from Liverpool to the coast of West Africa, or 'Guinea', then to the West Indies or the southern colonies of British North America before coming home. Taking trinkets, spirituous liquors, cheap muskets and other 'trade goods' she would have exchanged these for slaves, before running west to sell these in Cuba, Jamaica, Georgia or the Carolinas, returning with whatever cargo best offered. Her lines are noticeably fine. *(139)*

The British Merchant Marine of the Eighteenth Century

The Merchant Marine of Great Britain was the most numerous in the world during the eighteenth century and comprised a great variety of vessels. These ships carried most, if not all, of the world's trafficable commodities in relatively unsophisticated stowage. A merchant ship exists by selling its capacity, therefore the greater the space available to carry cargo, the greater potential a merchant ship has to capitalise upon her costs. In most trades, therefore, a full hull was required, with a deep hold which may, or may not have been subdivided by a single deck. In frigate-built ships, which often bore an armament, this was often referred to as a gun-deck, but it might also be called a 'between-deck', contracted to 'tween deck. Intermediate decks might, of course, be necessary for the safe carriage of the cargo itself, particularly so in the case of slavers, and other arrangements were occasionally adopted, such as the cutting of loading ports for timber low down in the hull, or the fitting of platforms within a hold. A few types were built with a definite eye on speed, most notably slavers, and such ships switched to privateering in time of war. But generally it was more important to haul a ship's lading safely across the ocean than to make a fast passage.

The care of cargo during a passage was something which often left a lot to be desired. The importance of ventilation was not fully understood and claims against masters and owners were frequent. As the century passed, matters improved, but all progress at sea tends to be slow, not merely from the innate conservatism of an industry in which unwise experimentation might cost lives, but also because innovation is costly and ships are neither quickly built nor easily modified.

1/400
40   30   20   10   0 ft
10   5   0 m

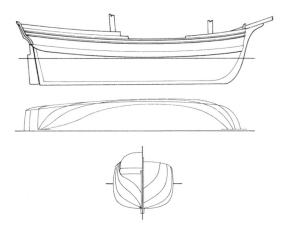

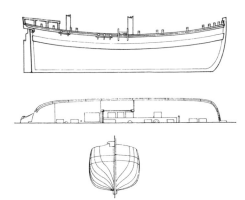

Herring buss. The name 'buss' has a very long and complex etymology, but by the eighteenth century it meant a small merchant ship, usually rigged as a ketch and often, as in this case, used for fishing. The characteristics were a round stern with a small flute-like transom and they were common on the coats of Schleswig, Hanover, The Netherlands and the east coast of England. *(34)*

Collier brigs, about 1760 (above) and 1800. One of the most important British merchantmen was the modest collier, trading between the Tyne and the Thames with her cargoes of 'sea-cole', so-called because it came by sea. There were hundreds of such vessels feeding London's insatiable hunger for coal, used for cooking and heating. Usually brig-rigged, the collier had a small, manoeuvrable and capacious hull. Seamen trained in this trade were highly regarded as potential ratings for the Royal Navy. Such a collier-brig as the *circa* 1760 vessel was James Cook's nursery. A slow increase in size and the refinement of the brig-rig produced a slightly larger vessel by the end of the century. Such a ship could be handled by a small crew and to this end the fore course is narrow-footed and significantly smaller than the topsails. It was often fitted with a Bentinck's boom across its foot between the clews, making tacking and stern boards relatively easy in confined waters. The rig was quite tall and powerful, driving a short, full hull to windward through waters renowned for their short, steep seas and strong tides. *(195/130)*

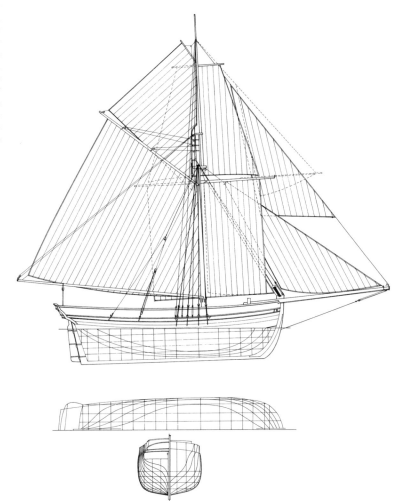

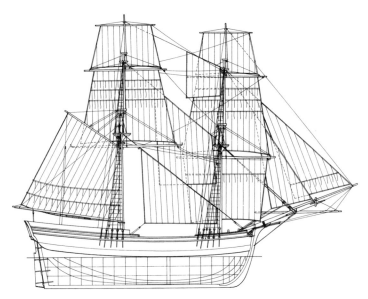

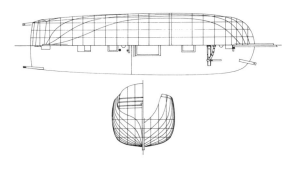

Leith smack, about 1825. Carrying passengers between the Thames, the Tyne and the Firth of Forth, the Leith smack made similar passages to the collier-brig. In the passenger trade speed was of some consequence, minimising the misery of the wretched 'cargo' for whom a run between London and Edinburgh was their only experience of the sea. Although road-building improved during the latter half of the eighteenth century and the Mail Coach became an icon of speed and service, the Leith smack retained a corner of the market into the next century. Cutter-rigged, her form differed from the naval equivalent in being somewhat fuller, with a more horizontal keel, and her sail-plan, extending some kites, was not quite so extravagant, for she carried a much smaller crew. *(129)*

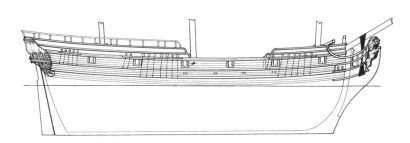

Dutch East Indiaman of the mid-eighteenth century. This shows a relatively small class of vessel trading to the Dutch East Indies, modern Indonesia, in search of high-value cargoes of spices. *(112)*

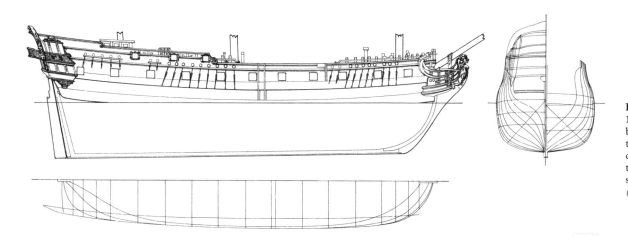

English East Indiaman of around 1750. The larger size of this frigate-built and armed Indiaman emphasises the grandeur of these vessels. Note the double stern gallery, the upper being the commander's cabin, the lower the saloon provided for the passengers. *(34)*

French East Indiaman of 1781. The plain lines-plan shows the more angular midships hull form favoured by French builders of the period. French possessions in the east were steadily eroded during the eighteenth century, but the temporary loss of superiority at sea by the British at the end of the American Revolution allowed an opportunistic expansion by French interests. *(130)*

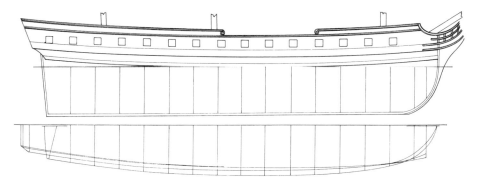

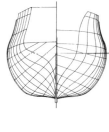

East Indiamen

The East Indiaman was not only the largest merchant ship of the era, she was also the least exposed to competition. East India Companies were founded in most major European maritime states, protecting their interests by monopolistic charters or statutes. Armed, they occasionally fought creditable actions with predatory cruisers of an enemy. The most notable of these was in 1804, when of a mixed force of British Indiamen and Indian-owned merchant ships commanded by Commodore Dance of the Honourable East India Company out-manoeuvred the French Admiral Linois. East Indiamen customarily made leisurely voyages, cosseting their passengers, but when the monopoly was partially lifted and competing vessels entered the trade, they made much better times. Invariably ship-rigged, few innovations were introduced during their dominance of the oriental trade and the East Indiaman was a by-word for conservative tradition. However, strict regulations governed the conduct and management of East Indiamen, and they were the first British merchant vessels to be navigated by properly qualified officers.

40 30 20 10 0 ft
1/400
10 5 0 m

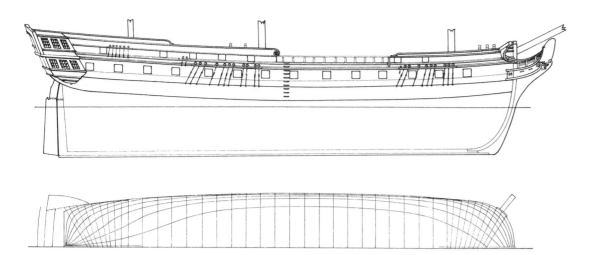

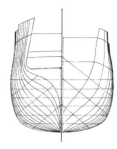

English Indiaman of 1800. By comparison with the mid-century example, the larger size of this Indiaman is clear, as is the less opulent decoration. But most significant is the loss of tumble-home, her sides being more vertical in an attempt to increase cargo capacity and to widen the spread of the vessel's standing rigging. (*170*)

Swedish East Indiaman, 1807. Both Denmark and Sweden owned Indiamen, but those of the former were victims of the British blockade during the Napoleonic War. Retaining a perilous neutrality, Swedish Indiamen, like this example of 1807, continued to trade. Of smaller tonnage than her British equivalent, this example was designed by the great F H af Chapman, his originality being manifested in the shape of her stem which hints at developments later in the nineteenth century. Her low ports are for loading ballast and were thoroughly caulked before sailing. **NB.** Sail plan is 1/600 scale. (*74*)

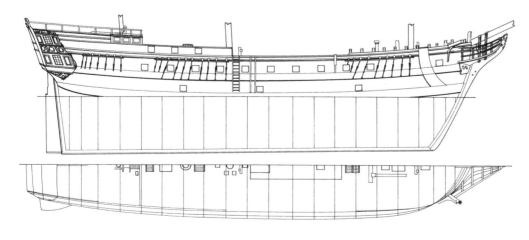

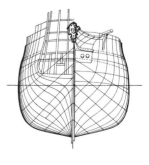

1/400   40 30 20 10 0 ft
        10   5   0 m

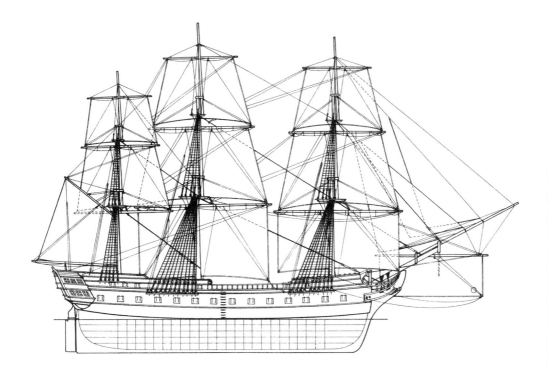

Trafalgar, British East Indiaman of 1820. The size and grandeur of this vessel reflects the confidence of the period. Even her name is redolent of British conviction and her hull form seems to pay little attention to the opening of her trade to competition. In fact, 'interlopers' had enjoyed profits under flags-of-convenience for many years, but the easing of the monopoly brought very much better passage times, even by traditional vessels such as the *Trafalgar*. Within a few years reform of British tonnage regulations rendered such magnificently ponderous merchant ships, with their standard ship rig, obsolete. **NB.** Sail plan is 1/600 scale. *(228)*

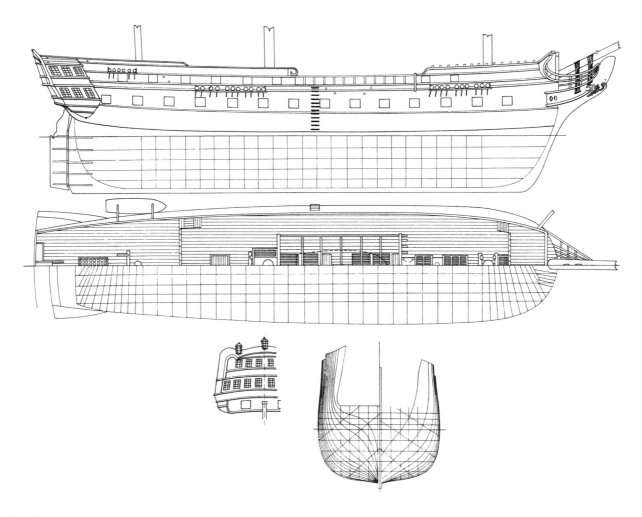

1/400   40   30   20   10   0 ft
10   5   0 m

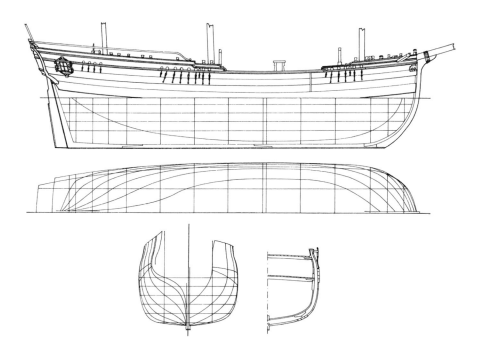

Exeter of 1776. Small West Indiamen were common; this example probably traded to North America as well as the West Indies. Her lines show a simple, unadorned vessel which would never-theless have borne a ship rig. *(130)*

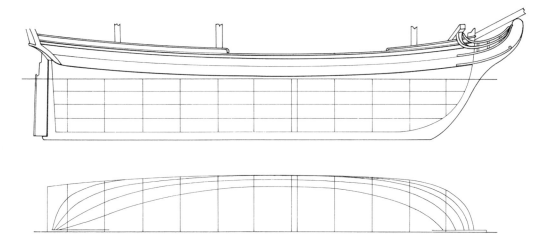

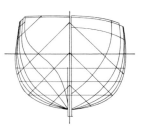

Hall of 1785. This shows a low hull with untypically vertical topsides and may have been built speculatively with the possibility of privateering in mind since, in 1785, there were signs that the sugar trade was past its peak. *(130)*

British West Indiamen

Built for the carriage of a homeward-bound homogeneous cargo of sugar, the British West Indiaman was a rather different ship from the East Indiaman. Unregulated, she owed her name to her trade, rather than any organisation. But this trade was of immense importance, generating revenue for the government, wealth for her owners, providing employment for seafarers, rich pickings for the gangs of 'tier-rangers' (as the robbers of the Thames were euphemistically known), and sugar for Britain's growing population. Carrying so valuable a cargo, the vessels employed in this trade were well-found and full-bodied, rather than fast.

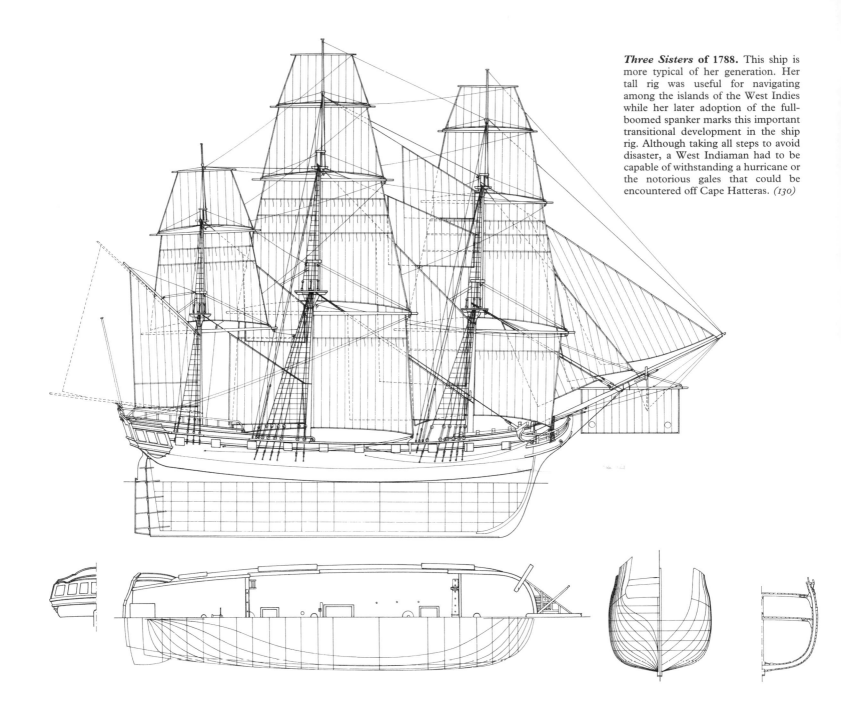

Three Sisters **of 1788.** This ship is more typical of her generation. Her tall rig was useful for navigating among the islands of the West Indies while her later adoption of the full-boomed spanker marks this important transitional development in the ship rig. Although taking all steps to avoid disaster, a West Indiaman had to be capable of withstanding a hurricane or the notorious gales that could be encountered off Cape Hatteras. *(130)*

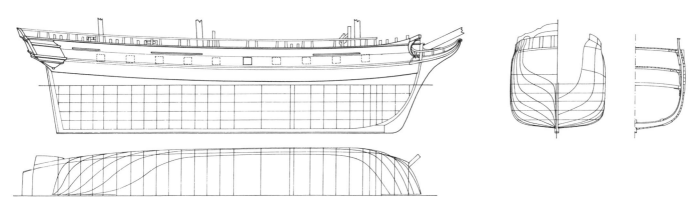

William Miles **of 1808.** Although the sugar trade was in irretrievable decline, this vessel demonstrates the capacity of a medium-sized British merchant ship of her day. Note the square midships section and the two full decks. It is most unlikely that all her gunports would have sheltered cannon and she would have sailed in a strictly regulated convoy, the system of which was extremely complex and efficient. *(130)*

1/300

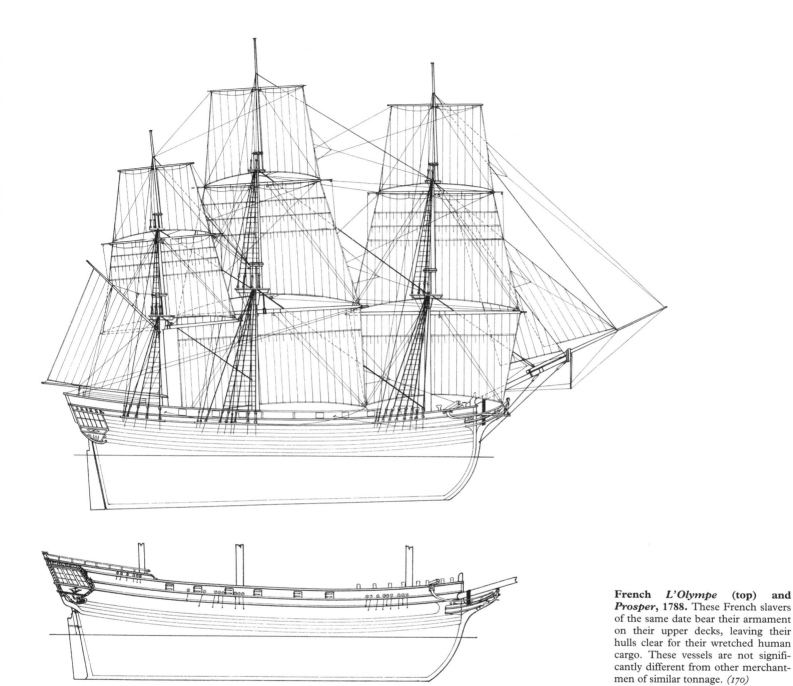

French *L'Olympe* **(top) and** *Prosper*, **1788.** These French slavers of the same date bear their armament on their upper decks, leaving their hulls clear for their wretched human cargo. These vessels are not significantly different from other merchantmen of similar tonnage. *(170)*

Slavers

This most notorious trade was engaged in by most major European maritime states. Although made illegal by the British parliament in 1807, wartime enforcement was a haphazard matter. British men-of-war charged with the duty were seen as underhand promulgators of British ambition and the vested interest in maintaining slaves in the Spanish colony of Cuba and the southern states of America kept the trade alive for a further half-century. Speed had always been an important component of a successful slaving ship, but the British proscription of the trade encouraged even faster ships. This created narrower hulls, greater experimentation with square rig and a number of fast schooners.

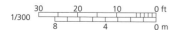

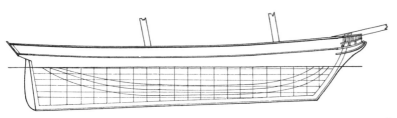

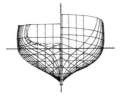

American slaving brig of about 1810. British 'interference' in the free trade between nations was anathema to the slave-dealers of the Carolinas and Georgia who regarded the declarations from London, rather as their fathers had a generation earlier, as something of a challenge to be flouted. Already developing fast schooners and brigs, speed was the governing consideration in the design of this vessel. *(27)*

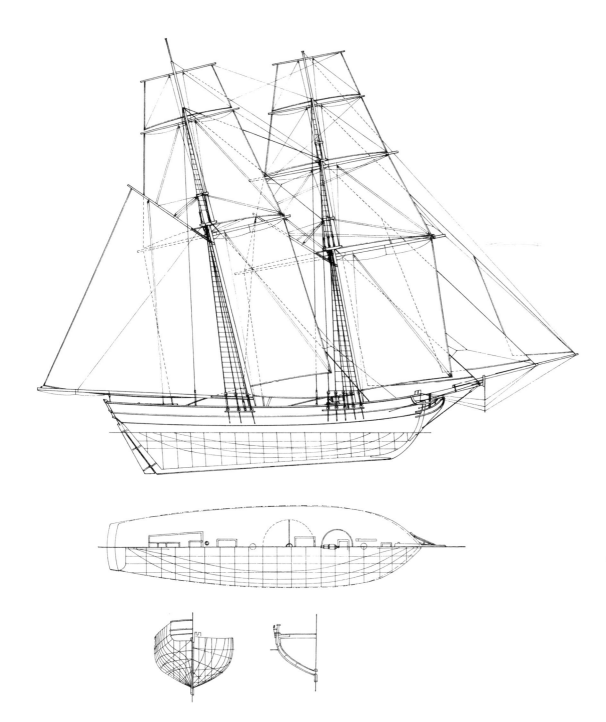

American slaving brig Dos Amigos, 1822. Amidships, mounted *en barbette*, she carries a large gun. This was not intended to intimidate African chiefs, but to engage an interfering British cruiser, and several sharp actions were fought between slavers and their pursuers. The *Dos Amigos'* tall, raked rig is noteworthy, particularly the return to deep courses. This predates the deep courses of the tea-clippers for, with their tacks hauled down, such sails drove a ship to windward remarkably efficiently. *(27)*

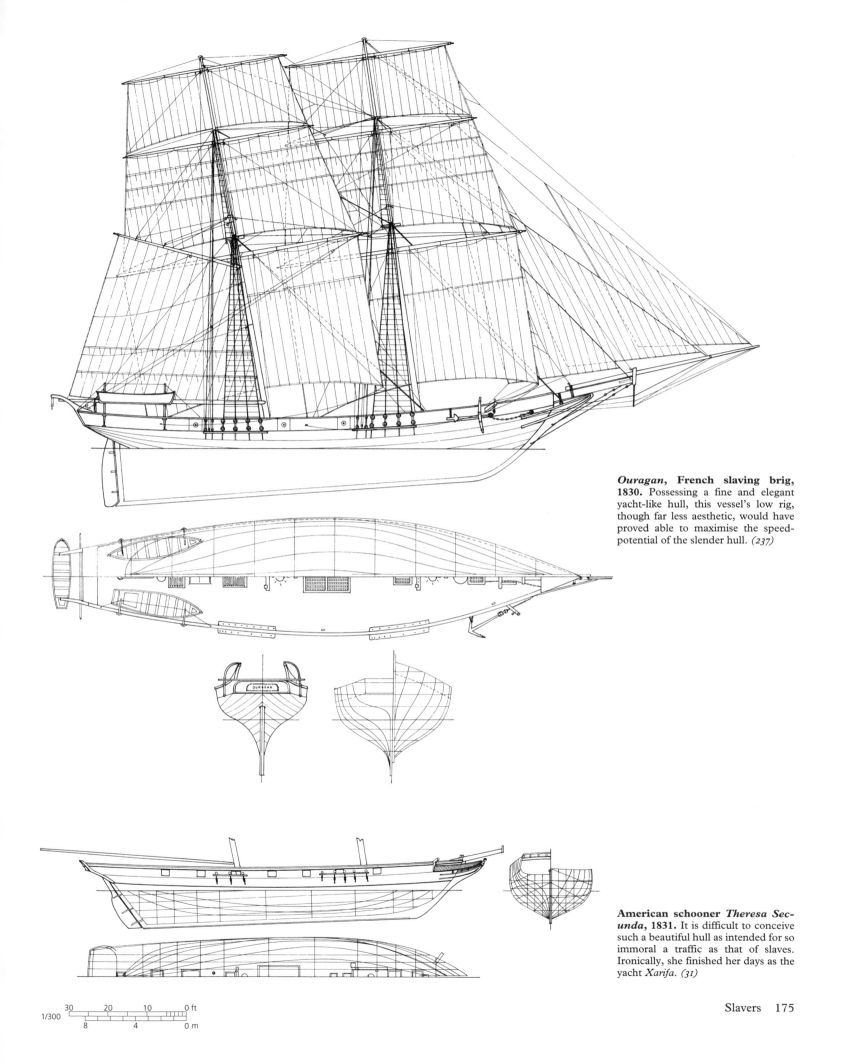

Ouragan, French slaving brig, 1830. Possessing a fine and elegant yacht-like hull, this vessel's low rig, though far less aesthetic, would have proved able to maximise the speed-potential of the slender hull. *(237)*

American schooner *Theresa Secunda*, 1831. It is difficult to conceive such a beautiful hull as intended for so immoral a traffic as that of slaves. Ironically, she finished her days as the yacht *Xarifa*. *(31)*

1/300

30   20   10   0 ft

8   4   0 m

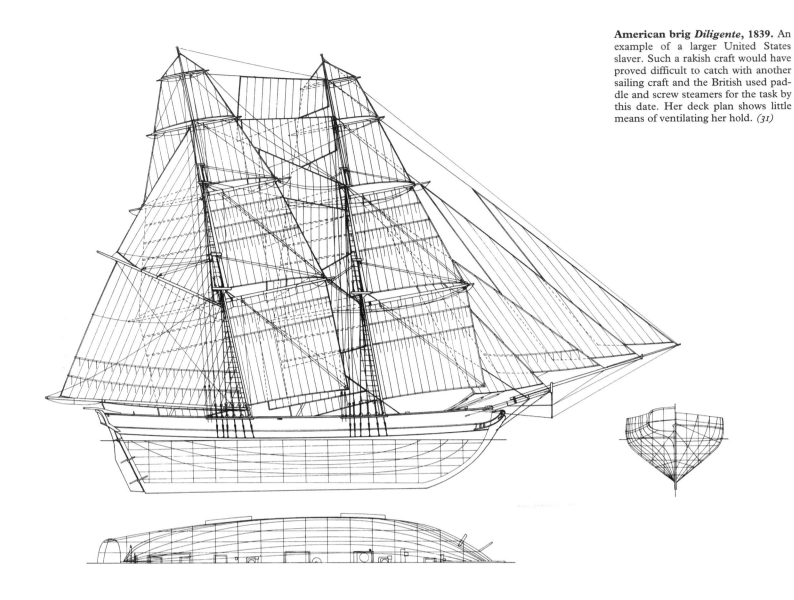

American brig *Diligente*, 1839. An example of a larger United States slaver. Such a rakish craft would have proved difficult to catch with another sailing craft and the British used paddle and screw steamers for the task by this date. Her deck plan shows little means of ventilating her hold. *(31)*

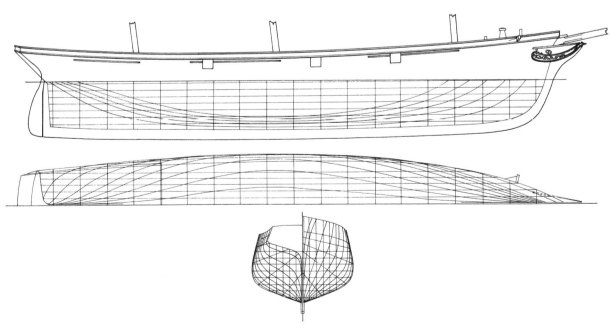

American clipper *Sunny South*, 1854. Right up until the Civil War, American slavers were engaged in their wicked trade, often buying their 'cargo' through Cuba, where they had close business connections. When the *Sunny South* proved too small for her intended China trade, she was sold to Havana interests and renamed *Manuela*, where she soon established a reputation as the fastest slaver out of that port. She was captured by the British screw sloop *Brisk* in 1861 off the African coast and renamed *Enchantress*. *(31)*

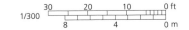

IX

British 74-gun ship, about 1780

Based on a number of sources including the original draught reproduced in 121

X
American frigate *Philadelphia*, 44 guns, 1799
Based on the original draught reproduced in 26

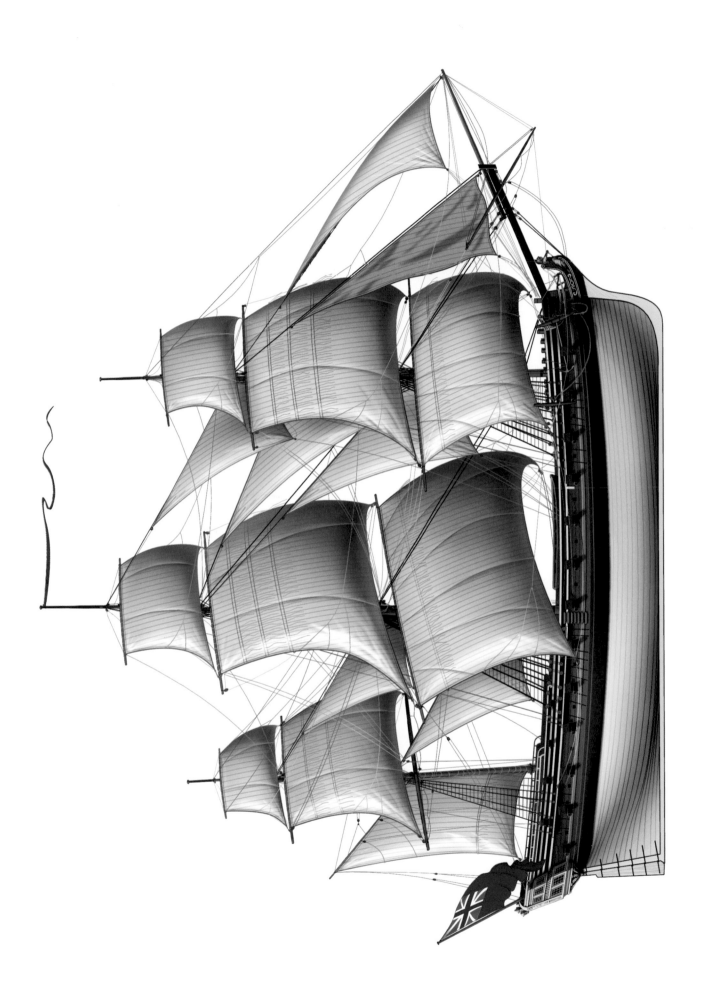

XI
British East Indiaman, 1782
Based on a Francis Holman painting of the General Coote
reproduced in 24

XII
British tea clipper *Thermopylae*, 1868
Hull based on model in 220; sail plan from 136

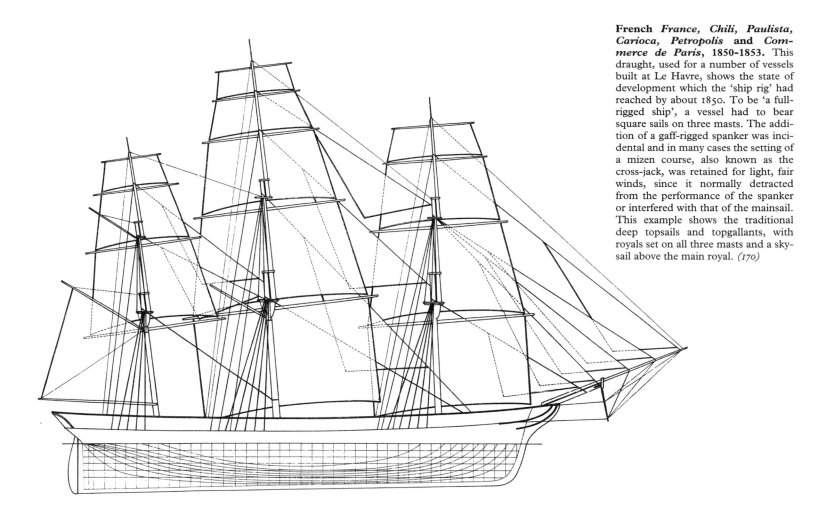

French *France, Chili, Paulista, Carioca, Petropolis* and *Commerce de Paris*, 1850-1853. This draught, used for a number of vessels built at Le Havre, shows the state of development which the 'ship rig' had reached by about 1850. To be 'a full-rigged ship', a vessel had to bear square sails on three masts. The addition of a gaff-rigged spanker was incidental and in many cases the setting of a mizen course, also known as the cross-jack, was retained for light, fair winds, since it normally detracted from the performance of the spanker or interfered with that of the mainsail. This example shows the traditional deep topsails and topgallants, with royals set on all three masts and a sky-sail above the main royal. *(170)*

The Nineteenth Century Proliferation of Rigs

As the world entered the industrial age, science and technology began to invade public perception. The enormous economic, military, philosophical, social and industrial upheaval of the late eighteenth century was the dawn of the modern era and out of the Age of Reason emerged societies dedicated to understanding the natural environment and the man-made world. Classification became important, and this applied to ships just as much as other things. At the same time harnessing the natural resource of the wind shifted from an empirical endeavour to an increasingly analytical and experimental matter. The result was a proliferation of rigs, each of which had a commonly understood name which, with one area of potential confusion, saw the age of sail to its mainstream commercial end. From this point, the term 'ship' has a prescriptive significance.

During the nineteenth century, construction changed from wood to iron and then to steel, with a brief period of composite building producing iron-framed, wooden planked vessels. The adoption of all-metal hulls encouraged longer and longer vessels. Since speed is a function of waterline length, this offered an incremental advantage to greater hull capacity. At the same time the ability of the sailing ship to triumph over the steam vessel in the long voyage was steadily eroded. To remain competitive, sailing vessels had to steadily reduce costs and this took the form of smaller and smaller crews.

To accommodate these changes, individual sail size was reduced, more masts were fitted and rigging incorporated steel wire and chain, reducing wear and tear, increasing rigging life and making a sailing ship theoretically less vulnerable to the elements. Steel was also used to fabricate masts and yards, while auxiliary power and mechanically efficient deck-machinery was introduced.

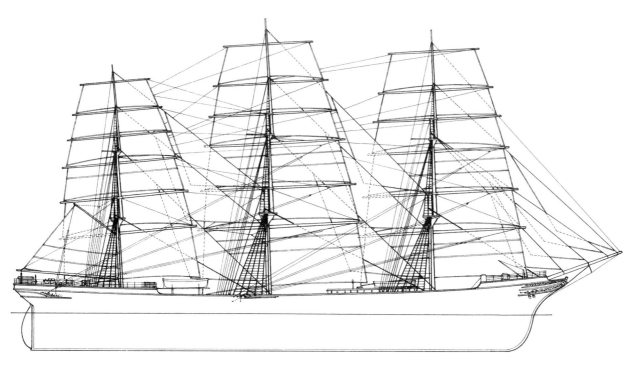

Ship rig with divided topsails, later nineteenth century. As the century advanced and ship-length increased, first the topsails and later the topgallants were split into upper and lower units. Such a sail was no longer reefed when the wind grew too strong, it was simply furled. Moreover the skysails and studdingsails so beloved of clipper masters were dispensed with, and yards were made wider, incorporating the lost area but making the whole spread more manageable. The ship rig shown here and dating from about 1870, therefore acquired a lower aspect ratio than her predecessor of 1850. This lower centre of gravity at first solved the problem of finding wooden spars of sufficient strength. Later steel spars were adopted. *(147)*

Four-masted ship, later nineteenth century. Increasing ship-length brought back the four-masted ship. The fourth mast, formerly called the 'bonaventure mizen', was now called the 'jigger mast' and rarely carried a royal. Such ships, beautifully proportioned though they were, were deficient in one important aspect: they required a significant increase in crew which was not paid back by the ship's earning potential. *(147)*

60 50 40 30 20 10 0 ft

1/600

15   10   5   0 m

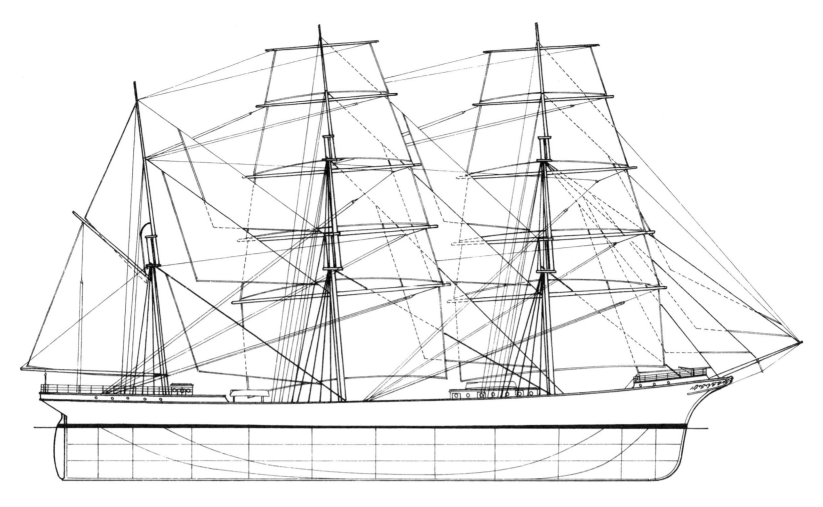

Barque rig, about 1850. Shrewd owners engaged in less profitable trafficking than the high profile tea and jute trades, found that where speed was not absolutely critical, a vessel's performance was little affected by removing the mizen yards. To some degree the loss of sail was made up for by a fore-and-aft topsail set above the spanker. As a consequence crew size could be reduced, securing a better profit margin. Such a vessel was called a 'barque', soon to be denominated a 'three-masted barque'. *(202)*

German polacre barque, about 1900. Although sailing vessels tended to follow orthodox principles, occasional experimentation sought the best means of combining the advantages of fore-and-aft and square rig, especially on short-sea trades without long runs with favourable winds. One solution was this German vessel which carries square topsails above a fore-and-aft rig, a mixture that borrowed the Mediterranean term 'polacre', or 'pollacca', to describe this hybrid barque. *(147)*

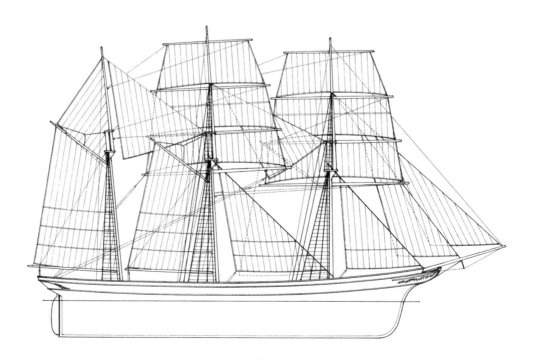

1/400   40   30   20   10   0 ft
         10   5   0 m

Bald-head barque, about 1890. The next development was to remove the royals and widen the span of the yards. Known in Britain as the 'jubilee rig' since it was introduced in 1887, the year of Queen Victoria's Golden Jubilee, it was also known as the 'stump-topgallant', or 'bald-headed rig'. It too meant a further reduction in crew numbers, but it proved successful and many existing ships were cut-down to it without great loss of performance. *(147)*

Four-masted barque, about 1900. By the end of the nineteenth century, large sailing ships were still able to hold their own in the tramping trades or where regular seasonal bulk cargoes were shipped, such as Australian grain or Chilean nitrate. Their optimum size was between 2400 and 3000 tons gross, a gross ton being hull capacity based on a 'ton' of 100 cubic feet. The standard barque rig was insufficiently powerful to drive a hull of some 90 metres length, and the first solution, the four-masted, full-rigged ship was proving too expensive. The solution was the four-masted barque, a handsome apogee which, in this example, sports royals above her double topgallants, even on her jigger. *(147)*

60 50 40 30 20 10 0 ft
1/600
15   10   5   0 m

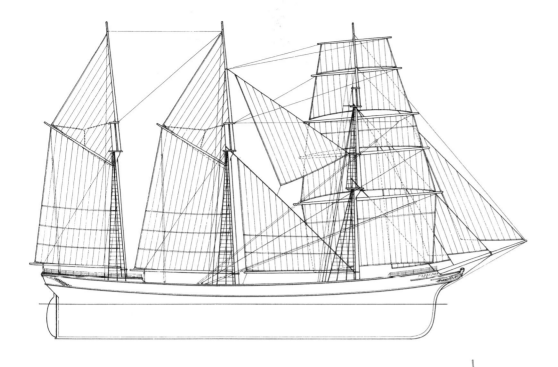

German barquentine of 1900. Smaller cargo ships needed smaller crews to be profitable and one of the best solutions for the medium-sized cargo-carrier was the barquentine rig, the largest of which were employed in the Cape Horn trade. The barquentine was usually three-masted and is distinguished by bearing square yards on her foremast only. The configuration of these conformed with the fashion of the day; this example has double-topsails, a single topgallant and a royal. She also has a boomed main staysail. (147)

German brigantine of the 1890s (below). In order to maintain competitiveness the brig rig was initially reduced by the removal of the main course, and the result was called a brigantine. This, however, was not a particularly enduring form of sailing vessel and its cousin, the hermaphrodite brig, with the main mast bearing all gaff sails, soon adopted the name without qualification. Thus by the 1890s this German two-master would have been called simply a brigantine. (147)

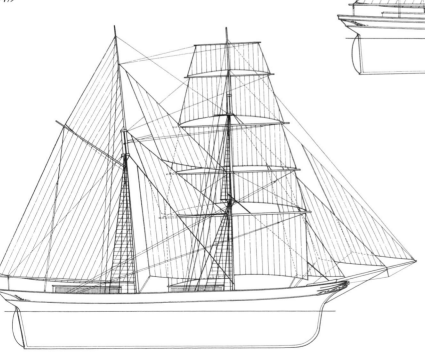

German brig, 1895. Still very popular as a small vessel's rig was the brig, despite the fact that she required a larger crew than a barquentine. The brig was, however, an extremely handy rig and often held onto older features longer than contemporary alternatives. The merchant brig had eclipsed the snow, but now carried a square main course. This example has double topsails, single topgallants and royals, but the upper topsails are on the deep side and furnished with reef points. Note too, that despite having a long spanker boom, this no longer overhangs the stern. (147/228)

1/400

40 30 20 10 0 ft

10 5 0 m

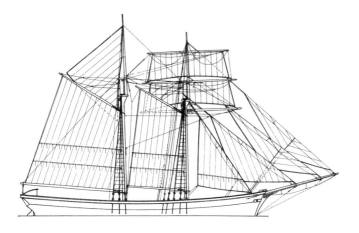

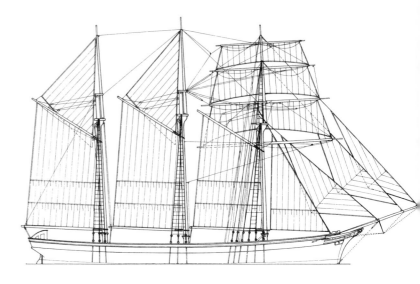

British topsail schooners, about 1900. A more economic and common form of coaster was the European topsail schooner which retained square topsails on the foremast. Depending upon size the topsail schooner had either two or three masts. In the former, it was common to refer to the square sails as 'upper' or 'lower' topsails, though larger versions might carry a topgallant. In fair winds a sail might have been set below the lower yard but this was in no sense a regular 'fore course'. *(207/208)*

British four-masted schooner, 1896. The schooner reached a maturity at the end of the days of sail which was quite astonishing, given her humble origins, particularly in North America. Here the purely fore-and-aft rig was popular. Multiple masts enabled the rig to keep up with hull-length, but capacity and low crew costs dominated the argument for rigging sailing ships as schooners, for speed no longer mattered. The last of the rig certainly did not 'scoon' upon the water. *(147)*

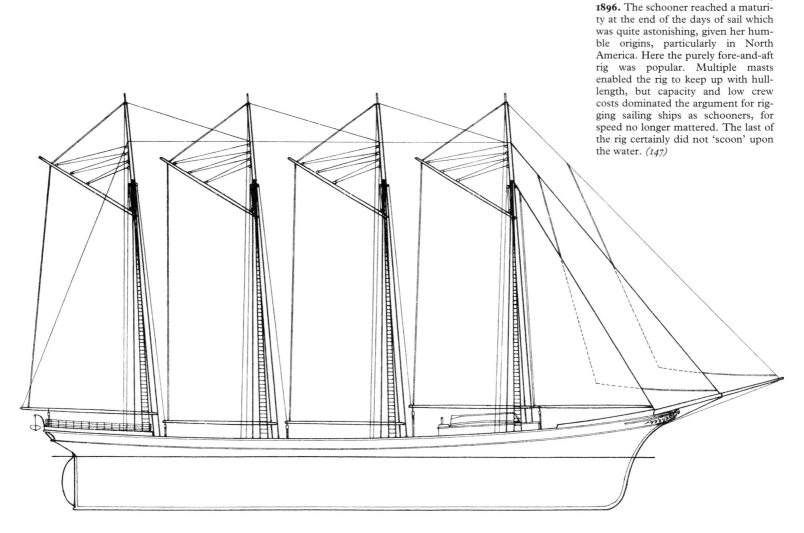

40 30 20 10 0 ft
1/400
10   5   0 m

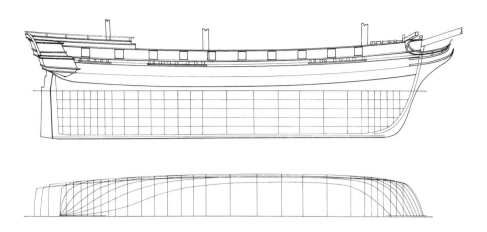

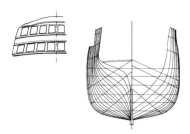

Coromandel, 1820. This ship-rigged vessel is fairly typical of the final generation of high-sided, flat-sheered East Indiaman. As the East India Company lost its monopoly on trade with India and China, their ships, never having been actually owned by the Company but chartered in, were easily employed in new trades. *(131)*

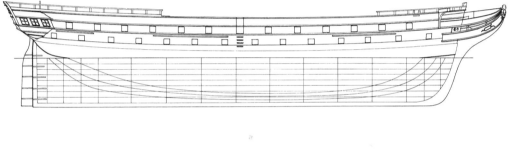

Seringapatam, 1837. Generally considered to be the 'first' distinct Blackwall Frigate, this ship dispensed with the double gallery, an innovation considered very daring at the time. Her hull form was also longer and leaner and she soon established a reputation for speed on her first passages to Bombay. She retained the flat sheer which had become a hallmark of the later Indiamen, but had dispensed with the long quarterdeck. *(131)*

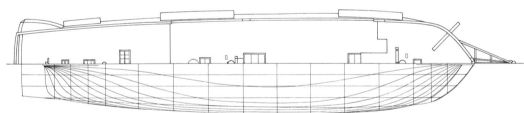

The Blackwall Frigate

It is ironic that the term 'frigate' was to apply to a merchant passenger vessel and to be almost spurious in its last manifestation as a sailing ship. Before the term disappeared, to be revived for the anti-submarine warship of the Second World War, it was applied to the fast passenger vessels that replaced the outdated East Indiamen in the 1830s. An increase in immigration, to Australia in particular, encouraged a new, competitive passenger trade and the ships built to accommodate it seemed initially at least very little different from their predecessors. In fact they were merely known by a different name and employed in a different trade. Frigate-built on the Thames, usually in the yard of Wigram

and Green at Blackwall which had built many pure Indiamen, substantial in form and ship-rigged, their lines were gradually refined as time passed. Nevertheless passenger comfort remained the dominating factor in their performance at sea. By the 1850s American influence had wrought significant change, but the name Blackwall Frigate clung to the imperial British passenger ship long after she had ceased to resemble an East Indiaman or be built at Blackwall. By this time they were being built at many other yards throughout the United Kingdom, but the convention of painting them in black with a chequered strake of white throwing out the illusion of gunports, maintained their 'frigate' image.

40   30   20   10   0 ft
1/400
10   5   0 m

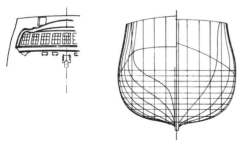

Blenheim, 1848. This 'Blackwaller' was built not on the Thames, but on the Tyne. Of 1314 gross tons, she was 53.5 metres long. With her sister ship, the *Marlborough*, *Blenheim* was presented with a silk ensign at the Great Exhibition in London in 1851 as being considered one of the two finest ships in the British Mercantile Marine. Note the uplift of the long bowsprit and jib-boom is countered by the martingale stay taken down round the 'dolphin-striker' and back to the stem. *Blenheim* was transferred from the Bombay to the Melbourne run in response to the gold rush. *(131)*

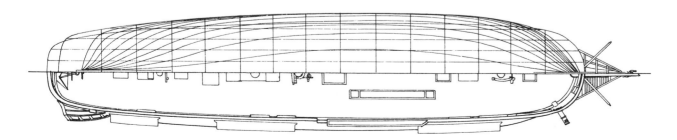

1/400

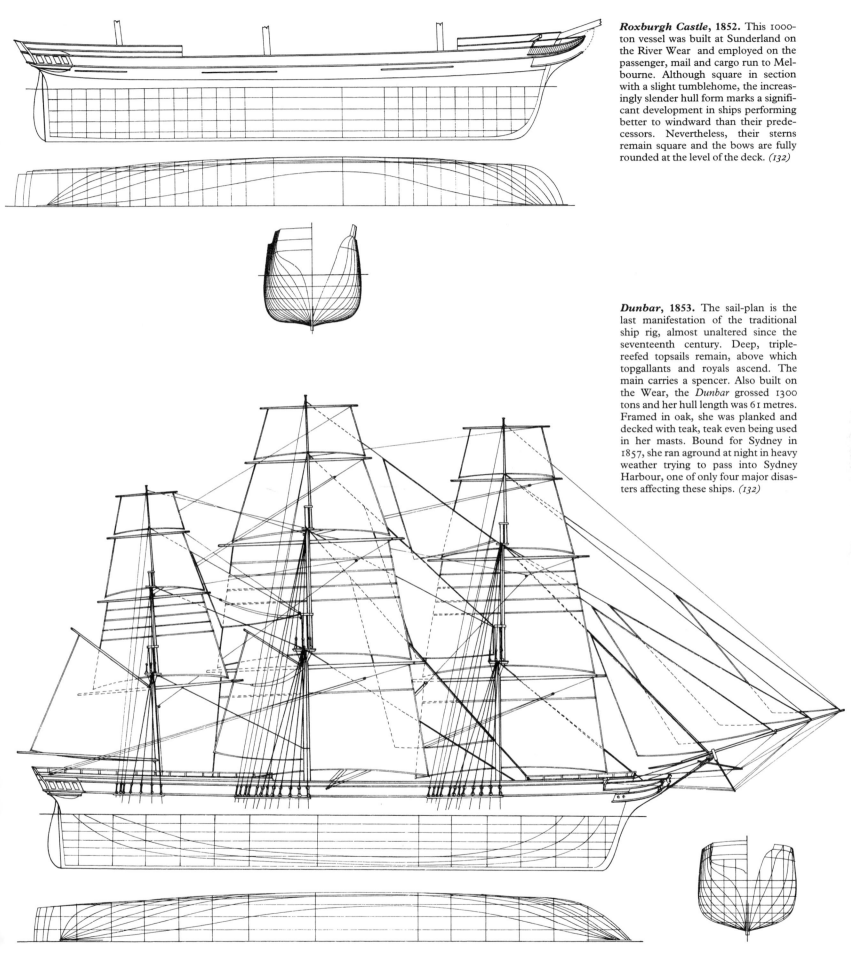

Roxburgh Castle, 1852. This 1000-ton vessel was built at Sunderland on the River Wear and employed on the passenger, mail and cargo run to Melbourne. Although square in section with a slight tumblehome, the increasingly slender hull form marks a significant development in ships performing better to windward than their predecessors. Nevertheless, their sterns remain square and the bows are fully rounded at the level of the deck. *(132)*

Dunbar, 1853. The sail-plan is the last manifestation of the traditional ship rig, almost unaltered since the seventeenth century. Deep, triple-reefed topsails remain, above which topgallants and royals ascend. The main carries a spencer. Also built on the Wear, the *Dunbar* grossed 1300 tons and her hull length was 61 metres. Framed in oak, she was planked and decked with teak, teak even being used in her masts. Bound for Sydney in 1857, she ran aground at night in heavy weather trying to pass into Sydney Harbour, one of only four major disasters affecting these ships. *(132)*

40 30 20 10 0 ft
1/400
10 5 0 m

The Blackwall Frigate   185

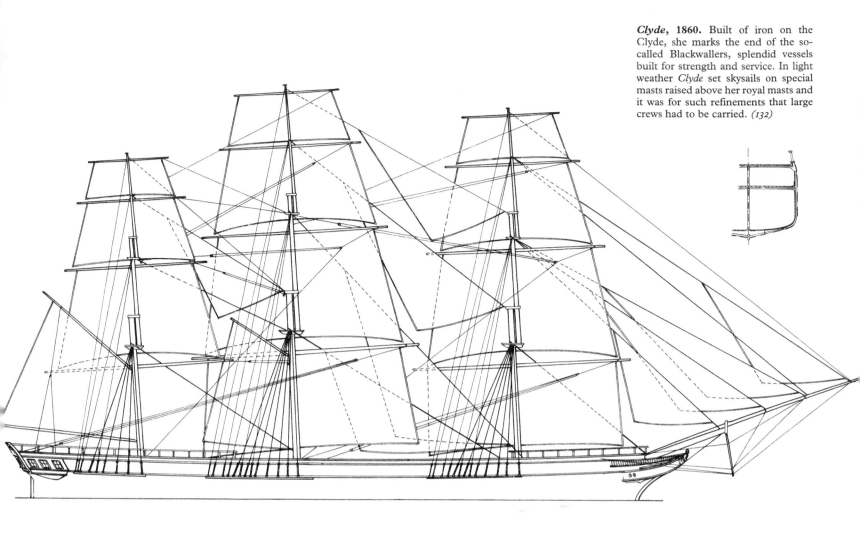

Clyde, 1860. Built of iron on the Clyde, she marks the end of the so-called Blackwallers, splendid vessels built for strength and service. In light weather *Clyde* set skysails on special masts raised above her royal masts and it was for such refinements that large crews had to be carried. *(132)*

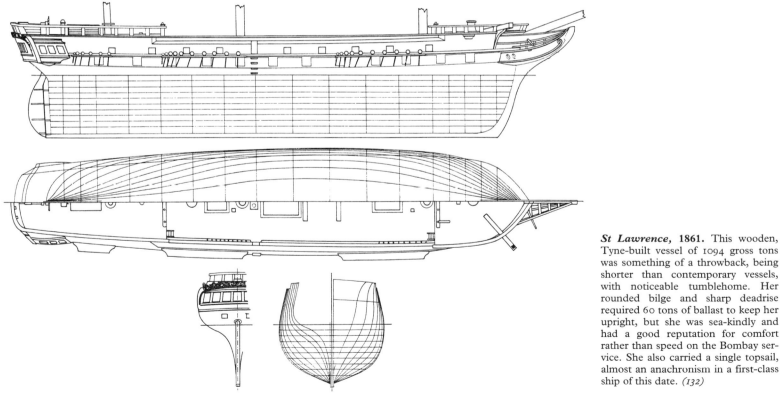

St Lawrence, 1861. This wooden, Tyne-built vessel of 1094 gross tons was something of a throwback, being shorter than contemporary vessels, with noticeable tumblehome. Her rounded bilge and sharp deadrise required 60 tons of ballast to keep her upright, but she was sea-kindly and had a good reputation for comfort rather than speed on the Bombay service. She also carried a single topsail, almost an anachronism in a first-class ship of this date. *(132)*

40   30   20   10   0 ft
1/400
          10   5   0 m

True Briton, 1861. A contemporary of *St Lawrence*, she was longer and drew less, but she too was already outmoded in 1861, retaining an over-canvassed conventional ship rig although she was fitted with patent roller reefing on her fore and main topsails. She was the last of three *True Briton*s built at Blackwall. Her profile shows clearly the 'painted ports' fashionable in Blackwall Frigates. *(207)*

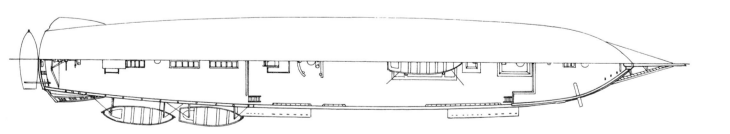

1/400   40   30   20   10   0 ft
         10   5   0 m

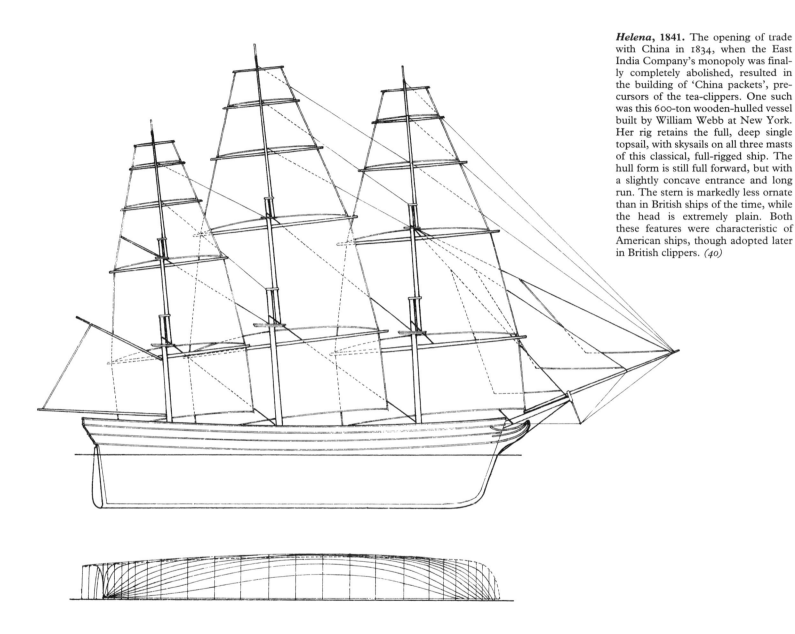

Helena, **1841.** The opening of trade with China in 1834, when the East India Company's monopoly was finally completely abolished, resulted in the building of 'China packets', precursors of the tea-clippers. One such was this 600-ton wooden-hulled vessel built by William Webb at New York. Her rig retains the full, deep single topsail, with skysails on all three masts of this classical, full-rigged ship. The hull form is still full forward, but with a slightly concave entrance and long run. The stern is markedly less ornate than in British ships of the time, while the head is extremely plain. Both these features were characteristic of American ships, though adopted later in British clippers. *(40)*

The American Packet Ship

Contemporary with the British Blackwall Frigate was the American packet ship, plying her trade across the North Atlantic, or on the newly-established run to China for tea. Here speed was of increasing importance, for more passages meant more passengers and more revenue, while tea was a perishable cargo and required swift delivery. American packet ships had to be sturdy, with good cargo-capacity and offer reasonable comfort. The making of smart passages engendered fierce competition between rival shipping companies and between America and Britain. This in turn fuelled a search for greater hull speed under sail.

40   30   20   10   0 ft
1/400
10   5   0 m

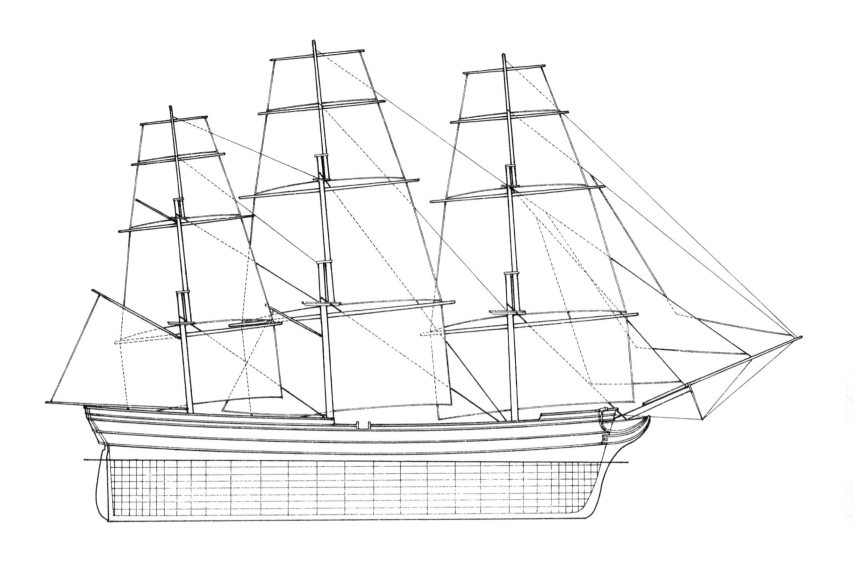

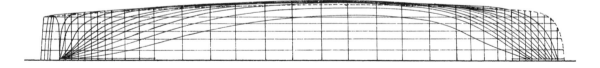

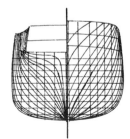

Yorkshire, **1843**. This ship was Webb's first packet to gross over 1000 tons and this is largely attributable to her high freeboard and fuller hull. Her less lofty rig still sports enormous topsails. *(40)*

1/400

40   30   20   10   0 ft

10   5   0 m

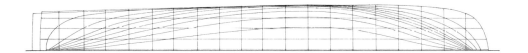

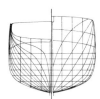

Rainbow, 1845. The *Rainbow* is generally considered to be the first true clipper, with a hollow entrance and fine run. Although only 47 metres on the waterline her hull form and tall rig, which included moonsails above her skysails, made her fast, but she sacrificed cargo-capacity for this. Built by John Griffiths, who had studied the shape of the *Ann McKim* (see below) and some of the principles of water resistance, *Rainbow* was launched in 1845. Her building had been beset by troubles, her backers threatening to withdraw. Not surprisingly, her long spars resulted in her being dismasted on her maiden voyage and she has to be regarded as an experimental, rather than a successful vessel. *(27)*

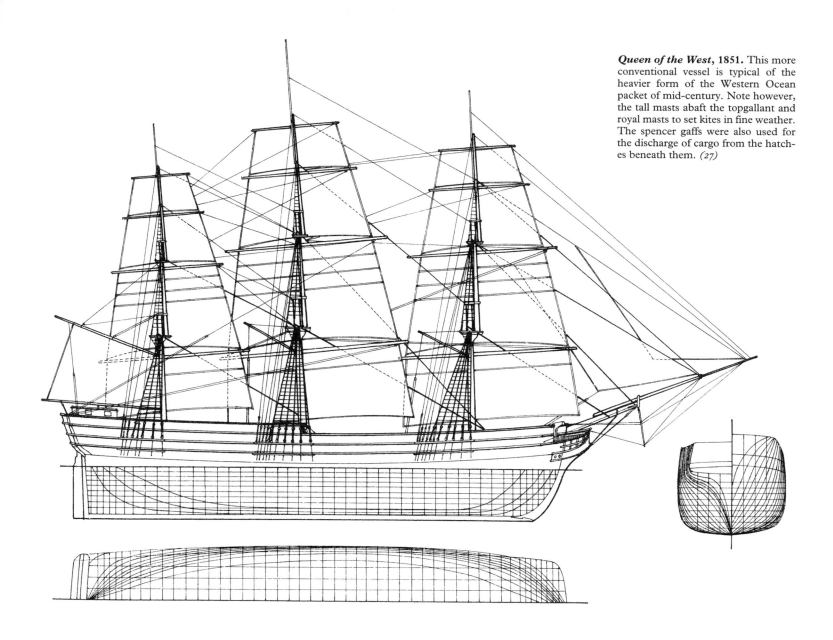

Queen of the West, 1851. This more conventional vessel is typical of the heavier form of the Western Ocean packet of mid-century. Note however, the tall masts abaft the topgallant and royal masts to set kites in fine weather. The spencer gaffs were also used for the discharge of cargo from the hatches beneath them. *(27)*

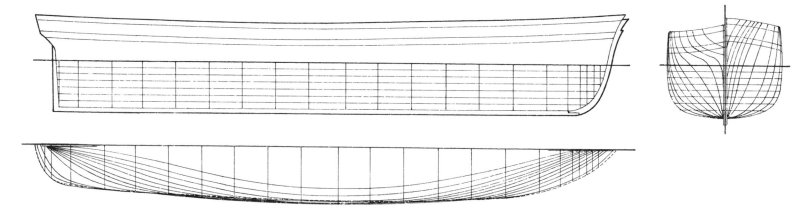

Andrew Jackson, 1851. The austere but sharp bow and rounded stern of the American packet hull are shown in this body plan. Short overhangs produce a beautiful, concave entrance while the after waterlines run up under an elliptical counter. Such a ship marks a true severance from the traditions lingering from the eighteenth century and the introduction of the clipper form. The *Andrew Jackson* ran from New York to San Francisco, via the Horn, in 89 days. *(40)*

1/400   40   30   20   10   0 ft
              10   5   0 m

The American Packet Ship   191

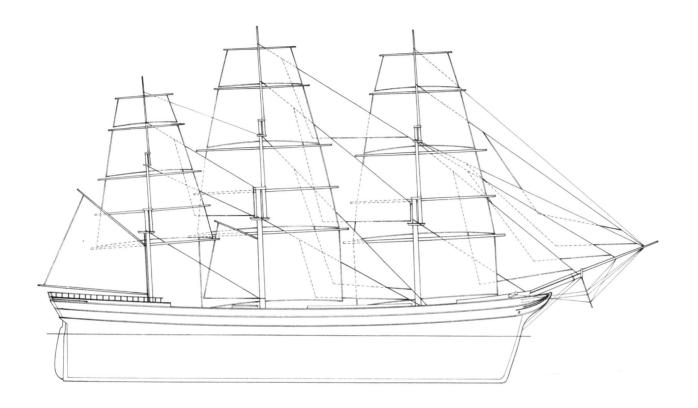

Ocean Monarch, 1856. This Webb-built ship was regarded as a medium clipper, retaining an unremarkable bow and stern. Her rig is significant in that it is lower than was customary in fast American ships and the original sail plan appears to show not an upper and lower topsail, but a topsail divided by an intermediate yard to facilitate its handling. Such a spar was fitted to the deep topsails of the *Donald McKay*. Nevertheless, the year of *Ocean Monarch*'s building was that of the widespread adoption of double topsails in North American vessels. **NB.** Sail plan is 1/600 scale. *(87)*

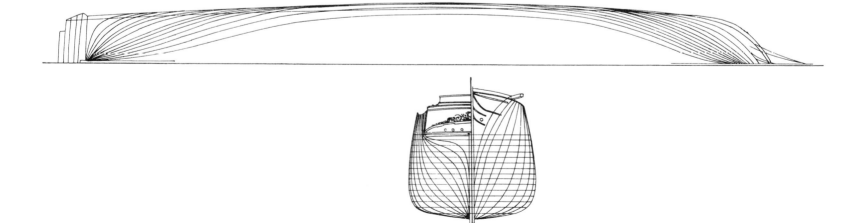

1/400

40 30 20 10 0 ft
10 5 0 m

XIII

German steel barque *Magdalene Vinnen*, 1921
Based on plans in 204

XIV
Dutch bol, 1940
Based on photographs and plans in 90

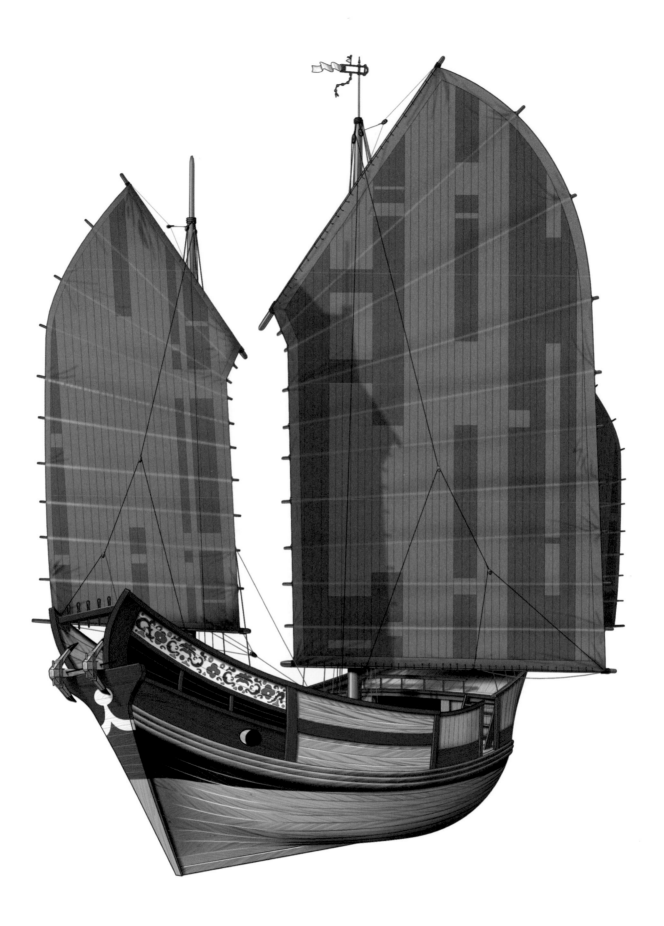

XV

Wenchow fishing junk, early twentieth century

Hull from sketch in 44; sails and details from other sources

XVI
Polish sail training ship *Iskra*, 1982
Based on plans in 231

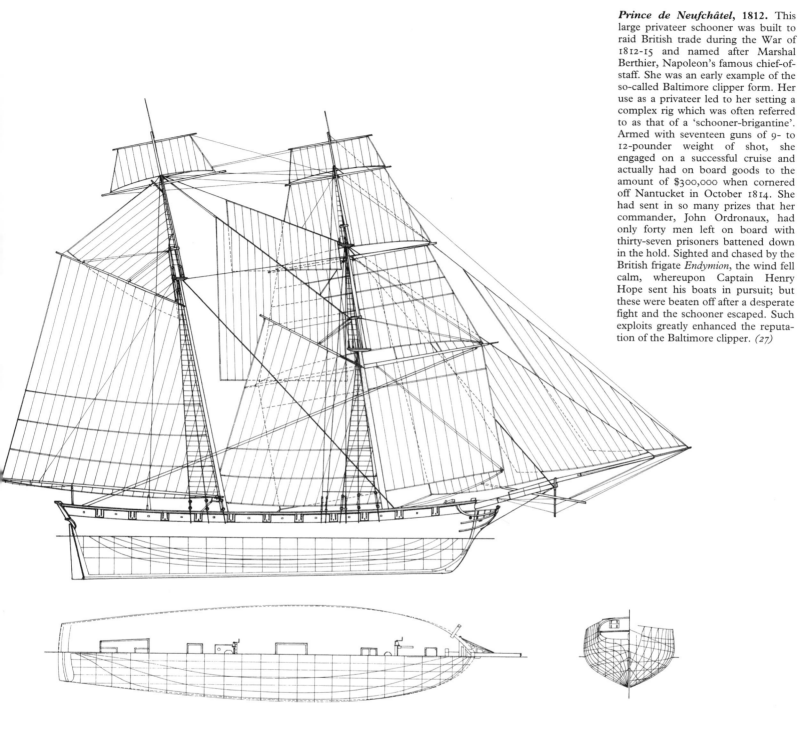

Prince de Neufchâtel, **1812.** This large privateer schooner was built to raid British trade during the War of 1812-15 and named after Marshal Berthier, Napoleon's famous chief-of-staff. She was an early example of the so-called Baltimore clipper form. Her use as a privateer led to her setting a complex rig which was often referred to as that of a 'schooner-brigantine'. Armed with seventeen guns of 9- to 12-pounder weight of shot, she engaged on a successful cruise and actually had on board goods to the amount of $300,000 when cornered off Nantucket in October 1814. She had sent in so many prizes that her commander, John Ordronaux, had only forty men left on board with thirty-seven prisoners battened down in the hold. Sighted and chased by the British frigate *Endymion*, the wind fell calm, whereupon Captain Henry Hope sent his boats in pursuit; but these were beaten off after a desperate fight and the schooner escaped. Such exploits greatly enhanced the reputation of the Baltimore clipper. *(27)*

The Baltimore Clipper, 1800-1840

The American clipper evolved from the experience of operating deep-water ships on the Atlantic, marrying this with the successful home-grown 'clipper' hull first developed on Chesapeake Bay and tried at sea in blockade-runners, slavers and privateers. The orthodox concept of ship construction was to build a full bow that would rise over the waves while transferring a relatively smooth flow of water aft, where this allowed the rudder to work efficiently. Thus the old maxim that a hull should be cod-headed and mackerel-tailed dominated the thinking of shipbuilders for generations. But the sheltered waters of the great bay had persuaded American builders that a sharper bow would cleave the water with ease. If, therefore, a compromise to permit a bow to both

cleave and yet ride an ocean wave could be found, then a ship could sail faster in the open sea. It was found unnecessary for the bow to be full at the waterline, only that it possessed sufficient 'reserve' buoyancy above the water to make it lift in heavy seas when pitching. Thus the bow had to be flared, and the extremely round bow at deck level was retained to keep the decks dry and provide adequate spread of deck to handle the foretack, important when going to windward. However, even this was gradually whittled away until a new compromise was found in the extreme clipper. This process started therefore with the Baltimore clipper.

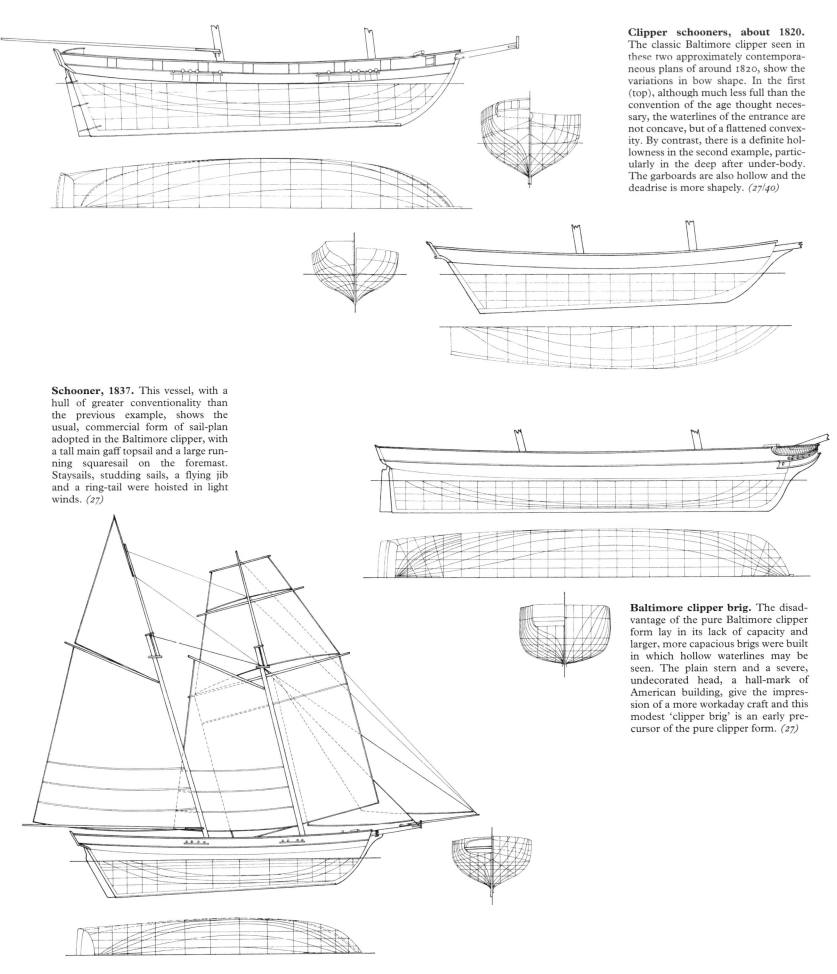

Clipper schooners, about 1820. The classic Baltimore clipper seen in these two approximately contemporaneous plans of around 1820, show the variations in bow shape. In the first (top), although much less full than the convention of the age thought necessary, the waterlines of the entrance are not concave, but of a flattened convexity. By contrast, there is a definite hollowness in the second example, particularly in the deep after under-body. The garboards are also hollow and the deadrise is more shapely. *(27/40)*

Schooner, 1837. This vessel, with a hull of greater conventionality than the previous example, shows the usual, commercial form of sail-plan adopted in the Baltimore clipper, with a tall main gaff topsail and a large running squaresail on the foremast. Staysails, studding sails, a flying jib and a ring-tail were hoisted in light winds. *(27)*

Baltimore clipper brig. The disadvantage of the pure Baltimore clipper form lay in its lack of capacity and larger, more capacious brigs were built in which hollow waterlines may be seen. The plain stern and a severe, undecorated head, a hall-mark of American building, give the impression of a more workaday craft and this modest 'clipper brig' is an early precursor of the pure clipper form. *(27)*

1/300   30   20   10   0 ft

8   4   0 m

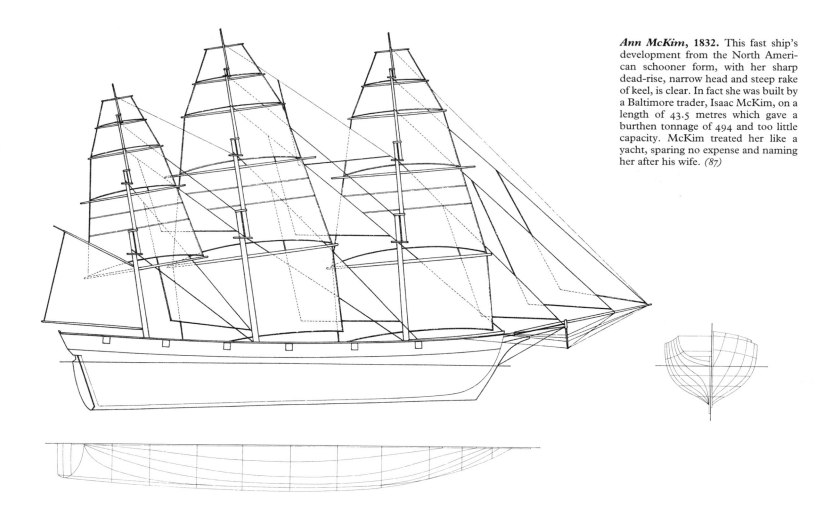

Ann McKim, 1832. This fast ship's development from the North American schooner form, with her sharp dead-rise, narrow head and steep rake of keel, is clear. In fact she was built by a Baltimore trader, Isaac McKim, on a length of 43.5 metres which gave a burthen tonnage of 494 and too little capacity. McKim treated her like a yacht, sparing no expense and naming her after his wife. *(87)*

Samuel Russell, 1847. By contrast the vertical ends of this ship, whilst still possessing considerable rise of floor, increase waterline length proportionately. The finer underwater body marks this design out as of similar concept to *Rainbow*, but she is remarkable in the steep angle of her deadrise. She was one of the vessels sent to California in 1849 and made her mark with a run to San Francisco, carrying 1200 tons of cargo, plus prospectors, of 109 days. This was a record soon broken. *(40)*

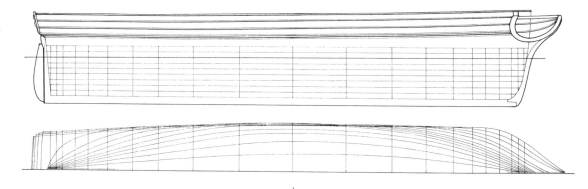

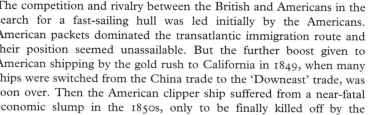

American Clipper Hull Forms

The competition and rivalry between the British and Americans in the search for a fast-sailing hull was led initially by the Americans. American packets dominated the transatlantic immigration route and their position seemed unassailable. But the further boost given to American shipping by the gold rush to California in 1849, when many ships were switched from the China trade to the 'Downeast' trade, was soon over. Then the American clipper ship suffered from a near-fatal economic slump in the 1850s, only to be finally killed off by the American Civil War. From about 1865, therefore, the British gained the upper hand.

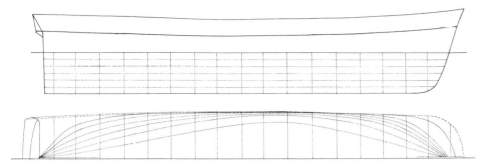

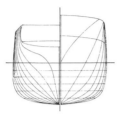

Mandarin, 1850. In order to accommodate the reserve buoyancy considered essential for sea-kindliness and dry decks, it was necessary to retain the full, flared bow. In this vessel the stem-post retains its angle, though the stern-post has now become vertical. *(40)*

Witch of the Wave, 1851. By stretching the length on the upper deck, and curving the cutwater, the bow becomes less flared and a compromise is sought, not entirely sacrificing reserve buoyancy, but allowing the ship to shoulder her way through heavy seas. This vessel is a medium clipper of deep draught, her length, compared with that of *Rainbow* or *Samuel Russell* enabling her to achieve relatively high speeds without excessively hollow waterlines. *(40)*

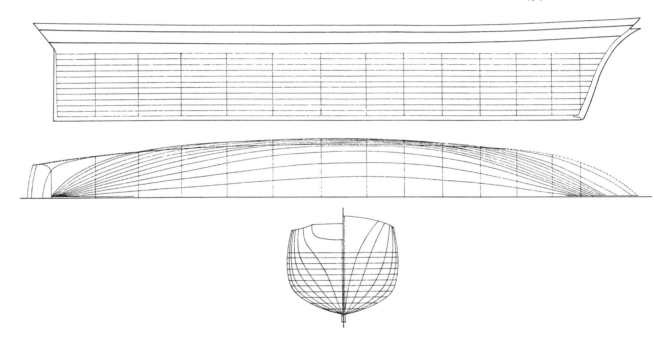

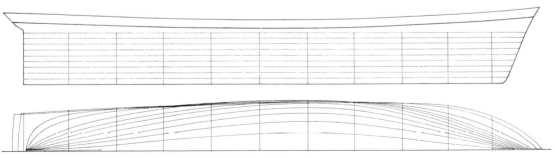

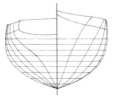

Nightingale, 1851. Built at Portsmouth, New Hampshire, and 56.3 metres in length, giving a burthen tonnage of 1100, she has somewhat vertical ends with notably steep deadrise, but a more elegant sheer than the *Samuel Russell*. She too made good passages, largely through being hard driven. *(40)*

1/400

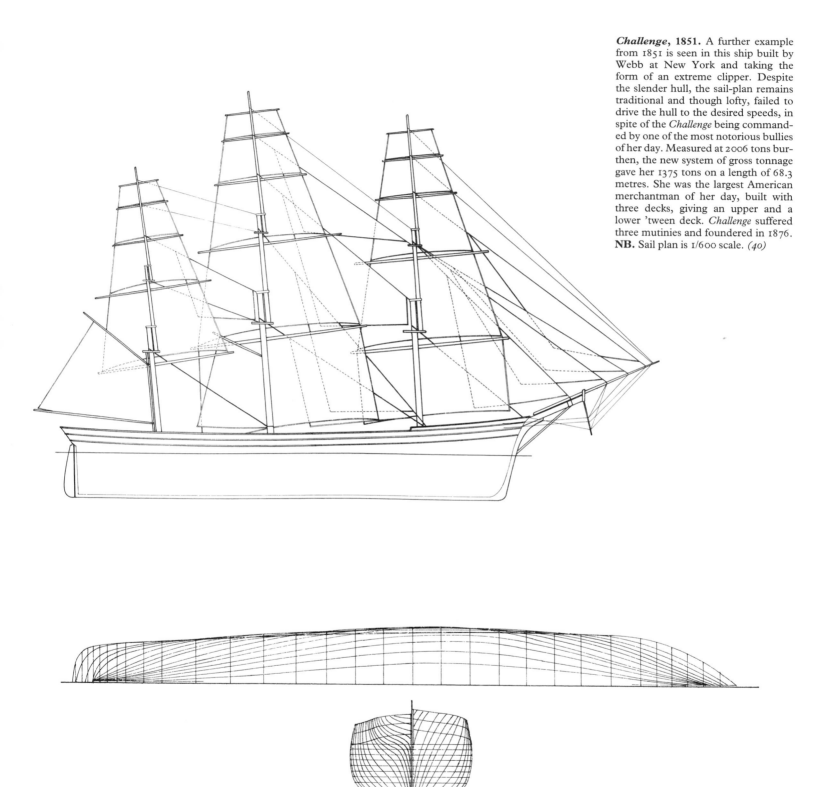

Challenge, **1851.** A further example from 1851 is seen in this ship built by Webb at New York and taking the form of an extreme clipper. Despite the slender hull, the sail-plan remains traditional and though lofty, failed to drive the hull to the desired speeds, in spite of the *Challenge* being command-ed by one of the most notorious bullies of her day. Measured at 2006 tons bur-then, the new system of gross tonnage gave her 1375 tons on a length of 68.3 metres. She was the largest American merchantman of her day, built with three decks, giving an upper and a lower 'tween deck. *Challenge* suffered three mutinies and foundered in 1876. **NB.** Sail plan is 1/600 scale. *(40)*

1/400

40   30   20   10   0 ft
     10   5   0 m

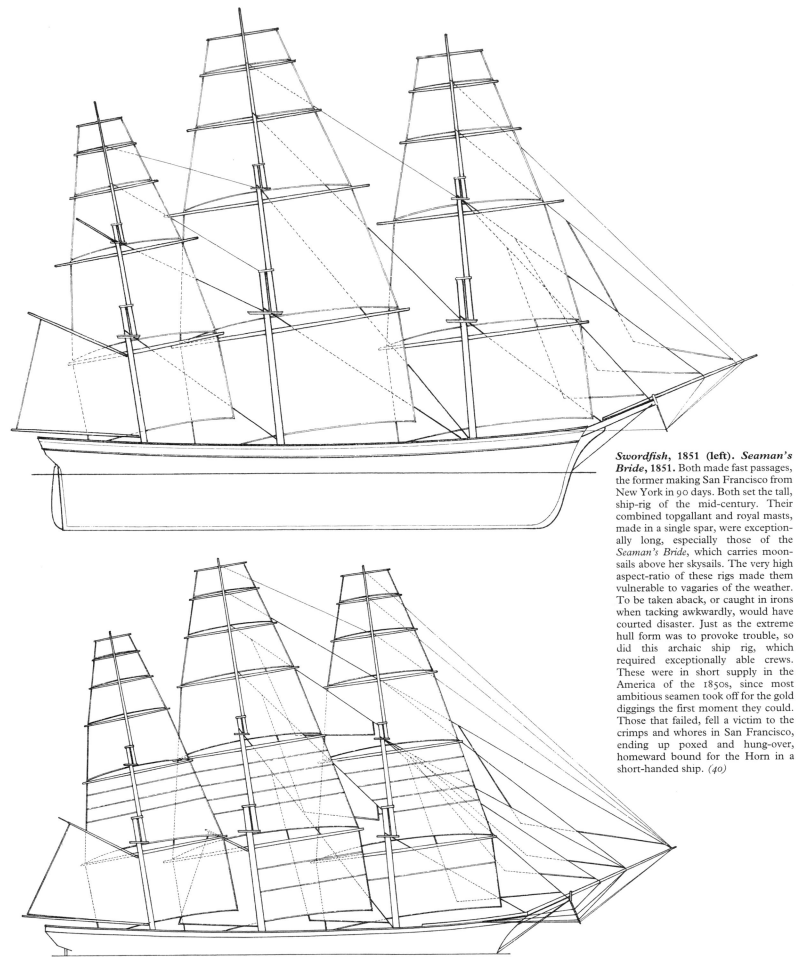

Swordfish, 1851 (left). *Seaman's Bride*, 1851. Both made fast passages, the former making San Francisco from New York in 90 days. Both set the tall, ship-rig of the mid-century. Their combined topgallant and royal masts, made in a single spar, were exceptionally long, especially those of the *Seaman's Bride*, which carries moonsails above her skysails. The very high aspect-ratio of these rigs made them vulnerable to vagaries of the weather. To be taken aback, or caught in irons when tacking awkwardly, would have courted disaster. Just as the extreme hull form was to provoke trouble, so did this archaic ship rig, which required exceptionally able crews. These were in short supply in the America of the 1850s, since most ambitious seamen took off for the gold diggings the first moment they could. Those that failed, fell a victim to the crimps and whores in San Francisco, ending up poxed and hung-over, homeward bound for the Horn in a short-handed ship. *(40)*

40 30 20 10 0 ft
1/400
10 5 0 m

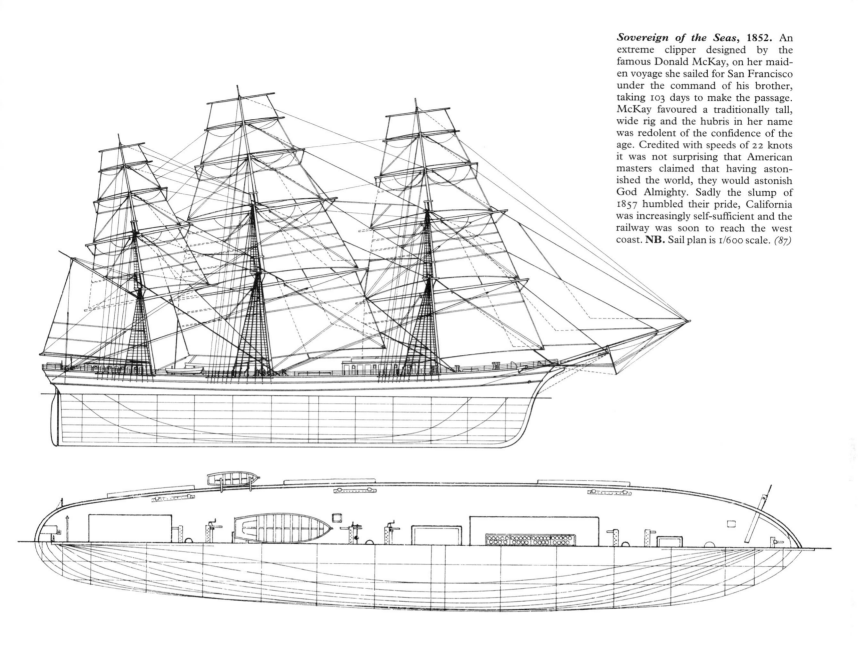

Sovereign of the Seas, 1852. An extreme clipper designed by the famous Donald McKay, on her maiden voyage she sailed for San Francisco under the command of his brother, taking 103 days to make the passage. McKay favoured a traditionally tall, wide rig and the hubris in her name was redolent of the confidence of the age. Credited with speeds of 22 knots it was not surprising that American masters claimed that having astonished the world, they would astonish God Almighty. Sadly the slump of 1857 humbled their pride, California was increasingly self-sufficient and the railway was soon to reach the west coast. **NB.** Sail plan is 1/600 scale. *(87)*

Herald of the Morning, 1853. The sheer beauty of the clipper form is exemplified in this lines plan. Full in her midships body, the smooth flow of waterlines run into her typical American squared stern, preserving a degree of reserve buoyancy aft where its loss caused pooping of ships with excessively fine sterns. Forward, her bow has a pleasing, though not excessive flare. *(40)*

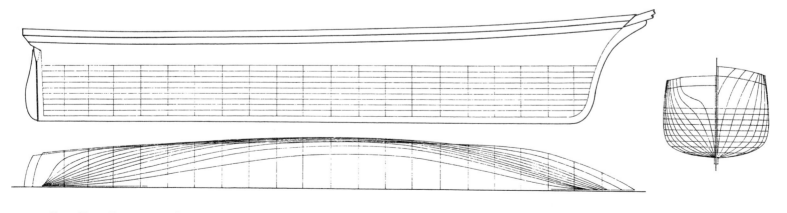

1/400

40 30 20 10 0 ft

10   5   0 m

American Clipper Hull Forms 199

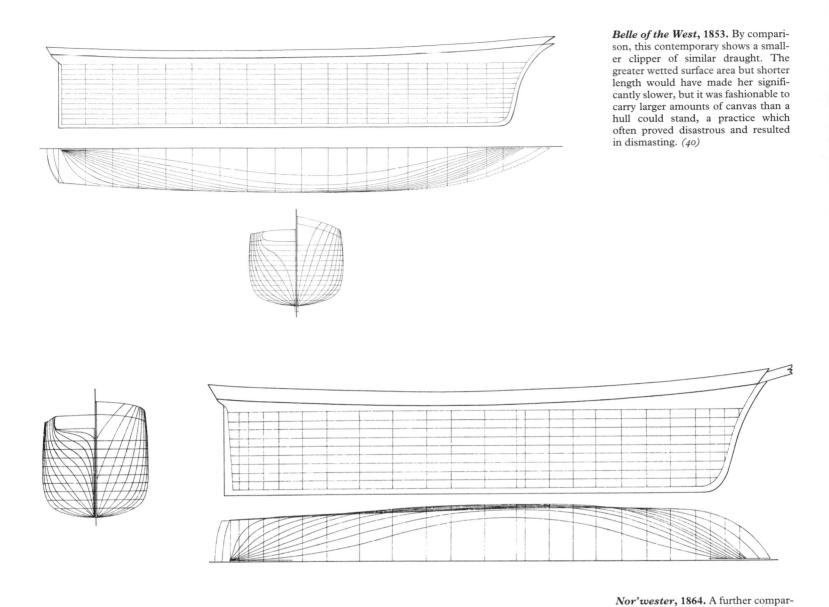

Belle of the West, **1853.** By comparison, this contemporary shows a smaller clipper of similar draught. The greater wetted surface area but shorter length would have made her significantly slower, but it was fashionable to carry larger amounts of canvas than a hull could stand, a practice which often proved disastrous and resulted in dismasting. *(40)*

Nor'wester, **1864.** A further comparison may be made with this exceptionally deep vessel which retains some characteristics of the earlier hull form, evidence that American owners and builders could prove as conservative as their British counterparts. *(40)*

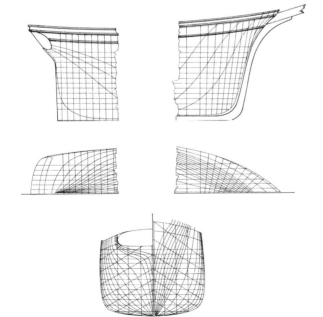

Downeaster, about 1880. The midships body and extremes of a typical American Downeaster show in some detail the form of these beautiful ships. The contours of the hull, in particular the flare of the bow, show very well in these enlargements. *(27)*

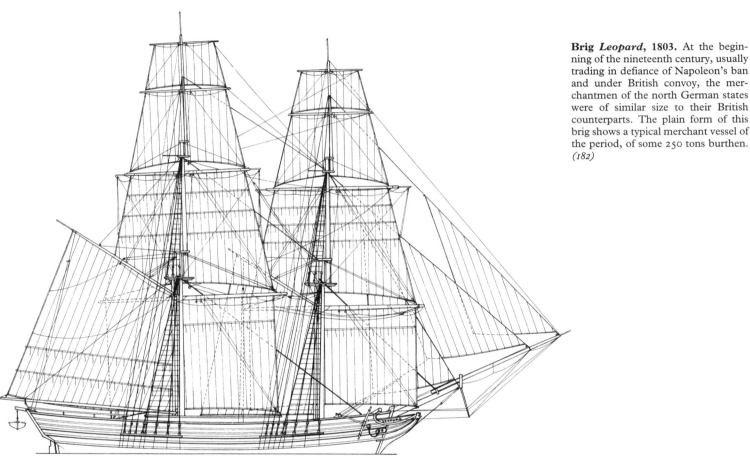

At the beginning of the nineteenth century, usually trading in defiance of Napoleon's ban and under British convoy, the merchantmen of the north German states were of similar size to their British counterparts. The plain form of this brig shows a typical merchant vessel of the period, of some 250 tons burthen. *(182)*

Growth of the German Merchant Marine

Before following the development of the fast clipper, it is appropriate to review contemporaneous shipbuilding elsewhere. After the Napoleonic War the German states remained fragmented, though Prussia was increasingly regarded as the leading Teutonic state and unification was completed by the formation of the German Empire in 1871. This political aggrandisement was of considerable significance in world affairs and produced a large merchant fleet under the new imperial ensign.

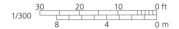

Brig *Auguste von Wismar*, 1840.
By the time this brig was built the sail-plan had reduced in area and she would have had a smaller crew than the *Leopard*. The lines of her hull show a full midship section, but despite her wide upper deck, her waterlines are surprisingly curved, giving relatively fine ends on a short hull. *(41)*

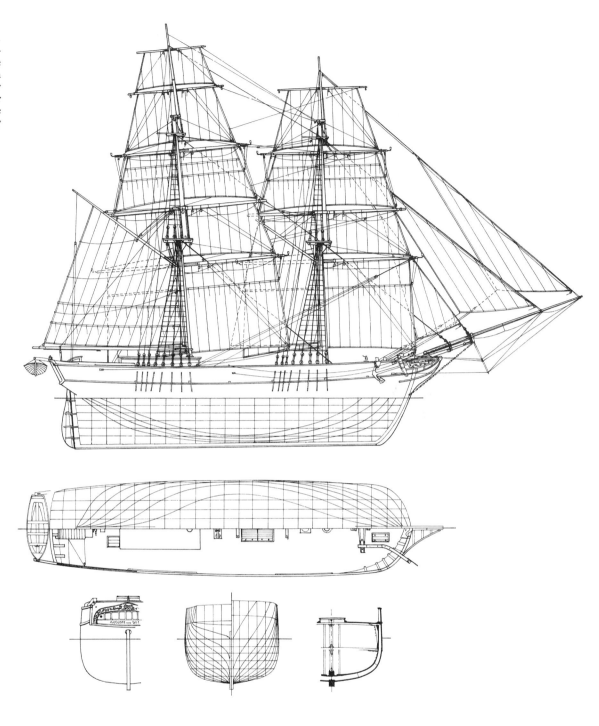

Schooner *Miranda*, 1855. A gradual improvement in the living standards of the populations of European states created new markets, and ship-owners expanded their fleets to accommodate the new demands. The fashion for fast 'clipper-schooners' employed in the wet fish and fruit trades had crossed the Atlantic by the time this vessel was built. *(178)*

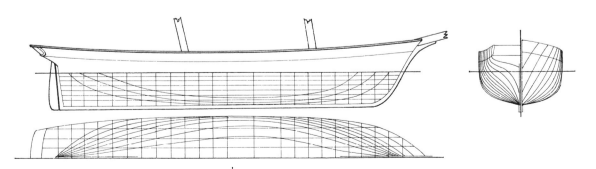

1/300

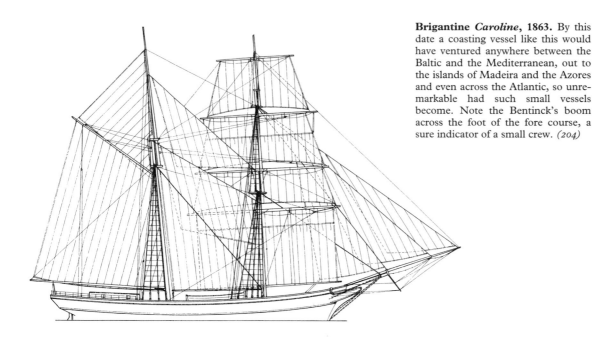

Brigantine *Caroline*, 1863. By this date a coasting vessel like this would have ventured anywhere between the Baltic and the Mediterranean, out to the islands of Madeira and the Azores and even across the Atlantic, so unremarkable had such small vessels become. Note the Bentinck's boom across the foot of the fore course, a sure indicator of a small crew. *(204)*

Brigantine *Regulus*, 1867. This slightly more rakish brigantine may well have been built specially for the fruit trade from Spain and Portugal to Hamburg, Bremen, Rotterdam or London. *(41)*

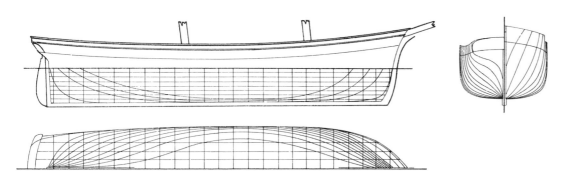

Schooner *Paul Grampp*, 1877. The lines are typical of thousands of medium-sized coasting vessels built throughout northern Europe in the last quarter of the nineteenth century. Road and rail links were still inadequate to fulfil all transport requirements, particularly in the garnering of relatively bulky produce from remote rural locations and the sailing coaster remained a cost-effective way of collecting it. *(178)*

30   20   10   0 ft
1/300
8   4   0 m

Growth of the German Merchant Marine   203

Barque *Go Ahead*, 1857. The bulk of deep-water European merchant ships remained relatively small by comparison with American vessels. Such modest craft were often barque-rigged, like this example, which shows no significant innovation in her lines beyond that exhibited in the hull of the *Auguste von Wismar*. Capacity of a hull and its ability to deliver its cargo in good condition were more important generally than speed. *(178)*

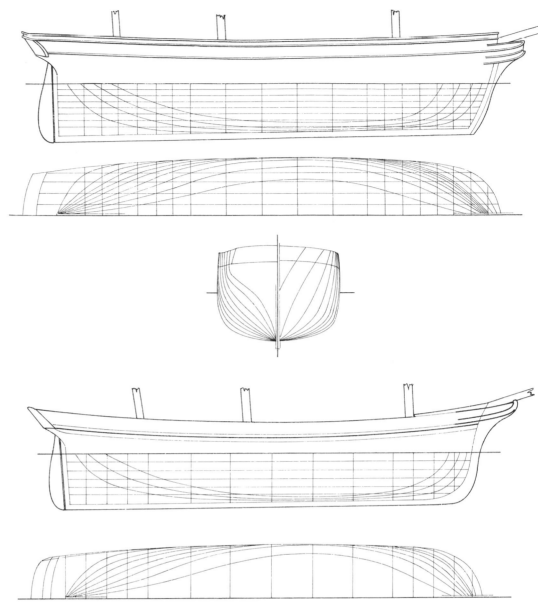

Barque *Tonnies Voss*, 1863. Inevitably, however, the influence of the clipper hull steadily impacted upon shipbuilding fashion and this is noticeable in this barque-rigged vessel of 1863. *(178)*

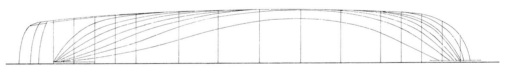

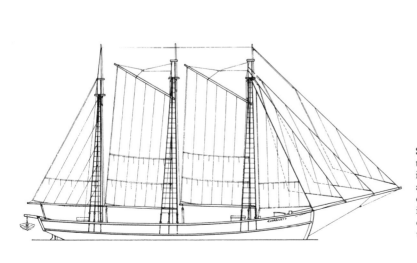

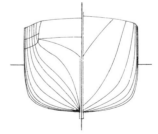

Schooner *Loreley*, 1930. The persistence of sail, particularly in the Baltic is seen here in this steel example of a twentieth-century German sailing coaster. She answered the same need in rural and insular communities that coasters had satisfied for many generations. *(204)*

1/300   30   20   10   0 ft
8   4   0 m

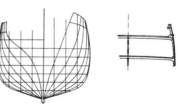

British Clippers – Composite, Iron and Steel

Until the 1850s, the British lagged behind the Americans in the development of the clipper. Despite innovations in hull design prompted by the revision of the tonnage regulations, the most extreme form of which was the long, overhanging 'Aberdeen bow', British clippers in the competitive China trade remained smaller vessels. Nevertheless, by mid-century they were making creditable passages and for a decade gave the Americans a good run for their money. British domination of the China tea trade began when many American ships responded to the Californian gold-rush and was then secured by the Civil War. It was in 1866 that the celebrated race between the *Ariel*, *Taeping*, *Fiery Cross*, *Taitsing* and *Serica* took place.

During this period composite construction enjoyed a brief vogue. Designed to benefit from the strength of iron framing, electrolytic action frustrated builders and in due course the all-iron ship achieved a beauty of her own. The economic production of steel further reduced costs and enabled ships of ever-increasing size to be built. An important consequence of the all-metal ship was the introduction of integral water and ballast tanks situated along a vessel's bottom between the ceiling of her hold and her outer shell plating.

Composite clipper *Ariel*, 1865. Built by Robert Steel at Greenock on the Clyde, and capable of 16 knots, she was 55.9 metres in length, and fully ship-rigged. She bore royals and single topgallants over double topsails, with a skysail on the mainmast, together with a full set of studding sails and light weather kites. To improve windward performance, clippers of her generation had deep courses and this enabled *Ariel* to make Hong Kong in an 'unbelievable' 80 days from London, against the prevailing monsoon in the South China Sea.

Ariel suffered a dismasting off Japan in 1870 and a year later she was posted missing. Her fate remains a mystery, but informed conjecture suggests the most likely reason was that she was pooped. Just as the tall ship rig was at the limits of its development in these lovely ships, the extremely slender lines of their hulls left them with insufficient reserve buoyancy at their ends. If a fine counter failed to rise to a following sea and the wave broke over the hull, as was not unknown, it could smash the afterpart of the vessel, flood her and cause her to founder. *(170)*

1/400 40 30 20 10 0 ft
        10   5   0 m

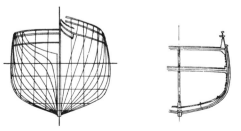

Composite clipper *Cutty Sark*, 1869. Also Clyde-built, by Scott and Linton at Dumbarton, she too was a composite ship, measured 64.8 metres in length and was registered at 921 tons. A fast ship, her sail plan was almost identical to that of *Ariel*, with the addition of a main spencer. It is a notable feature of British clippers that the length of spars had begun to widen significantly, when compared to the tall, narrow rigs of American ships. The small capacity of these tea-clippers was no disadvantage with a high-value cargo where profits rode upon the first consignment of each new season to reach the London market. When steamers took over the trade (the first British cargo-liner to open the China trade to steam did so in 1866 and the Suez Canal opened in 1869), the *Cutty Sark* and many other British clippers switched to the Australian wool trade where their lack of space was to work against them. The *Cutty Sark* is preserved today at Greenwich on the River Thames. *(229)*

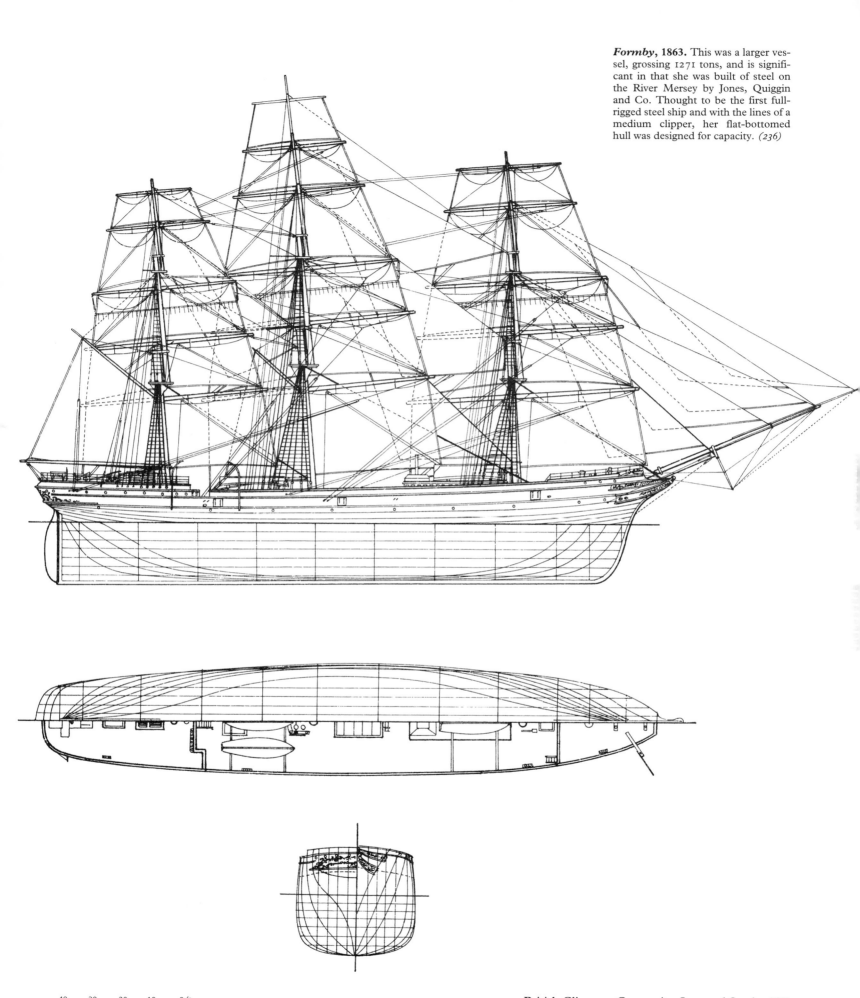

Formby, **1863.** This was a larger vessel, grossing 1271 tons, and is significant in that she was built of steel on the River Mersey by Jones, Quiggin and Co. Thought to be the first full-rigged steel ship and with the lines of a medium clipper, her flat-bottomed hull was designed for capacity. *(236)*

1/400   40   30   20   10   0 ft
        10   5   0 m

British Clippers – Composite, Iron and Steel   207

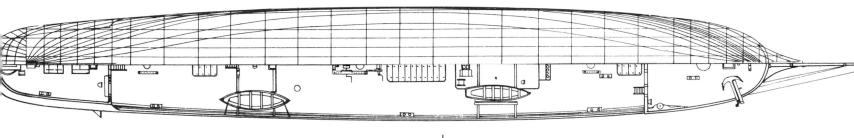

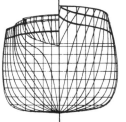

Mount Stewart, 1891. This 1903-ton ship, and her sister *Cromdale*, were the last ships designed and built for the Australian wool trade. A product of the Barclay, Curle yard on the Clyde, this relatively fine-lined steel-built vessel may represent the peak of development for the full three-masted ship rig. *(207)*

```
                              40    30    20    10    0 ft
                    1/400  └┴┴┴┴┴┴┴┴┴┴┴┴┴┴┴┴┴┴┴┴┤
                                   10        5        0 m
```

Development of the Barque

In the tea-clippers the ship rig reached its apogee and despite a few four-masted ships (and one five-masted), it was the barque which was favoured as the standard rig for the last generation of commercial sailing vessels. The four-masted barque was unquestionably the most numerous, but this had several variations. In Britain it was produced in two distinct types, the 'English' and 'Scottish' rigs, being further subdivided with the introduction of the bald-headed rig already mentioned. German barques, which included a number of five-masted vessels, were distinguished by the division of the spanker by twin gaffs.

The so-called English rig usually consisted of deep, single topgallants, above which royals were set. The spanker was a quadrilateral gaff sail, whereas in the Scottish rig, it was often a leg-of-mutton sail, while double topgallants were favoured under the royals. American four-masted barques were called 'shipentines' and often bore a leg-of-mutton spanker.

With the exception of the large American wooden shipentines, these vessels were steel, with steel spars and rigging. Lower and topmasts were usually fabricated from a single tube and the long bowsprit and jibboom of the clippers was replaced by a simple 'spike bowsprit'. In many cases too, the figurehead has gone, replaced by a simple fiddle-head.

 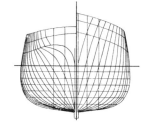

American *Great Republic*, 1853. Among the fast sailing craft built by Donald McKay was the largest wooden sailing vessel ever built. Intended to be of 4555 tons under the old measurement of tons burthen, she caught fire while building at Boston and her size was reduced when construction resumed. With a length of 99 metres, her final tonnage was 3356 and to drive this enormous hull she was given the rig of a four-masted barque, or 'shipentine'. This, however, has the general proportions of a ship rig, with the jigger mast well aft and the spanker boom extending over the stern. Note the very deep doublings of the topmasts. *(112)*

60 50 40 30 20 10 0 ft
1/600
15   10   5   0 m

British _Gloamin_, about 1870.
Although she has double-topsails, she
retains the single topgallants still common in the 1870s and '80s. However,
as a three-masted, or conventional
barque, it is clear that the reduction of
the spars on the mizen mast would
make her easier to maintain and work,
the chief attraction of the simplified
sail plan. *(208)*

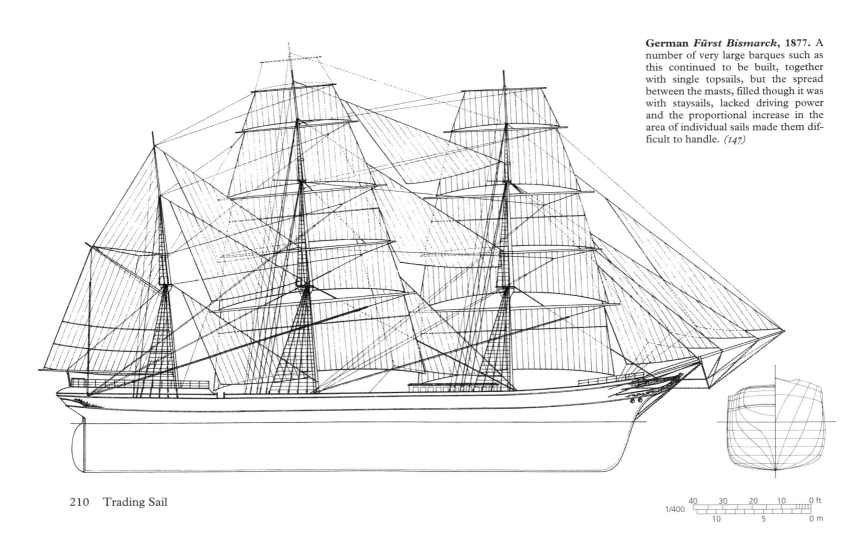

German _Fürst Bismarck_, 1877. A
number of very large barques such as
this continued to be built, together
with single topsails, but the spread
between the masts, filled though it was
with staysails, lacked driving power
and the proportional increase in the
area of individual sails made them difficult to handle. *(147)*

1/400   40   30   20   10   0 ft
         10   5   0 m

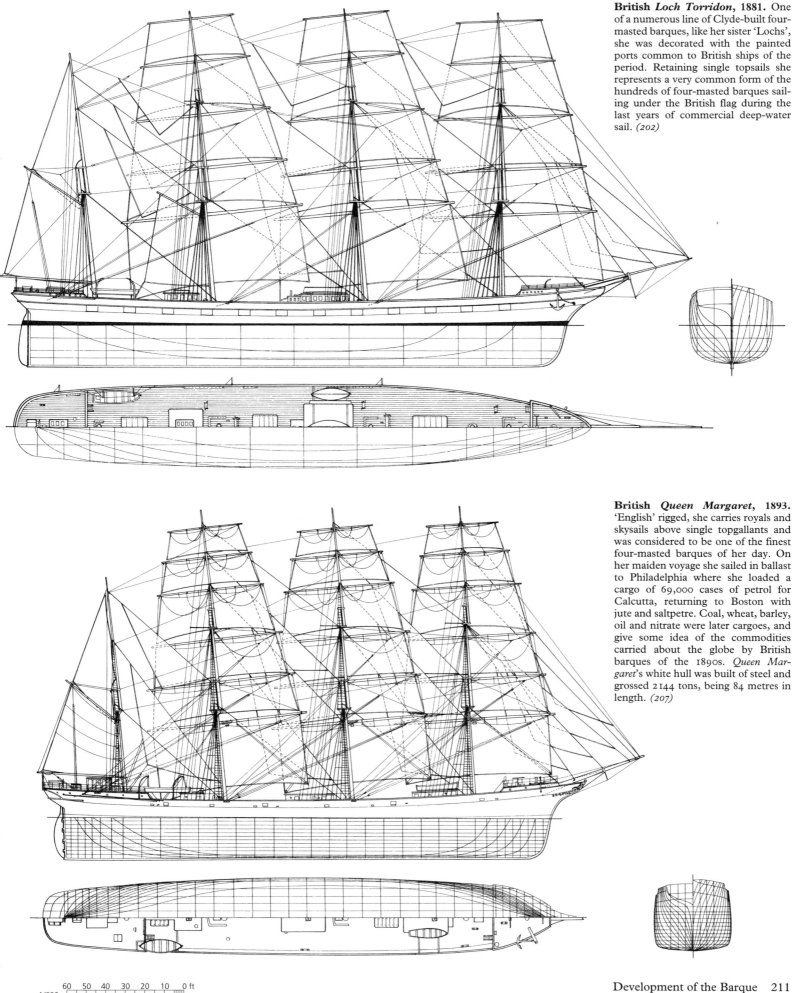

British *Loch Torridon*, 1881. One of a numerous line of Clyde-built four-masted barques, like her sister 'Lochs', she was decorated with the painted ports common to British ships of the period. Retaining single topsails she represents a very common form of the hundreds of four-masted barques sailing under the British flag during the last years of commercial deep-water sail. *(202)*

British *Queen Margaret*, 1893. 'English' rigged, she carries royals and skysails above single topgallants and was considered to be one of the finest four-masted barques of her day. On her maiden voyage she sailed in ballast to Philadelphia where she loaded a cargo of 69,000 cases of petrol for Calcutta, returning to Boston with jute and saltpetre. Coal, wheat, barley, oil and nitrate were later cargoes, and give some idea of the commodities carried about the globe by British barques of the 1890s. *Queen Margaret*'s white hull was built of steel and grossed 2144 tons, being 84 metres in length. *(207)*

60 50 40 30 20 10 0 ft
1/600
15 10 5 0 m

Development of the Barque 211

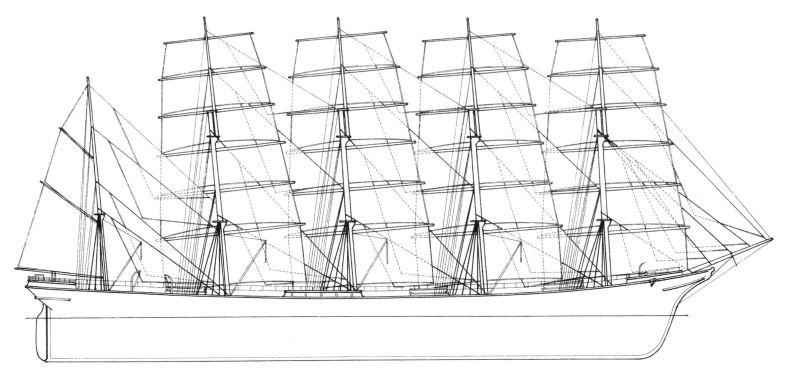

French *France*, 1890. Having been built in Britain by Hendersons of Glasgow, the steel five-masted barque *France* had painted ports and a split spanker, her upper boom being set well up the mast. Owned by A D Bordes of Bordeaux, with a gross registration of 3784 tons, she was relatively small by comparison with other vessels of the same rig. She carried double topsails, double topgallants and royals, along with a full gaff spanker. Note the jigger mast is a single steel spar and the other three consist of combined lower and topmasts. *(232)*

German *Potosi*, 1895. Regarded by many to be the epitome of the sailing vessel, this Hamburg-owned and registered vessel was built at Tecklenborg, on the Baltic, for the Chilean nitrate trade. Owned by F Laeisz, all of whose ships' names began with 'P', *Potosi* grossed 4026 tons and was 111.6 metres in length. An immensely powerful all-steel ship with steel spars and rigging she was able to keep enormous amounts of sail set even in extreme weather, so strong was this final generation of large sailing ship. The three-island construction, with a long midships centrecastle, provided excellent accommodation and dry working conditions for the crew. This was a hallmark of the Flying 'P' Line. Her double spanker was typical of German barques, and the division of the square sail plan into small, manageable individual sails was the final evolution of the deep-water sailing freighter. *(232)*

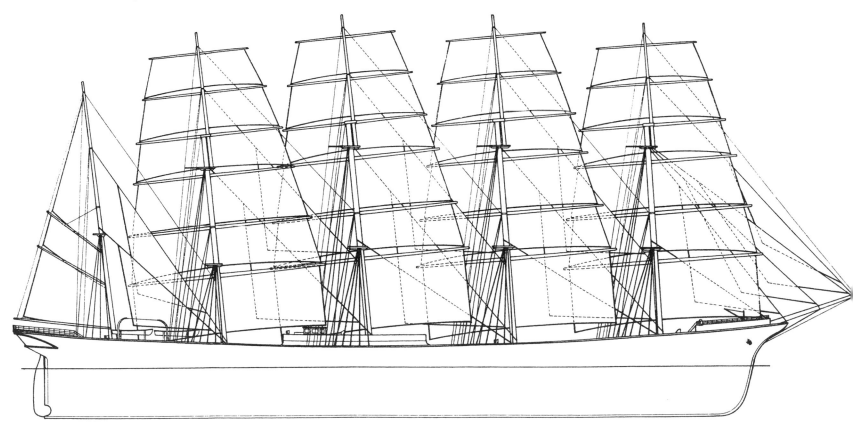

60 50 40 30 20 10 0 ft
1/600
15   10   5   0 m

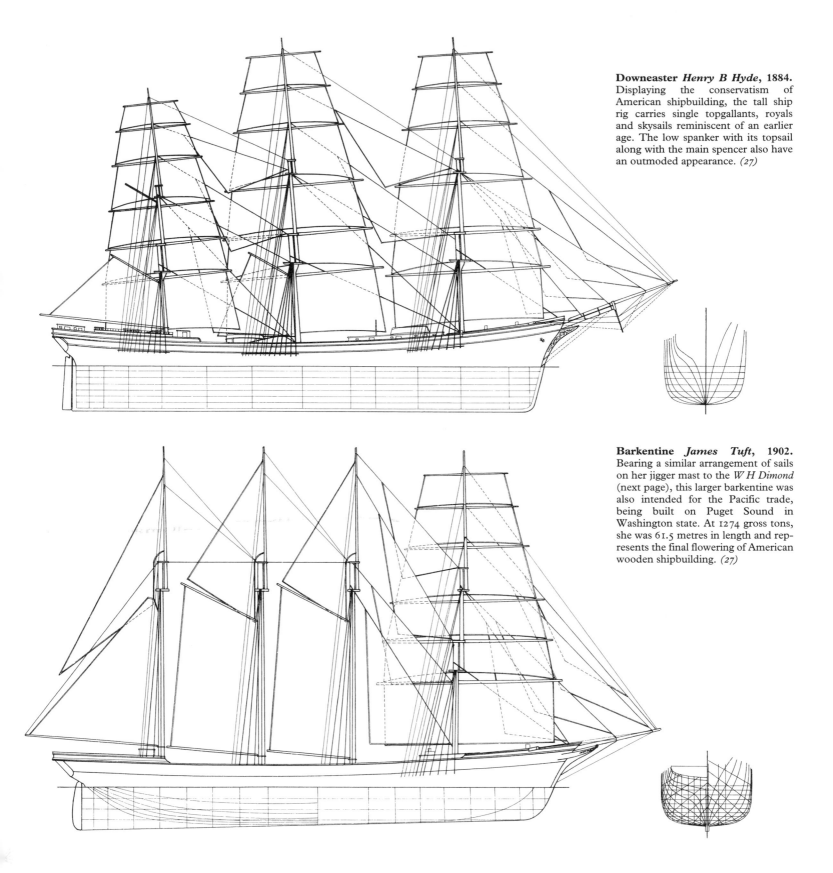

Downeaster *Henry B Hyde*, 1884.
Displaying the conservatism of American shipbuilding, the tall ship rig carries single topgallants, royals and skysails reminiscent of an earlier age. The low spanker with its topsail along with the main spencer also have an outmoded appearance. *(27)*

Barkentine *James Tuft*, 1902.
Bearing a similar arrangement of sails on her jigger mast to the *W H Dimond* (next page), this larger barkentine was also intended for the Pacific trade, being built on Puget Sound in Washington state. At 1274 gross tons, she was 61.5 metres in length and represents the final flowering of American wooden shipbuilding. *(27)*

America's Wooden Workhorses

The United States of America never recovered its place in the vanguard of sailing shipbuilding after the Civil War. The opening of the transcontinental railways was one factor, as was post-war depression and the filling of the market by British-flag ships. Nevertheless, an extensive coastal trade remained to American vessels while owners sought to repenetrate world trade, though largely with steam vessels. The primary material used in American merchant ship construction remained native softwood, while much emphasis was put on the production of very large schooners.

60 50 40 30 20 10 0 ft
1/600
15   10   5   0 m

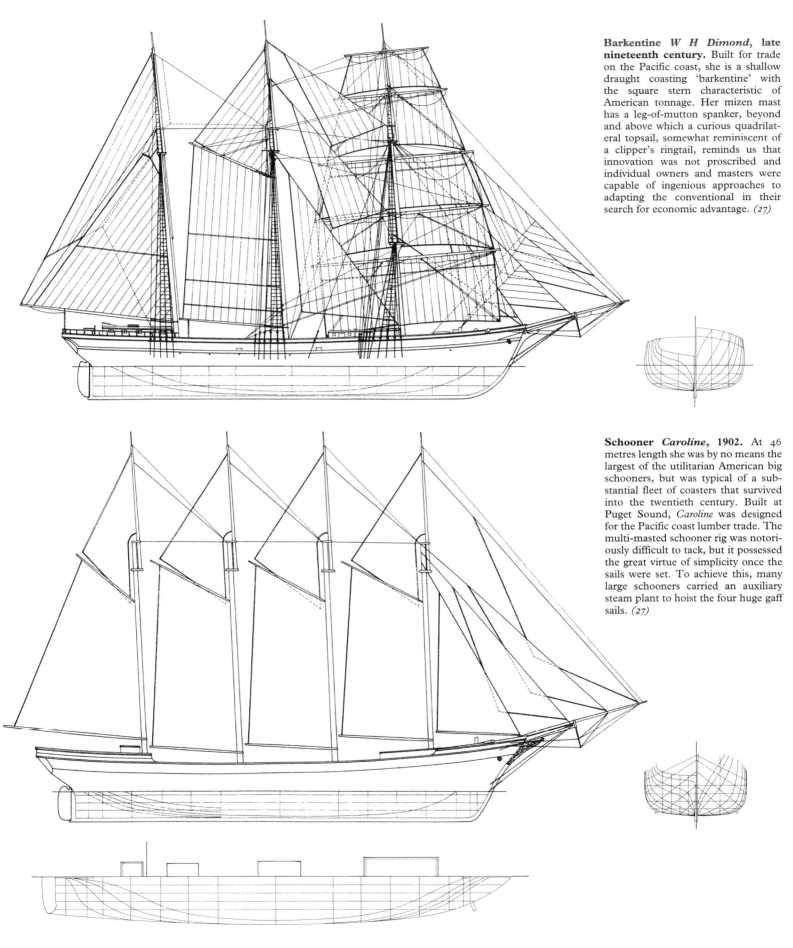

Barkentine *W H Dimond*, late nineteenth century. Built for trade on the Pacific coast, she is a shallow draught coasting 'barkentine' with the square stern characteristic of American tonnage. Her mizen mast has a leg-of-mutton spanker, beyond and above which a curious quadrilateral topsail, somewhat reminiscent of a clipper's ringtail, reminds us that innovation was not proscribed and individual owners and masters were capable of ingenious approaches to adapting the conventional in their search for economic advantage. *(27)*

Schooner *Caroline*, 1902. At 46 metres length she was by no means the largest of the utilitarian American big schooners, but was typical of a substantial fleet of coasters that survived into the twentieth century. Built at Puget Sound, *Caroline* was designed for the Pacific coast lumber trade. The multi-masted schooner rig was notoriously difficult to tack, but it possessed the great virtue of simplicity once the sails were set. To achieve this, many large schooners carried an auxiliary steam plant to hoist the four huge gaff sails. *(27)*

1/400

40   30   20   10   0 ft
10   5   0 m

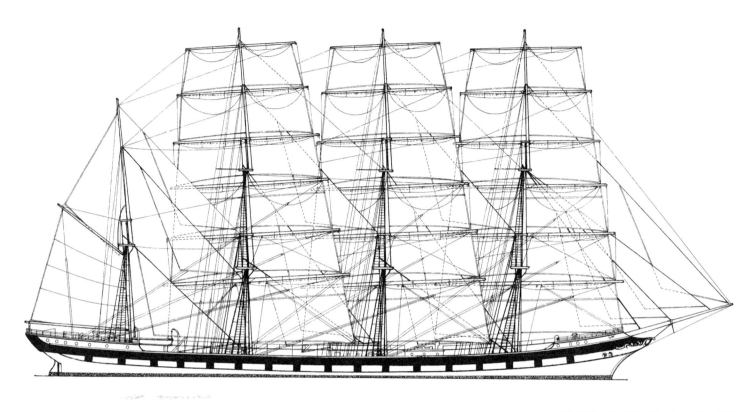

British *Archibald Russell*, 1905.
There was little exceptional in this vessel built by Scott & Co at Greenock; she was a standard steel Clyde 'four-poster' of 89 metres in length with a long and wet waist, painted ports and a plain fiddle under her spike bowsprit. Grossing 2354 tons, she was a maid of all work and, like many a Clyde-built barque, ended her days under the Finnish flag as part of Gustav Erikson's fleet, hauling Australian grain to Europe in the 1930s. She was broken up in 1949. *(112)*

The Last Deep-Water Sail

These last images exemplify the final days of deep-water sail, a period which, unsurprisingly, produced some very large and strong vessels, the masters of which understood the application of meteorological principles and made their passages where the prevailing winds were strong and steady. Although large and seemingly cumbersome, these big carriers were capable of consistent speeds rivalling the passage times of the much smaller clippers of an earlier generation. They bore neither studding sails nor kites and their rigs were wide by comparison with the large American packets of half-a-century earlier. These vessels often carried a steam engine for providing power on deck for sail handling. Brace-winches, devices which enabled the yards to be swung by a minimum of men, were common in all sailing vessels from the late nineteenth century onwards.

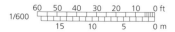

German *Preussen*, 1902. Built at Geestemunde, like all Laeisz's vessels, she was intended for the carriage of Chilean nitrate and thus a double passage of the Horn, the first against the prevailing winds of the Southern Ocean. This tremendous ship – and she *was* the world's only five-masted, full-rigged ship – was 124 metres in length, grossing 5081 tons. With her characteristic double spanker, double topgallants and topsails, royals, courses, staysails and jibs, she set in all forty-seven sails. She met her end in a collision off Dover in the English Channel with a cross-Channel steamer which misjudged her speed. *(147)*

German *R C Rickmers*, 1906. Of similar vintage, this German five-masted barque was built at Bremerhaven and named after her builder, who also owned her and her sisters. She was a very large ship, at 5548 gross tons and 125 metres in length. *(232)*

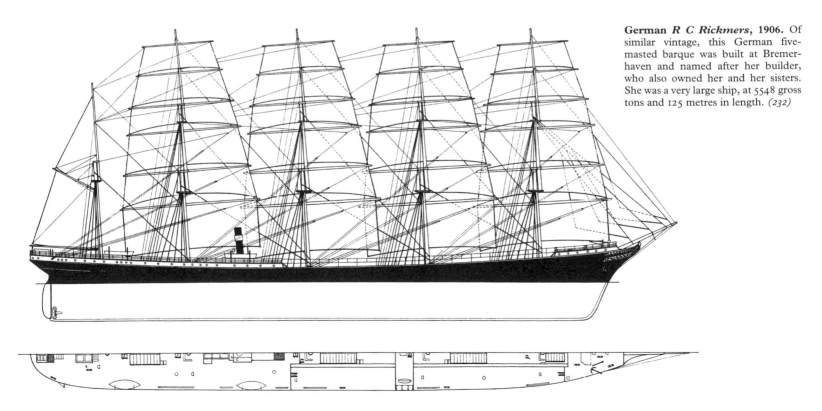

80   60   40   20   0 ft
1/800
20   15   10   5   0 m

French *France II*, 1911. To this vessel built at Bordeaux belongs the honour of being the largest ever sailing ship. She grossed 5633 tons, with a length of 127.5 metres and contained several modern innovations. Her owners, A D Bordes, had two auxiliary engines fitted to her to dispense with the cost of tugs in an age when even the subsidised sailing vessels of France were having trouble earning a living. A large proportion of her hull is parallel, emphasising the importance of maximising capacity, and her bald-headed rig is unglamorously practical. She had power-steering, an electric generator for lighting, pumps and her radio, large water-ballast tanks and stockless anchors. She was intended to make 17 knots but never succeeded, though her speed improved after the removal of her engines. In 1921 she lifted a record cargo of wool and tallow from New Zealand and achieved a passage of 90 days to London, including a day's run of 420 miles, but in 1922 she ran aground on the coast of New Caledonia and became a total loss. *(232)*

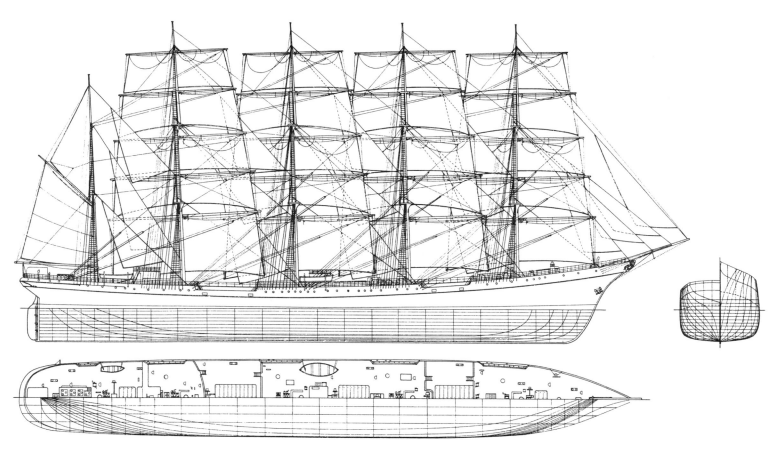

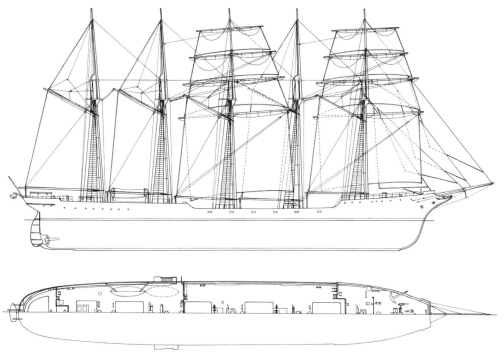

German *Carl Vinnen*, 1921. One of the last companies to own sailing ships was F A Vinnen, of Bremen, Germany. In the search for economic performance after the First World War, the Vinnens ordered a number of similar ships from Krupps. This vessel was five-masted and is variously regarded as a 'two-topsail schooner' or a form of 'jackass-barque', a rather widely used term for any sail-plan which stepped beyond accepted orthodoxy. Fitted with engines, the Vinnen ships, which grossed 1827 tons on a length of 79.5 metres, did not adopt the stockless anchor. *(208)*

80 60 40 20 0 ft

1/800

20 15 10 5 0 m

The Last Deep-water Sail 217

Local Coastal Sail

THE EXAMPLES in this section draw on historical tradition and review the final flowering of sail as it existed – and, in a few places, still exists – in coastal waters. Of course, in a historical perspective all sail was once coastal, but as we have seen, once ships were capable of venturing between continents, then size and speed governed their economic life. Coastal commerce, both arterial and distributive, was taken up by smaller vessels, often the lineal descendants of the precursors of sea-going prototypes. Coastal sail was important during the pre-railway age as being the only means to shift bulky commodities, and small ports, from whence distribution could take place, proliferated. In areas where railway development was impossible, such as archipelagos as diverse as the West Indies and the

Baltic, sailing coasters proved astonishingly durable, for their overheads were minimal compared with steam-propelled coasting vessels. Unlike the deep-sea ship which sought the great global winds to propel her on her long passages, the coaster must needs work in any direction, sometimes helped and sometimes hampered by tide, and avoiding the multitude of navigational hazards strewn in her way. These factors, and the fact that to make profits, coasters required to be manned by small crews, ensured they employed efficient and adaptable sail plans, most often fore-and-aft and based upon the schooner. It is therefore with the schooner of North America that we begin a review of the coasting sailing ship in the last two centuries.

St Ann, about 1730. The earliest identifiable schooner from Colonial North America is the *St Ann* of about 1736, the date that she was in England and her lines were taken off at Portsmouth. She was 17.7 metres in length and was only 36.5 tons burthen. *(31)*

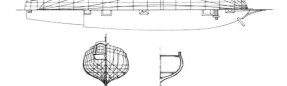

North American Colonial Schooners

The demands of trade and war in eighteenth century Colonial North America required a handy type of vessel, capable of coastal passages which might require a voyage to the West Indies, fast enough to outrun French or Spanish privateers, large enough to carry a cargo, yet able to enter and leave the relatively small, shallow ports of New England. She must, at least for general use, be manageable by a small, economical crew. Such a vessel was the schooner, the origins of the which have been

touched on earlier, as have the inherent versatility of the type, for she could become a privateer herself, slaver, cruising pilot vessel, revenue cruiser, or naval craft.

Not concerned with carrying bulk cargoes, colonial trade was usually confined to high-value commodities for which fast passages were often necessary and the rig soon migrated for the same purpose, copies of fast North American schooners being built for the Royal Navy.

30   20   10   0 ft
1/300
8   4   0 m

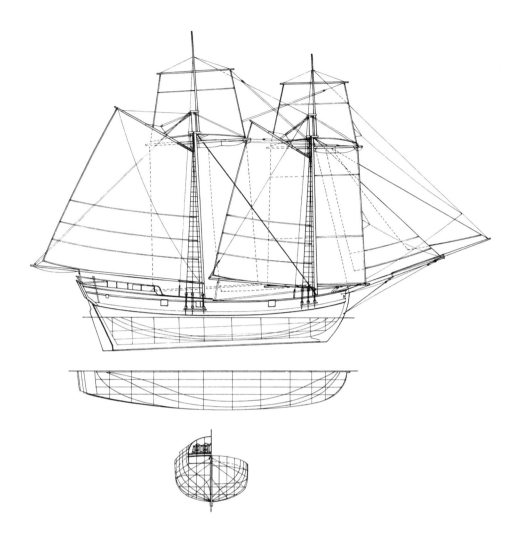

Chaleur, 1764. Royal Naval interest in the Colonial schooner began with the purchase of six of them in 1764 by the naval commander on the North America station, largely to enforce the unpopular revenue duties introduced by the home government. The largest of these was the newly-built *Chaleur*, a plain vessel with the bewildering array of square sails carried for light weather work. Although her lines show a tendency to fine her run and slightly hollow her entrance, she retains the 'apple-bow' then considered necessary to sea-kindliness. She measured 121 tons burthen, bore six guns and would have had a complement of about 30 men. *(97)*

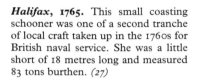
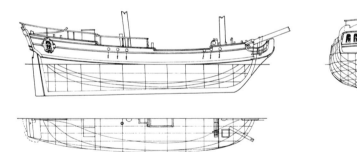

Halifax, 1765. This small coasting schooner was one of a second tranche of local craft taken up in the 1760s for British naval service. She was a little short of 18 metres long and measured 83 tons burthen. *(27)*

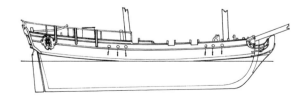

Halifax, as altered for Royal Navy service, 1768. When acquired by the British navy the schooner had a few low gunport-sills cut in the planksheer and swivel stocks added along the quarterdeck. *Halifax* was lost off Machias in 1775. *(27)*

30   20   10   0 ft
1/300
8   4   0 m

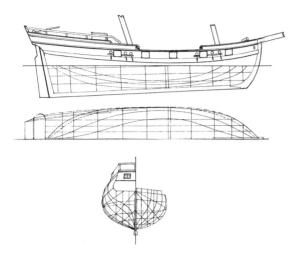

Marblehead, 1767. Built at New York, this schooner was one of those surveyed by the Royal Navy with a view to purchase for naval service. She is of a sharper model than the others taken up at the same time, and might be seen as a prototype of the later 'Baltimore clipper' model. *(27)*

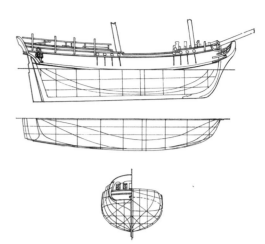

Sultana, 1768. The smallest Colonial schooner to see naval service was the 50-ton *Sultana*. Built at Boston by Benjamin Hallowell a year before being taken into the Royal Navy in 1768, she was 15.5 metres in length and armed with eight small swivel-guns. Her two topmasts set square sails. *(27)*

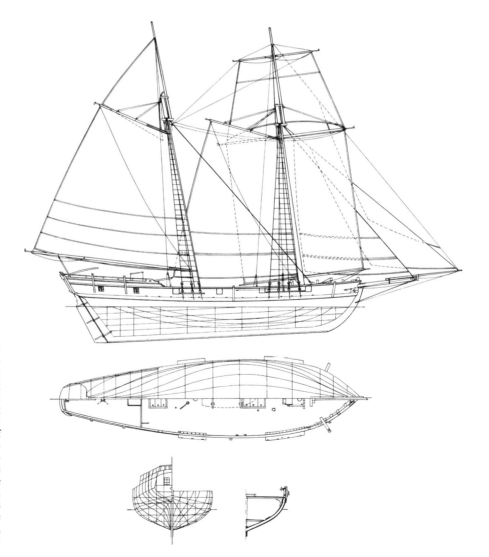

Berbice, 1780. The greater inclination of the keel, long fine run, hollow entrance and sharp deadrise of the *Berbice* provide an immediate contrast with the *Chaleur*. The raked masts and the lack of steeving in the bowsprit convey an air of urgency. The obvious desire for speed the original owners of this vessel required, suggest she was built for the slave trade, or as a privateer. Of identical tonnage to the *Chaleur* at 121 tons burthen, *Berbice* was 22 metres in length. Purchased into the Royal Navy in 1780, she was armed with six 3-pounder carriage guns and two 12-pounder carronades, eight swivels and six musketoons. *(31)*

1/300   30   20   10   0 ft

8   4   0 m

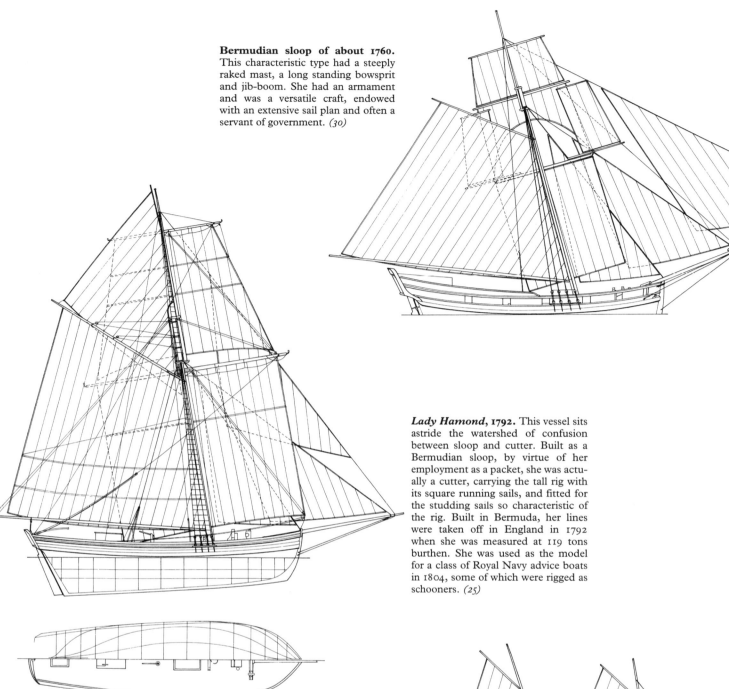

Bermudian sloop of about 1760.
This characteristic type had a steeply raked mast, a long standing bowsprit and jib-boom. She had an armament and was a versatile craft, endowed with an extensive sail plan and often a servant of government. *(30)*

Lady Hamond, **1792.** This vessel sits astride the watershed of confusion between sloop and cutter. Built as a Bermudian sloop, by virtue of her employment as a packet, she was actually a cutter, carrying the tall rig with its square running sails, and fitted for the studding sails so characteristic of the rig. Built in Bermuda, her lines were taken off in England in 1792 when she was measured at 119 tons burthen. She was used as the model for a class of Royal Navy advice boats in 1804, some of which were rigged as schooners. *(25)*

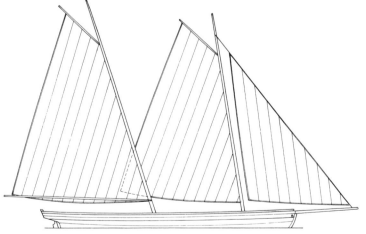

Fast-Sailing West Indies Craft

Similar conditions to the American coast pertained in the West Indies, where trade was particularly exposed to the depredation of privateers during times of war, producing a requirement for fast ships. But the privateers themselves were often built in the area, as were some slavers, while small naval cruisers, dispatch vessels and packets were all built for speed. Bermuda, a major source of small fast vessels for the Royal Navy, usually built in pencil cedar.

Bermudian 'ballahou' schooner, 1806. This two-masted type was a native, fair-weather craft, built cheaply for inter-island trade. She adopted the twin, narrow gaffed sail which emanated from The Netherlands, and was used in Britain and North America. *(30)*

30   20   10   0 ft

1/300

8   4   0 m

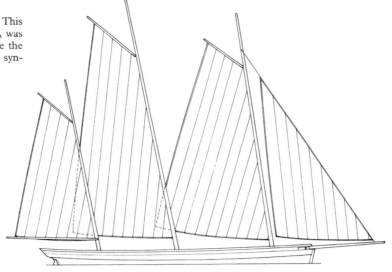

Bermudian gaff-schooner. This type, common between 1820-50, was extremely fast and in due course the adjective 'Bermudian' became synonymous with swiftness. *(30)*

Bermudian schooner. This variation of the rig, in service contemporaneously, outsailed the gaff version when heading to windward and ensured that this Bermudian schooner of the same period, between 1820 and 1850, became the eponymous dam of the rig we today call 'Bermudan'. *(30)*

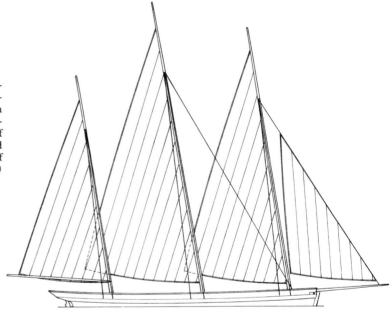

Bahamian fruit schooner of about 1860. The shallow form of the *Sarah E Douglas* shows a stable hull which could lift a modest cargo and convey it to a port for export. *(30)*

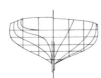

30   20   10   0 ft
1/300 ⊢─────────────────────┤
8   4   0 m

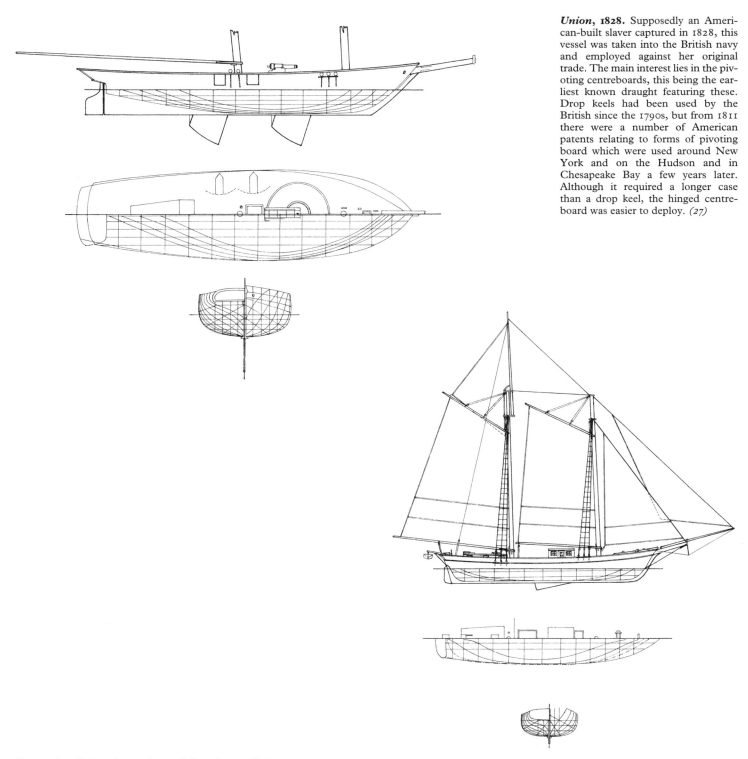

Union, **1828.** Supposedly an American-built slaver captured in 1828, this vessel was taken into the British navy and employed against her original trade. The main interest lies in the pivoting centreboards, this being the earliest known draught featuring these. Drop keels had been used by the British since the 1790s, but from 1811 there were a number of American patents relating to forms of pivoting board which were used around New York and on the Hudson and in Chesapeake Bay a few years later. Although it required a longer case than a drop keel, the hinged centreboard was easier to deploy. *(27)*

The Growth of the American Merchant Schooner

Until the end of commercial sail the schooner was the backbone of the United States' coasting fleet, a fact echoed in Canada. Even in their yachts, the Americans favoured the schooner, though they derived inspiration more from the superb fishing schooners than their more prosaic cousins in the coasting trade. Somewhat ugly in appearance, the simple wooden schooner was little more than a functional craft and a developmental dead-end, evolutionary only in terms of ever-increasing size.

Challenge, **1852.** The shallow coastal lagoons, bayous and bays of the east coast of the United States of America provided a natural highway for the carriage of cargoes and to accomplish this schooners such as this were built.

Shoal-draughted, the tall rig is supported by a beamy hull and this in turn is fitted with sliding centreboards to minimise leeway. Such coasters retained the implicit reference to speed in being called clipper-schooners. *(27)*

30   20   10   0 ft
1/300
8   4   0 m

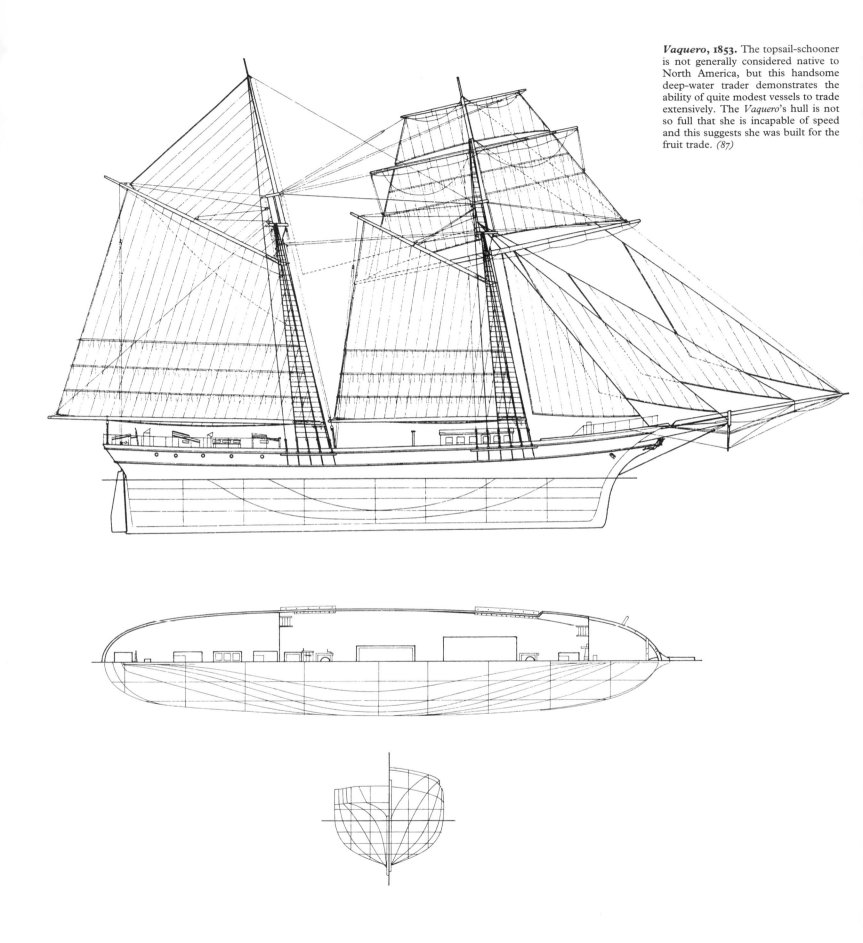

Vaquero, **1853.** The topsail-schooner is not generally considered native to North America, but this handsome deep-water trader demonstrates the ability of quite modest vessels to trade extensively. The *Vaquero*'s hull is not so full that she is incapable of speed and this suggests she was built for the fruit trade. *(87)*

1/200

20   10   0 ft

6   4   2   0 m

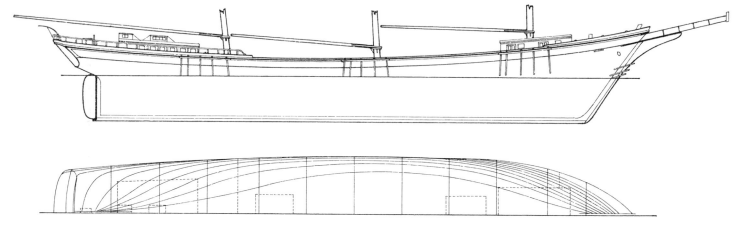

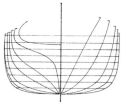

Maine-built coasting schooner.
Plain and square-sectioned, this wooden schooner of the late nineteenth century is typical of numerous vessels plying their trade on the eastern seaboard. Simple in form, her plain fiddle-head adds a touch of elegance to an otherwise utilitarian vessel. (27)

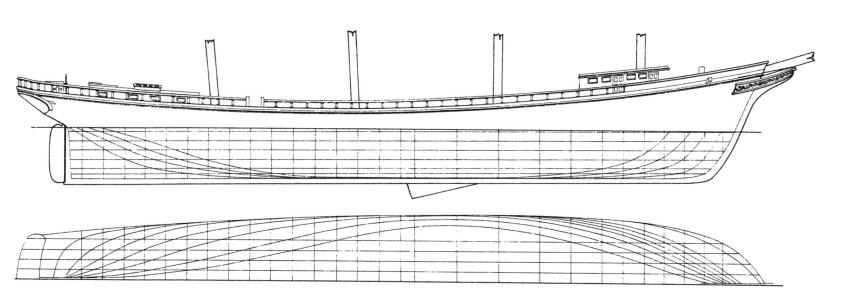

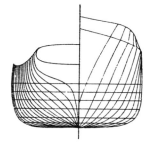

***Howard Smith*, 1888.** This shoal-draughted schooner has a centreboard to minimise leeway. The ever-increasing length of these wooden schooners, often built for the carriage of lumber, made for some very narrow hulls. With raised poop and forecastle, the extent of the low main decks could make them wet when caught offshore in dirty weather. Aesthetically, they contrast badly when set against the lovely fishing schooners of New England. Note the return to the full bow form at the weather deck. (27)

1/300 30 20 10 0 ft
       8   4   0 m

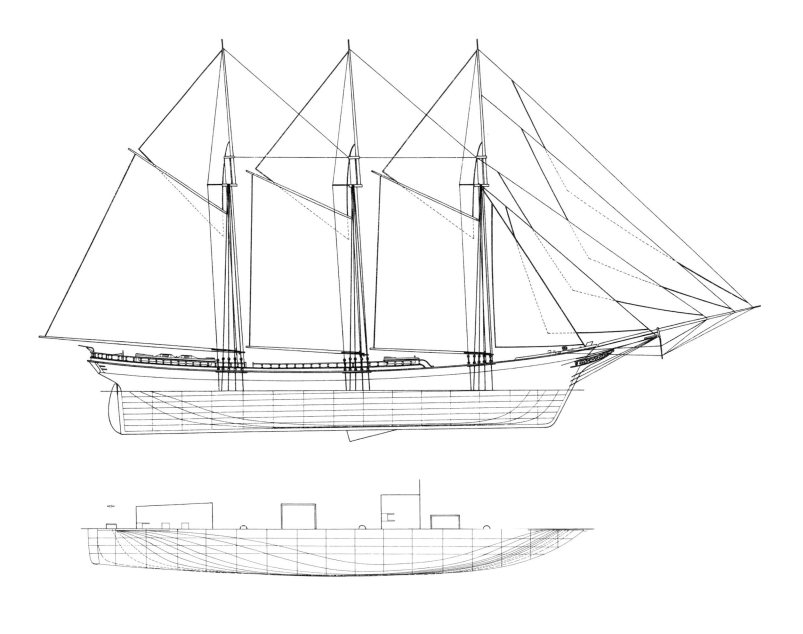

***Marion Sprague*, 1889.** This coasting three-master has a long quarterdeck, suggesting the provision of passenger accommodation. Of shoal-draught, she carries a centreboard and she sets several jibs on her long bowsprit and jib-boom. Note the triatic stay running between the caps of the lower mastheads and requiring especial attention when beating with the gaff topsails set. *(27)*

1/400

40   30   20   10   0 ft

10   5   0 m

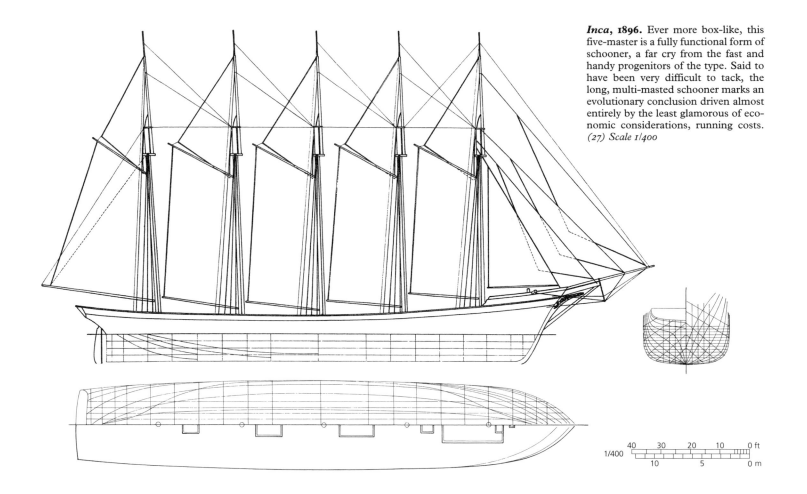

Inca, 1896. Ever more box-like, this five-master is a fully functional form of schooner, a far cry from the fast and handy progenitors of the type. Said to have been very difficult to tack, the long, multi-masted schooner marks an evolutionary conclusion driven almost entirely by the least glamorous of economic considerations, running costs. *(27) Scale 1/400*

40 30 20 10 0 ft
1/400
10   5   0 m

Thomas W Lawson, 1902. One of the largest sailing ships ever built, this seven-masted schooner was launched at Quincy, Massachusetts. Her gross measurement was over 5000 tons and her length 117 metres. Her masts all rose 58.8 metres above her long deck and her huge gaffs were hoisted by means of steam-powered halliard winches fore and aft, so that she needed a crew of only 16 men. Her life, however, was short, for she was lost in bad weather off the Isles of Scilly in 1907. *(147) Scale 1/600*

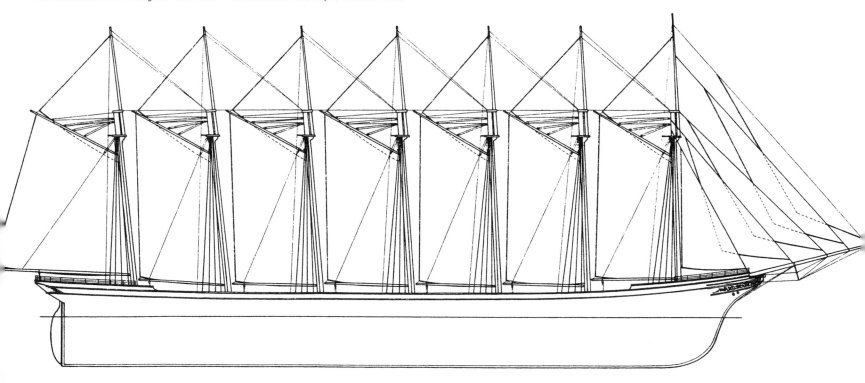

60 50 40 30 20 10 0 ft
1/600
15   10   5   0 m

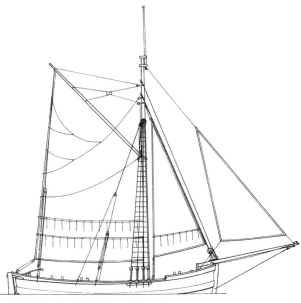

Sailing lighter. The simple sailing lighter was a barge used to literally lighten deep-water vessels of their cargo so that they could move up-stream into shallower water, or for redistributing the cargo to its destination. The rig was simple, a tall vertical and loose-footed mainsail with a stay-sail and jib. Typical of the Thames Estuary, it lingered on into the twenti-eth century in fishing bawleys. *(142)*

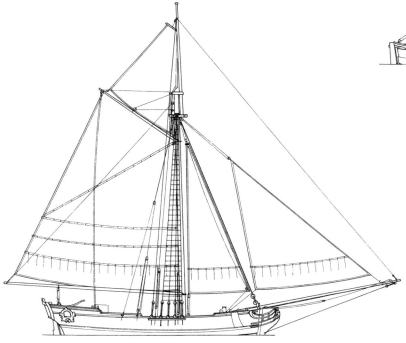

Sloop. Although often fitted with a square topsail, the single-masted 'sloop' not infrequently bore a gaff topsail as is shown here in an example from about 1800. Note the jib is set flying, run out to the end of the bowsprit on an iron traveller *(142)*

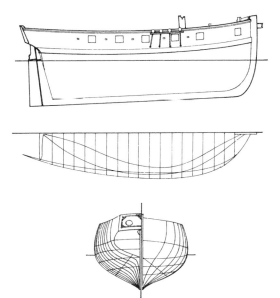

Cutters, Sloops and Hoys – British Single-Masted Types

The narrow but fiercely tidal and often stormy waters of the British home coasts produced some fine ships and fine seamen, but the often tiny ports that ensured the economic survival of coastal sail did not encourage the development of large hulls. Instead British small craft tended to be just that, producing a number of variants on a single mast for a variety of purposes.

English cutter. Where the American fashion extended the fast hull and fitted a second mast, and the French brought the lugger into being, the English persisted in the short-hulled cutter. A deep-draughted hull with an excellent grip on the water, the stoutly built cutter could mount up to four-teen guns and relied for speed on a huge press of canvas. This cutter dates from about 1760. *(34)*

1/300

Bermudian sloop. The Bermudian sloop has been referred to earlier, but the type was copied in English yards both for commercial and naval use, the latter as advice boats. *(30)*

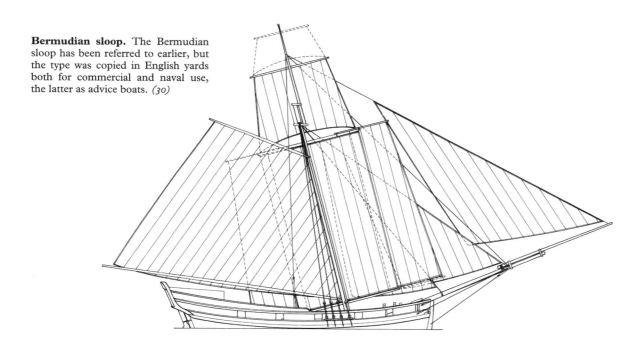

Grain barge. The simplest form of lighter is exemplified here in this eighteenth century grain barge. The hull is shallow but full with a high block co-efficient. *(34)*

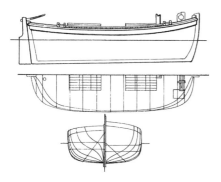

Hoy. Originally similar in function to the lighter, the hoy was often also a small passenger-cargo craft, some of which were fitted for the carriage of water or stores as these craft were used to attend and supply men-of-war anchored or stationed offshore. The afterbody retains vestigial signs of the flute, with its tiny overhanging stern and rounded shape. *(34)*

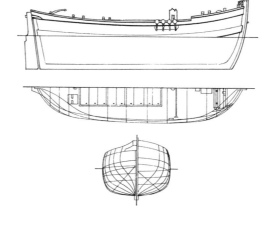

Smack. This eighteenth century smack was a fishing boat much used in the Thames Estuary. By the end of the period, the transom stern had been retained by the bawley, whereas the smack had developed a long, over-hanging counter. Essentially simple, this was a weatherly hull, not unlike the naval cutter. *(34)*

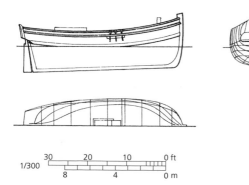

Swim-headed barge. One of the most basic forms of cargo-carrier developed on the Thames for use both in the river and along the coasts of the estuary. Fitted with leeboards and an easily-handled sprit rig, the flat-bottomed barge was intended to pene-trate narrow tidal creeks to load hay or bricks for London's horses and houses in return for outward cargoes of horse manure and garbage. The unrigged hull form can still be seen as a lighter. *(34)*

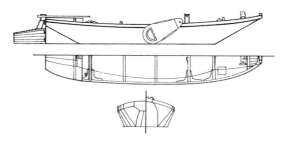

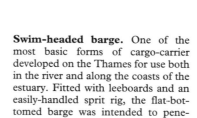

30 20 10 0 ft
1/300
8 4 0 m

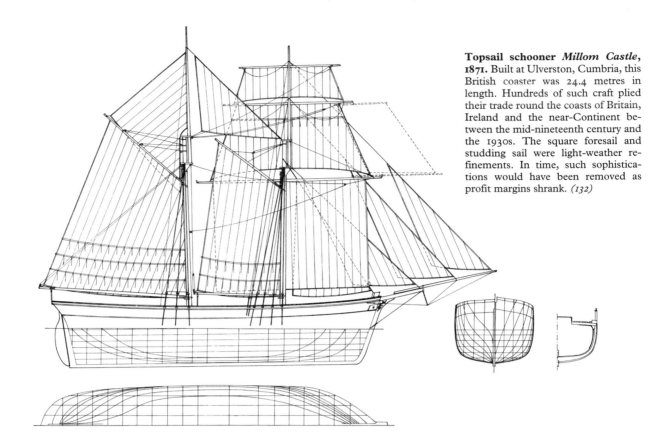

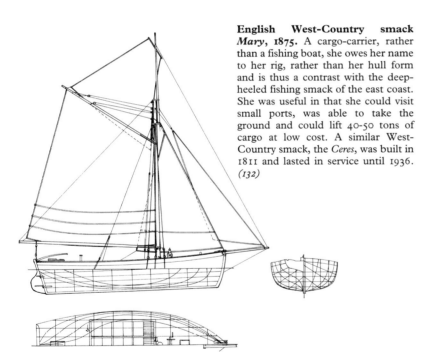

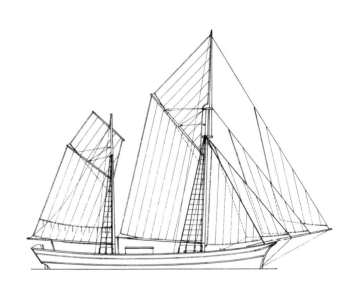

Topsail schooner *Millom Castle*, 1871. Built at Ulverston, Cumbria, this British coaster was 24.4 metres in length. Hundreds of such craft plied their trade round the coasts of Britain, Ireland and the near-Continent between the mid-nineteenth century and the 1930s. The square foresail and studding sail were light-weather refinements. In time, such sophistications would have been removed as profit margins shrank. *(132)*

English West-Country smack *Mary*, 1875. A cargo-carrier, rather than a fishing boat, she owes her name to her rig, rather than her hull form and is thus a contrast with the deep-heeled fishing smack of the east coast. She was useful in that she could visit small ports, was able to take the ground and could lift 40-50 tons of cargo at low cost. A similar West-Country smack, the *Ceres*, was built in 1811 and lasted in service until 1936. *(132)*

The Last British Coastal Traders

Despite Britain's early railway system and relatively good road network, the sailing coaster enjoyed a long twilight, lasting well into the twentieth century. The topsail schooner was a much favoured rig, since it enabled advantage to be taken of the wide variations in wind direction found on the British coast, with the gaff, or even the square-topsail ketch, runners up. These craft were owned and operated from West-Country ports well into the 1930s. The wide expanse of the Thames Estuary and shallower east coast of England was home of the extraordinary spritsail sailing barge which endured after the Second World War.

Coasting ketch, about 1880. Among the last British coasters, the ketch was an alternative to the topsail schooner. This example was some 25 metres in length and of around 100 gross registered tons. Some ketches bore a square topsail on the mainmast. *(27)*

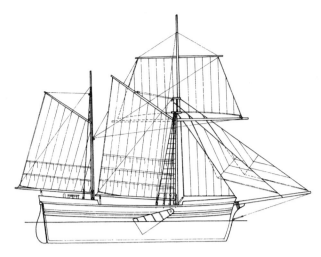

Ketch *Halcyon*, 1903. This British leeboard ketch was built at Hessle on the River Humber. Although she had round bilges, she was effectively a large sailing barge of 26 metres in length and 100 tons gross register. A small forecastle accommodates her crew, while the master (and probably his wife) lived aft. The majority of the hull was given up to cargo stowage, and the maindeck is largely taken up by the hatchway. The staysail is fitted with a boom making it self-tacking, like the main and mizen, the sheet running on a bar known as a horse which was fitted athwart the foredeck. *(207)*

English 'billy boy', about 1880. A sea-going development of the riverine barges of the Humber. As was customary in many British local craft, their barge antecedents tended to encourage the retention of type-names that rejected rig as the means of identifying them. Nevertheless, billy boys were either topsail schooners or ketches with a reefing or steeving bowsprit to allow them to reduce length in port. Square-sided and flat-bottomed, they worked cargoes off beaches, up creeks or in small ports, having a flat sheer and the long hatches common to most barges. *(230)*

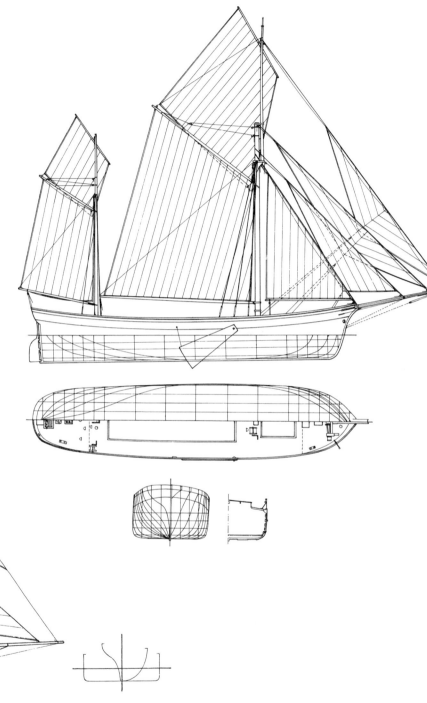

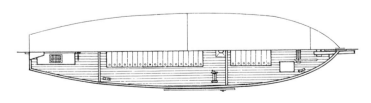

Thames spritsail barge. The Thames or spritsail barge was a remarkable craft, the largest of which grossed over 200 tons, could reel off 12 knots in a breeze and yet required a crew of only two men. A third was shipped just for shooting the bridges of the Thames and Medway, when the whole rig was lowered to the deck. The secret lay in the sprit rig and the control over the huge mainsail exerted by the brails. The standing sprit allowed the topsail to be set over a furled main, particularly useful when manoeuvring in a dock, while the mizen, sheeted to the rudder, guaranteed success when tacking. *(138)*

30 20 10 0 ft
1/300
8 4 0 m

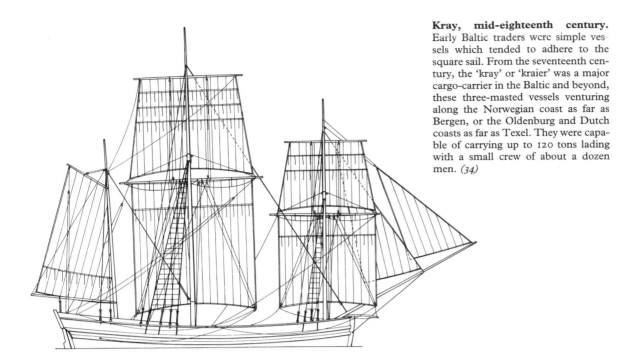

Kray, mid-eighteenth century.
Early Baltic traders were simple vessels which tended to adhere to the square sail. From the seventeenth century, the 'kray' or 'kraier' was a major cargo-carrier in the Baltic and beyond, these three-masted vessels venturing along the Norwegian coast as far as Bergen, or the Oldenburg and Dutch coasts as far as Texel. They were capable of carrying up to 120 tons lading with a small crew of about a dozen men. *(34)*

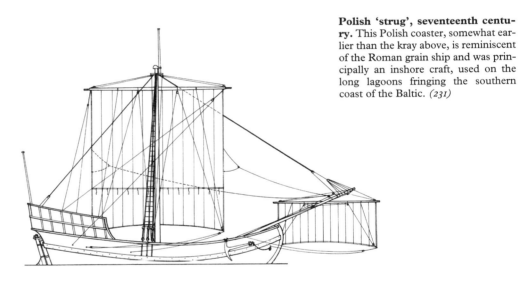

Polish 'strug', seventeenth century. This Polish coaster, somewhat earlier than the kray above, is reminiscent of the Roman grain ship and was principally an inshore craft, used on the long lagoons fringing the southern coast of the Baltic. *(231)*

Coastal Craft of the Northern Seas

The countries of Scandinavia developed highly individual forms of sailing vessels and retained these in a coastal capacity into the twentieth century. Traditions die hard and the relationship of the Norwegians, Swedes, Finns and Danes to the sea remains important. Despite freezing annually, the Baltic proved a stronghold of sail, due mainly to the isolation and insularity of much of its agricultural communities, but the Atlantic coast of Norway, with its fjords, archipelagos and the extensive inshore passages of the Leads, was also an environment nurturing some of the last examples of sailing craft descended from the Norse longship.

As elsewhere the etymology is confusing. The enduring and generic nouns 'schute', 'jacht' and 'galeass' each find several examples in these northern seas.

The name schute continued to refer to a simple, often open or half-decked barge-like craft, usually with only a single mast. Most commonly thought to arise from Dutch origins, the word's root, 'skuta', was actually Norse for a boat pulled by oars. By the eighteenth and nineteenth centuries, however, the term when used in the Baltic refers to a beamy, double-ended hull bearing a three-masted rig.

The 'jacht' or 'jagt' is an even less specific term, though its meaning is now well understood and it is difficult to imagine it once applied to anything other than a sailing vessel build for pleasurable cruising or competitive racing, but it is as well to remember its root derives from hunting, and is therefore applicable to speed. In Scandinavian waters the term referred to small commercial sailing vessels, most noted for their swiftness and used for passenger, livestock and mail transport.

The galeass or galeas has several qualifications, but after about 1750 and until its demise, was broadly a two-masted, flat-bottomed coaster, some 20 metres in length and displacing about 200 tons. Both masts bore gaff sails; the forward mast was usually the taller and in Sweden usually spread two or three yards, the Danish form being all fore-and-aft, as was the Finnish, though her after mast was the taller. Danish galeasses were slightly larger craft, more akin to the large British coasting ketch.

1/300

30 20 10 0 ft

8 4 0 m

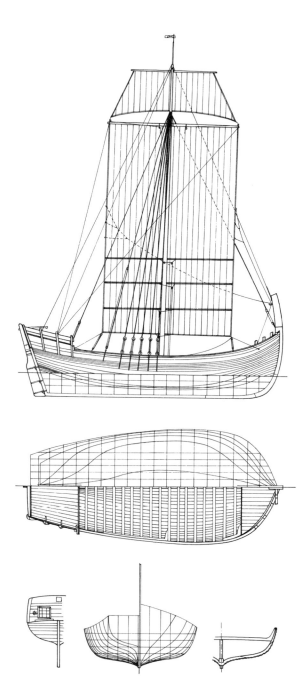

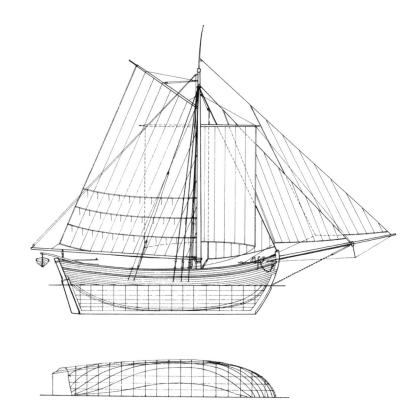

Norwegian Nordlandjagt, 1881.
This primitive Norwegian coastal type had a very full, shallow hull which was decked forward and aft, but open amidships. Suitable for conveying livestock and farm produce through the Leads or the fjords, elements of her Norse ancestry are present in her construction, which was clinker or lapstrake and rose forward to a great stem-post. She set a tall version of the square sail of the longship, often with a topsail above it. (*51*)

Danish jacht (above).
Danish galeass.
The heavy construction of these two Danish coasters, both simple cargo-carriers, marks them a stout, sea-going craft. The jagt, largely for use among the Danish islands of the Baltic, sports a smart cutter rig, with a running square sail. Some jagts carried a fore-and-aft topsail. The Danish galeass was a larger coaster, voyaging abroad, across the North Sea and throughout the Baltic. Many worked well into the present century and a few have been re-rigged as square-rigged brigs and barques for modern charter-work. The rounded transom stern was common in Danish coasters. (*27*)

1/300

30   20   10   0 ft
8   4   0 m

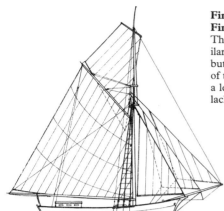

Finnish jagt (left).
Finnish galeass (right).
The Finnish jagt and galeass were similar in function to their Danish cousins but built for the more sheltered waters of the Finnish archipelago. They have a less robust look, bear taller rigs and lack the others' freeboard. *(112)*

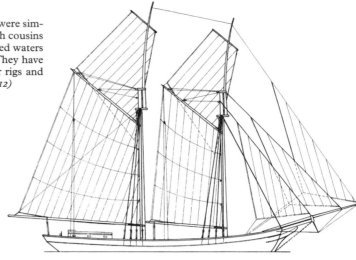

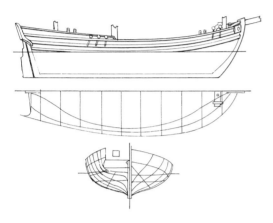

Baltic schutes, mid-eighteenth century. These two versions illustrate the wide variety of small vessels embraced by this generic term. One is clearly a cargo-carrier, the other has accommodation aft and a more sophisticated rig. *(34)*

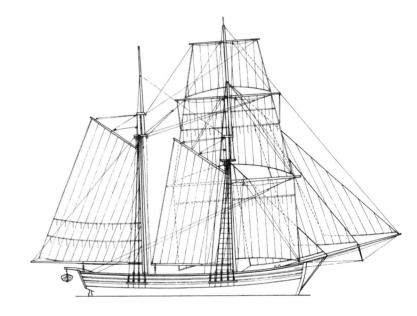

Swedish galeass. In Sweden the galeass was a kind of brigantine, a tall and handsomely-rigged vessel. Like its Danish counterparts, several have survived to be converted to less parochial square-rigs. Such craft could lift 80-100 tons and traded throughout the Baltic, being strongly constructed to withstand the winter icing. *(27)*

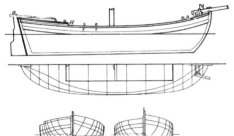

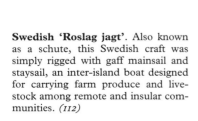

Swedish 'Roslag jagt'. Also known as a schute, this Swedish craft was simply rigged with gaff mainsail and staysail, an inter-island boat designed for carrying farm produce and livestock among remote and insular communities. *(112)*

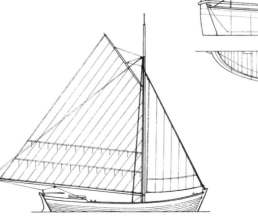

Swedish 'great sumpar'. Effectively a beamy barge for trafficking between the islands and skerries of the Baltic and the Gulf of Bothnia. Note the mitchboard for receiving the heavy boom when the sail was lowered. **NB.** 1/200 scale. *(34)*

1/300
30 20 10 0 ft
8 4 0 m

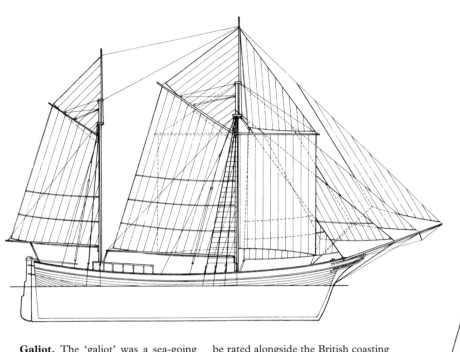

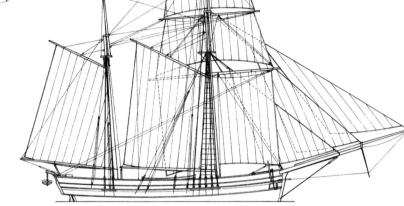

Galeass, 1837. The Pomeranian galeass is close kin to the Swedish version,
Pomerania having been a province of
Sweden and this nineteenth century
example shows the same form of rig as
is borne by its twentieth century
descendant. (204)

Galiot. The 'galiot' was a sea-going craft with two or three masts, many of which ventured much farther than the North Sea, but by the end of the nineteenth century the name applied to a large, ketch-rigged coaster which can be rated alongside the British coasting ketch and the Danish galeass in terms of trade and function. Like these vessels they proved very durable, examples existing into the 1930s. (147)

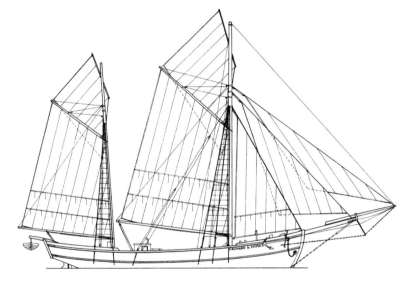

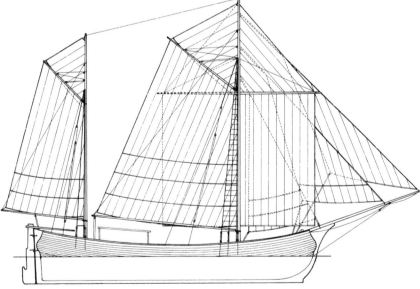

Galeass *Richard & Emma*, 1909. This twentieth-century German craft shows the influence of Danish building, perhaps because she was built in the former Danish provinces of Schleswig-Holstein conquered by the Germans in the 1860s. The name is retained by a sailing coaster, for there was nothing exclusive about its use. (204)

German Coastal Craft

Prior to unification, the individual German states naturally developed their own coastal craft, those of Oldenburg and Hanover able to cope with the North Sea as they plied their trade between Jutland and the Friesians, those of Holstein, Mecklenburg-Schwerin and Prussia being related to their neighbours across the Baltic.

Kuff. The 'kuff', or 'koff' was a Dutch or German coaster with two masts, usually basically a ketch. She bore the shallow, broad characteristics of Dutch origin, mainly owing to her trading area in the rivers Elbe, Weser, Ems and Jade, along the Friesian coast, and into the Zuider Zee. With sharply rising ends, the kuff had a good reputation for seakeeping and did not generally carry leeboards. Of anything between 50 and 90 tons burthen, the square topsails carried in the eighteenth century were gradually replaced by gaff topsails in the nineteenth, though a large squaresail was retained for running, as is seen here. They were gradually superseded by galiots during the second half of the nineteenth century, the last being built on the Weser in 1895. (147)

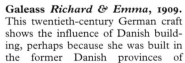

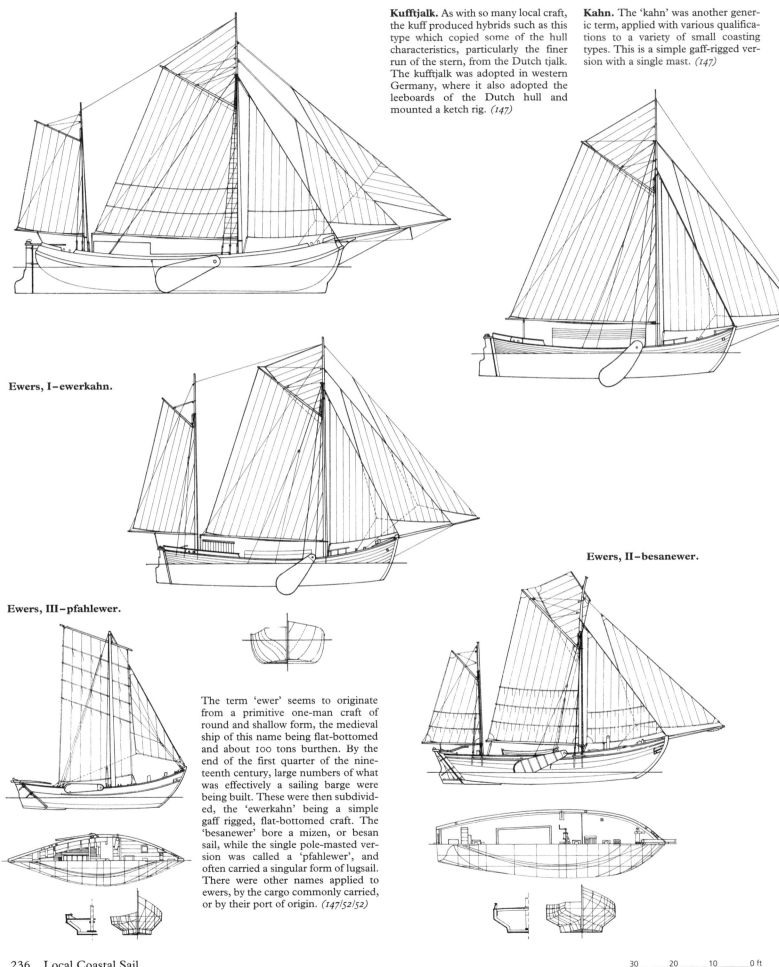

Kufftjalk. As with so many local craft, the kuff produced hybrids such as this type which copied some of the hull characteristics, particularly the finer run of the stern, from the Dutch tjalk. The kufftjalk was adopted in western Germany, where it also adopted the leeboards of the Dutch hull and mounted a ketch rig. *(147)*

Kahn. The 'kahn' was another generic term, applied with various qualifications to a variety of small coasting types. This is a simple gaff-rigged version with a single mast. *(147)*

Ewers, I–ewerkahn.

Ewers, II–besanewer.

Ewers, III–pfahlewer.

The term 'ewer' seems to originate from a primitive one-man craft of round and shallow form, the medieval ship of this name being flat-bottomed and about 100 tons burthen. By the end of the first quarter of the nineteenth century, large numbers of what was effectively a sailing barge were being built. These were then subdivided, the 'ewerkahn' being a simple gaff rigged, flat-bottomed craft. The 'besanewer' bore a mizen, or besan sail, while the single pole-masted version was called a 'pfahlewer', and often carried a singular form of lugsail. There were other names applied to ewers, by the cargo commonly carried, or by their port of origin. *(147/52/52)*

1/300   30   20   10   0 ft
         8   4   0 m

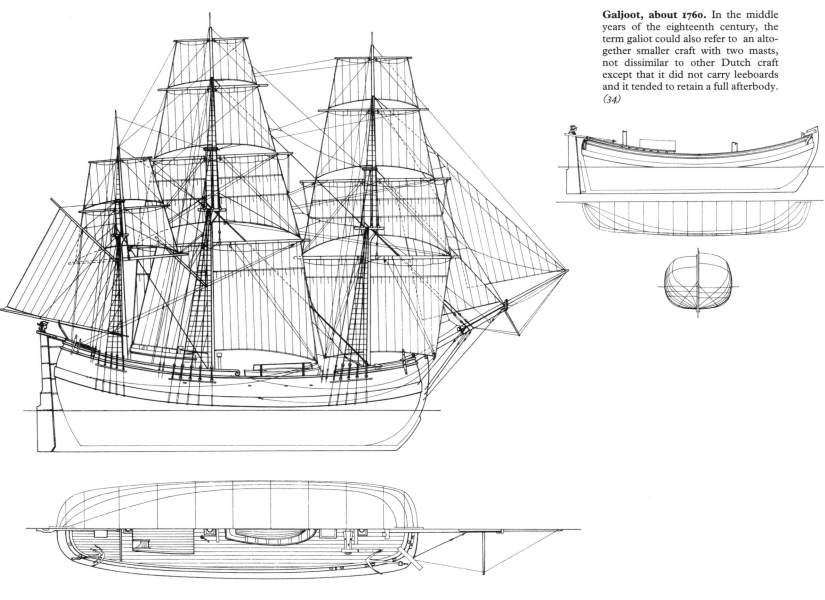

Galjoot, about 1760. In the middle years of the eighteenth century, the term galiot could also refer to an altogether smaller craft with two masts, not dissimilar to other Dutch craft except that it did not carry leeboards and it tended to retain a full afterbody. *(34)*

Galjoot, 1878. The Dutch galiot, or 'galjoot' had been a comparatively substantial craft in the eighteenth century and in The Netherlands as late as the 1870s the noun could apply to a sizeable craft of 200 or so tons. The hull form remained very rounded with rising ends and the stern more so than the bow. The square sails are relatively small in an endeavour to keep crew size down. Note the long doublings of the mast. *(170)*

Tjalk-rigged galjoot, about 1760. On occasions when such a hull bore leeboards it seems to have retained its title to being a galiot, but was referred to as being tjalk-rigged. *(34)*

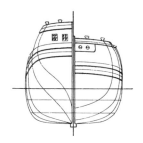

Dutch Coastal Ships

To the Dutch must go the laurels for bequeathing to history the most complex variety of rigs and hull-forms. The numerous types, with their names and their function, spread to their trading partners, so 'Dutch' types migrated along the Friesian Islands into Germany and beyond, into the Baltic. This selection is thus only representative of the craft existing in the eighteenth and nineteenth centuries.

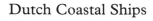

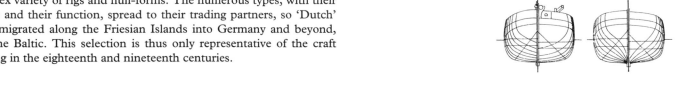

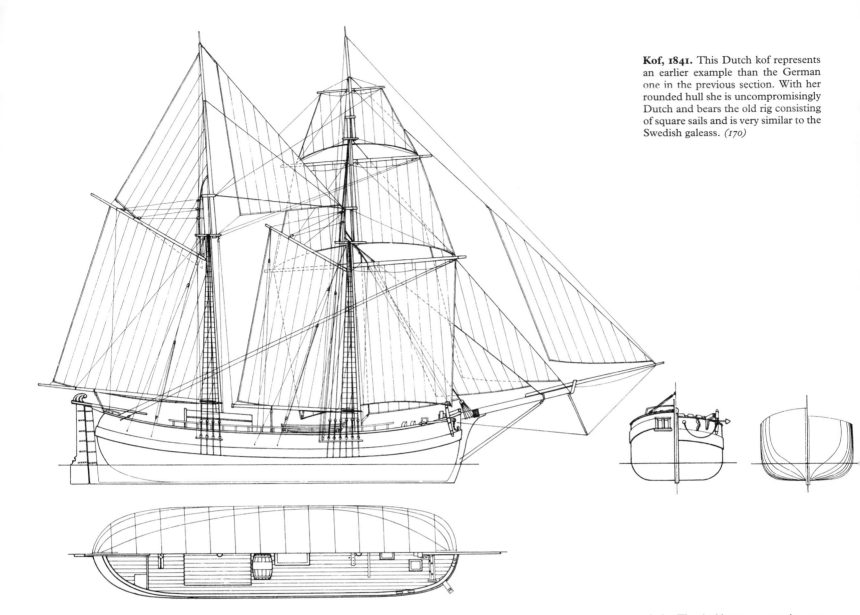

Kof, 1841. This Dutch kof represents an earlier example than the German one in the previous section. With her rounded hull she is uncompromisingly Dutch and bears the old rig consisting of square sails and is very similar to the Swedish galeass. *(170)*

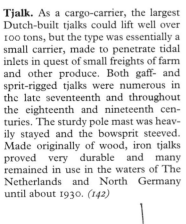

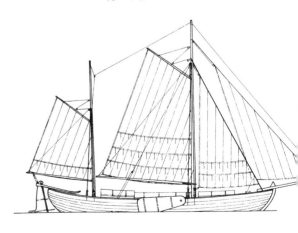

Aak. The 'aak' was a generic term referring to a riverine or coastal sailing barge built in North Germany, The Netherlands and Belgium. The term was widely used, prefixed by a local port name, or the river upon which the aak commonly traded. Aaks existed from Medieval times until the first years of the twentieth century and were ketch-rigged. Although steel aaks were built, this example represents a wooden example of the final form of the type. *(27)*

Tjalk. As a cargo-carrier, the largest Dutch-built tjalks could lift well over 100 tons, but the type was essentially a small carrier, made to penetrate tidal inlets in quest of small freights of farm and other produce. Both gaff- and sprit-rigged tjalks were numerous in the late seventeenth and throughout the eighteenth and nineteenth centuries. The sturdy pole mast was heavily stayed and the bowsprit steeved. Made originally of wood, iron tjalks proved very durable and many remained in use in the waters of The Netherlands and North Germany until about 1930. *(142)*

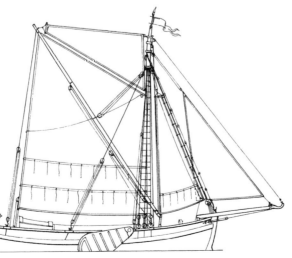

1/300   30   20   10   0 ft
        8   4   0 m

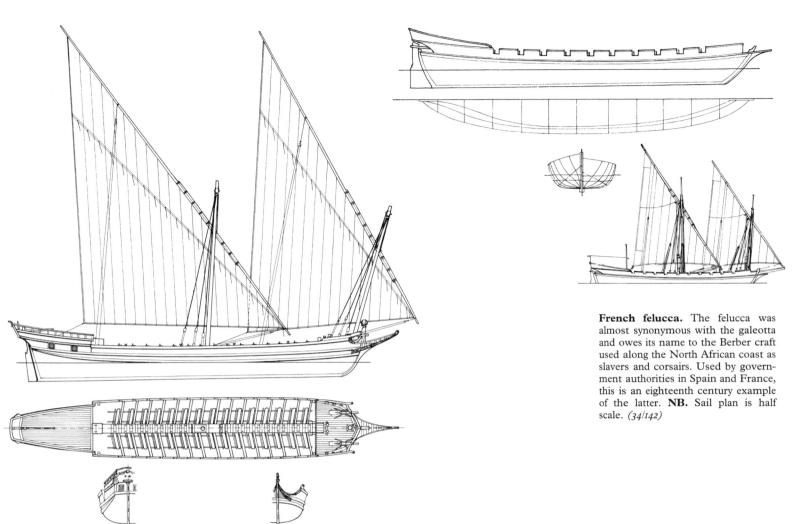

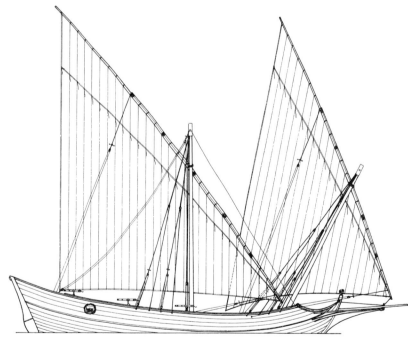

French felucca. The felucca was almost synonymous with the galeotta and owes its name to the Berber craft used along the North African coast as slavers and corsairs. Used by government authorities in Spain and France, this is an eighteenth century example of the latter. **NB.** Sail plan is half scale. *(34/142)*

Galeotta, eighteenth century. The fast, but relatively small galeotta with its twenty or so one-man oars, was suitable as a fast merchantman capable of conveying passengers. It was pulled by freemen, apprentices or bondsmen, and bore a defensive armament. Such craft were also operated by lawless elements along the Dalmatian coast and used to prey upon legitimate traders. *(127)*

Mediterranean Sailing Craft

Arab influence persisted long after the so-called Moors had been driven out of Spain, not least in the design of coastal craft, where it lingered long after the caravel and its successors had passed into history. Prime among these craft was the 'felucca', a noun altering its meaning with time. Originally a single-masted, oared sailing vessel, the lateen-rigged felucca began life as a ship of the Barbary coast, growing larger and, like the chebec, reaching respectability when adopted by the Spanish navy. The felucca had its equivalents in France and Italy, where they were called felouques and felucas. The 'tartane' also occurs in the vocabulary of these three languages as both coastal cargo-carrier and fishing vessel. Early tartanes were large enough to be used as horse transports and their hulls were full. Like the felucca they retained the lateen rig.

The evolution of the small sailing ship therefore retains many characteristics of the lateen, but also incorporated the square sail and some combinations have an exotic appearance seemingly at odds with the fact that they have been sailed by Europeans for centuries. Much of this is because of the persistent influence of the galley, both in its sail plan, but also its long hull form.

French tartane, about 1600. Like so many terms used in this story, the noun 'tartane' originally meant a small ship. The term is generic and was widely used, but the tartane was essentially a cargo-carrying coaster and fishing vessel. This French example dating from about 1600, carries a defensive armament of swivels and a pair of carriage guns. *(147)*

30   20   10   0 ft
1/300
8   4   0 m

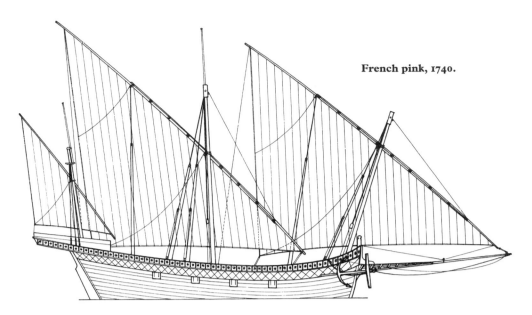

French pink, 1740.

Not to be confused with the north-European pink-built merchant ships of af Chapman's categorisation, the Mediterranean pink, pinque or pinke, was a contemporary of the caravel and is, in some ways, very similar. It outlasted the caravel, retaining its purpose as a 300-ton coasting vessel until the end of the nineteenth century, though this French example dates from 1740. Like the caravel, however, the pinke could convert its lateen rig to square sails when on a long passage, the lateen yards being lashed on deck. These latter examples are of Genoese vessels. *(152/61/61)*

Genoese lateen pink, about 1800.

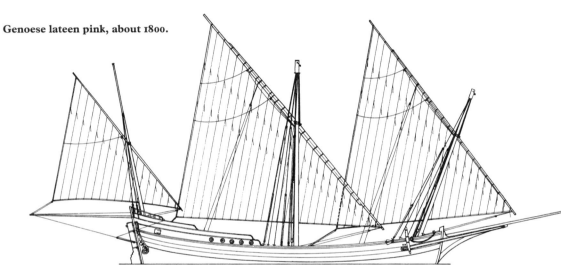

Genoese square-rigged pink, about 1800.

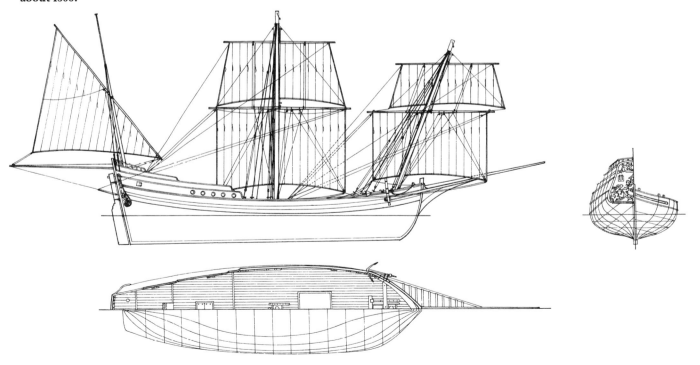

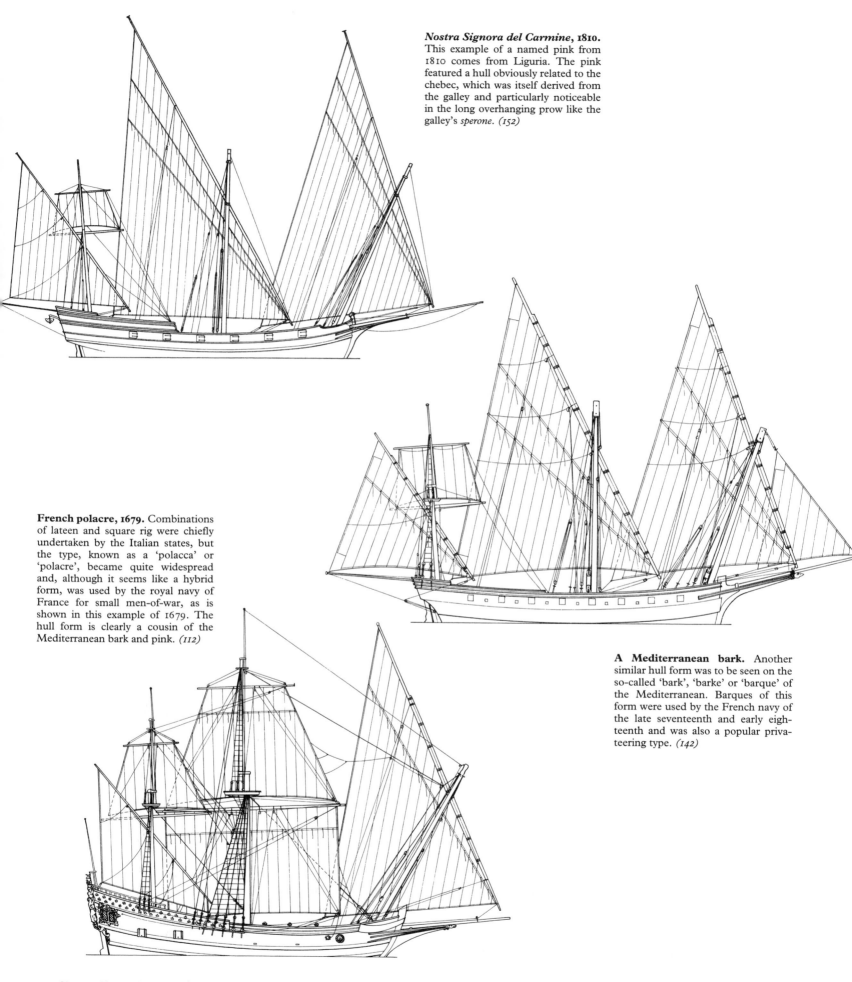

Nostra Signora del Carmine, 1810.
This example of a named pink from 1810 comes from Liguria. The pink featured a hull obviously related to the chebec, which was itself derived from the galley and particularly noticeable in the long overhanging prow like the galley's *sperone*. (152)

French polacre, 1679. Combinations of lateen and square rig were chiefly undertaken by the Italian states, but the type, known as a 'polacca' or 'polacre', became quite widespread and, although it seems like a hybrid form, was used by the royal navy of France for small men-of-war, as is shown in this example of 1679. The hull form is clearly a cousin of the Mediterranean bark and pink. (112)

A Mediterranean bark. Another similar hull form was to be seen on the so-called 'bark', 'barke' or 'barque' of the Mediterranean. Barques of this form were used by the French navy of the late seventeenth and early eighteenth and was also a popular privateering type. (142)

30 20 10 0 ft
1/300
8 4 0 m

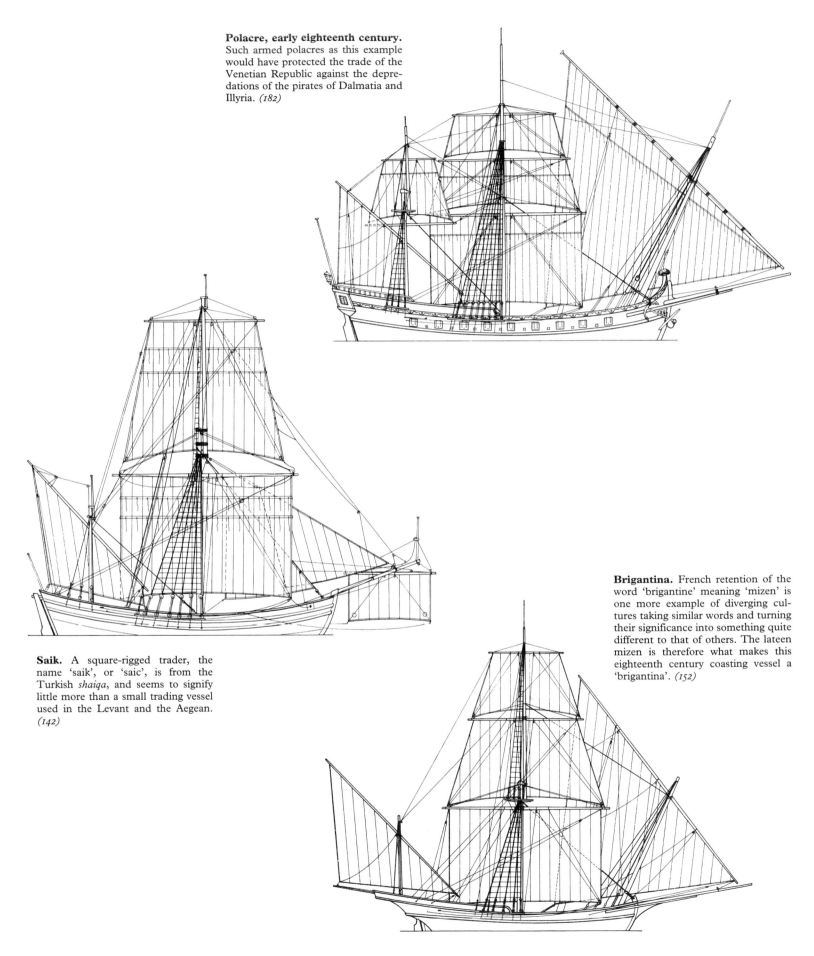

Polacre, early eighteenth century.
Such armed polacres as this example
would have protected the trade of the
Venetian Republic against the depre-
dations of the pirates of Dalmatia and
Illyria. *(182)*

Saik. A square-rigged trader, the
name 'saik', or 'saic', is from the
Turkish *shaiqa*, and seems to signify
little more than a small trading vessel
used in the Levant and the Aegean.
(142)

Brigantina. French retention of the
word 'brigantine' meaning 'mizen' is
one more example of diverging cultures taking similar words and turning
their significance into something quite
different to that of others. The lateen
mizen is therefore what makes this
eighteenth century coasting vessel a
'brigantina'. *(152)*

1/300

30   20   10   0 ft

8   4   0 m

French Mediterranean brig (right), 1762 .
French Mediterranean brigantine, 1762.
The ethnic differences in a country like France, with three distinctive shipbuild-
ing traditions on the Channel, Atlantic and Mediterranean coasts, produced
hybrids as the country expanded as a maritime power in the eighteenth century.
As a result this brig and brigantine of 1762, essentially northern rigs, have sharply
raked mainmasts and their foremasts are stepped well forward, both reflecting
Mediterranean practice. (130)

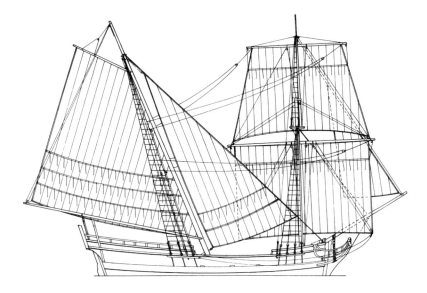

**Mediterranean schooner, about
1910.** As in northern Europe, the small
sailing vessel found it possible to turn
in economic returns for its owner
in the Mediterranean and elegant
schooners like this could be seen in
most harbours in the western basin up
until 1939, and even later on the coast
of the Levant. (228)

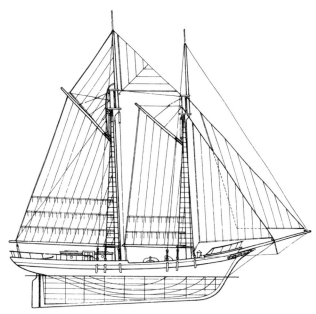

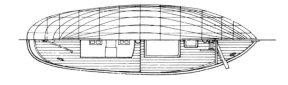

1/300 30 20 10 0 ft
        8   4   0 m

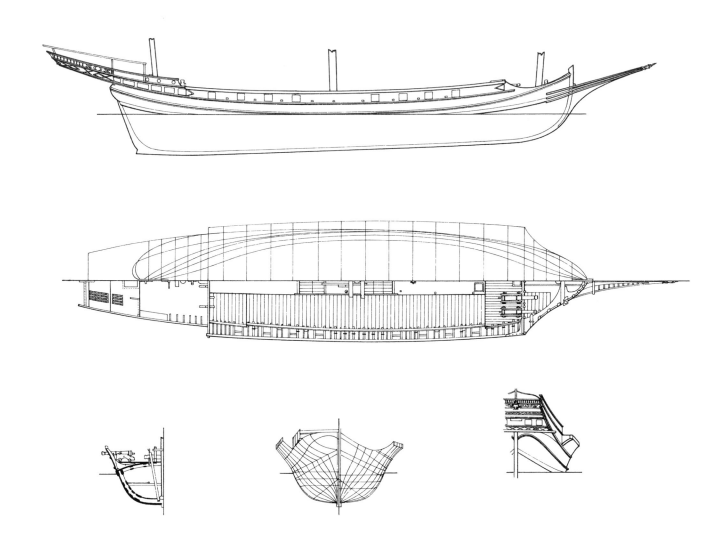

Algerine chebec. Chebecs like this, often generically described as 'Algerine', were favoured by the corsairs of all the Barbary states in the eighteenth and early nineteenth century. The galley ancestry is most clearly seen in this example's outrigger and the powerful forward-firing armament. *(34)*

The Chebec

Akin, perhaps, to the North American schooner in her versatility of application and derivatives, the chebec's name comes, as do so many such nouns, from a root meaning simply 'small ship'. In this case the word is Arabic and it has been rendered into several European languages, appearing in English in three forms, 'chebec', 'xebec' and 'zebec'. A three-masted craft much used by the rapacious corsairs of the Barbary coasts, the craft was copied or captured and used in the navies of France and Spain, the Royal Navy purchasing prize chebecs taken from the enemy. Some chebecs were quite large, mounting up to 40 guns and being ship-rigged when they were classed as 'chebec-frigates'.

But the chebec was also a cargo vessel and, with sizes up to 40 metres, its versatility is not surprising. The chebec was characterised by being fitted out with oars and oar-benches, and she is a logical extension of the galley and galleasse, though her great reputation was founded upon her qualities as a sailing vessel, usually lateen-rigged in full, but often, after about 1750, incorporating square rig, when they were called polacrechebecs. The extreme rake of the foremast was to exploit the hull's length and the chebec was well known for her extreme manoeuvrability. The success of the type as a descendant of the galley also ensured chebecs appeared in the Baltic.

30   20   10   0 ft
1/300
8   4   0 m

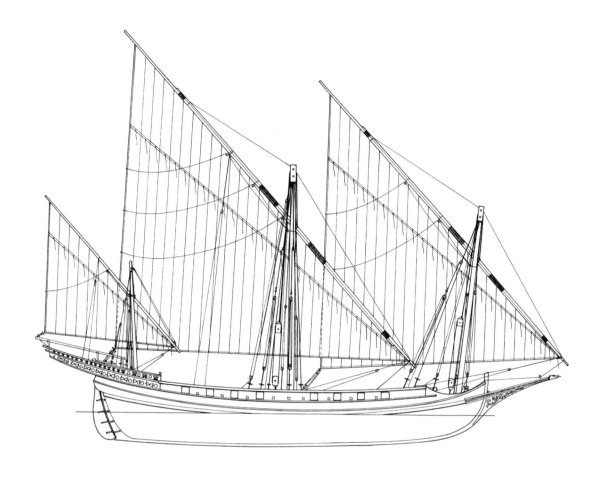

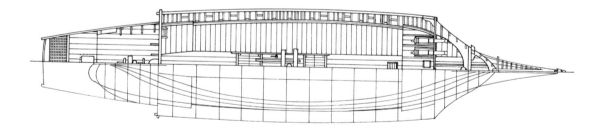

Spanish chebec, 1735. The French and Spanish navies of the eighteenth century used conventional chebecs to patrol their coasts and to raid an enemy's trade with considerable success. In this version the hull is a little more ship-like and the broadside armament more significant. *(152)*

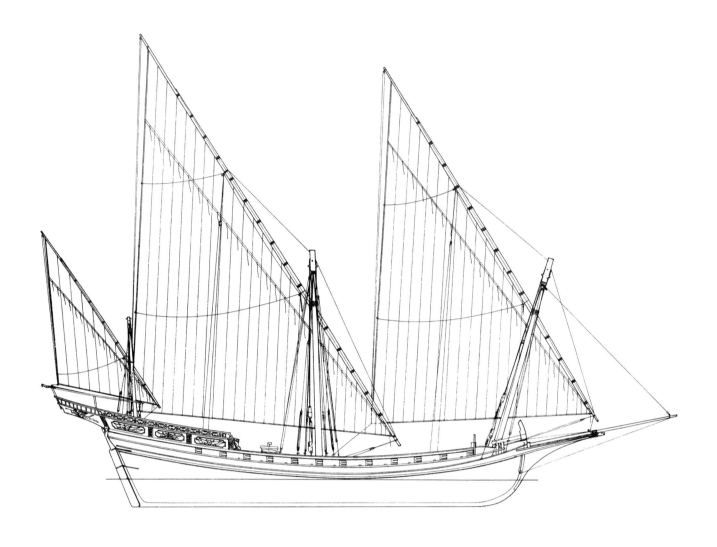

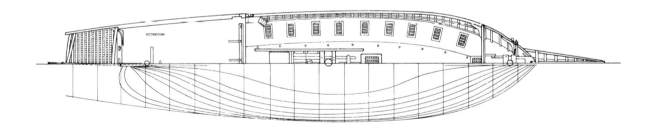

 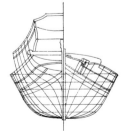

French chebec, 1750. Oar-ports have regained prominence in this French example, and the vessel has no heavy armament at all. *(237)*

1/300   30   20   10   0 ft
         8   4   0 m

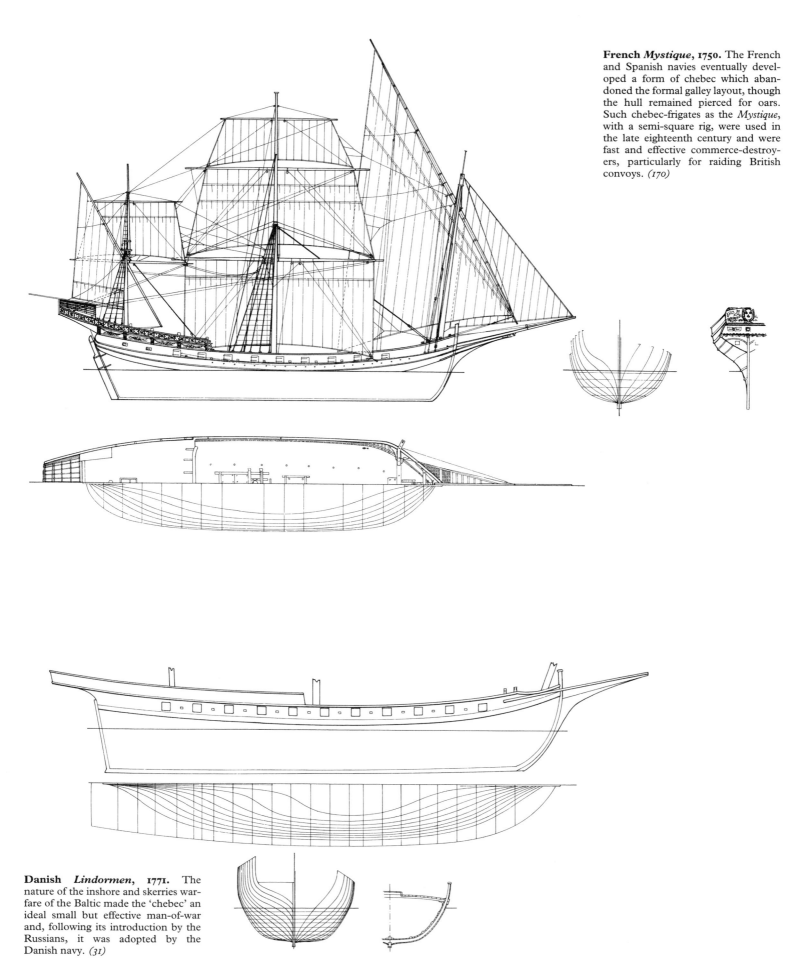

French *Mystique*, 1750. The French and Spanish navies eventually developed a form of chebec which abandoned the formal galley layout, though the hull remained pierced for oars. Such chebec-frigates as the *Mystique*, with a semi-square rig, were used in the late eighteenth century and were fast and effective commerce-destroyers, particularly for raiding British convoys. *(170)*

Danish *Lindormen*, 1771. The nature of the inshore and skerries warfare of the Baltic made the 'chebec' an ideal small but effective man-of-war and, following its introduction by the Russians, it was adopted by the Danish navy. *(31)*

30   20   10   0 ft
1/300
8   4   0 m

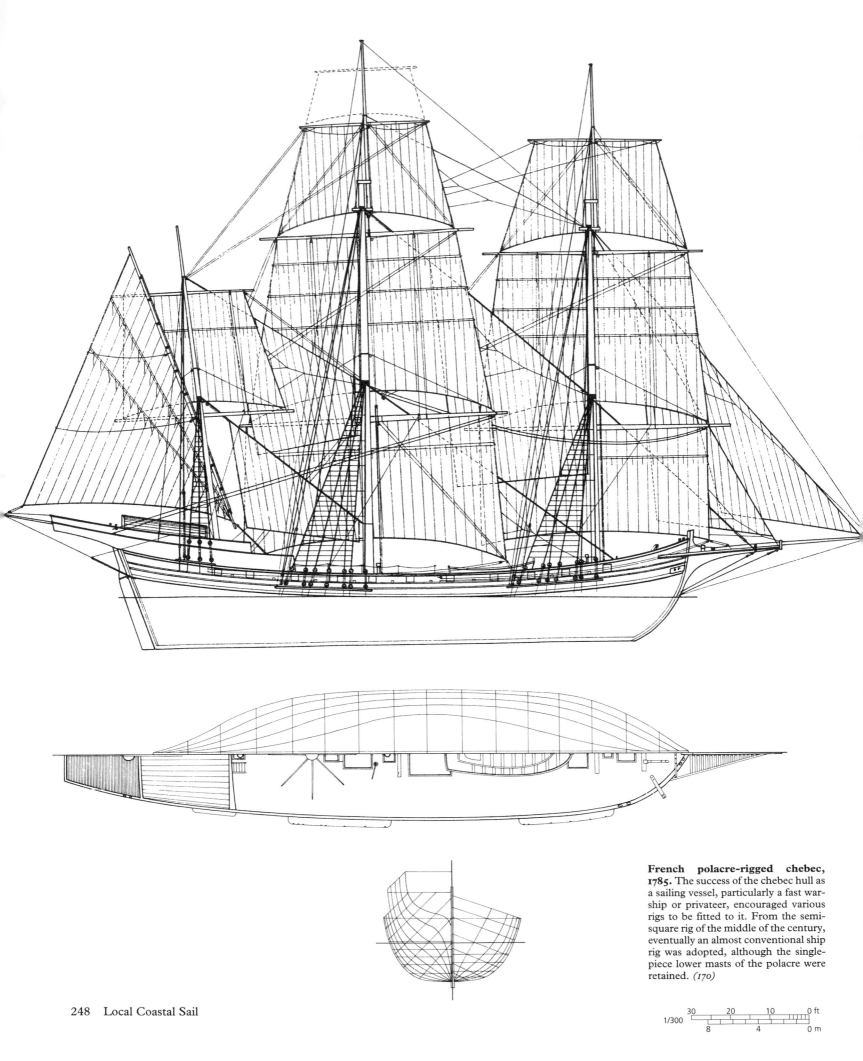

French polacre-rigged chebec, 1785. The success of the chebec hull as a sailing vessel, particularly a fast warship or privateer, encouraged various rigs to be fitted to it. From the semi-square rig of the middle of the century, eventually an almost conventional ship rig was adopted, although the single-piece lower masts of the polacre were retained. *(170)*

1/300

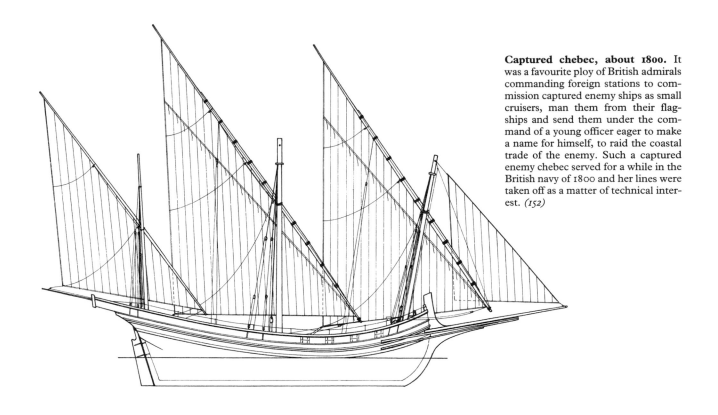

Captured chebec, about 1800. It was a favourite ploy of British admirals commanding foreign stations to commission captured enemy ships as small cruisers, man them from their flagships and send them under the command of a young officer eager to make a name for himself, to raid the coastal trade of the enemy. Such a captured enemy chebec served for a while in the British navy of 1800 and her lines were taken off as a matter of technical interest. *(152)*

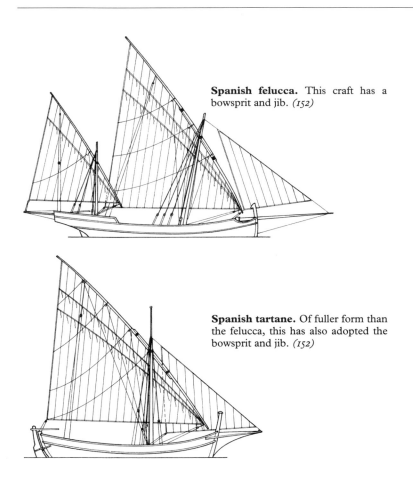

Spanish felucca. This craft has a bowsprit and jib. *(152)*

Spanish tartane. Of fuller form than the felucca, this has also adopted the bowsprit and jib. *(152)*

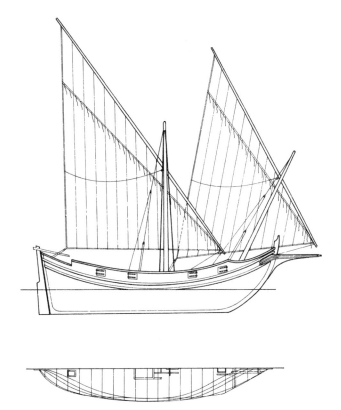

Western Mediterranean Local Craft

The terms felucca and tartane were widespread, and the boats they described varied from place to place, but there were many other local types and they all existed well into the twentieth century.

French tartane, eighteenth century. This version is fully decked, with hatches and still has the traditional beakhead, rather than a bowsprit. *(34)*

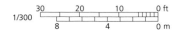

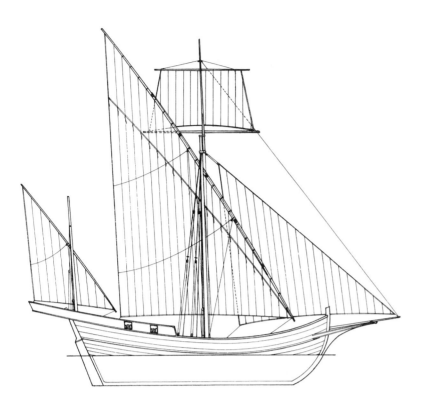

French tartane, 1810. A tartane such as this armed French example may have served as a privateer or a naval vessel covering the slow coastal convoys by which the French army laboriously moved military supplies. *(152)*

Tartane, mid-eighteenth century. This tartane is a cargo-carrier. *(142)*

Genoese vinco. A three-masted vessel, her hull of western ancestry, but setting a large lateen mainsail amidships, a smaller mizen aft, with square sails on her foremast. *(152)*

Tuscan liuto. A curious small passenger-carrying coaster, with a strange foresail which uses the bowsprit as a light foremast. The foresail sheets to the masthead and its lower clew to the deck. *(152)*

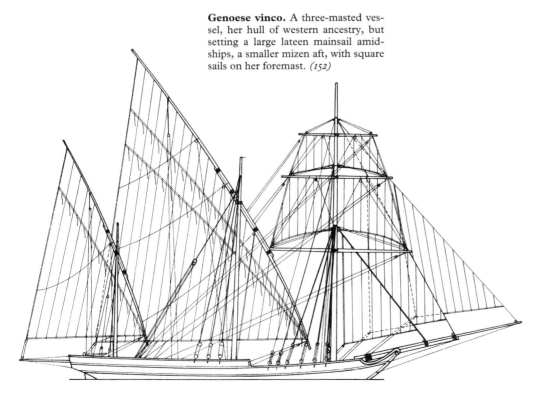

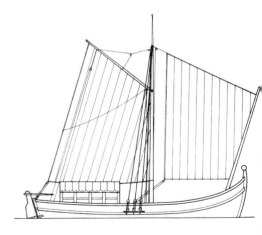

30   20   10   0 ft
1/300
8   4   0 m

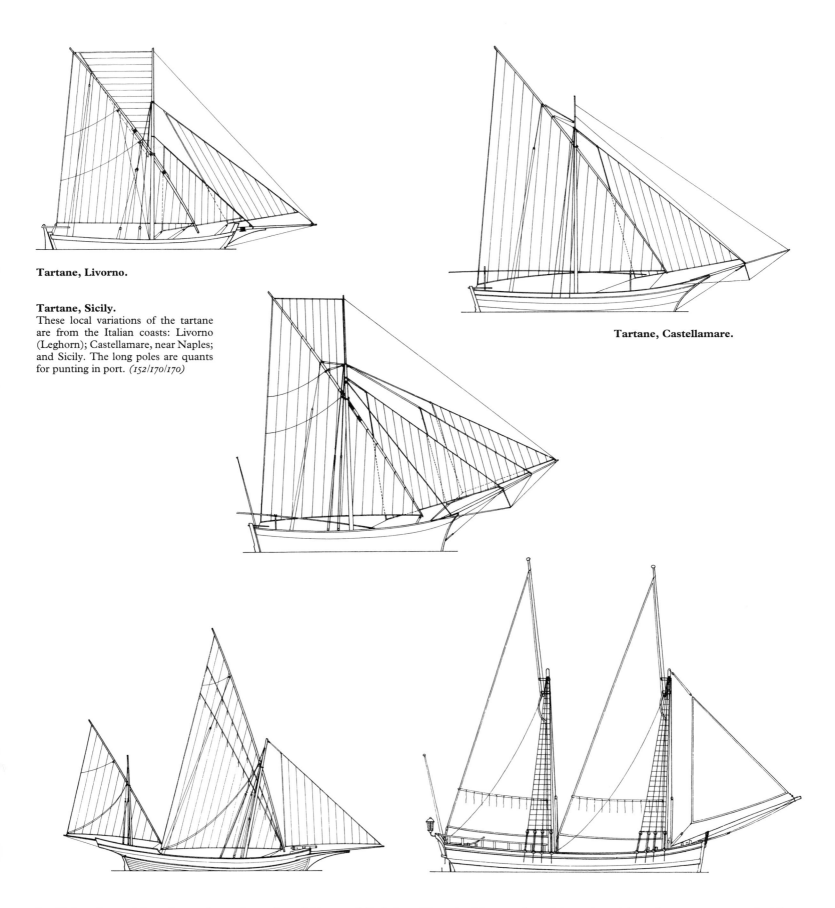

Tartane, Livorno.

Tartane, Sicily.
These local variations of the tartane are from the Italian coasts: Livorno (Leghorn); Castellamare, near Naples; and Sicily. The long poles are quants for punting in port. *(152/170/170)*

Tartane, Castellamare.

Sardinian bovo. The nineteenth century bovo, or bull-boat, was a sharp-lined and fast Sardinian coaster which could carry up to about 40 tons or be used as a fishing vessel. Both the tall main and small mizen mast carried lateen sails, with a staysail forward and a jib borne on a bowsprit. *(152)*

Houario. The name 'houario' actually derives from ferry but, as in the English 'wherry', craft so named also became working vessels, often used for fishing, though this example is an eighteenth century cargo craft. The vertical gaffs are early forms of gunterrig which was formerly sometimes known as the 'huari-rig'. *(142)*

30 20 10 0 ft
1/300
8 4 0 m

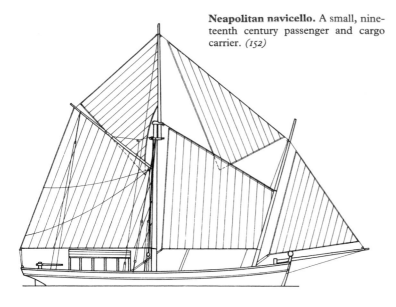

Neapolitan navicello. A small, nineteenth century passenger and cargo carrier. *(152)*

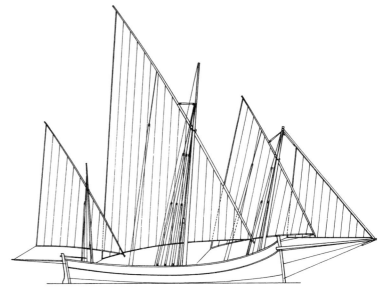

Sicilian great schifazzo. Sicilian produce was ferried to the mainland by way of the schifazzo, a lateen- rigged cargo or fishing boat which could lift 35 tons of grain or wine. *(170)*

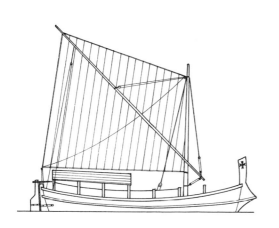

Speronaras. The speronara was equally at home in Sicily or Malta, being a small, open boat with a single mast fitted forward and setting a sprit- rigged sail. These are Maltese examples, one bearing the eye of Horus, the other the cross of the Knights of Malta. *(152)*

French allége, 1840. A flat-bottomed French sailing lighter, used to partially discharge loaded vessels in open road- steads to reduce their draught and allow them to enter ports in the tide- less Mediterranean. She has a rather elegant lateen rig with a bowsprit and large jib. *(45)*

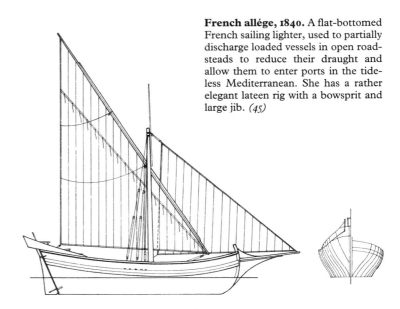

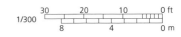

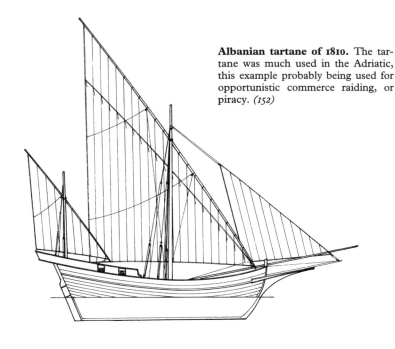

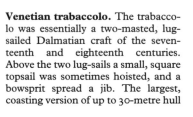

Albanian tartane of 1810. The tartane was much used in the Adriatic, this example probably being used for opportunistic commerce raiding, or piracy. *(152)*

Venetian trabaccolo. The trabaccolo was essentially a two-masted, lug-sailed Dalmatian craft of the seventeenth and eighteenth centuries. Above the two lug-sails a small, square topsail was sometimes hoisted, and a bowsprit spread a jib. The largest, coasting version of up to 30-metre hull length was fully decked with a capacious hold underneath. Her end posts were near vertical, but the all-purpose nature of the craft ensured the term was often applied to Italian boats and it was sometimes indistinguishable from the brazzera. *(152)*

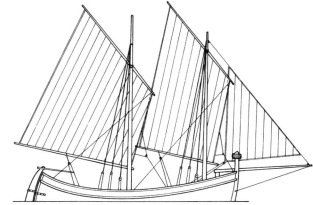

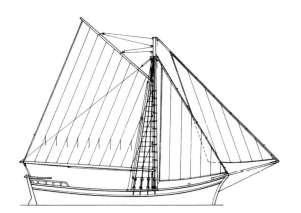

Adriatic brazzera, late nineteenth century. This was a fishing boat used on the Dalmatian coasts and by the Venetians into this century. Capable of carrying about 80 tons, the brazzera was fitted for oars. *(45)*

Greek sacoleva, 1844.

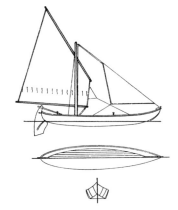

Venetian barco.

Widespread generic terms in this region are those of 'sacoleva' and 'barco'. Greek, Turks, Lebanese and Egyptian forms of the sacoleva have a hull of Arab origin with a main sail stretched by a sprit above which she carries a topsail on a forward raking mast. This may also set a square sail, with a jib extending to the end of the bowsprit. The sacoleva completes its outfit with a small, lateen-rigged mizen and sometimes a tiny jigger right aft. Even greater etymological confusion arises with names like 'barco' and 'barca', which is effectively rooted in one of the many synonyms for 'boat'. The barcane or barcone is a two-masted fisherman, whereas the barquetta or barchetta is a small, oared sailing boat usually engaged in fishing. The Venetian barco is clearly a very simple craft, as is also the barchetta. *(152/45/170)*

Barquetta, eastern Mediterranean.

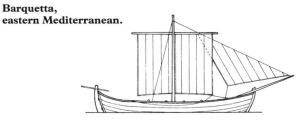

Adriatic and Eastern Mediterranean Local Craft

The greater influence of the Ottoman Turks persisted in the Levant, while the lingering memory of Venetian tradition and the innate conservatism of the Adriatic Balkans tended to create craft unique to this part of the Mediterranean basin.

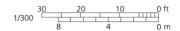

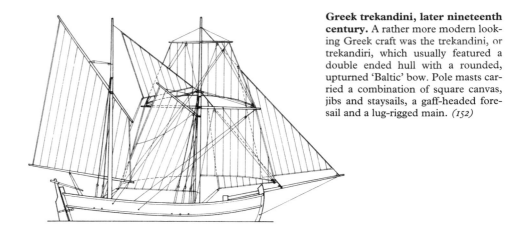

Greek trekandini, later nineteenth century. A rather more modern looking Greek craft was the trekandini, or trekandiri, which usually featured a double ended hull with a rounded, upturned 'Baltic' bow. Pole masts carried a combination of square canvas, jibs and staysails, a gaff-headed foresail and a lug-rigged main. *(152)*

The Greek scapho bore a simpler rig, a single sprit main and staysail, the former of which ran out along an outhaul on rings. It shared this with some Turkish coasters which, carrying a taller mast, set square sails on this. Another single-masted Turkish coaster, the tchektirme, set a leg-of-mutton sail with an array of jibs set on a long bowsprit. **NB.** 1/200 scale. *(152)*

Greek scapho.

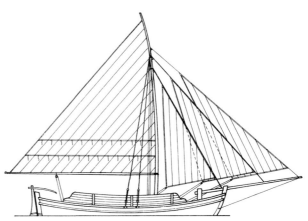

Turkish tchektirme.

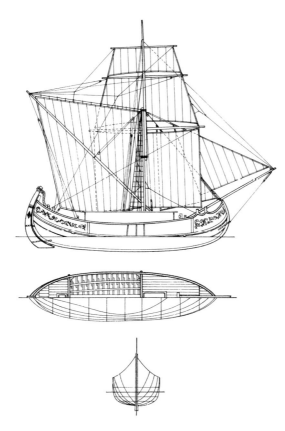

Turkish coasters. The variations of these craft owe much to each other, though whether the sacoleva borrowed from either of these Turkish coasting vessels, or vice-versa, is impossible to say. Both are cargo-carriers with a rig which draws on at least two traditions and is a mixture of easily handled sails and more complex canvas. The single-masted variant is known from at least the late seventeenth century. *(228/231)*

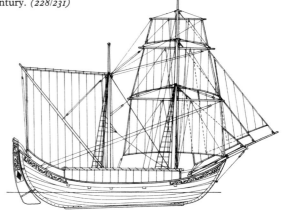

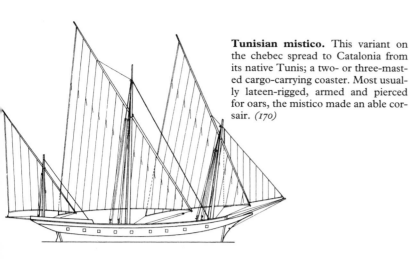

Tunisian mistico. This variant on the chebec spread to Catalonia from its native Tunis; a two- or three-masted cargo-carrying coaster. Most usually lateen-rigged, armed and pierced for oars, the mistico made an able corsair. *(170)*

Djerba chitiha. The Arab equivalent term for the European pink is chitiha and these craft were also used as corsairs. This example, from Djerba, combines both lateen and square sails, suggesting its piratical ambitions. *(170)*

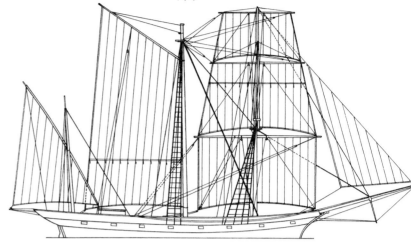

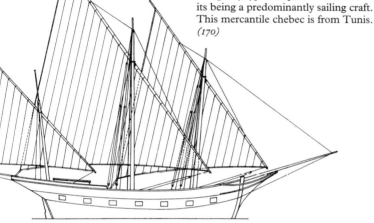

Tunisian chebec. By the nineteenth century the concept of the oared xebec as a galley type had passed in favour of its being a predominantly sailing craft. This mercantile chebec is from Tunis. *(170)*

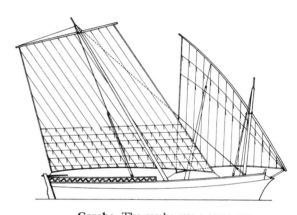

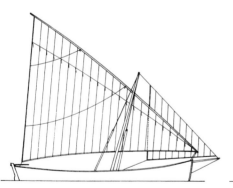

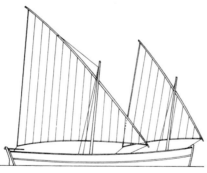

Carebe. The carebe was a cargo-carrier of the nineteenth century with an odd main lugsail set upon a steeply-raking mast. In the larger version, known as the great carebe (below), the fore and mizen masts bore lateen sails. A lesser carebe had only two masts, the odd raked mast still bearing its huge lugsail, the foremast carrying a lateen. These craft ran along the coasts of Tunisia and Tripolitania in the Gulf of Sidra. *(170)*

Sandale. Like the tartane, the sandale was a generic term for a lateen-rigged craft. The sandale was one- or two- masted, as in these two examples, both of which are from the Barbary coast, the single-master from Djerba. *(170)*

North African Local Craft

In the vessels of the former Barbary states may be traced the most influential craft in the Mediterranean, owing this to the ancient tradition of the Arab as navigators who have bequeathed much to modern arithmetic, astronomy, navigational and marine etymology. These examples are all based on a study published in 1882, but many had been in existence far earlier.

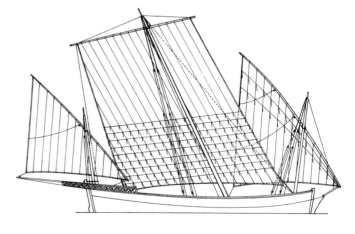

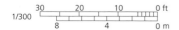

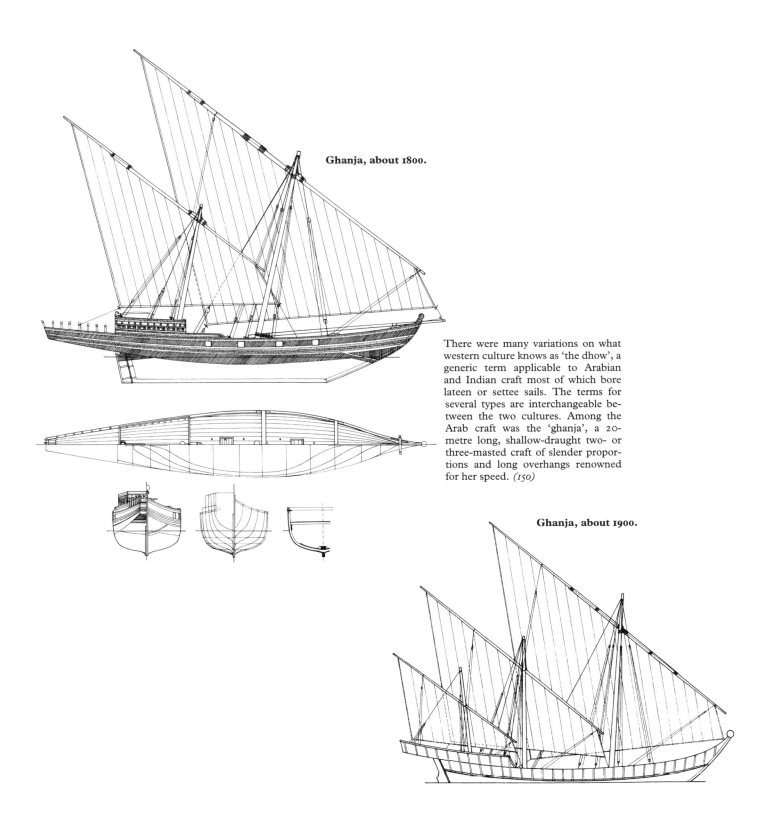

Ghanja, about 1800.

There were many variations on what western culture knows as 'the dhow', a generic term applicable to Arabian and Indian craft most of which bore lateen or settee sails. The terms for several types are interchangeable between the two cultures. Among the Arab craft was the 'ghanja', a 20-metre long, shallow-draught two- or three-masted craft of slender proportions and long overhangs renowned for her speed. (150)

Ghanja, about 1900.

Craft from the Coasts of Arabia and East Africa

For the Arabs, the monsoons of the Indian Ocean were a means of voyaging reliably, both across the Arabian Sea to the west coast of the Indian sub-continent and along the east coast of Africa. Sailing south along the coast of Africa during the North-East Monsoon between November and April, they could return with their slaves, ivory, ebony and other exotic luxuries which were much in demand throughout the rich and sophisticated Middle East of the Middle Ages, borne on the South-West Monsoon of May to October. Trade with India for general goods, cottons and spices was similarly governed. For this the lateen rig was ideal and it is borne on a variety of craft, from large cargo-carriers to fast vessels used by rival sheikhs to raid an enemy's traffic.

30   20   10   0 ft
1/300
8   4   0 m

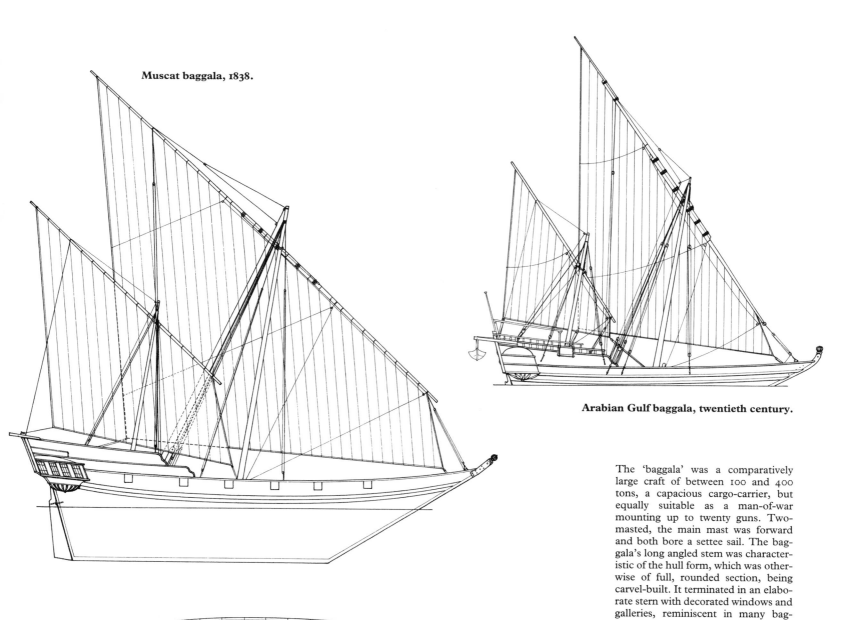

Muscat baggala, 1838.

Arabian Gulf baggala, twentieth century.

The 'baggala' was a comparatively large craft of between 100 and 400 tons, a capacious cargo-carrier, but equally suitable as a man-of-war mounting up to twenty guns. Two-masted, the main mast was forward and both bore a settee sail. The baggala's long angled stem was characteristic of the hull form, which was otherwise of full, rounded section, being carvel-built. It terminated in an elaborate stern with decorated windows and galleries, reminiscent in many baggalas that existed into the twentieth century, of western warships of an earlier age. Even without this, most dhows carried a degree of carved and painted work. *(170/142)*

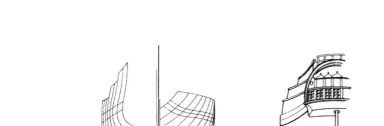

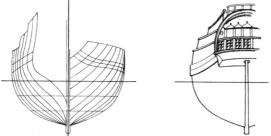

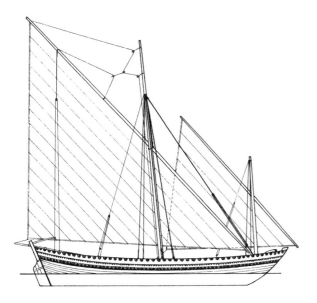

Arab thoni, or dhoni. Generally a light, fast dhow used along the east coast of Africa. *(150)*

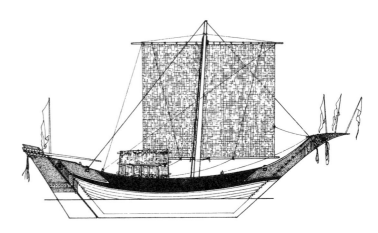

Lamu mtepe. Dhows remained in use throughout the greater part of the twentieth century, one of the most extraordinary being the 'mtepe' from the Kenyan island of Lamu which has a long overhanging stem, a short keel and narrow stern. Until modern times the strakes remained sewn together and the rudder was fastened to the stern-post by means of rope grommets. A square sail made of coconut matting replaced the more familiar settee shape and a deckhouse formed the mtepe's main accommodation. *(150)*

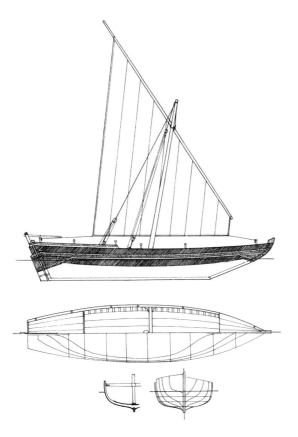

Khalissa. The 'khalissa' was a half-decked boat with a settee rig. *(150)*

Kuwaiti boom. While many types of dhow appear to have been widely distributed, most originated from one particular port and, as an example, the 'boom', or 'bûm', came from Kuwait. A cargo-carrier, booms can vary in size up to about 35 metres and sewn strakes were common, though not universal in boom construction. The mast was two-masted and settee-rigged. *(150)*

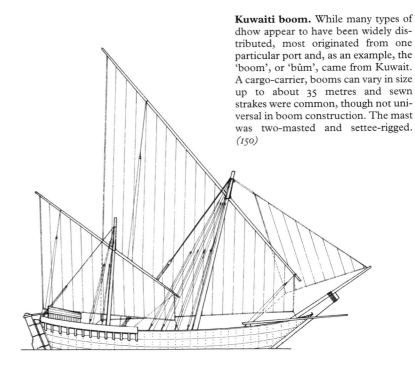

1/300

Red Sea sambuk. The 'sambuk' was a very fast, narrow-gutted craft, a close relation of the Iberian caravel, though whether as a cousin or a progenitor it is not possible to say with any certainty. Two-masted, the huge settee main was hoisted on the forward-raked mast common in most Arab craft. Used as a man-of-war and slaver, particularly in the Red Sea, the sambuk's capacity is relatively small, but she has a raised poop over a shallow transom which in turn fills out over a narrow stern section. *(112)*

Modern dhow. This twentieth century dhow might still be seen on the coasts of western India and Pakistan. *(150)*

Nurih. The oldest form of dhow is the 'nurih' which is said to date from the thirteenth century, a double-ended hull with a raked stern-post, but a more extremely angled stem, curving back on itself. A small elevated 'castle' was constructed above the stern and the tiller extended over this from a tall rudder stock. Two-masted and settee-rigged the sheer strake was often highly decorated. *(150)*

Batil. Another single-masted Arab and Indian dhow is the open 'batil' which is not to be confused with the larger Indian 'battela'. *(75)*

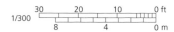

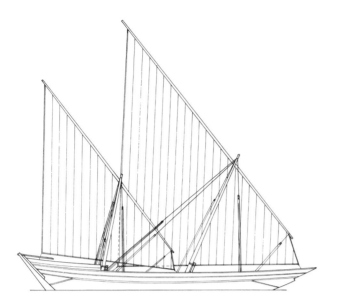

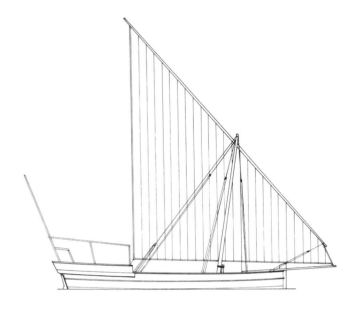

Zarook, Red Sea and Arabian Gulf. The 'zarook', or 'zarûk', was a small settee-rigged cargo-carrier or fishing vessel, though many were used as slavers. The rudder was originally operated by a rope yoke fastened to its lower part, but the tiller later replaced this. *(75)*

Jalbaut. A local craft mostly to be found around Bahrein and on the Saudi coast. *(75)*

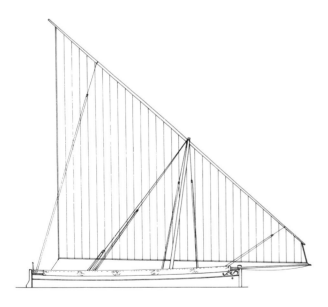

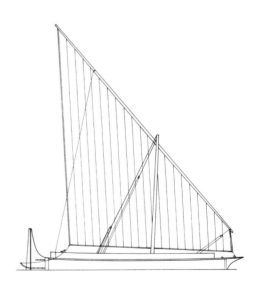

East African jahazi. A traditional coaster operating around Mombasa, Zanzibar and Dar es Salaam. *(75)*

Bedan. The 'bedan' was a primitive craft built by the Marsh Arabs of southern Iraq. Slender and lateen-rigged, with steering arrangements similar to the early zarûk, it is believed the bedan has altered little since pre-history. *(75)*

1/300   30   20   10   0 ft
8   4   0 m

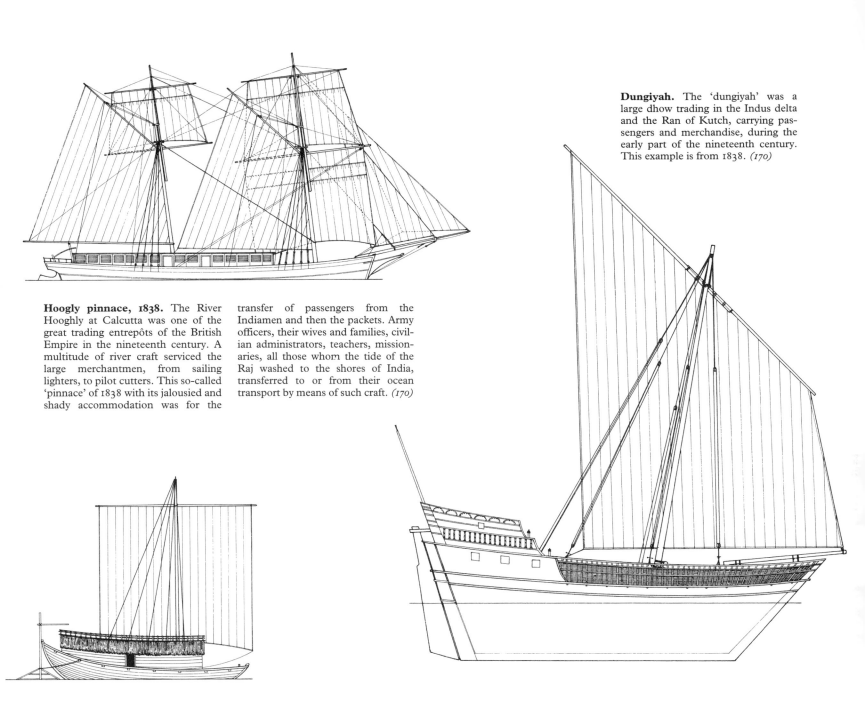

Dungiyah. The 'dungiyah' was a large dhow trading in the Indus delta and the Ran of Kutch, carrying passengers and merchandise, during the early part of the nineteenth century. This example is from 1838. *(170)*

Hoogly pinnace, 1838. The River Hooghly at Calcutta was one of the great trading entrepôts of the British Empire in the nineteenth century. A multitude of river craft serviced the large merchantmen, from sailing lighters, to pilot cutters. This so-called 'pinnace' of 1838 with its jalousied and shady accommodation was for the transfer of passengers from the Indiamen and then the packets. Army officers, their wives and families, civilian administrators, teachers, missionaries, all those whom the tide of the Raj washed to the shores of India, transferred to or from their ocean transport by means of such craft. *(170)*

Patile, 1838. There were, of course, many forms of riverine craft in India as elsewhere throughout the world and one such was the 'patile' from Mirapore, a freighting and passenger sailing barge used on the Ganges. *(170)*

Craft from the Indian Sub-Continent

Due to centuries of trade across the Arabian Sea, many Indian craft share similarities with their Arab cousins and the generic noun 'dhow' applies equally to sea-going craft of the sub-continent such as the 'dhangi', or 'dungiyah', a term common from the sixteenth century. As with most dhows, the stem is long, the stern squarely transomed over a narrow stern and the hull is shallow. Single-masted and settee-rigged, variants had a smaller mizen, and some bore a bowsprit and jib.

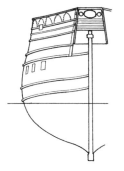
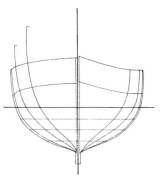

1/300 | 30 20 10 0 ft | 8 4 0 m

Batella (below and right). The inter-relationship between the Arab and Indian forms is exemplified in the 'batella'. This was a sea-going cargo-carrier which had imbibed European influences in having a bowsprit. Used in the coasting trade between Bombay and Karachi, the hull-form was similar to the zarûk, but with two masts and settee sails. The term, however, was loosely applied and could refer to smaller craft. *(217)*

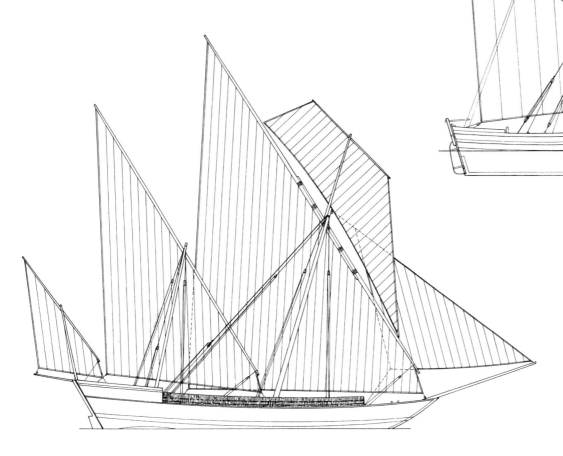

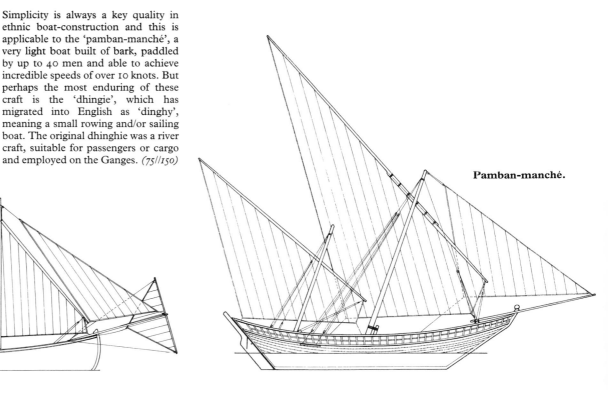

Dhingie.

Simplicity is always a key quality in ethnic boat-construction and this is applicable to the 'pamban-manché', a very light boat built of bark, paddled by up to 40 men and able to achieve incredible speeds of over 10 knots. But perhaps the most enduring of these craft is the 'dhingie', which has migrated into English as 'dinghy', meaning a small rowing and/or sailing boat. The original dhinghie was a river craft, suitable for passengers or cargo and employed on the Ganges. *(75//150)*

Pamban-manché.

30   20   10   0 ft
1/300
8   4   0 m

Dhangi.

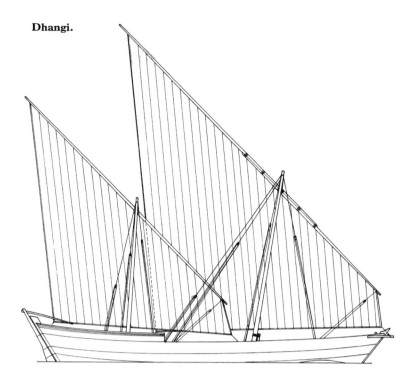

Padau.

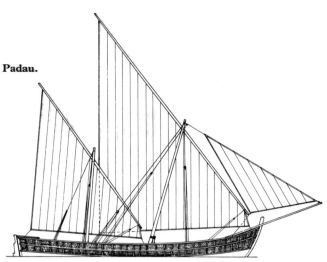

Odam.

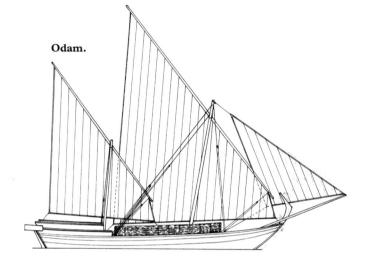

The 'dhangi' was a sea-going craft with settee sails which voyaged from the Indus delta across the Arabian Sea and occasionally to Oman and the Trucial States. The 'padau' and 'odam' also made similar coastal voyages, usually from Bombay to Dubai in the case of the former, and around the Laccadive islands and the Malabar ports for the latter. *(75)*

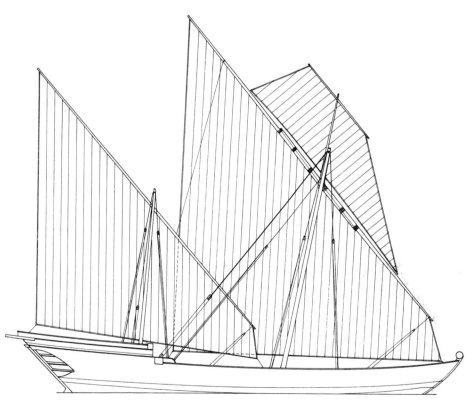

Kotia. The 'kotia' was the Indian version of the Arab ghanja, mainly used on the west coast of India and Pakistan and occasionally voyaging to East Africa and the Gulf. The generic nature of these Indo-Arab craft harks back to the confusion inherent in the Europe of the eighteenth century. *(75)*

30   20   10   0 ft
1/300
8   4   0 m

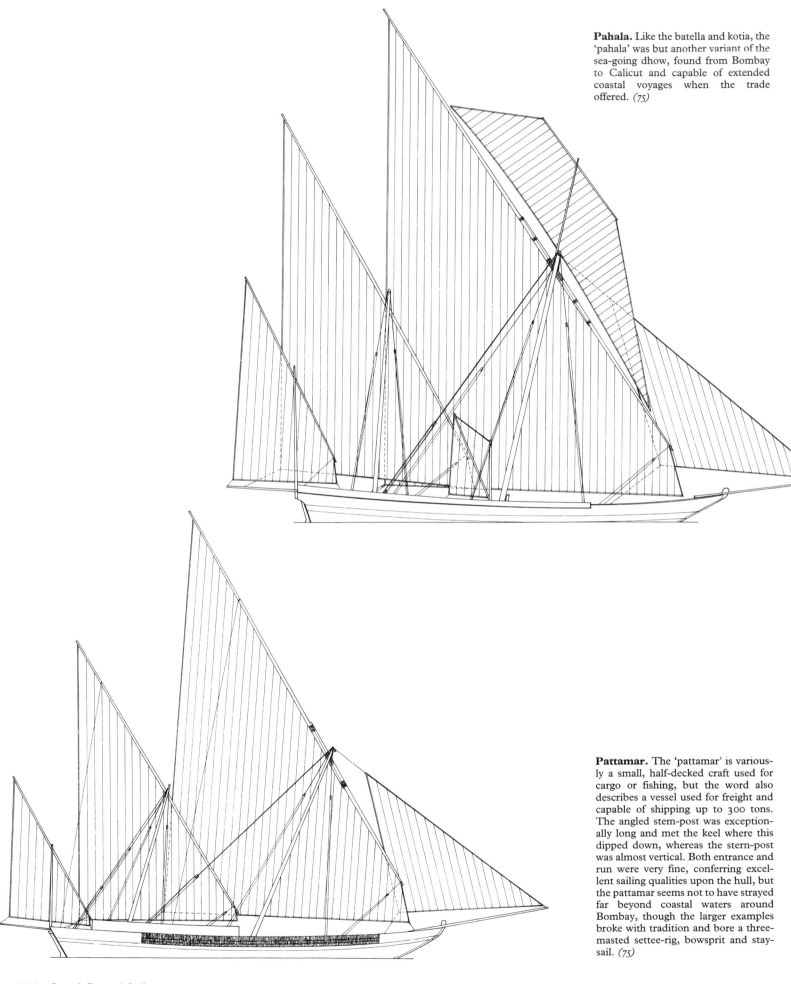

Pahala. Like the batella and kotia, the 'pahala' was but another variant of the sea-going dhow, found from Bombay to Calicut and capable of extended coastal voyages when the trade offered. *(75)*

Pattamar. The 'pattamar' is variously a small, half-decked craft used for cargo or fishing, but the word also describes a vessel used for freight and capable of shipping up to 300 tons. The angled stem-post was exceptionally long and met the keel where this dipped down, whereas the stern-post was almost vertical. Both entrance and run were very fine, conferring excellent sailing qualities upon the hull, but the pattamar seems not to have strayed far beyond coastal waters around Bombay, though the larger examples broke with tradition and bore a three-masted settee-rig, bowsprit and stay-sail. *(75)*

1/200 20 10 0 ft
6 4 2 0 m

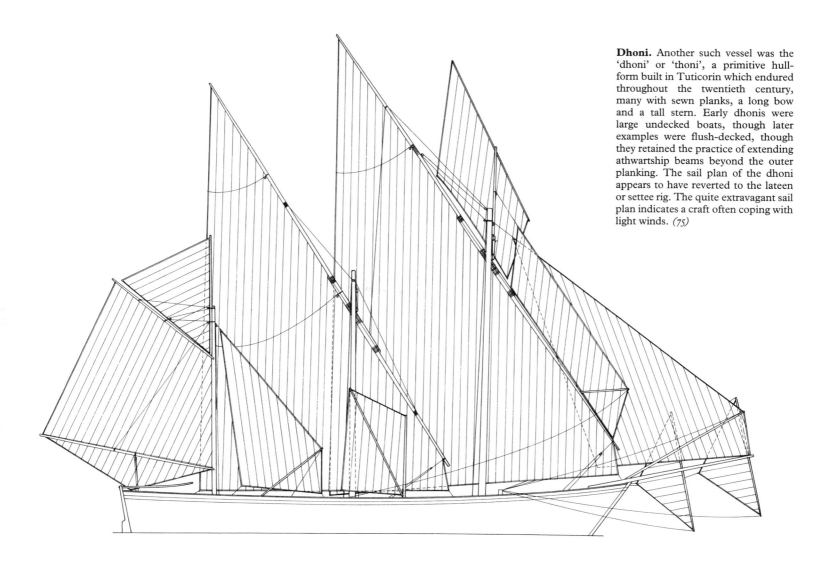

Dhoni. Another such vessel was the 'dhoni' or 'thoni', a primitive hull-form built in Tuticorin which endured throughout the twentieth century, many with sewn planks, a long bow and a tall stern. Early dhonis were large undecked boats, though later examples were flush-decked, though they retained the practice of extending athwartship beams beyond the outer planking. The sail plan of the dhoni appears to have reverted to the lateen or settee rig. The quite extravagant sail plan indicates a craft often coping with light winds. (75)

1/200

20   10   0 ft

6   4   2   0 m

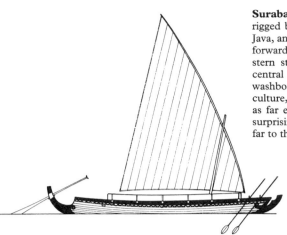

Surabaya boat, 1838. This lateen-rigged boat from Surabaya in eastern Java, and observed there in 1838, has a forward position for oars as well as a stern steering-cum-sculling oar. The central cockpit has removable raised washboards. The influence of Arab culture, especially in religion, reached as far east as Indonesia and it is not surprising to find this rakish craft so far to the east of the Red Sea. *(170)*

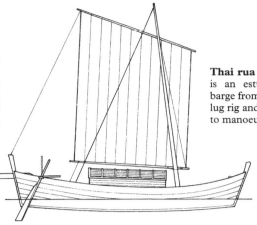

Thai rua chalom. The 'rua chalom' is an estuarine and coastal sailing barge from Thailand. It bears a simple lug rig and a pair of steering oars used to manoeuvre the craft. *(112)*

Vietnamese ghe ca vom. The hull of the 'ghe ca vom', also from Vietnam, is made from scarphed hardwood timbers. The ghe ca vom is a river barge, built as a cargo-carrier with what in European classification would rate as a lugsail. *(112)*

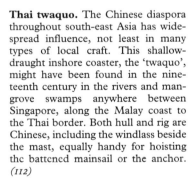

Vietnamese ghe luoi rung. The eastern gunter, or huari-rig, powers this swift 'ghe luoi rung' from Vietnam. The hull is decorated with an eye and the equally divided circle representing the balance of male and female, the ying and yang, in nature. *(112)*

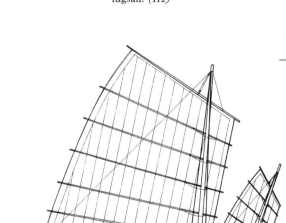

Thai twaquo. The Chinese diaspora throughout south-east Asia has widespread influence, not least in many types of local craft. This shallow-draught inshore coaster, the 'twaquo', might have been found in the nineteenth century in the rivers and mangrove swamps anywhere between Singapore, along the Malay coast to the Thai border. Both hull and rig are Chinese, including the windlass beside the mast, equally handy for hoisting the battened mainsail or the anchor. *(112)*

The Coastal Sailing Craft of South-East Asia

The extensive river networks among the low-lying deltas and plains of Indo-China have for centuries been highways of trade. Further afield, the extensive archipelagos of Indonesia and the Philippines have relied upon sea-borne trade maintaining intercourse between isolated communities. To these social imperatives must be added fishing as a mean of subsistence, all of which add to a series of powerful incentives to make limited voyages. A representative sample of the various riverine and estuarine craft is shown here. Many enjoyed an extremely long life, thanks to the great quantities of hardwood produced by the rainforests, but most of these craft have been replaced by diesel-engined vessels whose hulls, however, often betray their origins.

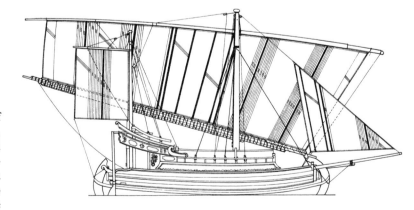

Malaysian prau mayang. The word 'prau' is the Malay for boat. The prau mayang was a large Malay and Indonesian cargo-carrier which ser-viced the East Indiamen, bringing produce to the anchorages at which the cargo-vessels loaded. *(142)*

1/300

30   20   10   0 ft

8   4   0 m

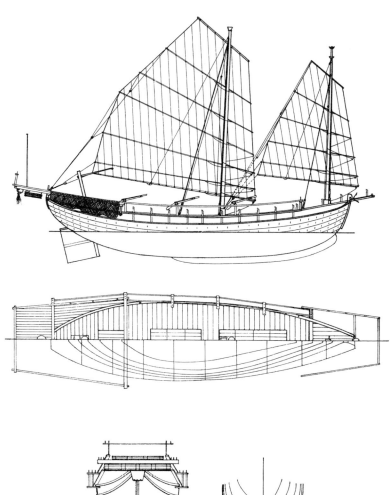

South China junk, nineteenth century. This example is of a sea-going junk from the southern provinces of Fukien or Kwangtung. She is armed and has very heavy, unstayed pole-masts. These were customarily made of teak, a heavy baulk of which was buried in boggy ground where it took up natural preservatives. All junks bore a measure of decoration which included symbolic emblems of good fortune, luck and appeasement to the gods and goddesses of the sea. Note the lozenge holes in the rudder. These make it easier to swing without much altering its directional function when the vessel is making way. *(27)*

South China junk, 1838. The junks of southern China were frequently used as pirate craft, preying particularly on British and American opium clippers, although this example of 1838 may be armed for self-defence. She bears battened sails which are easily reefed by simply lowering one or two battened sections. The arrangement of sheets attached to the after end of each batten ensures the set of the sail may be adjusted for maximum effect, and the rudder is adjustable. Of particular interest is the fact that although the deck arrangement is ungainly, the underwater body is of a very advanced form. (See Section 8, The History of Yachting.) *(170)*

The Junks and Sampans of China and Japan

China has a vast coastline, numerous rivers and a maritime culture which is probably as old as that of Egypt. Moreover, it is quite possible that rather than European nations dominating the modern world, China could have done so, for a few years before the Portuguese rounded Africa, the Chinese had been trading in the Persian Gulf and a major Chinese expedition had reached the East African coast. Stretching down to the south, its leader had concluded there was nothing warranting further investigation. The emperor decided to waste no more resources on marine exploration and China threw up an opportunity it had no way of knowing it had lost.

Nevertheless, the sea-going Chinese junk remains a remarkable craft. Many of its features have existed for years and were well ahead of west-

ern development. Watertight bulkheads, together with longitudinal sub-division were integral parts of Chinese ship-construction at least half a millennium before the concept was adopted in western vessels. The centreline rudder was known much earlier and lateral resistance was better achieved, as was windward performance, for the Chinese 'lug-sail', even when tattered and torn, can drive a heavily loaded hull to windward very efficiently.

The term 'junk' is generic; there are still a multitude of junks in existence, though they are dwindling. As recently as the 1960s the fishing fleets of ports such as Swatow were very large. Historically, ocean-going junks have been of considerable size, even allowing for the hyperbole considered necessary by the writers of chronicles.

1/300 30 20 10 0 ft
       8   4   0 m

Hang Chow junk. The islands of the Chusan archipelago and the great bight of Hang Chow Bay, like many areas of the Chinese coast, produced a local type of junk which was richly decorated, fitted with leeboards and between 20 and 28 metres in length. *(112)*

Chekiang junk, early 1900s. The province of Chekiang which borders Hang Chow Bay and includes the former treaty port of Ningpo, also produced a smaller junk. Such craft were in use during the first half of the twentieth century. Note the strong construction, the sophistication of the underwater body and the two windlasses. One on deck assists with the anchor and sail-hoisting, the other, mounted over the stern, adjusts the depth of the rudder which serves the dual purpose of acting as a leeboard. *(218)*

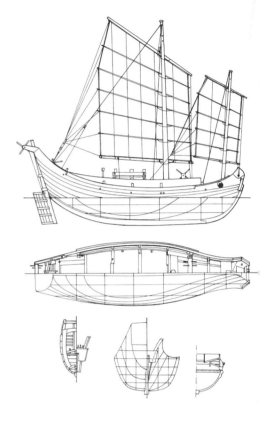

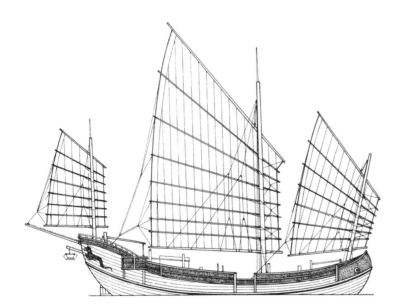

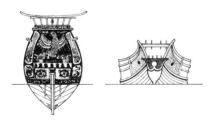

Foochow junk. The anchorage of Foochow on the Min River was a loading port for China tea and junks such as this were a familiar sight transferring cargo alongside the clippers. The richly embellished stern has a phoenix as a symbol of longevity. This was certainly true of the junks themselves, which were well built and incorporated natural preservatives like tung-oil. As with all multi-masted junks, having masts at the extremity of the hull made manoeuvring easier and Chinese seamen were extremely skilful at swinging their craft in confined waters. The Chinese thus avoided any significant use of oars as in the western galley. *(112)*

South China sampan. Small, riverine craft plied all over China, carrying produce and manufactures between trading markets and the great ports. They were simple and their crews generally consisted of whole families. Such small vessels, like the boats hoisted as tenders in the davits of larger junks, were called 'sampans'. Bamboo matting, which is produced in copious quantities in China, once made sails, but here either shelters the crew or the sampan's cargo. *(112)*

30   20   10   0 ft
1/300
8   4   0 m

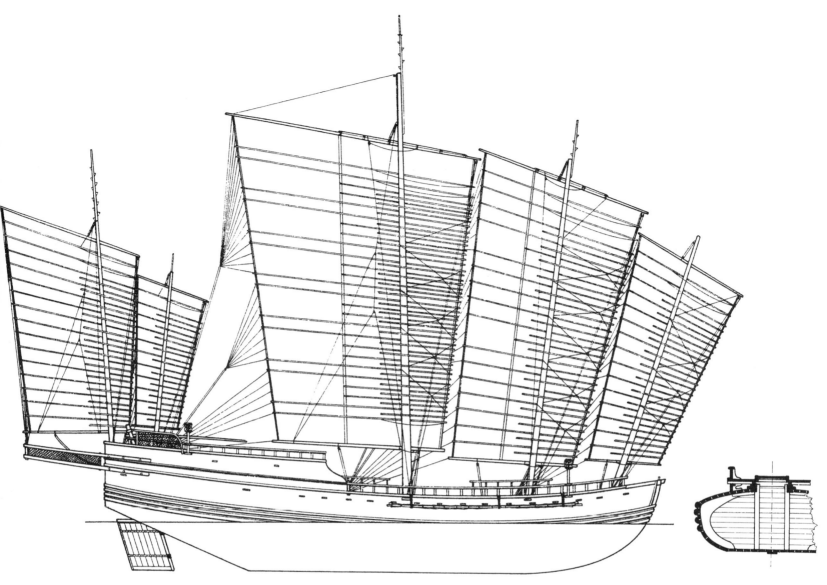

Petchili junk, early twentieth century. In the waters of northern China, such as the Gulf of Chihli, the angle of the upper sail battens is noticeably less steep than in their southern cousins. The Petchili junk, found here until the middle of the twentieth century, was the descendant of the great junks sent on voyages of exploration in the fifteenth century. These in turn were known to have developed from craft built at least two hundred years earlier. They were flat-bottomed, broad of beam and sub-divided into up to twenty watertight compartments on a hull some 55 metres in length. These enormous hulls naturally required a considerable sail area to drive them, but rather than build up height, in the western fashion, Chinese shipbuilders added masts, by which means the benefit one gained from another was helpful in working to windward in an area dominated by land-generated winds, but also allowed single-spar masts to be unstayed, the sails being uninhibited as they moved round them. (*112*)

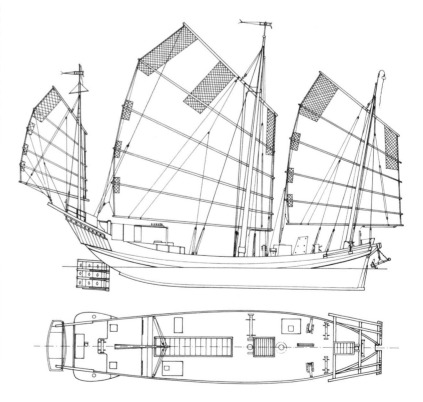

Kwantung junk. This junk might have been found anywhere along the southern coast of nineteenth or early twentieth century China, being used as a coaster, fishing boat, or opportunistic pirate, preying upon any hapless vessel, perhaps as a customs craft of a corrupt mandarin. The province of Kwantung includes the great Chinese port formerly known as Canton on the Pearl River. On either side of the estuary, lay the Portuguese territory of Macao and the British colony of Hong Kong. The junk is armed with muzzle-loading guns, and is a sea-going craft of considerable speed and weatherliness, despite her patched sails. Note the fish-shaped wind-vanes atop her masts. (*227*)

1/300   30   20   10   0 ft
         8   4   0 m

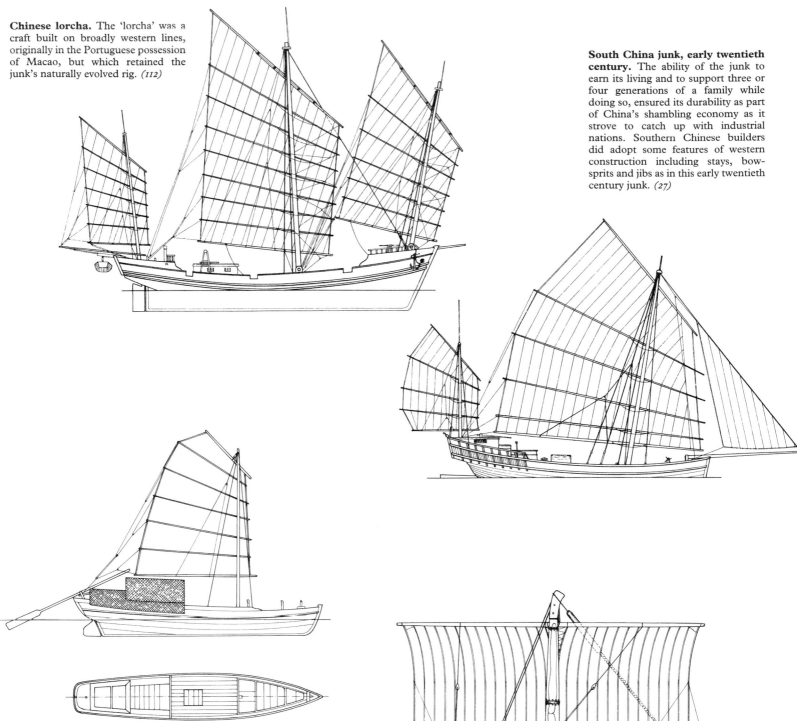

Chinese lorcha. The 'lorcha' was a craft built on broadly western lines, originally in the Portuguese possession of Macao, but which retained the junk's naturally evolved rig. *(112)*

South China junk, early twentieth century. The ability of the junk to earn its living and to support three or four generations of a family while doing so, ensured its durability as part of China's shambling economy as it strove to catch up with industrial nations. Southern Chinese builders did adopt some features of western construction including stays, bowsprits and jibs as in this early twentieth century junk. *(27)*

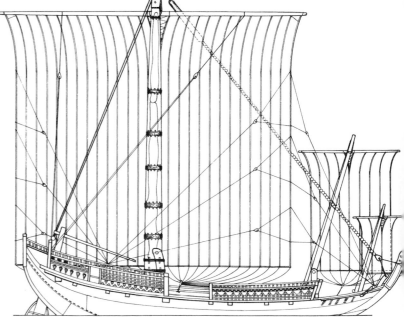

Hong Kong sampan. The simple sampan carried small parcels of cargo, acted as mail boat and taxi, agent's or pilots' craft, or even as a crew liberty boat to ships anchored in Hong Kong's large harbour. When the sail was lowered, the long stern-oar, or yuloh, was plied ceaselessly as a means of keeping way on the long and slender boat. **NB.** Twice scale. *(227)*

Japanese junk. Only in modern times were the Japanese a maritime people in the full sense of the word, though fishing has formed an important means of subsistence for many hundreds of years. Large Japanese cargo-craft possessed none of the finesse of the Chinese junk, though this sailing barge is often referred to as a junk. Like the Polish strug of the seventeenth century, it has an odd similarity to the Roman grain ship. *(142)*

30   20   10   0 ft
1/300
8   4   0 m

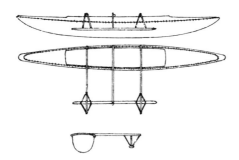

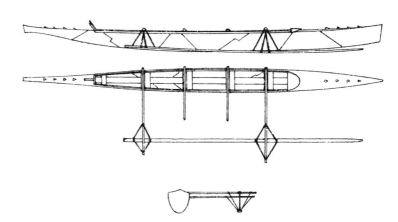

Boopaa (above) **and tafahanga, from Tongatabu.** Both are skin boats with stabilising outriggers from this mid-Pacific island. The tafahanga is the larger craft. *(170)*

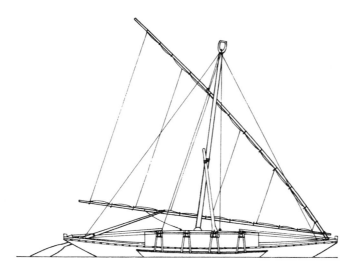

Fijian outrigger. In Fiji the outrigger canoe is fitted with a mast and sail, the latter of which shows an evolved, empirical understanding of aerodynamics. *(142)*

Craft of the Pacific and South America

The primitive indigenous populations of the archipelagos of the Pacific are now known to have made long voyages, using a method of stellar navigation. It seems inconceivable that they did not use the wind as well as oceanic currents, as was conjectured by Thor Heyerdahl when in 1947 the Norwegian scientist set out in a simple raft to prove the possibility of trans-Pacific migration from South America.

By the eighteenth century, when the Pacific was opened to Europeans, the islanders of Polynesia and Melanesia, revealed little obvious evidence of this adventurous genesis, though the variety of paddled canoes was impressive. Most significant to the story of sail was the outrigger canoe which, in due course, became the racing catamaran of the twentieth century yachtsman.

1/200 20 10 0 ft
6 4 2 0 m

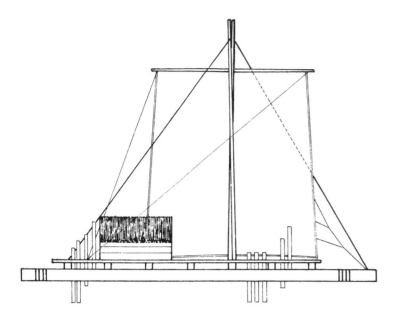

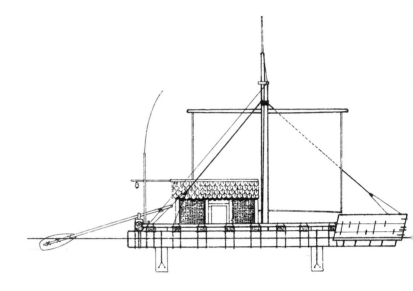

Kon Tiki, 1947. Thor Heyerdahl's balsa raft *Kon Tiki* was 13.7 metres long, by 5.5 metres in the beam. In 1947 Heyerdahl and his companions drifted and sailed 4300 miles from Callao, Peru, to the Tuamotos Islands in 101 days. *(138)*

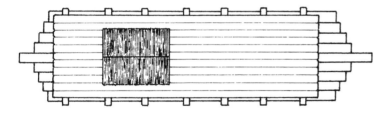

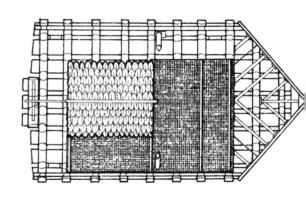

Peruvian balsa raft. On the Peruvian coast of South America, balsa rafts were observed in the early 1840s. *(242)*

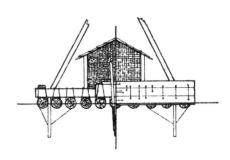

1/200   20   10   0 ft

6   4   2   0 m

SECTION EIGHT Small Fry and Fishermen

FROM THE EARLIEST days of sail, the infrastructure supporting the whole marine world was considerable. By the end of the eighteenth century, when the great sailing navies of Europe disputed command of the sea, not only did lesser craft attend the larger ships to which they might merely act as auxiliaries or be attached to, but they were frequently used as extensions of sea-power, many raids being made by the very boats of a warship herself. In addition, extended surveying voyages were accomplished in small craft and there occurred some epics of survival. In all cases, though oars were commonplace, sail was used to cover distances.

Furthermore, the maintenance of ports as well as battle-fleets required the services of small sailing ships, while the varied fishing traditions of several countries supported a highly individual development of fishing craft.

Many and varied are the types of craft in which men have shoved off from the shore to go fishing. In almost all cases the element of local demand, both in terms of the sea conditions likely to be met and the type of fishing intended, have governed their evolution. Of all seafarers, fishermen are perhaps the most resistant to change. In a highly dangerous profession, the tried-and-tested has the sanction of usage, whereas the new-fangled is always a matter for suspicion. Despite these limitations on innovation, some of the handsomest sailing craft ever produced have been fishing vessels, craft which combine strength and practicality with fitness-for-purpose to a remarkable and wonderful degree. In the Grand Banks schooner, built in North America, must surely be found one of the most beautiful sailing vessels ever produced anywhere on earth.

The plethora of fishing techniques used during the age of sail is staggering. Depending upon whether the fisherman was hunting pelagic species with seine net, drift net or long line and hook, or trawling for the benthic bottom-feeders, his craft had to be able to stand up to her task. While the smacks of the North Sea had to drag a trawl along the sea-bed, the Grand Banks schooner hardly soiled herself, sending out individual fishermen to lay their long lines from small dories. Most fishing boats had to carry out some form of processing on board, such as gutting and salting, and while many passed their catches to faster, specially designated craft which hastened away to market, some had to race home with full fish-holds. Others, such as prawners and shrimpers, often kept their catches live in wells open to the sea, landing their cargoes in a fresh state.

These relatively small vessels, while too insignificant to be made known to us by name, were of crucial importance both to human progress and to human survival. From the severely practical grew some of the most perfect sailing craft, transforming mere functionality to a rare and often unsurpassed beauty.

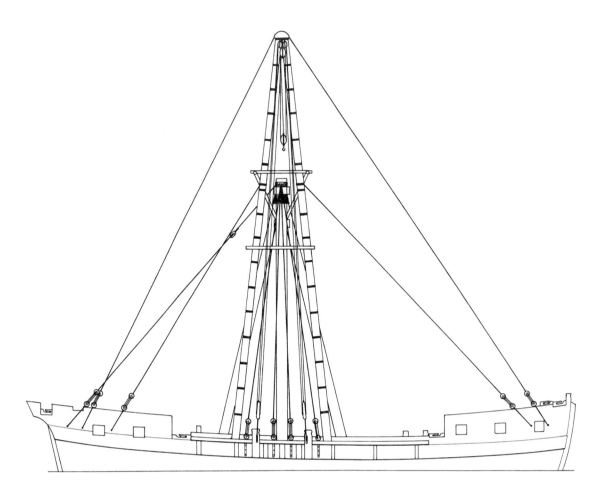

Sheer hulk. Usually a cut-down man-of-war or large redundant merchant-man, the 'sheer hulk' was a feature of any tidal port capable of fitting-out ships. The stepping of masts was accomplished by making the commis-sioning vessel fast alongside the per-manently moored sheer hulk. The hulk was so-named from its immo-bilised state, the meaning to which the noun had been reduced since it signi-fied a sea-going, medieval merchant-man. To carry out its task it carried a pair of huge, lashed spars, or sheers. These were lowered or raised by a heavy topping lift to the hulk's heavily stayed mast. (166)

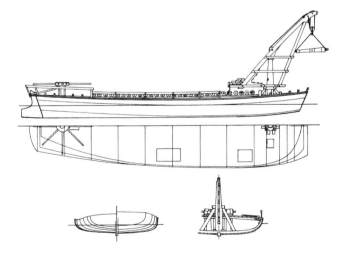

Harbour Service Craft

The servicing of individual ocean-going ships, whether merchant or naval, required the attentions of a number of lesser vessels, whilst the maintenance of ports, the provision of water and stores and the multi-farious complexities of moving large sailing ships in confined waters, generated a number of essential small fry.

Ordnance barge. When laid up out of commission, a man-of-war was emptied of her upper masts, spars, stores and guns. When re-commis-sioned the latter had to be returned to her and for this an ordnance barge was used. This Swedish example is from 1774 and bears a hand-operated crane. (74)

30   20   10   0 ft
1/300
8   4   0 m

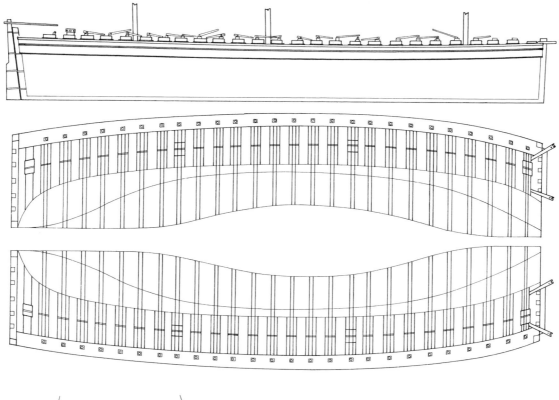

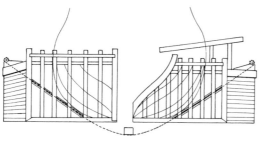

Dutch 'camels'. The draughts of laden Dutch East Indiaman and other large vessels were reduced by lifting the entire hull in 'camels' before towing them across the Zuider Zee for discharge. These camels, from 1778, were first flooded to submerge them beneath the ship's hull, which was then secured to the two pontoon halves. The water was then pumped out and the vessel rose with the camels. The device was used by other nations, like Venice, with similarly shallow coastal approaches. (78)

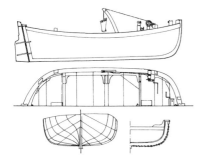

Trinity Lighter, 1786. The Corporation of Trinity House had been granted a monopoly to dredge the Thames at the beginning of the seventeenth century. This was not only to maintain the depth of the navigable channel, but also to give the Corporation a means of raising revenue by selling the shingle from the river bed as ballast in order to fund lighthouses, lightvessels, beacons, and buoys. A number of grab dredgers such as this one from 1786 were used. Stout wooden craft with a simple bucket grab, they changed little before the age of steam. (62)

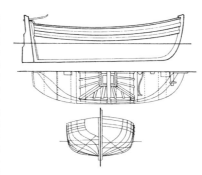

Newcastle ballast lighter. The River Tyne, in northern England was similarly dredged and this ballast lighter, or hopper, conveyed the spoil from the dredger to discharged sailing ships awaiting ballast before proceeding on a voyage. Fouled as it was with the waste products of the riverside conurbations, shingle ballast was a source of shipboard disease, so the cellular double bottom introduced with metal ship construction (allowing water to be used instead of shingle) was a great improvement. (34)

1/300 30 20 10 0 ft
       8   4   0 m

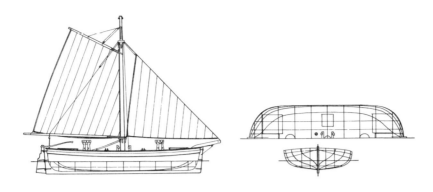

American anchor hoy, 1818. One of the most laborious tasks in a naval or commercial port was the provision of heavy ground moorings at which men-of-war or merchantmen could lie safely. Large warships might spend years at such moorings between commissions and sturdy craft such as this American mooring hoy of 1818, equipped with two capstans and a heavy davit which doubled as a bowsprit when the craft was in transit, laid out heavy anchors and ground cable in secure stream moorings. *(26)*

American tank lighter, about 1840. By the end of the Napoleonic Wars the British Royal Navy was no longer storing water in its new ships in barrels, but were using iron tanks. In the decades that followed the practice became widespread and water was conveyed to men-of-war in water lighters fitted with tanks and hand pumping arrangements. This flat-bottomed, schooner-rigged scow was an American water carrier of around 1840. *(26)*

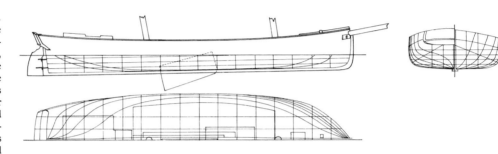

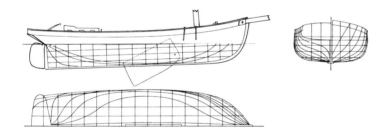

American powder boat, 1857. Gunpowder was taken out to men-of-war in conditions of great security, with special arrangements being made for its transport. A powder lighter, dedicated only to the carriage of gunpowder, was provided. *(26)*

American navy yard hoy, 1848. Some support craft were remarkably simple vessels, like this mooring hoy, which is little more than a pontoon. *(26)*

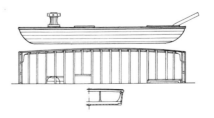

1/300
30   20   10   0 ft
8   4   0 m

***Swift*, Virginia pilot boat, 1803.** A schooner-rigged pilot 'cutter' from Virginia, her hollow lines show she would have lived up to her name servicing vessels entering or leaving the rivers and ports around Chesapeake Bay. *(27)*

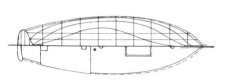

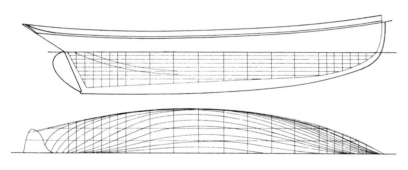

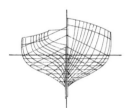

***Adams*, Boston pilot boat.** A yacht-like form may be easily discerned in this handsome New England pilot cutter, built at Essex in the late 1880s . *(27)*

***L'Henriette-Marie*, pilot cutter, 1866.** A number of very seaworthy pilot cutters were built in French and British ports during the period between 1850 and 1930. Many survived to become able cruising yachts. This is a Le Havre pilot cutter of 1866 and is, as were those of the Bristol Channel, rigged as a heavy gaff-cutter. Each pilot usually had his own cutter and solicited business by cruising out in the offing awaiting inward-bound ships. *(170)*

Pilot and Revenue 'Cutters'

By convention, the swift-sailing craft developed for the boarding and landing of pilots and for the interception and prevention of smuggling are known as 'cutters', irrespective of their rig. They have not only their speed in common, for such vessels had to be weatherly and therefore sea-kindly, but also robust and easily handled, varying demands which often imposed a rigour upon their builders which produced efficient, if not always beautiful, small sailing ships.

***Phantom* and *Pet*.** A pair of nineteenth century schooners, these were built for the New York pilotage service. *(27)*

1/300

30 20 10 0 ft

8 4 0 m

American revenue cutter of 1815–31-ton design. After the war with Great Britain, the United States government possessed a greater awareness of sea-power and the desirability of quashing the independence of native free-traders. A series of revenue cutters were designed for this purpose, of which this is an example of the 31-ton class built in 1815. Note the fast schooner rig and the heavy carronade mounted amidships, *en barbette*. (27)

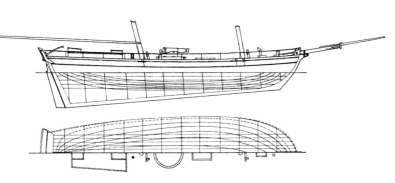

American revenue cutter of 1815–80-ton design. Of similar layout, this is one of the largest, 80-ton American revenue cutters of the 1815 programme. (27)

Morris, **American revenue cutter, 1831.** The next generation of American revenue 'cutters' carried a small broadside armament. (27)

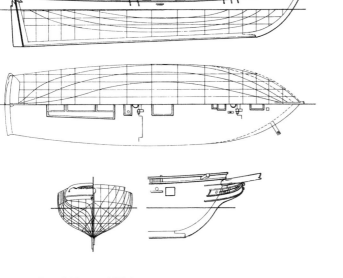

American revenue cutter of 1815–51-ton design. An intermediate class, of 51 tons, was also produced. (27)

1/300 30 20 10 0 ft

8 4 0 m

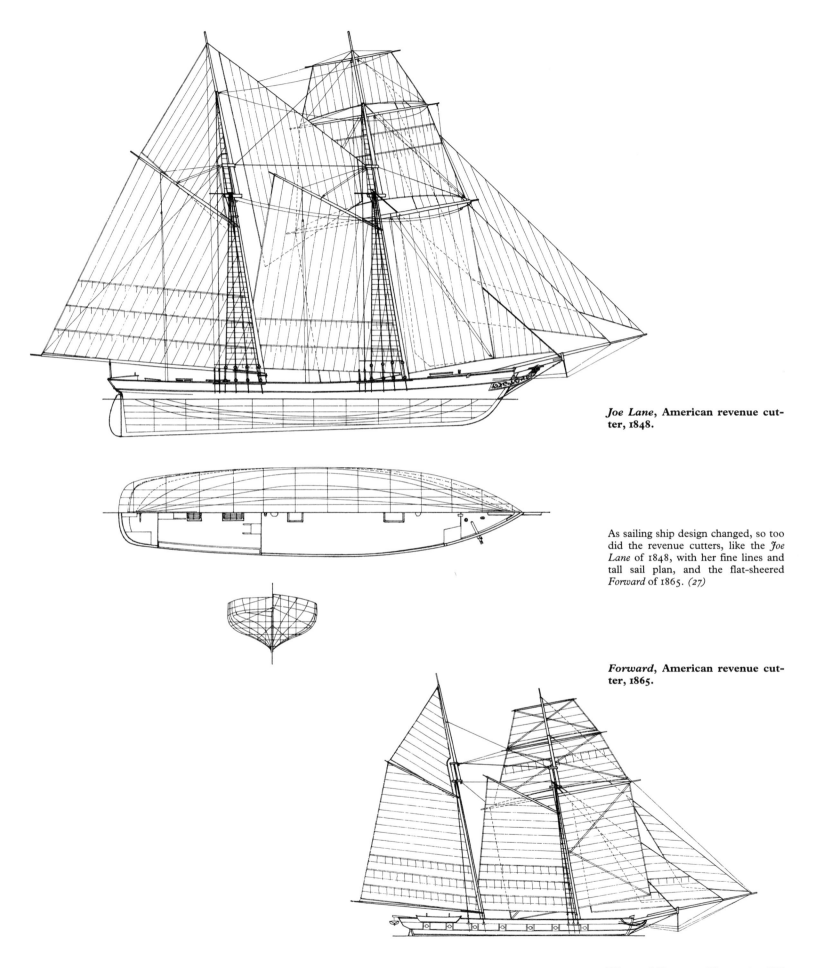

Joe Lane, **American revenue cutter, 1848.**

As sailing ship design changed, so too did the revenue cutters, like the *Joe Lane* of 1848, with her fine lines and tall sail plan, and the flat-sheered *Forward* of 1865. *(27)*

Forward, **American revenue cutter, 1865.**

30   20   10   0 ft
1/300 ————————————
      8   4   0 m

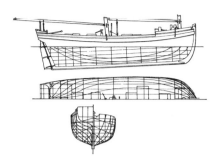

Chebacco dogbody, 1805. In re-building their fishing fleet after Independence, the Americans of Chebacco parish, Massachusetts, produced low-cost, two-masted fishing craft of about 10 metres length, called a dogbody. It was a square-sterned version of the usually pink-ended Chebacco boats. *(32)*

Manhattan, Noank well-smack sloop, 1854. Built in Noank, Connecticut for the New York fisheries market, she was one of the last of the fast-sailing sloops, the large sea-going vessels being replaced by schooners. These sloops had a wet fish well amidships, and set a powerful gaff-cutter rig with gaff topsail and two headsails; a square course and topsail could be set flying in favourable weather. *(28)*

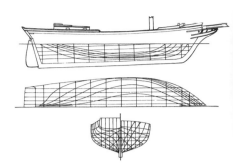

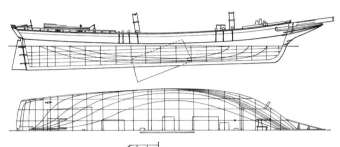

Sunny South, oyster schooner, 1855. Built at Baltimore, she was very fast, her role being to buy the oysters from the fishing craft and speed them to market. Her mainmast was offset to port of her centreline, with the centre-board just to starboard. Almost 22 metres in length, she drew 2 metres and being a long-keel craft was known as a 'pungy'. *(32)*

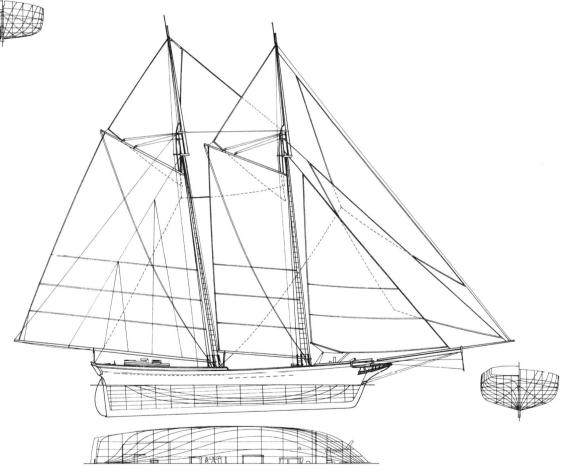

North American Fishing Boats

The extensive coasts of Canada and the United States, particularly on the eastern seaboard, provide considerable fishing grounds. A number of distinctive types of fishing boat were developed to hunt these extensive waters.

Flying Fish, mackerel schooner, 1857. Built in Massachusetts for the Gloucester mackerel fishery in 1857, the *Flying Fish* later went south on expeditions to Antarctica to hunt seals and sea elephants. Her tall rig and fine hull mark her as a 'clipper-fisherman' and she proved a fast sailer. It was necessary for fishing boats built for mackerel fishing to be efficient to windward, since their quarry frequently swam into the wind. *(32)*

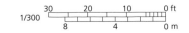

1/300 · 8 · 4 · 0 m · 30 · 20 · 10 · 0 ft

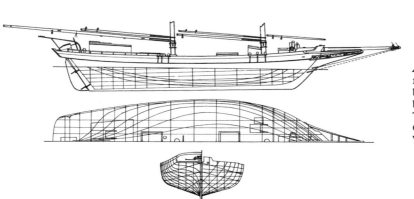

Amanda F Lewis, pungy schooner, 1884. A Chesapeake Bay schooner built with a deep keel and no centreboard was commonly called a 'pungy'. They were used as fishermen out of Gloucester, Massachusetts, and in the West Indian fruit trade. (28)

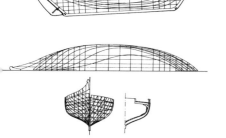

Dove, pinky, 1875. The pink-stern was favoured in some Chebacco boats and led to the development of the 'pinky', a slim-hulled, schooner-rigged fishing boat with considerable rake in both stem- and stern-posts. The *Dove* was built in 1875 and in fact used as a pilot boat for the port of Eastport, Maine. (32)

Lillie Sterling, bugeye, 1885. The Chesapeake 'bugeye' was a shoal-draught centreboarder which is thought to have derived from a log-canoe. (28)

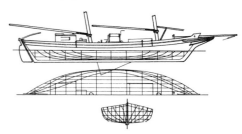

Florida sharpie, 1889. The flat-bottomed, hard-chined 'sharpie' was built for fishing but inspired a cheap and simply constructed form of yacht. This sharpie of 1899 from Florida is schooner-rigged. Note the balanced rudder and the extremely shallow draught for which a centreboard was essential. The sails were usually leg-of-mutton shaped. (28)

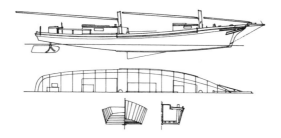

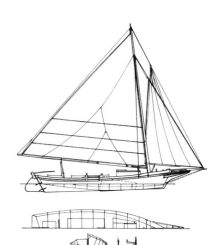

Albemarle Sound seine boat. Tucked in the extensive waters behind the margin of Cape Hatteras, the seine-netters of Albemarle Sound retained the sprit rig, with a detached gaff to stretch the foot of the topsail. (29)

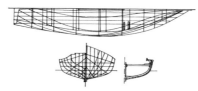

Chesapeake skipjack. The retention of the clipper bow on small craft is a feature of American inshore fishing boats like this Chesapeake 'skipjack'. Shallow draughted, the skipjack was a sloop-rigged, transom-sterned centreboarder, with a leg-of-mutton sail. Note the 'lazy-jacks' on the topping lift, fitted to gather the sail when lowered and avoid its filling the working well of the boat. The 'bowsprit' was not a single spar but a horizontal lattice of light sectioned timbers. (29)

30 20 10 0 ft

1/300

8   4   0 m

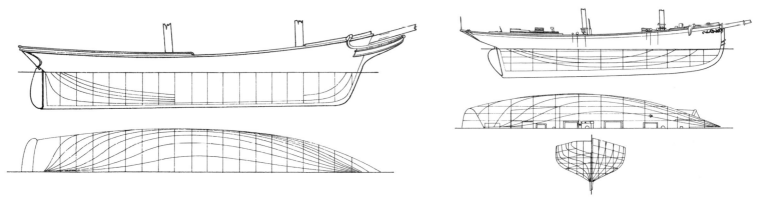

American clipper fishing schooner, about 1880. By the middle of the nineteenth century, the Chebacco dogbodies and pinkies, the pungy schooners and sharpshooters had evolved into the clipper-schooner. This vigorous development is clear evidence of the impetus given to design in a fishery where the economic rewards were apparently incremental. This clipper-schooner of the 1880s has the wide, square stern typical of North American craft, but her under-body is sharp forward and she was a 'market-schooner', taking her catch to market at speed. *(27)*

Nickerson, 1889. By the late 1880s, the long overhanging bow with its fiddlehead was being replaced by a straight stem, seen here on the *Nickerson*, built at Essex, Massachusetts in 1889. Arguments as to her name led her to being named 'for the whole damned family'! Yacht designers like the prolific, but tragically short-lived Edward Burgess, also designed fishing schooners and these were taking on a more yacht-like appearance for fast passages home with their catch. *(32)*

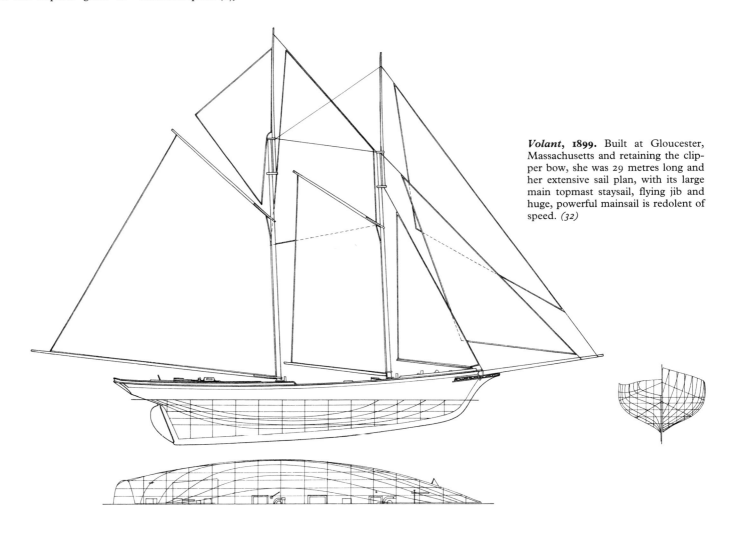

Volant, 1899. Built at Gloucester, Massachusetts and retaining the clipper bow, she was 29 metres long and her extensive sail plan, with its large main topmast staysail, flying jib and huge, powerful mainsail is redolent of speed. *(32)*

The Grand Banks Schooner

The great harvests of fish to be taken on the Grand Banks were known to Europeans before the end of the fifteenth century and by the eighteenth, the settlers of Massachusetts and Nova Scotia had joined the Portuguese, Dutch, French, British and Spanish fishing fleets for whom the vast shoals seemed inexhaustible. Catches were chiefly of cod and halibut though herring and mackerel were also taken.

1/300

30   20   10   0 ft

8   4   0 m

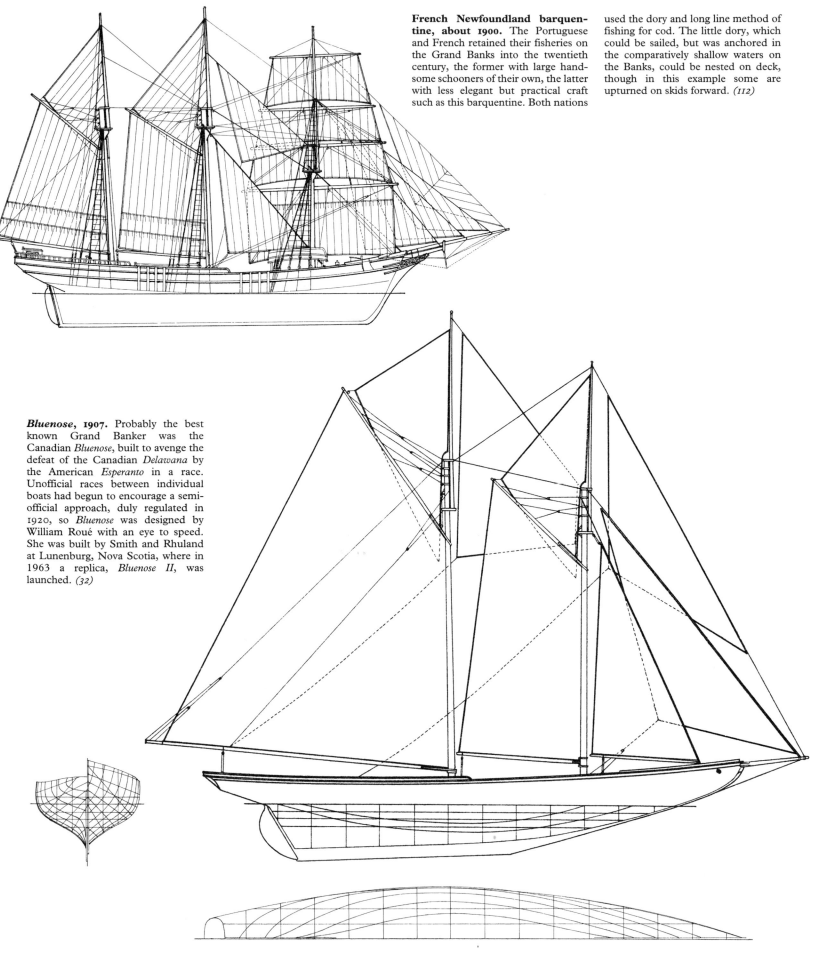

French Newfoundland barquentine, about 1900. The Portuguese and French retained their fisheries on the Grand Banks into the twentieth century, the former with large handsome schooners of their own, the latter with less elegant but practical craft such as this barquentine. Both nations used the dory and long line method of fishing for cod. The little dory, which could be sailed, but was anchored in the comparatively shallow waters on the Banks, could be nested on deck, though in this example some are upturned on skids forward. *(112)*

Bluenose, 1907. Probably the best known Grand Banker was the Canadian *Bluenose*, built to avenge the defeat of the Canadian *Delawana* by the American *Esperanto* in a race. Unofficial races between individual boats had begun to encourage a semiofficial approach, duly regulated in 1920, so *Bluenose* was designed by William Roué with an eye to speed. She was built by Smith and Rhuland at Lunenburg, Nova Scotia, where in 1963 a replica, *Bluenose II*, was launched. *(32)*

30 20 10 0 ft
1/300
8   4   0 m

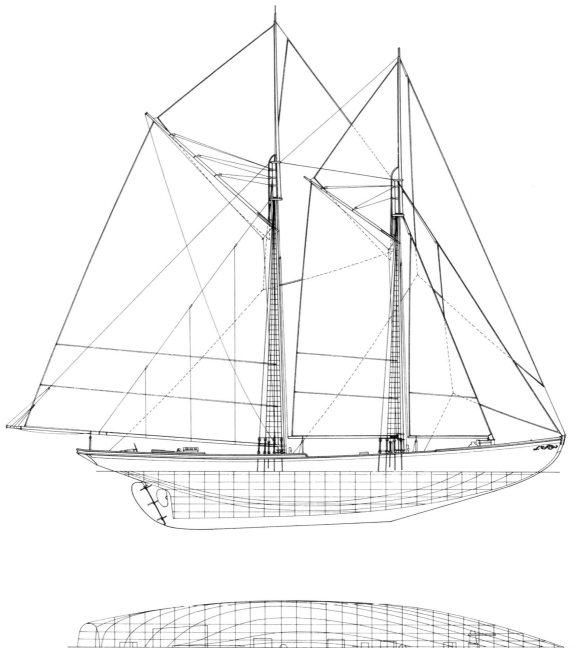

***Arethusa*, 1907.** While in 1907 *Blue-nose* was built for speed, the *Arethusa*, built by Tarr and James at Essex, was a more prosaic 'knockabout' fisher-man, with no bowsprit. However, she proved fast and weatherly and is reputed to have outrun a Canadian steam fishery protection vessel. With a bowsprit fitted she achieved a reputa-tion of some notoriety as a rum-runner during the Prohibition period. *(32)*

30   20   10   0 ft
1/300
8   4   0 m

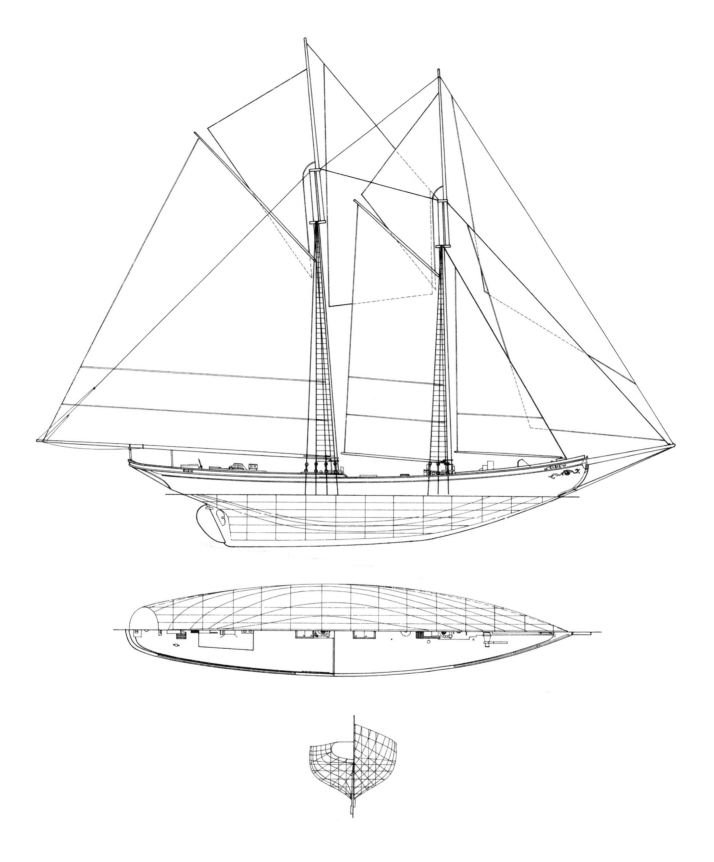

Elsie, 1910. A fishing schooner built in Massachusetts, she was fitted with an auxiliary engine at her building in 1910. She, more than *Bluenose* and the last few post-war race-built schooners, mark the high water-mark of the working Grand Banks schooner. Having beaten the home competition, *Elsie* was defeated by *Bluenose* in 1921, but this in no way detracts from her beauty which some may find more pleasing, particularly about her bow which lacks the over-eager reach of the Nova Scotian. The deck plan shows the break in the deck, giving a wide low forward area for the stacking of the dories. *(27)*

1/300 30 20 10 0 ft
8 4 0 m

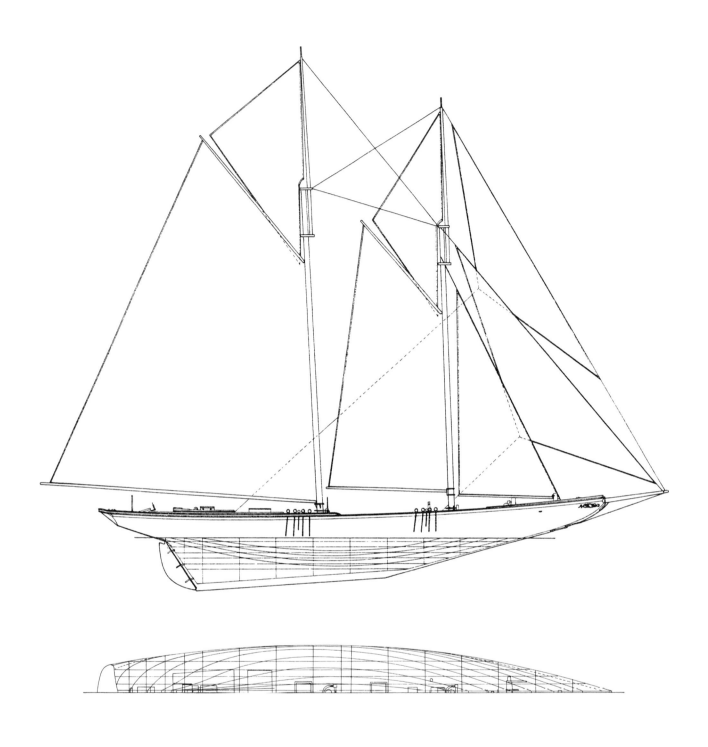

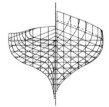

***Puritan*, 1922.** Designed as a racing fisherman by Starling Burgess, the Essex-built *Puritan* was measured at 42 metres on the deck. She was extremely fast and in June 1922, on only her third fishing voyage, when sailing on dead-reckoning, was ahead of this and ran hard aground on Sable Island. Only one man of her crew was saved. *(32)*

1/300

30	20	10	0 ft
8		4	0 m

Falmouth oyster dredger, present day. Half-decked and transom-sterned, the Falmouth oyster dredger not only worked in the River Fal, but also the Helford River. To conserve stocks, oyster dredging is illegal under power and these craft are therefore still working, though today made from GRP (Glass-Reinforced Plastic). *(101)*

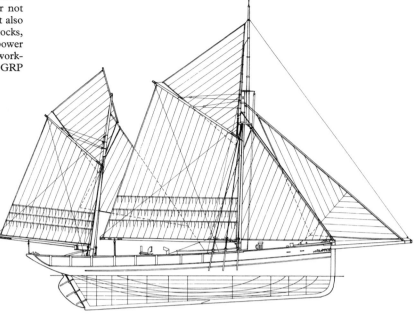

Master Hand, 1920. Typical of the big sailing trawlers of the British east coast port of Lowestoft and the Devon port of Brixham, the *Master Hand* is a powerful craft, capable of towing a heavy trawl along the sea-bed. *Master Hand* was built in 1920 to replace tonnage lost in the First World War. *(235)*

Norwegian Cap Stadt fishing boat.

Trondheim fishing boat.

The Norse tradition of lapstrake construction remained dominant in these two Norwegian fisherman of 1873. In the boat from Cap Stadt, the square sail has been retained, whereas the

boat from Trondheim, has a lugger rig. Note the steering arrangements and the slab reefing in the square sail of the Cap Stadt boat. *(170)*

Fishing Craft of Northern Europe

The coasts of Norway, Denmark, Germany, The Netherlands and the British Isles produced a huge variety of sailing fishing boats, each fitted for her particular task in the snaring of fish. Comprehensive coverage is beyond a single book, and what follows is a very small selection.

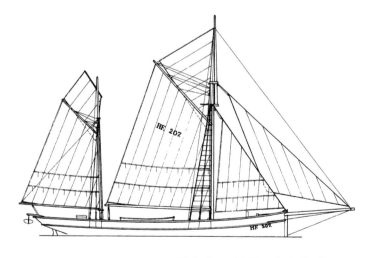

Victoria and Julius, 1888. The German North Sea coast produced this 'fischkutter'; actually ketch-rigged she is similar to her British cousins from Lowestoft. *(182)*

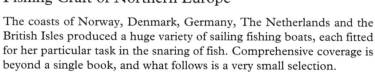

1/300 30 20 10 0 ft
       8   4   0 m

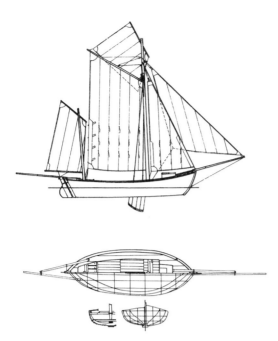

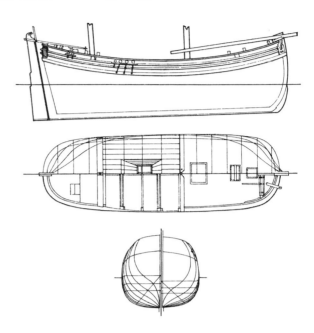

Dutch hummer-huker, mid-eigh-teenth century. Of the many types of Dutch craft the 'hummer-huker' was named originally from her venturing out beyond the sand spits of the Friesian Islands and many, as has already been noted, were used for freight. In fact fishing hukers also ventured much farther, as far as the Arctic, though they were chiefly used in the North Sea herring fishery. *(34)*

German zeesen boat, about 1920. There were two forms of 'zeesen' boat built and used on the Baltic coast of Germany. They were named for the type of trawl with which they fished for eels, which did not have conventional otter boards. This example built in about 1920 is from Mecklenburg and has a gaff mainsail, rather than a lug-sail. Beamy and shallow-draughted, they were centreboarders. *(52)*

Dutch bons. Another craft from the Zuider Zee was the little 'bons' used for catching anchovies and herring. *(90)*

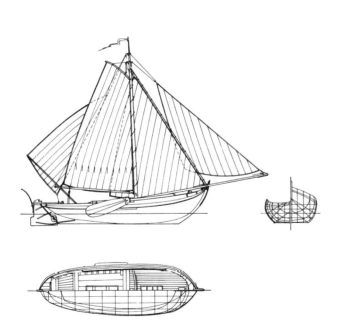

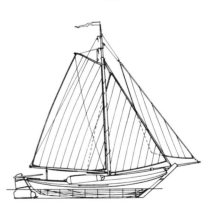

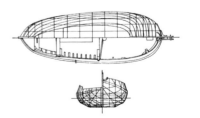

Vrouwe Cornelia, **Dutch botter, 1895.** The 'botter', originally from the island of Marken in the Zuider Zee migrated to other parts of The Netherlands. This example was fitted with an auxiliary engine. *(90)*

1/300

30   20   10   0 ft

8   4   0 m

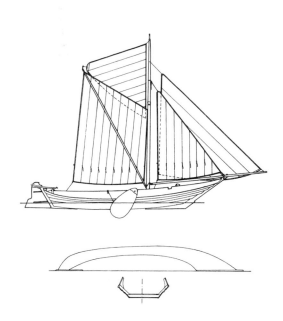

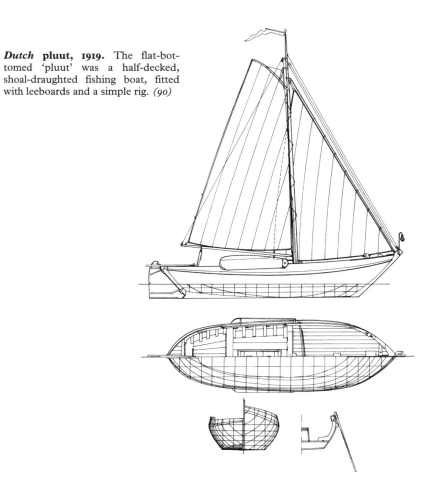

Dutch pluut, 1919. The flat-bottomed 'pluut' was a half-decked, shoal-draughted fishing boat, fitted with leeboards and a simple rig. *(90)*

Dutch hoogar, 1895. The 'hoogar', whose name derives from the same root as huker, was a sprit-rigged freight and fishing boat of wide-plank construction. This example from Kinderdijk dates from 1895. The hoogar is unusual in having her greater draught forward and possesses a lot of tumblehome. She was used in the Schelde for mussel fishing. *(15)*

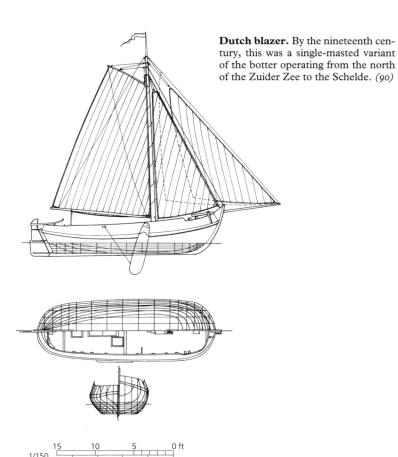

Dutch blazer. By the nineteenth century, this was a single-masted variant of the botter operating from the north of the Zuider Zee to the Schelde. *(90)*

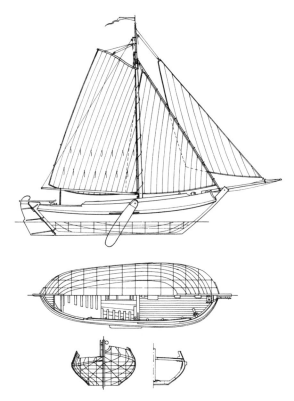

UK 110, Dutch schokker, 1883. A term of extreme longevity, by 1883, the 'schokker' was a humble sailing trawler coming originally from the Zuider Zee. Her boom was used to handle the trawl and the hull was massively built with wide planks and a heavy stem-post bearing a groove for her heavy grapnel anchor. *(90)*

15   10   5   0 ft
1/150
4   3   2   1   0 m

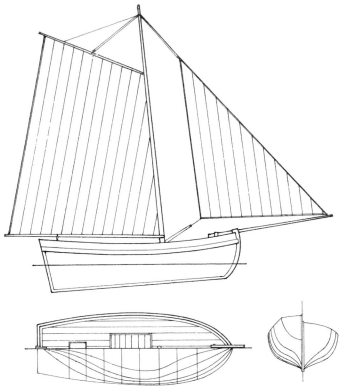

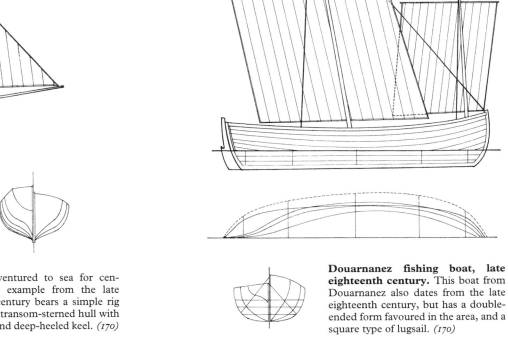

Ouessant fishing boat, late eighteenth century. The extremely hazardous, tidal and stormy waters of the north-west coast of France were nonetheless rich in fish and in the vicinity of the Île d'Ouessant fishing craft have ventured to sea for centuries. This example from the late eighteenth century bears a simple rig and a stout, transom-sterned hull with a full body and deep-heeled keel. *(170)*

Douarnanez fishing boat, late eighteenth century. This boat from Douarnanez also dates from the late eighteenth century, but has a double-ended form favoured in the area, and a square type of lugsail. *(170)*

Concarneau fishing boat, 1878. Almost a century later, the hull-shape has become more extreme, as is seen in this fishing boat from Concarneau on the southern side of the Brest peninsula. *(170)*

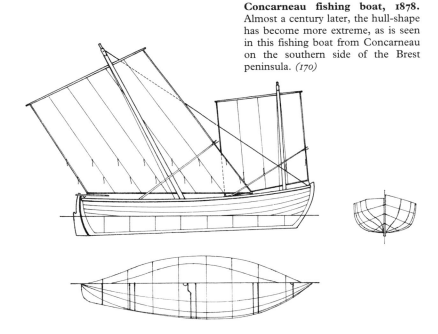

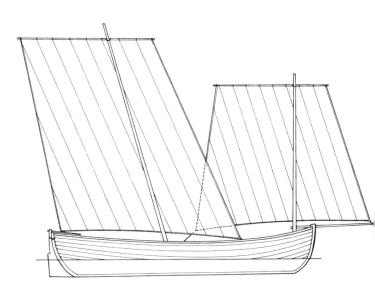

Traditional Fishing Craft of the French Atlantic Coast

It is interesting to contrast with the foregoing the craft developed on the wild north and west coasts of France which, outside their country of origin, are less well-known. There are obvious similarities with vessels of neighbouring areas, particularly the Celtic coasts of the British Isles.

Bayonne tricandour, about 1880. At the other, southern, end of the Biscay coast, this 'tricandour' from Bayonne also possesses a square, lugsail rig and a double-ended hull, suitable for net fishing, long-lining and passing through short, breaking seas. *(170)*

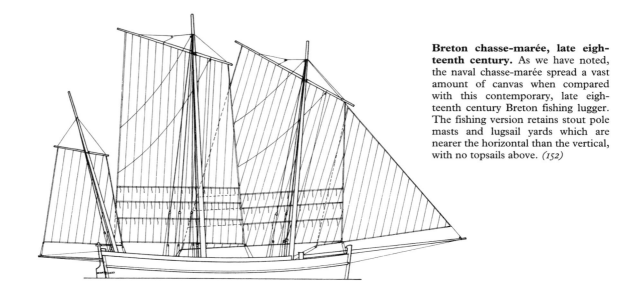

Breton chasse-marée, late eighteenth century. As we have noted, the naval chasse-marée spread a vast amount of canvas when compared with this contemporary, late eighteenth century Breton fishing lugger. The fishing version retains stout pole masts and lugsail yards which are nearer the horizontal than the vertical, with no topsails above. *(152)*

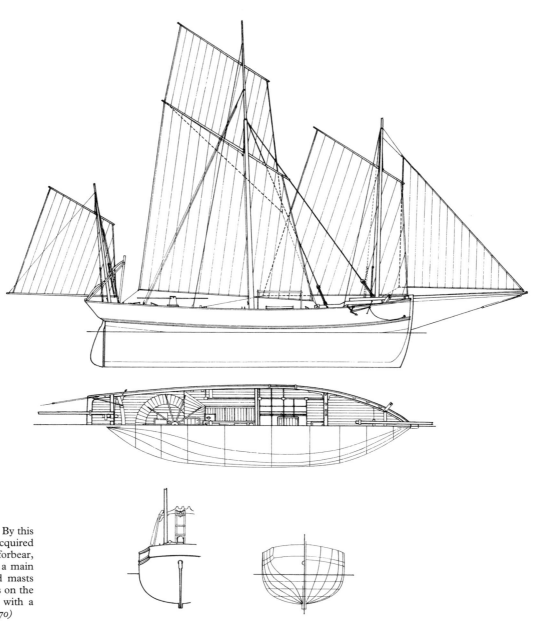

French fishing lugger, 1876. By this time the fishing lugger has acquired much of the look of her naval forbear, with higher peaked yards and a main topsail. However, her forward masts lower onto gallows when she is on the grounds and she is furnished with a capstan for rehoisting them. *(170)*

St Louis, Honfleur lugger, 1854.

The ancient port of Honfleur long supported a fishing fleet used to working the less vicious waters of the English Channel, or Le Manche. These luggers of 1854 are double-ended and have traditional cod-head and mackerel-tailed underbodies. The two-master *St Louis* of 1854, carries a light topmast on her main whereupon a topsail was set in good weather. Her mainsail is not sheeted to a bumpkin projecting over the stern, as was so common in many luggers, but uses a boom. The smaller version, *L'Espérance* of 1866, has a long pole-mast upon which a topsail could be set. Such sail plans were capable of hauling pelagic or benthic nets. *(170)*

L'Espérance, Honfleur fishing boat, 1866.

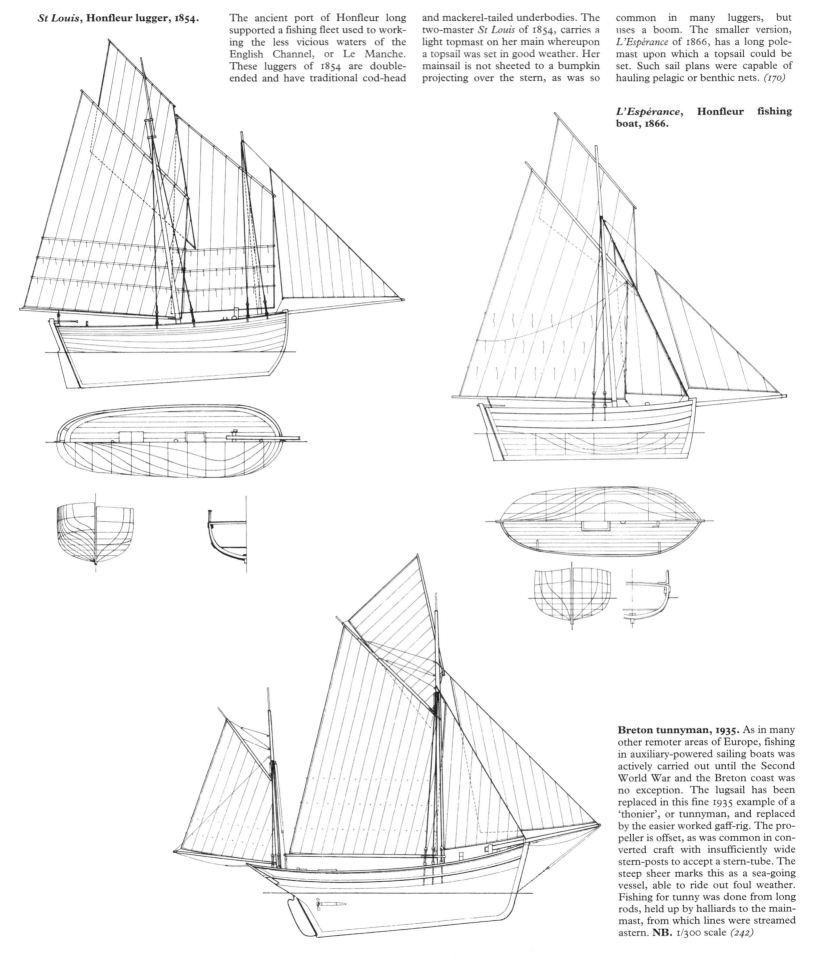

Breton tunnyman, 1935. As in many other remoter areas of Europe, fishing in auxiliary-powered sailing boats was actively carried out until the Second World War and the Breton coast was no exception. The lugsail has been replaced in this fine 1935 example of a 'thonier', or tunnyman, and replaced by the easier worked gaff-rig. The propeller is offset, as was common in converted craft with insufficiently wide stern-posts to accept a stern-tube. The steep sheer marks this as a sea-going vessel, able to ride out foul weather. Fishing for tunny was done from long rods, held up by halliards to the main-mast, from which lines were streamed astern. **NB.** 1/300 scale *(242)*

1/150   15   10   5   0 ft
        4   3   2   1   0 m

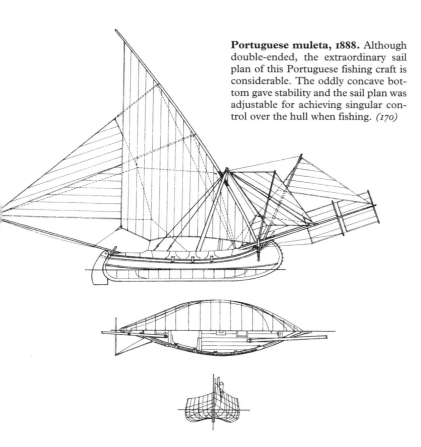

Portuguese muleta, 1888. Although double-ended, the extraordinary sail plan of this Portuguese fishing craft is considerable. The oddly concave bottom gave stability and the sail plan was adjustable for achieving singular control over the hull when fishing. *(170)*

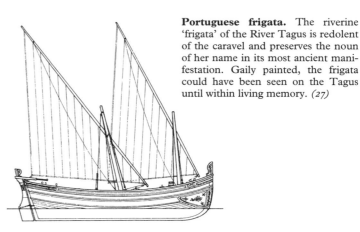

Portuguese frigata. The riverine 'frigata' of the River Tagus is redolent of the caravel and preserves the noun of her name in its most ancient manifestation. Gaily painted, the frigata could have been seen on the Tagus until within living memory. *(27)*

Rhône delta bette. The flat-bottomed 'bette' from the estuary of the River Rhône in southern France, was a fishing boat which adapted to use as a pleasure yacht during the nineteenth century. Its simple lateen rig was improved for windward work with a jib. *(45)*

Ligurian fishing craft, 1882.
The variety of local rigs is demonstrated here by two Italian fishing boats from the Ligurian coast around Genoa recorded in 1882. The larger 'bilancella' (right) was a long, decked craft which, like the bette, had adopted a jib which was tacked down to a bowsprit as her mast was raked forward to carry her large lateen mainsail. The general type was common along the coasts of Spain, France and Italy. The smaller open boat is sprit rigged and was known only as a 'batello peschereccia', translating simply as 'fishing boat'. **NB.** 1/150 scale. *(170)*

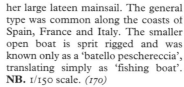

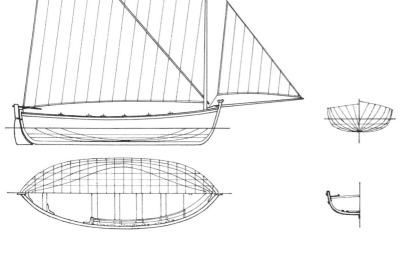

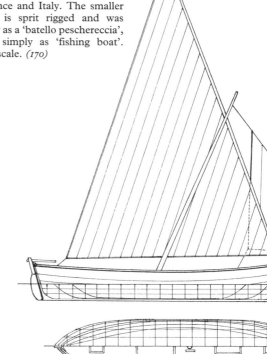

Southern European Fishing Boats

As with trading sailing vessels, the fishermen of southern Europe show their distinctive Arab inheritance. Their contrast with their northern cousins is therefore exotic and is marked almost exactly by the northernmost penetration of the Moors into the Iberian peninsula.

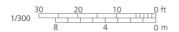

1/300

30   20   10   0 ft

8   4   0 m

Sicilian laoutello, 1882. The curious after rake of the stem which was characteristic of Sicilian shipbuilding did not prevent the 'laoutello' being built in large numbers or surviving into the twentieth century. Up to about 20 metres in length, the laoutello almost stubbornly seems to have retained the characteristics of a vessel from an earlier era. (170)

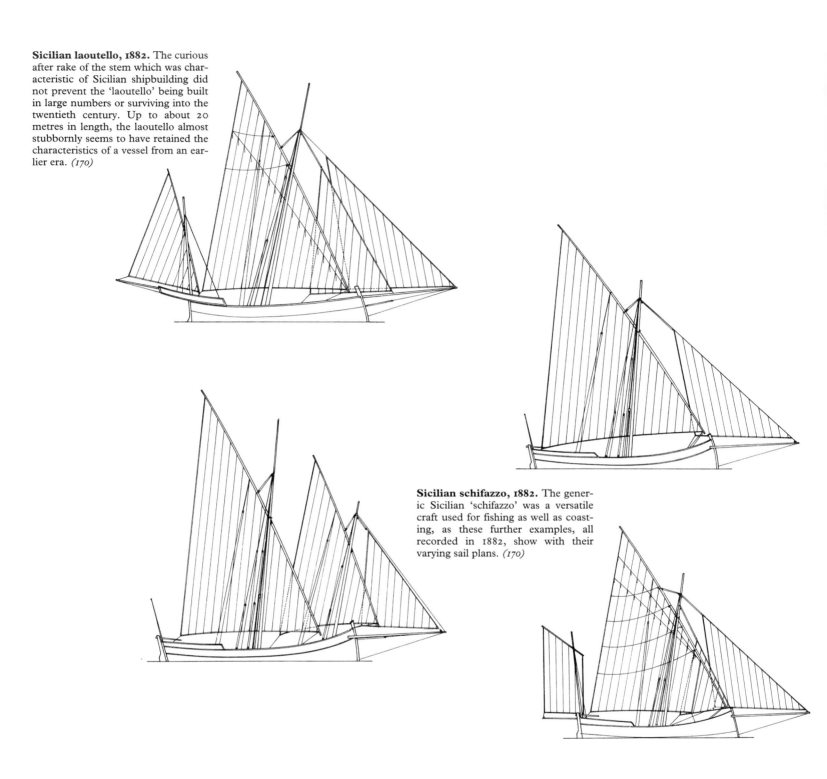

Sicilian schifazzo, 1882. The generic Sicilian 'schifazzo' was a versatile craft used for fishing as well as coasting, as these further examples, all recorded in 1882, show with their varying sail plans. (170)

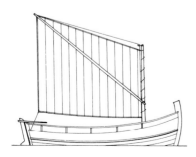

Maltese farella, nineteenth century. Used for both fishing and carrying cargo to and from the neighbouring coast of Tunisia, the crew of the 'farella' could fit additional washboards along her sides, raising her freeboard when necessary. Her sail plan was a very simple sprit-rig and her hull exhibited the exuberant colours common to many small Mediterranean vessels, but particularly characteristic of the Maltese. **NB.** 1/150 scale. (45)

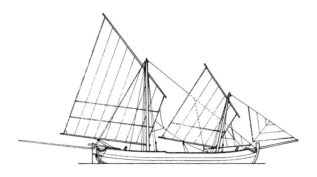

Adriatic bragazza, of the nineteenth century. In the Adriatic the lugsail was favoured over the lateen by the fishermen of Venice, Giulia, Istria and Dalmatia. The 'bragazza' was in existence into the twentieth century and was a large offshore fishing boat which was also fitted for pulling in calm weather. *(139)*

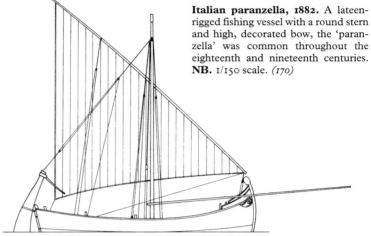

Italian paranzella, 1882. A lateen-rigged fishing vessel with a round stern and high, decorated bow, the 'paranzella' was common throughout the eighteenth and nineteenth centuries. **NB.** 1/150 scale. *(170)*

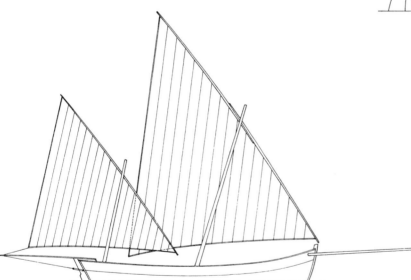

Italian paredgia, 1882. The less extreme form of the 'paredgia' marks her as a later development for although she is lateen-rigged, like other late nineteenth century Franco-Italian Mediterranean craft, she bears a bowsprit upon which a jib could be set. **NB.** 1/150 scale. *(170)*

Tunisian loude, 1882. The absolute simplicity of this 'loude' of the late nineteenth century from Sfax on the Tunisian coast, is an example of a craft developed for subsistence fishing. Oddly the rig has abandoned the lateen for a quaint quasi-lugsail reminiscent of the early fishing boats of Brittany. *(170)*

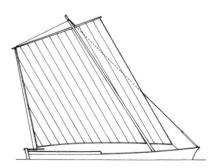

30   20   10   0 ft
1/300 ├──────────────────┤
      8   4   0 m

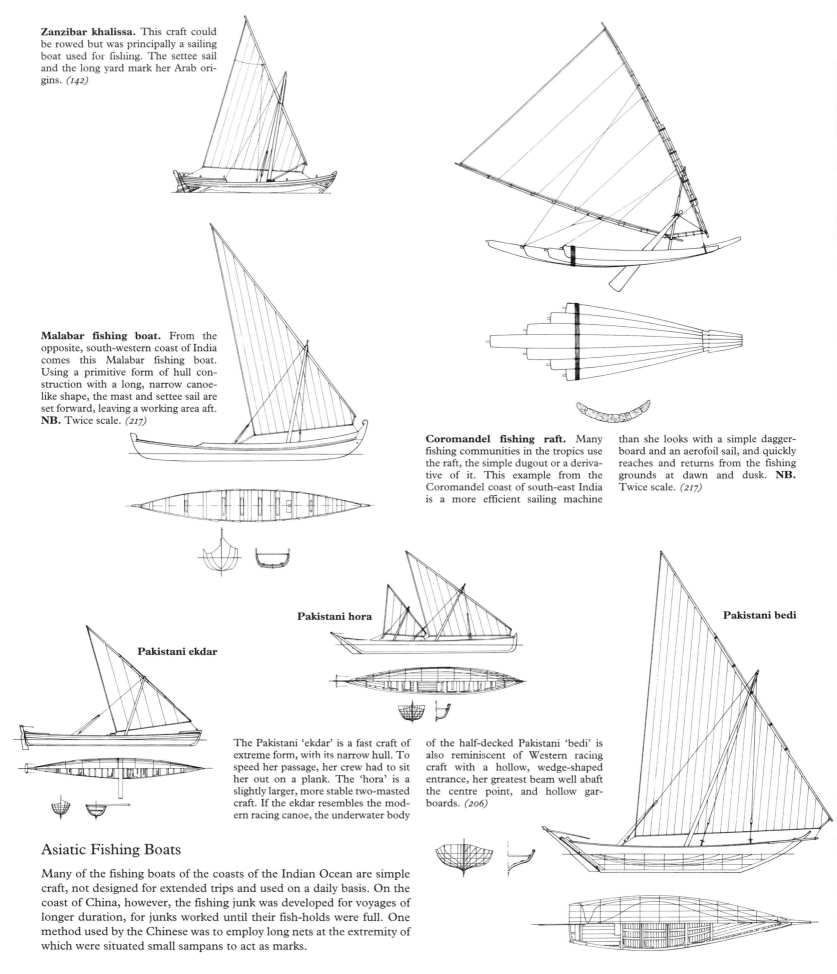

Zanzibar khalissa. This craft could be rowed but was principally a sailing boat used for fishing. The settee sail and the long yard mark her Arab origins. *(142)*

Malabar fishing boat. From the opposite, south-western coast of India comes this Malabar fishing boat. Using a primitive form of hull construction with a long, narrow canoe-like shape, the mast and settee sail are set forward, leaving a working area aft. **NB.** Twice scale. *(217)*

Coromandel fishing raft. Many fishing communities in the tropics use the raft, the simple dugout or a derivative of it. This example from the Coromandel coast of south-east India is a more efficient sailing machine than she looks with a simple daggerboard and an aerofoil sail, and quickly reaches and returns from the fishing grounds at dawn and dusk. **NB.** Twice scale. *(217)*

Pakistani ekdar

Pakistani hora

Pakistani bedi

The Pakistani 'ekdar' is a fast craft of extreme form, with its narrow hull. To speed her passage, her crew had to sit her out on a plank. The 'hora' is a slightly larger, more stable two-masted craft. If the ekdar resembles the modern racing canoe, the underwater body of the half-decked Pakistani 'bedi' is also reminiscent of Western racing craft with a hollow, wedge-shaped entrance, her greatest beam well abaft the centre point, and hollow garboards. *(206)*

Asiatic Fishing Boats

Many of the fishing boats of the coasts of the Indian Ocean are simple craft, not designed for extended trips and used on a daily basis. On the coast of China, however, the fishing junk was developed for voyages of longer duration, for junks worked until their fish-holds were full. One method used by the Chinese was to employ long nets at the extremity of which were situated small sampans to act as marks.

30   20   10   0 ft
1/300
8   4   0 m

Chusan fishing boat. The fishing craft of the Chusan archipelago are not intended for more than short trips to sea and although they appear to have 'European' spritsails, the complex sheeting arrangement is entirely Chinese in conception. *(142)*

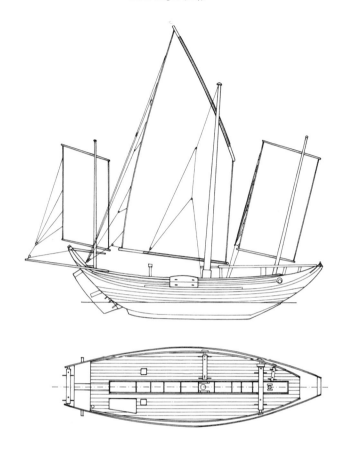

Amoy fishing junk. The fishing fleet of Amoy had fished the Taiwan Strait for generations and these modest fishing junks were remarkably seaworthy little ships. *(227)*

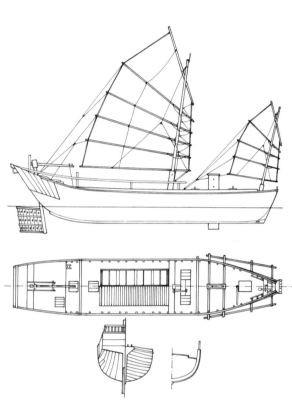

Tsat Pong trawler. This craft has the deep, but pierced, rudder and high-peaked sail plan typical of the junks of southern China. Note also her centreboard, enabling her to fish in shallow water. *(227)*

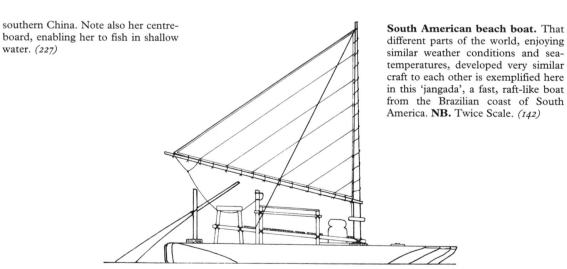

South American beach boat. That different parts of the world, enjoying similar weather conditions and sea-temperatures, developed very similar craft to each other is exemplified here in this 'jangada', a fast, raft-like boat from the Brazilian coast of South America. **NB.** Twice Scale. *(142)*

30   20   10   0 ft
1/300
8   4   0 m

German *Hoffnung*, 1780. Europeans pursued the Greenland right whale in the Arctic from the sixteenth century, when flutes were commonly sent north, but by the eighteenth century a form of vessel had been developed that was strong enough to voyage in loose pack ice, with a substantial freeboard and the ability to hoist her boats more efficiently than was the common practice in contemporary men-of-war and merchantmen. The *Hoffnung*, a German brig, shows how far this specialised vessel had advanced by 1780. Never built for speed, endurance and ease of handling when working through ice floes were of paramount importance in the waters of the Barents Sea and the Davis Strait. Note the barrel at the masthead from which the lookout not only searched for whales but indicated the leads, or passages of free water through the ice. *(243)*

Whale Ships

Initially regarded simply as very large fish, the whale was hunted from as early as the tenth century when the Basques harpooned the Atlantic right whale from small boats in the southern Bay of Biscay. The technique of harpooning from small rowing boats continued up until the twentieth century, though by the mid-nineteenth century, the harpoon was fired from a gun. During the late eighteenth century and greater part of the nineteenth, whaling was carried out entirely in sailing vessels, those whalers venturing to the Pacific after the sperm whale making voyages of up to four years duration. The shorter Arctic voyages, made during the summer season, occasionally resulted in whalers being beset in the ice. This risk and the lack of bunker space meant that sail was retained long after the introduction of steam. The steam whaler and her smaller sister, the sealer, achieved immortality by being used for polar exploration.

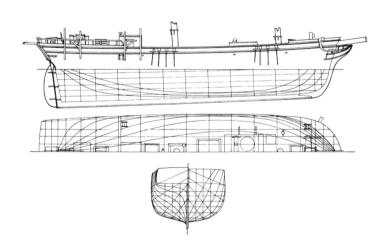

American *Agate*, 1853. The whalers of New England in the United States tended to concentrate on hunting the sperm whale of the Pacific. On such long voyages each whale had to be thoroughly treated at sea, the valuable oil 'tryed' out in brick boilers amidships and the blubber packed into barrels. Note the square stern typical of American ships in the whaler *Agate* of 1853, also the davits fitted on her quarters. *(32)*

30   20   10   0 ft
1/300
8   4   0 m

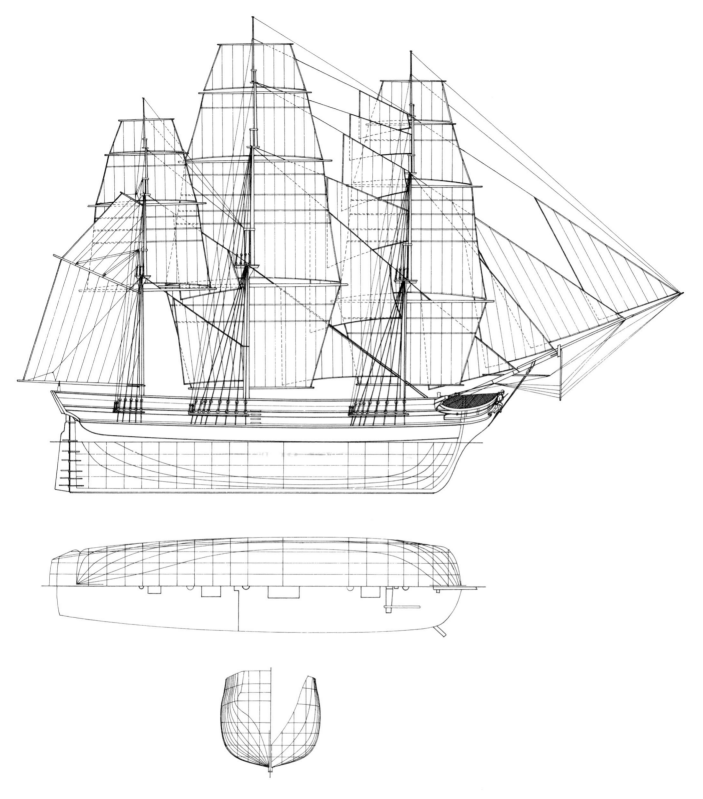

British *Baffin*, 1820. Built at Liverpool in 1820 for Captain William Scoresby, junior, the British whaler *Baffin* was highly successful under his command. A master with a strong scientific bent, Scoresby became a distinguished member of the British intelligentsia. The ship rig is specially modified for short-handed working when many of her crew were away in the boats chasing whales, while the ship had to be kept up with them. Note the smallness of the main and forecourses, and the fact that their feet are laced to Bentinck booms, which much eased their handling. The crossjack is entirely missing, replaced by a gaff topsail above the spanker. The deep single topsails are fitted with multiple reef bands and it was under these sails that the *Baffin* spent much of her time 'cruising' on the whaling grounds. Many British whalers abandoned the yards on the mizen in favour of the simple barque rig. *(131)*

30   20   10   0 ft
1/300
8   4   0 m

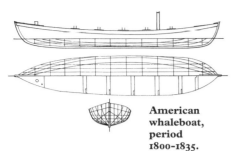

American whaleboat, period 1800-1835.

The graceful shape of the Nantucket whaleboat with its tapering stern sections is shown here in this example typical of the boats lowered from whalers between about 1800 and 1835. Note the heavy vertical timber in the stern. This was the 'loggerhead' round which the harpoon line was run as the boat was towed along, the line running forward and over the bow to the harpoon fast in the whale's body. The whaleboat was pulled up to an unsuspecting whale by oars, while a simple sprit rig was used to cover longer distances as shown in the later American arctic whaleboat used between 1850 and 1870. **NB.** Twice scale. *(29)*

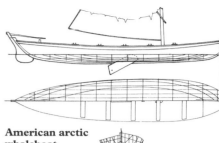

American arctic whaleboat, period 1850-1870.

British auxiliary whaler *Hope*, 1873. Built at Aberdeen by the famous clipper-builders Hall, the *Hope* was registered at Peterhead in Scotland. She was 45.5 metres long, measured 452 gross tons and her engines generated 98 horsepower. On her maiden voyage she encountered and slaughtered 9000 seals, which produced 200 tons of oil, but it was some time before she killed a whale – the following year, in fact. The *Hope* was wrecked in the Gulf of St Lawrence in 1901, her crew of 194 being rescued. The sail plan is interesting, lacking the hard driving power of contemporary deep-water merchant sailing ships, but is ideal for cruising on the whaling grounds. The fore and main possess double topsails, but carry only single topgallants above these. The mizen, though it crosses a single topsail, actually converts to a barque rig for ease of handling when the majority of the crew were away in the whaleboats, the davits for which line the *Hope*'s topsides. *(170)*

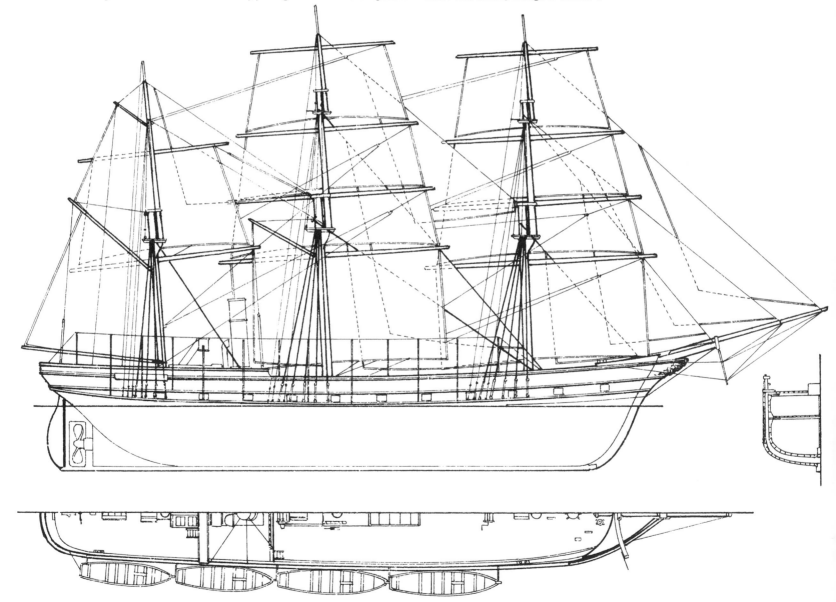

30   20   10   0 ft
1/300
8   4   0 m

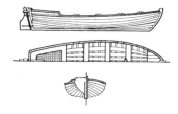

German jolle, 1669. The name derives from the Dutch, so it is not surprising that its use spread rapidly. The British Navy's 'yawl' which developed about this time was adapted from the beach-launched lapstrake yawls from Deal in Kent which serviced ships anchored in The Downs. By the late seventeenth century, British men-of-war carried these as part of their inventory. The warship's yawl pulled from four to eight oars and could also be sailed. *(176)*

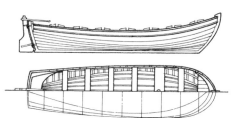

German barkasse, 1669. Another generic term, the 'barkasse' was a larger tender, similar to the British longboat, fitted for oars and sail and with a broad beam capable of conveying considerable loads. *(176)*

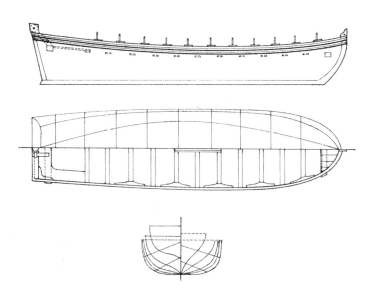

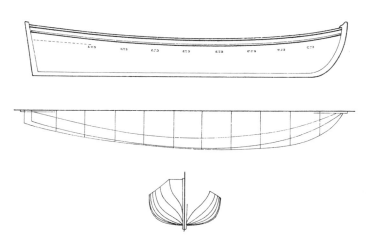

French longboat, 1769. For much of the eighteenth century the 'longboat' was a warship's major boat, used for a multitude of purposes. This example, a French longboat or *chaloupe* of 1769, shows a davit and sheave aft for handling anchor cables and warps, and twenty-two thole pins for oars. Such boats could load stores, land troops or carry out anchors and were vital to the management of a large First, Second or Third Rate ship-of-the-line. The longboat was superseded in the British navy at about this time by the 'launch'. *(168)*

French pinnace or *canot*, 1769. The 'pinnace', once the name of a light and fast warship, was by the eighteenth century a lighter and faster craft than the longboat, capable of being rowed and sailed and often sent away from her parent ship on expeditions, surveying and reconnoitring. This boat was sometimes associated with the commanding officer, as the larger but similar 'barge' was often considered a flag officer's boat. *(168)*

Ships' Boats

In an age which thinks of a ship's boats as being specifically intended for lifesaving, it is important to realise that until the twentieth century a ship's boats were intended for less dramatic purposes more closely associated with her everyday working life in port or when 'on the coast'. At sea, making a passage, they were usually well secured, for it was not until serious attention was paid to the development of davits that mass boat-lowering and evacuation of a payload of passengers was actually a realistic proposition. Sailing men-of-war bore a considerable number of boats which ranged from the captain's gig or barge, through various medium-sized boats for an assortment of duties, to the heavy launch which could be sent ashore to forage for wood and water, or load a carronade and lead an attack. Always a matter of fashion and usage, boat names such as 'cutter' and 'yawl' often used terminology we now associate with rig, but at the time had no connection either with their own, or any other rig. For instance, the 9.75-metre (32-foot) naval pulling 'cutter' used in the larger ships of the British Royal Navy up until the 1950s began life with a lugsail rig, but ended her service with a 'sloop' rig.

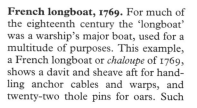

15   10   5   0 ft
1/150
4   3   2   1   0 m

The complex establishments of the French eighteenth century navy produced a range of 'chaloupes' for each 'rang', or rate, shown here in descending order. They were all effectively a warship's major tender, roughly the equivalent of her longboat, used for heavy lifting purposes and shipping a two-masted sailing rig. (170)

Chaloupe for First Rates.

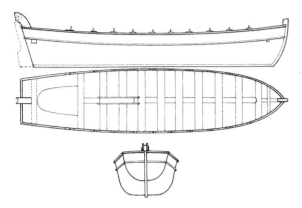

Chaloupe for Second Rates.

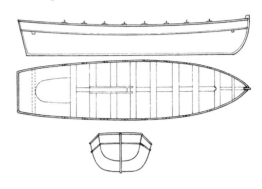

Chaloupe for Third Rates.

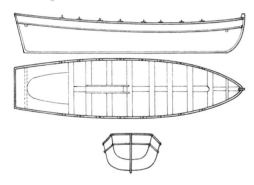

Chaloupe for Fourth Rates.

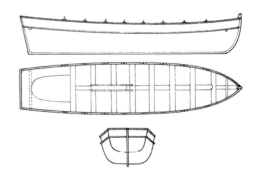

Chaloupe for Fifth Rates.

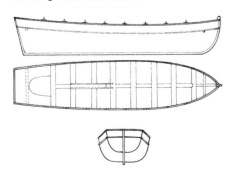

Chaloupe for frigates.

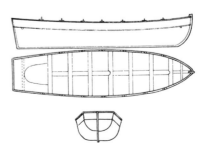

15   10   5   0 ft
1/150
4   3   2   1   0 m

Canot for First Rates.

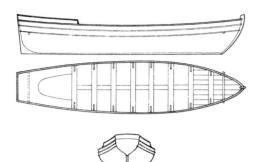

Canot for Second Rates.

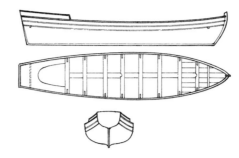

Canot for Third Rates.

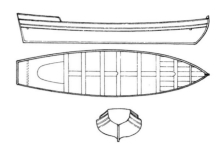

Canot for Fourth Rates.

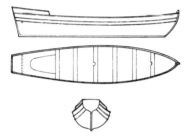

Canot for frigates.

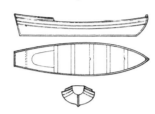

The 'canot' was the military boat, equivalent to the British yawl or cutter, and these too were built to a regulation pattern, a size for each 'rang'. (170)

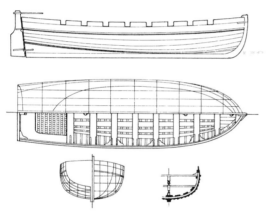

Launch, early nineteenth century. Originally a dockyard workboat, the heavily-built 'launch' superseded the longboat in the British navy during the last quarter of the eighteenth century. In such a boat Lieutenant Bligh made his trans-Pacific voyage of 3600 miles after the mutiny on the *Bounty* in 1789. This example is of lapstrake construction, but carvel-built launches were more common in ships-of-the-line. A launch, like a longboat, yawl or cutter, was double banked, with an oar being worked on either side. (236)

Naval whaler, nineteenth century. The British Navy adopted the Arctic whaleboat as the standard sea-boat, ready for duty at a moment's notice. The 'whaler's' double-ended hull made it an able boat for all duties, including landing in a surf. She was single-banked, with three oars to starboard and three to port, and hoisted a rig consisting of jib and gunter-rigged, loose-footed mainsail with a small, leg-of-mutton mizen. (236)

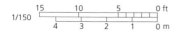
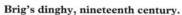

Brig's launch, nineteenth century. The needs of a man-of-war, whatever her size, were roughly similar. In fact small 'cruisers' acting independently, often made more contact with the shore than larger warships, and might land raiding and cutting out parties more frequently too. Thus even a brig-of-war required a heavy-duty boat and this is an early nineteenth century launch from such a minor cruiser. (236)

Brig's dinghy, nineteenth century. Space, however, curtailed the carriage of the variety of boats which a larger frigate bore and a brig might substitute a smaller oared boat like this lapstrake dinghy. In the Royal Navy the term was introduced about 1825; before that by naval convention the smallest boat (a cutter) was known as the 'jollyboat'. (236)

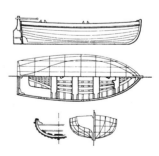

15 10 5 0 ft
1/150
4 3 2 1 0 m

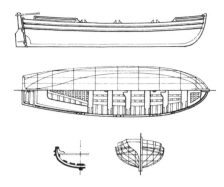

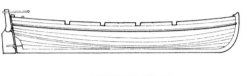

Warship's yawl, about 1800. Many men-of-war of the larger classes bore a wide variety of boats such as this yawl which, in addition to her oars, could ship a pair of short masts and sails. *(236)*

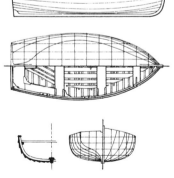

Warship's cutter, about 1800. A warship of consequence possessed two or three cutters. Their clinker construction making them relatively light, by the beginning of the nineteenth century these were slung on simple davits either side of the quarterdeck and across the stern, ready for use.

Used to put a prize-crew aboard a captured vessel, take part in cutting-out expeditions or carry the officers ashore for a dance, they were versatile craft capable of being sailed and were often dispatched on detached duties for days at a time. *(236)*

Working-boat's dinghy. The working fishing smack, like the sailing barge, ketch and schooner, always carried a working-boat for rowing out warps, taking the master ashore and painting the side. This twentieth century smack's dinghy is typical of a simple lapstrake tender. Steam tramps often carried a large dinghy which revived an ancient term, for they were usually called 'jollyboats'. **NB.** 1/100 scale. *(236)*

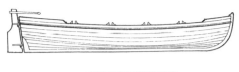

Warship's pinnace, about 1800. The pinnace or barge was a warship's smartest boat, often specially painted, with her crew decked out in a fancy rig at her captain's expense. Although used to convey senior officers, the pinnace or barge was equally at home leading a cutting-out expedition. They were usually of carvel construction. *(236)*

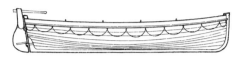

Merchantman's work-boat. The demands of a merchant ship for the services of a boat were much less, though sailing vessel masters often required ferrying ashore to attend to the ship's business. It was common therefore for a working-boat to be kept for this duty by the ship's apprentices who formed her crew when required. *(236)*

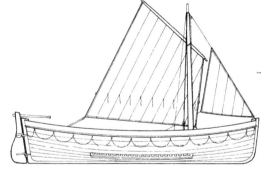

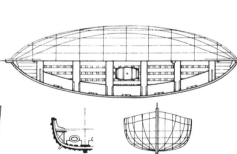

Ship's lifeboat. The dedicated lifeboat was essentially a feature of steamships, but the provision of a sailing rig and a number of epic voyages made by ship's lifeboats after the torpedoing of merchant ships justifies their inclusion in the story of sail. One remarkable peacetime voyage of survival in an open boat was made in 1923 when the British tramp steamer *Trevessa* was overcome by heavy weather in the southern Indian Ocean. Two of her lifeboats made voyages of 1700 miles to reach safety. Construction was simple, consisting of conventional lapstrake, the hull being double ended and with high freeboard, making them

clumsy boats to pull with oars. The rig was one designed for endurance rather than passage-making. A small, loose-footed standing lugsail was hoisted up a short pole mast, with a jib tacked down to the stemhead. Note the looped lifelines festooned round the boat's topsides and the bilge-keels pierced with hand-holds in case the boat capsized. Wooden 'barricoes' (pronounced 'breakers') were fitted on the bottom boards to hold water and galvanised tanks were clamped under the thwarts holding basic supplies: barley sugar, condensed milk and ship's biscuit. *(166)*

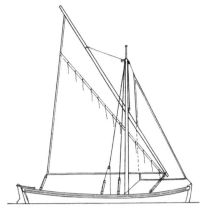

Lateen-rigged pinnace. The French and Spanish navies used the lateen rig for their pinnaces. *(142)*

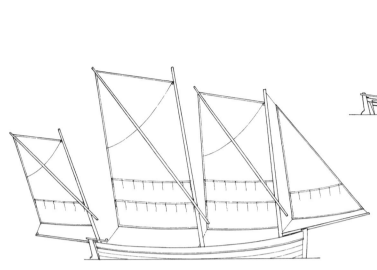

Sprit-rigged pinnace. In the eighteenth century, the British and Dutch favoured the sprit rig for their large pinnaces and longboats. The rig is quite complex with vangs to the sprit ends. *(142)*

Sprit-rigged cutter. The sprit rig was also used in British cutters and launches when they were sent on extended duties. This was more usual than is commonly supposed and boat's crews and parties of marines were sometimes engaged in actions far from their ships, up rivers, when raiding coastal shipping. *(34)*

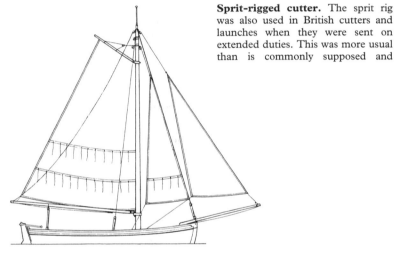

Sloop-rigged longboat. Large ships' boats, like British naval launches, were sometimes fitted with bowsprits and assumed the rig of eighteenth century 'sloops', particularly when sent on detached service. *(142)*

Gunter-rigged pinnace. By the late eighteenth and early nineteenth centuries, the spritsail had dropped from favour as a means of propelling the larger boats and the gunter-rig was widely adopted. This was largely because a tall sail could be set on spars short enough to be stowed easily in the boat concerned. Long after steam had replaced sail in men-of-war, a warship's boats were expected to be sailed with some skill by her junior officers. *(142)*

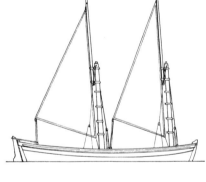

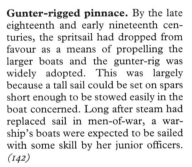

Yawl with leg-of-mutton sail. The smaller boats, such as this yawl, could use the leg-of-mutton sail and a jib. *(142)*

Dipping-lug. An alternative was the dipping lugsail. *(142)*

Settee rig. British officers serving in the Mediterranean and impressed with native rigs there, often had their boats fitted with settee sails. The fitting of boat rigs, while officially regulated, was often in practice a matter of personal preference. *(142)*

1/150 15 10 5 0 ft
4 3 2 1 0 m

SECTION NINE
Exploration, Experiment and the Enduring Tradition

By about 1850, the man-of-war had outgrown sail; a century later, so too had the commercial merchant ship. Man had mapped his planet, understood the physical causes of its great winds and invented weapons systems a very far cry from the brutal artillery of the Wooden Walls. The story of sail, it seemed, was over. Then, in 1956, the German four-masted sail-training barque *Pamir* was overwhelmed in the North Atlantic; her sister-ship, the *Passat* was confined to permanent moorings in a Baltic port. It was almost a challenge from nature: but that same year the first sail-training race was run from Torbay to Lisbon. It was apparent that young people could still find adventure under sail and that perhaps the story of sail was not yet finished.

It is appropriate that, despite the success of the steam vessel, the great age of exploration which ended with the discovery of the polar regions should incorporate ships which still carried sails. The vessels used in the last polar expeditions were usually auxiliaries which relied upon sail for endurance, but Arctic and Antarctic exploration had been born two centuries earlier and was initially undertaken entirely under sail.

But while mankind required sail to supplement his final endeavours to explore the uttermost reaches of the earth, he retains it to feed his competitive instincts, and thus the development of the yacht continues. Since this arises as much from the insatiable curiosity of human beings, a number of 'curiosities' attached to the search for ever more efficient sailing vessels have been included here. These inventive if odd craft are instructive. Some were bizarre, others sought to set a new norm, but all were sincere in their quest to improve performance under sail.

Nor has the commercial sailing ship quite vanished, for a small number of exotic types remain to feed the cruise sector of the leisure industry. Finally there are those remnants, rebuilds or replicas which serve as sail-training ships. Sail, it seems, still exerts a fascination over us, a fascination that is in tune with our new regard for the slender resources of our small, blue planet. This is an enduring tradition, for the wind is free and the ocean is limitless, as limitless as the dreams and aspirations of mankind.

Scientific and Exploration Ships

Running parallel with the development of the sailing ships traced throughout these pages was the concurrent exploration and charting of the globe and the advance of the natural sciences. The craft selected for such voyages were often unremarkable and typical craft from prosaic sources and they are examples of types found elsewhere in this book. There were, however, some vessels specially built for their tasks.

Barents' boat, 1596. Willem Barents set out in 1594 to discover the North East passage to India, reaching Novaya Zemlya where he was frustrated by ice. This occurred on his second voyage and in 1596 he set out on his third attempt. Rounding Cape Zhelania, he got no further, his ship being beset; taking to the boats the following spring, Barents perished. The ship's boat seen here was a simple sprit-rigged open craft. *(112)*

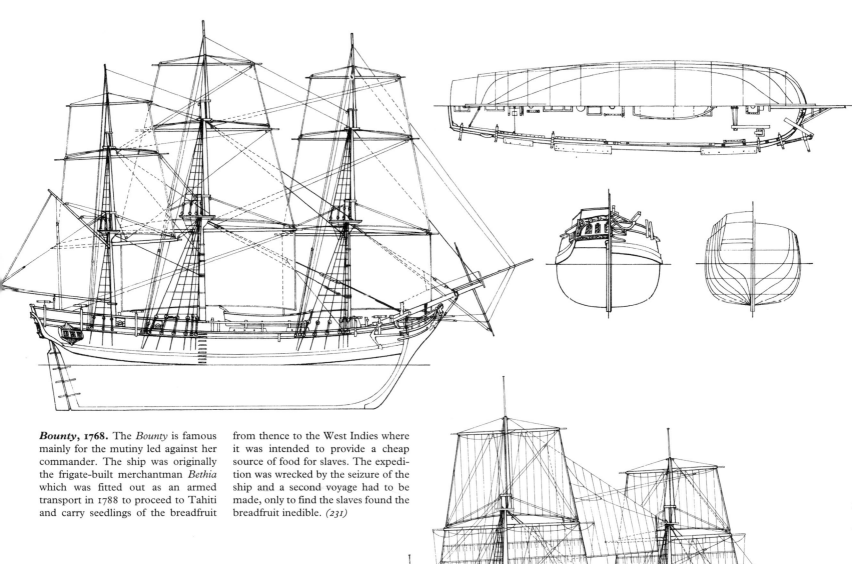

Bounty, 1768. The *Bounty* is famous mainly for the mutiny led against her commander. The ship was originally the frigate-built merchantman *Bethia* which was fitted out as an armed transport in 1788 to proceed to Tahiti and carry seedlings of the breadfruit from thence to the West Indies where it was intended to provide a cheap source of food for slaves. The expedition was wrecked by the seizure of the ship and a second voyage had to be made, only to find the slaves found the breadfruit inedible. *(231)*

Endeavour, 1768. The Whitby collier *Earl of Pembroke* was fitted out for James Cook's first voyage to the Pacific as the *Endeavour*. In her Cook made his remarkable voyage to Tahiti to observe the transit of Venus across the sun in 1769, carrying out running surveys along the coasts of New Zealand and eastern Australia before returning to Britain. A replica of *Endeavour* has shown the practicality of the vessel which, despite her bluff bow, was capable of over 6 knots. *(228)*

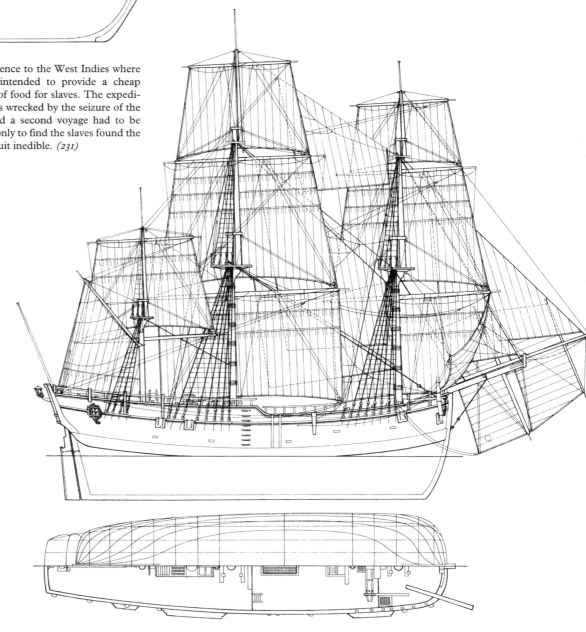

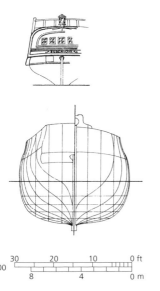

30   20   10   0 ft
1/300
8   4   0 m

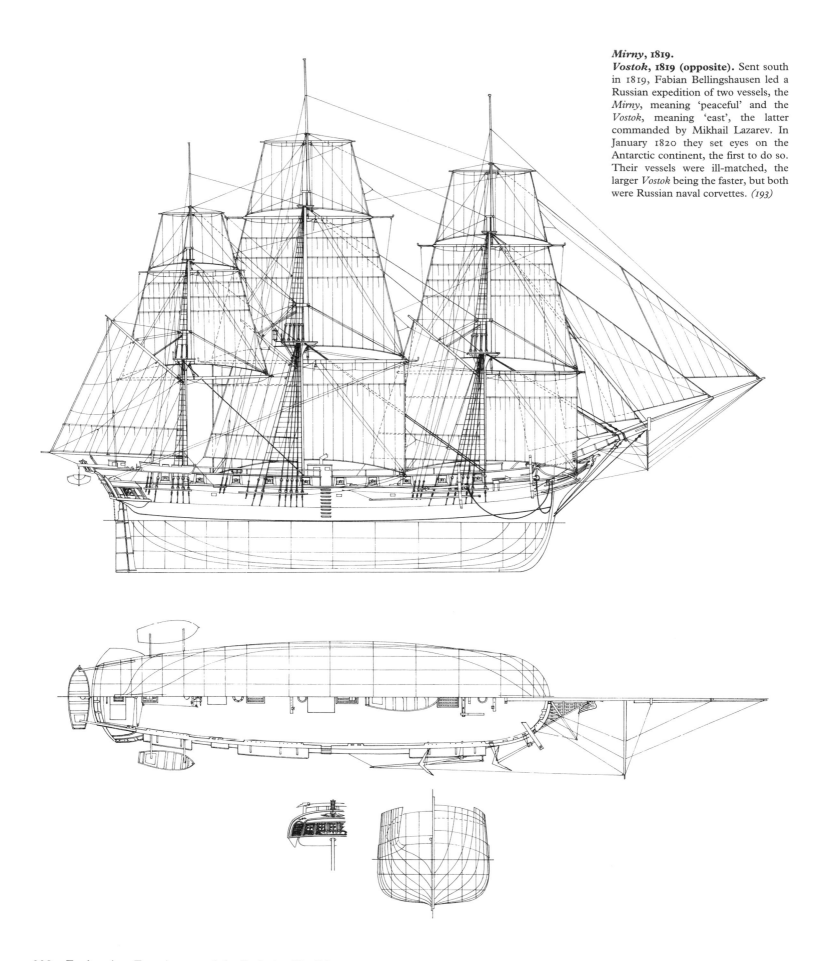

Mirny, 1819.
Vostok, 1819 (opposite). Sent south in 1819, Fabian Bellingshausen led a Russian expedition of two vessels, the *Mirny*, meaning 'peaceful' and the *Vostok*, meaning 'east', the latter commanded by Mikhail Lazarev. In January 1820 they set eyes on the Antarctic continent, the first to do so. Their vessels were ill-matched, the larger *Vostok* being the faster, but both were Russian naval corvettes. *(193)*

1/300   30   20   10   0 ft

8   4   0 m

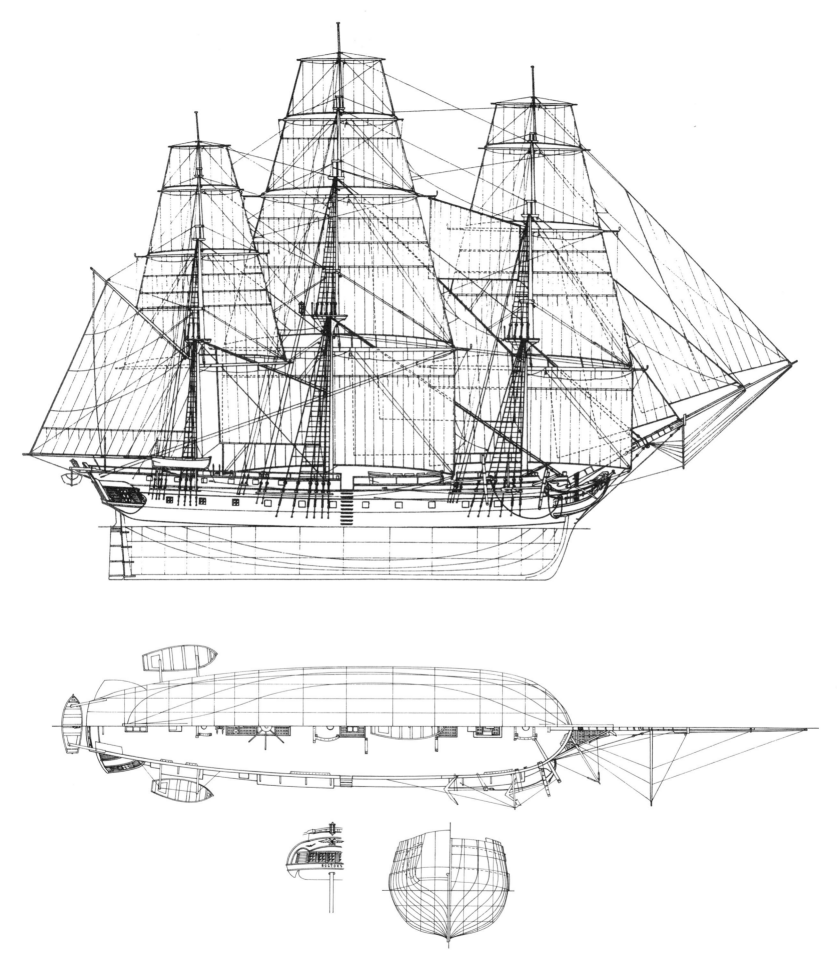

Beagle, 1820. Built as one of a large number of *Cherokee* class brig-sloops, in 1823 the 235-ton *Beagle* was specially fitted out for surveying. Her large spanker was removed, replaced by a small loose-footed spencer, and, with a mizen fitted, she was converted to a barque. In this guise she carried out a long surveying voyage under the command of Robert Fitzroy. In her company was Charles Darwin the naturalist, whose consequent work, the *Origin of Species*, challenged the accepted view of creation. Despite the number of gunports, for this voyage the ship mounted only 6 guns. She ended her days as a static coastguard vessel. *(166)*

Grönland, 1867. Built in Norway for the first German North Pole expedition of 1868, the *Grönland* was a version of the sturdy local 'jacht' type sailing coaster with an auxiliary engine. Although the expedition was unsuccessful, the 50-ton vessel survived and was later used for coastal trading. Since 1970 the vessel has been in the care of the Deutsches Schiffarhtsmuseum at Bremerhaven, where she is kept afloat. *(193)*

Pioneer and Consort, 1836. The United States Navy built *Pioneer* and *Consort* at the Navy Yards at Norfolk and Boston respectively. Both vessels were built for exploration of the South Pacific, the *Pioneer* being fitted out as a brig, the *Consort* as a barque, a rig then unique in the US Navy. Both mounted 6 guns, were 24 metres in length and measured 230 tons. On completion both were found to be too slow and their construction became something of a scandal. *Pioneer* and *Consort* were employed as salvage tenders until they could be quietly disposed of in 1844. *(26)*

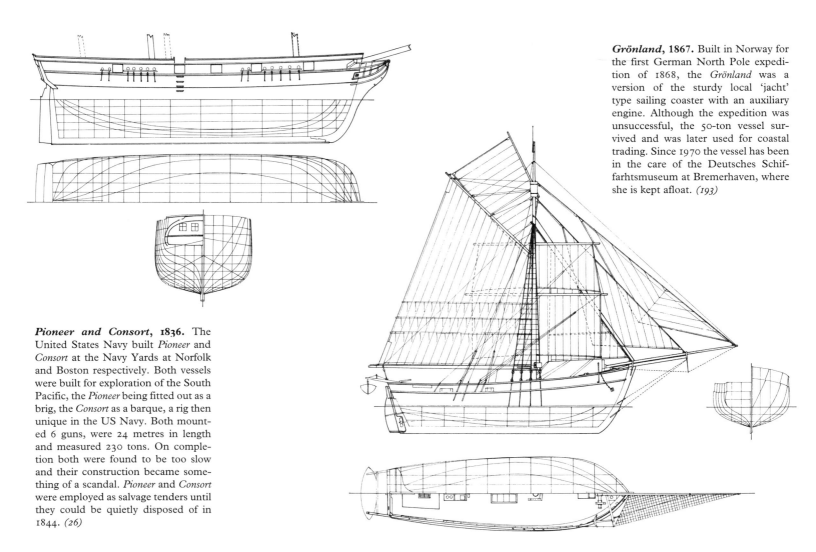

30   20   10   0 ft
1/300
8   4   0 m

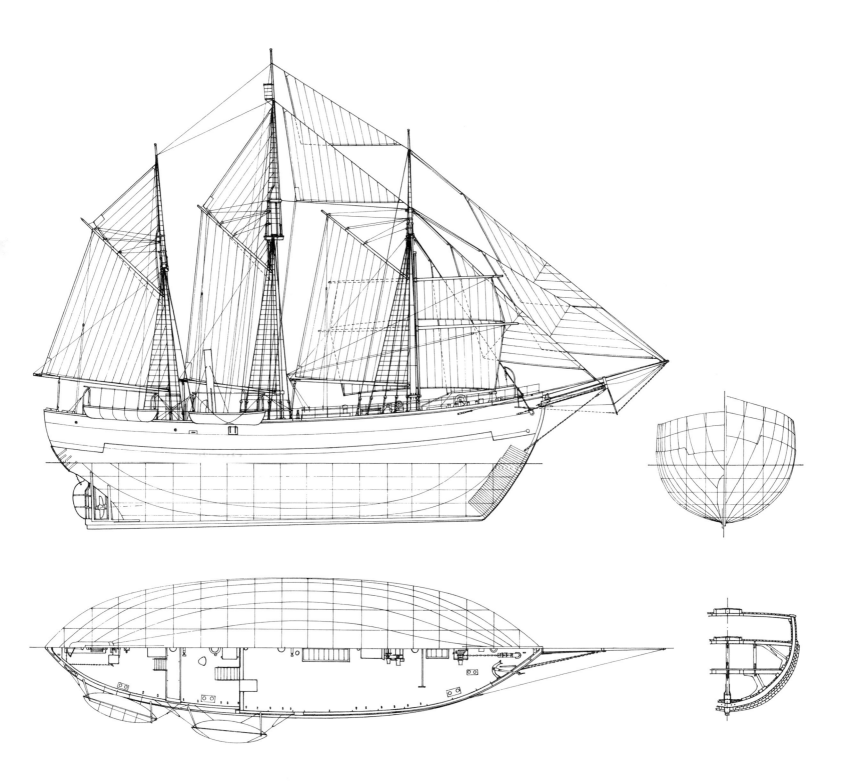

Fram, 1892. The *Fram* was the first vessel purpose-designed and built for Norwegian polar exploration. Designed in 1892 by Colin Archer, with a steam-powered auxiliary engine and of 402 tons, she was produced for the explorer Fridtjof Nansen. On the advice of his sailing master, Otto Sverdrup, *Fram* was rigged as a somewhat unconventional three-masted topsail schooner. Under Nansen, she completed a drift across the Arctic Ocean between 1893 and 1896, then between 1898 and 1902 she explored the north-west coast of Greenland under Otto Sverdrup. Finally, Roald Amundsen took her south and launched his successful bid to reach the south pole from her. Massively constructed, with reinforcing timbers of oak buttressing her full, round bilges, *Fram*'s double oak skin was sheathed with greenheart and the interstices were filled with insulating material set in pitch. Her bow was plated and her rudder and propeller could be retracted to avoid damage when beset in the ice. With the double-ended hull characteristic of Archer's designs, she was inelegant, but splendidly fitted for her purpose and remains preserved in Oslo today. *(193)*

30   20   10   0 ft
1/300
8   4   0 m

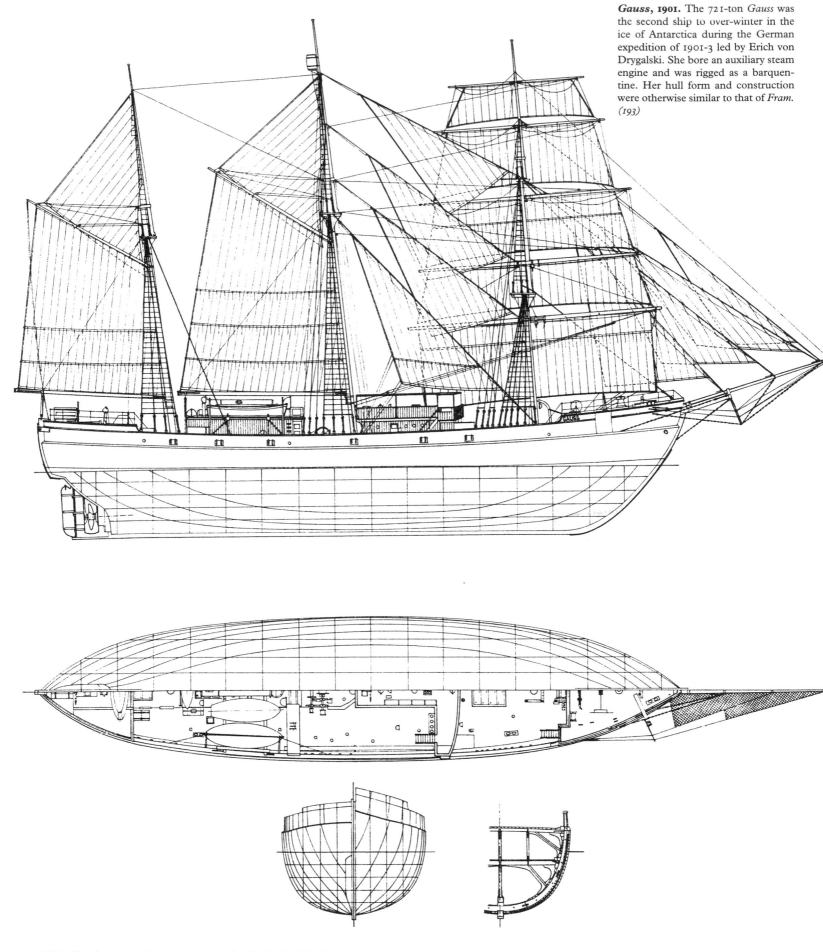

Gauss, 1901. The 721-ton *Gauss* was the second ship to over-winter in the ice of Antarctica during the German expedition of 1901-3 led by Erich von Drygalski. She bore an auxiliary steam engine and was rigged as a barquentine. Her hull form and construction were otherwise similar to that of *Fram*. (193)

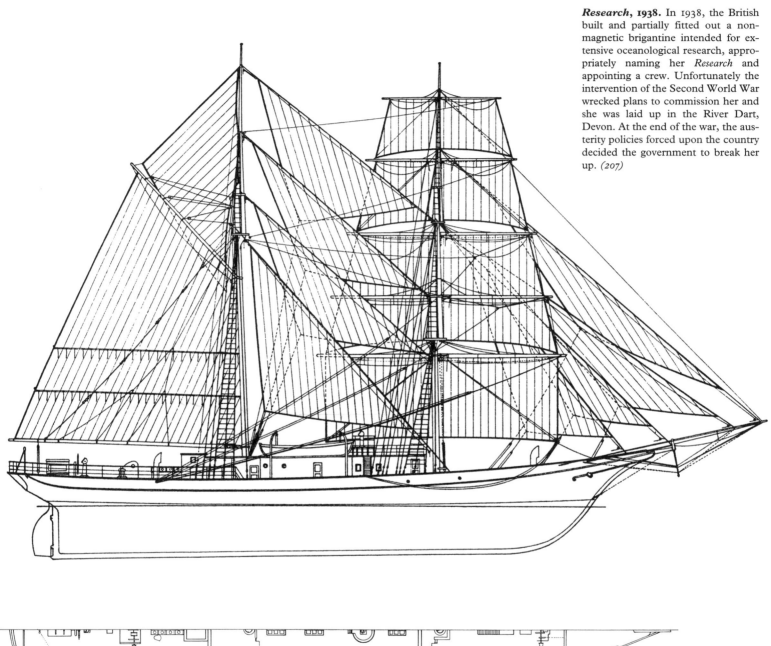

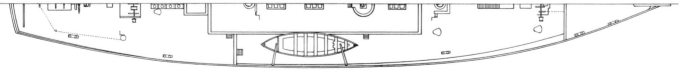

Research, 1938. In 1938, the British built and partially fitted out a non-magnetic brigantine intended for extensive oceanological research, appropriately naming her *Research* and appointing a crew. Unfortunately the intervention of the Second World War wrecked plans to commission her and she was laid up in the River Dart, Devon. At the end of the war, the austerity policies forced upon the country decided the government to break her up. *(207)*

1/300   30   20   10   0 ft
        8   4   0 m

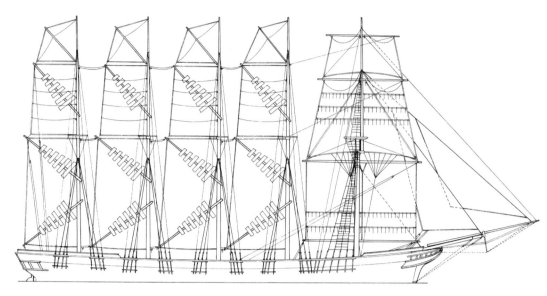

Transit **as conceived by Gower, 1800.**

The multi-masted *Transit* was conceived in 1800 by a Captain Gower of the East India Company. On a narrow hull with very hollow lines, reverse tumblehome and sharp dead rise, Gower designed a proto-barquentine with square sails on the foremast and on the remainder a fore-and-aft rig spread by battens substituting for gaffs and booms. The craft was actually built in 1808 as a dispatch vessel. Intended to go well to windward, she enjoyed a brief life in the Royal Navy, but failed to prove anything remarkable. Note the boom on the forecourse and the reefing points along the sail's foot. **NB.** 1/200 scale. *(208/129)*

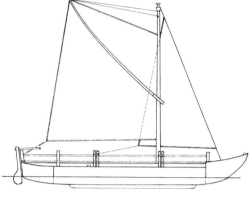

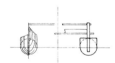

Catamaran *Simon & Jude*, 1662. Possibly inspired by descriptions of oriental multi-hulls – proas and the like – Sir William Petty, an English inventor and amateur naval architect, experimented with a series of catamarans, of which this was the first. They eventually reached 128 tons, but although they were fast, they did not handle well. At this time the Navy had a twin-hulled vessel used for towing large warships in the narrow confines of the Medway, and this may have been related to Petty's work. **NB.** 1/150 scale. *(230)*

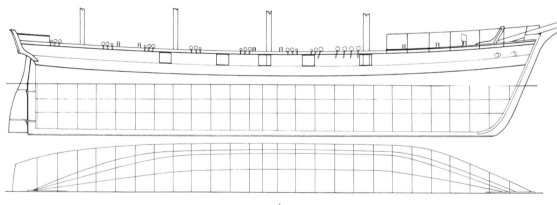

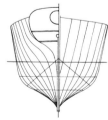

Transit **as built by the Royal Navy, 1808.**

Curiosities

Spread over a period of almost three hundred years, these oddities demonstrate the inventiveness of mankind. Some are derivative, but several show original thought.

30   20   10   0 ft
1/300
8   4   0 m

French privateer _L'Invention_, 1801. Possibly the first recorded four-masted full rigged ship was this vessel, built at Bordeaux in 1801 and designed by her captain, one M Thibaud, a leading member of the Society of Arts and Sciences and Belles Lettres. The four masts were made more or less obligatory by a very high length-to-breadth ratio of 5.44 (a conventional merchant ship was about 3.5), the hull measuring over 56 metres on the lower deck for a burthen of 486 tons. She was considered an outstanding sailer but was captured only nine days into her first cruise by two British frigates. **NB.** Sail plan is half scale. _(129)_

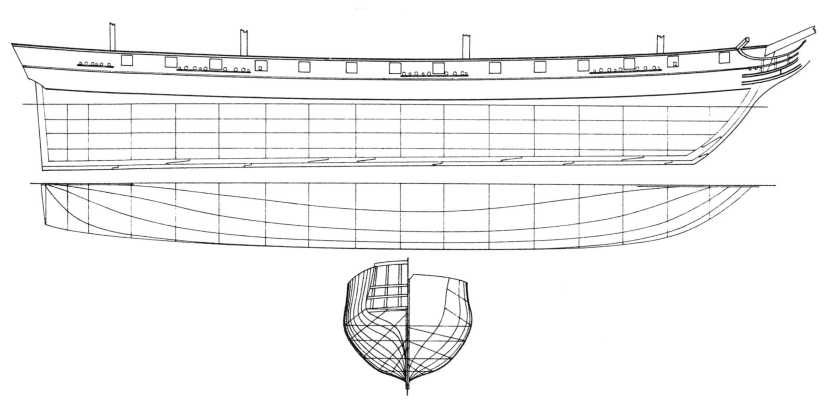

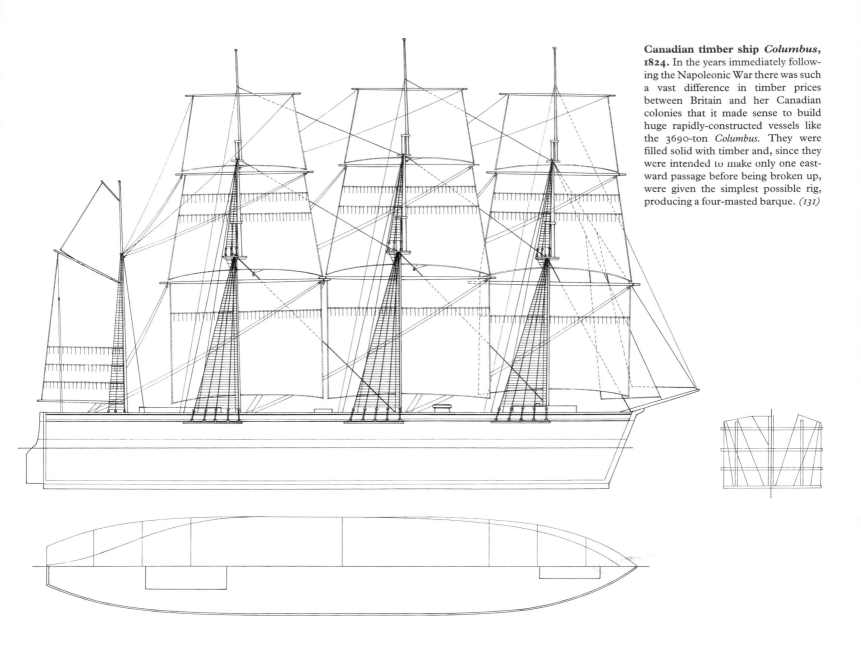

Canadian timber ship *Columbus*, 1824. In the years immediately following the Napoleonic War there was such a vast difference in timber prices between Britain and her Canadian colonies that it made sense to build huge rapidly-constructed vessels like the 3690-ton *Columbus*. They were filled solid with timber and, since they were intended to make only one eastward passage before being broken up, were given the simplest possible rig, producing a four-masted barque. *(131)*

John Christopher's improved rig, 1849. The nineteenth century was to see the patenting of many inventions and improvements to masting and rigging, generally useful in inverse proportion to their originality – after centuries of gradual evolution it was highly unlikely that any radical innovation would prove practical, except where new technology offered better materials. Christopher's ideas, which included small topsails and sliding topmasts housed abaft the lower masts, were published in 1850, but had little influence. **NB.** Not to scale. *(131)*

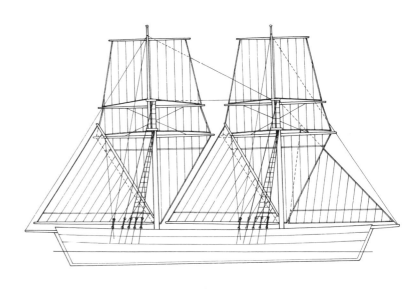

60 50 40 30 20 10 0 ft
1/600
15 10 5 0 m

'Jackass barque' *Ziba*, **1853.** Sailors employed the derisive term 'jackass' for anything out of the ordinary, including this odd configuration of sails. Jackass barques were attempts to square the circle of smart performance with small, economical crew size. In this the *Ziba* is a good example. She was built by Hall at Aberdeen in 1858 as a small tea-clipper of only 497 tons and 51.5 metres in length. Three-masted, she set square sails on her foremast, with gaff sails on main and mizzen. But instead of a gaff topsail, as borne on the mizen, the upper section of the mainmast set a square topsail, topgallant and royal. She was intended to be very fast, but was soon outclassed by the better British clippers of the 1860s. *(132)*

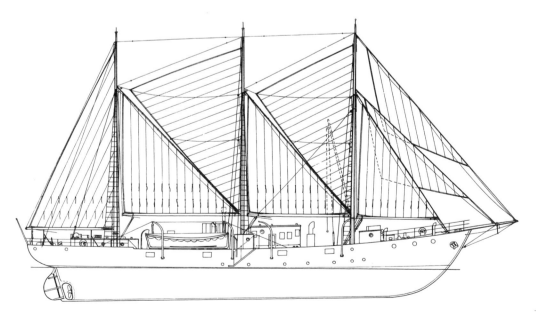

Staysail schooner *John Williams*, **1930.** The staysail schooner was an attempt to improve the performance of the conventional schooner, particularly in respect of the huge, gaffed sails fitted to the largest of the class. Making the last sailing vessels economic in the 1930s was a somewhat desperate gamble, but auxiliaries were already accepted as part of the equipment necessary to achieve this limited goal. In the *John Williams*, as in other staysail schooners, the mizen was made a leg-of-mutton sail, while the spaces between the fore and main, and the main and mizen, were fitted with boomed staysails. A triangular topsail which brailed to the mast ahead was supposed to make the vessel much easier to tack. *(210)*

30   20   10   0 ft
1/300
8   4   0 m

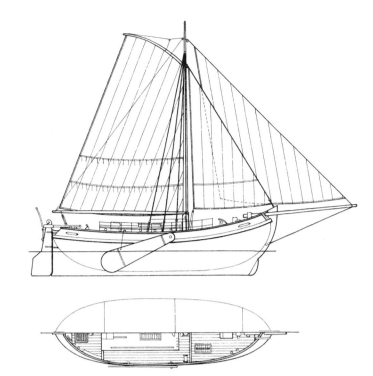

Dutch boier yacht, eighteenth century. The utility of the boier in executing numerous tasks from carrying small consignments of freight, laying buoys and their moorings, to acting as a passenger craft, naturally commended her for more pleasurable use. The beamy, double-ended hull with its simple sloop rig was capable of sailing in shallow water but, with the help of her leeboard, could work to windward. **NB.** 1/200 scale. *(45)*

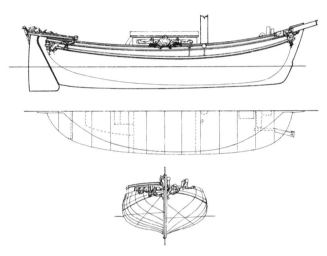

Dutch boier yacht, modern. These characteristics remain today, boierjachts being popular in the twentieth century Netherlands, offering capacious accommodation. The rig has acquired a bowsprit and competitive races are held on the wide waters of the Dutch meres. *(138)*

Swedish boyert, about 1750. In the eighteenth century, af Chapman found the boier had migrated all over Europe. This 'boyert' comes from his native Sweden where it was the plaything of a rich merchant or aristocrat who has lovingly embellished it as an indication of his material status. The leeboards have been dropped, but a small cabin and cockpit establish the layout that today's yachtsman would be familiar with. *(34)*

The Origins of Yachting – Early Pleasure Craft

While yachting ceased to be a preserve of the British court, during the eighteenth century it was certainly an activity exclusive to the aristocracy. In 1720 a 'water club' was formed in Cork, Ireland, and in 1760 a second, the Cumberland Society, later the Royal Thames Yacht Club, was formed in London. In 1815 the exclusive Royal Yacht Squadron was formed, with its headquarters at Cowes, on the Isle of Wight, owners intending their grand yachts as a supplementary naval reserve during hostilities. The era of gentlemanly cruising was born, but competitive racing did not really begin in Britain until after 1820. Races were not uncommon in The Netherlands, where water transport was widely used by all sections of society, but in America it was 1844 before the foundation of the New York Yacht Club.

Small craft had, however, long been used for pleasure, usually the languorous, rather than the sterner Corinthian variety. Slowly, however, the quest for speed produced an elegant hull form that in due course owed nothing to any other type of sailing vessel.

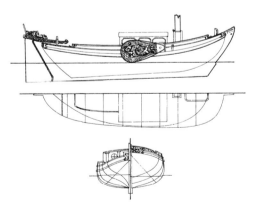

Dutch schuyt, eighteenth century. Originally an open barge, the 'schuyt' is a term that enjoys several meanings, but during the eighteenth century one was a simple yacht based upon a scaled down version of the larger barge. Note the tall cabin with its glazed windows and the decoration on head and stern, rudder, tiller and leeboard. *(34)*

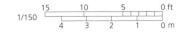

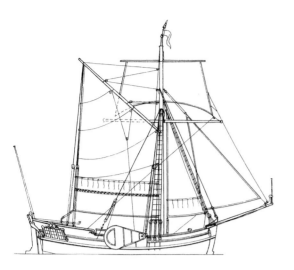

Dutch herrenjacht, eighteenth century. The sea-going rig, which incorporates the square topsail, marks this Dutch 'herrenjacht' as a craft capable of voyaging anywhere in The Netherlands, among the Friesian Islands of the north coast or further east towards the Weser and Elbe. *(142)*

Hungarian lake yacht *Phoenix*, 1796. Echoing the form of Danubian warships, this Hungarian yacht, the *Phoenix* is an unusual example of a pleasure craft. Capable of being worked by oars, the sail plan was designed to be moved round the masts on tacking. She was used on Lake Balaton, about sixty miles south-west of Budapest. *(138)*

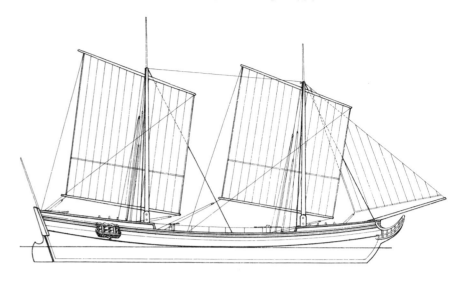

English yachts, about 1760. These English yachts from this time display the characteristics of small men-of-war, from which they differ only in their internal appointments. At the time the term 'yacht' applied not only to pleasure craft, but to small, specialised official vessels. Admiralty commissioners at Dockyard ports had yachts, as did the Viceroy of Ireland and several were owned by the Corporation of Trinity House. *(34)*

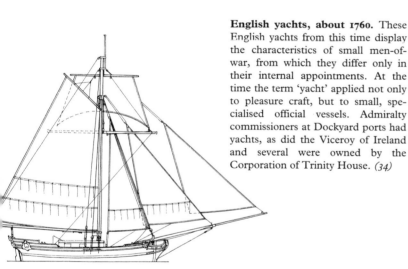

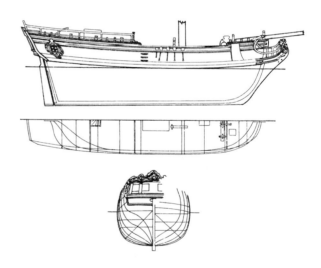

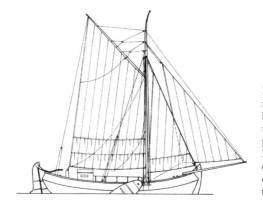

Dutch hecktjalk, eighteenth century. Like the term boier, that of 'tjalk' has a long and constantly evolving history which does not easily conform to precise definition. Like the boier, the Dutch tjalk was a broad, shallow-draught and flat-bottomed, lee-boarded craft. Middle-class families owned them as much to take them to church and their places of business, as for pure pleasure. Rigs varied slightly, but this form, with the standing gaff and loose-footed mainsail was easy to handle. The Dutch hecktjalk had a raised stern, through which, flute-like, the tiller passed. Others, like this with its conspicuous cabin, were called 'paviloentjalks'. *(27)*

30 20 10 0 ft
1/300
8 4 0 m

The Origins of Yachting–Early Pleasure Craft 319

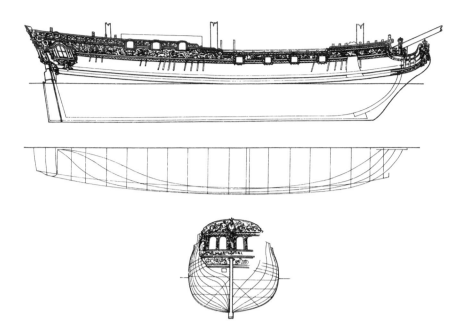

British royal yacht *Royal Caroline*, 1749. During the eighteenth century, the British monarchy had several yachts but in the *Royal Caroline* of 1749, the principle of one large yacht was established. Of 232 tons burthen, she was ship-rigged and regarded as a rated vessel, for command of a royal yacht was a highly political appointment. Renamed *Royal Charlotte* in 1761, she served as part of the anti-invasion barrage in the Thames between 1803 and 1805, and was broken up in 1820. *(34)*

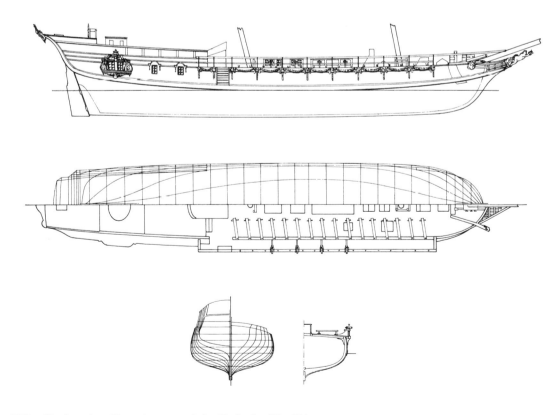

Swedish royal galley *Amphion*, 1778. Another of af Chapman's designs, the *Amphion* was an oar and sail-powered galley, with a light armament of swivel guns. She was occasionally used as the fleet flagship when the king himself was present in battle. *(74)*

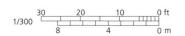

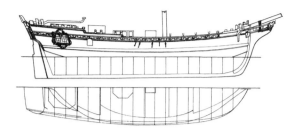

**Swedish *Esplendien* and *Amadis*,
1782.** These two Swedish royal yachts
are identical, single-masted and also
fitted for pulling. *(74)*

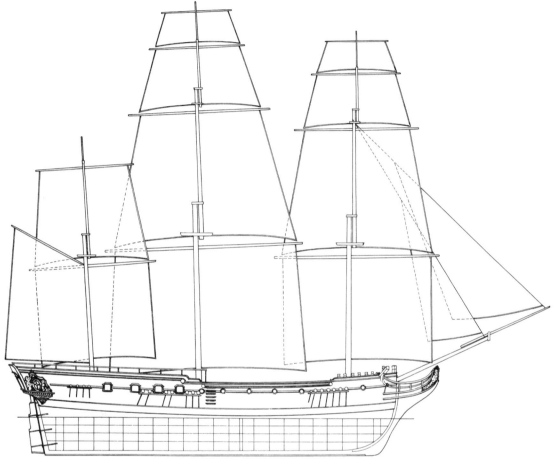

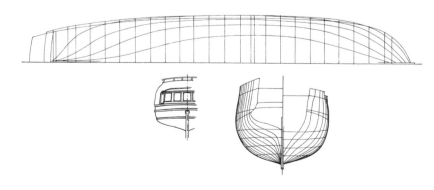

British royal yacht *Royal Sovereign*, 1804. Of some 278 tons burthen, this ship-rigged vessel was 29 metres on the gundeck. She was superseded as the principal yacht in 1817, but not broken up until 1850. During her life she became a familiar sight anchored off Weymouth when King George III went sea-bathing there, and she took King Louis XVIII back to France after the first abdication of Napoleon in 1814. *(129)*

1/300 30 20 10 0 ft
8 4 0 m

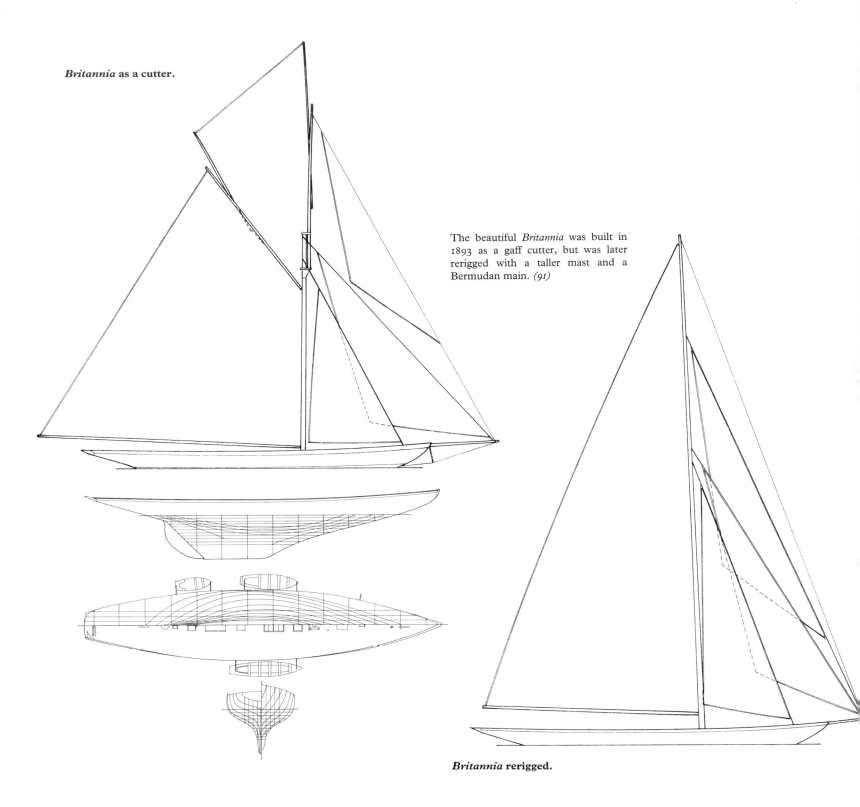

Britannia as a cutter.

The beautiful *Britannia* was built in 1893 as a gaff cutter, but was later rerigged with a taller mast and a Bermudan main. *(91)*

Britannia rerigged.

Yachting – the Sport of Kings

It was essentially the rivalry between King Charles II and his brother James, Duke of York, in setting their respective yachts against each other in races, that established yachting in Britain. Fed by a society obsessed with gambling in almost any form, the notion of possessing a yacht has become inextricably linked with great wealth and certainly the most magnificent and extravagant yachts have been built for the extremely wealthy, whether they were European kings or American multi-millionaires. Nevertheless, competition between rival monarchs held sway up until the First World War destroyed the world of aristocratic superiority. In the two decades before 1914, King Edward VII and Kaiser Wilhelm II, regularly raced at Cowes, in the Isle of Wight. As a grandson of Queen Victoria, Wilhelm was an honorary admiral of the British fleet but he secretly desired to excel and in the end the worldly Edward was disgusted by the ferocity of Wilhelm's competitiveness. The ancestry of these splendid yachts is a long one and, while it has been touched in an earlier section, merits a more detailed survey.

1/400

40 30 20 10 0 ft

10 5 0 m

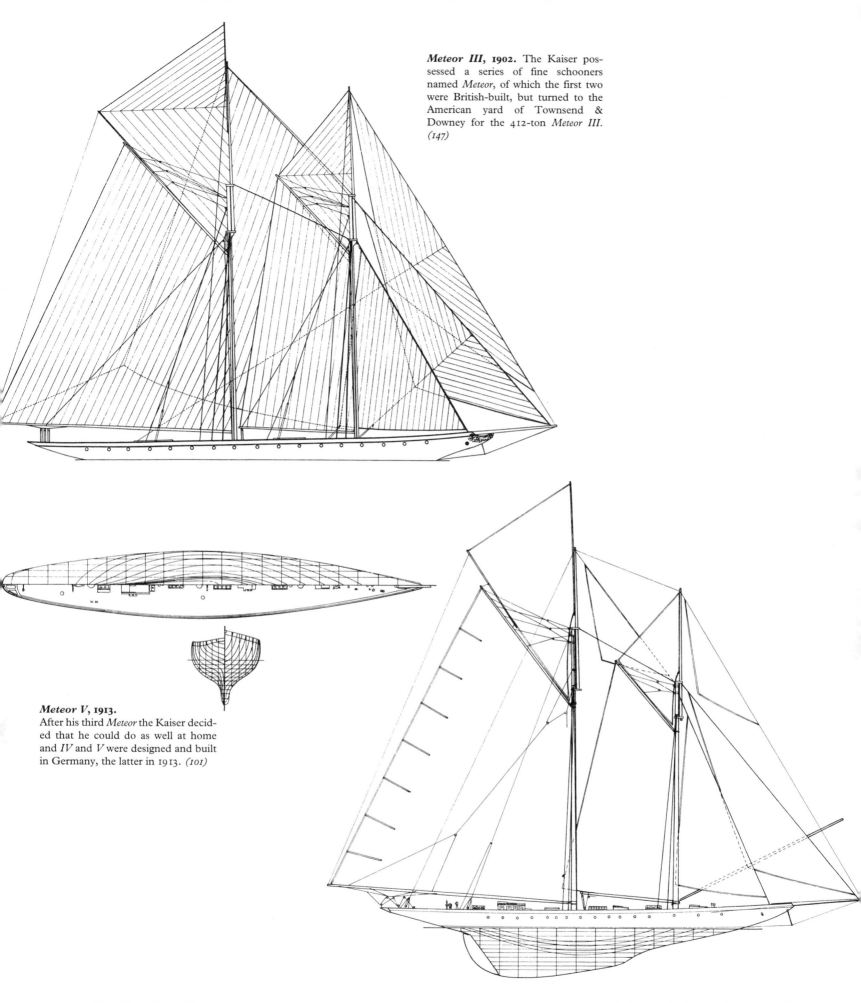

Meteor III, 1902. The Kaiser possessed a series of fine schooners
named *Meteor*, of which the first two
were British-built, but turned to the
American yard of Townsend &
Downey for the 412-ton *Meteor III*.
(147)

Meteor V, 1913.
After his third *Meteor* the Kaiser decided that he could do as well at home
and *IV* and *V* were designed and built
in Germany, the latter in 1913. (101)

1/400

40   30   20   10   0 ft

10   5   0 m

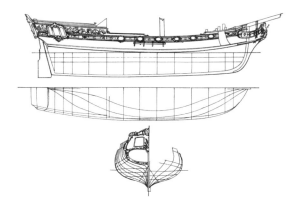

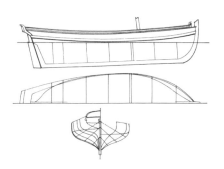

English yacht, about 1750. Early yacht hulls were very little different from small naval vessels of the period. Little real consideration was given to refined lines, but much to decoration and splendour, for these were craft essentially designed to give pleasure and when they did compete, often for high stakes, performance relied upon the skill of the helmsman and crew, rather than the innate qualities of the yacht herself. *(243)*

British *Cumberland*, 1780. The similarity between this very successful British racing yacht of the Royal Thames Yacht Club and the revenue and naval cutters of her day is clear. These were her model, for they were considered to be the swiftest craft of their day. The *Cumberland* has very hollow garboards and a sharp dead-rise. The deep heeled hull with its lighter draft forward, enabled her to tack smartly, an important matter in a strong tideway and a slow or uncertain business with a long keel. *(243)*

British *King's Fisher*, 1776. Half the size and of simpler, lapstrake construction, this yacht was half-decked, with a cockpit and would have carried a cutter rig. It was soon realised than speed could be gained if the hull was lighter than the contemporary heavy naval hull of the armed cutter, and clinker construction, often actually used at least in part in naval cutters, was adopted for this yacht. **NB.** Twice scale. *(243)*

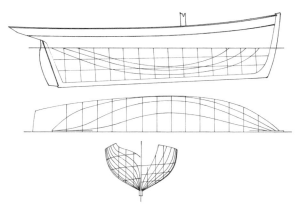

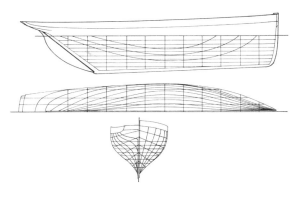

British *Corsair*, 1851. The requirement that a yacht must perform well on all points of sailing effectively meant that windward performance, being the most difficult to achieve, tended to outweigh other considerations. Craft that therefore found it necessary to press to windward, became the natural models for refinement. In the fishing smacks of the Thames Estuary there resided a fine, elegant form of working boat and the type was the originator of many early Victorian English yachts. The principle of building a full forebody with a tapering stern had begun to be eroded, as can be seen here in the *Corsair* of 1851, which has the almost vertical stem and overhanging counter characteristic of the smack. *(243)*

British *Volante*, 1851. Extreme rake in the stern-post and a deep forefoot made a long-keeled boat power to windward within the restrictions of gaff rig. Wet and difficult to tack she may have been, but the 48-ton British cutter *Volante* of 1851 was fast, particularly on a reach. She was built on the east coast of England at Ipswich by Thomas Harvey and was giving the *America* a hard race in 1851 when she broke her bowsprit. But she nevertheless remains somewhat cod-headed and mackerel-tailed, despite the performance of a British yacht called *Mosquito* which, in 1848, had adopted a radical new hull reversing these principles. Her designer, the engineer John Scott Russell, was a prophet unheard in his own country. *(243)*

The History of Yachting – the Hull

As can be inferred from the adaptations of King Edward VII's *Britannia*, the two elements of yacht development reside in the hull and the rig. While absolute fitness-for-purpose relies upon an intrinsic harmony existing between the two, reality often falls short of this ideal and it is convenient to review the changes in each component before concluding with a look at attempts to marry both and produce the ultimate sailing yacht.

In the development of hull form for yachts there are distinctions between a yacht intended for racing and one intended for cruising where speed is sacrificed for comfort. This is not hedonism; a cruising yacht is built to stand up to extremes of weather and extreme hull forms are not and never have been sea-kindly. Pursuit of misunderstood objectives has tragic consequences. The loss of the clipper *Ariel* may be attributed to her fine afterbody, just as the loss of the *Pamir* may be put down to her masts and rigging being too strong, so that instead of being dismasted and surviving, the entire ship foundered. This remains true, too, of modern ocean racing yachts. Despite the hi-tech materials at hand today, not a few powerful racing yachts have shed their fin keels in the grey wastes of the Southern Ocean.

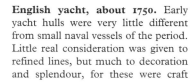

American *Magic*, 1857.

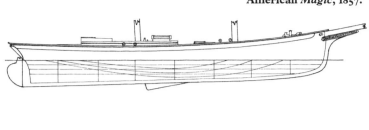

In 1851, the schooner *America* crossed the Atlantic to humiliate British yachts in a series of races for a cup presented by the Royal Yacht Squadron. Apart from raising an interest in the schooner rig in Britain, it was the revolutionary new hull form with a long hollow bow and the greatest width aft of amidships, that caused a greater furore, finally proving John Scott Russell correct. In the face of such convincing evidence, the new hull form was quickly accepted on both sides of the Atlantic. These two examples are American, the shallow-draught schooner *Magic* of 1857, and the larger *Enchantress* of 1870. *(27)*

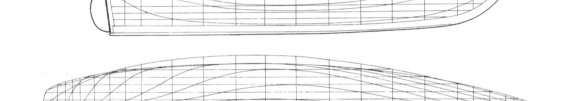

American *Enchantress*, 1870.

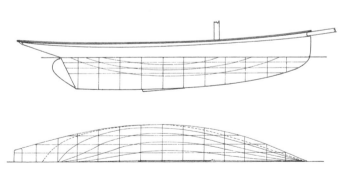

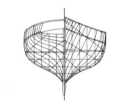

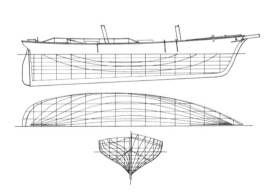

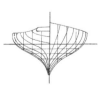

American *Titania*, 1888. The more rounded shape, already favoured in some fishing craft, was in vogue in North America by the 1880s. The emergence of an elegant spoon-bowed, counter-sterned hull which is unmistakable that of a yacht is seen her in this American centre-boarder. *(27)*

American *Volante*, 1855. Large American deep-draught yachts of this period were almost invariably schooners and this example very clearly shows the shift of the hull's greatest beam to aft of amidships. *(243)*

30   20   10   0 ft
1/300
8   4   0 m

The History of Yachting–the Hull   325

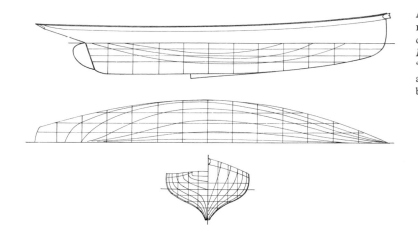

American cutter-yacht *Puritan*, 1885. Designed by Edward Burgess to defend the *America*'s Cup in 1885, the *Puritan* combined the virtues of the 'typical' American skimming hull with a deeper form. Though a centre-boarder, *Puritan* carried 27 tons of external ballast in her pierced keel, a fair proportion of her 105 tons displacement, and was narrower and deeper than the conventional Yankee form. She defeated the British threat of *Genesta*, making Burgess's name. *(173)*

By the last quarter of the nineteenth century yachts were no longer the privilege of the wealthy. The small, low-cost cruising yacht makes its appearance prior to the turn of the century. Although American, the *Shadow* of 1872 would have felt equally at home on the British Norfolk Broads with her low cabin and lifting centre-plate. Even more accessible, shoal-draught racing boats were being produced in America like this centre-board sloop, *Mischief* of 1897, while a simpler example is this cat-rigged American boat, *Truant*, from 1883. The hull provides a very shallow-draught hull, beamy enough to resist heel. **NB.** *Shadow* and *Truant* are twice scale. *(27)*

American *Shadow*, 1872.

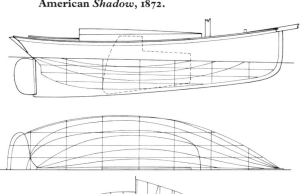

American *Mischief*, 1897.

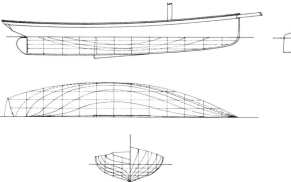

American *Truant*, 1883.

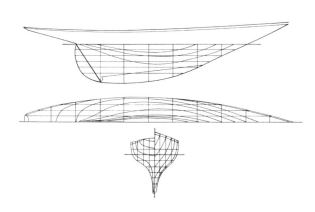

American *Gloriana*, 1891. The American yacht designer Nathaniel Herreshoff produced a masterpiece in the *Gloriana*, taking yacht design another important step forward. Fourteen metres on the waterline, *Gloriana* had long overhangs, but most notably her raked bow was almost straight, giving a cutaway forefoot and providing reserve buoyancy without undue flare being necessary. The deep hull, with its ballast keel proved stiff, performed well on all points of sailing, tacked easily and held a course. Unsurprisingly she wiped the floor with all opposition, representing the highly sophisticated compromise that all-round performance at sea demands. *(243)*

American *Elmina*, 1902. In United States waters, the schooner continued to dominate the upper end of the market and this hull, unsubtly named *Elmina* after a slaving depot on the African coast, shows both the influence of *America* and *Gloriana.* She is also fitted with a supplementary centre-board. *(27)*

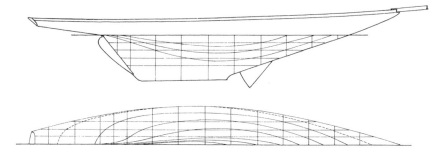
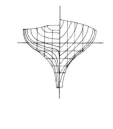

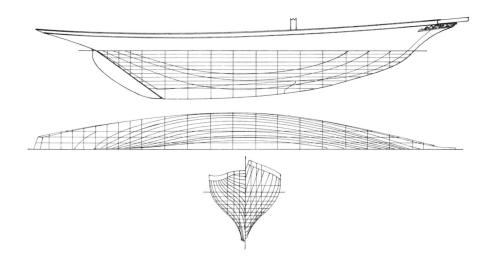

British *Iverna* 1890. The carriage of a cast-iron or lead ballast keel became increasingly necessary as yacht rig tended towards the extreme. It meant that a long narrow hull could be compelled to resist the heel induced in a yacht's sail's and this large cutter, the *Iverna*, shows a deep, narrow hull with long, elegant overhangs. *(173)*

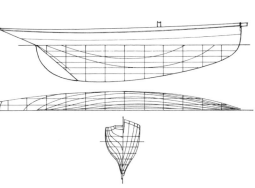

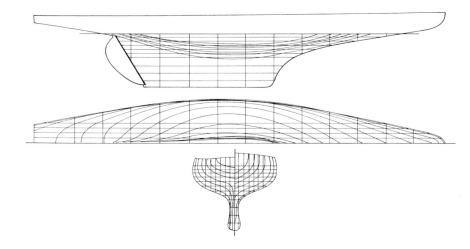

British *Clara*, 1894. The deep, narrow form shows the extent to which yacht design went to carry canvas. Such a craft would have been exceptionally wet when powering to windward. *(173)*

British *Shamrock IV*, 1914. Keen competition and social exclusion from the Royal Yacht Squadron for a mere grocer, howsoever rich he might be, spurred the owner of a series of five *Shamrock*s to race for the *America*'s Cup. Built by Sir Thomas Lipton, *Shamrock IV* was crossing the Atlantic when the First World War broke out.

The heavy ballast keel is here set on a shortened keel. Despite the long overhangs, the wetted surface of this yacht is kept to a minimum and so therefore is the friction and drag. Most important is the lack of lateral drag enabling *Shamrock IV* to answer her helm quickly, particularly when tacking. *(173)*

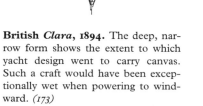

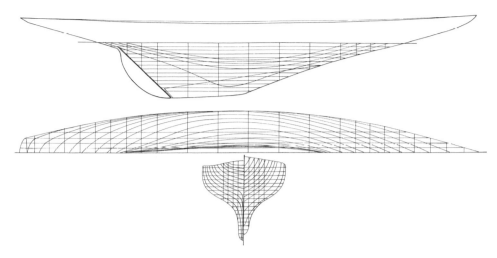

American *Enterprise*, 1929. The *Enterprise* was selected to defend the *America*'s Cup against the fifth and final challenge by the British yachtsman Sir Thomas Lipton in 1930, beating her fellow American contenders *Weetamoe*, *Whirlwind* and *Yankee* for the honour. Designed by Starling Burgess she was built for the millionaire Harold S Vanderbilt in 1929. The 24.4-metre long *Enterprise* was one of the famous J-class, measuring 128 tons

and setting a huge mainsail, a staysail, jib and jib-topsail. Renowned for their size and grace, as racing machines the J-class were flawed in their inability to cope with strong winds. *Enterprise* was conceived to perform at a speed of 10.75 knots in winds predicted to prevail over the race-course, predictions based upon wind studies derived from the United States Weather Bureau. Burgess incorporated considerable beam to enable *Enterprise* to stand up

to her rig, and full sections at the bow, which in practice caused the yacht to pound in a seaway. *Enterprise* bore a lightweight alloy mast and successfully defeated the heavier, more traditional British challenger, *Shamrock V*, winning four out of seven races. Lovely though these great yachts were, their limited performance parameters effectively consigns them to a cul-de-sac in terms of the development of the story of sail. *(173)*

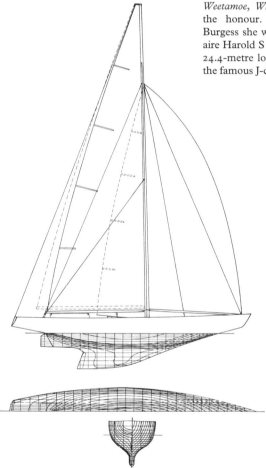

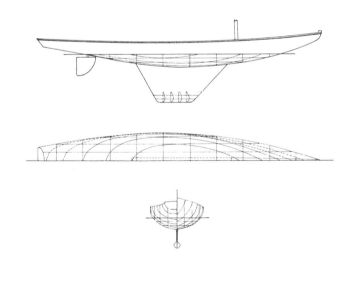

American *Intrepid*, 1967. By the 1960s, the *America*'s Cup was open to challenge from yachts other than from Britain. Australian challenges were accepted and defeated, twice by the American yacht *Intrepid*, built to a design of Olin Stephens in 1967. A 12-metre of 19.9 metres in length, the 58-tonner was of wooden construction,

with her rudder separated from her main keel. She was also fitted with a trim-tab on her main rudder, a device allowing her to point slightly higher when going to windward and to turn in a smaller circle. Other innovations included the situating of her winches and their handlers low in the hull to lower the overall centre of gravity. *(56)*

American *El Chico*. In one form or another, the fin-keeled yacht dominates the modern racing hull. The rudder is either a spade form, as here, or is set behind a skeg designed to afford it some protection. This reduces wetted surface whilst providing adequate stability and has been made possible through modern building materials. **NB.** Twice scale. *(27)*

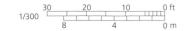

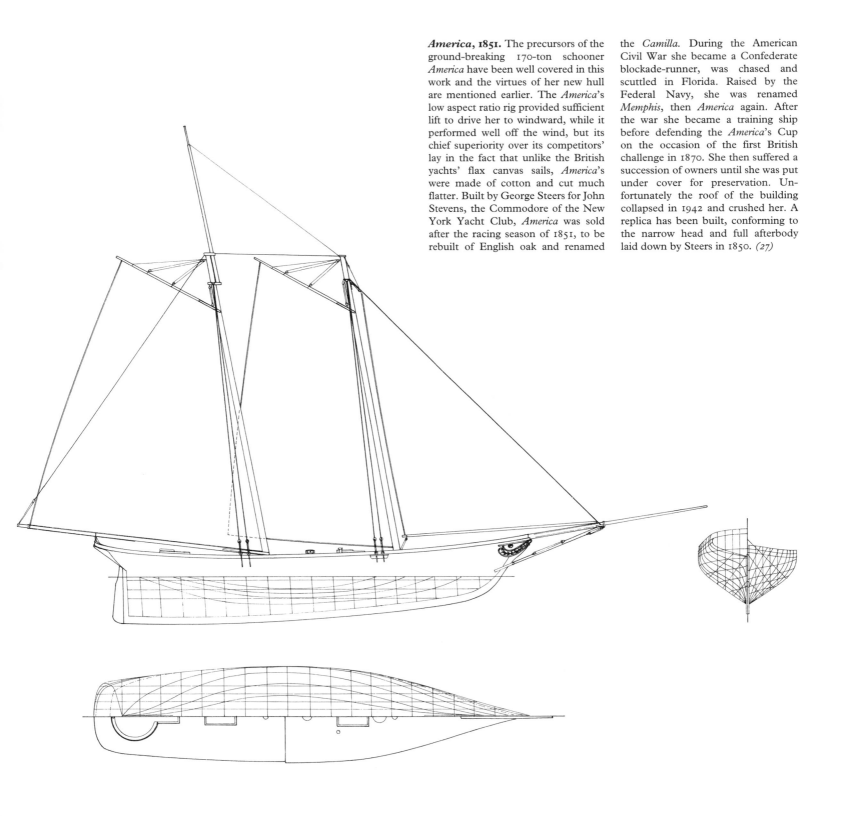

America, 1851. The precursors of the ground-breaking 170-ton schooner *America* have been well covered in this work and the virtues of her new hull are mentioned earlier. The *America*'s low aspect ratio rig provided sufficient lift to drive her to windward, while it performed well off the wind, but its chief superiority over its competitors' lay in the fact that unlike the British yachts' flax canvas sails, *America*'s were made of cotton and cut much flatter. Built by George Steers for John Stevens, the Commodore of the New York Yacht Club, *America* was sold after the racing season of 1851, to be rebuilt of English oak and renamed the *Camilla*. During the American Civil War she became a Confederate blockade-runner, was chased and scuttled in Florida. Raised by the Federal Navy, she was renamed *Memphis*, then *America* again. After the war she became a training ship before defending the *America*'s Cup on the occasion of the first British challenge in 1870. She then suffered a succession of owners until she was put under cover for preservation. Unfortunately the roof of the building collapsed in 1942 and crushed her. A replica has been built, conforming to the narrow head and full afterbody laid down by Steers in 1850. *(27)*

The History of Yacht Rig – the Schooner

Of all yacht rigs, the schooner, so prevalent in North American waters, represents the opulence attached to the public notion of the sport. In part this is attributable to the United States schooner-yacht *America*, which initiated a profound challenge to British yachting, the echoes of which resonate to this day. The simplicity of the *America*'s rig was per-haps the key to both her aesthetic appeal and her proven fitness-for-purpose, but her hull shape also marries the pragmatic with the extreme in a special form, and in considering rig, she must perforce be our starting point.

30   20   10   0 ft
1/300
8   4   0 m

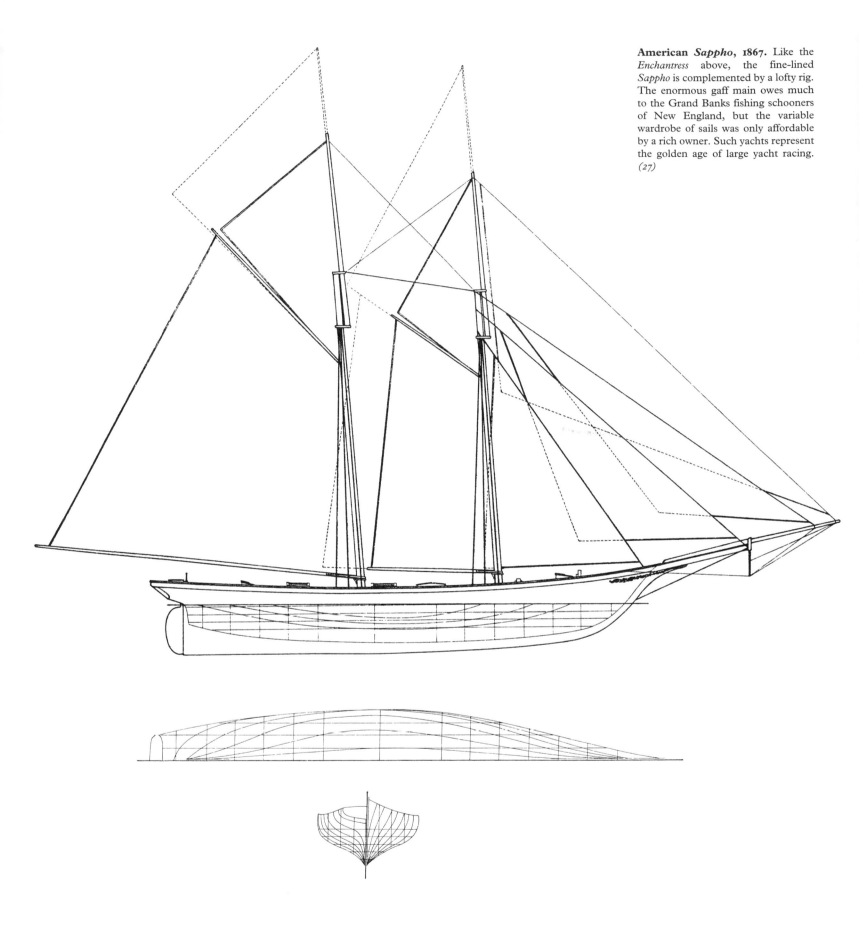

30   20   10   0 ft

1/300

8   4   0 m

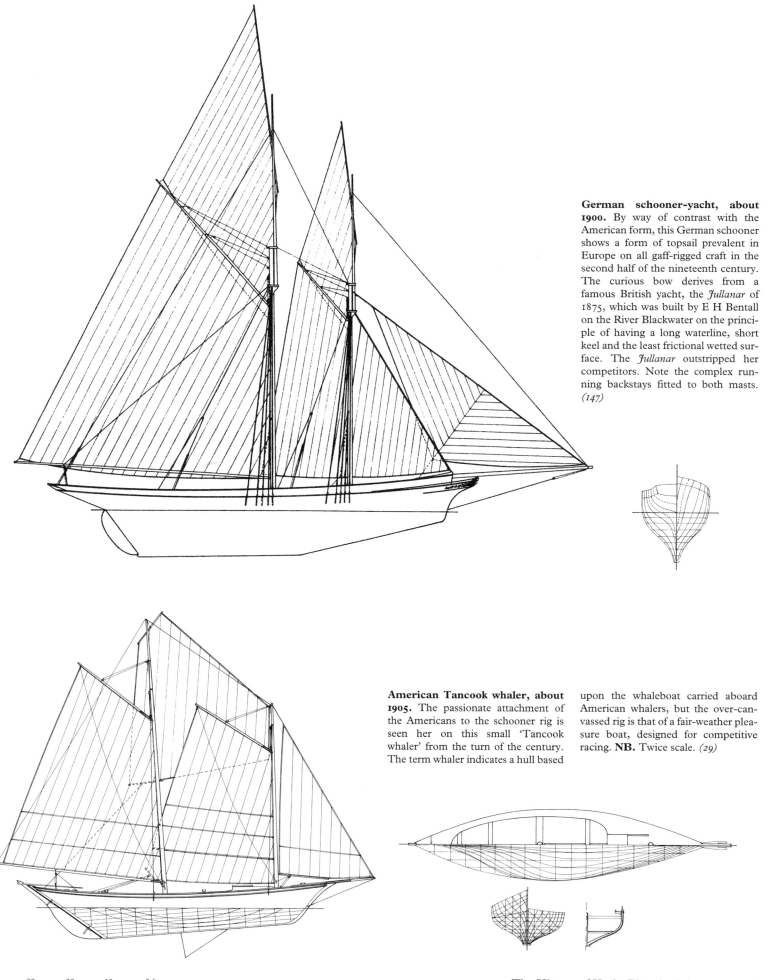

German schooner-yacht, about 1900. By way of contrast with the American form, this German schooner shows a form of topsail prevalent in Europe on all gaff-rigged craft in the second half of the nineteenth century. The curious bow derives from a famous British yacht, the *Jullanar* of 1875, which was built by E H Bentall on the River Blackwater on the principle of having a long waterline, short keel and the least frictional wetted surface. The *Jullanar* outstripped her competitors. Note the complex running backstays fitted to both masts. *(147)*

American Tancook whaler, about 1905. The passionate attachment of the Americans to the schooner rig is seen her on this small 'Tancook whaler' from the turn of the century. The term whaler indicates a hull based upon the whaleboat carried aboard American whalers, but the over-canvassed rig is that of a fair-weather pleasure boat, designed for competitive racing. **NB.** Twice scale. *(29)*

30 20 10 0 ft
1/300
8 4 0 m

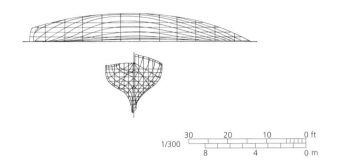

American *Nina*, 1928. The modern schooner rig comes in a variety of forms, most of which depend upon the configuration of sails between the fore and mainmast. This inter-war example, the *Nina* designed by Starling Burgess, employed the stay-sail schooner rig, which was then quite new. Note the consummate hull form: sea-kindly, able to tack without trouble, yet possessing stability and a compelling beauty, but the short overhangs were the result of the American Ocean Racing Rule. Such a craft stands near the peak of evolution, for it seeks not the extreme, but the all-weather competence of the versatile survivor. *Nina* won both the Transatlantic and Fastnet Races in 1928. *(56)*

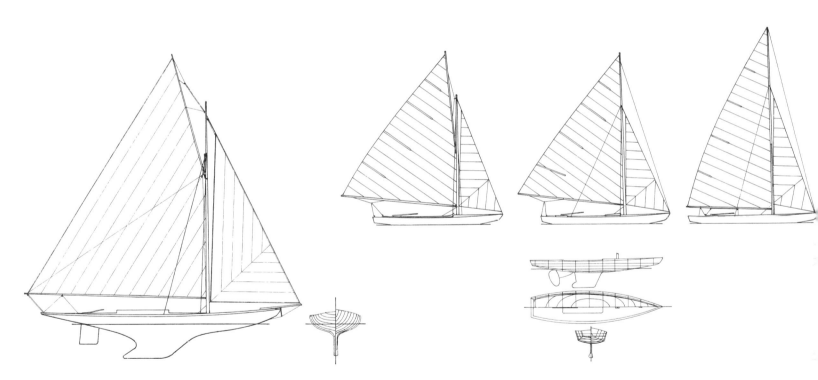

German sloop, about 1900. This example of an early twentieth century, high-peaked, gaff-rigged sloop comes from Germany. The mainsail has no topsail and the headsail fills the fore triangle in the classic form of the sloop-rigged yacht. *(147)*

The History of Yacht Rig – the Sloop

After a long travail the word sloop has come to mean a single-masted, fore-and-aft rigged sailing vessel which has a single headsail. This headsail is most commonly called a jib, but it should properly be termed a staysail, since it is not set flying, but is hanked to the forestay.

American *Star* class, sail plans 1911, 1921 and 1929. In order to race fairly, the concept of the class boat-pitted craft of identical design against each other, thus differentiating only in the skill of their crews. An early form of so-called 'one design' was the American *Star* class of 1911. These were sloop rigged and, being modern in 1911, eschewed the gaff rig. The original was gunter-rigged, a compromise that retained a short mast, extending the luff of the mainsail by means of a long yard which was hoisted almost parallel to, and beyond the mast (left). In 1921 the rig was changed to a Bermudan rig on a mast equal to the height of the hoisted gunter yard (centre). Finally, in 1929, this low aspect Bermudan rig was replaced by a much taller mast, extending the luff on a shorter boom (right). Note the fin keel and skegged rudder. *(56)*

American *Yankee*, 1924. The sloop was equally at home on far larger hulls. This is the *Yankee* of 1924 which possesses an inboard rig requiring a running backstay, and a 'three-quarter' rigged headsail. Variations on this configuration existed until about 1960, when the masthead rig became popular. Although superior to the gaff rig in going to windward, the Bermudan mainsail, with its long, tight luff, sacrificed area to this objective and performed less well downwind. A solution was found in introducing a balloon-like sail when running before the wind. A corruption of the name of the yacht on which an early example was fitted in 1870, the *Sphinx*, it has come to be known as a spinnaker. *(27)*

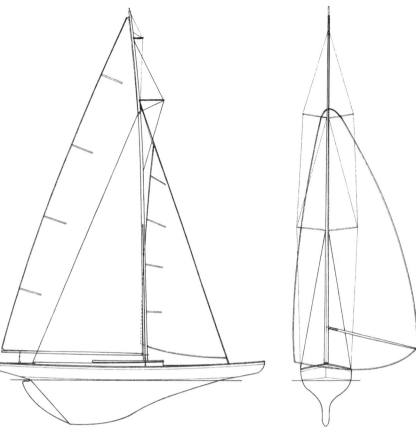

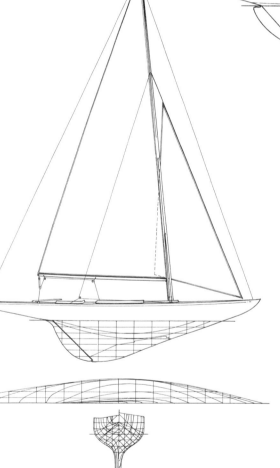

Cruising yacht, 1950s. Although a cruising yacht, this modern example shows how the mainsail is required principally as a windward engine, in concert with a large so-called 'Genoa jib' which, set upon the outer forestay, wraps round the luff of the main to produce lift. Down-wind performance relies increasingly upon the setting of a spinnaker and is countered by the standing backstay. The dotted lines show the steadily reducing jib achieved either by changing sails for a smaller, or by rolling up the genoa. Reefing of the mainsail may be achieved in a modern yacht through a number of options. A few still have reef points, more roll the sail up round the boom or reef in 'slabs', while the most modern furls the luff round a roller running up parallel to the mast inside a fairing. *(243)*

American *Nancy*, 1932. This example of a three-quarter rigged Bermudan sloop shows the mainsail boom well inboard so that it is possible to set up a standing backstay abaft the leech of the mainsail. *(243)*

1/150

British Moody 58 cruiser-racer, present day. With the introduction of glass reinforced plastic, it became possible to virtually mass-produce hulls for a range of cruising and racing yachts to suit most pockets. This standardisation made racing between boats possible and this British Moody 58 is typical of a multitude of masthead rigs. Note the slender profile of the mainsail and the large jib which provides a great deal of power for windward work. The hull has sufficient draught to provide ample accommodation, but is not excessive. A fin keel and skeg-mounted rudder are fitted. *(154)*

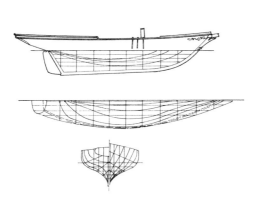

American Gloucester sloop, 1903. The influence of fishing boats persisted as in this small American yacht from Gloucester, Massachusetts, modelled on the basic shape of a Grand Banks fishing schooner. Built in 1903, the hollow lines forward swell out to form a full afterbody above the waterline. Her gaff topsail and flying or outer jib are light-weather sails and her long, overhanging boom is typical of the gaff-rigged racer of her day. Despite her local type-name, she is a true cutter. *(27)*

The History of Yacht Rig – the Cutter

The single-masted cutter sets at least two headsails, namely a staysail and jib. With the abandonment of gaff rig in racing and cruiser-racing yachts, the rig has likewise declined, but it has its adherents, particularly among a fraternity of diehards who refuse to relinquish the gaff.

German cutter, about 1910. Even without her gaff topsail and jib topsail, this early twentieth-century German yacht would be a cutter. With them, however, she proclaims the seductive glories of this tall and elegant rig. The gaff mainsail, the staysail set on the forestay and the jib which is set up flying, tensioned by its own halliard, confirm her as a cutter. *(147)*

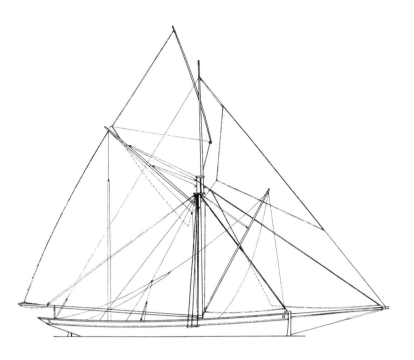

English smack, about 1900. This English smack yacht of the same period has a large topsail set upon a yard, a flying jib and a boom for stretching out a headsail abreast of the mast when running. Upper and lower running backstays, vangs and guys complicate the rig of the heavily-sparred gaff cutter so that the services of a professional sailing master and crew were common on such a 'gentleman's yacht'. *(27)*

British cutter, about 1930. Little has changed in the rig of this cutter from about 1930, though the spars and gear might be lighter and the topsail has a jack and jenny yard. The leech of the mainsail has been fitted with battens, an innovation borrowed from the Bermudan rig, otherwise, despite her spoon-bow and counter stern, she would have been complicated to sail, deterring many of those who could not afford a crew and wished to handle their boats themselves. Such considerations smoothed the acceptability of Bermudan rig. *(243)*

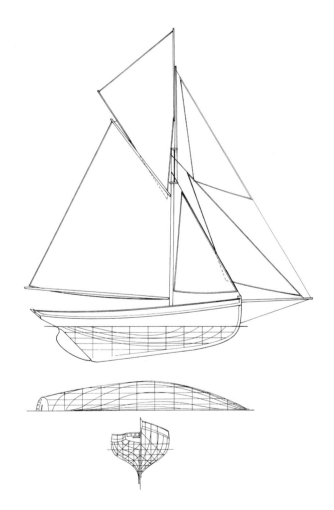

Pilot cutter *Jolie Brise*, as in 1928. The gaff-rigged pilot cutters of Le Havre on the Channel coast of France and of Cardiff and Bristol in Britain, made excellent cruising and racing yachts. The *Jolie Brise* was built for the Le Havre service in 1913 and was converted to a yacht. By 1925 she had passed to a Briton, Commander E Martin, who with her won the first Fastnet Race from the Isle of Wight, round the Fastnet Rock off south-west Ireland and back to Plymouth. In 1926 Martin won the Bermuda Race, making a passage of 10,000 miles to do so, being awarded the Blue Water medal from the Cruising Club of America. Under a later owner she again won the Fastnet in 1929 and 1930, and in the Bermuda Race of 1932 rescued the crew from the burning American yacht *Adriana*. Still afloat as a cruising yacht, *Jolie Brise* is universally admired as one of the handsomest forms of small sailing vessel. *(144)*

30 20 10 0 ft
1/300 8 4 0 m

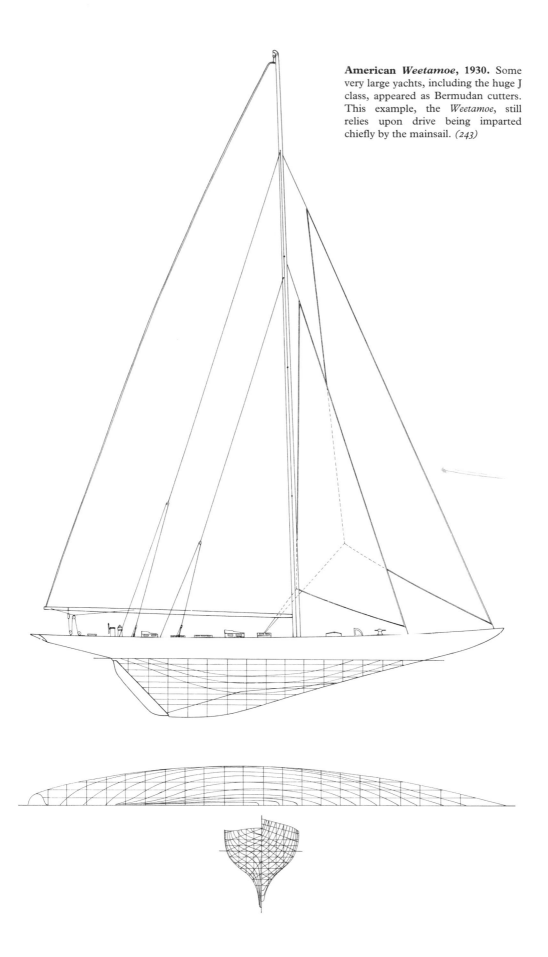

American *Weetamoe*, 1930. Some very large yachts, including the huge J class, appeared as Bermudan cutters. This example, the *Weetamoe*, still relies upon drive being imparted chiefly by the mainsail. *(243)*

1/300

30   20   10   0 ft

8   4   0 m

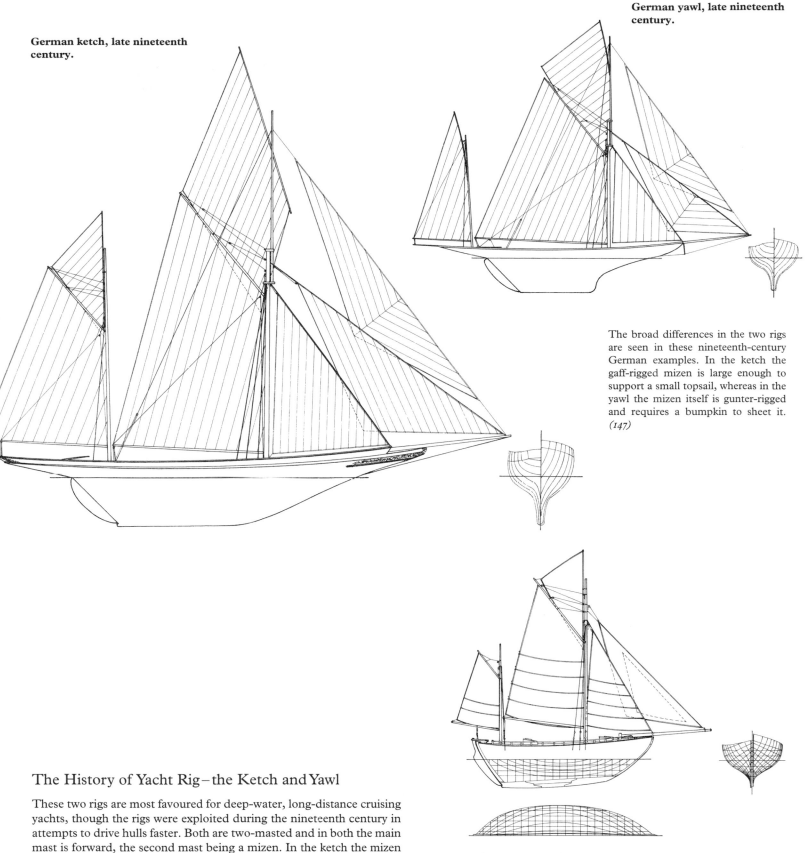

The broad differences in the two rigs are seen in these nineteenth-century German examples. In the ketch the gaff-rigged mizen is large enough to support a small topsail, whereas in the yawl the mizen itself is gunter-rigged and requires a bumpkin to sheet it. *(147)*

The History of Yacht Rig – the Ketch and Yawl

These two rigs are most favoured for deep-water, long-distance cruising yachts, though the rigs were exploited during the nineteenth century in attempts to drive hulls faster. Both are two-masted and in both the main mast is forward, the second mast being a mizen. In the ketch the mizen is stepped forward of the rudder-post. In the yawl it is stepped abaft the rudder post and the consequence of this arrangement is that proportionately, the ketch has a smaller main, but larger mizen than the yawl. The division of the sails reduces the otherwise huge mainsail of a cutter or sloop, giving alternative configurations when shortening down in heavy weather.

Norwegian Colin Archer lifeboat, 1909. One of the most admired twentieth century hull-forms is that of the Norwegian sailing lifeboats designed by Colin Archer, a Norwegian of Scottish extraction. Full-bodied and double-ended, these stout ketches have made an envied name for themselves and for many epitomise the durability and self-sufficiency of the true cruising yacht. Note the four rows of reef points, evidence that extremity of weather was to be no deterrent for vessels designed for life-saving. *(160)*

30   20   10   0 ft
1/300
8   4   0 m

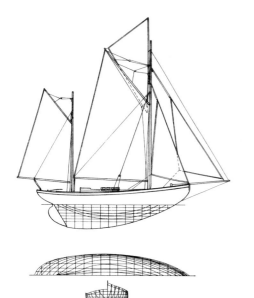

Cherub III. A double-ended, gaff yawl. Note the steeper angle to the mizen gaff and the bumpkin by which the mizen is sheeted in. Given a short bowsprit, *Cherub* sets either her No 1 jib to its end, or in bad weather, her No 2 jib to the stem-head. **NB.** Twice scale. *(56)*

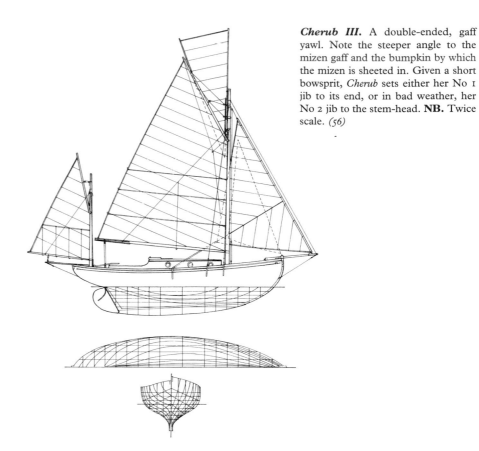

Maud, ketch yacht, 1889. If imitation is the sincerest form of flattery, the principles laid down by Archer are not far away in the design of the *Maud*. A gaff-ketch, her mizen is a little larger and her headsails, set upon a shorter bowsprit, of smaller area. *(166)*

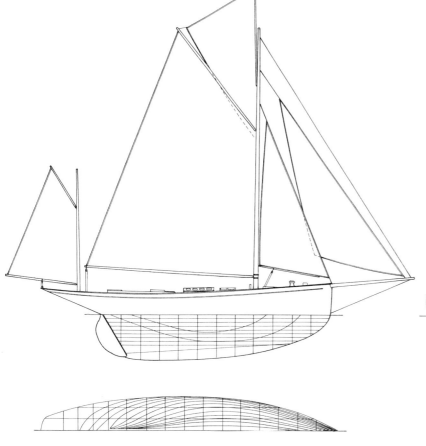

Tern II, 1899. Yawls are occasionally given the misnomer 'cutter-yawls' if, like this example they hoist more than a single headsail. This infelicity is encouraged when the mainsail is very large when compared with the mizen, for the terminology of sailing rigs is never an absolute matter! Yawls with this proportional difference sometimes hoist a small triangular, leg-of-mutton mizen, reducing the amount of gear on the after mast. The long counter of *Tern II* removes the need for a bumpkin. **NB.** Twice scale. *(166)*

Dorade, 1930. This more modern Bermudan yawl boasts two headsails and in fine weather sets a mizen staysail. This is a particularly useful sail when reaching and exploits the versatility inherent in a two-masted rig. *(56)*

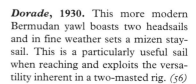

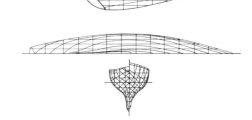

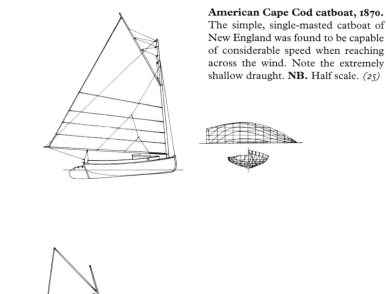

American Cape Cod catboat, 1870. The simple, single-masted catboat of New England was found to be capable of considerable speed when reaching across the wind. Note the extremely shallow draught. **NB.** Half scale. *(25)*

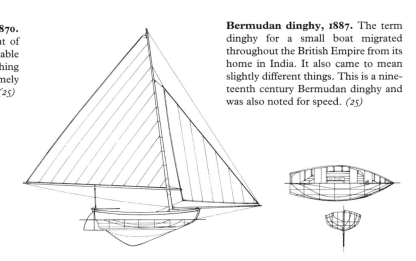

Bermudan dinghy, 1887. The term dinghy for a small boat migrated throughout the British Empire from its home in India. It also came to mean slightly different things. This is a nineteenth century Bermudan dinghy and was also noted for speed. *(25)*

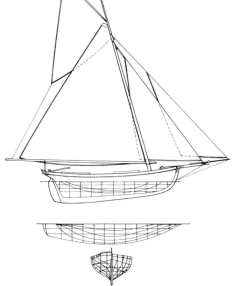

Bermudan racing sloop, 1870. It was clear to those racing these craft that increases in sail area gained extra speed and this Bermudan racing sloop of 1870 demonstrates the curious lengths gone to to exploit a fine hull and a steady breeze. **NB.** Half scale. *(25)*

Procyon, **1873.** Designed by R T McMullan, *Procyon* was one of the small cruisers that proved his contention that a small boat at sea, if properly handled, was as safe as a large yacht. The loose-footed dipping lug encouraged experimentation with tighter control of the aerofoil shape of the sails. *(166)*

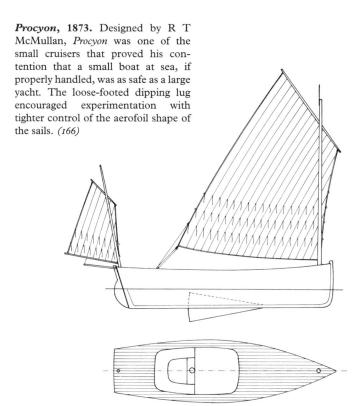

The History of Yachting – the Quest for Speed

In theory a hull can only be driven to a maximum speed above which effort has to be increased exponentially for small increases in forward motion. In due course this effort become unsustainable and an upper speed limit is reached. The first limitation, the hull's maximum theoretical speed, is a function of its waterline length and therefore greater length gives greater speed potential. To this, however, have to be applied other considerations, most notable that of block co-efficient. This is the ratio which a hull has with a solid block of identical overall dimensions. A cargo-carrying merchant ship might have a block co-efficient of about 0.75 to 0.8, though a fine yachts might whittle this down to 0.5. With this, of course, goes wetted surface area and the frictional drag caused by the flow of water past the hull as it is driven forward. In a sailing ship designed to carry cargo, only a press of sail can push the hull beyond its natural maximum, a technique known to clipper-masters as 'driving'.

A small hull, however, that of a boat rather than a ship, can exceed its hull speed by planing: that is it climbs up on the wave made by the progress of the hull and rides along in an exhilarating rush. Speeds of up to two-and-a-half times the hull speed can be achieved. The quest for very high speeds is therefore a matter for small craft.

15   10   5   0 ft
1/150
4   3   2   1   0 m

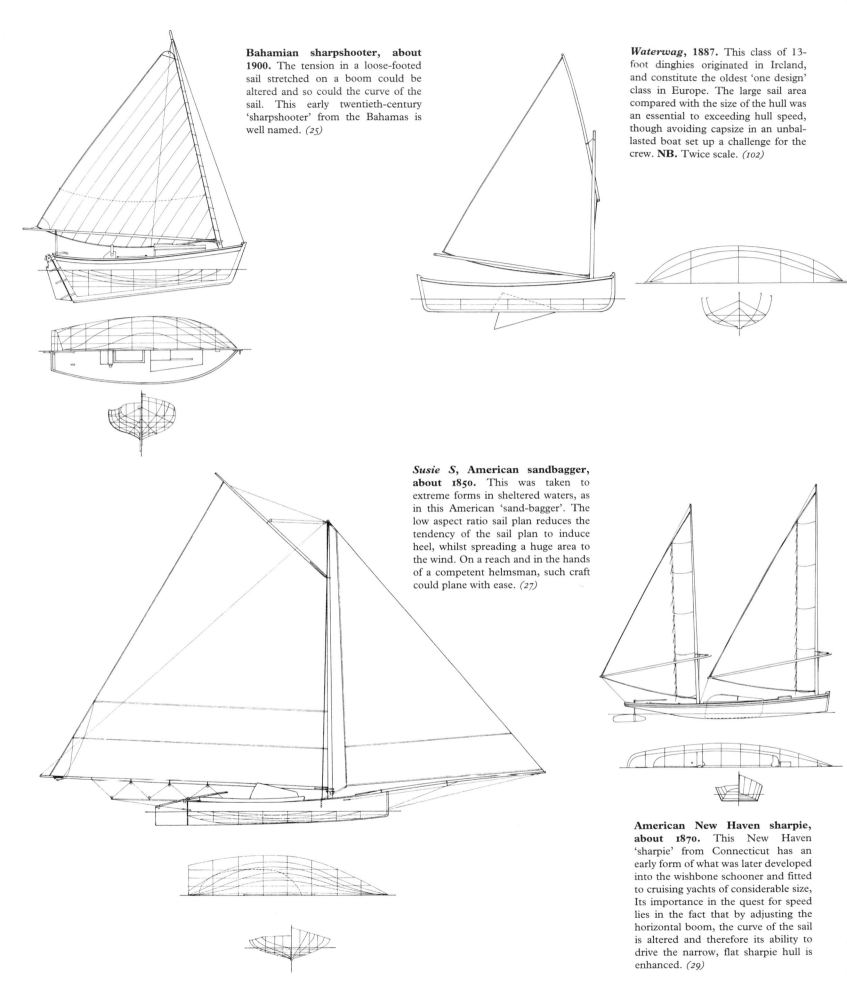

Bahamian sharpshooter, about 1900. The tension in a loose-footed sail stretched on a boom could be altered and so could the curve of the sail. This early twentieth-century 'sharpshooter' from the Bahamas is well named. *(25)*

Waterwag, 1887. This class of 13-foot dinghies originated in Ircland, and constitute the oldest 'one design' class in Europe. The large sail area compared with the size of the hull was an essential to exceeding hull speed, though avoiding capsize in an unballasted boat set up a challenge for the crew. **NB.** Twice scale. *(102)*

Susie S, **American sandbagger, about 1850.** This was taken to extreme forms in sheltered waters, as in this American 'sand-bagger'. The low aspect ratio sail plan reduces the tendency of the sail plan to induce heel, whilst spreading a huge area to the wind. On a reach and in the hands of a competent helmsman, such craft could plane with ease. *(27)*

American New Haven sharpie, about 1870. This New Haven 'sharpie' from Connecticut has an early form of what was later developed into the wishbone schooner and fitted to cruising yachts of considerable size, Its importance in the quest for speed lies in the fact that by adjusting the horizontal boom, the curve of the sail is altered and therefore its ability to drive the narrow, flat sharpie hull is enhanced. *(29)*

1/150

15 10 5 0 ft
4 3 2 1 0 m

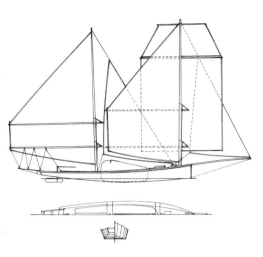

American racing sharpie, about 1884. The extreme simplicity and lack of wetted area over a long waterline length encouraged experimentation on the sharpie hull and this fantastic rig was just one. The sharpie continues to provide an excellent base for trial rigs. **NB.** Half scale. *(29)*

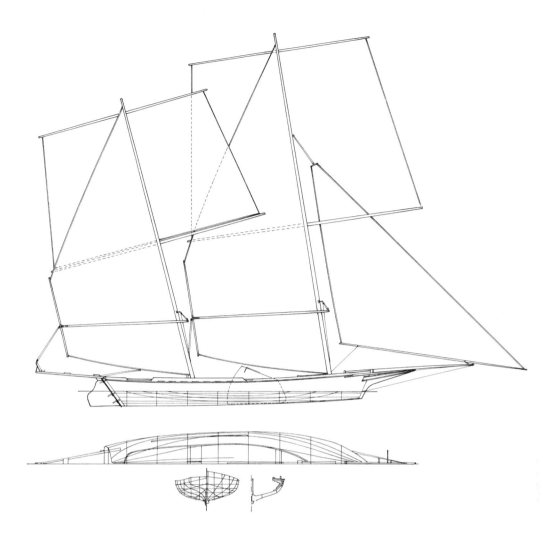

Jay Dee, **American Chesapeake Bay log canoe, 1931.** A similar rig is found a generation later on a slightly more sophisticated hull, not on Long Island Sound, but Chesapeake Bay, that nursery of the Baltimore clipper. This is a so-called 'log canoe' and would require an energetic crew to maintain stability. *(29)*

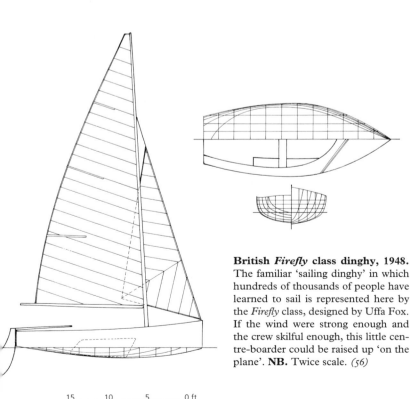

British *Firefly* class dinghy, 1948. The familiar 'sailing dinghy' in which hundreds of thousands of people have learned to sail is represented here by the *Firefly* class, designed by Uffa Fox. If the wind were strong enough and the crew skilful enough, this little centre-boarder could be raised up 'on the plane'. **NB.** Twice scale. *(56)*

British *Laser* class dinghy, 1970s. Competitive excellence can only be resolved by providing an absolute standard so that the sole difference in a race is the competence of the helmsman. With the single-handed *Laser*, all boats have an identical moulded plastic hull and individual skill decides the winner. The *Laser*'s unstayed mast and sleeved sail are set up aerodynamically and provide a 'gull-wing' aerofoil which is extremely efficient, the hull is shallow draughted and possesses a centeboard and drop-bladed rudder to resist leeway. **NB.** Twice scale. *(166)*

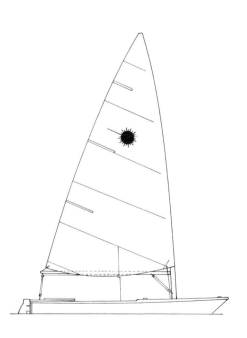

15 10 5 0 ft
1/150
4 3 2 1 0 m

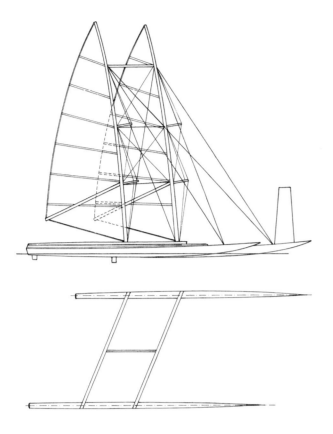

Crossbow II, world sailing speed record holder, 1976. High speeds of 22 knots in a 24-hour run have been achieved by catamarans since they maximise waterline length but minimise drag through wetted surface area. One of the fastest craft over a shorter course is the 18-metre 'flying proa' *Crossbow II*, seen here. In 1976 she raised the world record to 31.8 knots, 33 knots in 1977 and to 36 knots in 1980. Hi-tech materials in the hull, sail-fabric, rigging and spars make such a craft as near-weightless as possible. *(222)*

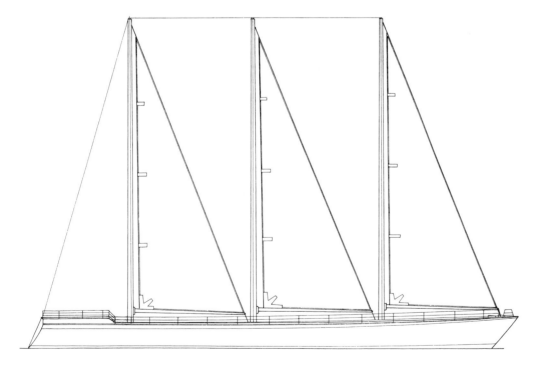

French *Vendredi 13,* **1972.** Only in the open ocean can the quest for speed be truly pursued and this French yacht, the *Vendredi 13* is designed for such an exacting environment. *(222)*

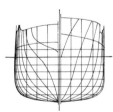

Russian *Kruzenshtern*, post-war. Built as *Padua* by Tecklenborg at Wesermunde in 1926 for F Laeisz of Hamburg, this four-masted barque was one of two post-war barques intended to re-establish the company and traded up to the outbreak of the Second World War. Of 3545 gross registered tonnage, 97.4 metres in length, she was taken as war reparation by the then Soviet Union and renamed *Kruzenshtern*, after the Russian circumnavigator. Considerably altered to suit her new task as a schoolship for the Ministry of Fisheries, she has been fitted with engines. She nevertheless remains typical of the big German four-masted barques built for the nitrate trade and designed to round Cape Horn twice a voyage. *(229)*

Sail-Training Ships

Many nations hold that training under sail is invaluable not only for cadets of their navies and mercantile marines, but for imbuing in their young citizens a sense of valuing their fellows, of learning to work as part of a team, and for the encouragement of leadership skills. Some of these ships have been specially built, others have a history of their own.

60 50 40 30 20 10 0 ft
1/600
15 10 5 0 m

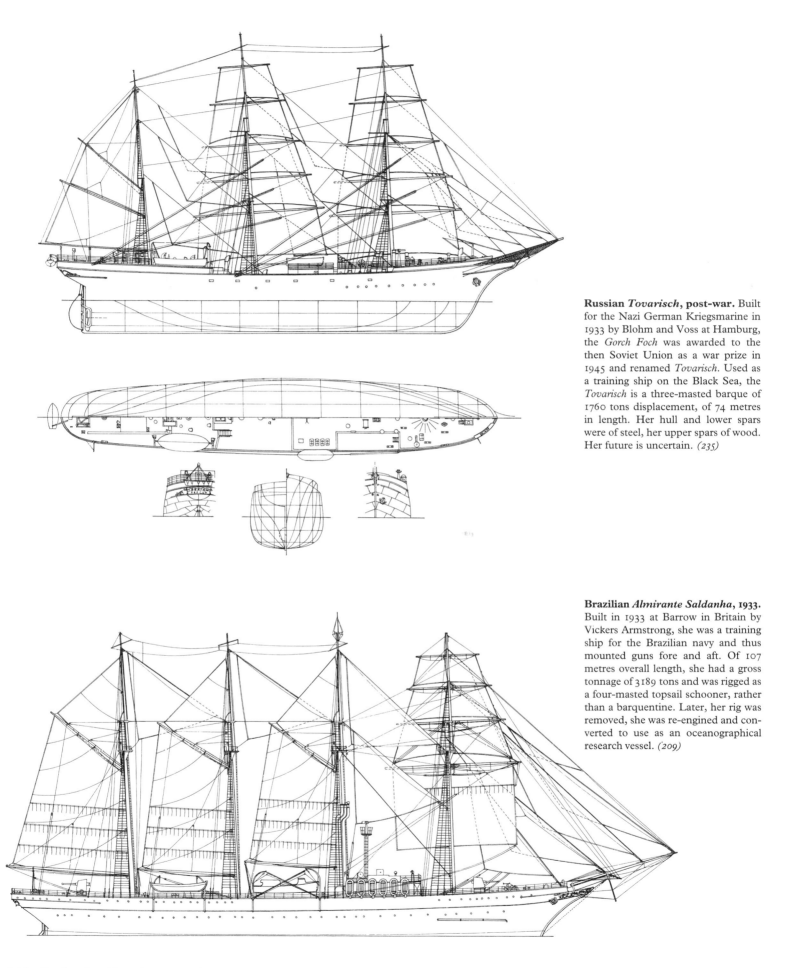

Russian *Tovarisch*, post-war. Built
for the Nazi German Kriegsmarine in
1933 by Blohm and Voss at Hamburg,
the *Gorch Foch* was awarded to the
then Soviet Union as a war prize in
1945 and renamed *Tovarisch*. Used as
a training ship on the Black Sea, the
Tovarisch is a three-masted barque of
1760 tons displacement, of 74 metres
in length. Her hull and lower spars
were of steel, her upper spars of wood.
Her future is uncertain. *(235)*

Brazilian *Almirante Saldanha*, 1933.
Built in 1933 at Barrow in Britain by
Vickers Armstrong, she was a training
ship for the Brazilian navy and thus
mounted guns fore and aft. Of 107
metres overall length, she had a gross
tonnage of 3189 tons and was rigged as
a four-masted topsail schooner, rather
than a barquentine. Later, her rig was
removed, she was re-engined and converted to use as an oceanographical
research vessel. *(209)*

60 50 40 30 20 10 0 ft
1/600
15   10   5   0 m

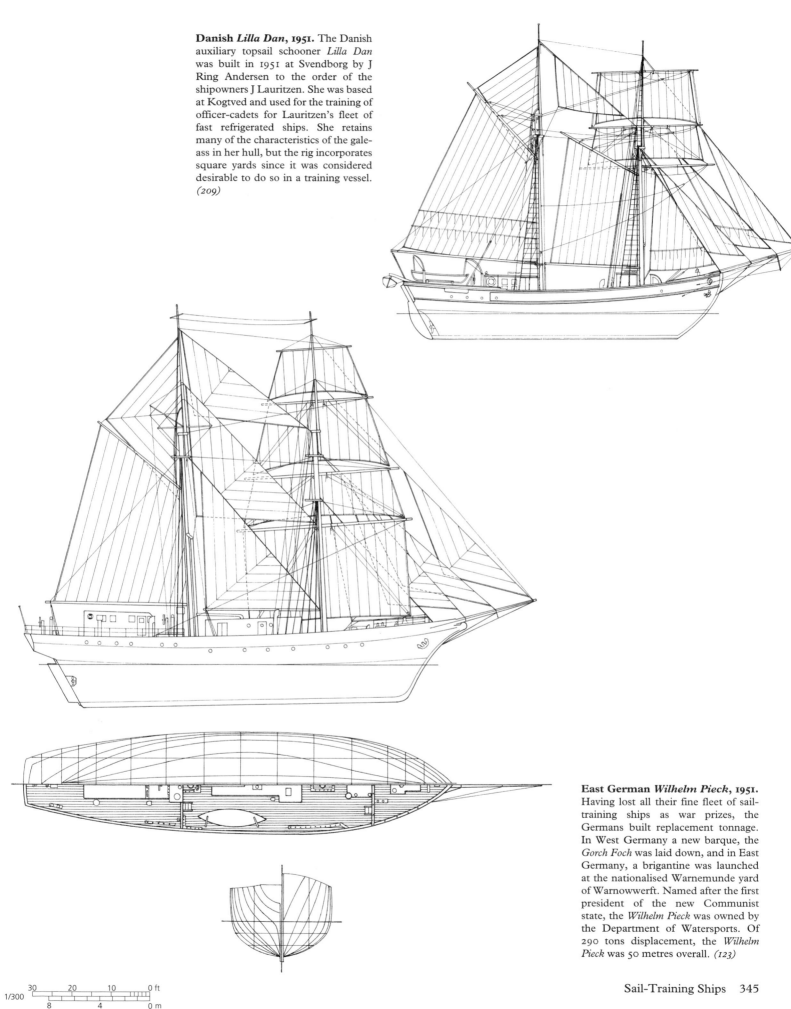

Danish *Lilla Dan*, 1951. The Danish auxiliary topsail schooner *Lilla Dan* was built in 1951 at Svendborg by J Ring Andersen to the order of the shipowners J Lauritzen. She was based at Kogtved and used for the training of officer-cadets for Lauritzen's fleet of fast refrigerated ships. She retains many of the characteristics of the galeass in her hull, but the rig incorporates square yards since it was considered desirable to do so in a training vessel. *(209)*

East German *Wilhelm Pieck*, 1951. Having lost all their fine fleet of sail-training ships as war prizes, the Germans built replacement tonnage. In West Germany a new barque, the *Gorch Foch* was laid down, and in East Germany, a brigantine was launched at the nationalised Warnemunde yard of Warnowwerft. Named after the first president of the new Communist state, the *Wilhelm Pieck* was owned by the Department of Watersports. Of 290 tons displacement, the *Wilhelm Pieck* was 50 metres overall. *(123)*

1/300

30   20   10   0 ft

8   4   0 m

British *Sir Winston Churchill*, 1966.
Having long since relinquished sail-training for either the Royal Navy or its mercantile marine, Britain fully rejoined the international sailing community with a number of large yachts and small sailing vessels. Among these is the Sail Training Association's *Sir Winston Churchill*. Built at Hessle on the River Humber by Richard Dunston in 1966, the vessel is a 41-metres long, three-masted auxiliary topsail schooner. *(228)*

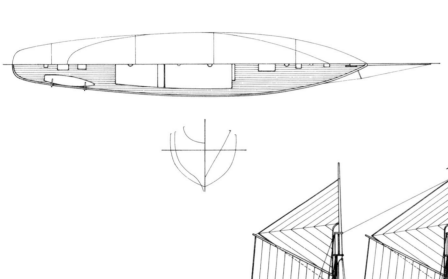

Polish *Iskra*, 1927. Used by the Polish navy before the Second World War, this 348-ton three-masted, auxiliary schooner, was built by G Muller in the Netherlands as the *Vlissingen* for the coastwise trade. She was sold to British owners in 1925 and renamed *St Blane*. In 1927 she was bought by the Polish navy, converted to a training vessel, and as *Iskra*, based at Gdynia. She was in a French North African port at the outbreak of war in 1939 and, on the Fall of France, was sailed to Gibraltar to become a depot ship for the duration. *Iskra* was returned to Poland after the war and has since been replaced by a modern barquentine of the same name. *(235)*

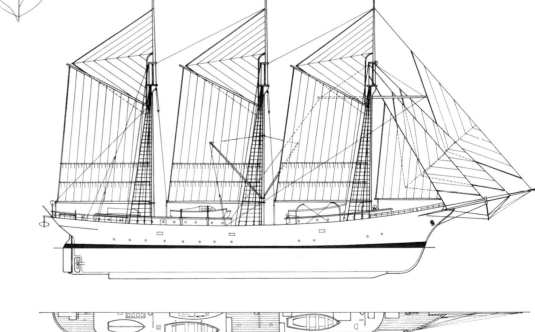

1/400

40   30   20   10   0 ft

10   5   0 m

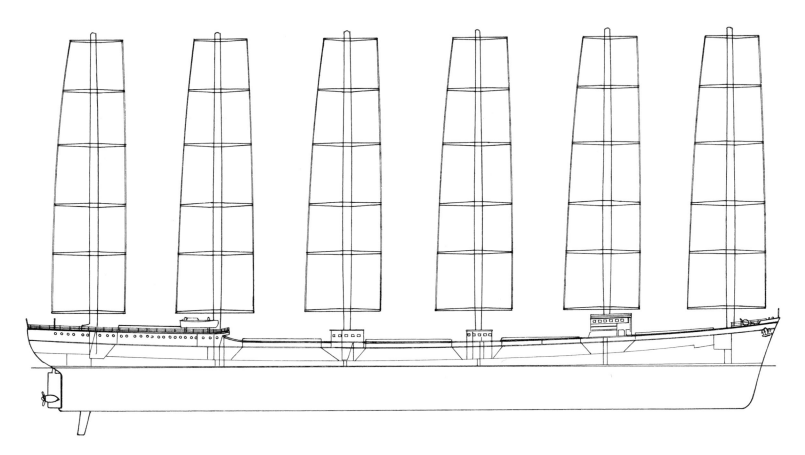

German Dynaship project, 1960-67. The fossil fuel crises caused by a succession of upheavals in the Middle East beginning with the Arab-Israeli War of 1967, focused attention on applying modern hi-tech solutions to exploiting the wind. A German team conceived the 'dynaship', a sail plan using modern materials to form aerodynamic square-rigged sails which would be handled mechanically, rather than by running rigging. The notion was to power bulk-carriers of up to about 17,000 gross tons. A diesel auxiliary would provide propulsion for moving through calms and in and out of port, while providing electricity to operate the control system for the sails. *(222)*

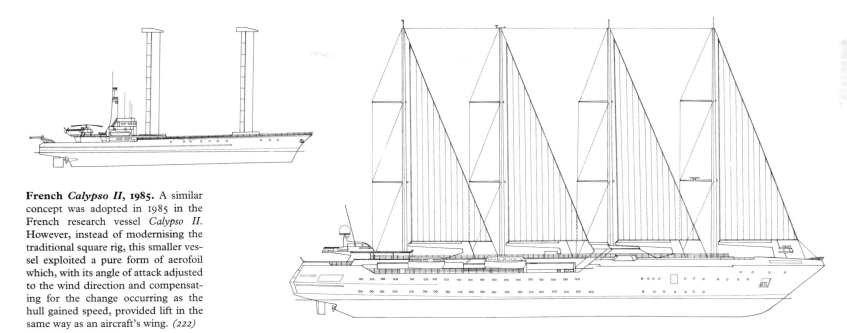

French *Calypso II*, 1985. A similar concept was adopted in 1985 in the French research vessel *Calypso II*. However, instead of modernising the traditional square rig, this smaller vessel exploited a pure form of aerofoil which, with its angle of attack adjusted to the wind direction and compensating for the change occurring as the hull gained speed, provided lift in the same way as an aircraft's wing. *(222)*

Contemporary Applications of Sail

A number of disparate applications of sail remain. A few examples are shown above.

Finnish sailing cruise ship, 1981. A number of sailing cruise ships have been built in recent years. All employ hi-tech materials in their spar and sail construction, as well as in highly sophisticated control systems. Since these can be operated by the watch-keeping officer, the notion of a working crew has been abolished, insofar as the handling of the sails are concerned. This example is of a Finnish sailing cruise ship, built in 1981. Such vessels are designed for leisurely passages in exotic locations. *(222)*

Sources and Bibliography

Books

1. Adney, E T & Chapelle, H I: *The Bark Canoes and Skin Boats of North America* (Washington, DC 1964)

2. Anderson, R C: *Oared Fighting Ships* (London 1962)

3. Anderson, R C: *Seventeenth Century Rigging* (Watford 1977)

4. Angelucci, E & Cucari, A: *Ships* (London 1977)

5. Audemard, L: *Les Jonques Chinoises: Ornamentation et Types* (Rotterdam 1960)

6. Audemard, L: *Les Jonques Chinoises: Construction de la Jonque* (Rotterdam 1959)

7. Audemard, L: *Les Jonques Chinoises: L'Histoire de la Jonque* (Rotterdam 1957)

8. Aufheimer, H: *Schiffsbewaffnung* (Rostock 1983)

9. Bak J, Csonkaréti K, Lévay G & Sárhidi Gy: *Hadihajók* (Budapest 1984)

10. Baker, W A: *Sloops and Shallops* (Barre, Mass 1966)

11. Bass, G F: 'A Byzantine Trading Venture', in *Scientific American* (Aug 1971)

12. Battson, R K: *Modelling Tudor Ships* (Hemel Hempstead 1972)

13. Battson, R K: *Period Ship Modelling* (Watford 1979)

14. Beylen, J van: *Schepen van de Nederlanden* (Amsterdam 1970)

15. Beylen, J van: *Zeeuwsche vissersschepen van de Ooster-en Westerschelde* (Amsterdam 1964)

16. Bjerg, H Ch & Erichsen, J: *Danske orlogsskibe 1690-1860*, 2 vols (Copenhagen 1980)

17. Boudriot, J: *La Frégate* (Paris 1992)

18. Brito, N de: *Caravelas, Naus e Galés de Portugal* (Porto nd)

19. Broby-Johansen, R: *Északi sziklarajzok* (Budapest 1979)

20. Brögger, A W & Shetelig, H: *The Viking Ships* (London 1953)

21. Bürms, J: *Lehrhefte für der Boots-und Schiffbau, Nr 2: Der Linienriss* (Hamburg nd)

22. Busch, F O & Docter, H: *Germanische Seefahrt* (Berlin 1935)

23. Busley, C: 'Schiffe des Altertums', in *Jahrbuch der Schiffbautechnischen Gesellschaft*, Bd 20 (Berlin 1919)

24. Calvocoressi, R: *Marine Painting* (New York 1978)

25. Chapelle, H I: *American Sailing Craft* (Camden, Maine 1975)

26. Chapelle, H I: *The American Sailing Navy* (New York 1949)

27. Chapelle, H I: *The History of American Sailing Ships* (New York 1935)

28. Chapelle, H I: *The National Watercraft Collection* (Washington, DC 1960)

29. Chapelle, H I: *American Small Sailing Craft* (New York 1951)

30. Chapelle, H I: *The Baltimore Clipper* (Salem, Mass 1930)

31. Chapelle, H I: *The Search for Speed under Sail 1700-1855* (London 1968)

32. Chapelle, H I: *The American Fishing Schooners 1825-1935* (London 1973)

33. Chapelle, H I: *The Constellation Question* (Washington, DC 1970)

34. Chapman, F H: *Architectura Navalis Mercatoria* (reprinted Burg bei Magdeburg 1957)

35. Christensen, A E jr: *Boats of the North* (Oslo 1968)

36. Crone, G C E: *Nederlandsche Binnenschepen* (Amsterdam 1944)

37. Crone, G C E: *Nederlandsche Jachten, Binnenschepen, Visschersvaartuigen* (Amsterdam 1926)

38. Csonkaréti K: *Hadihajók a Dunán* (Budapest 1980)

39. Curti, O: *Schiffsmodellbau* (Rostock 1972)

40. Cutler, C: *Greyhounds of the Sea* (Annapolis, Maryland 1960)

41. Däbritz, R & Quinger, W: *Die Brigg* (Rostock 1982)

42. Däbritz, R & Quinger, W: *Von der Fregatte zum Vollschiff* (Rostock 1987)

43. Dessens, H: *De Hazenberg modellen* (The Hague 1991)

44. Donnelly, I A: *Chinese Junks and other Native Craft* (Shanghai 1924)

45. Dudszus, A & Henriot, E & Krumrey, F: *Das Grosse Schiffstypenbuch* (Berlin 1983)

46. Editors of Wooden Boat Magazine, *Fifty Wooden Boats* (Brooklin, Maine 1993)

47. Eich, L & Wend, J: *Schiffe auf druckgraphischen Blätter* (Rostock 1980)

48. Evans, A C: *The Sutton Hoo Ship Burial* (London 1986)

49. Ewe, H: *Abbild oder Phantasie?* (Rostock 1978)

50. Ewe, H: *Schiffe auf Siegeln* (Rostock 1972)

51. Faerøyvik, O: *Inshore Craft of Norway* (London 1979)

52. Fircks, J von: *Ewer, Zeesenboot und andere ältere Fischereifahrzeuge* (Rostock 1982)

53. Fircks, J von: *Normannenschiffe* (Rostock 1986)

54. Fircks, J von: *Wikingerschiffe* (Rostock 1979)

55. Fonseca, Q da: *A Caravela Portuguesa* (Coimbra 1934)

56. Fox, Uffa: *Sailing, Seamanship and Yacht Construction* (Southampton 1981)

57. Friederici, G: *Die Schiffahrt der Indianer* (Stuttgart 1907; reprint Kassel 1975)

58. Fries Sheepvaart Museum en Oudheidkamer, *Jaarboek 1980*.

59. Furttenbach, J: *Architectura Navalis* (Ulm 1629; facsimile reprint Hildesheim, New York 1975)

60. Gardiner, R: *The First Frigates* (London 1992)

61. Gardiner, R: *The Heavy Frigate* (London 1994)

62. Gardiner, R (ed): *The Line of Battle* (London 1992)

63. Gardiner, R: *The Age of the Galley* (London 1995)

64. Goodwin, P: *The Construction and Fitting of the Sailing Man of War 1650-1850* (London 1987)

65. Gráfik I: 'A magyarországi fahajózás', *Néprajzi Közlemények* XXVI (Budapest 1983)

66. Greenhill, B: *The Archeology of Boats and Ships* (London 1995)

67. Greenhill, B: *The Merchant Schooners*, 2 vols (London 1951)

68. Greenhill, B & Manning, S: *The Schooner Bertha L Downs* (London 1995)

69. Gulás, S & Lescinsky, D: *Avitorlás hajók története* (Budapest 1985)

70. Hackney, N C L: *HMS Victory* (Rostock 1977)

71. Hagedorn, B: *Die Entwicklung der wichtigsten Schiffstypen bis ins 19 Jh* (Berlin 1914)

72. Halldín, G: *Svenska Flottans Historia*, 2 vols (Malmö 1943)

73. Hanke, H: *Az óceánok meghódítása* (Budapest 1965)

74. Harris, D G: *F H Chapman: The First Naval Architect and his Work* (London 1989)

75. Hawkins, C W: *The Dhow* (Lymington 1977)

76. Heide, G D van der: *Archeologie auf dem Meeresboden* (Düsseldorf 1971)

77. Heinsius, P: *Das Schiff der hansischen Frühzeit* (Weimar 1986)

78. Henriot, E: *Kurzgefasste illustrierte Geschichte des Schiffbaus* (Rostock 1971)

79. Henschke, W: *Schiffbautechnisches Handbuch*, 3 vols (Berlin 1952)

80. Hoeckel, R: *Das Wappen von Hamburg*, Vol I (Burg bei Magdeburg 1958)

81. Hoeckel, R: *Modellbau von Schiffen des 16 und 17 Jh* (Rostock 1971)

82. Hoeckel, R: *Risse von Schiffen des 16 und 17 Jh* (Rostock 1979)

83. Hoeckel, R: *Schiffsrisse zur Schiffbaugeschichte*, 2 vols (Burg bei Magdeburg 1957-58)

84. Hoheisel, W-D: *Die Bremer Hansekogge von 1380* (Bremerhaven 1996)

85. Hollander, N & Mertes, H: *Solange sie noch segeln* (Hamburg 1983)

86. Holmberg, G: *Svensk Skeppsbyggeri* (Malmö 1963)

87. Hölzer, W: *Klipperschiffe des 19 Jh* (Rostock 1976)

88. Hornell, J: *Water Transport: Origins and Early Evolution* (Newton Abbott 1970)

89. Howard, F: *Sailing Ships of War 1400-1860* (London 1979)

90. Huitema, T: *Ronde en platbodem jachten* (Amsterdam 1970)

91. Irving, J: *The King's Britannia* (London c1936)

92. Israel, U & Gebauer, J: *Kriegsschiffe unter Segel und Dampf* (Berlin 1988)

93. Israel, U & Gebauer, J: *Segelkriegsschiffe* (Berlin 1982)

94. Jaeger, W: *Das Peller-Modell von 1603* (Rostock 1973)

95. Jenkins, N: *The Boat beneath the Pyramid* (London 1980)

96. Joergensen, B E: *Les bateaux des vikings* (Rouen 1992)

97. Johansson, D: *Ein Schiffsmodell entsteht* (Berlin 1979)

98. Johansson, D: *Technologie des Schiffsmodellbaus* (Berlin 1976)

99. Kádár F: *Hajósmesterség* (Budapest 1961)

100. Kamminga, L: *Schepen van de Friese Admiraliteit* (Leeuwarden 1973)

101. Kelting-Eischeid, R: *Historische Schiffsrisse* (Kiel 1994)

102. Kemp, Dixon: *A Manual of Yacht and Boat Sailing* (7th ed, London 1891)

103. Kemp, P (ed): *The Oxford Companion to Ships and the Sea* (Oxford 1988)

104. Ketting, H: *Prins Willem* (Rostock 1981)

105. Kirsch, P: *Galleon: The Great Ships of the Armada Era* (London 1990)

106. Knoll, C & Winde, J: *Windjammer* (Leipzig/Jena/Berlin 1980)

107. Kooijman, J: *Tien platbodemjachten* (The Hague 1944)

108. Koop, G: *Die deutschen Segelschulschiffe* (Koblenz 1989)

109. Kühl, E & Vahlen, Th (ed): *Yachtbau und Yachtsegeln* (Berlin 1910)

110. Laas,W: *Die grossen Segelschiffe* (Berlin 1908)

111. Laird Clowes, G S: *Sailing Ships: Their History and Development*, 2 vols (London 1930)

112. Landström, B: *Das Schiff* (Gütersloh 1976)

113. Landström, B: *Die Schiffe der Pharaonen* (Munich/Gütersloh/ Vienna 1974)

114. Landström, B: *Segelschiffe* (Gütersloh 1970)

115. Lane, F C: *Venetian Ships and Shipbuilders of the Renaissance* (Baltimore, Maryland 1934)

116. Lanitzki, G: *Die Wasa von 1628* (Berlin 1986)

117. Laughton, L G C: *Old Ship Figure Heads and Sterns* (London 1925, reprinted New York 1973)

118. Lavery, B (ed): *Deane's Doctrine of Naval Architecture, 1670* (London 1981)

119. Lavery, B: *The Arming and Fitting of English Ships of War 1600-1815* (London 1987)

120. Lavery, B: *Nelson's Navy* (London 1995)

121. Lavery, B: *The Ship of the Line*, 2 vols (London 1983)

122. Lees, J: *The Masting and Rigging of English Ships of War 1625-1860* (London 1990)

123. Lienau, O: *Das grosse Kraweel der Peter von Danzig* (Danzig 1943)

124. Longridge, C N: *The Anatomy of Nelson's Ships* (Watford 1953)

125. Loon, F N van: *Beschouwing van den Nederlandschen Scheepsbouw* (Haarlem 1820, reprinted Haarlem 1980)

126. Lubbock, B: *The Western Ocean Packets* (Glasgow 1925)

127. Lusci, V: *Der Schiffsmodellbau nach historischen Vorbildern*

128. MacGregor, D R: *Clipper Ships* (Watford 1979)

129. MacGregor, D R: *Fast Sailing Ships* (London 1980)

130. MacGregor, D R: *Merchant Sailing Ships 1775-1815* (Watford 1980)

131. MacGregor, D R: *Merchant Sailing Ships 1815-1850* (London 1984)

132. MacGregor, D R: *Merchant Sailing Ships 1850-1875* (London 1984)

133. MacGregor, D R: *Schooners in Four Centuries* (London 1982)

134. MacGregor, D R: *Square Rigged Sailing Ships* (London 1977)

135. MacGregor, D R: *The China Bird* (London 1961)

136. MacGregor, D R: *The Tea Clippers* (London 1983)

137. MacGregor, D R: *Merchant Sailing Ships 1775-1815* (London 1985)

138. Marjai I & Kö T: *Történelmi hajók modellezése* (Budapest 1966)

139. Marjai I & Pataky D: *A hajó története* (Budapest 1973)

140. Marjai I: *Hajómodellez's* (Budapest 1980)

141. Marjai I: *Nagy hajóskönyv* (Budapest 1981)

142. Marquardt, K H: *Bemastung und Takelung von Schiffen des 18 Jh* (Rostock 1986)

143. Marquardt, K H: *Schoner in Nord und Süd* (Rostock 1989)

144. Martin, E G: *Deep Water Cruising* (London 1928)

145. May, W E: *The Boats of Men of War* (London 1974)

146. McKee, A: *Die Mary Rose* (Vienna & Hamburg 1983)

147. Middendorf, F L: *Die Bemastung und Takelung der Schiffe* (Berlin 1903)

148. Millward, C N: *Modelling the Revenge* (Hemel Hempstead 1972)

149. Mondfeld, W zu : *Historische Schiffsmodelle* (Munich 1990)

150. Mondfeld, W zu: *Die arabische Dau* (Rostock 1979)

151. Mondfeld, W zu: *Die Galeere* (Rostock 1977)

152. Mondfeld, W zu: *Die Schebecke und andere schiffstypen des Mittelmeeraumes* (Rostock 1980)

153. Mondfeld, W zu: *Schicksale berühmter Segelschiffe* (Munich 1993)

154. Moody, official company brochure

155. Moore, A: *Sailing Ships of War 1800-1860* (London 1926)

156. Morris, E P: *The Fore-and-Aft Rig in America* (London 1974)

157. Morrison, J S & Williams, R T: *Greek Oared Ships* (Cambridge 1968)

158. Müller, E: *Konstruktion und Bau von Segeljollen* (Berlin 1927)

159. Neukirchen, H: *Seefahrt Gestern und Heute* (Berlin 1979)

160. Neukirchen, H: *Seemacht* (Berlin 1982)

161. Nikula, O: *Svenska Skärgardsflottan 1756-1791* (Helsinki 1933)

162. Novouszpenszkij, N: *Aivazovsky* (Leningrad 1972)

163. Nowy, W: 'Egipski okret floty Ramzesa III', in *Modelarz*, Nov 1989 (Warsaw)

164. Oderwald, J: *Het Nederlandsche Zeilschip* (Amsterdam 1939)

165. Oderwald, J: *Nederlandsche Snelzeilers* (Amsterdam 1940)

166. Original draughts (copies of official or builders' plans)

167. Paris, F E: *Die grosse Zeit der Galeeren und Geleassen* (Rostock 1973)

168. Paris, F E: *Linienschiffe des 18 Jh* (Rostock 1983)

169. Paris, F E: *Segelkriegschiffe des 17 Jh* (Rostock 1975)

170. Paris, F E: *Souvenirs de Marine* (selections reprinted Magdeburg 1956; Rostock 1962)

171. Pataky D & Marjai I: *A hajó a mûvészetben* (Budapest 1973)

172. Petrejus, E W: *Modelling the Brig-of-War Irene* (Hengelo 1970)

173. Phillips-Birt, D: *The History of Yachting* (London 1974)

174. Pizzarello, U: *Boote in Venedig* (Venice 1984)

175. Prins, A H J: *Sailing from Lamu* (Assen 1965)

176. Quinger, W: *Wappen von Hamburg*, Vol I (Rostock 1980)

177. Quinger, W: *Wappen von Hamburg*, Vol II (Rostock 1983)

178. Rabbel, J: *Rostocker Windjammer* (Rostock 1983)

179. Rabbel, J: *Rostocks eiserne Segler* (Rostock 1986)

180. Ralamb, A C: *Skeps Byggerij eller Adelig Öfnings Tionde Tom* (Stockholm 1691, facsimile reprint Malmö 1943)

181. Rehbein, E (ed): *Einbaum-Dampflok-Düsenklipper* (Leipzig 1968)

182. Reich, K & Pagel, M: *Himmelsbesen* (Berlin 1981)

183. Risch, H: *Windschiffe* (Berlin 1988)

184. Robertson, F L: *Evolution of Naval Armament* (London 1921)

185. Romola, A & Anderson, R C: *The Sailing Ship* (New York 1963)

186. Rónay T: *Német-magyar, magyar-német hajós szétár* (Budapest 1917)

187. Rudolph, W: *Boote-Flösse-Schiffe* (Leipzig 1974)

188. Sannes, T B: *Die Fram* (Berlin 1986)

189. Scharnow, U (ed): *Transpress Lexikon Seefahrt* (Berlin 1981)

190. Schäuffelen, O: *Die letzten grossen Segelshiffe* (Bielefeld 1977)

191. Schmidt, G: *Der Schiffsanker im Wandel der Zeiten* (Rostock 1982)

192. Schmidt, G: *Schiffe unterm Roten Adler* (Rostock 1986)

193. Schmidt, I: *Polarschiffe* (Rostock 1988)

194. Schoerner, G: *Regalskeppet* (Stockholm 1964)

195. Serényi, P (ed): *A TIT Természettudományi Stúdió Hajózástörténeti és Modellezõ Klubjának Évkönyve* (Budapest 1983)

196. Steinhaus, C F: *Die Construction und Bemastung der Segelschiffe* (Hamburg 1869, reprinted Kassel 1977)

197. Steinhaus, C F: *Die Schiffbaukunst in ihrem ganzen Umfang*, 2 vols (Hamburg 1858, reprinted Kassel 1977)

198. Steusloff, W: *Votivschiffe* (Rostock 1981)

199. Szymanski, H: *Deutsche Segelschiffe* (Berlin 1934)

200. Szymanski, H: *Die Segelschiffe der deutschen Kleinschiffahrt* (Lübeck 1929)

201. Tenne, A: *Kriegsschiffen zu Zeiten der alten Griechen und Römer* (Oldenburg 1915)

202. Thiel, H: *Vom Wikingerboot zum Tragflächenschiff* (Berlin 1969)

203. Tiller, A: *Handbuch des Wassersports* (Ravensburg 1939)

204. Timm, W: *Kapitänsbilder* (Rostock 1978)

205. Torr, C: *Ancient Ships* (Chicago 1964)

206. Traung, J-O: *Fishing Boats of the World*, 3 vols (Farnham 1978)

207. Underhill, H A: *Deep-Water Sail* (Glasgow 1955)

208. Underhill, H A: *Masting and Rigging* (Glasgow 1946)

209. Underhill, H A: *Sail Training and Cadet Ships* (Glasgow 1956)

210. Underhill, H A: *Sailing Ship Rigs and Rigging* (Glasgow 1956)

211. Ürügdi Gy: *Hogyan utaztak a régi rómaiak?* (Budapest 1979)

212. Vermeer, J: *Het Friese jacht* (Leeuwarden 1992)

213. Viereck, H D L: *Die römische Flotte* (Hamburg 1996)

214. Vocino, M: *La Nave nel Tempo* (Milan nd)

215. Wachsmann, S: *Seagoing Ships and Seamanship of the Bronze Age Levant* (College Station, Texas & London 1998)

216. Ware, C: *The Bomb Vessel* (London 1994)

217. Wiebeck, E: *Indische Boote und Schiffe* (Rostock 1987)

218. Wieg, P: *Chinesische See-Dschunken* (Rostock 1984)

219. Wieg, P & Freyer, J: *Chinesische Fluss-Dschunken* (Rostock 1988)

220. Williams, G R: *Das grosse Buch der Schiffsmodelle* (Frankfurt am Main 1973)

221. Winfield, R: *The 50-gun Ship* (London 1997)

222. Winkler, H: *Zeesboote* (Rostock 1986)

223. Winter, H: *Das Hanseschiff im ausgehenden 15 Jh* (Rostock 1975)

224. Winter, H: *Der holländische Zweidecker von 1660-1670* (Rostock 1978)

225. Winter, H: *Die katalanische Nao von 1450* (Burg bei Magdeburg 1956)

226. Winter, H: *Die Kolumbuschiffe von 1492* (Rostock 1980)

227. Worcester, G R G: *Sail and Sweep in China* (London 1966)

Magazines and Journals

228. *Modellezés* (Budapest)

229. *Ezermester* (Budapest)

230. *Model Boats* (Hemel Hempstead, UK)

231. *Modelarz* (Warsaw)

232. *Marinekalender der DDR* (Berlin)

233. *Modelist Konstruktor* (Moscow)

234. *Köhlers Flotten-Kalender 1989* (Herford, Germany)

Commercial Plans

235. Plany Modelarskie (Warsaw)

236. H A Underhill (Baltonsborough, UK)

237. Assoc des Amis des Musées de la Marine (Paris)

238. Benczur L (Budapest)

239. V Lusci (Florence)

240. F Gay (Messina)

241. R I Collins (UK)

Original Sources

242. Unidentified material

243. After contemporary illustration

244. After a relief at Nineveh

Illustrator's Acknowledgements

With regard to those drawings derived from the work of Howard I Chapelle, the illustrator would like to thank Dr Paul F Johnston of the Smithsonian Institution, Washington DC for guidance. In matters relating to his own work Karl Heinz Marquardt was both co-operative and encouraging. Material from *Die römische Flotte* is now the copyright of, and is reproduced by courtesy of, Koehlers Verlagsgesellschaft mbH, Hamburg.

Index of Ship Names and Ship Types